2003

Year B 3

AN ALMANAC OF PARISH LITURGY

SOURCEBOOK

FOR SUNDAYS AND SEASONS

Paul Turner

LTP

LITURGY
TRAINING
PUBLICATIONS

Sourcebook for Sundays and Seasons 2003 is lovingly dedicated to Peter Mazar, who served as both author and editor of *Sourcebook* at various times. Every page of this book shows his influence. He was instrumental in shaping how it is arranged, he directed the artists whose images adorn the pages and the cover, and he edited the words. Peter died while *Sourcebook 2003* was in production, on April 22, 2002, at the age of 49.

The cover is a fitting tribute to him. He loved God's creation, and cooperated fully with God in making the world beautiful. He was an avid and talented gardener. He could give you the Latin name for every plant, tell you how Christians in different places and eras saw it as a revelation of the mystery of God, and then show you how to use it as a decoration, a food or even a toy! He decorated his office, the public areas of the offices at LTP, his parish church and every flat surface of his home for each feast and season. His Christmas trees and Halloween decorations were legendary, as were his generosity, his kindness and his wicked sense of humor.

As you read *Sourcebook* you may wonder if the lavish vision unfolded herein of keeping the church's calendar is possible. It is. Peter showed us how.

Sourcebook for Sundays and Seasons 2003: An Almanac of Parish Liturgy, copyright © 2002, Archdiocese of Chicago: Liturgy Training Publications, 1800 North Hermitage Avenue, Chicago IL 60622-1101; 1-800-933-1800; fax 1-800-933-7094; e-mail: orders@ltp.org; website: www.ltp.org. All rights reserved.

Printed in the United States of America

ISBN 1-56854-403-0

SSS03

Artist Julie Lonneman depicts the evangelist Mark with
his traditional symbol, the winged lion. The lion is here
surrounded by the images of Christ, the paschal lamb;
of God the Father, the strong and protective eagle; and of
the Holy Spirit, the dove. Framing them are the springtime
flowers traditionally associated with Easter, through which
slides the snake, often a symbol of Satan, who tempted
our ancestors to sin, the "happy fault which gained for us
so great a Redeemer," as the Exsultet proclaims.

CONTENTS

THE PASCHAL TRIDUUM

EASTER

SUMMER AND FALL ORDINARY TIME

RESOURCES

PUBLISHERS

From the Author

■ THANKS for your interest in *Sourcebook for Sundays and Seasons 2003*. I pray that it will help you pray throughout the coming year.

While I was writing this book for you, I accepted a call to a new ministry. After 12 years as pastor of St. John Francis Regis Catholic Church in Kansas City, Missouri, I have become the pastor at St. Munchin Catholic Church in Cameron, Missouri, its mission St. Aloysius in Maysville, and of the Western Missouri Correctional Center.

You may be wondering: Who is John Francis Regis? And who is Munchin? Or, as my former Latin teacher Reginald Foster wrote, "Quisnam cœlorum iste St. Munchin est?" Even John Page, the director of the International Commission on English in the Liturgy, admitted he had to pull Butler's *Lives of the Saints* off the shelf because the name of the parish patron had stumped him.

■ REGIS (1597–1640) was a Jesuit from southeastern France noted for his catechetical skill, commitment to workers' rights, and dedication to parish missions. He longed to come to North America along with other French Jesuit missionaries, but his superiors liked what he was doing at home—enlivening the faith in communities that had adopted Christianity but lacked leadership to keep them faithful.

In 1640 he agreed to give the parish pre-Christmas mission at La Louvesc. (Pronounce it "la loo-VAY.") He went first to Le Puy to settle some debts. (For all you francophiles, when you go to Le Puy you go "au Puy" and when you leave you go "du Puy.") The hagiographers do not further explain the debts, but the point is that Regis had to go du Puy to La Louvesc in late December when a winter storm kicked up. He and a companion got lost. Regis contracted pleurisy. He crawled the rest of the way, so the story goes, to La Louvesc and got there several days after Christmas.

The people still wanted to hear the mission talks, and they begged Regis to give them. One small problem—he was still down with pleurisy. So they put Regis in bed, went up the hill to the local mountain stream, fetched a pail of water, and—I guess from here there are two ways to conclude the story. Version A: On the strength of that water, he revived and preached for three days straight. Or, version B: Three days after drinking the water, he died. They named the stream after him.

Regis worked tirelessly and inspired many other Jesuits to do the same. When French Jesuit missionaries crossed the ocean to spread Christianity to the Americas, they brought the name of Regis with them. In the 1830s the missionaries, who passed through what would become northwest Missouri, dedicated a log cabin church in honor of Saint Regis.

This first church in the region stood on a bluff overlooking the confluence of the Missouri and the Kansas Rivers. (I still prefer calling it the Kaw River in the local patois, but they're asking us now to call it the Kansas.) Eventually that church was torn down and another one replaced it in the nineteenth century, but they changed the name to the Immaculate Conception, who was becoming all the rage as a patron in those days. Even that church proved to be too small. It has been replaced with the one known now as the Cathedral of the Immaculate Conception, the mother church of the diocese of Kansas City–St. Joseph. That cathedral stands on the site of the original log cabin church dedicated to Saint John Francis Regis. Regis is still the secondary patron of our diocese.

In the 1960s, as the population of Kansas City was growing out toward the southeast, Bishop Charles Helmsing, one of the fathers of the Second Vatican Council and a great supporter of liturgical renewal and ecumenical dialogue, established a new parish and named it after Regis. It's never been a Jesuit parish, but it has always had a Jesuit patron. It honors the pioneers who brought the faith to northwest Missouri as much as it honors the saint.

I claim to be the only person in the history of our diocese to have visited the site of Regis's death. As the pastor of St. Regis Church in Kansas City, I got to meet the pastor of St. Regis Church in La Louvesc. Going up the hill to the water source, I asked one of the local shopkeepers how much the water cost. "The water is free," he explained. I smiled, and he continued, "But this plastic bottle . . ." So I bought the bottle and brought some of the water home. We poured a portion of it onto the soil when we broke ground for a new parish church in 1996, sprinkled more of it on the cornerstone, and poured the rest into the baptismal font on Dedication Day.

■ SAINT MUNCHIN IS THE PATRON OF SNACK FOOD. No, seriously, and please do not call us the church of St. Munchkin. Munchkins are creatures who inhabit Oz. Munchin is the patron of Limerick in Ireland. That also sounds like a straight line, but it's true.

There once was a priest named Munchin
Who shooed away flies with a truncheon
  Then plunged into dips
  With fistfuls of chips:
He was bunchin' for munchin' at luncheon.

(Thought I'd better do it before you did.)

Among the founders of Cameron, Missouri, about one hundred fifty years ago were immigrants from Limerick, Ireland. They came here to build the railroad that ran between St. Joseph, Missouri (home to the Pony Express), and Hannibal, Missouri (home to Mark Twain, Becky Thatcher and Tom Sawyer). The Catholic founders of the town gave their new church here the name of their home church back in Ireland— St. Munchin. The church there is still thriving, along with a school named for the same saint.

So, who was Munchin? Well, nobody knows for sure, but we think he was a great religious leader of the seventh century, possibly a bishop, but maybe not; possibly an abbot, but maybe not; possibly of Germanic stock, but maybe not. In the Catholic church, this never stops us from honoring someone as a saint. Three early martyrologies call Munchin "the Wise." Unfortunately, this still leaves the rest of us as "the Ignorant." Nonetheless, Limerick claims him as its first bishop. Munchin appears in the Roman martyrology on January 2, but Limerick celebrates the feast on January 3, in case you want to observe it this year.

Here in Cameron, the locals are very proud that we have the *only* St. Munchin Church in all of North America. I think we have South America covered, too.

Depending on who you ask, we have about eight thousand people in town and several thousand more in the state prisons. Up at Maysville—the county seat of DeKalb County, *that* Maysville—we have even fewer. Some two hundred seventy Catholic families call Cameron home, and another thirty or so claim Maysville. We have a few dozen prisoners who come to the Masses in English and in Spanish at the jail. The organist at St. Munchin is also the mayor of Cameron. She sings a solo with the Cameron Municipal Band when it gives its free Thursday night concerts at McCorkle Park during summer. This is a great place to call home.

That's what's happened to me this year. While my move was underway I spent a long time living out of boxes and tapped out sections of this book on a tiny dining room table in the back of the rectory here in Clinton County. I hope the results are coherent.

Blessings on you in 2003! I hope the changes in your life this year result in much pleasure.

Paul Turner
www.paulturner.org

From the Editor

■ Many people move this book from being electronic impulses (the manuscript is sent to LTP via e-mail) to being a book. Jane Kremsreiter designed the 1991 edition. Mary Bowers made modifications to the design, and Ana Aguilar-Islas designed the cover.

As production editor, Carol Mycio has the task of crafting language to house style, checking facts, conforming manuscript to design, and proofing each stage along the way. Lucy Smith is the design artist and Mark Hollopeter is the production artist. Their work turns *Sourcebook* into a thing of beauty.

■ More and more parishes are recognizing the need for catechesis founded on the liturgy. To this end, note the bulletin inserts at the end of each seasonal chapter—something new last year in *Sourcebook* and very welcome. Pass them to the parish secretary or to whomever is responsible for weekly catechesis. The purchaser of this book has permission to reprint these inserts free of charge in a parish bulletin or other noncommercial publication.

■ New this year is attention to the saints' days, patronal festivals and other local liturgical observances of Central and South America. This information can be hard to come by, so it is provided as a service within each season's calendar.

■ You hold us accountable for the contents of this annual book, and we listen to you. We're interested in hearing your comments and suggestions at any time.

Peter Mazar

Welcome to 2003!

■ IT's 1,000 YEARS since the founding of the Bamberg Cathedral under Henry II. It's 500 years since Pedro de Cieza de Leon first described the potato in his "Chronicle of Peru." It's 100 years since the election of Pope Pius X. And it's 50 years since I was born.

Whatever anniversary you celebrate this year, may it be a happy one.

Sourcebook for Sundays and Seasons hopes to guide you through the year, to help you celebrate the special days and the seasons of life. This book follows the liturgical calendar of the Roman Catholic Church and helps you find your way through the liturgy of each day, but especially the liturgies for Sundays and seasons of the church year.

SOURCEBOOK 2003: ORGANIZATION

Sourcebook is divided according to the seasons of the liturgical year: Advent, Christmas, Lent and Easter. The Paschal Triduum, the center of the Christian life, also receives its own section. Ordinary Time will appear in two parts: winter and summer/fall.

Within each of those sections you will find two further divisions: the season and the calendar. The seasonal overview features several parts.

- *The Meaning:* the basic purpose of the season
- *The Saints:* how to celebrate days devoted to saints this season
- *The Liturgical Books:* how the lectionary, sacramentary and other ritual texts capture the season's meaning
- *The Art and Environment:* ideas for the seasonal appearance of places of worship
- *The Music:* the music that enhances the changing times of year
- *The Parish and Home:* prayer within the domestic church
- *Texts:* suggestions for seasonal adaptations

The calendar section is an almanac that takes you day by day through the year. You will find these four components each Sunday and solemnity:

- *Orientation:* the background to this particular day
- *Lectionary:* an explanation of the scriptures for the day

- *Sacramentary:* insights into our prayers, ideas for implementing options
- *Other Ideas:* more thoughts to keep in mind

■ BULLETIN INSERTS: Each seasonal chapter concludes with a section of reprintable bulletin inserts for the Sundays and principal feast days of the year. They reflect the first readings at Mass as the spark for catechesis on the liturgical year.

Inserts may be reproduced within the weekly bulletin, participation aid or other handout given to parishioners at no charge. Be sure the parish secretary knows about these! They are written to bring home something of the mystery of each Sunday's liturgy, to invite further reflection and study of the scriptures, and to assist parishioners in becoming more and more literate in the language of the liturgy.

CALENDAR OVERVIEW: DECEMBER 1, 2002, TO NOVEMBER 29, 2003

■ ADVENT AND CHRISTMAS: The new year begins over the long Thanksgiving weekend. The secular and sacred worlds will turn together this year. December 8 falls on a Sunday, so the Immaculate Conception—but not the obligation to attend Mass—gets transferred to the ninth. Christmas sits on a Wednesday, making this an Advent of average length.

■ THE WINTER WEEKS OF ORDINARY TIME last nearly two months, the final day of the Christmas season falling on January 12, the first day of Lent falling on March 5.

■ LENT, TRIDUUM AND EASTER: Easter is fairly late this year because the full moon will come and go just before the vernal equinox. We wait nearly a month for it to return.

The Triduum begins on April 17, coinciding with Passover, and concludes with Easter Sunday on April 20.

Ascension will fall on Thursday, May 29, or Sunday, June 1, depending on your region. Pentecost concludes the Easter season on June 8, followed by week ten of Ordinary Time.

■ FESTIVAL DAYS IN 2003: This is that rare year when a whole series of solemnities and feasts replace the Sunday Ordinary Time liturgy. The Presentation of the Lord (February 2), the Apostles Peter and Paul (June 29), the Triumph of the Cross (September 14), All Souls (November 2), and the Dedication of the Lateran Basilica (November 9) all fall on Sunday this year. This series of festivals will give several breaks in Ordinary Time.

■ SUNDAY, THE DAY THAT THE LORD HAS MADE: Sunday is the Lord's Day. It is the day we celebrate the resurrection. It is our primary day for gathering for worship and celebrating the eucharist. In regions where a priest is not available, the community should still gather on Sunday. A Mass during the week cannot replace it because of the symbolism of the first day of the week, the day on which God created light, and the day on which the Son rose.

The people who gather in your church on Sundays have made a special effort to be there. They have arranged their schedule and coordinated with loved ones. They come together in church to meet others who share a similar faith. Greet them warmly. Be prepared for their arrival. Be strengthened in your own faith by their commitment.

LECTIONARY OVERVIEW 2003: YEAR B

■ THE YEAR OF MARK: Mark's gospel is supposed to dominate the Sundays of 2003. After all, Matthew has Year A. Luke has Year C. And John opens his mouth wherever the church year gives him a chance, notably during the Easter season every year.

But Year B is never completely Marcan. Mark tells nothing about the infancy of Jesus, so the Sunday gospels that need to tell that story turn to Matthew and Luke. Mark's is also the shortest of the four gospels, and he does not have quite enough material to make it through the year. So he steps aside for five weeks of summer Ordinary Time, while John weighs in with the "Bread of Life" discourse from the sixth chapter of the gospel.

This year, though, Mark has another difficulty being heard. This year other solemnities and feasts that just happen to fall on a Sunday replace several of the Ordinary Time Sundays and their gospels. On average, this happens once every seven years. On average, it should happen to Mark once every 21 years. Well, this is the year. Poor Mark, for whom Year B should be his time to shine, keeps getting overshadowed by other needs throughout 2003.

What many consider to be a climax of Mark's gospel, Peter's confession of faith, will be omitted this year because of the Triumph of the Cross.

A list of resources for studying Mark are found on page 244.

■ THE AUTHOR OF MARK'S GOSPEL: The true author of the gospel we call Mark is unknown. The gospel itself never tells who the author is, and the title "Mark" was added after the earliest manuscripts had already been written. Mark is the name of a companion to Peter, and an early tradition ascribed the gospel to him, assuming he was Peter's scribe in Rome.

Scholars think it was written shortly after the fall of Jerusalem, around the year 70, making it the earliest of the four gospels. In fact, Mark apparently coined the term "gospel" in his opening verse.

The gospel seems to have a Gentile audience in mind. It was written in Greek and carries interpretations of some Jewish laws, as if the reader would need some explanation. It also contains some weird geographic references (7:31), suggesting the author had minimal knowledge of the region.

Both Matthew and Luke probably relied on Mark. This gospel's collection of stories about Jesus was apparently reworked to suit other needs.

■ THE IDENTITY OF JESUS: Mark's main point is to identify Jesus as the Son of God. He states this in his opening verse. The whole story builds to Peter's confession in the eighth chapter, and then the passion seals the good news about the kind of Messiah Jesus is.

The conclusion to Mark's gospel has long been a point of disputation. The original ending comes abruptly and stops with more doubt than faith. A longer ending was appended, collecting some of the later stories about the apparitions of Jesus, giving the gospel a more satisfying, if less original, close.

■ FIRST AND SECOND READINGS: As usual, Sunday's first readings shift from book to book throughout the year. The lectionary skips through the Bible to find passages that fit the theme of the gospel or of the season or feast.

Second readings during Ordinary Time of Year B come from five books. This year opens, as every year does, with part of Paul's First Letter to the Corinthians; in this case, chapters 6–10. Then the lectionary takes us through Paul's Second Letter to the Corinthians, the letter to the Ephesians, the letter of James, and the letter to the Hebrews.

■ THE *LECTIONARY FOR MASSES WITH CHILDREN:* This year you will find more comments about the Sunday lectionary for children. In the seasonal

overviews you will catch a glimpse of what to expect: which readings and psalms are included, omitted or altered.

SACRAMENTARY OVERVIEW

Although the Sunday lectionary spans a three-year cycle of readings, the sacramentary in use for the United States offers the same options year after year. The presider selects from one of two opening prayers, but otherwise the presidential prayers remain constant. There is greater variety in the prefaces for each weekend.

■ A RICH AND VARIED RESOURCE: The sacramentary also includes texts for the proper of saints, the commons, ritual Masses, Masses and prayers for various needs and occasions, votive Masses, and Masses for the dead. (Helping you steer your way through the many options within the sacramentary is one of the tasks of *Sourcebook*.) Among these, the ones most likely to appear on a Sunday are the ritual Masses, which are related to the celebration of certain sacraments and sacramentals.

If a wedding Mass takes place on a Saturday night in Ordinary Time, for example, the ritual Mass for marriage may replace the presidential prayers of the Sunday.

The local ordinary (usually the bishop of the diocese) may call for an appropriate Mass to be celebrated on a Sunday in Ordinary Time in cases of serious need or pastoral advantage. For example, the bishop could request the "Mass in Time of War or Civil Disturbance" or "For the Election of a Pope or Bishop" if these seem opportune. These texts from the lectionary and the sacramentary would replace the Ordinary Time Sunday texts at the bishop's direction.

In any case, most of these prayers can be rewardingly and easily used on weekdays in Ordinary Time.

■ THE CLOUD OF WITNESSES: The Roman martyrology lists about a dozen lesser-known saints for every day of the year. Unless it is already an obligatory memorial or feast or solemnity, you have the option of celebrating one of these as a memorial almost any day, and the parish's patrons would be observed as a local solemnity. The reason these saints are not on the general calendar is to give it some room to breathe and to return the celebration of certain saints to the localities where they have special significance.

Be sparing in exercising the option of these saints' days. If you do so, you choose the prayers for the saint from the sacramentary, and you may choose readings from the lectionary commons (although, as the lectionary itself suggests, it's best to leave the weekday course of readings intact, even on saints' days).

New to *Sourcebook* this year is an expanded set of references to important days on the calendar of countries in Latin America. Many of our parishes include people from these regions, and these references should alert you to their festivals. Even if your parish has no immigrants or lineage from Paraguay, for example, you may find it interesting to know which days have importance to our neighbors to the south.

■ ENTRANCE AND COMMUNION ANTIPHONS AND PSALMODY: *By Flowing Waters: Chant for the Liturgy* (Collegeville, The Liturgical Press, 1999) is the first complete edition in English of the Simple Gradual, one of the church's official songbooks. Of the 680 chants in *By Flowing Waters*, there are 63 entrance antiphons and psalms and 62 communion antiphons and psalms that provide seasonal music and propers for solemnities and feasts of the church year.

By Flowing Waters also has a complete set of commons for parishes celebrating the solemnities of their dedication and of their patron saint. (There is a wealth of information about how to use these chants in the performance notes—pages 417 to 428—and generous reprint permission for assembly editions—pages 429 to 432.)

LITURGY OF THE HOURS OVERVIEW

In addition to the Sunday eucharist, your community will gather for other types of prayer. These may flow from the eucharist and lead the faithful back there.

The full celebration of the Liturgy of the Hours includes an Office of Readings, Morning Prayer, Daytime Prayer, Evening Prayer and Night Prayer. Very few parishes offer the full range of this liturgy every day, but many of them offer some parts of the hours throughout the year.

■ FOUNDATIONAL PRAYER: The two hours on which the entire liturgy turns are Morning and Evening Prayer. They have a similar structure (although there are many local variations). Generally, after an opening versicle, the community sings a hymn. Then one, two, or three psalms are sung. These lead toward a short passage from scripture, followed by a responsory. A canticle from the gospels is sung. Then the community offers petitions and the Lord's Prayer. A prayer of the day (for instance, the opening prayer of Mass that day), blessing and dismissal conclude the liturgy.

■ REPEATED PRAYER: The Liturgy of the Hours gains its strength from the daily repetition of a predictable form. Like the rosary, its spirit comes not from variety but from its meditative pace. The prayer is so word-heavy that the traditional music for this prayer is usually understated. This allows the community to settle into the texts effortlessly. The construction of this liturgy assumes that the community prays some of it every day.

Wherever the Liturgy of the Hours is more occasional, the faithful may find help in more varied musical presentations of the psalms. If you're planning Morning or Evening Prayer, select a good hymn and psalm settings that will invite participation. The assigned texts may direct the type of music to seek: hymns that celebrate the time of day, the season or occasion, and psalms that do the same.

SACRAMENTS OVERVIEW

The primary celebration of the sacraments takes place at the Easter Vigil each year, when the community shares the celebrations of baptism, confirmation and eucharist.

■ THE BAPTISM OF CHILDREN: The Rite of Baptism for Children may be celebrated at a Sunday Mass or on some other occasion. Celebrating baptism at Mass will let the entire community witness the sacrament and will invite their support to the new life in their midst.

If baptisms take place apart from Mass, plan how to keep them celebratory and participatory in spirit. Greeters to welcome visitors, musicians to lead singing, prepared readers—these ministers will enhance the community's celebration of the sacrament on a day and occasion when visitors are many.

■ OTHER CELEBRATIONS OF CONFIRMATION AND FIRST COMMUNION: The parish may celebrate the Rite of Confirmation on diverse occasions. The bishop may visit, or he may delegate another priest to preside.

Baptized candidates may celebrate the Rite of Reception into the Full Communion of the Catholic Church at any time. When they do so, the priest who presides also confirms. In case of an emergency, a priest who baptizes may confirm at once, even if the candidate is an infant. More commonly, the public celebration of confirmation allows the entire community to renew its commitment to prayer and service.

If the candidate for confirmation is already a baptized Catholic, the bishop is the ordinary minister of the rite. So if you have some adult Catholics who have been away from the faith for a while and were never confirmed, the bishop is the ordinary minister for them. Many bishops will delegate the pastor to confirm in this instance, but permission must be received. One important exception to this rule is danger of death. A priest may confirm any Catholic who is dying. No further permission is needed.

First communion will be a highlight for families. The parish may celebrate this sacrament at a regularly scheduled Mass or at a separate occasion. You may observe the principles of the *Directory for Masses with Children,* including adaptations to the presidential prayers, readings, and the use of special eucharistic prayers.

■ RECONCILIATION AND HEALING: Our ministry of reconciliation surfaces most profoundly in the sacrament of penance. Most parishes schedule confessions once a week. Although Saturday afternoon remains the most popular day and time, other occasions may be chosen. Schedule communal celebrations of reconciliation well in advance. Are these already on the parish calendar? Have you coordinated the times with the times set by neighboring parishes?

Our ministry of healing extends also to the sacrament of anointing the sick. Be sure the homebound of your community have opportunities for this sacrament during the year. One or more of the faithful could accompany the priest when he visits the homebound, or he may set a time when family and friends of the parishioner may attend. Many parishes schedule a communal celebration of the sacrament at church or in nursing homes on one or more occasions yearly.

■ ORDINATION AND PROFESSION: A parish celebration of ordination is rare, but it does happen. Who in the parish is being called to ordination as a deacon or priest? Who is called to profession to religious life? What support is offered their families? Does your community have a vocations committee promoting careers in religious life? If you celebrate an ordination, careful planning will observe its spirit of servant leadership.

■ WEDDINGS: The Rite of Marriage calls for attention to liturgical details. Liturgical guidelines about music, the communion rite, and decorations should fit the general liturgical practice of the parish. If the avoidance of secular music and if the sharing of communion under both forms are norms for parish Masses, they should be norms for Masses of marriage as well.

■ FUNERALS: Of course, you never have much notice before celebrating a funeral. Decisions have to be made rapidly and efficiently. Some parishes become remarkably skilled at offering attentive care to the bereaved in their time of grief. It will help to have one or more people on your liturgy team familiar with planning and presiding over a vigil service and a funeral, knowledgeable about scriptures and music, and able to offer consolation and guidance.

More and more cantors are taking on the role of leading the liturgical vigil (wake). Plan these services with good music, observing the church's rituals. Many people assume you have to have a rosary for the wake service, but the word *rosary* never appears in the *Order of Christian Funerals,* which recommends a scripture service. We cannot reasonably rely on the judgment of those in mourning to plan the liturgy. Parish ministers can give careful direction to assist mourners in preparing the funeral liturgies.

The more and more frequent choice of cremation among the faithful calls for certain changes in funeral customs and attitudes. Is your community prepared for the celebration of the funeral rites with the ashes of the deceased?

ANNUAL CELEBRATIONS OVERVIEW

■ PATRONAL/TITULAR DAYS AND DEDICATION ANNIVERSARIES: Many services occur once a year. Your parish should observe the annual day of the dedication of its church and also its patronal solemnity. Are these marked on the parish calendar?

■ DAYS OF PRAYER: In place of rogation days, the church now invites us to set aside special days of prayer. In the United States, the Conference of Bishops suggests that each diocese determine days or periods of prayer for the fruits of the earth, prayer for human rights and equality, prayer for world justice and peace, and penitential observance outside Lent (*Appendix to the General Instruction,* 331). Does your diocese have these? Are they noted in your parish calendar for this year?

Your parish may have other traditional observances. Look ahead and see how they fit with the liturgical year. Sometimes a sudden crisis or tragedy within the parish or the wider community demands liturgical prayer. Who in the parish is able to make liturgical decisions as needed when the unexpected happens?

■ DEVOTIONS: Your parish may also have traditional devotional prayers. For example, how is First Friday observed each month? Do you offer Stations of the Cross during Lent?

Are there special celebrations in honor of Mary? Is there a celebration in connection with the Assumption on August 15 or with Our Lady of Guadalupe on December 12?

How are the saints honored? Are there occasions for drawing attention to the religious art and statuary that adorn your church? Given the particular mission and charism of your community, are there some saints who should be especially honored there as heroes?

■ BLESSINGS: Once or twice annually, review the parish's schedule of blessings. Coordinate the blessings with the liturgical calendar and with parish need. A blessing is a true liturgy and requires liturgical ministers to do it well. Each season *Sourcebook* suggests blessings (primarily chosen from the church's *Book of Blessings*) that can be part of the life of the local community.

About the Art

THE illustrations within *Sourcebook for Sundays and Seasons 2003* are by Corey Wilkinson, an Illinois artist. The art for Sundays and seasons employs zoological images, and art for feast days makes use of botanical ones.

The associations of such natural images with an occasion or season are drawn mostly from Christian folklore. Several associations are mentioned in the 1868 book *Flowers and Festivals* by W. A. Barrett of Saint Paul's Cathedral in London. Thanks to Peter Scagnelli for sending LTP a copy! The following explanations of the art were written by Peter Mazar.

■ SUNDAY—DOVE: On the first day, the Spirit of God brooded over the dark waters. Then God said, "Let there be light," and there was light.

The Lord's Day, the day of resurrection, is the day of the giving of the gift of the Holy Spirit.

■ ADVENT—OWL: In traditional art, Lady Wisdom, whom the scriptures describe as God's bride, sometimes is shown with a wise old owl nearby. During Advent we ask Lady Wisdom to "come and show your people the way to salvation."

■ CHRISTMAS—OX AND ASS: The gospels don't mention these animals. The opening chapter of the book of the prophet Isaiah does, however, which says that even the ox and ass know who feeds them. In a like manner we should recognize the Lord in our midst.

■ WINTER ORDINARY TIME—DEER: Psalm 42 has been a favorite for members of the church, especially during the procession toward the baptismal font: "As a deer longs for flowing streams, so my soul longs for you, O God."

■ LENT—SNAKE: Genesis tells us about a talking snake. Adam ate the forbidden fruit, gaining death for himself and his progeny. In a desert Jesus fasted, and through the obedience of Christ we are invited home to God's garden.

■ TRIDUUM—LAMB: John the Baptist called Jesus the lamb of God. The paschal lamb upon God's throne is also our Good Shepherd, who lays down his life for the sheep.

■ EASTERTIME—PEACOCK: Few things are more glorious than a peacock fully fledged. The molting of peacocks and the renewal of their plumage are ancient signs of resurrection.

■ SUMMER AND FALL ORDINARY TIME—LION: Folklore associates the sun with the zodiacal sign of Leo, perhaps because the warmest days in the Northern Hemisphere are during the weeks that the sun passes through this sign, perhaps also because the golden mane of a male lion is imagined to resemble the sun.

■ IMMACULATE CONCEPTION—WHITE PINE: Our ancestors were mystified about how conifers reproduce. Where are the flowers? And yet without flowers conifers produce abundant seeds. For this reason pines became symbols of the Virgin Mary.

■ CHRISTMAS—HOLLY: Christmas has a lot of Easter in it. Holly's prickly foliage has been called "Christ's thorn," and the red berries are compared to his blood. The evergreen foliage is a sign of the life that is stronger than death.

■ HOLY FAMILY—PAPERWHITE NARCISSUS: Winter-blooming flowers are signs of paradox, of the things (in the words of G. K. Chesterton) that "cannot be but that are," of the mystery of the incarnation in which immortality is wrapped within the mortal.

■ MARY, MOTHER OF GOD—ENGLISH IVY: The ivy vine using holly as its support is a sign of the Christian clinging to Christ. Ivy is transfigured in treetops from a flowerless vine into a fruitful and sturdy shrub, and for this reason has become a symbol of Mary, as well as of every Christian made fruitful in baptism.

■ EPIPHANY OF THE LORD—MISTLETOE: Mistletoe magically roots itself in tree branches and so seems suspended between earth and sky. No wonder that it, like the olive borne by Noah's dove, has become an emblem of the reconciliation of heaven and earth!

■ BAPTISM OF THE LORD—OLIVE: According to ancient laws even warfare is not an excuse to chop down an olive. Human societies come and go, olives live for centuries.

■ PRESENTATION OF THE LORD—SNOWDROP: These earliest of flowers are sometimes called "Candlemas bells." Like the day itself, they stir the heart for spring.

■ SAINT JOSEPH—CROCUS: Tradition holds that Joseph died on the final day of winter. On his grave the first flowers of spring erupted.

■ ANNUNCIATION OF THE LORD—MADONNA LILY: This day, Joseph's Day and Eastertide (and a host of other days) are celebrated with lilies, which along with roses, as emblems of purity and ardor, are imagined to fill heaven to the brim.

■ PALM SUNDAY—PUSSY WILLOW: Many northern Europeans call pussy willow "palm" since it's carried in today's procession. All sorts of willows, as water-loving trees, are associated with the elected catechumens preparing for baptism at Easter.

■ HOLY THURSDAY—FORSYTHIA: Even in the north this shrub comes into bloom about now. The crosswise, fragrant flowers, like all members of the olive family, have become emblems of the Christian Passover.

■ GOOD FRIDAY—HAWTHORN: Hundreds of species of plants have been imagined to be the kind used for Jesus' crown of thorns. This is one of the thorniest and most common.

■ HOLY SATURDAY—MYRTLE: According to Middle Eastern folklore, Myrrha mourned the death of her son. In pity the powers of heaven transformed her into the myrtle tree. Her tears became fragrant myrrh, a resin used to embalm the dead.

■ EASTER VIGIL—PASSION FLOWER: Few flowers are as complex in appearance as passion flowers, whose blooms hold five anthers (said to be Christ's five wounds), three stigmas (said to be the three nails), and a corolla of petals (said to resemble the crown of thorns).

■ EASTER SUNDAY—FLOWERING DOGWOOD: *Cornus florida,* a North American native, is imagined as the tree of the wood of the cross. The flowers bear crosswise bracts marked at the tips in bloody brown and centered by the true flowers, which some claim to resemble Jesus' crown of thorns.

■ OCTAVE OF EASTER—DAFFODIL: Is there a merrier flower than a daffodil? It seems to trumpet the Easter words of Christina Rosetti: "Spring bursts today, for all the world's at play."

■ ASCENSION OF THE LORD—LILY-OF-THE-VALLEY: "I am the rose of Sharon and the lily of the valley," says one of the lovers in the Song of Songs. Eastertime, the *al fresco* season, leads us from the fragrant valley up to the mountain of the ascension, from the confines of the upper room out into the streets of the city.

■ PENTECOST—PEONY: A central European title for the peony is "Pentecost rose." The intense fragrance of peonies and roses and other flowers has become a sign of the Holy Spirit in much the same way that sacred chrism is a sign of a God whose presence infuses creation.

■ THE HOLY TRINITY—IRIS: Late spring is when irises bloom in profusion. Many species favor water, and irises that blossom by waterside (sometimes called "flags"), with their three-part flowers, are signs of baptism in the name of the Trinity.

■ BODY AND BLOOD OF CHRIST—WHEAT: Now is the season when wheat ripens across the Great Plains of the United States. This most important harvest gives us "our daily bread."

■ BIRTH OF SAINT JOHN THE BAPTIST—DAISY: The "day's eye" is among the sunniest of flowers. It blooms in June and has become associated with Midsummer Day and the fiery prophet John.

■ SACRED HEART OF JESUS—ROSE: Roses are classic symbols of love and passion. A rose's richness, complexity, fragrance and even its thorns tell us something of love.

■ SAINTS PETER AND PAUL—POPPY AND BACHELOR BUTTON: Along with daisies, these "cornflowers" form a red, white and blue carpet alongside European wheat fields. Red poppies are Peter's flowers, and blue bachelor buttons, of course, are Paul's.

■ TRANSFIGURATION OF THE LORD—SUNFLOWER: Any of the flowers that turn their heads toward the sun as the day passes (the meaning of the word "heliotrope") are symbols of the Christian who follows the Lord, who on this day shone more brightly than the sun.

■ ASSUMPTION OF MARY INTO HEAVEN—GLADIOLUS: The flower's name means "sword." It has an association, thanks to Simeon's prophecy, with this "Mary's month" that includes the festivals of her assumption, birth and sorrows.

■ HOLY CROSS—BASIL: Legends tell of the herb basil, with its crosswise and fragrant foliage, covering Golgotha when Helen discovered the wood of the holy cross.

■ ALL SAINTS—CHRYSANTHEMUM: The Japanese especially use chrysanthemums in profusion during their autumn festivals. Mexican folklore claims that the pungent foliage of these and marigolds stir memories of the dead.

■ ALL SOULS—MUSHROOM: Autumn is a time to hunt for mushrooms—carefully. The deadliness of some species is infamous. Christian lore sees in mushrooms a sign of the mystery of abundant life arising from death.

■ DEDICATION OF THE LATERAN BASILICA—GOURD: Gourds are symbols of the Christian. From one seed can come an endless array of fruit, each crammed with hundreds of seeds. But the vines need support, and we need Christ.

■ CHRIST THE KING—OAK: Oaks have been associated with royalty even as long ago as Roman times, perhaps because they are so long-lived, and perhaps because they take so long to come to maturity.

ADVENT

The Meaning

MOST people think of Advent as the time of preparation for Christmas. It is, but it is something more. Advent also prepares us for the coming of Christ at the end of time.

Advent makes us think about the two comings of Jesus. He came first in a humble birth at Bethlehem. He will come again in glory at the end of time. While preparing for the annual celebration of the birth of Christ, we prepare our hearts for Jesus to return.

The season lasts through four Sundays. This year's Advent goes only a little farther, ending on a Tuesday.

The liturgical year wraps us in a cloak of birth and death. We close each year reflecting on the coming of Jesus Christ our King at the end of time. Advent begins with the same theme.

■ "THE HOLIDAYS": When you call a place of business this month, you're likely to hear a voice saying, "Happy holidays!" De-Christianized businesses seeking to appeal to a large audience will avoid references to the faith-filled term "Christmas" and simply call this season "the holidays," or, judging from catalogues, "Holiday 2002."

Just as Christianity has its holidays and moral codes, so does the business world. These holidays call for a specific code of behavior: shopping.

For faithful Christians, Advent is a season when sacred and secular jockey for attention. It falls especially to those who plan the Sunday liturgy to help the faithful keep their focus in the midst of a world that swallows them with sales.

The two worlds, the sacred and the secular, happily combine their goals in making this a season for charity. From Thanksgiving till Christmas people contribute well to causes that benefit the poor and the needy.

"God so loved the world," the famous passage of John 3:16 begins, "that we received the only Son, that whoever believes in him may have eternal life." The incarnation of God began with love. That love can inspire the world this season to similar acts of selflessness.

■ ADVENT'S FOCUS: Even as Advent raises our vision to the promised return of the eternal Son, it creates a place for the human heart to wait in hope and wonder.

Throughout this season the scriptures and antiphons create a vivid picture of this season's themes. Advent begins with a breathtaking vision of the end of time. It recalls the prophecies of promise to Israel in exile. It holds up John the Baptist, the bridge between the former and the new covenant, and it draws us into the private life of a virgin who enfolds the hopes of endless ages, the hopes of every heart.

From the general to the specific, from the heavenly to the homely, Advent sweeps us into its mystery.

The Saints

B Y happy coincidence, many of the saints we meet on our Advent journey shed light on the season. The days that honor them hold unequal importance, but they never draw our attention completely away from Advent.

In the United States and in Latin America the two most important saint days on the Advent calendar are December 8 and 12. Both days honor Mary, the Mother of God. The first, a solemnity, remembers her under her title of the Immaculate Conception. The second, a feast in the United States, honors her as Our Lady of Guadalupe. Because Mary is one of the central figures of this season, these days blend well with its character.

This year, however, the calendar makes one shift. December 8 falls on a Sunday. Prior to the Second Vatican Council, whenever this happened the Immaculate Conception took precedence

over the Second Sunday of Advent. Not any longer. Today the Sunday liturgy follows as usual and the solemnity is transferred to Monday. However when such a solemnity is transferred, the obligation to attend Mass does not transfer, and so December 9 is not a holy day of obligation.

■ SEVERAL OBLIGATORY MEMORIALS OCCUR DURING ADVENT. A martyr (Lucy) and a bishop (Ambrose) from the fourth century share time with a missionary (Francis Xavier) and a mystic (John of the Cross) from the sixteenth century. On each of these days the saint's vestment color and opening prayer take precedence. You may take the other presidential prayers (preface, prayer over the gifts, and communion prayer) from the Advent weekday, the saint's day, or the commons in the back of the sacramentary. (For Lucy, examine the common of one martyr or virgins; for John, consult the common of pastors or doctors, and so forth.)

Ordinarily, the Advent lectionary will supply the readings on these days. However, you could choose from the readings offered by the commons in the back of the lectionary. Guidelines do not advise this (see *Introduction to the Lectionary for Mass,* 8), but if you have some good reason, you may do so. What's a good reason? Is your parish named after one of Advent's saints (and so you have a patronal solemnity)? Would the regular Advent readings be inappropriate because of some local issue? If so, then turn to the commons.

■ THE OPTIONAL MEMORIALS OF ADVENT FALL INTO TWO GROUPS: those that occur before and after December 17. You may ignore the optional memorials, no matter which group they occupy. After all, you will want Advent to feel like Advent. But if you observe any of them, beware of some differences between the two groups.

An optional memorial observed prior to December 17 follows the guidelines for memorials in Advent. After December 17, if you take the option and celebrate Peter Canisius or John of Kanty, you may use their own opening prayers instead of the one for Advent, or use it as the conclusion to the general intercessions. But everything else (even Advent's violet vesture) comes from the Advent weekday.

In general, a community will benefit from honoring the season rather than the optional memorials. They are optional so that a community dedicated to these saints or their apostolate may celebrate them. The priest "should not omit the readings assigned for each day in the weekday lectionary too frequently or without sufficient reason, since the Church desires that a richer portion of God's word be provided for the people" (GIRM, 316).

■ VOTIVE MASSES: Liturgical books also supply texts for votive Masses and Masses for various needs and occasions. These texts are used during Advent only in cases of serious need or pastoral advantage. However, they may not be used on a Sunday or on the solemnity of the Immaculate Conception. Only a bishop can direct that they replace the texts for the feast of Our Lady of Guadalupe. The priest who presides for Mass can make the decision on any other day during the season. Ordinarily, though, it's not a good idea. The texts of Advent are well chosen, strong and beautiful.

The Lectionary

WE begin Year B, during which Mark's gospel is our Sunday companion. Throughout this season, the readings put us in touch with ancient Israel awaiting the arrival of the Messiah. They also awaken our hope in Jesus' return in glory.

The gospels of the four Sundays always follow the same pattern. The first week presents Jesus' vision of the second coming. The second and third weeks present John the Baptist, and the fourth week tells part of the story leading up to the birth of the Lord.

Isaiah dominates the first readings on the first three Sundays, but on the fourth we hear Nathan's prophecy from the Second Book of Samuel.

The second readings this year all come from undisputed letters of Paul, except for the second Sunday, which draws its text from the second letter attributed to Peter.

■ THE SUNDAY *LECTIONARY FOR MASSES WITH CHILDREN* offers most of these passages, but omits a few of them to simplify the liturgy of the word with children.

On the First and Fourth Sundays of Advent the first reading is omitted and the psalm is changed. The Second Sunday omits the second reading. The Third Sunday offers all three.

The weekday lectionary for children has four sets of readings for Advent. The first introduces a gospel not found in the regular lectionary for this season and pairs it with an abbreviated version of the first reading found in the second set. The second set draws both readings from the first Saturday of the season. The first reading for the third set comes from Wednesday of the second week; the accompanying gospel comes from Wednesday of the third week. The final set introduces a new first reading for the season and takes the gospel from December 22.

Children's Masses need not correspond with these dates, but you may want to avoid a duplication of readings for those attending daily Mass.

The Sacramentary

■ INTRODUCTORY RITES: If the visual images are strong, you may not need many words to introduce the Mass. The presence of the Advent wreath and the purple vesture will signal a change to people even without many words of introduction. After the sign of the cross, the presider may simply say, "The Lord be with you," pause after the response to establish eye contact with as many as possible, and then begin the Penitential Rite.

■ PENTITENTIAL RITE: Try opening the Penitential Rite with a text that reminds people of the season. It could come from the opening song or one of the scriptures. (See page 10 for an example.) If you plan to use Penitential Rite C, be sure to note the sample one for Advent in the sacramentary at C-ii. Option B is briefer, and if your community is unfamiliar with it, this could be a season to put it into repertoire. Some communities have blessed the wreath in place of the Penitential Rite on the First Sunday (but see the *Book of Blessings*).

■ THE GLORY TO GOD is omitted on the Sundays of Advent. This streamlines the entrance rites and drives the liturgy more directly toward the scriptures. When the hymn returns at Christmas, it will lift hearts high with joy.

■ ALL THE PRESIDENTIAL PRAYERS of this season first appeared in older liturgical books. The opening prayers for the first and second Sundays come from the Gelasian Sacramentary (eighth century). The prayer over the gifts and communion prayer for the first Sunday, the opening prayer of the third, and the communion prayer of the fourth all come from the Veronese Sacramentary (sixth century). The others appeared later in the Middle Ages.

The opening prayers are filled with allusions to the scriptures and themes of the Advent season. Part of the genius of the Roman Rite is its ability to pack a lot of thought into a few phrases of prayer.

■ THE GENERAL INTERCESSIONS are the texts of the Mass that allow the freest composition, but there are rules and principles and a customary order. A sample for Advent appears in the sacramentary's first appendix, #3. You will find additional samples in LTP's *Prayers for Sundays and Seasons, Year B.*

■ THE TWO PREFACES for Advent introduce the sacramentary's complete set of over eighty prefaces. These first two entries are intended for each of the two halves of Advent. Begin the first on the first Sunday, and switch to the second on December 17. That one is used until the morning of Christmas Eve.

The first preface perfectly presents the two main themes of Advent. It recalls the incarnation, when Christ humbled himself to come among us, and it announces that we watch for the day when he will return in glory.

The second preface focuses more on the coming commemoration of the birth of Jesus, as the scriptures of this part of the season do. This preface traces the line from the prophets through Mary and John the Baptist—all preparing the way for the coming of Jesus. Both prefaces are new to the missal but have antecedents dating back to the fifth century.

■ THE EUCHARISTIC PRAYERS FOR RECONCILIATION may be used with other prefaces that refer to penance and conversion (see *Notitiae* 19 [1983], 270). So if you want to highlight the penitential aspect of this season, you may choose one of these prayers and substitute an Advent preface. Prayer II speaks of "your Son who comes in your name" and pictures the great eschatological banquet "in that new world" at which are gathered "people of every race and language and way of life."

The Book of Blessings

ALTHOUGH this book has innumerable uses throughout the year, most people will find it helpful at the start of the year because the United States edition presents a blessing for an Advent wreath. The blessing does not appear in the sacramentary.

The *Book of Blessings* recommends blessing the wreath on the first Sunday of the season after the homily of the Mass (1509).

The wreath may also be blessed outside Mass in a celebration of the word of God, or even with a simpler rite of blessing. It is hard to imagine why this would be done because the blessing during Mass activates the symbol on behalf of the entire worshiping community. However, if this year you have other events on the schedule for this day, you could schedule a blessing of the wreath at some other time. Or if you had a group of people meeting for some other purpose, like a retreat day or an educational event, you could bless the wreath with them. Turn to the *Book of Blessings* for assistance.

During this season you might use this book for other blessings as well. For example, on the Fourth Sunday of Advent you could offer a blessing of those awaiting the birth of a child in their families (1–7). Let them step forward before the general intercessions and conclude the community's prayers with a blessing for parents before childbirth, on the day the gospel tells of Mary's pregnancy. You could also bless engaged couples (1–6) or travelers (9). (See page 10 in this *Sourcebook* for a blessing of travelers to use on the Third Sunday of Advent.)

The Rite of Christian Initiation of Adults

IF you have catechumens in your community, they may be dismissed at each Mass during this and every season of the year. Sample dismissals appear at number 67.

The First Sunday of Advent is not the ideal time to celebrate the Rite of Acceptance into the

Order of Catechumens and the Rite of Welcoming the Candidates. Some communities used to do this to parallel the Rite of Election on the First Sunday of Lent. The Rites of Acceptance and Welcoming should be celebrated two or even three times a year (RCIA, 18.3), depending on when the catechumens and candidates are ready for them. This means that some people will be joining a group where others have more experience. But those who need more time in formation can take it. With so much happening during Advent, this may not be the best season to schedule these liturgies, but if the catechumens and candidates are ready, you certainly may.

The Liturgy of the Hours

THE principle hours to honor are always morning and evening prayer. These are the two hinges on which the Liturgy of the Hours turns. If some in your community can gather for prayer apart from the eucharist, these are the most important celebrations to honor.

The format for the hours remains the same through every season of the year, but during Advent some psalms appear that we do not use during the rest of the year. These passages tell about the history of Israel. By introducing them into the liturgy during this season, our prayer can help us meditate on Israel's long wait for the promised Messiah.

The specific changes are as follows: Psalm 105 replaces Psalms 131 and 132 on the first Saturday; 106 replaces 136 on the second Saturday; and 78 replaces 55 and 50 on the Friday and Saturday of the fourth week. All the replaced psalms still occur in other spots of the cycle. If you are planning a celebration of the hours this month, try incorporating one of the psalms that develop the character of the season.

If you use the four-volume set, note that the *General Instruction of the Liturgy of the Hours* appears only in the first volume, the one set aside for Advent and Christmas. Why not add it to your seasonal reading this year?

■ THE "O ANTIPHONS" are a jewel of the Advent hours. These beautifully crafted texts serve as the antiphons for the *Magnificat* during evening prayer from December 17 through December 23. Each addresses Christ by a different title and begs him to come for salvation.

You are familiar with the idea of the antiphons if you have ever sung the popular, seven-verse Advent hymn "O Come, O Come, Emmanuel." The hymn puts the seventh antiphon first, then jumps back to the first and has the rest in order.

■ THE OFFICE OF READINGS includes some treasures from early Christian writers. For example, you'll find an excerpt from a treatise on the value of patience by Saint Cyprian of Carthage in Africa (Saturday, First Week of Advent). Peter Chrysologus reflects on love as the driving force of salvation history (Thursday, Second Week of Advent). And Ambrose helps later generations of Christians to insert themselves into the story of Mary's visitation to Elizabeth (December 21). Ambrose writes, "You also are blessed because you have heard and believed. A soul that believes both conceives and brings forth the Word of God."

■ AT NIGHT PRAYER, the concluding antiphon to Mary from Advent until Candlemas is "Alma redemptoris mater." You can find the beautiful chant setting in the *Liber cantualis*.

The Rite of Penance

MANY parishes offer a communal rite of reconciliation during the season of Advent. Be sure to schedule yours early.

The Rite of Penance also suggests a different kind of celebration during Advent, a non-sacramental liturgy of penitence. It envisions that the community would gather simply to reflect on their sins and to seek God's forgiveness on an occasion when the sacrament may not be offered. When celebrated by the faithful, children and catechumens—not all of whom are eligible for the sacrament—it will foster a spirit of penance in the community. The celebrations may also be useful in areas where no priest is available for sacramental absolution.

In other areas, the celebrations may be adapted to include the sacrament of reconciliation. In such cases, the Rite of Penance follows the homily. Readings recommended for Advent

(Appendix II, #II) are Malachi 3:1–7a, Psalm 85:2–14, Revelation 21:1–12, and Matthew 3:1–12 or Luke 3:3–17. Other readings may be chosen for a parish celebration of reconciliation in preparation for Christmas.

Be sure to consult the *Rite of Penance* when preparing your communal celebration of reconciliation. The order is straightforward and largely familiar, but intimidates some people who prepare the liturgy:

■ OUTLINE OF THE RITE FOR RECONCILIATION OF SEVERAL PENITENTS WITH INDIVIDUAL CONFESSION AND ABSOLUTION:

> Introductory Rites
> > Song
> > Greeting
> > Introduction
> > Opening prayer
> Celebration of the Word of God
> > First reading
> > Responsorial psalm
> > Second reading
> > Gospel acclamation
> > Gospel
> > Homily
> > Examination of conscience
> Rite of Reconciliation
> > General confession of sins
> > Litany or song
> > Lord's Prayer
> > Individual confession and absolution
> > Proclamation of praise for God's mercy
> > Concluding prayer of thanksgiving
> Concluding Rite
> > Blessing
> > Dismissal

The Pastoral Care of the Sick

THE sick in your community may be anointed at any time. The sacrament may be celebrated during or outside of Mass. It may take place in homes, hospitals or at church.

Some communities have celebrated this sacrament at a Sunday Mass during the Advent season, but this may not be advisable. Those who administer the sacrament during Advent and Lent accentuate its penitential aspect, and indeed, this sacrament does forgive sins. But because these seasons are filled with other themes and needs, it may be best to schedule the rite of anointing at one or two other times of the year on a Sunday. Guarantee that the sacrament will be available to those who need it at regular intervals during the year.

Anointings during Advent have no special form. If you schedule a communal celebration of the sacrament during a Sunday Mass in Advent, keep the scriptures and presidential prayers of the Sunday. They should not come from the Rite of Anointing within Mass. When celebrating apart from Mass, consider using the scriptures from the rite that fit the spirit of this season, such as the prophecies of Isaiah.

The Rite of Marriage

IF weddings take place during Advent, they should keep the spirit of the season. The promised joy that bubbles through Advent will itself lend a note of anticipation to the wedding.

If the wedding takes place on a Saturday evening during Mass, the readings and prayers of the Advent Sunday are used. The same applies to the celebration of marriage on any Sunday this season or on Monday, December 9, the solemnity. The couple or the presider may substitute one reading from the Sunday or solemnity with one from the *Rite of Marriage* (11), but otherwise the scriptures are set. Any Saturday night Mass fulfills the Sunday obligation.

If the wedding does not include a Mass, or if the wedding Mass does not take place on a Saturday night or Sunday or solemnity, the scriptures and prayers from the *Rite of Marriage* may be used in their entirety during the ceremony.

Decorations for the wedding should respect those already in place for Advent. (Photos of previous years' Advent environments are helpful to share during the preparation for the wedding.) Light the wreath before the ceremony. Let the season of the year speak to the ritual celebration.

The Order of Christian Funerals

A funeral may take place on any day during Advent. On ordinary Advent weekdays the funeral Mass may replace the readings and prayers of the day. If a funeral is celebrated on an Advent Sunday or on the solemnity of the Immaculate Conception (December 9 this year), the readings and prayers already assigned for that day take precedence.

When selecting readings for a funeral on an Advent weekday, consult the lectionary's daily proper texts first. They often offer a note of hope for the mourners. If you choose to replace them, look for ones that keep the spirit of the season. For example, there are passages in the funeral lectionary from the book of Isaiah.

In the United States we usually see white vesture for funerals, but violet may be worn (*Order of Christian Funerals,* 39). That color may not look out of place for an Advent funeral, but most still prefer white vesture.

The Art and Environment

I NSIDE and outside the church, decorations can give worshipers a sense for the season. The contrast between the long period of Ordinary Time and the sudden appearance of Advent can summon the faithful to prepare in their hearts a way for Christ.

Advent decorations "should be marked by a moderation that reflects the character of this season" (*Ceremonial of Bishops,* 236). Advent, more than anything, is a season for holding back so that the joy of Christmas can unfold. It is like a slow prelude that leads to an exuberant fugue.

Remember to decorate several areas. Put something outside the building, something inside the doors, and inside the worship space itself. Be sure to decorate the area where the people gather, not just the sanctuary, otherwise it looks like the ministers celebrate Advent while everybody else watches them do it.

■ THE VIOLET VESTURE for this season invites comparisons to Lent. Indeed, Advent has origins as a penitential season. The word *penitence* means more than sorrow for sin. It signifies reorientation and setting priorities straight, which is something Lent and Advent have in common.

Violet had been the color for vigils, and in our own day we focus less on the penitential nature of Advent and more on the double focus of anticipation: standing with ancient Israel as the chosen people await the Messiah, and standing with contemporary Christians as we await the Messiah's return. Both call for a spirit of vigilance and penitence wrapped inside a message of hope.

The rose-colored candle on the Advent wreath is reserved for the third Sunday. Some people still have not made the connection. The candle signifies that the season is half over. Christmas is coming soon. We may rejoice even in the colors we wear. So the candle wears rose. Presider and deacon also may wear rose vesture, signaling that the full joy of Christmas is drawing near.

If you have several sets of violet vestments, designate one of them for Advent. People will subconsciously make the association between that vestment and Advent's call to them for preparation. Some parishes prefer a more blue-hued violet for this season, to distinguish it from the purple of penitence in Lent.

You may also choose a similar shade of violet for other appointments in the church—altar frontals, tablecloths and wall hangings. But keep it subdued. Save something for Christmas.

■ CHRISTMAS DECORATIONS do not yet belong in church. Stores and streets and homes may be filled with lights, poinsettias and evergreen trees, but they do not enter our worship space until Christmas has arrived. Resist the temptation, just as musicians must do with carols, and save Christmas for Christmas. Give Advent its due.

■ PREPARE AN ADVENT WREATH. For ideas, see the *Book of Blessings* (1510–1512), but be sure to visit other churches in your area as time permits. Gather ideas from your neighbors and share some of yours. Explore the various ethnic customs that employ the images of light, of circles and of evergreens.

Customarily, the wreath is a circle of evergreen branches, and four candles stand upon it. Traditionally three candles are violet and one is rose, but four violet or four white candles may be used instead. Some communities add a fifth candle. They light this at Christmas.

The size of the wreath varies from place to place. But the ones useful at home will appear too small in church. In a public setting, the wreath should be large enough for all to see it. Some suspend it from the ceiling or place it on a stand. This creates a glorious impression and announces loudly the spirit of the season. If the wreath somehow extends into the area where the assembly gathers for prayer, it will draw them into the celebration of the season. But it should not obstruct people's view of the altar, ambo or chair.

■ Statues, paintings and other images of Mary and John the Baptist, or one of the prophets, already adorn many churches. This would be a beautiful season to draw attention to those images in your church. Some parishes erect a Jesse tree with symbols of the ancestors of Jesus, or a "giving tree" of gifts for the needy (see "The Parish and Home" below).

The Music

Advent comes with a vast array of hymnody from many parts of the Christian world. These traditional songs put the community in touch with the season as well as with all those who have celebrated it in every time and place.

■ Hymns about John the Baptist are especially fitting on the second and third Sundays of Advent. Those are the days when the gospel tells some aspect of John's life and ministry. This is true every year during Advent.

■ Hymns of the Virgin Mary will be especially appropriate on the feasts of the Immaculate Conception and Guadalupe, as well as on the fourth Sunday, when the gospel tells part of the story leading up to the birth of Jesus. Our music books brim with Marian hymnody. "Immaculate Mary" will come to mind, but consider other hymns and canticles that especially fit the feast or season: "Behold a Virgin," "Ave Maria," "Magnificat," and the classic Polish anthem, "Serdeczna Matko" or "Stainless the Maiden."

The skilled choir ready for a challenge will warm to David Conte's "Ave Maria" (E. C. Schirmer, 4729). Also worth a look is "Asi andando" by Tomás Pascual (Max Quin) (fl. 1595–1635), arranged for singers and instruments by Christopher Moroney (WLP, 12713). This piece tells part of the story of the miracle of Guadalupe and is sung in seventeenth-century Spanish.

By Flowing Waters (The Liturgical Press, 1999) has a fine English version (658) of the Advent Marian antiphon "Alma redemptoris mater," as well as a lovely setting (411–414) of the ancient entrance antiphon, "Beata Mater," with Psalm 46, "God is our refuge."

■ Gospel acclamation: Choose an alleluia that will last throughout the season. As always, the verses will change, but the lectionary groups them into those for the first (193–202) and second (202) parts of the season. The first set features scriptures that announce the coming of the Savior together with non-scriptural proclamations of the same hope. The second group represents the O Antiphons from evening prayer. These seven verses are completely interchangeable, but careful planning will unite them to the *Magnificat* antiphon sung that evening or the previous one.

■ Psalms: *By Flowing Waters* (The Liturgical Press, 1999) includes two settings for the Advent entrance and communion antiphons and psalms, as well as responsorial psalms.

■ For eucharistic prayer acclamations, choose one set and stay with it throughout Advent and on into Christmas. People will be able to sing these as true acclamations if they stop wondering which one it will be each week. This practice also gives the season an identifiable sound. You might even use the same set each year to help people make more associations between the music and the season. Any of the memorial acclamations may be sung, but the first three announce the theme of Christ's coming better than the last does.

■ Two Latin chants from the *Liber cantualis* are traditional for this season. The tune for *Conditor alme siderum* should be well known. *Rorate caeli* is less popular, but a good challenge for a choir or assembly to add to the repertoire. The chant O Antiphons are lovely pieces for a choir disciplined enough to sing them. Find them in the *Antiphonale monasticum*. Traditionally, a bell is rung while singing these antiphons at evening prayer.

■ HYMNODY: Traditional hymnody includes: "Wake, Awake," "Come, Thou Long Expected Jesus," "On Jordan's Bank" and "Comfort, Comfort, Ye My People." These, of course, are useful for any liturgical gathering during the season.

You might also take a look at two fine Advent hymns by Steven C. Warner. "Take Comfort, My People" is based on Isaiah 40 (WLP, 8653) and "Maranatha! Come, Lord Jesus" is based on 1 Corinthians 16:22 (WLP, 7221). Both are arranged for choir, assembly and instruments.

An index of music that reflects the scripture passages can be found in good hymnals and other resources from publishers.

■ CHOIR MUSIC: Let your choir shine during this season with music that will prepare hearts for the coming of Christ. J. Michael Thompson's arrangement of the popular hymn "Redeemer of the Nations, Come" (WLP, 5793) and Richard DeLong's arrangement of "Come, Thou Long-Expected Jesus" (E. C. Schirmer Music Company, 4852) are fine compositions. A three-part choir will enjoy Alan J. Hommerding's arrangement of the spiritual "Keep Your Lamps Trimmed and Burning" (WLP, 5739).

■ YOUTH: The prolific Ed Bolduc has written two songs that should especially please young voices during Advent. "Rain Down" (WLP, 7412) and "Look to the One" (WLP, 7418) will add energy and punch.

■ CHILDREN: For even younger voices, don't overlook the pieces in the Music for Children Series from World Library Publications. Dolores Hruby's "Lamps for a Wedding" and Julie Howard's "Two Psalms for Advent and Christmas" are childlike but not childish. These pieces will engage the children with songs that will satisfy more advanced musical tastes in the assembly.

■ A POPULAR ORGAN SOLO for the Advent season is the chorale prelude on "Wachet Auf" by J. S. Bach. A good tenor and accompanist may bless the assembly with a rendition of the opening movements to G. F. Handel's *Messiah*: "Comfort Ye" and "Every Valley."

■ BE ALERT TO THE NEEDS OF MUSICIANS. This time of year demands a lot from them. Make sure they can keep the meaning of these days in their hearts.

The Parish and Home

■ THE GIVING TREE: A giving tree takes some coordination, but it is well worth it. The basic idea is that people buy gifts for the poor and place them under the tree. It's a tree where churchgoers are *giving* gifts, not getting gifts.

Set up a tree in a public place like the gathering space, vestibule or reception area. Staff members who know the needy can solicit from them a list of gifts that would help. Volunteers write the needed gift on an ornament and place it on the tree, keeping confidential the name of the person it will benefit. Members of the community then take an ornament, purchase the gift, wrap it, and place the ornament on the outside so the staff and volunteers who distribute the gifts will know who gets what. Households learn the importance of sharing with those in need at a time of year when the satisfaction of gift-giving runs high and our Dickensian attention to the poor is strong.

■ ADVENT WREATH: The wreath in church should encourage people to set one up at home. Let people know how to obtain an evergreen wreath and to turn it into an Advent wreath. Perhaps a group in the parish could take orders and make the wreaths available. Prepare prayer cards for use at home throughout the season. Those who gather at home at the start of the day or for the evening meal may light the candles and join in prayer.

■ SAINT NICHOLAS: There are many delightful stories about Saint Nicholas. Look for him in lives of the saints or on websites. The marvelous cantata "Saint Nicolas" by Benjamin Britten with a text by Eric Crozier includes congregational song and covers many of the important legends about the holy bishop. Coming to know this saint will help everyone recover the origins of Santa Claus. Exchange gifts on his memorial, December 6. Nicholas is a patron of children, and in many cultures the saint makes an appearance to children and households on this day or its eve.

■ FAMILY ADVENT DAY: The parish could host a day for families early this month. You could offer educational activities related to the season. Information about Advent's history, scriptures, themes and customs might be welcome, especially by parents who want to hand on Catholic traditions to their children.

You can help parents of young children by sponsoring a Saturday event for children so parents are free to go Christmas shopping. Gather everyone at the beginning or at midday for prayer, sing the hymns of Advent, make wreaths and prayer cards for mealtime rituals. The day could conclude with all joining in a parish celebration of evening prayer.

You could also distribute copies of useful resources. LTP's *Take Me Home* and *Take Me Home, Too* contain activity pages for families for each week of the season.

■ CALENDARS: LTP's *Year of Grace 2003* is a large poster families will enjoy hanging at home. They can track the entire liturgical year. Clear the refrigerator door! In 2003 the calendar features the story of Noah and the ark.

LTP's calendar for Advent and Christmas comes with perforated doors and windows that reveal drawings to match the prayer for each day, found in an accompanying booklet. It will delight all ages.

Texts

■ GREETING:

God, who shows us mercy and love, the Lord,
    be with you.

From the one who is, who was, and is to come,
    grace and peace be with you.

■ INTRODUCTION TO THE PENITENTIAL RITE:

God is the potter. We are the clay. Let us place
    ourselves in the hands of our merciful Creator.

Lord, make us turn to you. Let us see your face
    and we shall be saved.

■ RESPONSE TO THE GENERAL INTERCESSIONS:

Lord, come and save us.

Come, Lord Jesus.

The United Church of Canada recommends the following prayer for Advent (1G004). It could conclude the general intercessions:

God, our Father,
the One who comes in your name comes again
with grace and power,

with forgiveness and strength,
with truth and imagination,
with gentleness and love.
May the Coming One enter the hearts
of those who wait with quiet expectation
for all that is good and holy and just.
[We make our prayer in the name of Jesus,
who is Lord for ever and ever.] Amen.

■ DISMISSAL OF CATECHUMENS:

Sisters and brothers, we send you forth to reflect upon the word we have shared. As you wait, God will keep you firm to the end, irreproachable on the day of our Lord Jesus Christ. Go in peace.

■ A BLESSING FOR TRAVELERS ON THE THIRD SUNDAY OF ADVENT (ADAPTED FROM THE *BOOK OF BLESSINGS*): After the communion prayer, the parish announcements are made as usual. Then the deacon, cantor or presider begins in these or similar words:

Deacon: We offer a blessing today for all those who will be traveling over the Christmas holidays. Please step forward and face the assembly.

(*Pause while those who will be traveling come forward.*)

Presider: The Lord be with you.

All: And also with you.

Deacon: Let us extend our hands in blessing over our brothers and sisters.

Presider: (cf. *Book of Blessings,* 631)

All-powerful and merciful God,
you led the children of Israel on dry land,
parting the waters of the sea;
you guided the Magi to your Son by a star.
Help these, our brothers and sisters,
    and give them a safe journey.
Under your protection
    let them reach their destination
and come at last to the eternal haven
    of salvation.
We ask this through Christ our Lord.

All: Amen.

Presider: May almighty God bless you all, the Father, the Son, and the Holy Spirit.

All: Amen.

Deacon: Go in peace.

All: Thanks be to God.

December 2002

Lectionary #2 (Lectionary for Masses with Children [LMC] #2)   violet

First Sunday of Advent

ORIENTATION

Announce the new liturgical year in many, subtle ways. You want people to get the idea, but this is Advent, so you want to save something for Christmas. The music and the environment for this day will help set the tone.

What people see can draw them into the season. Set the Advent wreath where it will be visible. Make sure something calls attention to the season wherever people will be: outside the church, in the gathering area, near their places in the worship area, and in the sanctuary.

What people hear will also draw them into the season's spirit. The voices of cantors and greeters can show an attitude more business-like than before. Let people know that the work of the season has begun. The music of the season will bring back memories of Advents past.

LECTIONARY

The particular spirit of the first Sunday can be found in the gospel of the day. Jesus says, "Be watchful! Be alert! You do not know when the time will come." Obviously, he is not talking about Christmas, because we all know when that is. He is instead talking about his death, exaltation and return, or perhaps about the impending death of his disciples. This passage signals Advent's big theme. During this season we do not just prepare mangers to remember the baby Jesus; we prepare our hearts and our world for the return of Jesus in glory.

In the first reading we meet people who are hoping for God to appear. Unlike the gospel, where Jesus implies we should be fearful about meeting God, Isaiah's passage indicates that the people have had enough of sin and sorrow and wish God would "rend the heavens and come down." The description of their sins is woeful in its remorse: Even good deeds are like polluted rags.

The psalm refrain is a cry for salvation, a very subtle allusion to Jesus, whose name means "Savior." The psalmist sings with the same desire we met in the first reading, "Rouse your power, and come to save us."

The opening of Paul's first letter to the church at Corinth affirms the people as a community that waits. They wait for the revelation of our Lord Jesus Christ. That is our stance this season as well. Paul assures the church of his day and of ours that God will keep them firm to the end, irreproachable "on the day of our Lord Jesus Christ." Taken together, these texts focus our gaze on the return of Jesus in glory.

SACRAMENTARY

The sacramentary offers a selection of presidential prayers for each Sunday of the year and on many weekdays. They do not follow the three-year cycle of lectionary readings. Look over the two opening prayers and choose one that speaks to your community.

The sacramentary recommends Psalm 24 for the entrance antiphon: "No one who waits for you is ever put to shame." A verse from Psalm 84 is suggested for communion, a provocative image of God showering the earth with gifts and the land yielding fruit. The greatest gift showered upon us, of course, will be the incarnation.

The *Book of Blessings* places the blessing for the Advent wreath after the homily. Some communities move it to the position of the Penitential Rite instead. They open with the hymn, sign of the cross, and greeting, then continue with the wreath ceremony and conclude it with the opening prayer for the Mass. See the *Book of Blessings* (47) for the primary texts.

If the blessing of the wreath follows the homily, Mass opens as usual with the Penitential Rite. Note that the second option under rite C was written with Advent in mind. The Glory to God is omitted.

Advent Preface I applies today. It may be used with Eucharistic Prayers I, II or III, or with either of the prayers for reconciliation. Alan Griffiths published another translation of this in his collection of eucharistic prefaces from the Ambrosian Rite (Sunday 1 of Advent), *We Give You Thanks and Praise* (Sheed & Ward, 2000).

The solemn blessing suggested for this day looks for the coming of Christ in glory. Still, it is only one option. Consider substituting a prayer over the people, such as #4, which prays that they may find in God "the fulfillment of their longing."

OTHER IDEAS

The new liturgical year begins as we end Thanksgiving weekend. You may wish to acknowledge visitors who have joined you for worship.

Begin Volume I of the *Liturgy of the Hours* today.

Mail out a parish Christmas card or letter, giving times for the communal reconciliation service, private confessions, and the Christmas Mass schedule. Include an examination of conscience and one or more of the new forms of the prayer of the penitent (act of contrition) from the *Rite of Penance,* #45. Promote the same events in the bulletin.

The celebration of evening prayer this weekend and throughout the season can help people pray in the gathering darkness for the coming of the Light.

This past Friday night our Jewish sisters and brothers began Hanukkah. This festival celebrates fidelity to the covenant in the face of tyranny and forced cultural assimilation. (See 1 and 2 Maccabees.) Include a prayer for our Jewish neighbors, that God's light may shine through their witness to the covenant. See LTP's publication, *Teaching Christian Children about Judaism.*

Late this coming week, when the crescent of the new moon is first spotted in the west after sunset, Muslims conclude their observance of Ramadan, the holy month of fasting and prayer, and celebrate Eid al-Fit'r, the most joyful days of the Muslim year. Let us include them, too, in our prayers.

M O N 2 — #175 (LMC #172–175) violet — Advent Weekday

From today through Wednesday next week, the weekday lectionary features a series of readings from Isaiah. We hear these prophecies in a semicontinuous order. This means that if you look them up in Isaiah, you will find them in this order. But we skip over a lot of passages from Isaiah in between the ones that appear in the lectionary. The psalms and the gospels are chosen because they echo a theme from the first reading. The gospel passages during this part of the season are not semicontinuous. They jump around the synoptics because the first reading sets the pattern for this part of the season.

Because this is Year B, select the customary first reading (Isaiah 2:1–5). Isaiah presents a glorious image of all the nations streaming toward the Lord's mountain. There they will experience unity and peace. "They shall beat their swords into plowshares."

The psalm develops the theme of the mountain. It is a processional psalm, sung by pilgrims on their way to the mountain of God, Jerusalem. We Christians sing it in anticipation of our ascent to the New Jerusalem.

The gospel develops the theme of inclusion. In his conversation with a Gentile centurion, Jesus observes that people will come from the east and the west and find a place at the banquet in God's reign. This faith-filled Gentile will have his place with the ancestors of Judaism. Advent's opening theme is big.

Start using the first Advent preface today. The recommended antiphon for the introductory rites echoes the theme of the readings. It invites the nations to hear God's message and make it known to the ends of the earth.

■ TODAY IS THE 22ND ANNIVERSARY of the martyrdom in 1980 of American missionaries to El Salvador: Maura Clarke, Ita Ford, Dorothy Kazel and Jean Donovan. Missionaries in Central America continue to lay down their lives for the sake of the poor. Remember them in prayer and imitate their example of love.

T U E 3 — #176 (LMC #172–175) white — Francis Xavier (+ 1552), presbyter, religious, missionary — MEMORIAL

In a passage that inspired the Jesse tree and the list of gifts of the Holy Spirit, Isaiah prophesies that a great leader, filled with the spirit of justice, shall descend from the family of Jesse. Even the Gentiles shall seek him. Psalm 72, favored throughout Advent, echoes the theme of the just ruler. In the gospel, Jesus, filled with the Holy Spirit, tells the disciples that prophets and kings longed to see and hear what they are witnessing.

■ TODAY'S SAINT: Francis Xavier, a Spaniard of noble descent, became a disciple of Ignatius of Loyola and a driving force behind the missionary activity of the Jesuits in the Orient. His celebration draws an obligatory memorial, so the presidential prayers come from the proper of saints, not the Advent weekday. But you could use the Advent prayer or one from the Masses "For the Spread of the Gospel" with a shorter ending ("We ask this through Christ our Lord") to conclude the general intercessions.

W E D 4 — #177 (LMC #172–175) violet — Advent Weekday

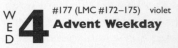

Optional Memorial of John of Damascus (c. + 754), presbyter, monastic, doctor of the church / white ▪ Isaiah envisions a bounteous feast on the Lord's mountain. The prophecy, supported by the ever-popular Psalm 23, foreshadows the heavenly banquet.

Jesus gives depth to this vision by feeding a multitude. Your parish's efforts to supply food for the hungry make this work of Jesus present again.

■ TODAY'S SAINT: John of Damascus served as a financial officer before becoming a monk near Jerusalem. His dogmatic theology served as a textbook for the Greek church. He vigorously defended the use of images in worship. His life blended the secular, academic and spiritual worlds, and, because of his work with the Muslim leaders in his area, he might be considered a patron of Muslim-Christian dialogue. The texts of hymns like "The Day of Resurrection" and "Come, You Faithful, Raise the Strain," are based on John's work. His memorial is optional; unless your community has a special devotion to John of Damascus, celebrate the Advent weekday.

THU 5 #178 (LMC #172–175)   violet
Advent Weekday

Isaiah's prophecy salutes a city built strong on its firm purpose. Other cities will be trampled by the needy and the poor. The psalmist invites us to take refuge in God, not in people. Jesus praises those who build their city on the rock of his words. Justice, not might, provides civic strength.

FRI 6 #179 (LMC #172–175)   violet
Advent Weekday

Optional Memorial of Nicholas (+ 399), bishop / white ▪ Matthew alone records Jesus' cure of two blind people at once. The story perfectly illustrates the fulfillment of Isaiah's prophecy of a miraculous day on which, among other marvels, the eyes of the blind shall see. With new sight we sing Psalm 27, "The Lord is my light and my salvation."

▪ TODAY'S SAINT: The saint revered as Santa Claus appears today in the Advent calendar. Nicholas served as bishop of Myra in modern day Turkey, and became the subject of innumerable legends and icons. Patron of sailors, scholars, travelers, thieves, virgins and children, his generosity continues to inspire the giving of gifts. According to the story, he rescued three virgins from prostitution by an anonymous gift toward their dowries. Provide some activities for children today, recalling stories from the life of Nicholas and supplying gifts for the needy.

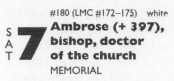

SAT 7 #180 (LMC #172–175)   white
Ambrose (+ 397), bishop, doctor of the church
MEMORIAL

Isaiah's prophecy promises a day when God will hear the people of Zion, give them bread and water, teach them, guide them, fatten their herds, fill their streams, brighten the very light of day and give them no more cause to cry. The psalm praises the goodness of God who rebuilds Jerusalem. Its refrain comes from the same chapter of Isaiah that provides the first reading today. In the gospel, Jesus cures the illnesses of the crowds and sends his disciples to do the same.

▪ TODAY'S SAINT: A soldier and administrator by profession, Ambrose was still a catechumen in Milan when the people chose him as their new bishop. His influence in the court repressed the spread of Arianism and forced Emperor Theodosius I into public penance for a massacre at Thessalonica. Several of Ambrose's Latin hymns still appear in the *Liturgia horarum,* including the first hymn of the week, *Deus, creator omnium.* In English, another text survives as the Advent hymn, "Savior of the Nations Come."

Ambrose's prayer of preparation for the eucharist is in the sacramentary's first appendix. The presidential prayers come from the texts for his memorial.

8 #5 (LMC #5)   violet
Second Sunday of Advent

ORIENTATION

John the Baptist plays the central role today and next Sunday. As an Advent figure, John points not to the birth of Christ, but to his ministry, and ultimately to his death. Advent prepares us for the coming of Christ in many ways. Light a second candle on the wreath today.

LECTIONARY

The opening words of today's first reading bring wondrous consolation. We hear the voice of God speaking through the prophet Isaiah, "Comfort, give comfort to my people." This passage opens the second part of the book of Isaiah. Many scripture scholars believe that this section was composed sometime after the first section of the book by a different hand. It is sometimes called The Book of Consolation, or Deutero-Isaiah, or Second Isaiah. The poetic prophecies of this section must have warmed the hearts of the returning exiles who first heard them. They never fail to inspire the faithful today. George Frideric Handel opens his 1742 oratorio *Messiah* with a lyrical setting of this text. This prophecy of restoration perfectly fits the tone of Advent, a season that anticipates the coming of God with power.

The responsorial psalm today is also one of the common psalms for the season of Advent (#174/2). If you learn a setting of this, you may sing it every Sunday throughout the season. The refrain prays for the coming of "salvation"—a key word that signifies our longing for the coming of Jesus, whose name means "Savior." The psalm envisions that the virtues of heaven and earth will meet.

The Second Letter of Peter makes its only Advent appearance today. The letter, widely regarded as pseudonymous, is directed to a general ("catholic") audience, not to a specific local church. In today's passage the author treats the problem of the delay in Jesus' return. The early church expected Jesus' imminent return, and his delay was causing problems. Today's text says this is not a delay, but a sign of God's patience. The readers are expected to conduct their lives blamelessly while awaiting the coming day of God. We read this appropriate passage during the season that marks our waiting for the coming of our God.

In the gospel, John the Baptist makes his entrance. John wears camel's hair and a leather belt. He dresses like Elijah in 2 Kings 1:8. He appears as a prophet, the last of the old prophets and the bridge to the new covenant. He calls people to repentance and prepares them to watch for someone more powerful coming soon. John heralds the arrival of Jesus and becomes a star figure of this season.

SACRAMENTARY

Today's opening prayer is based on an Advent prayer from the eighth century. The alternative prayer levels a timely holiday caution against greed. To conclude the general intercessions try one of the opening prayers for June 24. An excerpt from the Advent prayers of the United

Church of Canada could also work well: "O God, we pray that in our hearts your way may be prepared, that the path among us, by which your Spirit comes, may be made straight (1T006). The solemn blessing over the people is brief, but you may use the generic threefold one for Advent.

The sacramentary suggests opening the celebration with music based on Isaiah 30: "The Lord will come to save all nations." The recommended communion refrain from Baruch heralds the joy that is coming from God.

OTHER IDEAS

Call attention to the images of John in your church. Many places of worship have one at least in the baptistry. You need not move the image to highlight it. The focus of Mass should always be the table and the word.

Be sure to announce tomorrow's solemnity. It may surprise some people who do not know it gets moved back a day this year. Assure people that the solemnity transfers, but the obligation does not. Even so, Mary is the patron of the United States and many other countries under this title. It is most appropriate for the community to gather for prayer tomorrow.

An Advent penance service this week can build on John's call to repentance.

#689 (LMC #429)   white

MON 9 The Immaculate Conception of the Blessed Virgin Mary
SOLEMNITY

ORIENTATION

Ordinarily we celebrate this day on December 8. This year December 8 is an Advent Sunday, so we move the celebration to the next available day on the calendar.

The Solemnity of the Immaculate Conception is the patronal feast for the United States. Other countries claiming the same patronage include Nicaragua and Panama. But this year the solemnity is not a holy day of obligation because the day has been transferred.

The mystery we celebrate this day is widely confused with the virginal conception of Jesus, a confusion underscored by the choice of gospel passage for this solemnity, Gabriel's annunciation to Mary. The Immaculate Conception refers to the belief that Mary was conceived without sin. The idea was first expressed in the earliest Christian centuries, and in 1854 Pope Pius IX proclaimed it a dogma. Many new parishes established about that time adopted this title of Mary. The date of course is nine months before the feast of the Birth of Mary, September 8. (She will arrive one day premature this liturgical year!)

This is liturgical trivia but reveals something important about the thought processes of framers of the liturgical year: Eastern Rites observe the Conception of Mary on December 9 every year. Mary's birth is observed, as in the west, on September 8. John the Baptist's conception is observed on September 23 and his birth, as in the west, is celebrated on June 24. For Mary and for John eastern liturgical calendars make sure that the periods between conception and birth are not perfectly nine months long. In contrast, as in the west, the conception of Jesus is celebrated on March 25 and the birth on December 25—which to their way of thinking indicates the "perfection" and unique status of Christ.

Today is the patronal feast of Paraguay, but under the title Our Lady of Caacupé. Tradition holds that a newly converted Indian escaped after an attack by pagans and carved a wooden statue of Mary, which has been enshrined at Caacupé. This solemnity is observed as a holy day of obligation in all Latin American countries except Costa Rica, the Dominican Republic, Ecuador and Mexico.

LECTIONARY

The Bible is silent about the precise dogma. The gospel of the annunciation, though, remembers Mary as a person who cooperates with God's plan. Read as prophecy, the Genesis passage anticipates the coming of a woman whose offspring will oppose the serpent of temptation. For this reason, Mary the Immaculate Conception is frequently depicted in iconography trampling a snake. Paul speaks of our predestination for glory, a mystery made personal in Mary's preservation from sin. The marvels of the God who can accomplish these things are sung in today's psalm.

SACRAMENTARY

The alternative opening prayer asks God to "prepare once again a world" for the Son. Otherwise, no hint of Advent appears in the prayers. The Glory to God and the Creed are said or sung. Note the special preface for this solemnity. Eucharistic Prayer III was composed with days like this in mind. Consider using the Advent solemn blessing instead of the optional one that appears in the sacramentary for this day. If you prefer the blessing for the feast, you can find it with inclusive language in the *Book of Blessings,* Appendix II, #20.

OTHER IDEAS

Sing the same gospel and eucharistic prayer acclamations throughout the Advent season, including today. They will add cohesion to the season and simplify matters for the assembly. Sing a setting of the Glory to God that you plan to use at Christmas, to help everyone sing it well on that special day.

By Flowing Waters (393–402) has a complete suite of antiphons and psalms for this solemnity.

Decorate the images of Mary in and around your worship space with flowers and candles. Introduce the liturgy with an explanation of the feast's meaning. Find model general intercessions and concluding collects in *Prayers for Sundays and Seasons.* Consider intercessory prayers for those awaiting the birth of a child, those yearning for justice, and the development of the charisms of women in church and society.

■ THIS CELEBRATION IRONICALLY SUPPRESSES the optional memorial for Juan Diego (Cuatitlatoatzin), who saw the vision of Our Lady of Guadalupe. You may refer to the event in the general intercessions or commentary for today.

Ordinarily, Juan Diego's memorial is obligatory in Ecuador and Mexico, and optional in Argentina, Bolivia, Chile, Colombia, Costa Rica, Cuba, the Dominican Republic, Ecuador, El Salvador, Guatemala, Honduras, Nicaragua, Panama, Paraguay, Peru, Puerto Rico, Uruguay, Venezuela—and, of course, the United States.

Ecuador lists this date as an obligatory memorial for Blessed Narcisa de Jesús Martillo Morán (+ 1869), who devoted her life to prayer and painful penance. Its observance is suppressed this year.

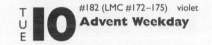
T U E 10 #182 (LMC #172–175) violet
Advent Weekday

Our first reading today, the consoling opener to Isaiah 40, repeats the one we heard on Sunday. Nonetheless, it is such a gloriously famous passage of comfort that no one should mind. Boisterous Psalm 96 draws its confident refrain from the first reading today: "The Lord our God comes in strength." The immense care God offers even individuals shines through Jesus' parable of the hundred sheep.

■ TODAY IS THE ANNIVERSARY of the death of the Cistercian monk and spiritual writer Thomas Merton (+ 1968). Consult his writings and audiotapes for spiritual advice that relates even to people outside a monastery's walls.

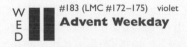
W E D 11 #183 (LMC #172–175) violet
Advent Weekday

Optional Memorial of Damasus I (+ 384), pope/white ■ Those feeling exhausted already by holiday preparations will find comfort in today's texts. Isaiah says God "does not faint nor grow weary." The Almighty gives strength to the fainting and makes vigor abound for the weak. The gospel answers this theme with Jesus' supportive words, "Come to me, you who find life burdensome, and I will refresh you." Today's psalm blesses God, who is slow to anger and abounding in kindness.

■ TODAY'S SAINT: Damasus was the son of a priest and eventually served the same parish his father administered in Rome. A poet, reformer, and pious man, he served the poor and won the esteem of the irascible Saint Jerome, who served as his secretary when Damasus became pope.

T
H 12 #707–712 (LMC #447–451) white
U **Our Lady of Guadalupe**
FEAST

ORIENTATION

Today's feast honors the mother of Jesus as mother also of the Americas. Mary appeared to a local Indian, who then presented himself to the bishop. At first doubtful, the bishop believed in the apparition after Juan Diego returned, his tilma filled with roses from the snowy heights of Tepeyac. When the roses fell to the ground they revealed the image of Mary on the tilma, now enshrined in Mexico City. Mary resembles a *mestiza,* a woman of Native American and European heritage, representing God's affirmation of all American natives. She wears the blue band of expectant Aztec women, and on her womb appears a flower, the Aztec symbol for new life and a new era. She blocks the sun, which the natives had worshiped as a god. Like the church in Advent, she awaits the birth of Christ who will usher in a new era of peace and justice.

This is the patronal feast of Mexico, where it is a holy day of obligation. Mexico and Guatemala observe today as a solemnity. Today's observance does not appear on the church's universal calendar, but it is kept as a feast in the

United States, and also in Argentina, Bolivia, Chile, Colombia, Costa Rica, Cuba, the Dominican Republic, Ecuador, El Salvador, Honduras, Nicaragua, Panama, Paraguay, Peru, Puerto Rico, Uruguay and Venezuela.

LECTIONARY

Any readings from the common of the Virgin Mary may be used today, although in making choices, keep an eye toward the readings heard on December 8 and those to be heard on the Fourth Sunday of the season. Recommended are Zechariah 2:14–17 (707.11) or Revelation 11:19a; 12:1–6a, 10ab (708.2); and Luke 1:26–38 (712.4) or Luke 1:39–47 (712.5). Two readings will suffice, but you may choose three.

SACRAMENTARY

The Mass calls for the Glory to God, but not the Creed. Today's presidential prayers can be found in the 1994 Sacramentary Supplement. Either preface of Mary (P 56 or P 57) may be used. The second echoes Mary's *Magnificat.* A third preface can be found in Appendix X, #4, for the Mass of Mary, Mother of the Church. A solemn blessing may be taken from those for Advent (#1) or Mary (#15).

OTHER IDEAS

Today, as a feast, provides another opportunity to sing the Glory to God you will use at Christmas. Your community may provide a bilingual celebration, fiesta or music that will highlight the ethnic origins of the feast. Honor the image of Our Lady of Guadalupe in your church.

F
R 13 #185 (LMC #172–175)   red
I **Lucy (+ 304), martyr**
MEMORIAL

Starting today the daily lectionary turns its full attention to John the Baptist. From now through December 16 we have a series of gospels that all mention this prophetic figure. Jesus reveals the obstinacy of his contemporaries by complaining of their treatment of himself and of John the Baptist.

The semicontinuous series of readings from Isaiah concludes today with a similar complaint: Israel would enjoy prosperity if only the people would hearken to God's commandments. Psalm 1 describes the two ways of responding to God's law.

For the remainder of the season, the first readings will now follow the gospel's theme, reversing the pattern of the first part of Advent, during which the semicontinuous passages from Isaiah set the theme for the day, and the gospels answered.

■ TODAY'S SAINT: The Sicilian Lucy took a silent vow of virginity early in her life, prayed to Saint Agatha for the healing of her mother's hemorrhage, was arrested during a persecution of Christians, and martyred. Because her name means "light," her feast appropriately falls during Advent, and Christian art depicts her holding her eyes. According to one legend, her tormentors removed her eyes; according to another, the virgin herself gouged them out and presented them to a disappointed suitor.

The opening prayer comes from the common of saints. You may choose the other presidential prayers from the Advent weekday or the commons of virgins or martyrs. The preface for martyrs (P 66) may be used. Lucy is among the saints listed in the first eucharistic prayer.

#185 (LMC #172–175)   white

S A T **14**

John of the Cross (+ 1591), presbyter, religious, doctor of the church
MEMORIAL

Today's gospel continues the series of references to John the Baptist from Matthew. Jesus connects him with Elijah, one of the greatest prophets. Because the Bible never reports Elijah's death—only that he left in a fiery chariot—speculation abounded that he would return, as reported in today's first reading. Psalm 80 calls upon God to save, a frequent Advent theme that will be realized in the birth of a child whose name means "Savior."

■ TODAY'S SAINT: John of the Cross is still admired as a mystic and poet. A Carmelite reformer, he befriended Teresa of Avila. Your community might appreciate a bilingual presentation of one of his poems in the bulletin.

✸ **15** **#8 (LMC #8)   rose or violet**

Third Sunday of Advent

ORIENTATION

John the Baptist continues his central role as the prophetic figure whose life and ministry points the way to Jesus. The optional rose vestments and rose candle on the wreath announce that the season of waiting nears its end. This is one of the Sundays that used to be identified by the first Latin word of its entrance antiphon, and hence the first word of the day's Mass. Some people still call it *Gaudete*.

LECTIONARY

The cause of joy today is not merely the approach of celebrating Christmas. The joy also pertains to the kind of Messiah God will bring to Israel. Isaiah speaks in the person of one anointed with the spirit of God. With this anointing the prophet brings glad tidings to the poor, heals the brokenhearted, and releases prisoners. The Messiah of God will bring justice. That is the kind of coming we await this Advent.

The refrain from today's responsory comes from the first reading. But the rest of the text is Mary's *Magnificat* from Luke. Its appearance advances the gospel story of the birth of Jesus, an account we will hear in loving detail over the next few weeks. It also echoes the theme of the first reading when it stresses God's care for the hungry and the poor.

Throughout the New Testament letters, we can find references to the spiritual predicament of the early Christians who expected the swift return of Jesus but needed to behave in the meantime. The Advent lectionary locates these texts and lets us hear from them in the second reading. If you're listening for something pertaining to Christmas, you'll miss the point, but once you start listening for expressions like "the day of the Lord" or "the coming of our Lord" you'll see the connection immediately. Today's text is a fine example. Paul's First Letter to the Thessalonians may be the earliest book composed among the Christian scriptures. Today's passage opens with the theme of this Sunday, "Rejoice!" and closes with a reference to the coming of Jesus. Paul calls on us Christians to perfect ourselves in holiness and to rejoice as we await the coming of our Savior.

John the Baptist appears as expected in the gospel. However, today's passage is from the fourth gospel, by the evangelist who never calls John by the popular appellation "the Baptist." He's just "John." But we know who he is because this story parallels those we find in the other gospels. In this episode, people question John about his identity. They want to know if he is one of the promised figures from the scriptures whose return was expected some day: the Messiah, Elijah, or a prophet like Moses. John points toward Jesus.

SACRAMENTARY

The Glory to God is omitted. Both versions of the opening prayer highlight the theme of rejoicing. The first has roots in the fifth century. The message of either prayer will convince if the presider's face and voice radiate joy. The liturgy calls for the first Advent preface again today, even though the second says more about John the Baptist. A solemn blessing appears in the sacramentary, identical to the one for the first Sunday. The prayers over the people provide other suitable options, like #5.

OTHER IDEAS

You may open the liturgy with a song that recalls the entrance antiphon from Philippians 4:4–5: "Rejoice in the Lord always; again I say, rejoice! The Lord is near." The recommended communion antiphon comes from one of the most-quoted passages of the season: "Our God will come to save us." The source passage, this day's first reading, inspires both the recommended psalm and communion antiphon of the day. Festive music will help keep the spirit of this Sunday consistent with its prayers.

MON 16
#187 (LMC #172–175)   violet
Advent Weekday

The popular story of the Magi has some background in the lesser-known story of Balaam. In the prophecy we hear today, Balaam envisions a star advancing from Jacob, one that Christians believe later guided the Magi to the coming Savior. You can almost hear an echo of this application in the psalm for the day: "Your ways, O Lord, make known to me." This is one of the common psalms for Advent and may be used throughout the season.

We have already heard the principal texts about John the Baptist, but the lectionary serves up any reference it can find during this period of Advent. Today's comes from a controversy between Jesus and the chief priests and elders. The interpretation of John's baptism becomes a source of dispute. Here, John points the way to Jesus as the Messiah so focused on his mission that he will cause division.

TUE 17
#193 (LMC #172–175)   violet
Late Advent Weekday

Today begins the final stage of this season. The octave before Christmas shifts Advent into a reflection on the coming celebration of the birth of our Savior. We leave John the Baptist behind after following parts of his story for the past week. Note that the proper lectionary and sacramentary texts are the ones entitled "December 17"—not "Tuesday of the Third Week of Advent." The lectionary directs us to the solemn opening of Matthew's gospel, a text that requires practice and patience, impressive in proclamation more by its overall effect than by its details. It is paired with a prophecy from Genesis that the scepter of governance shall never

depart from Judah. Psalm 72 returns, a prayer for the coming of a ruler who is just.

The opening prayer of the day recalls the humanity and divinity of Jesus, a perfect preparation for the gospel. The second Advent preface should now be proclaimed. Alan Griffiths published another translation of this (Weekdays before Christmas 2) in *We Give You Thanks and Praise* (Sheed & Ward, 2000).

THE O ANTIPHONS

These antiphons provide the most strikingly beautiful feature of these days before Christmas. Composed for the *Magnificat* at evening prayer, they now also appear as versicles for the gospel acclamation at Mass (although the lectionary fails to distinguish which antiphon is assigned to which day). Each of the antiphons calls for the coming of Christ by a different title, and sometimes multiple titles pile up in profusion. The antiphons receive a distant but profound echo on the Solemnity of the Ascension, when the antiphon calls for the coming of the Spirit. That Ascension chant follows the same musical formula as the Advent antiphons do.

This final week of Advent is truly "solstice," "sun-stand-still," as the day lengths hover at their shortest (in the Northern Hemisphere) before beginning their slow increase at Christmas.

You may mark the seven holy evenings with a seven-branched candelabrum. Light one more candle each evening until all are lit the evening before Christmas Eve. The seven-branched menorah of the Jewish Temple signified God's presence on earth, a presence Christians celebrate in Christ.

The antiphons begin this evening with *"O Sapientia,"* "O Wisdom": "teach us to walk in the

paths of knowledge." If your community has one or more persons who can sing chant, they will beautify the liturgy by singing this classic antiphon. If you decide to sing a verse of "O Come, O Come Emmanuel" with the alleluia each day, begin today with verse two. Other settings include Marty Haugen's "My Soul in Stillness Waits" (GIA, 2652); Michael Joncas's "Let the King of Glory Come"; and the chant adaptation in *Worship: Liturgy of the Hours, Leader's Edition.*

■ JOURNEY TO BETHLEHEM: To mark this week in sympathy with the liturgy, each day this upcoming week some parishes move the nativity-scene statues of Mary, Joseph and the donkey through the church bit by bit, closer to the empty manger each day. In some places the stable with the empty manger is set up for this final week of Advent and its straw is blessed and distributed this coming Sunday.

WED 18
#194 (LMC #172–175)   violet
Late Advent Weekday

Matthew's account of the infancy of Jesus continues from yesterday's genealogy. In a story much briefer than Luke's, Matthew tells of the betrothal, annunciation, virginal conception, prophecy, naming and even the birth of Jesus. More verses from Psalm 72 announce the justice of God's reign, a theme explored in the prophecy from Jeremiah. The birth of this child will bring justice to the earth.

■ O ADONAI: Adonai, a sacred title for the ineffable name of God, translates most commonly into English as "Lord." When the O Antiphon assigns this title to the coming of Christ, it proclaims the incarnation. The God who redeemed Israel with an outstretched arm comes in human form.

THU 19 #195 (LMC #172–175) violet
Late Advent Weekday

We turn now to Luke's account of the events leading to the birth of Jesus. His story guides the daily Mass lectionary from today's celebration through the octave of Christmas. It begins with the birth of John the Baptist. The angel announces John's birth in today's passage, showing him to be the forerunner of Christ even in the manner of his birth. The consecration of a child to God from the mother's womb appears also in Psalm 71. In the first reading the angel's annunciation of Samson's birth and spiritual discipline prefigures the annunciation of John.

■ O RADIX IESSE: The image of today's O Antiphon is the root of Jesse, prophesied in Isaiah 11, a passage we have already heard twice this season.

FRI 20 #196 (LMC #172–175) violet
Late Advent Weekday

Luke's poetic account of the annunciation is one of his finest literary creations. The proclamation of the good news of salvation meets the perfect recipient, a servant of God, ready to follow the divine will. Bernard of Clairvaux's homily in today's Liturgy of the Hours perfectly complements the religious spirit surrounding the annunciation to Mary. Isaiah prophesies to Ahaz that a young woman shall bear a son, Emmanuel. The gospel and the liturgy see beyond that ancestral prophecy all the way to the birth of Jesus. Pilgrims on their way to the Jerusalem temple sang what is now called Psalm 24. We sing it today, bidding the Lord to enter the temple, bidding the Word to enter the womb of Mary.

■ O CLAVIS DAVID: The one who holds the key of David (Isaiah 22:22, Revelation 3:7) opens and closes with absolute authority. Today's O Antiphon salutes the key of David, the personification of authority, and the one whose judgment we both fear and welcome.

SAT 21 #197 (LMC #172–175) violet
Late Advent Weekday

Optional Memorial of Peter Canisius (+ 1597), presbyter, doctor of the church / violet ▪ The shortest day of the year, the first day of winter, draws a surprising scripture passage: "See, the winter is past." The Song of Songs, which the lectionary mines infrequently, remains an option for today's first reading. The love poem expresses the spirit of joyful longing that the new Israel feels for the coming of Christ, its divine spouse. That joy bursts through the darkness of a wintry dawn. The alternative passage for today's first reading summons similar joy, for God is in the midst of Israel. This spirit continues through Psalm 33: "Our soul waits for the Lord." Why all this happiness? The gospel proclaims that when Mary and Elizabeth met—one a virgin, the other too old to conceive, both pregnant—Elizabeth's baby, John the Baptist, in imitation of all the faithful at the nearness of Jesus, leapt for joy.

■ O ORIENS: Singers of today's O Antiphon in Latin relish the opening phrase, "O Oriens." It has the biggest O of all the antiphons. It applies the image of the rising sun, "the East," to the coming of the Savior. On the darkest day of the year, it calls for the sun to shine with the light of life, a light strong enough to pierce the grave.

■ TODAY'S SAINT: Peter Canisius, a Jesuit serving the church in the wake of the Reformation, challenged the church to reform and summarized our teaching in a much-used catechism. Because these final days of Advent take precedence in the same way the days of Lent take precedence over the memorials of the saints, if you observe Peter's memorial, vesture stays Advent violet and the texts for December 21 are used without substitution, except that the opening prayer at Mass can be the prayer for the saint. Or use the saint's prayer at the conclusion to the general intercessions.

☼ 22 #12 (LMC #12) violet
Fourth Sunday of Advent

ORIENTATION

Lighting the last candle on the wreath sets the full symbol ablaze with light, alerting us to the imminent celebration of the coming of Christ. For many weeks the secular culture has been celebrating "the holidays" while we have been celebrating Advent. We have heard the prophecies that proclaim the coming of Jesus not just at Bethlehem, but as judge at the end of time. Today for the first time our Advent scriptures tell the events that led to the birth of Christ.

In the lectionary, the sacramentary, and the *Liturgy of the Hours,* the texts for December 22 yield to those for the Fourth Sunday of Advent.

LECTIONARY

Today's prophecy comes from Nathan, who appears as a character in this passage from the Second Book of Samuel. David's desire to build a house for God occasions Nathan's advice to wait. God will build a house for David instead. That "house" is the kingdom that endures forever and reaches its perfection in the coming of the Son of David, Jesus.

The royal psalm that answers this reading remembers the same event. God promised David to confirm his posterity forever.

At the conclusion of Paul's letter to the Romans, he gives a final word of praise to God. In it, Paul remembers that God's revelation of the mystery of Jesus Christ was kept secret for long ages. Advent is the season that commemorates those long ages of the hidden mystery.

Luke's account of the annunciation appeared in the weekday lectionary just a couple days ago, but it is hard to find a more fitting gospel to proclaim on the Sunday before Christmas. Here is the point toward which the lectionary has been working. We have traced the mystery of God's love from the big Advent theme of the Second Coming through the appearance of John the Baptist who points the way to Jesus' public ministry. Now we finally step back into the story that tells of Jesus' birth. Mary says yes to God, and in that breath of the Spirit she becomes a model for the loving response of all creation to God's revelation.

SACRAMENTARY

Turn back a few pages from yesterday's celebration to find today's. We still omit the Glory to God. Today's opening prayer, which appeared in the missal for the first time after the Council of Trent, also concludes the recitation of a popular devotional prayer, the *Angelus.* The alternative recalls how Mary placed her life at the service of God's plan. The second Advent preface (P 2) continues throughout the second half of the season, even though the *Collection*

of Masses of the Blessed Virgin Mary includes one for the Annunciation (2). The entrance and communion antiphons today present two classic texts for the season, the *Rorate caeli* and the Emmanuel prophecy. A simple prayer over the people is provided after the communion prayer, but the seasonal solemn blessing may also be used.

Today's entrance antiphon, *Rorate caeli,* comes from Isaiah 45, "Let the clouds rain down the Just One, and the earth bring forth a Savior." Some translations say "justice" for "Just One" and "salvation" for "Savior," but the antiphon personifies these virtues to help us recognize the prophetic anticipation of the Messiah's birth. The suggested communion antiphon comes from Isaiah's prediction of the birth of Emmanuel (7:14).

OTHER IDEAS

A busy, rich week is ahead! Be sure everyone receives a printed copy of the liturgical schedule for Christmas, or e-mail it to parishioners today. Invite people to assist with decorations. Provide refreshments or simple gifts for those who do. If you offer first vespers on Christmas Eve, the office of readings or a vigil preceding midnight or late evening Mass, be sure people know when these events will occur.

In some parishes manger straw is blessed and distributed today, a task made less messy if the straw is bagged first, a job done earlier in the week by maybe a youth group.

■ O REX GENTIUM: Today's O Antiphon calls for the coming of the king of all the nations and the cornerstone that binds together the "mighty arch" of humankind. Even though Jesus kept his focus on Israel throughout his ministry,

his apostles took the message to the ends of earth, to fulfill the prophecy that the messiah would unite the world's peoples.

MON **23** #199 (LMC #172–175) violet
Late Advent Weekday

Optional memorial of John of Kanty (+ 1473), priest / violet ▪ The sequence of events leading up to the birth of Jesus reaches a climax in the birth of John the Baptist. John, who will point the way to Jesus in his ministry and death, is shown preparing us for Jesus also by his birth.

We finally hear from Malachi one of the reasons why Elijah figures into the story of John the Baptist. The prophecy says that God will send Elijah before the day of the Lord comes. John resembles Elijah not just in dress, but also as God's messenger. The seasonal psalm calls out for God the Savior, and its refrain comes from Jesus' own words predicting the coming of the Son of Man.

■ O EMMANUEL: Not surprisingly, the O Antiphons conclude this evening with this great title of Jesus, Emmanuel. It sums up the theme of Matthew's gospel: Jesus appears by this title at the beginning and promises to "be with" his followers at the end. This, the last of antiphons, is better known as the first verse of the popular hymn based on the series.

In Latin, the antiphons form a reverse acrostic. Take the first letter of each of the titles of Jesus, spell them backwards, and you get *ero cras,* "I will be [there] tomorrow."

■ TODAY'S SAINT: John studied at the University of Kraków, was ordained a priest, and lived a very ascetic life in imitation of the desert monks. Unable to adapt to parish life, he had a successful teaching career in the field of scripture. He died on Christmas

Eve. Because these are the final days of Advent, if you observe this memorial, the vesture must remain Advent violet, and the only change in the Mass is that the opening prayer for the saint may replace the opening prayer of December 23 (or else be used as the collect for the general intercessions). That's how important these Advent days are.

TUE 24
#200 (LMC #172–175)   violet
Late Advent Weekday

There is no O Antiphon because this evening will begin the celebration of Christmas. Many parishes with a full evening liturgical schedule do not offer Mass this morning, but those who do will find it a beautiful conclusion to the celebration of Advent.

Luke's account of the events leading up to the birth of Jesus concludes with the prophecy of Zechariah, a hymn know as the *Benedictus,* sung at morning prayer every day of the year. The text, which rejoices in the salvation arriving "in the house of David," is paired with a prophecy about the permanence of David's "house," a theme echoed in Psalm 89. The gospel acclamation today may repeat any of the O Antiphons, but those for the Dayspring or Emmanuel are most appropriate.

The opening prayer for this morning is a rare oration addressed directly to Jesus, not through Jesus. It sums up Advent's mighty call, "O come, O come."

■ AN OLD TRADITION commemorates our first parents today, "Saints Adam and Eve." These holy ancestors express our longing to embrace all our human family in the wedding of heaven and earth, consummated in the incarnation and paschal mystery of Jesus, in the potential sanctification of all people.

DECEMBER 1, 2002
First Sunday of Advent

It Must Be God's Fault
Isaiah 63:16b–17, 19b; 64:2b–7
"Oh, that you would rend the heavens and come down!"

IT must be God's fault. That's the conclusion Isaiah reaches. And who of us hasn't thought the same? If things don't go our way, if someone hurts us, if someone leaves us—even if the mess is our own fault—we blame God.

People sin, but Isaiah asks God, "Why do you let us wander from your ways?" People show no remorse, but Isaiah asks God, "Why do you harden our hearts so that we fear you not?" It must be God's fault.

Isaiah's prayer opens the season of Advent because of a specific request it makes: "Rend the heavens and come down." In the midst of our misfortune, sorrow and sin, when we realize our own strength fails to make life any better, to eliminate hurt, or to erase the past, we finally turn to God for a solution. Let there be no veil concealing heaven from earth. Let God rip it open, come down here, and save us from the messiness of life.

God did just that on the first Christmas Day.

As we stand on the threshold of another Advent, we ask God to do it again. Even if our mess isn't God's fault, we need God's help to set us free.

Written by Paul Turner. © 2002 Archdiocese of Chicago, Liturgy Training Publications; 1-800-933-1800; www.ltp.org.

DECEMBER 8, 2002
Second Sunday of Advent

Paving a Direct Route
Isaiah 40:1–5, 9–11
"In the desert prepare the way of the Lord!"

WHENEVER a highway changes from two lanes to four, you can often see the improvements. The old highway follows the dips and curves of the landscape. The new highway better controls the landscape. It is straighter and more level. The engineers have figured out how to improve the road, and citizens have supported the additional expense.

People like straight highways. They are quicker, safer and more pleasant.

In the prophecy of Isaiah, a voice cries out, "In the desert prepare the way of the Lord!" John the Baptist quoted this passage to prepare people for the coming of Jesus.

Make a straight highway in the wasteland. Fill in the valleys and lower the mountains. Make a smooth, direct road in your spiritual life.

During Advent we prepare our hearts for the coming of Christ in our lives. In the past we formed habits as sturdy as two-lane roads. They get us where we want to go, but sometimes not by the most direct route.

We have only a few weeks till Christmas. It is time to move the roadblocks and detours that keep us from encountering Christ. Hardness of heart, stinginess of time, or unbending habits: Which of these need repair on your highway toward Christ?

Written by Paul Turner. © 2002 Archdiocese of Chicago, Liturgy Training Publications; 1-800-933-1800; www.ltp.org.

DECEMBER 9, 2002
The Immaculate Conception of Mary

Mary, the New Eve
Genesis 3:9–15, 20
"The man called his wife Eve, because she was the mother of all the living."

HAVE you ever seen an image of Mary standing on a snake? Look at statues or paintings around your church or in your home. One of the most popular depictions of Mary, the mother of Jesus, shows her standing on a snake.

You don't have to be an expert in the gospels to know that there is no record of such an episode in Mary's life. Rather, the image depicts the fulfillment of a prophecy from the book of Genesis.

After Adam and Eve sinned, God punished both of them, as well as the serpent. God predicted that Eve's offspring would strike at the serpent's head and the serpent would strike at the offspring's heel.

Christians see in this passage a prediction of the mission of Jesus. Mary is the new Eve and her son would crush the power of sin, temptation and death. Whenever you see Mary standing on a snake, you know she is the one who bore the One that put an end to death and revealed the resurrection.

Is there a snake tempting you? Is there a sin that bothers you? You can find in Mary and Jesus the strength and power to resist temptation. You can find in Mary, the mother of the living. You can find in the Lord, the giver of life.

Written by Paul Turner. © 2002 Archdiocese of Chicago, Liturgy Training Publications; 1-800-933-1800; www.ltp.org.

DECEMBER 15, 2002
Third Sunday of Advent

A Christmas Wish List
Isaiah 61:1–2a, 10–11
"The Lord GOD will make justice and praise spring up before all nations."

YOUNG children sit on Santa's lap to answer the question that consumes them these days: What do you want for Christmas?

The child in each of us still wants stuff like toys and new clothes. But deep inside us we have more basic needs. We need security, fairness and love. We want something huge for Christmas. We want peace on earth and justice for the oppressed. We want poverty eliminated and wars ceased.

Isaiah promises we will not be disappointed. He promises that God will do such wondrous things that justice and praise will spring up in every nation. When God is the joy of our soul, Isaiah says, a robe of salvation clothes us and a mantle of justice enfolds us. When God is our joy, we feel as rich as royalty, no matter how poor our state.

What does the earth want for Christmas? It wants good news for the poor, healing for the brokenhearted, liberty for captives, and release for prisoners. The earth wants what God alone can provide.

What do you want for Christmas? Is it something for you, or something for the earth? Will it hinder or help the earth to get what it needs?

Written by Paul Turner. © 2002 Archdiocese of Chicago, Liturgy Training Publications; 1-800-933-1800; www.ltp.org.

DECEMBER 22, 2002
Fourth Sunday of Advent

God Loves a Cheerful Giver—and Receiver
2 Samuel 7:1–5, 8b–12, 14a, 16
"The LORD will establish a house for you."

DAVID and God were not exactly equals. David was king, of course, but that still gave him no leverage over God. Even when David wanted to do God a favor, God had complete control over the success of the king's intent.

David had a great idea. He saw how beautiful the house was where he lived, and how simple the cedar house was for the ark of God. David wanted to build God a glorious temple. But God said no.

God had other ideas. It was not David's position to provide a home for God. It was God's position to provide a home for David. Eventually God gave David more than a home. God promised that David's throne would stand firm forever.

God's promise was fulfilled in two ways. David did not build God a temple, but David's Solomon did. And, according to members of the church, David's throne would last forever because of a child born into the house and lineage of David, a holy child born in the city of David, Bethlehem.

In preparing for Christmas, you may have tried to do God favors through your prayers and through your charity toward others. But God is doing you the favor. God gives you the gift of salvation in the mystery of Christmas.

Written by Paul Turner. © 2002 Archdiocese of Chicago, Liturgy Training Publications; 1-800-933-1800; www.ltp.org.

CHRISTMAS

The Meaning

THE responsorial psalm for Christmas sings its meaning: "Today is born our Savior, Christ the Lord!"

Christmas is a celebration of the birth of Christ, the eternal Word who became flesh for us. The psalm has us singing that "today" is when this happens. Not "Today is the anniversary of the birth of our Savior," but "Today is born our Savior." Through the mystery of God and religious belief, we enter into God's eternal presence in this remarkable season. All time becomes collapsed into an eternal now. When we celebrate Christmas Day, we celebrate the birth of Jesus today, in our hearts, in our community, and in our world.

Our belief and actions bring Christmas to life. Whenever we give a gift of charity, sing of God's goodness, or support the needy, we are the body of Christ, newly born, bringing life and redemption to a wary world.

■ CHRISTMAS CRIES OUT FOR COMMUNITY. We are saddened whenever we hear of someone celebrating Christmas alone. This time of year is meant to be shared. People travel great distances to be present with those they love, and others telephone or send cards to family and friends. This celebration of love, symbolized in the custom of giving gifts, sits within the framework of the incarnation. God's love for us inspires us to show love for others.

■ A FESTIVAL OF MANY DAYS: The liturgical celebration of Christmas extends for several weeks beyond Christmas Day. The mystery is so deep that it requires a series of occasions to explore.

Epiphany and the Baptism of the Lord are celebrations of the implications of Christmas Day. It is not enough that God became one like us. This mystery must be shared with the world. This manifestation (epiphany) of Jesus to the nations shows how important Christmas is. It also shows the global significance of the incarnation. Jesus comes not just for a few people, not just for one race. His arrival announces salvation to all the nations of the world.

■ A FESTIVAL AT THE ONSET OF LENGTHENING DAYS: The date of Christmas coincides with the time of year in the northern hemisphere when the days begin to lengthen. The return of the sun's rays symbolizes the birth of the Son of God, who radiates the light of eternal life upon the entire world. In some works of art, the light seems to shine from the baby Jesus upon the faces of those gathered around. He is the source of light for all who believe.

■ THE DATE OF JESUS' BIRTH IS UNKNOWN. No accurate records tell us the day of the year or even the year on the calendar. The Bible seems to have a prejudice against the celebration of birth anniversaries—the only ones mentioned are of the Pharaoh of Egypt in the days of Joseph (who had his baker strangled after the birthday party), King Antiochus the madman, and King Herod, the murderer of John the Baptist.

The observance of December 25 evolved probably because it falls nine months after the Solemnity of the Annunciation, March 25, a date that had already been observed on the calendar. March 25 was selected for the Annunciation because that had been presumed as the date of the crucifixion, calculated as Passover in the year Jesus died.

Among the ancients, some regarded it a sign of greatness if an individual died on the anniversary of the day she or he was born. A slightly different tradition formed that Jesus died on the day he was conceived, giving him status as the divine and perfect human.

So, the theory goes that our ancestors thought Jesus died on March 25 because that was Passover, and that he was conceived on March 25 because he was perfect enough to die on the day of his conception, and that in his perfection he was born nine months to the day after he was conceived. March 25 and December 25, the day of the conception and the birth, are a perfect octave before the calends of the respective months, which is also, to the ancient way of thinking, an emblem of perfection.

Our ancestors regarded it as good news— that even the calendar proclaims Jesus' identity, Christ our God, the Lord of time and of history.

The year of Jesus' birth was determined by Dionysius Exiguus ("Dennis the Short"), a learned scholar engaged by Pope John I to perform this task. Using the best data at hand, Dionysius computed that Jesus was born 753 years after the founding of Rome. For various reasons, scholars believe he fixed the date four to six years too late. The most devastating argument against Dionysius' reckoning concerns Herod the Great. The two stories of the birth of Jesus (from Matthew and Luke) do not agree on many details. Whenever the two do agree, the detail becomes important. One of those points of agreement is that Jesus was born during the reign of Herod the Great. Modern dating of Herod, though, places his death around 4 BC. That is why it is generally thought that Jesus was born in the period of time we ironically call "before Christ."

■ CHURCH ATTENDANCE ON CHRISTMAS DAY IS HIGH, largely because it is socially acceptable and expected. People come for different reasons. Some genuinely want to celebrate their faith. Others want their children to experience Christmas. Still others want to keep peace in the family. Be prepared to offer hospitality to everyone who comes. This is not the day to gripe about "where are all these people the other 364 days of the year?" Have extra greeters on duty so that everyone who enters the building receives a cheery "Merry Christmas!"

Be church. Be joy. Be welcoming to all as Jesus, who came to save all.

After Christmas Mass, hand out copies of the parish bulletin and the diocesan newspaper. Include lots of information in the bulletin this day, including the address for the parish website and a list of activities and opportunities for the faithful, as well as phone numbers for various needs. Have visitor's cards available in places easily accessible. Make sure that those who want to leave a message for the parish have a simple way to do so. If your music ministry is preparing a special printed program for Christmas, see to it that it includes at least the address, phone number and website of the church, so those who want to contact you later can do so easily.

The most important evangelization we give is a joyful celebration of Christmas. From presider to greeter to choir, the face of every liturgical minister can glow with the joy of salvation.

The Saints

THE saints and festivals of Christmastime keep the spirit of joy alive throughout this season. The saints of the Christmas season have been called *comites Christi*, Christ's companions, a privileged retinue joined around their Savior. The octave of Christmas shares time with them, and the liturgy serves up a peaceful interchange of prayers among the feasts needing recognition at the Liturgy of the Hours and at the eucharist. You may sing the Glory to God many times during this period.

■ OBLIGATORY MEMORIALS OCCUR DURING THE CHRISTMAS SEASON, but, by design, not during the Christmas octave. On a memorial, its opening prayer takes precedence over the seasonal prayer. So does its vestment color, but it will not be noticed when it calls for white in a season that already does so. Christmas is too short a season for distractions. The preface, prayer over the gifts, and the communion prayer may be drawn from the Christmas weekday, from the saint's day, or from the relevant commons. The scriptures may be taken from the lectionary common, but it is better to observe the sequence of seasonal weekday readings.

■ WHEN AN OPTIONAL MEMORIAL OCCURS ON A WEEKDAY IN THE CHRISTMAS SEASON following the Christmas octave, you may celebrate the Mass of the Christmas weekday or of the saint. You may also choose a memorial from the martyrology. In doing so, you may choose the prayers for the saint from the sacramentary as well as readings from the lectionary commons. But normally you will observe the seasonal day to lend unity to these weeks. Another possibility is to use the saint's opening prayer as the conclusion to the general intercessions.

During the Christmas octave itself, if you choose to observe an optional memorial (Thomas Becket or Sylvester), it is treated as a commemoration like those of the last week of Advent. You may use the opening prayer of the saint in place of the seasonal opening prayer, or else use the saint's prayer as the conclusion of the general intercessions, and the vesture remains Christmas white even for Thomas. Otherwise, the prayers and readings for the octave take precedence.

■ VOTIVE MASSES and the Masses for various needs and occasions are used sparingly during Christmas. During the weekdays of the octave, only the bishop may direct their usage for serious need or pastoral advantage. On other weekdays, the presider may choose them only for serious reasons.

The Lectionary

THE mystery of salvation becomes clearer to us as we hear the extraordinary collection of passages from the Christmas lectionary. Most people will think of the infancy narratives when they think of Christmas, as those passages will surely warm the heart. The postnativity narratives are few, and most of these associate with a particular feast. Matthew and Luke relate the birth of Jesus. Luke records the events of the eighth day remembered on the Christmas octave, and Matthew tells of the visit of the Magi. All four gospels refer to the baptism.

The prophecies, sermons and letters of the Christmas lectionary sing out a full-throated proclamation of salvation. As we move through the season, the readings advance to later events in the life of Jesus: the miracles, or epiphanies, which support our belief in the power of the Word made flesh.

■ ON WEEKDAYS, Luke's story predominates the first part of the Christmas season because he tells more than others about the events following the birth of Jesus, like the presentation in the temple and the finding of the child there. John's first letter, so filled with ideas basic to Christian belief, accompanies these passages.

After Epiphany we hear about the manifestation of Jesus in a variety of gospel stories, notably the miracle accounts. The first readings return to the spirit of Advent. Together, the passages from the close of the Christmas season show the fulfillment of Advent's dreams.

■ THE COMMON PSALMS for Christmas and Epiphany are 98 and 72 respectively. Psalm 98 sings of God's salvation, a central theme to the season because the name Jesus means "Savior." Psalm 72, a royal psalm, appeared frequently in Advent. It returns now to celebrate the fulfillment of its prophecy.

■ GOSPEL ACCLAMATION: Versicles for the gospel acclamation are found in lectionary #212 and #219. In general they announce the coming of Christ and his manifestation to the world.

■ THE SUNDAY *LECTIONARY FOR MASSES WITH CHILDREN* makes only a few adaptations. It offers one set of readings for Christmas Day. The first reading and gospel come from the Mass at midnight. The second reading, however, comes from the Mass at dawn.

For the feast of the Holy Family, the children's lectionary offers only the options for Year A, readings which may be used at the parish Mass all three years of the cycle.

For Mary, Mother of God, the children's lectionary omits the second reading, as it does for the Epiphany. For the Baptism of the Lord, it includes the gospel from Year C (Luke's account), even though it is Year B.

The Sacramentary

■ THE ASSEMBLY: Whenever people gather at church they come for a common purpose. Sometimes they behave like a single body of believers. Other times they act like a gathering of individuals. At funerals and weddings, for example, people who are frequent churchgoers often forget when to stand, sit, and kneel, and even how to answer the responses. They behave more like individuals at prayer than as a single body. At Christmas, though, you will probably have an assembly that yearns to act as one.

You can help people form this community. They already have a common experience. They have made time to worship together on a day they have been anticipating for weeks. Give them a chance to meet one another. Give them songs to sing. Give them a beautiful experience to share.

On Christmas Day, and throughout this period, our churches welcome many visitors. Consider inviting the assembly to stand and greet those around them before the opening hymn this season. Ask parishioners to welcome visitors, and encourage people to exchange names and the greetings of the season.

If your space permits, you could even invite your regulars to introduce their guests, or ask visitors to announce where they come from. On Christmas, this noninvasive question can make visitors feel welcome and give the regulars an opportunity to rejoice in the gathering of faithful far and near.

■ GREETING: For the opening greeting of this season try something that announces the feast: "Christ was born for our salvation. The peace and love of God our Father, which has been revealed in Christ, be with you." Or: "The grace of the Lord Jesus, who became human for us, be with you."

■ THE PROCLAMATION OF THE BIRTH OF CHRIST may introduce the Christmas Eve Mass. A chanted version of this proclamation (along with some advice) is found on page 46 of this *Sourcebook,* and it's also found in the 1994 *Sacramentary Supplement* for the United States, which suggests it follow the greeting of the Christmas Mass during the night. In this case, the Penitential Rite is omitted, and the Glory to God forms a joyous sung response.

J. Michael Thompson has composed a simple but effective setting of this text for SATB choir and cantor (WLP, 5747). It's a fine piece, even though it carries an inexact title: "The Christmas Martyrology." It's the proclamation of the birth of Christ from the Roman martyrology.

■ PENITENTIAL RITE: Among the sacramentary's options for petitions in the Penitential Rite, C-iii focuses on the mystery of the incarnation and the role of Mary. The blessing and sprinkling of holy water might effectively replace the Penitential Rite on the feasts of Epiphany and Baptism of the Lord, or even on all Sundays of the season. As we celebrate the birth of Jesus, we remind ourselves of our rebirth in baptism.

■ THE GLORY TO GOD, after its Advent hiatus, returns on Christmas and throughout its octave, as well as on Sundays of the season. The opening words come directly from the Christmas story. As the angels sang this phrase on the first Christmas Day, it is most fitting to sing the Glory to God throughout the Christmas season.

■ REGARDING PRESIDENTIAL PRAYERS, almost all are based on texts from older missals. One of the oldest is the opening prayer for the Christmas Mass during the day, which appeared at least by the sixth century. The opening prayer and the prayer over the gifts for the Baptism of the Lord, in contrast, are new compositions.

Suggested texts for the season appear in Peter Scagnelli's *Prayers for Sundays and Seasons* (LTP). You will find introductions to the Lord's Prayer, invitations to communion and dismissal texts, as well as collect-style prayers especially useful at the conclusion to the general intercessions.

■ THE PROCLAMATION OF THE DATE OF EASTER may be made on Epiphany after the homily or after the communion prayer. A chanted version of this text is found on page 48.

■ SAMPLE FORMULAS FOR THE GENERAL INTERCESSIONS appear in the sacramentary's first appendix. See #4 for those suggested for the Christmas season.

■ THE CREED is recited or sung on Sundays and solemnities. Although the octave of Christmas calls for the Glory to God even on weekdays, it does not call for the Creed. On Christmas Day, we genuflect during the words that recall the incarnation. Ordinarily, we bow at this time. We used to genuflect at these words every time we recited the Creed, so the bow is a recent practice.

This particular bow, incidentally, is a profound bow from the waist, not a head bow. This may be a good season to catechize people about this simple gesture, which provides an opportunity for all the assembly to express the unity of their faith.

■ SAMPLE GENERAL INTERCESSIONS can be found in the sacramentary's first appendix. See #4 for the ones for Christmas.

■ THERE ARE FIVE PREFACES FOR THE CHRISTMAS SEASON. The first three are for Christmas and its octave, as well as the weekdays of the season. The second of these is a new text based on a fifth-century sermon by Pope Leo. Another translation can be found among the Ambrosian prefaces (weekdays between Epiphany and the Baptism of the Lord, Tuesday). See Alan Griffiths, *We Give You Thanks and Praise*. The same collection offers another translation of the Roman Christmas Preface III (Seventh Day in the Christmas Octave). The fourth Roman preface (P 6) is for Epiphany and may be used as an alternative for the first three during the weekdays following that feast. (For another translation, see the Ambrosian Preface for the Vigil of the Epiphany.)

The last Roman preface concludes the Christmas season with the celebration of the Baptism of the Lord. It also appears as the second preface for the same feast in the Ambrosian tradition.

Additional prefaces for this season can be found in the *Collection of Masses of the Blessed Virgin Mary* (4–9).

■ WHEN EUCHARISTIC PRAYER I is used at Christmas and during its octave, look for the special insert in the text at the phrase that begins, "In union with the whole church." It may be used even on weekdays of the octave. On Epiphany you will find another insert for the same phrase. The sacramentaries of other language groups suggest a seasonal insert for Eucharistic Prayer III as well. If the nature of your celebration calls for using one of the eucharistic prayers for reconciliation, you may use a preface from the season. If you use Eucharistic Prayer IV, however, you retain its own preface.

Christmas will be a good season to use the third eucharistic prayer for Masses with children, which suggests that all sing "Glory to God in the highest" as an acclamation during the prayer. If your community sings the Glory to God during Christmas, you could use the opening notes as the acclamation of this eucharistic prayer.

■ ACCLAMATIONS DURING THE EUCHARISTIC PRAYER may be the same you used during Advent. Add to the instrumentation or part-singing for the choir. Some communities choose a new musical setting for the eucharistic prayer during Christmas to set off the season. It is a short season, though, so it may be simpler on assembly and musicians to stay with the Advent set.

■ BLESSINGS for the season include Solemn Blessing #2 for Christmas, #3 for the Beginning of the New Year, and #4 for Epiphany. Among the prayers over the people, #14 especially fits the time of year.

The Book of Blessings

THE *Book of Blessings* includes words for a manger or nativity scene (48), a Christmas tree (49) and homes (50). You could incorporate blessings over the environment to begin or end the time for decorating the church. Or make these texts available for families to use at home.

Other blessings that fit this season include those over a family (1-1), a married couple (1-3), children (1-4) and travelers (9).

The Rite of Christian Initiation of Adults

AS usual, catechumens may be dismissed after the liturgy of the word at every Mass. Sample formulas appear at #67 and in texts on page 34.

Many catechumens enjoy the time after dismissal to reflect on the word with a catechist, but Christmas Day may not provide a good opportunity because of family responsibilities. Consider offering another time when catechumens can reflect on Christmas and its scriptures together. Or try a different form of catechesis this season: Give catechumens the option to spread Christmas cheer by donating time to the needy. Be sure to invite college students who are catechumens. Those who spend the school year away from home can make a connection with their parish over the Christmas break and continue their catechumenal formation.

One tough topic for catechumens and for all who struggle with living the Catholic way of life is the keeping of the Christmas season in tune with the liturgical year. It can be news to people that there is such a thing as the Christmas season and that it reaches its crescendo at Epiphany. Better than talking about such things is to provide opportunities to celebrate the season "with heart and soul and voice."

The Rites of Acceptance and Welcoming may be celebrated at any time of year, whenever the candidates are ready. But this season, so filled with solemnities and symbols, may not provide the best opportunity.

In many traditions east and west, Epiphany was one of the few days during the year marked for baptism or at least for the blessing of baptismal water. While Easter is the premier season for the sacraments of initiation, Epiphany also has a long-standing association with baptism. You might incorporate infant baptisms at Mass on Epiphany or on Baptism of the Lord. Although recent calendar reform makes the Baptism a separate feast from Epiphany, longstanding tradition understands Jesus' baptism as one of the great events celebrated at Epiphany and in the days that follow.

The Liturgy of the Hours

THE historical psalms added to the Advent office of readings continue through the brief Christmas season. Morning and evening prayer during the Christmas octave juggle the season with the feast days from the cycle of saints.

Among the treasures in the office of readings is Pope Paul VI's homey reflection on Nazareth, from his address there in 1964. Look for an opportunity to share a longer passage like this one with your community, either in written or oral form. Open choir practice with it or use it for part of a Christmas gathering of staff.

The Rite of Penance

THE busy time for the sacrament of reconciliation is before Christmas, not after. But some in your community will want to come. You may even have some visitors on Christmas Eve or Christmas Day whose hearts are moved to seek reconciliation. Be sure to include the times for this sacrament in the bulletin for Christmas and on the parish website. If the reconciliation room is hard to find in your church, post signs to show the way to visitors. Are times posted near the door of the church? If the church is locked when visitors arrive, will they know what time to come back for reconciliation?

The Pastoral Care of the Sick

THE sacrament of anointing may be celebrated at any time this season for those in need. With so much else going on at this time of year, it may not be the best season to offer the communal celebration. If you do choose to celebrate anointing within the context of Sunday Mass, the texts come from the Mass of the day, not from the Mass of the sacrament.

The Rite of Marriage

AS in Advent, the Rite of Marriage may be celebrated, but be mindful of which Mass may be used on what days. If the wedding takes place on the evening before or on the day of Christmas; Mary, the Mother of God; or Epiphany, the readings and prayers for the Sunday or solemnity take precedence. One reading may be substituted with one from the *Rite of Marriage*.

If the wedding does not include a Mass, or if the wedding Mass does not take place in conjunction with a solemnity this season, the scriptures and prayers for marriage may be used. The celebration of the Holy Family (December 29 this year) falls into this latter category. A Saturday evening wedding Mass (that is not a parish Mass for the Sunday) on December 28 may use the Mass of marriage in its entirety.

When decorating for the wedding, be sure to work with the Christmas decorations already in place. What point is there in adding a standard florist wedding arrangement of white gladioluses to a church already overflowing with poinsettias? Keep a photo album of seasonal decorations. Let the couple see what the church will look like at Christmas when they are preparing their details in summer.

The Order of Christian Funerals

A funeral may take place on any day during the Christmas season. If for some extraordinary reason the funeral needs to happen on Christmas Day, the Mass of Christmas must be celebrated. On other days the funeral Mass may replace the readings and prayers of the day, but consider using the scriptures of the day. Some of them may help the family integrate their loss into the promise of this season.

In guiding a bereaved family in making choices for music and readings, you need not ignore the season. The church will be filled with signs of Christmas, and the music and texts can complement these. There are few lovelier hymns for a wake or funeral at this season than "Hark the herald angels sing"—"born to raise us from the earth, born to give us second birth."

The Art and Environment

NO other season demands more of the art and environment crew. Everyone is busy. You will need extra hands. Get the word out early to potential volunteers. Which parishioners do a great job decorating their home at Christmas? Make a few phone calls to invite the help you need. Post appeals in the bulletin and on the website. Be prepared with a list of responsibilities so that when people walk in to help, you know exactly what task to assign to whom.

■ OUTDOOR DECORATIONS will put worshipers in a festive mood before they sing their first carol at church. Do you have trees you can brighten with floodlights or strings of bulbs? Some churches line the walk with luminarias, paper bags weighted with sand holding small candles. If you do so, be very careful of fire hazards. Other communities will set up banners with a seasonal greeting. Remember, "Merry Christmas" or "Christ is born" will evangelize better than "Season's greetings."

■ CANDLES inside the church will announce the coming of the Sun of Justice (Malachi 4:2) and the Light of the World (John 8:12). Arranged in patterns and colors, candles create a visual appeal that touch the heart.

■ EVERGREENS, by their very title, announce the eternal promise of life. The Christmas tree will profess our belief in eternity and in the power of God. Uprooted from its place of life, the tree comes indoors where all can enjoy its beauty, protected from the elements. It gives up its life for our enjoyment and becomes the place for our gifts, the symbols of our self-sacrifice. The tree dies in decorated splendor, giving hope to all mortals who yearn for the salvation of the eternal Christmas.

Become aware of civil restrictions regarding evergreens and work with local authorities to observe them while expressing the freedom of religion.

Holly brightens at its best in the winter. Its thorny leaves and red berries have made it a symbol of the passion in the midst of Christmas joy. The poinsettia serves a similar purpose. Wreaths and garlands symbolize victory and union, the victory of Christ and the union of the Savior with the church, of God with the human race.

■ THE NATIVITY SCENE WILL DRAW MANY VISITORS. Some people go from church to church to pray at each manger. The gathering of the poor, the foreigner, the angelic, and the animal invites every viewer into the scene. More than any other symbol of Christmas, the scene shows how we have fused the stories of Christmas into the popular imagination. The shepherds appear only in Luke. The Magi arrive only in Matthew. The ox and ass symbolize faith in the opening chapter of Isaiah. Yet they all find happy company under a roof in Bethlehem. Our church doors will open this Christmas to faithful and sinner, rich and poor, dark- and light-skinned.

Be careful about the size and placement of the scene. If indoors, it should not distract attention from the altar. It belongs in areas of more private worship, like the blessed sacrament chapel or a side area of the church. A larger scene may be constructed outside the church, to draw attention to the place and the season.

Some churches set the manger out early, but without the infant and with the Magi at a distance from the rest of the scene. They set the infant in the manger on Christmas Eve. They move the Magi closer for Epiphany. In some tra- ditions, the presider carries a statue of the infant in the opening procession Christmas Eve and places it in the manger. But many unfamiliar with this custom might find it idolatrous.

■ WHITE VESTURE (or gold or silver) adorns the presiding ministers this season. If you have several sets of white vestments, select one that can be identified each year with the season and with corollary days through the year, such as Presentation of the Lord, Saint Joseph, Annunciation of the Lord, and the Nativity of John the Baptist.

The Music

SING carols. Everything else seems secondary. Traditional carols awaken old memories for believers and unbelievers alike. The powerful message of God's love touches the human heart in extraordinary ways through the singing of a Christmas carol.

■ CAROLS: For a church reveling in its universal appeal and diversity of membership, Christmas carols provide a natural opportunity to celebrate our catholicity and the global implications of the incarnation. Learn carols from other countries, and sing some in other languages. The assembly that sings "Adeste Fideles" and "Stille Nacht" will expand its appreciation of the season.

The useful collection of "Descants for Christmas" by James J. Chepponis makes a worthy addition to your repertoire (WLP, 7971). The score is for full choir, descant, guitar and keyboard. But even if God has blessed you with only one coloratura instead of a full choir, or even a high schooler learning the trumpet, you can add more splendor to the five popular carols in this folio.

The merriest Christmas Mass will absolutely drench worshipers in their favorite Christmas carols. They have abstained from singing these throughout the season of Advent, even though carols have been piped into every supermarket, elevator and waiting room they've entered. Now is their chance. Let the people sing!

■ THE RETURN OF THE GLORY TO GOD to the liturgy expresses the joy of the season as the celebration opens. Use the same setting throughout the season, on all its Sundays and solemnities.

You don't have one in your repertoire? Or you'd like to learn a new one? This is the perfect season to learn, because you will have many opportunities to repeat it over a few weeks.

■ CHOIRS WILL FORM FOR CHRISTMAS more easily than for other times of the year. There are terrific opportunities for them to sing a simple four-part arrangement of a traditional carol or a thrilling rendition of the Hallelujah Chorus from Handel's *Messiah.*

Publishers continually produce new music for Christmas. You'll be tempted to try some and will have success adding to your repertoire. See Steven C. Warner's "Watchman, Tell Us of the Night" (WLP, 8643), Timothy Dudley-Smith and Steven R. Janco's "Wood Is for the Manger" (WLP, 8707), John M. Neale and Richard Proulx's "Here Is Joy for Every Age" (WLP, 5784), and Robert Lau's "Ave, Ave, the Angel Sang" (Wayne Leupold Editions 100023). Proulx has a lovely setting of a traditional Czech carol, "Hearken, Hearken, Mother Dear" (WLP, 5785) for the rare choir with too many basses, scored for SATBB, flute and oboe.

■ YOUTH: Some songs popular with youth will also fit the season. These could include "Lord, I Lift Your Name on High" by Rick Founds (WLP *Voices as One,* 60).

■ CHILDREN: Julie Howard's "Two Psalms for Advent and Christmas" (WLP, 7129) includes a jolly refrain for Psalm 96. Kids can also shake maracas and beat bongos for this number.

■ MUCH SOLO MUSIC based on Christmas carols has been written for organists. Whether it's "Gesu Bambino" or "Quelle est cette odeur agréable?" people will hum along not knowing why the tune is familiar.

The organist or handbell players who prepare a festive postlude for Christmas will reward worshipers with an extra measure of seasonal joy.

■ INTERESTED IN A SERVICE OF LESSONS AND CAROLS? Remember that this is a participatory liturgy, not a concert, and is modeled after the office of readings and after the extended liturgy of the word of the Easter Vigil. The United Church of Canada gives a model with excellent ideas in *Celebrate God's Presence* (pages 105–110).

The Parish and Home

PEOPLE should not need much encouragement to bring the spirit of Christmas to their homes, but it never hurts to promote the obvious. Outdoor lights and seasonal displays can evangelize an entire neighborhood. Indoor customs of the Christmas tree and manger scenes will remind the family of the season and create enthusiasm among children. Sending cards connects people more personally at this time of year.

Remember, the Christmas season lasts well into the new year. When are parish and parish-school parties and concerts scheduled, during Advent or during the Christmas season?

Some parishes provide an affordable alternative to high-priced New Year's celebrations. Through concerts and other entertainment, in churches or parish halls, in tandem with the chamber of commerce or other civic organizations, parishes participate in town-wide New Year's Eve "first night" celebrations that are family-friendly. More simply, New Year's Eve seems a marvelous occasion for watchnight prayer and caroling and, at midnight, some joyful noisemaking and refreshments.

In particular, Epiphany is a day to make what was homey and private about Christmas Day into a community-wide celebration that brings households together. One way to do this, borrowing Hispanic tradition, is to stage a public procession of the Magi and their retinue through the streets of town, in some places complete with camels! Through a concert, dance or party, and through communal prayer at Epiphany, many parishes have been successful in bringing entire neighborhoods together.

You can provide households with texts for blessing seasonal religious articles at home and for praising God for the family meal. Have children draw pictures for them. Put some texts and drawings in the bulletin or on the parish website. Table prayer for Christmas Day might be drawn from the *Book of Blessings* (#1038ff, 1048), or the simpler version in *Catholic Household Blessings and Prayers.*

More ideas for families to celebrate this season can be found in LTP's annual series *Welcome, Yule!* (written by Peter Scagnelli this year), as well as in Peter Mazar's *Winter: Celebrating the Season in a Christian Home* (LTP, 1996).

Texts

■ GREETING:
(Adapted from the sacramentaries of other language groups.)

Christ was born for our salvation. The peace and love of God our Father, which has been revealed in Christ, be with you.

The grace of the Lord Jesus, who became human for us, be with you.

■ INTRODUCTION TO THE PENITENTIAL RITE:

The kindness and generous love of God our Savior appeared not because of any righteous deeds we had done but because of his mercy. Let us call to mind our sins.

■ RESPONSE TO THE GENERAL INTERCESSIONS:

Word made flesh, hear our prayer.

Hear us, Savior of the World.

■ DISMISSAL OF CATECHUMENS:

In times past, God spoke in partial and various ways to our ancestors through the prophets; in these last days, God has spoken to us through the Son. May the Word made flesh resound in your hearts. Go in peace.

December

#13–16 (LMC #13)   white

WED 25
The Nativity of the Lord: Christmas Day
SOLEMNITY

ORIENTATION

The liturgy offers four sets of texts for the Christmas Mass, pertaining to different times of day. The vigil Mass is intended for use in the evening of December 24 and sets the stage for celebrating the great mystery. The Mass *in nocte* means "during the night" and need not take place at midnight. Yes, Jesus spoke of the coming of the bridegroom at midnight, but it's not like they wore watches in those days. Mass at dawn remembers the arrival of the shepherds to greet the newborn king. Mass during the day is a celebration of a deeper reflection on the Christmas mystery. The faithful may participate fully in more than one Mass (including the sharing of communion), but no parish is obliged to celebrate all four. In fact, the scriptures for any Mass may be proclaimed at any time. The general outline of the four Masses, however, is helpful for planning the community's prayer for Christmas Day.

Today is a holy day of obligation in the United States (including the diocese of Honolulu) and throughout Latin America.

LECTIONARY

The lectionary offers a completely distinctive set of readings for each of the four Masses of Christmas. The first set really has a vigil in mind. That is, it presumes the faithful will be back to celebrate Christmas Mass the next day. The other three sets of readings, even though they have recommended designations, may be proclaimed at any Mass on Christmas Day, judging from pastoral need. The most "Christmasy" of all the readings are those for midnight, with dawn running a close second. The gospels of the genealogy (vigil) and the prologue to John's gospel (day) fail to resonate as well with the worshiper who participates in only one Mass at Christmas.

■ VIGIL: Matthew's genealogy has to be the most boring passage in the lectionary, but in the hands of a skilled homilist it can come to life. Raymond Brown treats the genealogy in eye-opening detail in *The Birth of the Messiah*. The passage from Isaiah draws on the metaphors of the dawn and a marriage. The light of Christ will break forth like the dawn, and God will espouse Israel, even as the Word becomes flesh. Acts offers us part of Paul's preaching in which he proclaims that Jesus has descended from David. Psalm 89, a royal hymn about David, relates more to the readings that follow it than to the one before. Together, these scriptures, collected with dusk in mind, announce a new dawn: the coming of Christ through the line of David.

■ MIDNIGHT: Luke's marvelous account of the birth of Jesus proclaims the heart of today's mystery. Not only does it tell the story of the birth, but it also involves the census, the shepherds and the multitude of angels. It's the big

story most people are yearning to hear when they come to Mass at Christmas. Paired with it is the short passage from Titus, which urges the people to act temperately as they await the appearance of Jesus in glory. This brief but significant passage reminds us that the meaning of Christmas goes beyond Bethlehem to the anticipation of our redemption at the final and glorious coming of Christ. The prophecy from Isaiah, proclaimed in the middle of the night, announces that the people who walked in darkness have seen a great light. That light, we believe, is Jesus. Psalm 96, a hymn exulting the coming of the judgment of God, takes its refrain from the gospel. Note the word *today,* the *hodie* of the birth of Christ here and now, here among us.

The first reading and the gospel in the children's lectionary come from the Mass at midnight.

■ DAWN: The lectionary continues the story from Luke's gospel, focusing now completely on the shepherds, who go, presumably at dawn, to see the child born during the night. Paul explains to Titus why God our Savior has appeared, and Isaiah announces in joy that the Savior comes. Psalm 97 proclaims the kingship of God, and the dawning of light for the righteous. These passages all celebrate the coming of our Savior and the honor due to him.

The second reading in the children's lectionary comes from this Mass.

■ DAY: Theologically the deepest of the Christmas readings, John's prologue announces the mystery in language we hear often, "The Word became flesh." Isaiah proclaims that all the ends of the earth will behold God's salvation, indicating the full extent of the mission of the body of Christ. Psalm 98 takes up the same theme. The three psalms recommended for Christmas Day (96, 97 and 98), appearing sequentially in the Psalter, all sing praise to God. The letter to the Hebrews speaks of the coming of the Son, the refulgence of God's glory, and looks already to his ascension to the right hand of God. These scriptures focus on the mysterious incarnation and the glorification of the Son.

SACRAMENTARY

Complete texts for four Masses appear here. They bear the same titles as the Masses in the lectionary, but in this case the prayers are more carefully constructed to fit the time of day. You would not read the prayers for the Mass at dawn while celebrating Mass at the vigil.

All the Masses call for a genuflection during the Creed at the words of the incarnation. If the deacon, priest or cantor introduces the Creed with an invitation to genuflect, the assembly will be more likely to do so together. For example, "As we recite our Creed today, let us genuflect together during the words that recall the incarnation." Why not take a longer pause? Let everyone kneel to meditate a moment on the birth of Christ, as they perhaps do during the passion on Good Friday, in awe over the death of Christ.

If you use Eucharistic Prayer I at any of these Masses, you insert the special form of the prayer that begins "In union with the whole church."

■ VIGIL: As in the lectionary, the vigil is intended for those celebrating a late afternoon or evening Mass on December 24, but with the idea that they will return for Christmas Mass the next day. If the community gathering in your church on the night of the twenty-fourth is really celebrating Christmas, it makes more sense to use the prayers for midnight. Both opening prayers for the vigil Mass suggest that we are still waiting for the birth of the Son, not actually celebrating it. Any Christmas preface may be used, but the second may better fit the readings that tell of David's lineage. If you prefer to conclude the Mass with a more solemn or pertinent blessing, see solemn blessing #2 for Christmas.

Israel's Exodus from Egypt inspired the antiphon recommended for the introductory rites. At that time, God promised Israel that they would behold the glory of the Lord "in the morning." The communion antiphon recalls an Advent prophecy of Isaiah, that all would see the salvation of God.

■ MIDNIGHT: Even though the Mass is called "Midnight" it need not begin at that hour. Some communities start the Mass earlier, still in the dark of night, for the convenience and safety of the assembly. You may begin this liturgy with a vigil of psalms, silence, readings and prayers. It gives the choir an opportunity to share the wealth of music for the feast, and invites the assembly to enter into the spirit of the day, even if they get there early just to find a good seat.

The *Liturgy of the Hours* offers a suggested celebration of the office of vigils (vol. I, p. 399 and pp. 1622ff.) It could happen this way:

Procession: After the people have gathered in a semi-dark church, members of the community process in with the candles from the Advent wreath. The ministers follow. They might light candles held by the assembly. A setting of the invitatory psalm (95, 24, 67 or 100 for example) could accompany the procession. More candles may be lit at the altar.

Greeting: V. Light and peace in Jesus Christ our Lord. R. Thanks be to God.

Office of Readings: The *Liturgy of the Hours* recommends "What Child Is This?" for the hymn, followed by a selection of psalms. The readings themselves include a classic Christmas passage by Leo the Great.

The Office of Vigils: One or more canticles may be sung, as indicated (vol. I, pp. 1622ff). Then the gospel of the resurrection may be proclaimed. Since this is Year B, most fitting would be Mark's version (16:1–8). Then follows the gospel of the Christmas vigil, Matthew 1:1–25 or just 1:18–25.

Proclamation of the Birth of Christ: This announcement may be chanted. The text and music are found on page 46 of this *Sourcebook* and also in the 1994 *Sacramentary Supplement.* Acolytes with lighted candles might lead a procession. A deacon, cantor or reader may lead the proclamation from the ambo. All stand, but all kneel for the words "having passed since his conception, was born in Bethlehem of Judea of the Virgin Mary." Then all rise for the final sentence. Make sure the ministers know this so they can cue everyone else by their posture.

Mass: Mass begins with the Glory to God.

Some communities, not wanting to observe the entire vigil outlined above, may select some of its elements, or replace some with alternative scriptures and favorite carols.

If there is no celebration of the office of vigils, Mass begins in the usual way. Carols may be sung as preludes. The Proclamation of the Birth of Christ may follow the greeting.

Both opening prayers assume that this Mass takes place in the dark of night. Surprisingly, it is the alternative opening prayer for the Mass at dawn that makes the Christmas liturgy's only allusion to a passage from the book of Wisdom about God's Word leaping down from heaven "in the silent watches of the night." In Wisdom, the story concerns the exodus, but at Christmas, that line feeds the tradition of having Mass at midnight, the traditional time for the birth of Christ.

Two antiphons are offered for the introductory rites. One comes from the second psalm, a text that seems a natural for Christmas, but that the New Testament frequently applies to the resurrection, "You are my son; this day I have begotten you." The version from *By Flowing Waters,* 19, (The Liturgical Press), is especially effective with handbells. The alternative antiphon is nonscriptural, but acclaims the spirit and meaning of the celebration. The communion antiphon comes from the gospel of the Mass during the day and proclaims the central doctrine of Christmas: The Word of God became flesh.

From the Latin, the opening line of the solemn blessing "When he came to us as man" is more literally translated, "By his incarnation." Similarly, in the third part, "When the Word became man" renders the same Latin expression, literally, "becoming flesh."

■ DAWN: The prayers that open the liturgy are in celebration of the coming of light into the world. The prayer over the people that appears in the sacramentary may be replaced by the solemn Christmas blessing, #2.

The opening antiphon blends passages from Isaiah and Luke, to announce the shining of God's divine light this day. Another text associated with Advent appears in the communion antiphon, to announce that the Savior, the one we have awaited, has come.

If the early Mass at your parish lamentably includes no music, this is the day to repent and change your ways! Haul out a couple of familiar carols and acclamations.

Every scrooge will happily sing on Christmas Day.

■ DAY: The opening prayer for this Mass is the oldest of the set. The Latin text praises God for creating "the dignity of human substance" or "being." The prayer over the gifts recalls the great gift of peace.

The entrance antiphon echoes a prophecy heard at midnight Mass. The communion antiphon repeats the refrain from the responsorial psalm. (The citations appear to be different because the lectionary follows the Hebrew numbering of the psalms and the sacramentary observes the vulgate numbering.)

OTHER IDEAS

Publicizing the Mass times is essential, and the parish office will still receive innumerable phone calls. When recording the message, wish everyone a Merry Christmas and tell the Mass schedule first, or give the caller a mailbox number to press. People are calling for Mass times. They don't need to hear a long list of extensions.

Use the website, the Christmas card, the bulletin, signs in front of the building—whatever means you have to make the times public.

If you know some Masses will be overcrowded, for example on the vigil of Christmas, consider not publicizing those on the telephone recorder or the website, but only through the parish bulletin. It might encourage the visitors to come at a time when you have more room and more opportunity to greet them, and allow the faithful churchgoers better seats at the most crowded Mass.

If you publish a participation aid for Christmas, include the parish phone number and website for easy access, and don't be shy about publishing upcoming events to which visitors will be welcome.

You may want to celebrate evening prayer as a community, or at least as a group of ministers. If so, the best time would probably be before the first vigil Mass. But reserve your strength. You'll need it for the full schedule of Masses and visitors.

If you use incense only rarely, this is the day to get it out. If you use it regularly, reserve a special fragrance for today's celebrations.

Given the importance of today's gospel, the procession cries out for candles and incense. The deacon or priest may chant the good news. See *Chants for the Readings* (Joseph T. Kush, GIA, G-2114) and *Liturgical Music for the Priest and Deacon* (Columba Kelly, St. Meinrad's Archabbey, St. Meinrad IN).

Announcements at the end of Mass should acknowledge the ministers who made it possible, especially musicians and church decorators—and, of course, the assembly! Carefully choose a few additional parish announcements, so visitors hear about other opportunities to return to the community.

Leave the church open today, if possible. Announce it at Mass and invite people to return with visitors to show off the local worship space and to spend some time in prayer before the manger.

If some people wish to return to the church for vespers, you may offer evening prayer to conclude the day's activities.

T H U **26** #696 (LMC #437, 458–460)
red
Stephen, first martyr
FEAST

The joy of Christmas gives way to the shock of martyrdom. Stephen, known as the protomartyr, the first witness, reminds us of the price paid by those who place their faith in the newborn king. The first reading recounts the story of Stephen's martyrdom, an event foreshadowed in the gospel where Jesus predicts that his followers will suffer persecution. A quotation from the psalm for the day appears on the lips of Stephen at his death, as it did on the lips of Jesus at the crucifixion. The children's lectionary offers a different option for the gospel.

For the next three days the readings for the Mass are in the back of the lectionary with the saints, but the presidential prayers are in the front of the sacramentary with the seasons.

Today is "Boxing Day" in the United Kingdom and in Canada, a day for sharing gifts of charity. The custom reflects Stephen's care for needy members of the church.

You may be exhausted from the past few days, but keep up the Christmas spirit. Sing the Glory to God today, reprising the one from Christmas Day. If you're using Eucharistic Prayer I, which includes the name of today's saint, see the special insert for the octave of Christmas. Sing Christmas carols at Mass this week and next. Even those who rarely sing will welcome the invitation to join enthusiastically in the music of the season.

#697 (LMC #452–454 and 438) white

27
FRI
John, apostle, evangelist
FEAST

On the feast of John we begin the semicontinuous reading of the first letter that bears his name. The opening words remind us of the beginning of the fourth gospel, also attributed to John. "The disciple whom Jesus loved" experiences a defining moment in today's gospel, becoming a witness to the resurrection. Wondrously we hear the story of Easter dressed in Christmas finery. It honors the memory of the beloved disciple while unfolding the whole mystery of salvation in Christ.

Scholars insist that the John of the gospels, the beloved disciple, the evangelist, the author of three

New Testament letters, and the seer of the book of Revelation may not be the same person, but church tradition has conflated them into one, all recognized as the saint of this day. Today's psalm is seasonal, expounding nothing further about John, but singing of the joy of the coming of Christ at Christmas. The versicle for the gospel acclamation is the opening of the classic hymn *Te Deum*. Its most familiar adaptation in English is "Holy God, We Praise Thy Name." The chant is in the *Liber cantualis*.

Sing the Glory to God today in honor of the feast. Eucharistic Prayer I includes an insert for the Christmas octave as well as the name of today's saint.

#698 (LMC #456–459, 439) red

28
SAT
The Holy Innocents, martyrs
FEAST

The unspeakably sorrowful tale of the slaughter of the innocents drapes mourning over the octave of Christmas joy. This event goes unrecorded in other historical accounts of the period, but it unquestionably fits the personality of the murderous Herod. Matthew composed the story to parallel that of the birth of Moses, subtly establishing the role of Jesus as the new leader, guiding God's chosen people into freedom.

The gospel recalls the sober event, and the psalm lets us imagine the innocents singing its words of hope in the midst of tragedy. The first reading continues yesterday's passage and pertains more to the Christmas octave than to today's feast. It begins with the Christmas theme of God's light.

Prayers today may remember children who lose their lives through abortion, infanticide, neglect, abuse and hunger.

Sing the Glory to God today, and don't forget about the insert for Eucharistic Prayer I.

#17 (LMC #14) white

✸29
The Holy Family of Jesus, Mary and Joseph
FEAST

ORIENTATION

This feast, with roots in the seventeenth century, was added to the universal calendar in 1921 to build up devotion in family life. It upholds Jesus, Mary and Joseph as the ideal family. We now celebrate this feast on the Sunday within the octave of Christmas. (It used to fall during Epiphany's octave.) This feast comes at a time when our thoughts turn to the creation of the holy family at the birth of Jesus, as well as the gathering of our families and loved ones this season of the year.

Regardless of the particular feast, this is a Christmas day within the Christmas octave, and everything of this Sunday can shout the good news that Jesus Christ is born.

LECTIONARY

The arrangement of readings is hopelessly complex. The first set of readings may be used in all years—A, B and C. It includes a first reading from Sirach and a psalm. The second reading from Colossians has a longer and shorter form marked A and B, which do not refer to the year of the cycle. Then the lectionary offers a selection of three gospels, marked A, B and C, which do refer to the year of the cycle, but the one for year B, this year, has a longer and shorter form marked A and B, which again do not refer to the year of the cycle.

The potential confusion does not end there. After this complete set of readings the lectionary offers optional readings for years B and C of the cycle. The gospel for year B, this year, is the same one that appears in the first set of readings in a longer and shorter form. It shows up both ways here, too, marked A and B, referring to the length of the forms, not to the years of the cycle. Got it?

All this means you have a choice. You may choose the first two readings from either Year A or Year B. The gospel should come from Year B. You have a choice of longer and shorter readings with that gospel and with the second reading if you opt for the one from Year A.

Importantly, you will get the most variety over the three-year cycle (and skip some confusion) if you observe all the readings for Year B this year.

The first reading of Year B comes from Genesis (15:1–6; 21:1–3). By leapfrogging across six chapters, this text links God's promise that Abraham and Sarah will have offspring with the fulfillment of that promise in the birth of Isaac. In response we sing the opening verses of a lengthy psalm that extols God's faithfulness to the covenant.

The second reading of Year B comes from Hebrews (11:8, 11–12, 17–19). It praises the faith of Abraham, whom God rewarded with a family.

Luke's account of the presentation of Jesus in the temple serves as the gospel for Year B. Among the evangelists, Luke alone tells this story. It significantly places the temple into the life of Jesus, foreshadowing his role as sacrificial victim and eternal priest. If you choose the short form of the gospel, you shamefully exclude the prophet Anna from the Sunday scriptures. (All along in his infancy narrative Luke has been introducing female and male pairs, beginning with Elizabeth and Zechariah.)

You may decide to use the first two readings from Year A. The passage from Sirach extols the honor due to parents. The Canadian lectionary translates the last few verses in the plural, demonstrating that the child owes care not just to the father but to both parents. Psalm 128, one of the options in the wedding lectionary, praises God for the blessings of family. The letter to the Colossians invites the Christian community to put on its virtues like clothing, and bind them all with love. The shorter version of this passage eliminates the concluding verses, which sound abusive. Other solutions, like changing "Wives, be subordinate to your husbands" to "Wives, love your husbands," would not be faithful to what the letter says.

SACRAMENTARY

The presidential prayers today all mention the holy family, making it hard for anyone to miss the theme of the feast. No special preface is provided, though. Choose from the three prefaces for Christmas, but you may want to look at the *Collection of Masses of the Blessed Virgin Mary* for one called Our Lady of Nazareth (P 8). The special insert for the octave of Christmas may be used with Eucharistic Prayer I. Alternate blessings include the one for the Christmas season (solemn blessing #2) and prayers over the people #2 or 9.

The suggested chants for entrance and communion present a prophetic passage from Baruch and a fulfillment from Luke: God establishing a home among the people. The prayer for the holy name of Mary in Appendix X of the sacramentary might conclude the general intercessions today.

OTHER IDEAS

The *Book of Blessings* offers a full array of blessings for families, and *Catholic Household Blessings and Prayers* includes one for "a Family or Household." Religious articles received as Christmas gifts could be included as part of the final blessing for Mass, or afterwards in a gathering at the manger. See *Book of Blessings,* 44, shorter rite.

The day's themes are captured in two choices for the entrance antiphon in *By Flowing Waters,* 28 or 29, with the "family psalm," Psalm 128.

MON 30 #203 white
Sixth Day in the Octave of Christmas

Both readings come from the front part of the lectionary now. The first few days of the Christmas octave are also feast days, so those readings were located among those for December's saints. Today, though, turn back to the weekday readings of the season, located just after those for the last days of Advent.

You will discover that the sequence of first readings begun last week with Saint John continue this week. All are taken from the letters of John. The author addresses listeners of every age group, urging them to forsake the enticements of this world. We sing several verses of Psalm 96, a hymn of praise to God that fits the Christmas season.

The gospel concludes the story of Jesus' infancy with part of Luke's account of the presentation in the temple. The full account appeared as the long form of the gospel yesterday. Today, Anna the prophetess thanks God and tells everyone about Jesus. She is a model of prayer and evangelization.

Sing the Glory to God. You may use the insert for the Christmas octave in Eucharistic Prayer I.

TUE **31** #204 white
Seventh Day in the Octave of Christmas

Optional Memorial of Sylvester I (+ 335), pope/white ▪ Today's gospel presents the prologue of John. One of the alternate passages for Mass on Christmas Day, it appears here in a more subdued setting for peaceful reflection, apart from the hectic demands of Christmas Day. The first reading recalls division within the early church amid a somber proclamation of the coming of the antichrist in the final hour, an ominous text for New Year's Eve. Psalm 96 is seasonal.

▪ ONE OF THE LONGEST REIGNING POPES in the history of the church, Sylvester served during a time of great councils, including Nicea, which clarified our belief in the divinity of Christ.

Still within the octave of Christmas, the liturgy calls for the Glory to God and the optional insert to Eucharistic Prayer I.

January

WED **1** #18 (LMC #15) white
Octave of Christmas
Mary, the Mother of God
SOLEMNITY

ORIENTATION

We celebrate many events today. The octave day of Christmas brings our weeklong celebration to a close. The Roman Catholic calendar names this day as the solemnity in honor of Mary's motherhood, her role and title as "Theotokos," "Dei Genitrix," the "Bearer of God."

The civic calendar celebrates New Year's Day. Many Eastern (and the former Western calendar) churches emphasize the circumcision of Jesus, an event the gospel notes on the eighth day of his birth. Some churches of the Reformation honor the holy name of Jesus because Luke says that Jesus received his name on the day of his circumcision. Paul VI designated this as a day of prayer for world peace. Many of the faithful will participate at Mass today simply as a good way to start the year.

This is a holy day of obligation in the United States (except in the diocese of Honolulu) and throughout Latin America, except in Chile, Paraguay and Uruguay.

No matter how you keep this day, it is a Christmas day, the capstone of the Christmas octave and one of the great days of the season. Carols, carols and more carols!

LECTIONARY

The gospel explains the original cause of this celebration. Luke records the circumcision and naming of Jesus on the octave day of his birth. The same text mentions Mary, whom we honor today as "Theotokos," mother of God, reflecting in her heart on the birth of Jesus.

The lectionary adds a blessing from the book of Numbers for those who invoke the name of God, and a passage from Galatians. Paul's letters tell us nothing about the life of Mary, but in this one passage he alludes to God's son, "born of a woman." He never reveals her name, but the lectionary adopts this lonely reference from Paul on this and other days in honor of Mary. Psalm 67 echoes the theme of blessing from the first reading.

SACRAMENTARY

All the presidential prayers express the theme of Mary's motherhood. The liturgy calls for the first preface of the Blessed Virgin Mary (P 56), but notice the one for Mary, the Mother of the Church, in Appendix X of the sacramentary, and Mother of the Savior in the *Collection of Masses of the Blessed Virgin Mary* (P 5). All the eucharistic prayers refer to Mary by this title, Mother of God. This could be a good day to reflect on its paradoxical meaning. (How can God have a mother? Only with the incarnation.) On this last day of the octave, the special insert for Eucharistic Prayer I may still be used. The sacramentary suggests a prayer over the people, but the solemn blessing for the new year (#3) would also be appropriate.

The communion antiphon, "Jesus Christ is the same yesterday, today, and for ever," seems to have the new year in mind. The entrance antiphon combines a prophecy from Isaiah with a fulfillment in Luke. The alternative text comes from the works of Sedulius, a fifth century Roman who authored a poetic version of the gospels.

OTHER IDEAS

You might conclude the general intercessions with the collect for the Mass of "Beginning of the Civil Year" (Various Needs and Occasions, #24), from texts that otherwise cannot be used today.

Music for today should continue the singing of Christmas carols. Good choices include "What Child Is This?" and "Of the Father's Love Begotten." Christopher Walker's stately gospel version of "At the Name of Jesus" from the collection of the same name is available from Oregon Catholic Press. Fitting for the day is the *Te Deum*, most popularly sung as "Holy God, We Praise Thy Name." The original chant is in the *Liber cantualis*.

Among the prayers of thanksgiving after Mass in the sacramentary's first appendix is one to the Virgin Mary, acknowledging her as Mother.

NEW YEAR'S EVE

Some parishes merge a New Year's Eve party with liturgical celebration. Many members will appreciate a safe and sober family event. A party could follow the evening eucharist, or lead up to a midnight prayer of vigils or eucharist.

A celebration of vigils inspired by the *Liturgy of the Hours* (vol. I, 479ff and Appendix I, 1622ff) could happen as follows:

Entrance procession: While the church is in semidarkness, ministers may light the candles of the altar and assembly while a version of the invitatory (Psalm 96, 24, 67 or 100) is sung.

Greeting: V. Light and peace in Jesus Christ our Lord. R. Thanks be to God.

Office of Readings: The *Liturgy of the Hours* suggests "Virgin-Born, We Bow Before Thee" for the hymn, followed by a selection of psalms. The readings include a passage from a letter of Saint Athanasius, concerning Mary's role in the incarnation.

Office of Vigils: One or more canticles may be sung, as indicated (vol. I, pp. 1622ff). Then the gospel of the resurrection may be proclaimed. You may repeat Mark's version (16:1–7) if you used it at Christmas vigils, or perhaps use John's (20:1–8). Then follows the recommended gospel (John 20:19–31). The office of vigils says that this text may be substituted by

another gospel from the feast "which is not read at Mass this year," but those do not exist. Tonight, John's prologue, from the Mass during the day on Christmas Day, seems perfect: "In the beginning . . ."

Mass: If Mass follows, omit the *Te Deum* and begin with the Glory to God.

If you do not want to observe the entire vigil outlined above, select some of its elements, or replace some with alternative scriptures and Christmas carols.

Celebrate God's Presence offers the following prayer for New Year's Day (30G001):

Holy God,
  as we enter this new year,
we thank you for your presence
  with us
in all the years of our lives.
We have known joy, and
  also sorrow,
success and failure,
and through it all,
  you have been with us—
the companion of all our journeys.
Much of life is fleeting
and so we thank you for things
  that endure:
the love of faithful friends,
wisdom gained from experience,
the reliability of nature,
and your steadfast love.
We thank you for this new year
  which awaits us;
Take us by the hand,
  and lead us on. Amen.

#205   white
Basil the Great (+ 379) and Gregory Nazianzen (+ 389), bishops, monastics, doctors of the church
T H U 2
MEMORIAL

The First Letter of John urges the readers to be faithful to the teachings they have received, to the promise of eternal life, and not to fall subject to false teaching. Psalm 98 is seasonal, repeating the text from Christmas Day. The gospel verses follow those we

heard on December 31. This week's continuous reading from the first chapter of John marks the events accompanying the appearance of Jesus. Today, John the Baptist announces his coming. Incidentally, the fourth gospel never calls this prophetic figure "the Baptist." He is simply John.

■ TODAY'S SAINTS: Basil and Gregory, both great theologians of the Eastern tradition, were also the best of friends from school days in Athens. Basil's monastic rule serves as the ideal for monastic life in the East. An anaphora attributed to Basil is a direct ancestor to Eucharistic Prayer IV. Gregory's remains lie in St. Peter's in Rome. His tribute to Basil is in today's office of readings.

#206   white
F R I 3
Christmas Weekday

More verses of the seasonal Christmas psalm (98) follow today's passage from the First Letter of John, which proclaims that we are children of God. John the prophet introduces Jesus as the "Lamb of God who takes away the sin of the world." Today's passage also presents John's description of the Baptism of the Lord, almost parenthetical by comparison with the stories in the other gospels. This account never even says explicitly who baptized Jesus. These scriptures reveal more about the child born in Bethlehem and the implications of his birth for believers.

#207   white
Elizabeth Ann Seton (+ 1821), married woman, educator, religious founder
S A T 4
MEMORIAL

At the recognition of the Lamb of God, the Messiah, the first disciples follow Jesus. According to John's first letter, those who are begotten of God behave accordingly, living lives free of sin. We hear yet more verses from the seasonal Psalm 98.

■ TODAY'S SAINT: Elizabeth Ann Seton, Episcopalian at birth and later a Catholic, a wife, a mother of five, a founder of a religious community, and an educator, left her native Italy to serve the church in the United States. Her efforts to establish Catholic schools achieved enormous success. A special celebration involving Catholic school children would be very appropriate today, even at the Saturday evening Mass.

☀ 5 #20 (LMC #16)   white
The Epiphany of the Lord
SOLEMNITY

ORIENTATION

Although most of the rest of the Christian world celebrates Epiphany on January 6, Catholics in countries where the day is not a holy day of obligation transfer the celebration to the nearest Sunday. Our custom lends absurdity to singing "The Twelve Days of Christmas"—it's only eleven between Christmas and Epiphany this year. But it allows everyone to celebrate this festival in a Sunday gathering.

Epiphany means "manifestation," or the appearance of Jesus. The significance of this day is not just the arrival of the Magi, but the coming of Gentiles to adore the newborn King of the Jews. The event recognizes Jesus' lordship over the entire world.

Many traditions about the Magi have evolved. The influence of Psalm 72 on the seasonal liturgy led to the belief that they were kings. An alternate translation calls them astrologers. The blessing today calls them wise men. The Bible says there were three gifts, but never says how many Magi brought them. Nonetheless, many traditions claims there were three and even ascribed them the names of Melchior, Balthasar and Caspar. In iconography, one is often depicted with dark skin. Their remains are said to be contained in an elaborate reliquary in the cathedral of Cologne, Germany.

LECTIONARY

Use the readings for the Epiphany of the Lord. Texts for the Second Sunday after Christmas are for countries that celebrate the Epiphany liturgy tomorrow.

Matthew alone tells the story of the Magi. It contrasts the innocent newborn king with the deceitful Herod, while it recalls prophecies about the Messiah's birth. The refrain for Psalm 72 announces the universal theme of Jesus' kingship, even as it foretells the arrival of kings who will pay homage to God's own just king. Because of this psalm, the Magi often appear in iconography wearing crowns. Isaiah prophesies the arrival of caravans of camels bearing gold and frankincense to praise the Lord. But the short passage from the letter to the Ephesians states the main theme of this day most clearly: The Gentiles are coheirs and copartners in the promise in Christ Jesus.

SACRAMENTARY

The Proclamation of the Date of Easter may follow the homily or communion prayer. You'll find this proclamation on page 48 of this *Sourcebook.* The text and music also are in the 1994 *Sacramentary Supplement.* Adjust the dates as follows: the Triduum celebrated between April 17 and 20, Ash Wednesday on March 5, Ascension on May 29 or June 1, Pentecost on June 8, and the First Sunday of Advent on November 30.

The opening prayer recalls the revelation of Jesus to the Gentile nations. The prayer over the gifts refers directly to the gifts of the Magi. The communion prayer asks that we might recognize Christ in the eucharist, presumably as the Magi recognized him by the light of the star.

The preface is proper for the day (P 6) and refers to the revelation of Christ by the star's light. The preface for "Mary and the Epiphany of the Lord" from the *Collection of Masses of the Blessed Virgin Mary* (P 6) develops the same themes. If you use Eucharistic Prayer I, you may insert the special form of the prayer "In union with the whole Church." The second eucharistic prayer for reconciliation concludes with an Epiphany theme: "Gather people of every race, language and way of life to share in the one eternal banquet with Jesus Christ the Lord."

The solemn blessing is eloquent, but you may substitute another text, like prayer over the people #3 or 7.

The communion antiphon comes directly from the gospel, and the entrance antiphon recalls two prophecies fulfilled on this day.

OTHER IDEAS

The *Ceremonial of Bishops* suggests that there be a "suitable and increased display of lights" (240). An ancient title for this day is "festival of lights." Coptic Christians keep Epiphany with an array of ornamented lanterns and candles (a custom borrowed by Egyptian Muslims for their observance of Ramadan). At Mass, additional candles and candle bearers for the entrance procession can set this feast ablaze in light from its beginning.

Be sure to sing all the verses of "We Three Kings," and enjoy the elaborate catechesis of the text.

The priest or deacon may sing the gospel to a simple tone, to highlight the importance of its message and this day.

Make a special presentation of gifts. In place of gold, funds for the poor; in place of frankincense, letters to legislators on behalf of the needy; in place of myrrh, gifts for the homebound and dying. Use your imagination, or rely on local traditions. This idea is also based on the *Ceremonial of Bishops,* 240.

■ YOU COULD BLESS CHALK at the conclusion of the Mass. Prepare small pieces of chalk in envelopes that bear the inscriptions:

20 +C +M +B 03

The number of the new year is split at the beginning and end. The initials C, M and B represent Caspar, Melchior and Balthasar, and the three crosses stand for "saint." The letters also abbreviate the prayer *Christus mansionem benedicat,* "May Christ bless the house." As part of the blessings at the conclusion of Mass, include a text like this:

May God, who provided a safe
    dwelling for the eternal Word,
bless this chalk, the homes of
    the faithful, and the people
    who live there,
through Christ our Lord.

Then give one piece of chalk to representatives of every household as people leave. They may take it home, gather around the inside of the front door, and use the chalk to inscribe the numbers and letters on the lintel while saying, "May Christ bless the house." Throughout the year those who come and go through that door will enjoy the blessing of Christ.

Coincidentally, the month of January takes its name from the Roman god Janus, the guardian of thresholds (*ianua* is Latin for "doorway"). This ritual casts a Christian interpretation over the threshold we cross at the beginning of the calendar year.

Another blessing for homes on Epiphany is in the *Book of Blessings.* (See the shorter rite at #50.) Yet another is in *Catholic Household Blessings and Prayers,* p. 126.

■ YOU MAY CONCLUDE THE CELEBRATION OF EPIPHANY with vespers or a concert by the parish choir. They may present again the music they have practiced for so long. Candlelight, incense and carols for everyone will create a festive gathering. Add a parish supper or open house. Show appreciation to all who worked to make Advent and Christmas a time of beautiful, glorious prayer. If you offer this event on Saturday night, you may celebrate the office of vigils, as outlined in the *Liturgy of the Hours.* See Christmas and Mary, the Mother of God above for ideas.

M O N **6** #212 white
Christmas Weekday

Optional Memorial of Blessed André Bessette (+ 1937), religious ■ Readings for today are located in the lectionary under the title "January 7 or Monday after Epiphany." That means these readings should be proclaimed the day after Epiphany, whenever it is celebrated in your country.

The gospels this week take us through the four evangelists to show the coherence of evidence concerning Jesus' divinity as Messiah. In today's passage from Matthew Jesus succeeds the ministry of John the Baptist, fulfills a prophecy about the rising of a great light, announces the theme of his preaching, and cures great crowds in demonstration of his power and mission. Continuing the First Letter of John, today's first reading asserts the union of belief and love in the life of the Christian. Psalm 2, from a collection of royal poetry, states the Epiphany themes of the reign over all nations and the manifestation of Jesus as ruler.

This week's presidential prayers are in the sacramentary under a different title: "After Epiphany to the Baptism of the Lord." The opening prayer and suggested antiphons especially highlight the Epiphany theme. Use any Christmas preface or the one for Epiphany. Reviewing the Christmas prefaces this week enables us to pray them with Epiphany vision.

■ THE TWELFTH DAY OF CHRISTMAS: January 6 is too sacred a day, in our tradition, to leave unnoticed. Many parishes schedule something today—a Christmas concert, a parish potluck supper, a visit from the Magi or even hot chocolate and cookies after a morning Mass. Puerto Rico, the Dominican Republic, and Uruguay observe Epiphany today as a holy day of obligation.

■ TODAY'S SAINT: André Bessette, Canadian by birth, lived a while in the United States before joining the Brothers of the Holy Cross. He spent most of his ministry in or near Montreal, where he lived a life of humility and service.

TUE 7 #213 white
Christmas Weekday

Optional Memorial of Raymond of Peñafort (+ 1275), presbyter, religious / white ▪ In performing the miracle of the loaves, Jesus establishes himself as the promised one and just ruler who provides for the hungers of his people. The first reading reminds us that God loved us first and calls us to love in turn. This season especially encourages believers to share their love for all. Psalm 72, which appeared in Advent to prophesy the coming of the just king, reappears after Epiphany in fulfillment.

In the sacramentary the opening prayer and suggested antiphons restate the revelation of Christ among us. Use any Christmas or Epiphany preface.

▪ TODAY'S SAINT: Raymond balanced careers of preacher, canonist and confessor to Pope Gregory IX. His treatment of canon law became foundational in the development of the church's discipline. He died at age 100.

WED 8 #214 white
Christmas Weekday

Jesus walks on the water, an event the lectionary presents as a manifestation of his divinity. Gospels this week are showing "epiphanies" of who Jesus is. More verses of yesterday's psalm express the same mystery. John invites us into the mystery of God's love but also into acknowledging that Jesus is the Son of God, a proclamation that appears strongly here.

The opening prayer sustains the theme of the light of the nations.

THU 9 #215 white
Christmas Weekday

Moving into Luke's gospel, we hear Jesus reveal himself as God's anointed one, as he reads a passage from Isaiah in the synagogue. The psalm of the past two days, acclaiming God's just king, continues. The First Letter of John develops the expectations on the one who believes in God. If you love God, you must love your neighbor.

The antiphons for today are two classic passages from John's gospel, proclaiming the Word made flesh and God's promise of eternal life. The opening prayer again elaborates the theme of light.

▪ TODAY GUATEMALA OBSERVES an optional memorial of the ninth century Spanish martyr, Eulogius of Córdoba.

FRI 10 #216 white
Christmas Weekday

To proclaim Jesus' fulfillment of messianic prophecies, the lectionary chooses a miraculous cure of a leper from Luke. There is nothing distinctive about the cure of this leper compared with that of others in the gospels, except that this one otherwise appears nowhere in the lectionary. Today's psalm of praise again captures the theme of the season more than the specific themes of the readings. In the first reading we hear of the testimony of life in the Son of God.

The opening prayer makes a direct reference to Epiphany's star, and the antiphons repeat the themes of the season.

▪ IN PERU TODAY is a memorial of Blessed Anne of the Angels of Monteagudo (+ 1686), a Dominican who suffered physical ailments and spiritual trials.

SAT 11 #217 white
Christmas Weekday

Finally entering John's gospel, the week's readings about the manifestations of Jesus as Messiah conclude with a statement from John the Baptist, setting the stage for tomorrow's feast. This passage makes the claim that Jesus performed baptisms, a practice that the same evangelist elsewhere denies (4:1–3). The readings from the First Letter of John conclude today with the affirmation that the Son of God has come and given the faithful the ability to recognize the One who is true. Another psalm of praise joyfully concludes the Christmas weekdays.

The antiphons recall the divinity of Jesus and the sharing of his riches with the faithful. The opening prayer blends the themes of incarnation and new creation.

☀ 12 #21 (LMC #17) white
The Baptism of the Lord
FEAST

ORIENTATION

The Baptism of the Lord is another epiphany, a manifestation of Jesus' identity to the public. Last week, Gentile Magi recognized him. Today, God proclaims him the beloved Son before the witnesses to the baptism. This feast concludes the Christmas season, which means the Christmas environment and its service music, and even some carols, if only a final "Joy to the World," are part of this day.

The baptism of Jesus became difficult to explain early on. If baptism represents the forgiveness of sin, and if Jesus is sinless, why should he be baptized? You can see some growing embarrassment with the baptism as the gospels unfold. The synoptic gospels all present it rather plainly, and even the Acts of the Apostles refers to the event. But John's version, which appeared in the weekday lectionary on January 3, gives a more oblique account of the event. The baptism could not be ignored. It seems that everyone tried to make sense of it.

On the simplest level, the baptism functions as a beginning of Jesus' public career and a manifestation of his true identity. That identity comes not from the washing of sins but from the booming voice of the Father: "You are my beloved Son."

LECTIONARY

Mark's account of the baptism is probably the earliest in the New Testament. It makes the ceremony look like a private affair. Jesus comes from Nazareth to the Jordan, and John baptizes him there. Coming up from the water, Jesus sees the heavens open and the voice of God speaks directly to him: "You are my beloved Son."

The lectionary offers an option for the first two readings. The ones for Year A may be used every year, but in Year B you may choose alternates. This offers a wider range of texts for the celebration of this feast during the cycle.

The first reading for the Year B option comes from Isaiah (55:1–11). It is one of the readings offered for the Easter Vigil, the church's premiere celebration of baptism. This prophecy invites God's people to "come to the water" and receive from God's goodness. As at the Easter Vigil, a canticle from Isaiah 12 follows, assuring the faithful they will draw water joyfully from the springs of salvation.

The second reading for the Year B option comes from the First Letter of John (5:1–9). It proclaims that Jesus came through water and blood, and that the Spirit, water and blood testify.

You may choose the first readings from Year A instead. Peter's speech in the house of Cornelius recalls the baptism as the time when God anointed Jesus with the Holy Spirit and with power. The frequency with which this story appears in the New Testament gives testimony to its historicity. We hear from Isaiah the passage to which the voice of God in the gospel alludes. Psalm 29 is chosen because of its reference to the voice of the Lord thundering over the waters, an image made real in the gospel.

SACRAMENTARY

The entrance antiphon refers to Matthew's account of the baptism, and the communion antiphon mentions the testimony of John.

In place of the Penitential Rite today, consider using the rite of sprinkling with holy water. You may take this option on any Sunday, but today it will especially unite the themes of baptism and body of Christ.

There are three options for the opening prayer today. The first, a new composition, expresses the significance of the feast most clearly and remains free of the non-inclusive language that mars the alternative opening prayer. The extra prayer recalls strongly the image of the incarnation and may help conclude the season with a reflection on the meaning of Christmas. The preface marvelously blends the themes of the baptisms of Christ and of the faithful, as well as the images from today's scriptures concerning the dove, the anointing and the gospel of salvation for the poor. The recommended prayer over the people provides a good blessing, but other choices could be made, like solemn blessing #2, 3 or 4.

OTHER IDEAS

Keeping the Christmas decorations in place till today may make people wonder if you have been postponing the task, but it is appropriate. You may catechize those who complain that the Christmas season continues through today.

By Flowing Waters (38–46) (The Liturgical Press) has a complete suite of antiphons and psalms for Epiphany and the Baptism of the Lord. At the sprinkling rite, you can sing "Springs of Water," from the Easter Vigil, with verses from 199 (see the performance note on p. 420).

Sing the Glory to God today, the same version you have used throughout this season. It will bring the celebration to a joyful conclusion. You may also sing Christmas carols, since it is still the season of Jesus' birth. Conclude also the singing of the acclamations you have used throughout the seasons of Advent and Christmas.

You may want to conclude the Christmas season with evening prayer tonight, a prayer of thanksgiving for the mystery revealed in a manger. You might use it to rally volunteers to change the decorations in the church.

PROCLAMATION OF THE BIRTH OF CHRIST

To - day, the twenty - fifth day of De - cem - ber,

unknown ages from the time when God created the heavens and the earth

and then formed man and woman in his own i - mage.

Several thousand years after the flood,

when God made the rainbow shine forth as a sign of the cov - e - nant.

Twenty - one centuries from the time of Abra - ham and Sarah;

thirteen centuries after Moses led the people of Israel out of E - gypt.

Eleven hundred years from the time of Ruth and the judges;

one thousand years from the anointing of David as king;

in the sixty - fifth week according to the prophecy of Dan - iel.

In the one hundred and ninety - fourth O - lympiad;

the seven hundred and fifty - second year from the foundation of the city of Rome.

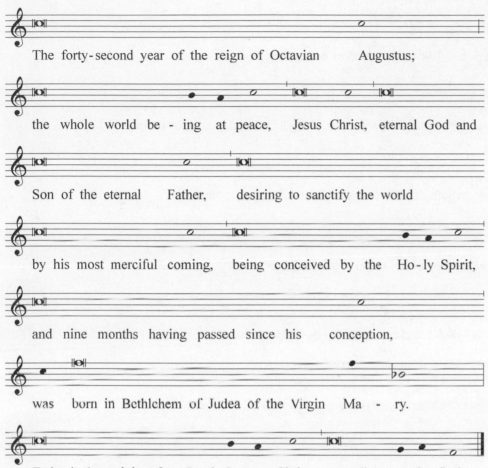

The forty-second year of the reign of Octavian Augustus;

the whole world be-ing at peace, Jesus Christ, eternal God and

Son of the eternal Father, desiring to sanctify the world

by his most merciful coming, being conceived by the Ho-ly Spirit,

and nine months having passed since his conception,

was born in Bethlehem of Judea of the Virgin Ma - ry.

Today is the nativity of our Lord Je - sus Christ according to the flesh.

PROCLAMATION OF THE DATE OF EASTER

Dear broth-ers and sis-ters, the glory of the Lord has shone up-on us,

and shall ever be manifest among us, until the day of his re-turn.

Through the rhythms of times and sea-sons

let us celebrate the mys-ter-ies of sal-va-tion.

Let us recall the year's cul-mi-na-tion, the Easter Tri-du-um of the Lord:

his last supper, his cruci-fix-ion, his burial, and his rising,

celebrated be-tween the eve-ning of the seventeenth of April

and the eve-ning of the twentieth of April. Each Eas-ter

as on each Sun-day the Holy Church makes present the great and sav-ing deed

by which Christ has for ev-er con-quered sin and death.

From Eas-ter are reckoned all the days we keep ho-ly.

Ash Wednesday, the beginning of Lent, will occur on the fifth of March.

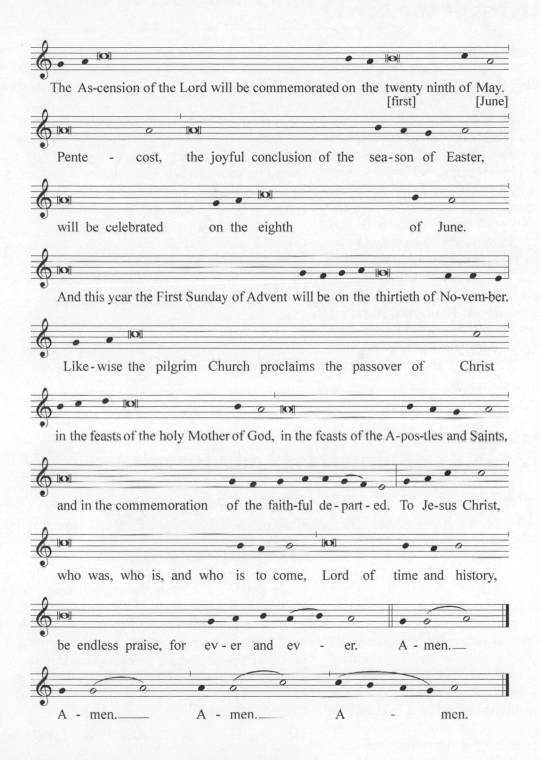

The As-cension of the Lord will be commemorated on the twenty ninth of May.
[first] [June]

Pente - cost, the joyful conclusion of the sea-son of Easter,

will be celebrated on the eighth of June.

And this year the First Sunday of Advent will be on the thirtieth of No-vem-ber.

Like - wise the pilgrim Church proclaims the passover of Christ

in the feasts of the holy Mother of God, in the feasts of the A-pos-tles and Saints,

and in the commemoration of the faith-ful de - part - ed. To Je-sus Christ,

who was, who is, and who is to come, Lord of time and history,

be endless praise, for ev - er and ev - er. A - men.

A - men. A - men. A - men.

DECEMBER 25, 2002
The Nativity of the Lord

Always Open for Business
Isaiah 62:1–5
"You shall be called 'My Delight' and your land 'Espoused'."

GOING-OUT-OF-BUSINESS signs spell good sales for the consumer and sad days for the seller. Businesses close when they can no longer turn a profit. Unemployment and poverty bring sadness to the families of workers. If several businesses close in one region, it disturbs the whole community. No one likes to go out of business. No one likes feeling empty and forsaken.

This Christmas Day, through the mouth of Isaiah, God promises that the chosen people will not go out of business. They shall be called "Frequented," a nickname that would make any store proud. God proclaims this message not just to ancient Israel but to all the ends of the earth.

At Christmas we reflect on our blessings but we are also disturbed by our losses. God enters these days with joy, to keep us from brooding over sorrow.

In the past year, have you ever felt that God abandoned you? If so, then Isaiah's message is for you. This message goes to the whole world, including you. You are a city that is not forsaken. You are called "Frequented," God's delight. God comes to be with you and to rejoice in you.

In you!

Written by Paul Turner. © 2002 Archdiocese of Chicago, Liturgy Training Publications; 1-800-933-1800; www.ltp.org.

DECEMBER 29, 2002
The Holy Family of Jesus, Mary and Joseph

The Miracle of Birth
Genesis 15:1–6; 21:1–3
"Sarah became pregnant and bore Abraham a son in his old age."

No matter whose child you are, you are a blessing. The miracle of your existence is a gift from God.

On this first Sunday of the Christmas season we remember the relationships that exist among family members. We celebrate with family and friends during these days of Christmas, we tell once again the family tales, we look to the Holy Family as an example for our lives, and we thank God for the family we have received.

One of the stories we remember today is about Abraham's family. God promised him that he would father a child. But Abraham was old. He complained that his inheritance would pass to his steward because he had no son.

God told Abraham that he was wrong. There would be a son. So even in his old age, Abraham put his faith in God's promise. Only then did Sarah conceive Abraham's child.

The birth of Isaac was a miracle. The birth of every child is a miracle. Your birth was a miracle too.

Do you know the circumstances of your own birth? Were your parents hoping for you? Were you a surprise? Even if you surprised them, you did not surprise God, who promised you life in the eternal plan of salvation. You are part of God's holy family.

Written by Paul Turner. © 2002 Archdiocese of Chicago, Liturgy Training Publications; 1-800-933-1800; www.ltp.org.

JANUARY 1, 2003
The Blessed Virgin Mary, Mother of God

A Blessed New Year!
Numbers 6:22–27
"The LORD bless you and keep you!"

WE begin the new year with hope. It is filled with possibility. Our calendars may look empty, but they will soon be filled with activity and events. We already have plans for some of them. Other events will surprise us. We realize this year will bring a measure of sorrow, but we trust it to also bring a measure of joy.

Let this day and this year be a blessing. Today we hear the words of blessing spoken by God to Moses. "The Lord bless you and keep you." They are words of protection. "The Lord be gracious to you." They are words of favor. "The Lord give you peace!" They are words that wish the finest blessing, the gift of peace.

This new year, with all its promise, gives us the possibility of blessing. Perhaps you have withheld blessing from someone you know. Perhaps you especially need God's gift of peace. Perhaps you fear the absence of God's protection. Let this blessing calm your heart. Let it inspire you to breathe God's gift of peace to all you meet this day and this new year.

In early January we're still enjoying the season of Christmas. We have many more days to sing carols, to invites guests over, to share the peace of the season. In this bright new year let the blessing of God, first spoken to Moses, echoing throughout the ages, enter your home and warm your hearth.

JANUARY 5, 2003
The Epiphany of the Lord

Caravans of Camels
Isaiah 60:1–6
"Arise, shine; for your light has come."

ABOUT those camels—we're not too sure about them. Yes, nearly every nativity scene shows the Magi seated on stately dromedaries, or leading their beasts of burden by bit and rein. But, honestly, the story of the Magi never tells us how they got there. They could have traveled on foot, in chariot, or by camel, on horseback, even on an elephant—but we just don't know.

The reason we keep putting them on camels in our art is because of Isaiah's prophecy. He predicted that caravans of camels would fill Jerusalem, and that people from the east would come bearing gold and frankincense.

"Rise up in splendor, Jerusalem!" Isaiah proclaims. "Your light has come."

In Matthew's story, the Magi realize that Jerusalem's light has come. They follow the star and bring their gifts of gold, frankincense and myrrh. By telling about these gifts, Matthew turns our attention back to Isaiah. Reading that prophecy, we realize that the light Isaiah mentioned is the Light of the world, Jesus Christ.

When we see the Magi seated on camels, we are remembering Isaiah. When we remember Isaiah, we remember the light that came to shatter the darkness of our world. Those camels carry hope.

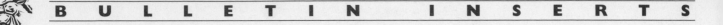

Simple Gifts
Isaiah 55:1–11
"Come, without paying and without cost, drink wine and milk!"

THE best things in life are free. The sun, the rain, the wind and the ground on which we tread are given to us without measure.

We buy products that we think will bring pleasure. Often they do, but sometimes they don't. Sometimes we squander our money and time on what we think will bring us relief. But it only causes us remorse. Perhaps the product is not as good as we thought. Perhaps we were being selfish. Perhaps we denied other people an opportunity for enjoyment by taking some for ourselves.

We forget about the simple pleasures of life: breathing deeply, being with a friend, or humming a tune.

Through the prophet Isaiah, God invited thirsty Israel to come to the water. Why spend money on what fails to satisfy? Come to the water of God's wisdom, mercy and goodness. Drink from God's water source and slake your thirst.

Today we remember how Jesus went to the waters of the Jordan, how he heeded God's voice and took delight in God's favor. He invites us to do the same: Throughout this new year of grace, drink deeply from God's wisdom in prayer and sacred conversation. It's one of the best things in life. And it's free.

WINTER ORDINARY TIME

The Meaning

ORDINARY Time appears each year in two periods of unequal length. The precise dates and length of this time is based entirely on the seasonal cycles of Christmas and Easter. The first period of Ordinary Time begins as Christmas closes and ends as Lent begins. We resume Ordinary Time after the Easter season, when it remains in force until the close of the church year and the beginning of Advent.

This time is ordinary in the sense that it lacks the seasonal focus of other periods and that it keeps pace with the order of time.

■ ORDINARY TIME BEGINS with the Baptism of the Lord. The lectionary explains that the Baptism, which closes the Christmas cycle, is the First Sunday of Ordinary Time. As John the Baptist bridges the Old and New Testaments with his prophetic testimony, so the Baptism of the Lord bridges two seasons. It is a further manifestation of Jesus in a season marked by epiphanies. It is the beginning of the public ministry of Jesus whose gospel story we will follow in sequence throughout both parts of Ordinary Time.

■ THIS YEAR WINTER ORDINARY TIME IS COMPARATIVELY LONG. Between the years 2001 and 2010, Winter Ordinary Time extends into March only twice. This gives us a sizeable break between seasons and should allow liturgical planners more opportunity to ready themselves and the community for Lent.

■ THE CARNIVAL SEASON BEGINS at Epiphany and reaches its crescendo on the night before Ash Wednesday, Mardi Gras. Parades and parties increase in the days before Lent as people make festival before making fast. An amazing number of traditions have evolved in celebration of Carnival, but most of these stand outside the church door, and some poke fun at or even challenge the church and other human institutions. Winter needs its cheer and hospitality, and while the liturgical texts do not always support a prelenten season resembling the joy of Easter, people bracing themselves for the rigors of Lent enjoy Carnival.

■ FEBRUARY IS BLACK HISTORY MONTH. Intercessions, homilies and music from the African American Tradition will help the community recognize this observance.

The Saints

D URING Ordinary Time, the celebration of the saints may progress unfettered by seasonal restrictions.

■ TWO DAYS RANKED AS "FEAST" can receive full attention and replace the other days of Ordinary Time. Feasts this year are the Conversion of Paul, January 25; the Presentation of the Lord, February 2; and the Chair of Peter, February 22.

Ordinarily, when a feast falls on a Sunday, the Sunday liturgy prevails. However, feasts of the Lord take precedence over Sundays in Ordinary Time. This year, when February 2 lands on a Sunday, we interrupt the sequence of Ordinary Time Sundays to celebrate the Presentation of the Lord.

■ WHEN AN OBLIGATORY MEMORIAL COMES UP (and there are many of these ranging from the virgin and martyr Agatha, February 5, to the priest John Bosco, January 31), use its vestment color and presidential prayers, including the preface. If the saint comes without a complete set of proper prayers, turn to the relevant common of martyrs, pastors, doctors, virgins or holy men and women.

On memorials the scriptures should generally continue the semicontinuous readings of Ordinary Time, but you may take them from the lectionary common appropriate for the saint.

■ WHEN AN OPTIONAL MEMORIAL OCCURS ON A WEEKDAY (and there are many of these too, ranging from the pope and martyr Fabian, January 20, to the virgin Angela Merici, January 27), your community may elect to celebrate the Ordinary Time Mass or the Mass of the saint. You may also choose from the list of many lesser-known saints in the martyrology.

One bit of caution: When there are options among two or more memorials on a given day, you may choose one but not choose to keep all the options at once.

You may then choose the prayers for the saint from the sacramentary as well as readings from the lectionary commons. But, ordinarily, follow the readings of the Ordinary Time weekday. That allows those who participate in daily Mass to hear the semicontinuous course of readings, to unite themselves with those at home whose daily prayer incorporates the lectionary, and to observe the recommendation of the lectionary.

When a Saturday in Ordinary Time calls for the weekday liturgy, a Mass from the *Collection of Masses of the Blessed Virgin Mary* or from the commons may be used. During this period, the only days that block such a Marian Mass in the average parish are the feasts of the Conversion of Paul, January 25; and the Chair of Peter, February 22; both falling on Saturdays this year.

■ SPECIAL CONCERNS, DEVOTIONS AND CIVIC EVENTS: The lectionary and sacramentary also supply the texts of Masses for various needs and occasions. These texts may be used throughout Ordinary Time. On Ordinary Time weekdays and optional memorials, you may freely but sparingly choose from these Masses (GIRM, 327). On obligatory memorials during this period, the presider may authorize a Mass for various needs and occasions only for serious need or pastoral advantage. For example, if the community fears the threat of a serious winter storm, the presider may offer the appropriate Mass (#37), even on Scholastica's Day, February 23. Only your bishop may authorize the same Mass for a Sunday in Ordinary Time.

Included during these weeks each year is the national holiday in remembrance of the life and work of Martin Luther King, Jr. Two events span a series of days during this period: The Week of Prayer for Church Unity and Catholic Schools Week call for some kind of liturgical recognition. You may find inspiration in the Masses and Prayers for Various Needs and Occasions: #13, For Unity of Christians; #14, For the Spread of the Gospel; #18, For Those Who Serve in Public Office; #21, For the Progress of Peoples; or #22, For Peace and Justice. Schedule times of prayer to recognize these events on the parish calendar.

The Lectionary

THE gospel for the Second Sunday of Ordinary Time always comes from John in all three years of the cycle. After that weekend, though, the year's featured evangelist settles in. All the gospels of Mark in Winter Ordinary Time will come from his first two chapters. The exception, of course, is February 2, when we celebrate the Presentation of the Lord instead of the Fourth Sunday in Ordinary Time.

As with every Winter Ordinary Time, the second readings open with passages from the First Letter of Paul to the Corinthians. During Year B, we hear the middle chapters of this important epistle. This year, because of the length of Ordinary Time before Lent begins, we will also hear some passages from Second Corinthians.

The first readings for this set of Sundays come from a wide range of Old Testament collections: historical books, prophets and the wisdom literature. They are chosen, of course, because each carries a theme that foreshadows the gospel.

Each Sunday comes with its own responsorial psalm, but your community may build its musical repertory by selecting one from the common psalms for Ordinary Time. They may be used on any Sunday throughout the season. These psalms (19, 27, 34, 63, 95, 100, 103 and 145) explore the greatness of God, the wonders of God's word, and the thirsty spirit yearning for divine union.

■ THE SUNDAY *LECTIONARY FOR MASSES WITH CHILDREN* follows the same course of readings. Typically, the children's lectionary omits the second of Sunday's three readings. This will be the case on the Second, Third, Seventh and Eighth Sundays of Ordinary Time. However, the first reading is omitted on the Sixth Sunday. The Fifth Sunday offers all three readings.

The second reading will also be omitted from the children's lectionary for the Presentation on February 2, and you will find those readings not in the Year B volume, but in the volume of readings for weekdays.

The Sacramentary

■ SAMPLE FORMULAS FOR THE GENERAL INTERCESSIONS appear in the sacramentary's first appendix. (See #1–2 and 9–10 for those suggested for Ordinary Time.)

Ordinary Time is a good time to evaluate some of the things we do ordinarily. Consider, for example, the preparation of the altar and gifts.

■ "OFFERTORY" is a word that keeps appearing in liturgical conversation, but it poorly describes what the main purpose of this part of the Mass is: preparing the altar and gifts for the sacrifice and eucharist. Many people still think of it as "offertory" in keeping with the former title and because this is when they make their offering to the church. But much more is going on.

The actions and words of this part of the Mass prepare the gifts for the sacrifice, and those gifts include the hearts of the assembly. At the beginning of the preparation we gather what is needed for the prayer to continue. At the conclusion of the preparation we are ready to begin the heart of the eucharist, the great eucharistic prayer.

During the eucharist, the Holy Spirit changes the bread and wine we present into the body and blood of Christ. The gathering of these gifts allows them to be transformed, and then we will be transformed by the gift of God that we share in communion.

Linens are set out to prepare the altar. Prior to this, the altar should be fairly bare and open. The altar receives attention now as we move from the liturgy of the word to the liturgy of the eucharist. The corporal should be broad enough to receive the vessels. If the corporal is large enough only for the priest's host and chalice, it becomes a symbol of a clerical culture that makes the priest's communion more important than that of the assembly. The purificator is also set out at this time. This cloth will catch any drips of the precious blood of Christ from the chalice.

The chalice and missal are also brought to the altar. Prior to this point, is the chalice kept on the side at your church? Or is it brought to the altar even before the liturgy of the word, as was the former custom? By bringing the chalice to the altar now, the vessel draws our attention to the altar of sacrifice, the principal furnishing of this part of the Mass.

The missal is also brought to the altar now. Some communities still place the missal on the altar from the beginning of the service, or move it there after the opening prayer. Having the server place the sacramentary on the altar after the opening prayer may save a few steps, but it draws attention to the altar too soon, when our attention should be riveted on the word. The missal is placed on the altar during the preparation of the altar and gifts.

In arranging the chalice and missal, consider placing the missal closer to the presider and the chalice closer to the assembly. This may help the presider see the texts and keep the visual impact of the cup unobstructed for the assembly.

Note also that ministers place these items on the altar. They are not part of the procession of the gifts.

The procession includes bread, wine and gifts for the church and the poor. It does not include extra cups, the water cruet, the finger bowl, or the hand towel. Many communities assume that you simply process up the aisle with the things that belong on the side table. No, process with the gifts of the people. Process with what will be transformed at Mass, the symbols of the sacrifice of Christ and of the community. In a similar way, communities should be wary of processing with textbooks, basketballs, photographs and other symbols of academic or personal pursuit. The primary symbols of this eucharist are bread, wine and offerings for the church and the poor.

A "sufficient" amount of bread and wine should be prepared. A sufficiency means enough bread so that no one receives communion from the tabernacle. The symbol is that we receive in communion the very gifts we have offered, now consecrated by God. A sufficiency also means enough wine so that all may participate under both forms. If you consistently run out of the precious blood during communion, or consistently do not even offer communion under both forms, the quantity of wine carried in procession should be increased.

The collection of fiscal offerings is an important part of the ceremony. It demonstrates our willingness to support the church with our means, and to share what we have with others, no matter how great or small our resources. Do you encourage your community to make a sacrificial tithe, a gift of ten percent to charities?

How does the collection take place? Ushers need not be the same ministers as the greeters at the door, but many communities combine the functions. Are ushers participating in the entire Mass, or are they gathering in the usher's room until their time of service? Do you use baskets on poles or pass a basket through the room? Is the ministry of usher restricted to adult men? Do youth or families ever serve as ushers?

On some Sundays you may have a second collection. Some communities take it up after communion, to separate it from the first collection, but this also separates it from the preparation of the altar and gifts and the part of the Mass that most signifies our personal sacrifice. If you have designated envelopes for a second collection, you may include them in a single collection and let the money counters sort it out after the service. Or if you prefer two collections, you may start the second once the first has begun. People can have their separate contributions ready and make the distinction as the baskets come by in sequence.

Members of the assembly process with the gifts. Their presence symbolizes the entire community's offering. If ushers help collect the gifts, they need not be the same ones who present them to the altar. By inviting different members of the assembly to this action, you broaden the participation of the people and better symbolize that the gift comes from everyone.

Who receives the gifts at the altar? The rubrics indicates it is the priest or deacon. Or do those who bring the gifts place them directly on the altar? What does this symbolize?

The presider raises the bread and cup "slightly," according to the rubrics. The gesture is one of taking or receiving the gifts. At the Last Supper, Jesus took, blessed, broke and gave. All these actions unfold in our celebration of every Mass. At this point the priest is simply receiving the gifts. The offering will come later, during the eucharistic prayer. When he lifts the bread and cup here, does the presider use a small gesture?

The "Blessed are you" prayers may be said audibly or inaudibly. Most people in the assembly feel left out if the priest says them inaudibly, but that may be the better solution when music accompanies these actions. If there is instrumental music, does the presider recite these prayers inaudibly, wait until the music is over to say them aloud, or shout down the music to get the prayers in? There is a time and a place for everything.

Incense may be used. If so, the offerings, priest and people may be incensed. The altar was probably incensed at the beginning of the service and need not be incensed again now. The difference is that the gifts are now on the altar, and they receive the incense. Whenever incense is used throughout the Mass, you honor the various presences of Christ in the eucharist: in the altar, the gifts, the priest and the people. Throughout the year, on what occasions do you use incense?

The priest washes his hands at the side of the altar. This secondary, semiprivate action does not take place in the same way as the other parts of the preparation of the altar and gifts. Does the washing of hands appear subdued in your celebration?

A song may be sung by all, by the choir, or by a soloist. Instrumental music may fill the air. Or no music may be heard at all. Formerly, the liturgical books gave a text for an "offertory song," but it no longer appears in the liturgy. You may sing something, but it may also be a nice time for a break.

The Book of Blessings

BE aware of some of the blessings the community may wish to observe. These include a mother before and after childbirth (1-VIII), parents after a miscarriage (1-IX), parents and an adopted child (1-X), birthdays (1-XI), the sick (2), pilgrims (8) and travelers (9). There are also blessings for a new school (14), a new library (15), a parish hall or catechetical center (16), a gymnasium or athletic field (20), means of

transportation (21), technical installations and equipment (23), tools (24), fields and flocks (26), seeds (27), an athletic event (29) and meals (30).

These blessings may be incorporated into the community's Sunday worship, or take place on some other special occasion.

The Rite of Christian Initiation of Adults

■ FOR THOSE LOOKING TOWARD BAPTISM THIS EASTER, Winter Ordinary Time becomes a crucial period. During these weeks the community should be making its final assessment, discerning who is called to the sacraments this spring. This discernment should precede the Rite of Election, which usually coincides with the First Sunday of Lent. All ministers, including the entire community, "should, after considering the matter carefully, arrive at a judgment about the catechumens' state of formation and progress" (RCIA, 121). You might consider a special evening of prayer to help those who are making this deliberation.

■ OTHER LITURGIES OF THE CATECHUMENATE may take place in full force during this time. The Rite of Acceptance into the Order of Catechumens may take place two or three times a year (RCIA, 18.3). Schedule the celebration for some Sunday this season if you have inquirers this year. Most likely, these will not be baptized this Easter, but will remain catechumens through this year until next, in order to complete their formation (*National Statutes for the Catechumenate*, 6).

■ YOU MAY ALSO CONDUCT CELEBRATIONS OF THE WORD OF GOD (RCIA, 81–89). These may include minor exorcisms (90–94), blessings of the catechumens (95–97), or even an anointing with the oil of catechumens (98–103). If the community does not often witness the use of the oil of catechumens, this provides a good opportunity for catechesis and celebration. If the supply is low, the local priest may bless more, a ritual that could also take place in the presence of the community.

A priest may bless oil of the sick and the oil of catechumens, but only a bishop consecrates chrism. If you run out of chrism, get more from the bishop. But if you run out of the oil of catechumens, your priest can increase the supply himself, starting with any vegetable oil.

The Liturgy of the Hours

Turn to Volume III of the set for this season's *Liturgy of the Hours*. New users will find this the perfect season of the year to become acquainted with the format. The feasts and seasons of the year require many ribbons just to keep the flow of the liturgy, but the Ordinary Time prayer lays out rather neatly. You could introduce morning and evening prayer at different occasions of this season to celebrate any of its special events. Follow the liturgy in the book, or adapt it with a sung celebration in the parish involving cantors, musicians and ministers.

Don't forget about the beautiful collection of religious poetry in Appendix IV. These compositions by Augustine, Dante, Saint Theresa and John Donne, among others, will enrich your people. Provide the texts as a live meditative reading or as a printed poem in the bulletin or on the website.

The Rite of Penance

The way pastoral practice has unfolded, this is usually "off-season" for reconciliation. Advent and Lent become primary times for the celebration of this sacrament. Still, sin knows no season, and opportunities for reconciliation will challenge the community toward its continuous spiritual development.

Make sure the regular celebration of individual confession of sins and absolution is well advertised. Use the bulletin, the signage at the church and the website. If you plan a communal reconciliation service, expect it to be poorly attended. Most Catholics will wait for Lent, but some will take advantage of the opportunity.

If you are affiliated with a Catholic school, this may be a good season to celebrate the sac-

rament communally. It will spare the confessors who have a busy season coming up in March and April. When celebrating the sacrament with children, try to keep the service brief. Do several short communal services in a row for small groups of children, rather than one large one that keeps all the children waiting. With several confessors, you can celebrate for each group of children in 30 minutes or less.

The Pastoral Care of the Sick

If you have not celebrated this sacrament communally at Mass, this would be a good season to do so. Those beleaguered by winter weather, yet freed from the demands of Christmas and Lent, might appreciate an opportunity to celebrate the sacrament. The introduction to this rite (1–4) opens with a beautiful meditation on human sickness and its meaning in the mystery of salvation. It deserves much reflection to help people distinguish between sickness and sin. Illness does not mean God's punishment. It can be an opportunity for grace. Care should be taken that the faithful understand who is eligible for the anointing (8–15). The illness should be serious.

The Rite of Marriage

Throughout Winter Ordinary Time, there is little restriction on the celebration of the Rite of Marriage at Mass. If the wedding takes place on a Saturday night or Sunday, the wedding Mass may be used with its prayers and scriptures. This includes February 1 this year, when the parish community may celebrate the Presentation of the Lord at a Saturday evening Mass. The wedding Mass may be celebrated in its entirety that evening, without alluding to the feast. Any Saturday night wedding Mass fulfills a Sunday obligation.

This could be a good season to evaluate the parish wedding celebration. How do the entrance rites flow for the wedding? Do couples ever take advantage of the description of the procession in the *Rite of Marriage* (19), which indicates that they come in together? There is no rubric for a father giving away a daughter. There is an option for parents (in the plural) to be part of the procession.

How is the sanctuary arranged? Can the bride and groom be seen by the faithful when they give their consent? If the presider stands between them and the assembly, all will see their faces. Can the bride and groom be heard by the faithful? Attach a wireless microphone to the groom, and all will hear the words of both.

The Order of Christian Funerals

WINTER funerals may require some accommodations. If the assembly arrives wearing coats, is there a visible place to hang them up? If snow covers the ground, will assistance be needed at the cemetery?

Evaluate the celebration of funerals at your parish. How is the wake service conducted? The Order of Christian Funerals gives a beautiful outline for a scripture service. Is it observed or does your community expect someone to lead a rosary at the wake? Who leads this service? It need not be a priest. If lay ministers lead it, have they received training and evaluation? Where does the wake service take place? It may be celebrated at the church, where the faithful are accustomed to gather, where hymnals are present, sanctuary furniture is in place, musical instruments are always prepared, and the spirit of prayer already abounds. Is there a secure place to keep the body of the deceased overnight at church? Are there volunteers who will truly keep vigil?

Many people find it easier to attend the vigil service rather than the funeral Mass the next day because of their work schedules. Has your community made the vigil a real liturgy? Are ministers of music available? Readers? Greeters?

The Art and Environment

THE look of the church should reflect the simplicity of Ordinary Time, but not the barrenness of Lent. Transitional environment will help people make the shift out of the Christmas season, lulling them into the commonplace before the severity of Lent. Use the winter plant life of your region. If possible, duplicate the shade and fabric of the vesture in appointments for the church. Be sure to give attention to the nave. Simple decorations where the assembly enters and gathers are just as important as those that adorn the sanctuary.

The Music

■ EUCHARISTIC ACCLAMATIONS: Choose a set of acclamations for the eucharistic prayer. Use them throughout this season. This could be a good time to learn a new set of acclamations. If the assembly has been singing a familiar set throughout the Christmas season, they may be ready for something new. It will also help establish the new season.

■ YOU MIGHT ALSO EXPAND THE ASSEMBLY'S REPERTOIRE in a different way. For example, the people might learn a setting of the general intercessions or of the Our Father. Steven C. Warner's "The Lord's Prayer" (WLP, 7204) could become a weekly staple in your parish, singable and prayerful.

Take a look through the indexes of your hymnal and participation aids. Use this period to become more familiar with the way you can reference scripture passages and the themes that emerge from them. Does your repertoire of hymnody need expansion to include songs of discipleship, service, mission or social concern?

Collections of hymns are available from a variety of publishers, and not many of these selections appear in popular participation aids. You will find it worthwhile to become familiar with books like these: *Worship & Praise Songbook,* a collection of folk and contemporary music available from Augsburg Fortress, 1999; *Voices:*

Native American Hymns and Worship Resources, a remarkable resource for hymns and prayers that speak to the heart, available from Discipleship Resources in Nashville TN; *Swift Currents and Still Waters* by John A. Dalles, 65 hymn texts you can use with tunes in the book or to tunes your community knows (GIA, G-5366); *Awake Our Hearts to Praise!,* by Herman G. Stuempfle, another collection of hymn, song and carol texts that can be sung to a variety of tunes (GIA, G-5302); and Randall Sensmeier's *Teach Our Hearts to Sing Your Praise* (GIA, G-5632), more hymn tunes, songs and carols. All these resources will offer your community fresh texts to sing and new tunes to learn. No one should be overburdened with too much new material, but you may find just the text you'd like for a special occasion.

You can add new life to old hymns by adding choir and instruments. See "Sent Forth by God's Blessing" by Omer Westendorf and John Schiavone (WLP, 8517); "We Are Your People," a text that fits the tune of "For All the Saints," arranged by Steven R. Janco (WLP, 8623); "Concertato on Ellacombe," better known as "Go Make of All Disciples" and "The Day of Resurrection" by Charles Thatcher (WLP, 8656); and a "Concertato on Hymn to Joy," an arrangement of Beethoven's most popular hymn by Paul M. French (WLP, 8698). See also "Jesus Christ, Bread of Life" by Steve Schaubel" for a setting of the Largo from Dvořák's New World Symphony (WLP, 5230).

Broaden the ethnic appeal of your repertoire with James V. Marchionda and Mark Rachelski's setting of "Just a Closer Walk with Thee" (WLP, 8576) and Steven R. Janco's fine and fun arrangement of "Is There Anybody Here Who Loves My Jesus?" (WLP, 8609). Henry Mollicone's "Hear Me, Redeemer" (Schirmer, 4511) borrows a similar style. There is no end to the reflective, useful music from Taizé (GIA). In Spanish, it is hard to top "Nada te turbe," a confident hymn of trust, based on words by Saint Theresa of Avila.

Psalmody: Settings of the psalms appear in almost every participation aid, but you may want to give attention to some fine octavos.

When it comes to responsorial psalmody, a very simple chant-like setting may be the very tonic to draw more attention to words than to music. See the very simple, practical and spiritual "Six Psalms for Sundays and Seasons" by Thomas M. Cosley (WLP, 6208). Paul Lisicky's

"You Are My Guide" (WLP, 6204) accomplishes the same kind of result.

If you want something a little more interesting, try Alan J. Hommerding's "Psalms in Canon" (WLP, 6235), which enable choirs to sing in parts just by learning one melody. Michael Hay's "We Will Rest in You" (WLP, 6246) is as effective a setting of Psalm 134 as you will find, and Paul Inwood's "Search Me, O God" (WLP, 6217) is a moving rendition of Psalm 139.

If you want something even more jazzy, look for Paul A. Tate's "Glorify the Lord with Me!" based on Psalm 111 (WLP, 7487). "Show Us Your Way, Lord" by Ed Bolduc (WLP, 7358) is syncopated enough for youth but relaxed enough for more settled tastes. "You Are My Rock" by Michael T. Pierce (WLP, 6229) sounds like a spiritual.

Psalm settings in Spanish and English include Julie Howard's "Here I Am, God" (WLP, 7128); Pedro Rubalcava's "Alaben Todos" (WLP, 12678); and Peter M. Kolar's "El Señor Es Compasivo" (WLP, 12670).

Choir: Your parish choir may use this season to expand its repertoire. The classical literature is endless, but some recent reprints by composers of historical importance make this music even more available to you. Look for "Dixit Maria ad angelum" (WLP, 5791) by Hans Leo Hassler (1564–1612); "I Will Not Leave You Comfortless" (Schirmer, 1676) by William Byrd (1543–1623); "Hallelujah, Amen" (Schirmer, 304) by George Frideric Handel (1685–1759); and "How Lovely is Thy Dwelling-Place (Schirmer, 1713) by Johannes Brahms (1833–1897).

From the contemporary literature for choir, consider "I Believe in the Lord" by William A. Wollman (WLP, 8617), a beautiful hymn of trust; "God, Be Merciful Unto Us" by David Seitz, a setting of Psalm 67 that is mostly in unison, unaccompanied; "Canticle of Daniel" by Jeffrey Honoré (WLP, 8690), a difficult setting of a useful text; and an arrangement of the popular song "The Gift to Be Simple" by Robert W. Schaefer (WLP, 8687). The youth will enjoy "Give Us Your Peace" by Michael Mahler (GIA), a quiet, but insistent appeal to "Let All the Fighting Cease."

Let your children's choir explores pieces like "Children of the Lord" by James V. Marchionda (WLP, 7848) and the delightful "Two Copper Coins" by Dolores M. Hruby (WLP, 7119).

The Parish and Home

ENCOURAGE reflection on the Sunday scriptures at home by providing people with references to them or to resources where they can be found. The United States Conference of Catholic Bishops website is useful. Become acquainted with LTP's *At Home with the Word* and *Palabra de Dios.*

Your religious education ministry could sponsor a table of resources making scripture study and commentaries available. Consider offering additional information about Mark's gospel, as we work through its early chapters.

■ RECOMMEND USE OF *CATHOLIC HOUSEHOLD BLESSINGS AND PRAYERS* for a wide variety of home celebrations. These include blessings for waking, washing and dressing, going out from home each day, at noon, and coming home. Table prayers for Sundays can also be found.

LTP's *Blessings and Prayers* can be used for teaching children to pray.

The more ambitious may want instruction on praying the *Liturgy of the Hours* at home. You could provide catechetical sessions for those who are interested in the one volume edition.

■ THE FEAST OF THE PRESENTATION OF THE LORD, February 2, comes during this season. This year it falls on a Sunday when all are called to worship. Encourage people to bring candles from home for the blessing. They may light them for family prayer throughout the year.

Texts

■ GREETING:
(Adapted from the sacramentaries of other language groups.)

Grace and peace in the holy assembly of God's church be with you.

The grace of our Lord Jesus Christ,
the love of God,
and the communion of the Holy Spirit be with you always.

■ INTRODUCTION TO THE PENITENTIAL RITE:

Brothers and sisters, before we hear the Word of God and celebrate the sacrifice of Christ, we should prepare ourselves and ask God for the forgiveness of our sins.

Let us prepare for the celebration of the eucharist by recalling that we are sinners.

■ RESPONSE TO THE GENERAL INTERCESSIONS: The *Order of Christian Funerals* uses a formula with which many Catholics are unfamiliar. You could acquaint people with it by using it for the Sundays of Ordinary Time. Each petition concludes with "Lord, in your mercy." All respond, "Hear our prayer."

■ DISMISSAL OF CATECHUMENS:

Catechumens, the kingdom of God is at hand. Repent and believe in the gospel. Go forth now as disciples of the One who makes us fishers of people.

■ EUCHARISTIC PRAYER: The Spanish sacramentary includes inserts for Sundays in two eucharistic prayers. In Prayer II, after the words "Lord, remember your church throughout the world," the presider adds, "and gathered here on Sunday, the day on which Christ conquered death and made us partakers of his immortal life." The same expression appears in Prayer III after the words "the entire people your Son has gained for you."

The German sacramentary has a similar practice. On Sundays, in Eucharistic Prayer II, following the words "You are holy indeed, the fountain of all holiness," the presider adds these words: "We come before your presence and celebrate in communion with the whole church the first day of the week as the day on which Christ rose from the dead. Through him, whom you have raised up to your right hand, we pray." The same sentence occurs in Eucharistic Prayer III on Sundays, after the words "a perfect offering may be made to the glory of your name."

January

#305 (LMC #193–227)   green

MON 13 Weekday (First Week in Ordinary Time)

Optional memorial of Hilary (+ 367), bishop, doctor of the church/white ▪ The readings for Ordinary Time weekdays appear in the lectionary right after those of the Easter season.

The gospels of Ordinary Time weekdays present semicontinuous readings of the synoptics in the order in which, scholars believe, they were written. We start with Mark, progress to Matthew, and conclude the year with Luke. Mark's comparatively terse account presents a Jesus more rough-hewn than the other gospels describe. Mark's narrative moves swiftly, and his Jesus is the kind of character about whom we want to know more. We pick up the gospel today not at its beginning, but after the opening episodes of John the Baptist's proclamation, the baptism of Jesus, and the test in the desert. We begin with the Galilean ministry of Jesus, as he summarizes his entire message and calls his first disciples.

The first readings over the next two months come from three different books: Hebrews, Genesis and Sirach. The letter to the Hebrews is a cerebral work demanding much attention to understand its passages. The opening chapters of Genesis are well-known and delightful to hear. Sirach takes us into the Bible's wisdom literature with lyrical reflection.

The author of the letter to the Hebrews is unknown. The style differs considerably from that of Saint Paul, whose letters this book follows in the New Testament. The readers were probably Jewish Christians, familiar with the Old Testament scriptures. The book resembles a sermon more than a letter.

Hebrews opens with a proclamation of the divinity of Jesus, the Son of God, who reigns even above angels. The psalm invites angels and lesser divinities to prostrate before God. On the lips of Christians who have just heard the opening of Hebrews, the psalm invites angels to worship Christ.

The sacramentary offers a set of presidential prayers for the first week in Ordinary Time, following those for the Easter season. You may choose any other Ordinary Time prayers you wish. Consider also the text for the Spread of the Gospel (Various Needs and Occasions, #14). The entrance antiphon draws on images from the book of Revelation. The communion antiphons present Jesus as the source of life.

▪ TODAY'S SAINT: Hilary was born in Poitiers, nearly contemporary with a baptismal font still visible in the city. He defended the church against Arians and suffered exile under Constantine.

#306 (LMC #193–227)   green

TUE 14 Weekday

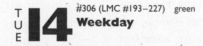

Hebrews comments on Psalm 8, which serves as today's responsorial psalm. It interprets the line, "You made him for a little while lower than the angels." Hebrews sees there a prophecy that the eternal Son of God took on human form.

Early in his ministry, Jesus exorcises an unclean spirit from a man in the synagogue. From the beginning of Jesus' ministry, Mark shows us the real enemy of the Son of God: the forces of evil. Jesus, who is all-good, stands in contrast to the unclean spirit.

Among the sacramentary texts, consider those for the Mass of Angels (Votive #9).

#307 (LMC #193–227)   green

WED 15 Weekday

Jesus continues his ministry of healing, giving new life to those suffering from physical infirmity as well as those possessed. Mark establishes Jesus' authority over various forces of nature at the beginning of the narrative.

Hebrews explains the purpose of the incarnation. Jesus took on human form so that through his death humans might have life. He became human so that he might be a merciful high priest, having suffered what people suffer. Today's psalm recalls God's faithful covenant with the children of Abraham, the people Jesus came to save, according to today's text from Hebrews.

The Mass for the Sick (Various Needs and Occasions, #32) might be appropriate today.

▪ THE PEOPLE OF GUATEMALA celebrate their patronal feast today, Jesus Christ of Esquipulas (*Santísimo Jesucristo Señor Nuestro de Esquipulas*).

#308 (LMC #193–227)   green

THU 16 Weekday

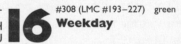

Yet another miracle story is reported in today's gospel. A leper kneels to request a cure. Characteristic of the Jesus of Mark's gospel, the healer tells the leper to keep the cure secret.

Once again, today's passage from Hebrews comments on a psalm, in this case 95, which predictably serves as the responsorial psalm. The pertinent verses from this psalm lament ancient Israel's infidelity with God and caution those believing in Christ not to succumb to the same temptation.

The Mass for Persecuted Christians (#15) includes prayers for those remaining faithful in time of trial.

FRI 17 #309 (LMC #193–227)   green
Anthony (+ 356), abbot
MEMORIAL

The first reading promises the faithful the reward of rest. God rested after creation. God promised rest to ancient Israel. God has promised eternal rest for those who accept Christ in the new covenant. The psalm challenges God's chosen people not to be like the wayward and rebellious generations of the past.

After a few days, Jesus returns to Capernaum to preach. When believers present a paralyzed man to him for a cure, his first thoughts are to cure the sinful soul.

■ TODAY'S SAINT: Heralded as the founder of monasticism, Anthony gave away his possessions, fled to the desert, and attracted a band of followers. Use the texts in the sacramentary for today's memorial. The preface for virgins and religious (P 68) suits the day well.

SAT 18 #310 (LMC #193–227)   green
Weekday

Optional Memorial of the Blessed Virgin Mary / white ▪ The letter to the Hebrews explains its method. So far the work has delivered interpretations of several scripture passages to encourage the readers to faithfulness. Today it announces that God's word is a two-edged sword that penetrates and divides soul and spirit, joints and marrow. God's word sees all and becomes the principle of judgment. A psalm in honor of God's word follows.

God's often-incomprehensible choice appears in the gospel as well, as people question the pedigree of the followers of Christ.

■ TODAY BEGINS THE WEEK OF PRAYER FOR CHRISTIAN UNITY. Under the old calendar, the octave began on this day with the celebration of the Chair of the Apostle Peter at Rome, now transferred

to February 22. The octave still concludes with a feast of Saint Paul. You may choose texts from the Mass for the Unity of Christians in the sacramentary (Various Needs and Occasions, #18A, B and C; and preface P 76) and even the lectionary. Include this intention among the intercessions. Use the first version of the eucharistic prayer for various needs and Occasions with this Mass if you wish, "The Church on the Way to Unity." *By Flowing Waters* (p. 292) has a complete suite of antiphons and psalms for the Votive Mass for the Unity of Christians.

☀19 #65 (LMC #60)   green
Second Sunday in Ordinary Time

ORIENTATION

Although we have been celebrating Ordinary Time on weekdays, this is the first green-vestment Sunday. Simpler church decorations and green vesture will signal the gathered assembly that the ordinary days of winter have arrived. But something special is needed to keep these days from being cheerless, something more than leftover poinsettias.

Some parishes keep most of the poinsettias (as long as they remain handsome) until February 2 (this year falling on a Sunday), then send them to loving homes.

The framers of liturgical texts chose to keep Epiphany in the forefront this Sunday. The gospel tells the manifestation of Jesus to his first followers. The antiphon for the introductory rite acknowledges that all the earth should give God worship and praise.

LECTIONARY

Each year the Sundays in Ordinary Time open with a passage from John's gospel. These three passages appear sequentially, but few will notice their interrelationship from year to year. Today's passage makes a seasonal transition. John the Baptist points out the Lamb of God to two of his own disciples. They engage Jesus in conversation and follow him in faith. This text is recommended for the Rite of Acceptance into the Order of Catechumens because it unveils the ancestry of all who seek to become disciples of Christ.

Today's first reading tells the story of Samuel, called into God's service while sleeping. With the help of a spiritual guide, Eli, Samuel recognizes the voice of the Lord. The psalmist sings what must have been also in the heart of Samuel and the disciples of John who first saw Jesus: "Here am I, Lord, I come to do your will."

The second reading begins this year's semicontinuous passage from Paul's First Letter to the Corinthians. No one will remember this, but we pick up the letter where we left off last February. Each year of the lectionary cycle turns to this letter for the second readings that open Ordinary Time. In today's passage, Paul says the human body is a temple of the Holy Spirit. As part of the body of Christ, we are called to conduct ourselves accordingly.

SACRAMENTARY

The alternative opening prayer includes the theme of following God's call. The prayer over the gifts cites 1 Corinthians 11:26—not today's lectionary passage, but from the same New Testament book that serves as the second reading this season. The entrance antiphon's universal theme fits with the Week of Prayer for Christian Unity. Although the first communion antiphon comes from one of the most popular psalms, the rendering of the second phrase, "[The Lord has] given wine in plenty for me to drink," will cause those dealing with alcoholism to shudder. Any of the prefaces for Sundays in Ordinary Time may be used (P 29–36), but you might consider one that presents the mission of Jesus, like P 32, or the one for Christian unity (P 76). Or, if your community has not heard Eucharistic Prayer IV in a while, you may revive it today. For the final blessing, solemn blessing #14 for Ordinary Time offers a generic possibility. But consider a simple prayer over the people, like #13.

OTHER IDEAS

During the Week of Prayer for Christian Unity, the eucharistic prayer for various needs and occasions offers a beautiful text. The first version, "The Church on the Way to Unity," is especially fitting. Since this long weekend honors Dr. Martin Luther King, you may include petitions for racial harmony and the developing of the nation's moral conscience.

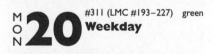

M O N **20** #311 (LMC #193–227) green
Weekday

Optional Memorial of St. Fabian (+ 250), pope, martyr/red • Optional Memorial of St. Sebastian (+ c. 250), martyr/red • U.S. Civil Observance: Martin Luther King, Jr. • The readings assigned for this day resume the early ministry of Jesus from Mark's gospel. Jesus finds himself in controversy over the behavior of his disciples, makes a pronouncement that distances himself from rote application of the law, and offers two sayings about cloth and wineskins to drive home the point.

The letter to the Hebrews compares Jesus to the Jewish high priest. The high priest offered sacrifice for sins because he himself was beset by weaknesses. He did not take the office onto himself, but received it as an appointment. Jesus received his appointment as the great high priest from God. We sing a psalm that recalls the ministry of high priesthood.

■ TODAY'S OPTIONAL MEMORIALS are of martyrs who suffered under the persecution of Diocletian. Fabian was chosen pope when a bird landed on him. Little is known of Sebastian, but he is a popular subject in the history of Christian art because his persecutors shot him with arrows. Both are buried in Roman catacombs.

■ THE DAY FOR THESE SAINTS falls fittingly this year on the day we observe the life and work of Dr. Martin Luther King, a martyr for the causes of civil rights. Educational and worship materials in English, Spanish and Vietnamese are available from the National Catholic Conference for Interracial Justice, 202-529-6480. Liturgy Training Publications offers two resources for commemorating Dr. King: "Evening Prayer Commemorating the Birthday of Dr. Martin Luther King, Jr." (*Plenty Good Room* September–October, 1993) and "Amazing Days: Martin Luther King's Birthday," a handout with quotations, prayers and commentaries that can be used as a bulletin insert.

All the prayers for Mass may be replaced with a set recalling the work of Dr. King; for example, For the Nation (#17), For the Progress of Peoples (#21) or For Peace and Justice (#22). Even the scriptures may be taken from an appropriate celebration in the lectionary, like the Mass for Peace and Justice.

Remember to pray for church unity.

T U E **21** #312 (LMC #193–227) red
Agnes (+ c. 304), virgin, martyr
MEMORIAL

The virtue of hope is sometimes represented as an anchor. The idea comes from today's first reading from Hebrews. God offers a sure promise so that we might seize the hope placed before us. That promise is remembered in today's psalm about the covenant.

Controversy continues as Jesus supports the morality of his disciples' behavior, superficially contrary to the law.

The church unity octave continues today.

■ THE DOMINICAN REPUBLIC celebrates its patronal feast today, Our Lady of the Altagracia, or "full of grace." It is a holy day of obligation there. An image of Mary bearing this title was venerated in Santo Domingo as early as 1502. The painting was probably made in fifteenth-century Spain, but tradition holds a different story about a young girl who saw the image in a dream and begged her father for a copy. He was unable to locate one, but a mysterious old man with a white beard produced one from a satchel and then disappeared. Mary wears what will become the national colors of the Dominican Republic.

■ TODAY'S SAINT: Agnes died in the persecution of Diocletian at the age of 13. Sentenced to a house of prostitution for being a Christian, she maintained her virginity and her sanctity until her death. The acts of her martyrdom, dating from the fifth century, are unreliable.

The opening prayer comes from the proper of saints. Draw the other texts from the many available options. If you used martyrs' prayers yesterday, consider those for virgins today. Agnes is among the saints listed in the first eucharistic prayer.

Optional Memorial of Vincent (+ 304), deacon, martyr / red ▪ Jesus again meets opposition, this time for curing on the Sabbath. Already a plot develops to stop his ministry.

Melchizedek appears in the letter to the Hebrews today as a symbol of Jesus. His name means "king of justice" and his title means "king of peace." He appears also in the responsorial psalm, and, if you choose to use it today, Eucharistic Prayer I.

▪ TODAY'S SAINT: Vincent suffered under the persecution of Diocletian, as did Agnes, Fabian and Sebastian. Deacon to Bishop Valerius of Saragossa, his name appears in sermons by Augustine.

This is also the anniversary of the Supreme Court's decision legalizing abortion in the United States. The public witness to the church's belief in the sanctity of life should also appear in prayer today.

Chile, the country of her birth, and Argentina, the country of her death, have an optional memorial today for Blessed Laura Vicuña (+ 1904), a child who labored to earn tuition, suffered refusal to join a religious order, and who was beaten by her mother's lover. At 13, she is the youngest person not a martyr to have been beatified.

The letter to the Hebrews portrays Jesus as the high priest of the heavenly court, who has no need to offer a repeated sacrifice. His one perfect sacrifice fulfilled all others, as the responsorial psalm seems to foreshadow.

The darkness of controversy gives way to a bright day at the lake, as Mark's gospel begins a new section. Jesus preaches and cures great numbers.

This is the last opportunity this week to use the sacramental texts from the Mass for the Unity of Christians.

▪ IN GUATEMALA today is the optional memorial of the Spanish saint Ildephonse (+ 667), pupil of Isidore of Seville and bishop of Toledo.

According to the letter to the Hebrews, just as Jesus is a new kind of high priest, so he has obtained a new kind of covenant between God and the faithful. This insight prompts the New Testament to include its longest single citation from the Old Testament, a prophecy from Jeremiah. The psalm asserts the mercy of God, whose justice looks down from heaven.

In Mark's gospel, Jesus appoints a group of companions known as "the Twelve." He gives them authority to preach and to expel demons. Throughout the New Testament, the names of the Twelve suffer some variation, but they always begin with Peter and end with Judas.

Remember to pray for Christian unity.

▪ TODAY'S SAINT: A devout bishop and strong defender of the faith, Francis de Sales preached tirelessly, ministered to the needy and wrote about spirituality. He died with the name of Jesus on his lips. Prayers come from the proper of saints, recalling Francis's compassion, gentleness and love.

▪ IN ARGENTINA today is the optional memorial of Mary, Queen of Peace.

The Week of Prayer for Christian Unity concludes today. Originally spanning the days between the celebrations of the chair of Peter and the conversion of Paul, the week sat under the patronage of the apostles most responsible for the spread of the Christian faith.

The reason for the choice of this date for this feast is not clear. It appears in liturgical books in the early Middle Ages. Prior to that there is some evidence for a celebration of the transfer of Paul's relics on this date from the church of St. Sebastian in Rome to that now called St. Paul outside the Walls. Paul's remains are believed to be beneath this church that bears his name.

The lectionary offers two choices for the first reading, both telling the story of the feast. The gospel and the psalm announce the theme of Christianity's universal mission, which Paul embodied by his journeys and preaching.

Prayers from the sacramentary come from the proper of saints. Either preface for the apostles may be used, but the second (P 65) seems more fitting. Paul is mentioned in the first eucharistic prayer. Both the entrance and communion antiphons for the day come from autobiographical passages in the Pauline corpus.

The Glory to God is sung today, in keeping with the tradition of honoring apostles with days ranked as feasts.

☀26 #68 (LMC #63) green
Third Sunday in Ordinary Time

ORIENTATION

Mark, the featured evangelist of Year B, finally makes his appearance today, only to disappear again next week.

LECTIONARY

As we begin Mark's story, John the Baptist is already in prison. It appears that Jesus began his public ministry as a result of the conclusion of John's. It is possible that Jesus numbered himself among John's followers. He proclaims the core of his message: "This is the time of fulfillment. The kingdom of God is at hand. Repent and believe in the gospel." Mark probably coined the word *gospel,* which has come to mean the content of the message (good news) as well as the literary form of his work. Note how quickly the story moves. We go from John's arrest to Jesus' proclamation and to the call of disciples in just a few verses.

The first reading tells about an Old Testament prophet who preached a message of repentance. Most of us think of Jonah as the guy in the whale, but the excerpt from his book that we hear today tells of his actual prophetic mission. Jonah is sometimes likened to John the Baptist because of the similarity of their names and of their preaching. For example, Caravaggio's painting of Saint John the Baptist in the desert (on view at the Nelson-Atkins Museum of Art in Kansas City) places him in the same pose Michelangelo used for Jonah on the ceiling of the Sistine Chapel. Today, however, the lectionary compares the prophet to the Messiah. Like that of Jesus, the message of Jonah is short and to the point. People respond to him, just as the disciples respond to Jesus. A wisdom psalm, seeking to know the ways of God, follows.

Paul warns the Corinthians that the world as we know it is passing away. Not one of the most famous passages from this important letter, today's verses carry the blunt impact we sense in the preaching of Jonah and Jesus.

SACRAMENTARY

A general chorus of praise appears as the entrance antiphon. In the face of the serious messages from Jonah and Jesus, the first option for the communion antiphon serves up jovial defiance: "Look up with gladness and smile." The opening prayer implies that the power of God should impel us toward efforts of making peace. Any preface from Ordinary Time may be used, but P 30 dwells on the mission of Jesus. Eucharistic Prayer IV with its own preface unfolds a full picture of Jesus' life and ministry. Among the prayers over the people, #6 asks for a complete change of heart.

OTHER IDEAS

If you repeat the same musical acclamations throughout this period of Ordinary Time, you will help people grasp the unity of the season. You could also build your repertoire with a new Glory to God to highlight its absence when Lent arrives. Many communities, though, recite the Glory to God during Ordinary Time. It gives the assembly an opportunity to speak a common text of praise.

Next Sunday we celebrate the Presentation of the Lord. The Mass begins with a blessing of candles. Invite people to bring from home any candles they would like blessed to accompany their prayer. Put the word out in the bulletin, the announcements at Mass, the telephone answering machine and the website. Procure extra candles this week for those who do not have the means or the memory to bring their own.

MON27 #317 (LMC #193–227) green
Weekday

Optional memorial of St. Angela Merici (+ 1540), virgin, religious founder/white ▪ The letter to the Hebrews contrasts Christ the high priest with the earthly high priest. The earthly priest enters the temple that is a copy of the one in heaven, whereas Christ has entered heaven itself. This text also gives scriptural foundation for our belief that Christ will come again at the end of time to save those who await him. The psalm sings of God's salvation, which we Christians believe is accomplished through the priesthood of Jesus.

Questions about the origins of Jesus' power appear in the gospel. He rebukes the accusation that he colludes with Satan.

The sacramentary's prayers for priests (Various Needs and Occasions, #6) refers to Christ the eternal high priest.

■ TODAY'S SAINT: Desiring to provide better education for children, Angela Merici organized a group of young women to live in poverty, chastity and obedience, but in their own homes rather than as a convent. The Ursulines became a formally approved religious congregation a few years after Angela's death.

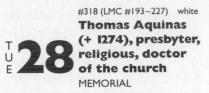

#318 (LMC #193–227)   white

Thomas Aquinas (+ 1274), presbyter, religious, doctor of the church

TUE **28**

MEMORIAL

Questions about Jesus' origins appear again today. This time, he restates who are his true relatives: those who do the will of God.

The letter to the Hebrews offers a commentary on yet another psalm. The former covenant, it says, was unable to cleanse people from sin, but Jesus is able to cleanse sin because he came to do God's will. Psalm 40, upon which this passage comments, follows today's reading.

■ TODAY'S SAINT: Italian by birth, Dominican by vocation, Thomas Aquinas became a philosopher of unparalleled importance for the church. Reputed to be a terrible student as a child, he became an undisputed intellectual giant. Catholic Schools Week generally includes his feast. You may find hymns by Thomas in your participation aid. Thomas's prayers of preparation for Mass and of thanksgiving after Mass are in the first appendix of the sacramentary.

The opening prayer for the Mass comes from the proper of saints. Among the options for the other prayers, those from the common of doctors of the church, #2, are especially fine today.

#319 (LMC #193–227)   green

WED **29** Weekday

The letter to the Hebrews sums up its recent arguments by saying Jesus' one sacrifice took away sins and perfected those who are being sanctified. The prophecies cited here tell of God's new covenant and the complete forgiveness of sins. We pray again the psalm that refers to the eternal priesthood of Melchizedek.

Mark's collection of parables begins the same way as the one in Matthew, with the sower. Jesus, who has already revealed his power to cure, now demonstrates his skill at making parables. Jesus interprets the meaning for his followers.

The Mass texts for the spread of the gospel (#14) pray for workers in the great harvest of the gospel.

#320 (LMC #193–227)   green

THU **30** Weekday

The letter to the Hebrews turns its attention to the effect of Jesus' eternal priesthood on the believer. Jesus' blood has opened heaven to us, so we may draw near in sincerity and absolute confidence. Some have been absent from the gathering of the faithful, and the letter encourages believers to encourage one another as God's Day draws near. The psalm explains that those whose hands are sinless, whose heart is clean, may ascend the mountain of God.

Mark has collected several brief sayings demonstrating Jesus' wisdom and compacted them in a few brief verses. In the midst of the parables, these "mini-parables" are easily remembered words to live by.

The sacramentary includes prayer texts for all the dead (3C), that they may enjoy the vision of eternity promised to the faithful followers of Christ.

#321 (LMC #193–227)   white

FRI **31** John Bosco (+ 1888), presbyter, religious founder, educator

MEMORIAL

The letter to the Hebrews includes an exhortation to those tempted to forsake their faith. It urges believers to recall the perseverance they already demonstrated in the face of sufferings, and to draw upon that strength again to build their confidence in God's promise. The psalm offers the same reassurance: The salvation of the just comes from God.

Returning to parables, Jesus, the master teacher, labors to explain the reign of God with lively, everyday images.

■ TODAY'S SAINT: John Bosco founded the Salesian Society of St. Francis de Sales and the Daughters of Mary, Help of Christians. He cared for children by founding a kind of "boys town" and also a center for girls, training them for life in the church and the world.

The opening prayer is found in the proper of saints. You may draw the others from those for teachers, among the common of holy men and women, #10.

February

#322 (LMC #193–227)   green

SAT **▮** Weekday

Optional Memorial of the Blessed Virgin Mary/white ▪ Justly famous is today's passage about faith from the letter to the Hebrews. Faith is confident assurance concerning hope. Abraham and Sarah are models of those who did not obtain what had been promised, but saw and saluted it from afar. As a response today, the lectionary offers us a section of the Canticle of Zechariah from Luke's gospel, which recalls the promise God made through prophets and directly to Abraham.

A few of the miracle stories of Jesus demonstrate his power over natural forces. Today's gospel is an example. It challenged the Gentile belief that the gods who governed nature held the most powerful sway.

Eucharistic Prayer IV gives a swift overview of salvation history, God's role as creator and God's promise of salvation.

■ IF YOU CELEBRATE THE OPTIONAL MEMORIAL OF MARY, consider the Blessed Virgin Mary and the

Presentation of the Lord (7) from the *Collection of Masses of the Blessed Virgin Mary.*

⊛2 #524 (LMC #252)   white
**The Presentation
of the Lord**
FEAST

ORIENTATION

Forty days after the birth of a child, the people of Israel presented the newborn to the temple. The gospels say that the parents of Jesus obeyed this law. In doing so, they revealed him as the fulfillment of the law.

Forty days after our celebration of the birth of Jesus, the church remembers his presentation in the temple. Today's feast used to close the Christmas cycle. Although that season now ends with the Baptism of the Lord, today's feast is still calculated from Christmas Day. Formerly called the Purification of Our Lady and regarded primarily as a Marian feast, the day is now honored as a feast of Christ. Eastern tradition names today as the "Meeting," of Christ and Simeon and Anna, of Christ and his expectant people.

Whenever a feast of the Lord falls on a Sunday in Ordinary Time, it replaces the texts for that day.

■ TODAY IS ALSO THE PATRONAL FEAST OF BOLIVIA, OUR LADY OF COPACABANA. The title honors a wooden statue of Mary carved in the form of an Inca princess by the Indian Francisco Tito Yupanqui. The statue is venerated in Copacabana, on an isthmus on Lake Titicaca in the Andes.

LECTIONARY

The readings are found under Solemnities and Feasts of the Lord and the Saints. Luke's account of the event is selected for the gospel. The long form completes the story with the prophetess Anna.

Malachi prophesies that God will send a messenger, bringing the divine presence into the temple. The surprise here is that the fiery messenger comes under the guise of an infant.

The psalm remembers the arrival of the ark of the covenant in Zion, as we remember the arrival of Jesus in Zion's holy temple.

The second reading appeared in the daily Mass lectionary a couple of weeks ago. This passage from the letter to the Hebrews states that Jesus' acceptance of humanity enabled him to redeem humanity. This feast celebrates that saving incarnation.

If you are using the *Lectionary for Masses with Children* today, you will need the volume of readings for weekdays. The Year B volume does not include today's readings.

SACRAMENTARY

This Mass begins in an unusual fashion, and it is important to be prepared beforehand. The assembly needs candles, like those for the Easter Vigil, as they gather outside the church. They may supply their own, or you may provide them. The presider will need holy water and a sprinkler. Prepare incense if you like.

The blessing follows one of two forms. Given the nature of the feast, it would be preferable to use the first, the procession of all the faithful. If those arriving early for Mass have already taken their seats in the church, gently but firmly invite them outside the main doors for the opening ritual. The opportunity to hold lighted candles for the entrance rite will please many a churchgoer and strengthen the celebratory nature of the feast. Catholic spirituality has strong roots in rituals like this. Today you can engage people anew in the traditions of the faith.

When all are in place, the candles are lighted. Unlike the Easter Vigil, it is not necessary that these be lit from a single source. The symbol is the candles, not the fire.

A short refrain may be sung, either the one proposed in the sacramentary or another using the theme of light. The presider makes the sign of the cross, greets the people, introduces the feast and blesses the candles, sprinkling them with holy water.

The procession enters the church at the invitation of the presider (or deacon). The censer, the cross between two candles (two glorious candles, preferably), and the book of the gospels lead the way. The presider follows, and the assembly of the faithful then enters with song.

When all have taken their place, the Glory to God is sung, perhaps using the one from Christmas, as a faint reminder of the solemnity we recall today. Since any hymn may be sung in the procession, some communities use the Glory to God as the processional song, to avoid singing two substantial pieces of music in immediate succession. The opening prayer for the Mass follows the Glory to God.

There is no instruction for extinguishing the candles. It may be impractical for all to keep them lit throughout the Mass. All will probably extinguish their candles as they are seated for the liturgy of the word, but they could be lighted for the gospel or even the eucharistic prayer. The rest of Mass continues in the usual way.

The sacramentary includes a text for the entrance antiphon, but it is not clear when this might be sung. It perhaps works best as an alternate suggestion for other music in the introductory rites. The presidential prayers eloquently express the significance of the feast, as does the proper preface (P 49).

The German sacramentary provides inserts to the eucharistic prayers for this day. For example, in Prayer III, after the words "a perfect offering may be made to the glory of your name," the prayer continues, "And so we come into your presence, and in union with the whole church we celebrate that day when your only-begotten Son was presented in the temple. Through him, the Light of your Light, we bring you these gifts. We ask you to make them holy . . ."

MUSIC

The Latin chants for this day are among the most beautiful in the repertoire. The community might enjoy hearing or singing *Lumen ad revelationem gentium* as the processional hymn or even as the gathering refrain. Find it in the *Liber cantualis*. Another good choice would be a sung version of the Canticle of Simeon, the *Nunc dimittis,* which comes from today's gospel. It appears in the *Liturgy of the Hours* every night for night prayer. Check the hymn index under temple, Mary, church and Christ for more suggestions. *By Flowing Waters* (302–315) has a complete suite of processional chants, antiphons, psalms and the sung Canticle of Simeon.

OTHER IDEAS

A Hispanic custom gaining in popularity throughout North American parishes is the "presentation of the Christ Child": people bring with them to church the figure of the infant Jesus from their home nativity scenes. The figures are wrapped in lace and held up at Mass for a blessing this day.

The presider may wear the vestments from the Christmas season. This is a premier day each year for celebrating a school liturgy— but it's a Sunday this year. Creative pastors, teachers and parish liturgical ministers will bring something of the celebration into the school year, will invite students to participate today, will join with the religious education program in preparing a celebration that unites the parish. LTP's *School Year, Church Year* and *Preparing Liturgy for Children and Children for Liturgy* offer ideas for keeping this feast in the parish school and among students in religious education programs.

If your community offers the blessing of throats on St. Blase's Day, make the announcement today and prepare the candles for tomorrow.

M O N **3** #323 (LMC #193–227)   green
Weekday (Fourth Week in Ordinary Time)

Optional Memorial of St. Blase (+ c. 316?), bishop, martyr/red ▪ Optional Memorial of St. Ansgar (+ 865), bishop/white ▪ Today's gospel is part of a group of miracle stories collected by Mark. Jesus drives unclean spirits from a man into a large herd of swine. The number of spirits only serves to demonstrate the extent of Jesus' power. The location of the miracle in Gentile territory foreshadows the opening of Christianity to all the nations.

The letter to the Hebrews recalls more heroic ancestors whose faith helped them persevere through times of trial. Faith did not remove their hardship, but it kept them strong when they longed to see the fulfillment of God's promise. The psalm, like the reading, assures comfort to those who hope in God.

The first eucharistic prayer's list of martyrs accomplishes a goal similar to that of this passage from Hebrews: It reminds the faithful of those who kept faith strong in the face of difficult suffering.

For the blessing of throats today, prepare candles ahead of time. Traditionally, two crossed candles are tied with a red bow. Prepare also cards with the text of the blessing for those who need one for reference.

It is best if the ministers memorize the text of the prayer. Priests and deacons who find memorization difficult may place the printed text in the hand that holds the candles (practice this!) so their other hand is free to make the blessing.

The blessing of throats generally takes longer than communion does. If you have more throat ministers than communion ministers, the assembly will not need to wait long for the ceremony to conclude. Lay ministers may invoke the saint with the proper text, but they should not conclude it with the sign of the cross.

After the intercessions, ministers go to their stations. The faithful process forward. Place the crossed candles onto the neck and pray the blessing.

Alternatively, the blessing may be given once over the entire assembly.

▪ TODAY'S SAINTS: Blase (also spelled *Blaise,* and pronounced like blaze and not *blasé*), is said to have been a bishop in Armenia, but little can be known for sure. Legend holds he suffered a brutal martyrdom under Diocletian, having his flesh ripped open by metal wool combs, then decapitation. The legend that he removed a fish bone from the throat of a boy has made him patron for those with sore throats, and a blessing may be given to the faithful today in his honor. Blaise is also the patron of wool combers. He is patron of Paraguay.

Ansgar was born in Amiens, became a monk at Corbie, developed a talent for preaching, then went on mission to Denmark, where he is remembered as the patron. He not only preached the gospel, he lived it. He washed the feet of the poor and waited on them at table. The prayer that concludes each psalm in the *Liturgy of the Hours* was his idea.

■ TODAY IS ALSO THE PATRONAL FEAST FOR HONDURAS, Our Lady of Suyapa. Indian laborers sleeping by the roadside on a Saturday night in February 1747 discovered a small statue of Mary buried in the dirt. They built a small church for it, and it has been a popular pilgrimage site ever since.

T U E **4**
#324 (LMC #193–227)   green
Weekday

Mark interweaves two miracle stories, the healing of a woman's hemorrhage and the raising of the daughter of Jairus from death to life. The second of these, the most dramatic miracle thus far in Mark, seems to require two proofs of the cure: The girl walks and eats.

The letter to the Hebrews exhorts the faithful to resist sin. As models, they have the great crowd of faithful witnesses and Jesus himself, who endured the cross because of the joy that lay ahead. Those who do not suffer the threat of persecution still require perseverance to avoid abandoning the struggle against sin. The psalm acknowledges the generations of those who seek God.

The sacramentary's prayers for any need (#38) ask God's help in time of suffering.

■ IN MEXICO, today is an optional memorial for Águeda (Agatha), virgin and martyr.

W E D **5**
#325 (LMC #193–227)   red
Agatha (+ c. 251), virgin, martyr
MEMORIAL

In spite of the miracles he worked and the wisdom he preached, many of Jesus' own people still reject him. Mark concludes this section of his gospel with a reminder that Jesus faced controversy throughout his life, even among his own people.

The letter to the Hebrews sees suffering as discipline. God uses it to help us grow like children. The psalm, after a passage that comes from a context of suffering, praises the mercy of God.

■ TODAY'S SAINT: Agatha, one of the earliest Christian martyrs, died during the persecution of Decius. Her tortures included the removal of her breasts (according to a sixth-century legend), and so she is now a patron of women with diseases of the breast.

The opening prayer for Mass comes from the proper of saints. Options exist for the other prayers, but consider the common of martyrs (#7). Agatha is among the saints named in the first eucharistic prayer.

■ IN MEXICO AND VENEZUELA, today is the feast of Philip [de las Casas] of Jesus (+ 1597), protomartyr of Mexico. The day is an optional memorial in Honduras. Philip, the oldest of 11 children, was born in Mexico of newlywed parents who had emigrated from Spain. As a youth, he learned to work with silver, and at age 20 he traveled to Manila, where he decided to join the Franciscans. Seeking ordination to the priesthood, he boarded a ship from the Philippines back to Mexico, but the boat ran ashore at Japan,

where the persecution of Christians was in force. Philip was crucified on this date together with 25 other Christians, including Paul Miki, on a hill outside Nagasaki.

T H U **6**
#326 (LMC #193–227)   red
Paul Miki (+ 1597), presbyter, religious, missionary, martyr; and his companions, martyrs
MEMORIAL

Having contrasted high priests and covenants, the letter to the Hebrews now contrasts mountains. Moses drew near a mountain untouchable with its fire, darkness and storm. But the faithful approach a mountain of angels, festival and the presence of Jesus. The psalm praises Jerusalem, the mountain of God, but we Christians sing it in praise of the new Jerusalem, the eternal destiny toward which we march.

Beginning a new section of the gospel dealing with discipleship, Mark tells how Jesus sent the Twelve out on mission to preach repentance and to cure the sick. Our practice of anointing the sick is partly inspired by the testimony of this passage.

■ TODAY'S SAINT: Caught in the midst of political machinations and fear of national conquest, Paul Miki and his companions, including some altar servers, were crucified at Nagasaki. Celebrating this obligatory memorial of martyrs from Japan reminds Catholics from other places of the global witness to the faith.

The opening prayer comes from the proper of saints. Choose the other presidential prayers from the common of martyrs. There are five groups of texts for days that honor a plurality of martyrs. Use any you wish, but note that the communion prayer of the first set makes a reference to the cross.

■ IN BOLIVIA, today is the memorial of Philip of Jesus, Paul Miki and companions. The country combines yesterday's Mexican feast with today's universal memorial.

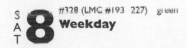

F R I 7 #327 (LMC #193–227) green
Weekday

Near its conclusion, the letter to the Hebrews exhorts Christians with a variety of advice: Love one another. Be hospitable to strangers. Visit the imprisoned. Be faithful in marriage. Share wealth. The choice for the opening verses of the psalm is inspired by the close of this reading.

By placing the story of John the Baptist's death after the story of the mission of the Twelve, Mark foreshadows the crucifixion of Jesus and the suffering of those who followed him. The account of John's martyrdom is especially poignant.

The Masses for Various Needs and Occasions include a prayer for prisoners (#31).

S A T 8 #328 (LMC #193–227) green
Weekday

Optional Memorial of Jerome Emiliani (+ 1537), presbyter, religious founder / white • Optional Memorial of the Blessed Virgin Mary / white • Having sent the Twelve in the passage we heard on Thursday, Jesus receives the apostles back from their mission. He invites them to some time away, but a large crowd interrupts the plan. Service continues.

We conclude four weeks of the letter to the Hebrews today. The upbeat farewell makes a final plea for generosity and obedience, then prays that God will grant the faithful all that is good.

Prayers for charity (#41) might be useful today.

■ TODAY'S SAINT: A veteran of war who had suffered imprisonment, Jerome Emiliani of Venice turned his life to service to God after his miraculous liberation. He is remembered as the founder of orphanages and for his technique of teaching children the faith in a question and answer format.

9 #74 (LMC #69) green
Fifth Sunday in Ordinary Time

ORIENTATION

Since Christmas we have had only two Sundays of Ordinary Time. Last week's feast returned us to the cycle of Christmas stories. Today, once again, green-vesture Ordinary Time resumes its place, together with a gospel from Mark.

■ IN ECUADOR, today is the feast of San Miguel Febres Cordero (+ 1910), a Christian Brother, and of his martyr companions. Miguel is remembered as an educator, scholar and grammarian. The day is an optional memorial in Venezuela.

LECTIONARY

Mark gives us an overview of Jesus' amazing ministry. He cured the mother-in-law of Simon, and then healed everyone the people brought to him. He left early the next morning to pray alone, but people arose early in search of him. He moved on, demonstrating that his ministry was not to one town, nor just to the sick, but to all towns, where he preached and expelled demons. In the midst of his busy ministry, Jesus still made time for prayer.

Today's passage from Job is one of the most depressing in the lectionary. It opens the liturgy of the word today in bleak despair. The automatic response of the assembly, "Thanks be to God," will sound incongruous after hearing Job say that his life is like wind and that he will never see happiness again. The psalm tries to cheer things up by praising God, who heals the brokenhearted. Job asserts the universal human condition that Jesus has come to redeem. We draw reassurance only from hearing the gospel of Jesus' healing ministry.

Paul explains his service to the gospel with the often-quoted line, "I have become all things to all people." He preaches because it is his duty, and the preaching is its own reward. By enslaving himself to the gospel, Paul appeals to the weak and the strong.

SACRAMENTARY

The first communion antiphon praises the kindness God shows to people. The first opening prayer says all our hope is in God. Among the prefaces for Ordinary Time, P 31 remembers that God came to our rescue. The second solemn blessing for Ordinary Time (#11) prays for the peace of God that is beyond all understanding.

OTHER IDEAS

It's not too soon to make announcements about Lent. Invite people to bring last year's palm branches to church over the next few weekends. They may be burned for this year's ashes.

M O N 10 #329 (LMC #193–227) white
Scholastica (+ 547), virgin, religious founder
MEMORIAL

Today the first reading turns to the first part of the first book of the Bible, Genesis. This book will supply scriptures for Mass for the next two weeks. This sequence of readings comes at a time of the year in the northern hemisphere when nature is preparing to reveal again the glory of spring. Scholars doubt the historicity of this section of Genesis, but its stories speak the truth of God's presence and action.

The story of creation is much loved and much disputed. Although we hear about four days of creation today, there is no need to assume these are literal days. The scientific discoveries of evolution will continue to lead us to affirm the creative action of God. Here, God is depicted in full command of creative energy. The psalm that follows tells another version of creation, devoid of days, with a different explanation for the origins of water, but affirming the same truth: God is creator.

Mark provides a summary statement of Jesus' ministry with his disciples. People came primarily to benefit from his power to heal.

■ TODAY'S SAINT: Scholastica, the sister of Benedict, joined him in dedicating her life to prayer and work and is the patron of Benedictine nuns. All the information about her comes from the *Dialogues* of Gregory the Great. In a famous story, Benedict refused to extend his visit with Scholastica one evening, in spite of her entreaty. So she prayed and God sent a storm that required her brother to remain. They enjoyed spiritual conversation, a pastime too rarely pursued in a high-speed world.

The opening prayer comes from the proper of saints. Choose the other presidential prayers from the common of virgins. There are four sets from which to choose. But avoid the fourth, which is for days that honor more than one virgin.

TUE **11** #330 (LMC #193–227) green
Weekday

Optional Memorial of Our Lady of Lourdes/white ▪ We resume the story of creation interrupted after yesterday's account of the first four days. Today's passage from Genesis tells of God's creation of animals that inhabit the air, the sea and the land, including the glory of God's creation, people. The psalm says that God has made us little less than angels and has crowned us with glory and honor.

Jesus confronts the Pharisees on ritual purification and hypocrisy. Instead of being warm and comforting, Jesus has harsh words for the religious leaders of his day.

■ TODAY'S MEMORIAL: On this date in 1858 is recorded the first of a series of apparitions of Our Lady to Bernadette Soubirous at Lourdes. Clothed in white, she identified herself as the Immaculate Conception. The popular shrine has been a place of pilgrimage and miraculous healing.

Consider offering the sacrament of the anointing of the sick at the daily Mass.

WED **12** #331 (LMC #193–227) green
Weekday

The opening of the book of Genesis actually has two separate creation stories. Today we hear from the second version, in which God creates humanity before creating plants and animals. As wise as the humans will be, God forbids them to eat from the tree of knowledge of good and bad, a sign that all moral judgments will never be clear to the human mind. We sing more verses from the psalm we started on Monday. All creatures look to God for food and breath.

After his jeremiad against the Pharisees, Jesus explains more to his disciples. Impurity has more to do with right intention than with compulsive action.

Prayers for those unjustly deprived of liberty (#30) may help us appreciate the freedom of choice God gives humanity.

THU **13** #332 (LMC #193–227) green
Weekday

God creates animals in today's passage, and stands back to watch what the human creature would call them. Finally, God creates woman. Genesis explains the origins of marriage in the ready companionship of man and woman. We sing a psalm about the blessedness of marriage and family life.

In parts of Mark's account, Jesus appears more rattled than we customarily think of him. After dealing with the religious leaders in passages earlier this week, Jesus now meets the Syro-Phoenician woman who asks him to cure her daughter. He refuses, because she is a Gentile. But he finally relents at her clever persistence.

The third preface for marriage (P 74) refers to God's creation of humanity in love.

FRI **14** #333 (LMC #193–227) white
Cyril (+ 869), monk, missionary; and Methodius (+ c. 884), bishop, missionary/white
MEMORIAL

The newly created man and woman succumb to the temptation of the serpent and eat forbidden fruit. The temptation resembles those we all face: the fruit is nutritious, beautiful and a source of wisdom. We can talk ourselves into the sin of disobedience by rationalizing its benefits. In the psalm that follows, the singers acknowledge their sin and God's mercy.

Jesus cures a deaf man with a speech impediment. Aspects of this cure make it a model of initiatory discipleship: The man is brought by believers, who ask Jesus to lay a hand on him. He prays that the man will be opened, and the man then speaks plainly. Through testimony and prayer, people will be opened to catechesis and discipleship.

■ TODAY'S SAINTS: Cyril and Methodius are patrons of Europe. Missionaries to Bulgaria, Moravia and Dalmatia, these two brothers tirelessly served the church. They translated the scriptures into Slavic, developing its "Cyrillic" alphabet. Formerly optional, this day is now an obligatory memorial.

Most people, of course, would assume we celebrate Saint Valentine today, but the information on that Roman martyr is not reliable enough to win him a spot in the universal church calendar. Vestment color should be white today. Wrap chocolates in red. There's a useful blessing of valentines in LTP's annual *Children's Daily Prayer.*

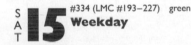

S A T 15 #334 (LMC #193–227)   green
Weekday

Optional Memorial of the Blessed Virgin Mary / white ▪ The names of Adam and Eve appear for the first time in the Genesis account today. God converses with them about their sin and punishes them. But the church sees in God's curse of the serpent the promise of redemption through Christ, born of a woman, who will strike at the head of the source of all evil. In spite of this fearsome conversation, the psalm states confidently our trust in God who provides refuge in every generation.

Mark tells of the miracle of the loaves. Four thousand people eat from seven loaves and a few fish. Jesus' actions (taking, thanking, breaking and giving) foreshadow the eucharist.

Texts for a votive Mass for the Holy Eucharist appear at #3.

☀ 16 #77 (LMC #72)   green
Sixth Sunday in Ordinary Time

ORIENTATION

So much happens in the first chapter of Mark's gospel that it takes weeks for it to unfold. We hear the final verses of that chapter today.

■ IN THE OLD CALENDAR TODAY WOULD HAVE BEEN SEPTUAGESIMA SUNDAY, which, if anything, was a strong sign of the nearness of Lent. The onset of Lent is relatively late this year, March 5. Lent should not sneak up on a parish. Begin to make everyone aware of the coming of the season of grace. Begin distributing materials to help the parish pray, fast and give alms.

LECTIONARY

In curing the leper today, Jesus not only demonstrates his power over illness, he asserts his authority over the law. He touches the unclean. Then, as if to make up for his boldness, he asks the former leper to observe the law by offering to the priest what Moses prescribed. The man seems to disobey Jesus' request for secrecy, and spread widely the report of his cure.

The first reading gives some background to the gospel's story. The book of Leviticus asked the leprous to make their disease and uncleanness known, and to live apart from the community. This double burden—illness and banishment—Jesus doubly lifts.

The psalm celebrates God's forgiveness of the guilty. It falls short in naming the leper's difficulty, but it correctly identifies the God who helps in time of trouble.

"Imitate my example," is advice few of us could give without meeting resentment. It seems to work for Paul, who does all for the glory of God and avoids giving offense by seeking the benefit of others.

SACRAMENTARY

The seventh preface for Ordinary Time Sundays (P 35) prays to see and love in us what God sees and loves in Christ. The line resembles the attitude of Saint Paul.

The fourth solemn blessing for Ordinary Time (13) prays for peace and freedom from anxiety.

OTHER IDEAS

Lent is drawing near. Remind people of upcoming programs that will help them prepare for the season.

Does your parish offer any ministry to those whom society considers as outcasts? Remember them in prayer on this day we recall Jesus' ministry for lepers.

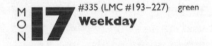

M O N 17 #335 (LMC #193–227)   green
Weekday

Optional memorial of the Seven Founders of the Order of Servites (+ 13th century) religious / white ▪ The joy of the birth of Eve's first son gives way to the horror of the enmity he bears toward the second. Cain and Abel are ancestral symbols of humanity's potential for the gravest evils, sins against life. God offers mercy to the guilty Cain, threatening vengeance on anyone who kills him. This thought-provoking story unsettles a society that condones capital punishment. The psalmist hears God making accusations against those who speak against their own siblings. God reads the human heart. Humans should unite their heart with their sacrifices. To do less is to create empty ritual.

A sigh rises from the depths of Jesus' spirit as the Pharisees demand some heavenly sign from him. He refuses, exasperated at their lack of faith, and leaves town.

Eucharistic Prayer I mentions the sacrifice of Abel.

■ TODAY'S SAINTS: Internal feuding and immoral behavior plagued their society. But the seven young men who joined the Confraternity of the Blessed Virgin devoted themselves to spiritual renewal, recruited new members, and evangelized by their prayer and penance. The seven were Buonfiglio Monaldi, Alexis Falconieri, Benedict dell'Antela, Bartholomew degli Amidei, Ricovero Uguccione, Geraldino Sostegni and John Buonagiunta. It is easier to remember them as the seven founders.

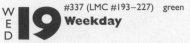

T U E **18** #336 (LMC #193–227)   green
Weekday

The evil nature of humanity persisted, according to the book of Genesis, and God determined to wipe out creation. Somehow, Noah found favor with God. Letting Noah in on the plan, God has him build an ark for his family and pairs of animals. No one knows why God let the second mosquito go on board.

The psalm of praise we sing speaks of the voice of God resounding over the waters. The psalm mentions God's throne "above the flood," making it a fit response for today.

Jesus chooses the wrong metaphor to explain to his disciples how exasperated he is with the Pharisees. Be on guard against their yeast, he says. The disciples were short on food and missed the point altogether. Jesus finds that neither friend nor foe fully understands him.

If you pray for those who suffer famine (#28), also remember those who suffer from spiritual hunger.

W E D **19** #337 (LMC #193–227)   green
Weekday

As the story of Noah continues, the waters recede, and God promises never again to doom the earth in the same way. Noah builds an altar to God, and we sing with the psalmist, "To you, Lord, I will offer a sacrifice of praise."

Only Mark reports this instance of Jesus curing the blind by stages. Jesus touches the eyes of a blind beggar with spittle, imposes hands, and the man sees people but they look like walking trees. Jesus tries a second time and the man sees perfectly. This story threatens to make Jesus appear ineffective in his first attempt. The other gospels, probably written after Mark, do not include it in their depictions of the Son of God.

The fourth eucharistic prayer summarizes the ministry of Jesus.

T H U **20** #338 (LMC #193–227)   green
Weekday

As a sign of God's covenant with humanity, a rainbow appears in the sky. God's covenant with Noah prefigures the greater covenant on its way when Abraham enters the story. The psalm says that God looks down on earth from heaven and releases those doomed to die.

Mark's gospel reaches its turning point with Peter's affirmation that Jesus is the Messiah. This episode takes place in the northern reaches of Palestine, Caesarea Philippi, and from there, as Jesus alludes, the story moves to Jerusalem. Peter, having received good marks for identifying the Messiah, fails when it comes to interpreting his affirmation. Jesus calls him Satan.

A prayer to avert storms is included in the Masses for Various Needs and Occasions (#37).

F R I **21** #339 (LMC #193–227)   green
Weekday

Optional Memorial of Peter Damian (+ 1072), bishop, monastic, doctor of the church/white ■ Still displeased with the actions of humanity, God unleashes another punishment. When people erect a tower to try to reach heaven, God jumbles their language so they cannot understand each other. This story, still part of the opening chapters of Genesis that have little historical foundation, was told to help explain the multiplicity of languages in the world. It also serves as the backdrop for the miracle of Pentecost, in which all from every nation could understand the speech of the apostles. The confusion before the first covenant gives way to illumination after the second. The psalmist says that God foils the designs of peoples, but the divine plan stands forever.

Just after predicting his passion to his disciples, Jesus summons the crowd to tell them what discipleship will cost: take up a cross, he says, and follow. Life with Jesus is not all loaves and fish. It will include suffering.

Prayers from the Triumph of the Cross (September 14) may drive home the point.

■ TODAY'S SAINT: Peter Damian, a Benedictine abbot, bishop and doctor of the church, worked with the great reformer, Pope Gregory VII.

S A T **22** #535 (LMC #263)   white
Chair of Peter, apostle
FEAST

Originating as a feast for Peter's leadership in Antioch, distinct from the celebration of his leadership in Rome (which used to be kept on January 18 and so began the octave of prayer for Christian unity bracketed by a feast of Peter and then of Paul), this feast uses the image of the chair as the seat of authority. Its universal celebration today, interrupting the seasonal texts of Lent, celebrates the unity of our church.

The gospel tells of Jesus' choice of Peter as leader. The first reading, ascribed to Peter, appeals for good qualities among church leaders. The psalm remembers the shepherd-like leadership of God.

The sacramentary texts proclaim the unity of the church, founded on the rock of Peter's faith. Other Petrine passages appear in the antiphons for the day. The preface comes from one for the apostles, and the first (P 64) serves the feast well. Eucharistic Prayer I includes a mention of the apostles, but Prayer IV has Antiochene antecedents.

◉ 23   #80 (LMC #75)   green
Seventh Sunday in Ordinary Time

ORIENTATION

Today concludes the series of second readings from Paul's First Letter to the Corinthians. A second series of readings begins next week from Paul's Second Letter to the Corinthians, but it will be truncated by the abrupt arrival of Lent.

LECTIONARY

Today we open the second chapter of Mark. As with last Sunday, we hear a lengthier treatment of a single story, rather than a series of shorter episodes. Today's miracle details Jesus' cure of a paralytic. The comical scene depicts four men ripping off the roof of a house to drop the hapless patient into the room crowded with admirers of the miracle-worker.

Jesus trumps the expectations of everyone by saying words the friends were surely not expecting: "Your sins are forgiven." You can almost hear the four guys shout back in shock, "That's not why we came here!"

God's power to forgive sins is the theme that closes today's first reading from Isaiah. Ancient Israel had burdened God with sins, wearied God with crimes. But now God was freeing them from exile, and wiping out their sins forever. Humans who need relief from their burdens often have wayward expectations of God. But God relieves burdens by forgiving sin.

There were probably at least three letters from Paul to the church at Corinth. In the one we call the second, he refers to another letter, and Paul's description of it does not fit the themes of the letter we call the first. Furthermore, scholars think the second letter may itself be a combination of two or more epistles. But it is Paul's style, and its authorship is not generally questioned. Today Paul says that there is no prevarication in God. You do not get yes and no. You only get yes. Jesus Christ was God's yes. When we pray, Paul explains, we pray to God through Jesus by saying Amen. Throughout the history of liturgy, we have maintained the habit of concluding prayers with "through Christ our Lord, Amen," as inspired by this text. That conclusion clears a straight highway of affirmation from our lips to God's ear.

SACRAMENTARY

One of the eucharistic prayers for Masses of reconciliation would be appropriate today because of the theme of God's mercy that predominates the first and third readings.

Prayer over the people #21 asks for help in avoiding evil pleasures so that we might delight in God alone.

OTHER IDEAS

The readings highlight forgiveness of sins. You might promote opportunities for the sacrament of reconciliation during the upcoming season of Lent.

M O N 24   #341 (LMC #193–227)   green
Weekday

Our first readings now turn to the book of Sirach. In some Bibles it is known as the book of Ecclesiasticus, not to be confused with the book of Ecclesiastes, which is different. This book of Wisdom and Proverbs dates from around 180 BCE. The lectionary chooses some excerpts from this lengthy book for daily Mass readings during the seventh and eighth week of Ordinary Time every other year. Our sequence will be shortened further this year when Lent begins next week.

The beginning of the book serves as today's first reading. Some people deduce from creation the existence of the creator. Sirach deduces from creation the *wisdom* that orders creation. Then the book acclaims the God who existed before the wisdom that drives creation. Psalm 93 praises God who made the world firm.

Mark's gospel enters its second half. Today's passage comes after Peter's confession that Jesus is the Messiah and the transfiguration of Jesus. These events form a centerpiece of Mark that answers the foundational question of the gospel, "Who is Jesus?" Throughout the second half, Jesus works his way toward Jerusalem and the cross. Today Jesus cures a possessed child. The father states both his belief and his dependence on Jesus to sustain it. The pair of stories—the transfiguration and the cure of the possessed boy—is depicted in Raphael's famous painting of the transfiguration.

The second preface of the Holy Spirit (P 55) praises God for the gift of the Spirit and for helping us trust.

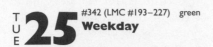

TUE 25 #342 (LMC #193–227) green
Weekday

Sirach tells those who serve God to be prepared for trials. He advises acceptance of whatever befalls them, for God will help those who are tested in misfortune. The psalm urges us to trust in God, who will grant our heart's desires.

Following the transfiguration and the cure of the possessed child, Jesus again warns the disciples about his upcoming fate. They do not get his meaning, and talk tastelessly about which of them was the most important. Jesus uses a child to teach a lesson.

Eucharistic Prayer II's own preface affirms the humility of Christ who took on flesh and opened his arms on the cross.

■ IN MEXICO, today is the optional memorial of Blessed Sebastián of Aparicio (+ 1600), who fled Spain and undesirable romances, settled in Puebla in Mexico, worked the land, built highways, married at the age of 60, lost his wife, joined the Franciscans at the age of 72 and died at 98.

WED 26 #343 (LMC #193–227) green
Weekday

Those who seek wisdom will receive the reward, Sirach says. We seek wisdom like a servant. If we trust her, he says, we will possess her. The longest psalm of the psalter is a praise of God's wisdom. We sing several verses in response.

The disciples object to a nonbeliever's use of Jesus' name to expel demons, but Jesus does not mind. His attitude might foster better inter-religious dialogue today.

The sacramentary includes several sets of prayers for Christian unity (see 13C, alternate, for example).

THU 27 #344 (LMC #193–227) green
Weekday

Sirach warns those who think too much of their wealth and strength and too little of God's anger. They lull themselves into thinking God forgives many sins while delaying their own conversion. The first psalm makes our response today, instructing us to choose between the two ways of those who delight in sin and those who delight in God's law.

Some of Jesus' strongest words are leveled against those who cause scandal to others. Hypocrisy among believers cannot be tolerated.

One of the eucharistic prayers for reconciliation will strengthen the theme of conversion.

FRI 28 #345 (LMC #193–227) green
Weekday

Let your acquaintances be many, Sirach advises, but let your confidant be one in a thousand. His treatment on friendship is a classic piece of wisdom. Again, verses from the longest psalm supply our response.

Jesus speaks strong words again, this time about marriage and divorce. He holds up the ideal of a loving union.

Presidential prayers for the relatives and friends (44) might be appropriate.

March

SAT #346 (LMC #193–227) green
Weekday

Optional Memorial of the Blessed Virgin Mary/white ▪ Sirach describes the wondrous creation of humanity. Another author might praise the scientific marvels of human attributes, but Sirach ascribes their awesomeness to God. A creation psalm praises God's kindness in spite of the brevity of life.

Jesus' love for the powerless and oppressed extends even to children. The story could have justified the inclusion of children among the baptized in the post-apostolic church.

The fourth eucharistic prayer praises the creation of God. "All your actions show your wisdom and love."

■ IF YOU CHOOSE THE OPTIONAL MEMORIAL OF MARY TODAY, consider Mary, Mother and Teacher in the Spirit (32), with its reference to baptismal promises in the prayer over the gifts.

2 #83 (LMC #78) green
Eighth Sunday in Ordinary Time

ORIENTATION

This is the last Sunday of Ordinary Time this winter. Farewell to the Alleluia! Although the readings draw their primary focus from the sequence in which they fall, they will help remind people of the upcoming season of repentance and grace.

LECTIONARY

Occasionally the gospels leave the impression that there was some mild conflict between the disciples of John the Baptist and the disciples of Jesus. You can hear why this suspicion arises in the opening line today where the disciples of John are mentioned in the same breath as the Pharisees. Jesus distances himself from the religious practices of both groups.

His disciples do not fast while he, the bridegroom, is with them. But when he is gone, the time for fasting will come. Obviously, this reading comes at an opportune moment to remind the faithful today why we fast as part of our observance of Lent. We anticipate the day of the bridegroom's return.

The image of Jesus as bridegroom will provoke much thought. In today's first reading God takes on the role of bridegroom for Israel. "I will espouse you to me forever," God promises. This spiritual marital relationship was a stormy one, due to the infidelity of ancient Israel. That is why the psalm reaffirms that no matter what the circumstances, God is kind and merciful.

Throughout his career, Paul battled with those who doubted his authority and credibility. No surprise. He formerly persecuted Christians. Today he tells the Corinthians that they are his letter of recommendation, written not in ink, but on human hearts.

SACRAMENTARY

The alternative opening prayer asks God to send us as witnesses of gospel joy.

You may wish to avoid using Eucharistic Prayer IV during Lent in order to make the most of the lenten and Easter prefaces. The preface for the fourth eucharistic prayer should not be changed with any other. If you plan to use it less or not at all, you may want to pray it this weekend with the community, one last time before Lent and Easter.

Prayer over the people #11 asks for the heavenly gifts that make us ready to do God's will.

OTHER IDEAS

This is the last Sunday that the assembly will sing alleluia until the Easter Vigil. In the Middle Ages, some communities buried scrolls bearing the word *Alleluia* to symbolize the dying and rising of Christ. Some communities today perform a variation on the custom. Sing a strong alleluia for the gospel acclamation today and include hymns that repeat the word. See the hymn tune index for versions of LASST UNS ERFREUEN, for example.

LTP's *School Year, Church Year* provides ideas for making much ado of saying goodbye to the Alleluia and also for making ashes from burnt palms. Included is a version of the traditional hymn, "Alleluia, Song of Gladness."

Be prepared with announcements about Ash Wednesday and opportunities for spiritual growth during Lent. LTP has many materials available. Catholic Relief Services Rice Bowl provides a handy way to remember the social dimension of fasting. The money we do not spend as a result of our fast can provide food for the needy. Provide ways people can give food to the hungry.

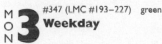

M O N **3** #347 (LMC #193–227)   green
Weekday

Optional memorial of Katharine Drexel (+ 1955), virgin religious founder / white ▪ After praising God's creation of humanity, Sirach acknowledges that people sin. To the penitent, he says, God provides a way back. The psalm knows the happiness of those whose sin is forgiven.

The cost of discipleship becomes painfully clear to the rich young man. Jesus looks at him with love, the only description of such a gaze in the gospels, and invites the man to give up everything to follow him. It makes one wonder how impressed Jesus would be with tithing.

One of the eucharistic prayers for reconciliation will fit the theme of today's first reading.

▪ TODAY'S SAINT: Born in Philadelphia to an affluent family, Katharine became devoted to society's poor and to American Indians. She founded the Sisters of the Blessed Sacrament and pursued the ministry of evangelization. After a heart attack in 1935 she spent her last 20 years of life in prayerful retirement.

T U E **4** #348 (LMC #193–227)   green
Weekday

Optional Memorial of Casimir (+ 1482) / white ▪ God knows no favorites, Sirach says. We close our reading of passages from his book with his reflections on the importance of observing the law in a spirit of charity. It is a perfect passage to use while preparing for Lent. The psalm affirms God's gift of salvation for the upright of heart.

Peter seems disturbed by yesterday's "good news" about the need to give up possessions to follow Jesus. He voices the followers' concern that they receive something for their sacrifice. Jesus promises good and ill.

The prayers for religious (#10) remember those who renounce worldly possessions to follow Christ.

▪ TODAY'S SAINT: Casimir, son of the king of Poland, led an austere, celibate life. His religious devotion meant more to him than the national crown. The beginning of Lent makes a fitting setting for the remembrance of his asceticism.

▪ SHROVE TUESDAY: On this last day before Lent, some communities will celebrate Mardi Gras. Celebrate with a parish party, a pancake breakfast, or some other way to say goodbye to whatever the faithful may choose for fasting. LTP's *School Year, Church Year* includes ideas for celebrating this occasion with children.

JANUARY 19, 2003
Second Sunday in Ordinary Time

Sleep on It
1 Samuel 3:3b–10, 19
"Speak, Lord, for your servant is listening."

MANY of the problems that seem unsolvable by day disintegrate with the dawn. It's almost as if God speaks to us when we sleep.

This happened to Samuel. Even while he was a young child, Samuel heard the voice of God calling him. But he did not know that it was God. He told Eli the priest. Eli did not know that it was God.

Not until God spoke for the third time did Eli figure out the mystery. God was speaking to Samuel in his sleep.

Eli gave Samuel some very simple advice: Listen. If God is trying to speak to you, listen. Tell God you are listening.

Too often our world is cluttered with unnecessary noise. We leave the television on when no one is watching. We turn on the radio behind our conversation with a friend. We disturb our neighbors by playing music loudly in public or using car horns instead of doorbells. Sometimes we create so much noise it is hard to sleep.

What do you do when God is trying to speak to you? Follow Eli's advice. Listen.

Written by Paul Turner. © 2002 Archdiocese of Chicago, Liturgy Training Publications; 1-800-933-1800; www.ltp.org.

JANUARY 26, 2003
Third Sunday in Ordinary Time

God's Change of Heart
Jonah 3:1–5, 10
"God repented of the evil that he had threatened to do to them."

DOES anything ever change God's mind? Today's story from Jonah answers yes.

Most of us know Jonah as the prophet who was swallowed by a whale. Not everyone remembers the rest of the story.

Jonah didn't want to be a prophet. When God asked him to bring a message to Nineveh, Jonah refused. He ran away, boarded a ship, and tried to hide from God.

It didn't work. The ship hit turbulent waters. The sailors believed that God was coming after someone on the boat. They figured out it was Jonah, so they threw him overboard and into the jaws of the giant whale. After three days, the whale delivered Jonah safely to land. Surely, Jonah was relieved to see the earth again. But it probably shocked him to find out where he was. The whale had brought him to Nineveh, the very city where God wanted him to go in the first place.

So Jonah gave up. He prophesied destruction to Nineveh, as God had asked him to do. God was determined to punish the people for their sins.

But then something happened. The people repented, and they changed God's mind. God decided not to punish them after all.

Sometimes what changes God's mind is changing ours.

Written by Paul Turner. © 2002 Archdiocese of Chicago, Liturgy Training Publications; 1-800-933-1800; www.ltp.org.

God Bleaches Us to the Bone
Malachi 3:1–4
"Lo, I am sending my messenger to prepare the way before me."

AT first glance, the presentation of the infant Jesus in the temple appears to be a peaceful scene. His parents present him. They bring along an offering. Prophets ooh and aah over the baby Jesus. They predict marvelous things. The parents are very proud. You can almost feel their hearts flutter.

But hearts shudder at the scene from Malachi. God says, "Suddenly there will come to the temple the Lord whom you seek." He comes like a refiner's fire or like fuller's lye. He comes able to burn you to ash and bleach you to the bone. In Malachi, the Lord's coming to the temple is not at all peaceful.

For Malachi, this terrifying appearance corrected a problem. The priests of the temple were not offering a due sacrifice to God. Perhaps they were unclean themselves. Perhaps they did not observe God's commands. They needed correction, so God prophesied that the Lord himself would appear in the temple to set things aright.

That tiny baby gurgling in the arms of his parents grew up to be the Savior who reads the thoughts of hearts and calls us to conversion.

In baptism we were anointed as a priestly people. Let God's fire purge whatever keeps us from sincere prayer.

God's Restlessness
Job 7:1–4, 6–7
"Job spoke, 'My days come to an end without hope.'"

ALMOST everyone experiences depression. Some people struggle with it throughout their lives. Others have days or months when life seems hopeless.

No one in the Bible experienced despair as much as Job. Job lost his livestock, his servants, his children and their homes due to the forces of nature and enemy troops. In swift succession, Job lost everything that was dear to him.

At first, Job accepts this. He knows he came into the world with nothing and will leave this world with nothing. What he has belongs to God. God determines whether or not Job will keep it: "The Lord gave and the Lord has taken away. Blessed be the name of the Lord."

But later, as the reality of his loss sinks in, Job experiences despair. "I have been assigned months of misery, and troubled nights have been allotted to me," he says. "My days come to an end without hope. I shall not see happiness again."

When we experience those emotions we may feel far from God. The security we once felt in God's presence departs.

But Job's raw emotions appear uncensored in the Bible and in the Sunday readings. All human experience finds its place under the mantle of God's farseeing care. Even depression.

FEBRUARY 16, 2003
Sixth Sunday in Ordinary Time

Making Misery Public
Leviticus 13:1–2, 44–46
"The leper shall dwell apart."

LEPERS lived in misery. At the time of Moses, people showing symptoms of leprosy had to present themselves to Aaron the priest. If he diagnosed that they had contracted the disease, the law had very specific expectations. They had to live apart from everyone else, wear tattered garments, keep their head exposed, and cry out, "Unclean!" wherever they went.

Having an illness is bad enough. But calling attention to it is worse. Most of us try to hide our conditions. We medicate ourselves before going to work. We apply makeup over blemishes. We conceal hair loss. We prefer to have people think we're "normal." We don't want them to stare. We don't want them to know.

Lepers could not do that. Their contagion threatened the life of the community. Defeated by illness, embarrassed by publicity, shamed by society, they lived in misery.

Still, they observed what the law required. They made their condition public. They did it in service to others, who needed to know.

We all have something wrong with us. We may get very skilled at hiding it. But sometimes it helps people to know. It may help them know they are not alone. It can help them help us overcome the feelings of defeat.

Written by Paul Turner. © 2002 Archdiocese of Chicago, Liturgy Training Publications; 1-800-933-1800; www.ltp.org.

FEBRUARY 23, 2003
Seventh Sunday in Ordinary Time

God Remembers
Isaiah 43:18–19, 21–22, 24b–25
"Your sins I remember no more."

SOMETIMES we are the last ones to forget the sins of our past. We said words we regret. We did things we wish we had not. Many of the people we hurt have long forgotten what happened. But sometimes the memory stays deep within us. We are the last ones to forget the sins of our past.

Actually, not quite the last. God remembers. God remembers even when we have forgotten. But God does not desire to hold a grudge, to torment, or to punish. God desires, above all, to forgive.

Through the prophet Isaiah, God told ancient Israel to forget the events of the past. Their sins had cost them dearly, but now they could start over. God permitted them to forget that they had abandoned prayer and burdened God with sins. God was ready to forgive.

In rescuing the chosen people from their place of exile and restoring them to Jerusalem, God offered them something new. With a new beginning, they could establish their covenant more strongly.

Significantly, God wanted to forget the past. "Your sins I remember no more."

Even when it is hard for us to forget our sins, God stands ready to forgive—and to forget even what we remember.

Written by Paul Turner. © 2002 Archdiocese of Chicago, Liturgy Training Publications; 1-800-933-1800; www.ltp.org.

MARCH 2, 2003
Eighth Sunday in Ordinary Time

Wedded to Mercy
Hosea 2:16b, 17b, 21–22
"I will espouse you to me forever."

IT'S not easy being husband and wife. Marriage begins in romance, with dreams of a perfect future where the beloved will be the source of every joy.

But many couples face disappointment. Some never overcome it. Others get beyond the difficult days and deepen their love for each other in spite of them. When couples conquer disillusions, their love reaches new levels beyond where it began.

God's love for ancient Israel was like a determined person's love for an unreliable partner. Even though the partner had drifted away, God was ready to resume and strengthen the relationship.

Love is more than infatuation. God knew what love would demand. God said of Israel, "I will espouse you in right and in justice, in love and in mercy."

Love requires faithfulness and justice. It requires prudent decisions and moments of mercy.

Love can mysteriously include the imperfections of relationships, because virtues are stronger than sins. A commitment to the godlike attributes of love and mercy is stronger than the inadequacies of human effort.

Whether you are single, married, separated, divorced or widowed, God's relationship with you is like a determined, faithful spouse. God's covenant does not break.

Written by Paul Turner. © 2002 Archdiocese of Chicago, Liturgy Training Publications; 1-800-933-1800; www.ltp.org.

LENT

The Season

The Calendar

The Meaning

Lᴇɴᴛ is our time for spiritual renewal. For many people summer is the time for physical renewal, Christmas is the time to renew friendships and family. In Lent we renew our spirit.

This spiritual renewal takes on specialized form for two different groups in the parish. The faithful recommit themselves to life in Christ. The elect prepare themselves for baptism. Both groups undergo Lent as a season of preparation, and the experience of one group feeds the other. The elect see in the faithful the ideal of sacramental life toward which they strive. The faithful see in the elect the strengthening of a spiritual commitment that they strive to renew.

To these mutual ends, all those in the household of the church use Lent as a season of prayer, fasting and almsgiving, to arrive at Easter purified of heart and renewed in spirit.

Lent used to be marked by an intense obligatory daily fast. Now only Ash Wednesday, the day the season begins, is a day of obligatory fast. The fast reappears after Lent on Friday and Saturday of the Triduum. Abstinence from meat is practiced on all the Fridays of the season. Many Catholic-based organizations sponsor a Friday night fish fry to help the community socialize while observing the spirit of the season.

■ Tʜɪs ᴄᴏᴍᴍᴜɴɪᴛʏ ᴅɪᴍᴇɴsɪᴏɴ ᴏғ Lᴇɴᴛ should not be overlooked. This season is not just a matter of personal renewal. It is a time of communal renewal. We do not enter it alone, preparing as we might for a job interview. We enter it as a community, like blood donors, recyclers and highway cleanup volunteers. Our efforts make us feel like better persons, but they give us an experience of mutual sacrifice, building up the community, and making the world better for everyone. Although one's personal observance of Lent may seem like a private matter, it takes place within the context of an entire community seeking to renew hearts and souls together.

■ THE ELECT have a central place in the liturgies of Lent. As they make their preparation for baptism, they undergo a series of rites to purify their intention and enlighten their faith.

Parish organizations will probably want to keep meeting during Lent, but you might be able to combine their gatherings with occasions for worship, catechesis or service.

■ THROUGHOUT THE SEASON the liturgy makes a few adjustments: We omit the Glory to God on all Sundays of the season. We continue to recite the Creed. We substitute another gospel acclamation for the Alleluia, a word suppressed throughout Lent.

The Saints

Two solemnities fall during Lent almost every year: St. Joseph (March 19) and the Annunciation (March 25). Both call for the Glory to God and for white vesture, which otherwise are not part of the liturgy throughout Lent. The gospel acclamation remains lenten for both days. Solemnities call for the Creed, just as the Sunday liturgy does.

■ THREE OBLIGATORY MEMORIALS appear during the next six weeks: Perpetua and Felicity (March 7), John Baptist de la Salle (April 7) and Stanislaus (April 11). However, because they occur on weekdays of Lent, they are treated as optional, the same as other optional memorials of this season. If they have special significance for your community these saints may be celebrated according to the lenten rules, but otherwise the lenten weekdays take precedence.

■ WHAT ARE THE LENTEN RULES FOR CELEBRATING A SAINT'S DAY? If you wish to celebrate a memorial during this season, you may choose

the opening prayer for the saint from the sacramentary as a replacement for the opening prayer of the lenten weekday. Or you may use the saint's prayer to conclude the general intercessions. In any case the vesture remains lenten violet and all the other orations and readings remain those of the lenten weekday. That's how important the lenten course of weekday texts is to the life of the church.

■ VOTIVE MASSES and the Masses for various needs and occasions are used only for real need or pastoral advantage.

The Lectionary

■ THE SUNDAY LECTIONARY DURING LENT follows the same structure each year. The gospels on the first two Sundays tell of the temptation of Jesus in the desert and the Transfiguration. We hear these stories as told by the evangelist who dominates the gospels of that year. The gospels of weeks three, four and five offer stories of repentance and renewal.

During Year A the gospels for these middle weeks bear special significance for the elect who are completing their preparation for baptism: the woman at the well, the man born blind and the raising of Lazarus. Consequently, these may be used in any community any year. They make the most sense if you have elect preparing for baptism, for they celebrate scrutinies on those Sundays.

■ THE FRAMERS OF THE CATECHUMENATE restored the scrutinies to these Sundays with gospel texts that probably accompanied them in the early church. Their idea was not just to restore an ancient practice, but to show a progression of sin over which Jesus had power: individual sin, social sin and the effects of sin in human death. The first readings trace significant events in salvation history, and the second readings refer to a theme that arises from one of the other two each Sunday.

■ RESPONSORIAL PSALMS FOR THE SEASON ARE 51, 91 AND 130. These may be used for any seasonal Mass. The first is a classic psalm of repentance. The last carries a similar theme. Psalm 91 includes a text that Jesus cites in his temptation, according to Matthew and Luke. It relates most to the First Sunday of Lent in Years A and C, but it may be sung any time.

■ ON WEEKDAYS the scriptures develop various themes of Lent throughout the first half of the season. But during the second half we begin to hear a semicontinuous reading of John's gospel. The lectionary chooses those passages that lead up to the death of Jesus. The first readings for the second half of Lent are chosen to match the gospel's theme each day.

■ THE SUNDAY *LECTIONARY FOR MASSES WITH CHILDREN* adheres closely to the lenten scriptures. If a scrutiny is involved, consider using the readings from Year A for weeks Three, Four and Five of Lent.

The children's lectionary omits the second reading on all the Sundays of Lent except for the Second and the Fourth, when it omits the first reading instead. In this way, it omits the painful stories of the sacrifice of Abraham's son Isaac and of the destruction of the temple in Jerusalem.

The Sacramentary

■ USE A SIMPLE GREETING to open the Mass. Fast from words.

■ AMONG THE OPTIONS FOR PENITENTIAL RITE C, iv and v are especially good for Lent. Option A makes a good choice for this season, because it allows the community to confess its sins together.

Some communities kneel for the Penitential Rite during Lent. One of the roles of the deacon is to indicate a change of posture with the traditional phrases "Let us kneel" and "Let us stand."

Although the sprinkling rite is permitted on Sundays throughout the year, you may wish to avoid it during Lent. If you sprinkle on Sundays of the Easter season the symbol of water will speak more clearly.

Does your community know a sung setting of the Penitential Rite? This would be a good season to sing it. Use a setting of the Lord, Have Mercy or invite people to sing one of the traditional chants for the Kyrie. These may be incorporated into Rite C.

■ THE GLORY TO GOD is omitted during Lent. It will be sung, however, for the two solemnities, St. Joseph on March 19 and the Annunciation on March 25.

■ GOSPEL ACCLAMATION: Characteristic of this season is the change in the text for the gospel acclamation. In a spirit of penitence, the liturgy "abstains" from the Alleluia. We replace it with texts like "Praise to you, Lord Jesus, Christ, king of endless glory." Or else we employ silence. If the gospel acclamation is not sung, it may be omitted.

Because *Alleluia* means "praise God," the substitute acclamation is a kind of English translation of the Hebrew, which seems strange. Still, this alteration of the usual pattern in greeting the gospel remarkably creates a sense of the season, because the Alleluia remains "buried" even on Sundays and solemnities until Easter.

■ SAMPLE FORMULAS FOR THE GENERAL INTERCESSIONS appear in the sacramentary's first appendix. See #5 and 6 for those suggested for the lenten season.

■ THE SACRAMENTARY OFFERS A VARIETY OF SEASONAL PREFACES (P 8 to 19), a broader selection than was formerly available. Together they catechize the faithful about the demands of the season while lifting our praise to God.

The Ambrosian Rite has several prefaces that parallel those in the Roman. Translations by Alan Griffiths appear in *We Give You Thanks and Praise.* (P 8 resembles Wednesday 5 of Lent; P 9 resembles Sunday 2 (2); P 10 resembles Thursday 1; P 14 resembles Sunday 2 (1), P 17 resembles Wednesday of Holy Week; P 18 resembles Tuesday of Holy Week; P 19 resembles Palm Sunday.)

■ THE EUCHARISTIC PRAYERS FOR RECONCILIATION I AND II are both appropriate for this time of repentance. The first one seems to suggest Lent when it prays, "Now is the time for your people to turn back to you and to be renewed in Christ your Son, a time of grace and reconciliation." The second is especially fitting for a time of war or civil unrest.

■ INSERTS IN THE EUCHARISTIC PRAYER: Under the ritual Masses for Christian Initiation, the one for the scrutinies (#2) adds the names of the godparents for the elect to the text of Eucharistic Prayer I. The *Rite of Christian Initiation of Adults* says that the names of the godparents as well as those of the elect may be included in the eucharistic prayer (156), and it does not limit this to Prayer I. The sacramentary provides no text for the other eucharistic prayers. If using Prayer II, invert the order of the phrases. After "In memory of his death and resurrection, we offer you, Father, this life-giving bread, this saving cup," add the phrase "We offer them especially for the men and women you call to share your life through the living waters of baptism." Similarly, before the phrase "Lord, remember your Church throughout the world," it would be fitting to hear "Remember, Lord, these godparents who will present your chosen men and women for baptism," and then the list of their names.

■ FOR THE SOLEMN BLESSING on Sundays, the sacramentary on the First and Third Sundays suggests the one that the collection of solemn blessings envisions for the passion, at the end of Lent. Because other blessings may replace this one, better choices can be found in the prayers over the people, #6, 16 or 24. A solemn blessing for the season appears in the *Book of Blessings,* Appendix II, the fifth option at #2047. Near the end of Lent, the solemn blessing for the passion will prepare people for the Triduum. So will prayer over the people #17.

The prayer over the people, with its bow of the head, was once the traditional form of blessing during Lent.

■ DISMISSAL: The Roman Rite never calls for a recessional hymn at the end of Mass, and yet this has become a much-observed custom. During Lent, you could end the Mass in silence, for a feeling of austerity. You will also lend more weight to the words of dismissal, because people will leave promptly upon being dismissed, without the intervening song.

The Book of Blessings

YOU may wish to offer some other blessings during the season, to draw attention to some aspects of parish and community life. You may bless organizations concerned with public need (7), or bless pilgrims (8), seeds (27), meals (30), ashes (52) or a Saint Joseph's table (53). The solemn blessing for Lent at #2047 may also be used for other liturgical events.

The Rite of Christian Initiation of Adults

DURING this season of purification and enlightenment, the rites for the elect come frequently and intensely. The liturgy provides no less than eight ceremonies for them, which can be augmented by many more. In some traditions of the early church, those preparing for baptism took part in daily liturgical prayer during the weeks before their initiation.

The number of rites we offer during Lent highlight the importance of the interior transformation guided by the Holy Spirit.

■ THE RITE OF SENDING is the first of the series. It should precede the Rite of Election, normally celebrated on the First Sunday of Lent. The date for the Rite of Election varies from one diocese to the next. Therefore, some communities may anticipate the Rite of Sending even before Lent begins.

In many dioceses, the signing of the Book of the Elect takes place at this parish celebration. In other dioceses, the signing takes place at the cathedral as part of the Rite of Election. If catechumens sign the Book of the Elect during the Rite of Sending at your parish, they should not be confused into thinking that the signature constitutes their election. Rather, it is the proclamation by the bishop during the Rite of Election that achieves this status for them.

Because the giving of the name is a pre-baptismal ritual, it pertains to the unbaptized catechumens to do so, not the baptized candidates for the Rite of Reception into the Full Communion of the Catholic Church. Their names are already numbered among God's chosen people. Writing down the names and submitting them to the bishop is a practical and symbolic means of preparing for baptism.

■ THE RITE OF ELECTION takes place at the cathedral church, ideally on the First Sunday of Lent, either as a service of the word or during the liturgy of the word of a Mass.

In the early church, all the rites took place at the cathedral, including baptism. The demographic distribution of a large number of the elect makes this difficult today, so the liturgy assigns only one rite for the cathedral, election. Ideally, all those preparing for baptism should celebrate this rite, and it is imperative that their godparents be present for it. It is the godparents who make the all-important testimony on behalf of those who desire baptism.

If for some reason a catechumen is unable to attend the Rite of Election at the cathedral, the pastor could request delegation from the bishop to conduct the rite in the parish church on a subsequent occasion, as soon as reasonably possible.

■ THREE SCRUTINIES for the elect take place on the Sundays of Lent. These are offered on the Third, Fourth and Fifth Sundays for those who are preparing for baptism.

Given the nature of the texts for this service, it is not appropriate to pray them over those who are already baptized. The purpose of the scrutinies is to drive away from the elect whatever might keep them from baptism, and to strengthen what is good within them.

Throughout the American edition of the *Rite of Christian Initiation of Adults,* the baptized and unbaptized may be invited to celebrate stages together in combined rites. However, there are no combined rites for scrutinies.

When celebrating the scrutinies at a parish Mass, note the change in the order of service. Petitions for the elect may be combined with the general intercessions, and all these may precede the Creed. Or the general intercessions and the Creed may be omitted. Probably the ones who most need to know this are the ushers because it changes their cue for when to start the collection.

■ THE PRESENTATIONS OF THE CREED AND THE LORD'S PRAYER should take place apart from the Sunday Mass, during the third and fifth weeks of Lent. They may even be anticipated to another time of year, but historically they took place in the weeks preceding baptism.

You might consider having these presentations as part of an evening lenten Mass or Stations of the Cross or evening prayer, or in conjunction with another event at the parish— an adult education night, for example. In that way members of the faithful may be present for these rituals.

It is especially important that the faithful be represented at the Presentation of the Creed. After all, they are the ones making the presentation. In the liturgy, the presentation of these texts is made orally, not in calligraphy on parchment.

■ IF THERE ARE CANDIDATES FOR THE RITE OF RECEPTION INTO FULL COMMUNION, they may celebrate a Penitential Rite on the Second Sunday of Lent, a ceremony resembling a scrutiny, but with texts that honor their baptism. For those who have never professed the Nicene Creed, a case can be made that they should receive the Presentation of the Creed as well when that is offered later in the season.

■ THROUGHOUT THIS PERIOD, blessings and minor exorcisms may continue to be offered for the elect during their catechetical sessions.

A parish may also have unbaptized inquirers or catechumens who will not be expecting baptism this Easter because their preparation thus far has been too short. The other rites and stages of the catechumenate still pertain to them. In other words, you may have inquirers, catechumens and elect all in the parish at the same time. Not every catechumen becomes one of the elect during this season.

■ INFANT BAPTISM: Many parishes refrain from offering the Rite of Baptism for Children during the season of Lent. The *Circular Letter concerning the Preparation and Celebration of the Easter Feasts* ("*Circular Letter*") says, "It is not fitting that Baptisms and Confirmation be celebrated [during Holy Week]" (27). But it would help heighten the anticipation for baptism if infant baptisms could be deferred from Lent to the Easter season. There are exceptions, of course, and in an emergency baptism should be administered without delay.

The Liturgy of the Hours

THE same psalm changes that occurred in Advent and Christmas return for Lent and Easter. Psalm 105 replaces Psalms 131 and 132 on the first Saturday; 106 replaces 136 on the second Saturday; and 78 replaces 55 and 50 on the Friday and Saturday of the fourth week.

Some beautiful texts appear in the office of readings. Note especially the one by Aelred of Rievaulx on Friday of the first week of Lent. There he warns those who have suffered injuries that they can keep the fire of divine love from growing cold if they meditate on the serene patience of the Savior. If your parish is looking for some kind of prayer to add during the season, consider a Sunday night vespers, or morning prayer on a day there is no early Mass.

The Rite of Penance

LENT is a beautiful season to celebrate the sacrament of reconciliation. The prayers and practices of this season help us call to mind our sins and God's forgiveness. As we grow in awareness of our faults, we can bring them to God in a spirit of repentance, open to growth in grace, awaiting the full expression of mercy and love.

The experience of the faithful parallels that of the elect. Through the scrutinies, we ask God to purify those preparing for baptism. Through reconciliation, we seek the same goal.

Many parishes offer a communal celebration so the faithful can bring their lenten penance to a sacramental moment. If several parishes are all planning a communal service, publish announcements about them together in the bulletin and on the website. Start all the services at a common time.

■ IF CHILDREN IN CATHOLIC SCHOOLS ARE TO CELEBRATE THE SACRAMENT, offer communal services for them early in the season to avoid scheduling confessors for too much work at the end. For children, a series of short services is better than one long one. Although many adults have patiently tolerated what might be called "communal waiting services," children have a shorter attention span.

■ INDIVIDUAL RECONCILIATION SHOULD ALSO BE AVAILABLE. Publish the times in a prominent space in the bulletin, and encourage all to include the sacrament in their lenten regimen. Publish also the times the sacrament is available at neighboring parishes. Advertise all opportunities well so the parish knows when reconciliation will be offered.

■ NON-SACRAMENTAL PENITENTIAL SERVICES for Lent can be found in Appendix II of the *Rite of Penance.* They may be used with any group wanting to express sorrow and pray for forgiveness. They also offer readings and prayers that could be incorporated into a communal sacramental celebration. The first suggests sprinkling with holy water as an act of repentance, but without proper catechesis it will seem like a prolepsis of Easter. The second suggests adoration of the cross or Stations of the Cross to conclude the service. Because the veneration of the cross is a highlight of the Good Friday liturgy, it may seem odd to anticipate it. Stations, however, might make a fitting conclusion to the celebration.

Seen another way, a penitential service might make a good prelude to stations. The custom of Friday stations is observed throughout the Catholic world, although there is no universal liturgical rite for the prayer. Many publishers make quality materials available.

The Pastoral Care of the Sick

THE sacrament of the sick may be given at any time during this season, but because of the large number of other liturgical prayers vying for attention, it may be best to celebrate communal anointing of the sick during another season of the church year.

The penitential services in the *Rite of Penance* include an example of one for the sick. This option offers a time of prayer with the sick when the sacraments are not administered.

The Rite of Marriage

MARRIAGES may take place during Lent. The parish priest is asked to advise the couple to take into consideration the special nature of the season (*Rite of Marriage,* 11 and *Ceremonial of Bishops,* 604).

If the wedding takes place during a Saturday evening Mass, the readings and prayers for the Sunday in Lent take precedence. The couple is not free to select alternative scripture passages for the wedding Mass during Lent.

If the wedding does not include a Mass, or if the wedding Mass does not take place on a Saturday evening or Sunday, the scriptures and prayers for marriage may be used. No other special texts or scriptures apply to weddings during Lent.

When decorating for the wedding, the couple should honor the seasonal appearance of the church. It will contribute to the ecclesial context in which the wedding takes place.

The Order of Christian Funerals

FUNERALS may take place on any day of Lent. On weekdays, consult the daily lectionary. Sometimes the daily readings of Lent seem suitable for a funeral Mass. But the funeral lectionary may be used. If a funeral needs to take place on a Sunday in Lent, the Sunday Mass is used with its prayers and scriptures.

Purple vesture is permitted for funerals throughout the year. Although most parishes celebrate the Mass in white, the color of Lent may also be used.

The Art and Environment

THE spare use of materials in this season will inspire the spare use of food, drink and extraneous activity. A sober environment fits the season of Lent.

■ CONSIDER THE OUTSIDE AS WELL. There may be something you can remove during the season to restore it later. Less is more.

■ DROUGHT: Some communities empty the holy water stoups or the baptismal font during the season. The practice has some grassroots support, but it does not appear in the liturgical books. We sign ourselves with water upon entering the church as a reminder of baptism, but it can also function as an act of ritual cleansing in harmony with the spirit of the season and the nature of the eucharist.

The Easter candle continues to reside near the font, but perhaps in a less prominent place. It will look rather stubby by now.

■ IF CATECHUMENS SIGNED THE BOOK OF THE ELECT at your parish, you may display it someplace where the faithful can observe it. Names and faces of the elect should be on bulletin boards, if not in the weekly bulletin and on the website during Lent. Have kids cut out crosses and print the name of one of the elect on each one. Stuff them in the bulletin so they can end up on refrigerators at home, to remind each household to pray for at least one of the elect by name.

■ THE COLOR FOR VESTURE IS VIOLET. If you have a set more purple than the bluish tint used during Advent, use it to distinguish these seasons. The Fourth Sunday permits the use of rose vestments. The final Sunday of Lent takes red vesture.

The Music

A rich heritage of music for Lent has evolved in every age.

■ CHANT: Some of the Latin chants are especially lovely. Your community could sing "Attende, Domine" and "Parce, Domine" (found in the *Liber cantualis*), "Vexilla Regis," "Pange, lingua," and all will hold up well with repeated use during the season. Consider using a set of chant acclamations for the eucharistic prayer. Has your community learned the one in English in the sacramentary?

■ ENTRANCE AND COMMUNION ANTIPHONS AND PSALMS, as well as the responsorial psalms and other chants between the readings, appear in *By Flowing Waters* (The Liturgical Press). These can be especially effective at daily Mass when only a cantor is available to lead the singing. This collection of unaccompanied song for assemblies, cantors and choirs includes settings for the Penitential Rite (606, 611 and 612), eucharistic acclamations (578–581), a threefold Great Amen (583) and the fraction rite (605, 610, 615, 616, 621 and 622).

■ HYMNS: The classic hymns for Lent include "Lord, Who Throughout These Forty Days" and "This Is Our Accepted Time." Your community could really belt out "Lift High the Cross" using William Ferris's arrangement for choir, descant, trumpets and organ (WLP, 8688). Michael Ward has a fine arrangement of the traditional spiritual "Near the Cross" (WLP, 8526).

■ YOUTH: The entire community may also learn songs meaningful to teens and expressive of the season, like Rich Mullins's "Awesome God" (WLP *Voices as One,* 7) or Bob Hurd's "Be With Me" (OCP, *Spirit and Song*). Henry Mollicone's

"Hear Me, Redeemer" (Woodland Hills Music Press, 4511) is in a gospel style. Ed Bolduc's "If Today You Hear the Voice of God" (WLP, 7352) has a relaxed, rock style.

■ PSALMODY: Richard Proulx's "Six Choral Introits for the Church Year" (WLP, 5783) includes a beautiful one for Lent, with the text from Joel, and the tune based on the haunting *Tonus peregrinus*. William Ferris has a simple setting of Psalm 91, "Be With Me, Lord" (WLP, 6221). Christopher Walker's "O Lord, Heal Us," works for Lent and Passiontide (OCP, 10799). Robert Schaefer's choral setting of Psalm 51, "Be Merciful, O Lord," is in English and Spanish (WLP, 6241).

Other noteworthy settings of lenten psalms include Psalm 137: "Let my Tongue Be Silenced" by Mike Hay (WLP, 6224) and "Beside the Streams of Babylon" by Paul Lisicky; Psalm 91: "God Has Put the Angels in Charge of You" by Kathy Powell (WLP, 6234); and Psalm 51: "Psalm for Mercy" by Stephen Pishner (GIA, G-4707), based on the hymn "Wondrous Love."

■ THE SCRUTINIES AND PRESENTATIONS will also demand music. Be sure to plan for involvement of musicians and assembly in these events. J. Michael Thompson's piece for unison choir, "God, Give us Grace These Lenten Days," blends the themes of Noah's ark and baptismal rebirth (WLP, 5777). Jerry Galipeau's "Three Litanies for the Scrutinies" (WLP, 5235) will help you incorporate local petitions into a sung framework.

And do not overlook the oddly named "RCIA Suite" by Omer Westendorf and Robert E. Kreutz (WLP, 8551), the same team that brought us "Gift of Finest Wheat" and a number of other singable, creditable compositions. The suite alternates instrumental and choral music. The texts are remarkably poetic. (Whoever thought you could sing the word catechumen!) Plus, the choral writing is superb. Use the entire suite as part of a lenten prayer service, or use bits of it throughout the season for Sunday worship.

■ THE AVOIDANCE OF INSTRUMENTAL MUSIC IN LENT, a longstanding tradition, causes its own penance for a community who would love to hear J. S. Bach's chorale preludes like "O Mensch, bewein' dein' Sünde groß" or one of the many versions of the Passion Chorale "O Sacred Head" for organ, like "Herzlich tut mich verlangen" by Johannes Brahms.

The Parish and Home

THE parish will do all families a service by providing texts for prayer at home. Lent is a season when families may build a spirit of communal prayer. Provide mealtime prayer cards and suggestions for decorating the table. You will find several good suggestions in *Catholic Household Blessings and Prayers,* like the Ash Wednesday blessing of the season and a place for prayer (pp. 132ff), the blessings of lenten disciplines (pp. 137ff), and the passion Sunday placing of branches in the home (pp. 140ff).

LTP's two-volume *A Lent Sourcebook* (1990) is an outstanding resource of texts useful for prayer and meditation. *What Am I Doing for Lent This Year?* (2000) will help individuals and communities think about the spiritual growth they wish to attain and make a practical plan for the season.

Start planning the Easter Sunday bulletin. You may have to submit the copy early in Holy Week to get it back while the office is still open. Brainstorm the information you want visitors to know about. What's coming up after Easter that they could return for? What opportunities for community life should they know about?

Texts

■ GREETING: The German sacramentary suggests this alternative greeting:

> The grace of the Lord Jesus, who suffered for us, be with you.

■ INTRODUCTION TO THE PENITENTIAL RITE:

> My sisters and brothers, let us repent and believe in the gospel.

■ RESPONSE TO THE GENERAL INTERCESSIONS:

> Lord, have mercy.
>
> Be merciful Lord, and hear our prayer.

Among the texts recommended for Lent in the United Church of Canada's *Celebrate God's Presence* is this one, which could conclude the general intercessions or be incorporated in some other seasonal prayer:

Beginner of all things,
begin in us again:
take these tired limbs
and rouse them to dance your joy
from sunbreak to sundown.

Help us,
O Blessed One,
to shake off our weariness
that we may know new life in you
and offer it to one another. Amen. [17T004]

■ DISMISSAL OF CATECHUMENS AND ELECT:

We do not live on bread alone, but on every word
that comes forth from the mouth of God.
    Catechumens and elect, feast yourselves on God's
word until you come again to feast at this table.
    Go in peace.

March

#219 (LMC #176–184) violet
Ash Wednesday

ORIENTATION

"Come and admit you are wrong" is hardly an invitation the typical American would find favorable. But the power of Ash Wednesday calls believers to their place of worship in droves to confess their sin, and even to wear a public sign of their repentance.

The blessing and administration of ashes opens this season of sorrow and mercy. Ash Wednesday has been observed throughout the universal church for over nine hundred years. It invites the baptized faithful into a spirit of repentance. Even those who do not frequent the Mass come to express their sorrow and to receive the symbol of repentance.

This is a day of fast and abstinence. After a light breakfast, the other meals should not equal a full meal. There should be no snacking. The faithful are asked to abstain from meat today. That includes poultry and amphibians, but not fish and seafood. Still, the idea is to eat simply, not lavishly.

Other services may be offered in addition to Mass—the Liturgy of the Hours, for example, or even a word service that includes the giving of ashes. [See the *Book of Blessings* for a complete order of service (52).] Some parishes offer a simple fasting evening meal following Mass or vespers to accommodate those coming from work. Ashes are distributed only as part of communal prayer. Those who wear ashes this day signify their acceptance of penance and their participation in community.

LECTIONARY

The gospel outlines three divisions of penitential disciplines: prayer, fasting and almsgiving. Through the prophet Joel, God invites the people to turn from sin with fasting. Paul tells the Corinthians that now is the time of their salvation. The psalm invites us all into a confession of our sins before God. Overall, the readings proclaim the existence of sin, the need for repentance and the means to execute it. They should inspire a 40-day response.

SACRAMENTARY

Ashes are made from the previous year's palm branches. There is no liturgical ceremony that accompanies their burning. This can be done simply well in advance of the liturgy. Parishioners who don't know what to do with leftover palm branches will appreciate the opportunity to bring them to church for this purpose.

Set the ashes someplace visible before the service begins. If necessary, provide cards for the ministers with the text they will recite. Washing bowls, pitchers of water and slices of lemon will help ministers clean up after the distribution of ashes. (See notes on this day in G. Thomas Ryan's *The Sacristy Manual,* available from LTP, pp. 194–195.)

Mass begins with a hymn or song based on the entrance antiphon acclaiming God's mercy. A simple refrain, chanted *a capella,* may be effective, or a hymn that establishes the theme of the 40 days. The presider makes the sign of the cross, greets the people, and then immediately offers the opening prayer. There is no Penitential Rite and no Glory to God today. The giving of ashes replaces the Penitential Rite.

After the homily comes the blessing and giving of ashes. No introduction is offered, but one could be devised based on a text in the *Book of Blessings* (#1663) either at this point or after the greeting before the opening prayer. The presider invites all to silent prayer, and then blesses the people or the ashes (depending on which version of the prayer you use), sprinkling the ashes with holy water. One need not be a priest or deacon to distribute ashes. The presider and other ministers then rub ashes onto the foreheads of all who come forward, reciting one of the texts provided. A song of repentance is sung. Psalm 50 is recommended. That is the alternate numbering for the psalm marked 51 in the lectionary, the same one used for the responsory at this Mass. After the ministers wash their hands, the general intercessions are prayed.

The preface recommended for Ash Wednesday (P 11) is entitled "The Reward of Fasting," but actually treats the "observance of Lent," not just fasting.

The liturgy today makes no allusion to the catechumens who will become elect. Ash Wednesday developed at a time in our history when catechumens were few and the church needed to begin this season with a penitential service for all the faithful. The catechumens, of course, make their entry into the season with the Rite of Election this coming Sunday.

OTHER IDEAS

As with the communion procession, it is cumbersome for people to process with a hymnal in hand. Choose music with an easily memorized refrain for the distribution of ashes. Good options include "My Soul Is Longing for your Peace" and "Grant to Us, O Lord" by Lucien Deiss (World

Library) and "Give us, Lord, a New Heart" by Bernadette Farrell (OCP, 710). For liturgies celebrated with children, consult *Preparing Liturgy for Children and Children for Liturgy,* 81.

Since the sixth century the text from the book of Wisdom has been sung as the entrance song for Ash Wednesday; it may be found in *By Flowing Waters* (50–51). All 19 verses of Psalm 51 are available for singing during the distribution of ashes at 55–56.

Among the prayers of thanksgiving after Mass in the sacramentary's first appendix is the universal prayer attributed to Pope Clement XI. It may make a good prayer for Lent.

THU 6
#220 (LMC #176–184)   violet
Lenten Weekday

The first reading sets out the two ways, life or death. Moses enjoins the people to choose life by following God. The same two ways appear in the psalm. During this time of renewal, we will be called to observe more closely which path we have chosen.

Already in the gospel the shadow of the cross falls across this season. We who follow Christ will take up his cross.

The third preface (P 10) uses the theme of self-denial.

■ IN URUGUAY, the votive Mass of the Virgin Mary, Mother of Reconciliation, is encouraged during Lent.

FRI 7
#221 (LMC #176–184)   violet
Lenten Weekday

Optional Memorial of Perpetua and Felicity (+ c. 203), martyrs/ violet ▪ We abstain from meat today. The opening prayer seems to allude to this lenten custom.

In the gospel Jesus speaks of the need to fast when the bridegroom is taken away. This is Matthew's version of the passage we heard from Mark this past Sunday, when we concluded Ordinary Time. In the first reading, Isaiah explains the full implications of a fast—a discipline not just concerning food, but an entire way of life. The penitential Psalm 51 returns. The first preface (P 8) relates charity to prayer.

■ TODAY'S SAINTS: Perpetua and her slave Felicity, both catechumens in North Africa, both either a mother or a mother-to-be, were baptized shortly before their martyrdom in Carthage. Thrown to wild beasts and slain by the sword, they died in the embrace of Christian peace. The Felicity who appears in Eucharistic Prayer I was probably the second-century martyr from Rome, not the third-century martyr from Carthage. However, it appears that the Carthaginian Perpetua found her way into the same eucharistic prayer by association with Felicity's name. That may explain why the names appear in reverse among the saints of the Roman Canon.

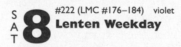
SAT 8
#222 (LMC #176–184)   violet
Lenten Weekday

Optional Memorial of John of God (+ 1550), religious founder/violet ▪ Jesus invites a sinner into discipleship, giving hope to all. Isaiah gives advice for the authentic practice of belief. The psalm expresses a sinner's aspiration to overcome evil and do good.

The suggested communion antiphon quotes from Matthew's version of today's gospel. The second preface (P 9) expresses the goals of this season of repentance.

■ TODAY'S SAINT: Portuguese by birth, shepherd and warrior by profession, John changed professions at the age of 40 and devoted his life to caring for the sick.

#23 (LMC #19)   violet
☀9 First Sunday of Lent

ORIENTATION

Although Lent started several days ago, this will be the first day many in the community become aware of it. It is also the day when the elect begin their period of purification and enlightenment, after celebrating the Rite of Election.

The time frame within which one must fulfill Easter duty begins today. It hardly seems necessary to remind people, but they are expected to share communion at least once between today and Trinity Sunday.

LECTIONARY

The gospel each year tells of the temptation of Jesus in the desert. His 40 days there gives us the length of Lent. In fact, some people count the 40 days of Lent beginning today and ending on Holy Thursday.

Mark's version of the temptation story sounds abrupt if you are accustomed to hearing Matthew and Luke. Commentators believe Mark's account was written first, and that Matthew and Luke expanded on Mark with another document, now lost, called "Q," short for *quelle,* the German word for "source." The Q document probably contained a list of the sayings of Jesus, including his dialogue with Satan, in which they each quote scripture at each other. Mark, who probably did not have access to Q, does not include the dialogue. But the tradition of Jesus spending time in the desert was well established in Christian tradition from its earliest days.

Apart from the 40-days-in-the-desert motif, this passage befits the opening of Lent for another reason. It gives us the first words of Jesus' ministry, a lenten-sounding saying that could be called Jesus' motto: "The kingdom of God is at hand. Repent, and believe in the gospel."

Throughout the season, the first readings will trace principal events in salvation history. The series begins today with Genesis. The story of Noah makes a rare Sunday appearance. In today's passage, God has rescued Noah, his family and the animals from the flood and established a covenant with them. This covenant predates the one God made with Abraham. It shows from early in the Bible God's intent to rescue us from sin. In the psalm we sing about faithfulness to the covenant.

The second reading makes a reference to Noah. The First Letter of Peter says God waited patiently in the days of Noah and saved eight people, prefiguring baptism. Baptism cleanses not just the body, but the conscience. Early Christian writers pointed out that the eight saved people symbolize the eighth day, a time outside of time in which God brings our ordinary week to an extraordinary perfection. Sunday, when we baptize, is not just the first day of the week, but also the eighth. This is one reason why many baptismal fonts have eight sides. If the reader stresses the word *Noah,* people may make the connection.

SACRAMENTARY

The Glory to God is omitted. The suggested texts for the entrance and communion antiphons rely on the gospel of today. The preface for the First Sunday (P 12) recalls the temptation, but other choices

may be made. Given the theme of sinful humanity in the other scriptures today, a eucharistic prayer for reconciliation would also make a good choice. You may use either of them with the lenten preface if you wish. For the final blessing a better choice might be prayer over the people #24.

OTHER IDEAS

The *Circular Letter,* 23 (reprinted in LTP's second volume of *The Liturgy Documents*), recommends a penitential procession to open the Mass for the First Sunday of Lent. The *Ceremonial of Bishops* (261) suggests a procession for all the lenten Sundays wherever the bishop presides. The community gathers someplace outside the church and a procession forms. The presider may wear a violet cope. During the procession the Litany of the Saints is sung. Upon entering the church, all take their places, the presider reverences the altar, and then goes to the chair. The opening prayer for Mass follows immediately. If the Kyrie was not incorporated into the litany, it may precede the opening prayer.

By Flowing Waters includes a solemn form of the Litany of the Saints (663–675) for this Sunday (see Performance Note on pp. 419 and 426–427). See also Richard Proulx's "Litany for the Season of Lent" (WLP, 5228), based on texts from the *Book of Common Prayer.* Not a litany of the saints, but a litany worth considering at the beginning of Lent.

Psalm 91 (62 and 63) has been traditionally the psalm of the First Sunday of Lent. In 64, the rapid return of the refrain, "Because I have sinned against you," after every verse of the psalm illustrates the disastrous effects of our sinfulness on all of our relationships.

If your community has not yet celebrated the Rite of Sending for

the Rite of Election, you may do so today. It should take place, of course, before the Rite of Election.

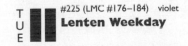

MON 10 #224 (LMC #176–184) violet
Lenten Weekday

The demands of Christian charity are no more eloquently explained than in Jesus' image for the last judgment in Matthew 25. Everyone knows what the final exam will be. Whatever we do for the least of our brothers and sisters we do for Jesus.

Proper treatment of neighbors is also the theme of today's passage from Leviticus. Because it is drawn from the Torah, we sing a psalm in praise of God's law. The refrain comes from Jesus' own description of his discourse on the bread of life. His words are spirit and life.

The suggested communion antiphon today comes from the gospel.

Preface IV (P 11) explains the rewards of a faithful lenten observance.

TUE 11 #225 (LMC #176–184) violet
Lenten Weekday

Prayer, one of the topics of the gospel from Ash Wednesday, returns in today's gospel. In fact, this is the passage excised from the gospel that day. Jesus teaches the Lord's Prayer.

The first reading explains the effectiveness of God's word, implying the effectiveness of the Lord's Prayer. The psalm recalls that the Lord will hear the cry of the just.

Preface II (P 9) invites us to purify our hearts.

WED 12 #226 (LMC #176–184) violet
Lenten Weekday

Hearing the Jonah story today makes us think of it as a foreshadowing of Jesus' burial and resurrection. But the lectionary has something else in mind. Jesus says the point of the story of Jonah was the conversion of the people. That is its lenten message today. Psalm 51 returns to round out the theme of repentance.

Eucharistic Prayer I for Reconciliation makes a good choice today.

THU 13 #227 (LMC #176–184) violet Lenten Weekday

Another text on the benefit of prayer pairs nicely with Tuesday's scriptures. Jesus invites us to ask God for what we want. Queen Esther prays for guidance before she appears before the king to plea for the freedom of her people. The psalm gives thanks for prayers answered. The first preface (P 8) acknowledges our spirit of reverence for God.

FRI 14 #228 (LMC #176–184) violet Lenten Weekday

The message of reconciliation sounds clear this Friday in Jesus' plea for those who cannot get along. Make peace on your way to the altar, he says. Whenever possible, settle disputes outside of court.

Ezekiel encourages a similar conversion of heart. The wicked who turn from their sins will find forgiveness. We pray for forgiveness with one of the greatest psalms of human sorrow and divine mercy.

The second eucharistic prayer for reconciliation says, "Your spirit changes our hearts: enemies begin to speak to one another."

SAT 15 #229 (LMC #176–184) violet Lenten Weekday

Jesus' command to love enemies is a measure of Christian perfection. This season calls us to charity as part of its discipline. Moses reminds the people of the importance of observing God's commands, and the first verses of

Psalm 119 meditate on the same. Service to neighbors is highlighted in the first lenten preface (P 8).

☀️ 16 #26 (LMC #22) violet Second Sunday of Lent

ORIENTATION

We hear the annual story of the Transfiguration of Jesus, a glimpse of what is to be. With the apostles we climb the mountain of Lent to behold Jesus at the summit in glory. If there are baptized candidates for the Rite of Reception at Easter, they may celebrate a Penitential Rite at Mass today (RCIA, 459).

LECTIONARY

Mark's account of the Transfiguration brings Peter, James and John to a high mountain, apart from Jesus. As Jesus is transfigured, Moses and Elijah appear at his side. Significantly for the season we have entered, Moses, Elijah and Jesus each spent 40 days fasting during part of their ministry.

The first reading on the Second Sunday of Lent each year tells some part of the story of Abraham. This year we hear about the sacrifice of Isaac. Hearing about Abraham the week after Noah, we trace the unfolding of God's covenant with humanity, which reaches its promised fulfillment in the paschal mystery. This particular episode from Abraham's life is among the scriptures for the Easter Vigil because Christian commentators believe it prefigured the sacrifice of Jesus, the only Son of God, who was rescued

from death. The psalm has this theme in mind when we sing, "I will walk in the presence of the Lord, in the land of the living." For Christians, those living in Christ are found in that land.

"If God is for us, who can be against us?" Paul's rhetorical question comforts the believer in the midst of frustration and persecution. We hear this text during Lent because Paul argues that the death of Jesus is a sign of God's immeasurable love. God did not spare the only Son, Paul argues, and this weekend we remember that Abraham did not spare his only son either.

SACRAMENTARY

Begin simply in the spirit of the season. Perhaps you will sing the Penitential Rite. The Glory to God is omitted. Both versions of the opening prayer build on the theme of light. The preface recommended for today (P 13) is a good choice, but others suit the season just as well. A prayer over the people is suggested, but consider also #7.

OTHER IDEAS

The Rite of Reception for baptized candidates may take place any time of year. It need not happen at the Easter Vigil. The timing pertains more to their readiness than to a season of the year. Even if they are received into the full communion of the church at Easter, the rite offered today is optional. However, if your community chooses to celebrate it, it may serve as a prelude to the scrutinies over the next few Sundays. You might invite the assembly to extend their hands over the candidates during the presider's imposition of hands. The deacon, or a representative from the Christian Initiation team, may impose hands as well. The liturgy encourages catechists to take a strong liturgical role (RCIA, 16).

MON 17 #230 (LMC #176–184)   violet
Lenten Weekday

Optional Memorial of St. Patrick (+ 461), bishop, missionary / violet ▪ Among the charitable attitudes Jesus commends to his followers is nonjudgmental pardon. In the first reading Daniel confesses the sins of the people to God, speaking himself the words of a communal expression of sorrow. The psalm asks God not to treat us as our sins deserve.

The second eucharistic prayer for Masses of reconciliation fits the themes today.

▪ TODAY'S SAINT: Patrick came from Great Britain and served a period of slavery in Ireland. After a dramatic escape, he became a priest, then a bishop, returned to Ireland, and preached the gospel there. If the parish gathers today in his honor, your choir might want to sing his Lorica, "Christ Be Near at Either Hand" (WLP, 7200) arranged by Gerard Gillen and Steven C. Warner. Note that the vestment color for today is purple, even if celebrating Patrick, as in other lenten memorials.

TUE 18 #231 (LMC #176–184)   violet
Lenten Weekday

Optional Memorial of Cyril of Jerusalem (+ 386), bishop, doctor of the church / violet ▪ Jesus condemns hypocrisy and invites people into authentic religious observance. The psalm asks in a similar vein, Why do people profess the covenant with their mouth but cast God's words behind them? The passage from Isaiah is a little more generic in its call to renewal, but in the context of the other readings, it also challenges formalism—those who merely go through the actions of worship without any heart.

In this spirit of repentance, the first eucharistic prayer for reconciliation would serve well today.

▪ TODAY'S SAINT: Cyril served as bishop in Jerusalem about the time Egeria made her pilgrimage there. Together their testimonies reveal a great deal about the fourth-century Holy Week liturgy of the church in Jerusalem. Cyril participated in the council of Constantinople, which finalized the Creed we use each Sunday.

▪ TODAY IS THE JEWISH FEAST OF PURIM, celebrating the defeat of the plot to destroy the Jews of Persia.

WED 19 #543 (LMC #272)   white
Joseph, Husband of the Virgin Mary
SOLEMNITY

ORIENTATION

We interrupt Lent for this special celebration. Foster father of Jesus, a patron of the universal church, Joseph enjoys widespread devotion among the faithful. Although his influence has been enormous, the New Testament records not a single word that issued from Joseph's mouth.

Joseph is patron of Costa Rica.

LECTIONARY

Two choices appear for the gospel today. In the first, a puzzled Joseph learns of the pregnancy of his betrothed and receives advice from an angel. In the second, he searches for the child he lost in Jerusalem. Both stories show very real examples of a man trying to do his part while dealing with the struggles of family life.

The first reading and the psalm that follows it concern the lineage of David, out of which Joseph will come. The second reading pushes the lineage back all the way to Abraham, and we also find in him an example of the faithful father realized later in Joseph.

SACRAMENTARY

Today's solemnity calls for the Glory to God and the Creed. A preface for the day is provided (P 62). Eucharistic Prayer I includes Joseph's name, the last change made to the Roman Canon before the opening of the Second Vatican Council.

The gospel acclamation of Lent continues. Hymnody to Joseph is rare, but useful. Check the indices of your hymnals.

The suggested antiphons today recall the faithfulness of Joseph's service.

OTHER IDEAS

For the white vesture, you may want to use a set from the Christmas season, recalling Joseph's role in the story of the incarnation.

Your community may host a St. Joseph's Table. The Italian tradition combines a meal for the faithful with donations for the poor. The Book of Blessings includes an Order for the Blessing of St. Joseph's Table (53).

See *Catholic Household Blessings and Prayers* for domestic prayer (165) and a litany (36).

T H U **20** #233 (LMC #176–184)   violet
Lenten Weekday

The parable of Lazarus and the rich man forms a graphic illustration of the importance of sharing one's gifts with the needy. Jeremiah suggests that those who trust in God will demonstrate that in peaceful, steadfast behavior. The psalm repeats the theme of the tree that receives life because it is planted beside the water of God's word.

The third preface (P 10) fits these themes.

F R I **21** #234 (LMC #176–184)   violet
Lenten Weekday

The readings give us another somber Friday in Lent. Jesus' parable of the wicked tenants reads like an omen of his own suffering and death. Yet, as the first reading shows, we have seen it all before in the story of Joseph, sold for 20 pieces of silver. That story is retold in the psalm. The Joseph story's happy ending is hidden from view as we are made to face the horror of sinful human behavior in need of redemption.

The first eucharistic prayer for reconciliation will put this into perspective.

S A T **22** #235 (LMC #176–184)   violet
Lenten Weekday

"A man had two sons." So begins one of the most famous stories in the history of the world. The Prodigal Son is a masterful tale woven by Jesus, artfully recounted by Luke. It moves the reader to repentance. Paired with this is Micah's beautiful reflection on the mercy of God, who casts our sins under the sea.

The communion antiphon today quotes the gospel. The second eucharistic prayer for reconciliation will fit this liturgy.

#29 or 28 (LMC #25 or 24)
violet

○**23** **Third Sunday of Lent**

ORIENTATION

This Sunday and the next two form a unit, especially in communities where members of the elect are preparing for baptism. On all three Sundays we have the option of proclaiming the scriptures from Year A. Although this option is not restricted to communities with elect, it makes most sense to exercise it when you celebrate the scrutinies. You may use the Year A readings only at scrutiny Masses, or you may replace all the Year B readings with those from Year A. You may even use the Year B readings at a scrutiny Mass, but they will not fit as well with the theme of their prayers.

On this date the churches of Bolivia, Ecuador, Colombia and Honduras normally celebrate the memorial of Turibio of Mogrovejo (+ 1606), bishop and missionary.

LECTIONARY

■ YEAR A READINGS: The gospel of the woman at the well forms the centerpiece of the scriptures this weekend and gives shape to this part of Lent. She does not approach Jesus. Jesus approaches her. He has living water. She asks for some. He reveals his knowledge of her. She becomes a believer. She

also becomes an apostle, proclaiming that Jesus is the Messiah. For all these reasons, she becomes a kind of patron for the elect, whom God has approached, who have asked for the living water of baptism, who are expressing their belief, and who must become apostles of the Good News.

The first reading continues the series summarizing salvation history. Each year the first reading on the Third Sunday of Lent gives us a story of Moses. This year's recalls Israel's thirst in the desert and God's gift of water from the rock. The psalm sings critically of the same event, when Israel tested God at Massah and Meribah, even though the people had seen God's work.

The second reading reinforces the theme of Christ dying for all sinners.

■ YEAR B READINGS: The gospels for the next three Sundays come from John, not Mark. We hear from John at special seasons of the year, notably during the Lent and Easter cycle.

When John tells the story of Jesus driving the money changers out of the temple, he places it near the beginning of his gospel. The other evangelists place it later, where it becomes one of the events that provoke the arrest of Jesus. In John's version, Jesus says, "Destroy this temple and in three days I will raise it up." This is the main reason we hear this text today. The words prophesy the death and resurrection of Jesus' body.

The second reading likewise reflects on the death and resurrection of Jesus. Paul says the crucifixion of Jesus was a stumbling block to those looking for signs of God's power and wisdom. But we enter the mystery of human suffering and of the crucifixion with confidence and proclaim it proudly. The promise of life untangles the mystery of death.

The first reading continues giving us highlights of salvation history. After hearing of the covenant with Noah and the faithfulness of Abraham, we now hear about the giving of the covenant to Moses. This text includes the famous Ten Commandments, easier to pick out in the shorter form of the first reading. Several of the psalms sing praise of God's word. Today's responsorial is one of them.

SACRAMENTARY

The prayers for the Third Sunday appear where you expect to find them, but if you are celebrating the scrutinies at one or more Masses this weekend, you may also use the prayers under Ritual Masses: Christian Initiation, the Scrutinies (2). The text frequently refers to the "chosen ones," a translation for the same Latin word that is rendered "elect" in the *Rite of Christian Initiation of Adults*. The eucharistic prayer may include a mention of the names of the elect and their godparents. Print out the names of each group so the presider can include them at the appropriate place in the prayer. The prayers under the Third Sunday of Lent are more appropriate when no elect are present. Two communion antiphons are suggested, depending on which gospel is proclaimed.

The preface for today is proper (P 14), but its references to the gospel of Year A make it a better choice if you are celebrating scrutinies. Otherwise consider the first lenten preface (P 8). The suggested solemn blessing perhaps too soon anticipates the passion. prayer over the people #6 offers a better text.

OTHER IDEAS

Plan out how people should be arranged for the scrutiny (RCIA, 150–156). Visibility and audibility are important. One option is to have the elect in the sanctuary, but facing the assembly, with the priest in the center aisle facing them. Another is to place the elect and their godparents throughout the church so the faithful can see at least one of them up close. Churches with antiphonal seating can line up the elect on both sides of the altar and assembly.

The rite never explains how the elect get there. Perhaps the deacon or catechist could read their names and invite them to come forward.

The presider invites first the assembly and then the elect to silent prayer. The elect bow their heads or kneel. After a period of silent prayer, the elect should stand again. Some have them kneel or prostrate throughout, but physical demands should not get in the way of the prayer.

Two options for intercessions exist. The first offers prayers for the elect, their families, the assembled community and the whole world. The second uses imagery from the gospel. If you wish, the general intercessions may also be invoked at this time.

These intercessions conclude with the exorcism. There are two options for the text. The presider says the first part, hands joined, to God. He imposes hands on the elect in a gesture calling on the Holy Spirit. He prays to Jesus Christ with hands outstretched over the elect. All these prayers ask for the banishment of whatever keeps them from accepting Christ, and for the gift of the Spirit to strengthen their resolve.

In some communities the deacon, the director of the catechumenate, the godparent, a catechist or members of the faithful join the imposition or extension of hands.

A song may be sung, and then the elect may be dismissed. If there are catechumens preparing for initiation the following year, they are not included in the scrutiny prayers, but they may be dismissed at this time.

There are three ways of handling the Creed and the general intercessions. If the general intercessions were added to the scrutiny invocations, you may recite the Creed after the dismissal of the elect and catechumens, and then begin the preparation of the altar and gifts. If you choose this first option, alert the ushers that the collection will follow the Creed, not the intercessions today. In the second option, if general intercessions were not included in the scrutiny invocations, they may follow the dismissal. In the third option, the Creed and the intercessions may both be omitted. Pick one way of doing it and repeat it for the three weeks.

Be sure to rehearse the scrutiny. It is best if the presider, catechist, godparents, servers, musicians and others involved in the ceremony meet at the church at least one day before the scrutiny to review cues so the ceremony can flow smoothly.

The lectionary offers an optional Mass for the third week of Lent, with texts borrowed from the Year A readings of today. In the rare event that scrutinies take place apart from Sunday, these texts may be used. Or if you have not heard these texts on Sunday, you may use them at another Mass this week. For example, if you have an evening Mass on a weeknight during Lent, you may choose the readings from the optional Mass.

The Presentation of the Creed takes place sometime this week, not on Sunday. You may wish to choose an evening when other members of the community will be on site to profess their faith on behalf of the elect. If committees are meeting, or if there is an adult education session some weeknight, make the Presentation of the Creed the prayer for the event. It does not take long, but it will involve the faithful in the all-important task of handing on their belief.

M O N 24 #237 (LMC #176–184) violet
Lenten Weekday

Today's passage from Luke records a little-remembered attempt on Jesus' life. He very nearly died by being tossed from a cliff. One of the stories that lies behind the uproar is told in today's first reading, the healing of Naaman the Syrian in the waters of the Jordan. The psalmist expresses thirst for the streams of the living God. The passages appear today because they tell the severe consequences of the prophetic ministry and prepare us for the more effective attempt on Jesus' life that we recall at the end of this season.

Preface of Lent II (P 9) stresses the discipline that nurtures a prophetic stance. Although it is a bit early to use a preface for the passion, the gospel text makes a case for using P 18, with its phrase, "the days of [Jesus'] life-giving death and glorious resurrection are approaching."

■ TODAY IS THE TWENTY-SECOND ANNIVERSARY of the martyrdom of Oscar Romero, archbishop of San Salvador, whose defense of the poor cost him his life.

T U E 25 #545 (LMC #274) white
The Annunciation of the Lord
SOLEMNITY

ORIENTATION

More a feast of the Lord than a feast of our Lady, the Annunciation recalls the appearance of the angel Gabriel to Mary to announce the immediate coming of the Messiah. Mary agrees to God's will, and then sets into motion the events of our salvation.

LECTIONARY

Luke alone records the event we celebrate today and it is his gospel we hear. (Matthew reports an angel's annunciation to Joseph instead.) Even though it is Matthew, not Luke, who draws a parallel to a passage from Isaiah, that prophecy appears as today's first reading. Psalm 40, "Here am I, Lord; I come to do your will," and the selection from the letter to the Hebrews, perfectly capture Mary's disposition.

SACRAMENTARY

Lines from the first two readings appear as suggested opening and communion antiphons today. All the presidential prayers reflect on the mystery of the incarnation. There is a preface for the feast (P 44).

The white vestments today might be those of Christmas.

Sing the Glory to God. During the Creed, all are to genuflect at the words describing the incarnation. You may cue the faithful immediately before this begins with a statement like "In our church's tradition, we genuflect during the Creed today after the words 'born of the Virgin Mary'." You could extend the genuflection into a full change of posture, allowing people to kneel and pause for a while in humble recollection of the good news of our salvation, as they kneel and pause at the news of the death of Christ during the passion accounts of Holy Week.

You might use the solemn blessing for Advent (1) or for the Blessed Virgin Mary (15) to conclude the celebration.

OTHER IDEAS

Celebrate evening prayer today as a way of extending the feast and showing its difference from the season of Lent. Today is a day for flowers.

The annunciation is one of the most popular images of religious art. If you have such a representation in your church, call attention to it today. You might also open a book of art reproductions to display one by Leonardo da Vinci or Fra Angelico.

The German sacramentary includes a special insert for Eucharistic Prayer I: "In union with the whole church we celebrate that day when Mary received your eternal Son through the Holy Spirit. We praise her above all the saints, for she is the glorious ever-Virgin mother of Our Lord and God Jesus Christ."

The chant "Ave maris stella" is a beautiful hymn for today. Find it in the *Liber cantualis*.

WED 26 #239 (LMC #176–184) violet
Lenten Weekday

In other passages, Jesus seems to take the law into his own hands, but today he insists he has come not to abolish the law, but to fulfill it. Devotion to the law also appears as the theme of the first reading, and the gift of God's law to Israel is praised in the psalm. Within the context of Lent, we know that the first law is charity, and that obedience to the law establishes a pattern of discipline that keeps us focused on a lenten renewal of heart.

Preface of Lent IV (P 11) stresses the importance of observing Lent.

THU 27 #240 (LMC #176–184) violet
Lenten Weekday

In casting out a devil, Jesus distances himself from those who claim he received this power from Satan. The passage alerts us to a growing enemy faction swelling around Jesus during his ministry. God's disappointment in the people's response to the covenant becomes obvious in the passage from Jeremiah. The psalm invites people to return to God. The readings foreshadow the passion even as they invite us to recommit ourselves to Christ.

Preface of Lent III (P 10) remembers the disciplines that sustain our resolve, and you might use Eucharistic Prayer I, the Roman Canon.

FRI 28 #241 (LMC #176–184) violet
Lenten Weekday

On a Friday when our lenten penance draws our attention to the crucifixion, we hear Jesus explaining the two great commandments. Good Friday is good because of Jesus' act of love. Hosea calls Israel to return to the one God. "There shall be no strange god among you," says the psalmist, "no worship of an alien god." Our celebration of Lent reinvigorates our practice of love of God and neighbor.

Preface I (P 8) recalls the two great commandments. The suggested communion antiphon cites the gospel.

SAT 29 #242 (LMC #176–184) violet
Lenten Weekday

In a parable, Jesus recommends humility in prayer. Israel, guilty of the formalism of insincere prayer, hears Hosea say love is a higher call than empty ritual sacrifice. That request from Hosea becomes the refrain to today's psalm, a song from a penitent who promises to offer not a sacrifice, but a contrite spirit.

Preface III (P 10) says we should conquer our pride. The communion antiphon comes from today's gospel.

30 #32 or 31 (LMC #28 or 27) rose or violet
Fourth Sunday of Lent

ORIENTATION

Today is the second of three Sundays reserved for scrutinies during Lent. The halfway point of Lent, this Sunday permits wearing rose vestments and the use of flowers. Once again, you have a choice of following the readings of Year A or Year B. If you have elect for the scrutinies, the Year A readings will be more appropriate, but you are free to choose either set, whether or not you will have adult baptisms at Easter.

LECTIONARY

■ YEAR A READINGS: The gospels include several stories of Jesus healing the blind. They all carry an undertone of movement from the darkness of unbelief to the light of faith. None of the stories reads as eloquently as John's masterful telling. Along the way, Jesus corrects assumptions about the relationship between sin and health, while pointing out the problems of religious blindness in his contemporary society. The story became a natural to accompany prayer for the elect on their journey of purification and enlightenment toward Easter.

The light metaphor appears also in the second reading, where the writer of the letter exhorts the readers with baptismal images to act like Christians: "You were once darkness, but now you are light in the Lord."

The first reading continues the story of salvation history leading up to the meaning of Jesus' coming. We hear the choice and anointing of David as king of Israel, a prototype of Jesus, the anointed one of God. Psalm 23, often chosen for its shepherd theme, appears today because of the royal phrase "You anoint my head with oil."

■ YEAR B READINGS: The gospel, as last week's, comes from John. Today we hear part of the conversation between Jesus and Nicodemus. Nicodemus, a member of the Sanhedrin, symbolically comes to Jesus at night. In the darkness, they discuss the light of the world. The passage includes one of the most often quoted lines of the entire Bible: "God so loved the world that he gave his only Son." This same verse is part of the gospel acclamation today.

The first reading continues its sweeping survey of salvation history. The Second Book of Chronicles tells of the infidelity of God's people, the sending of the prophets, the captivity in Babylon, and the freedom granted by Cyrus, king of Persia. This one passage covers several hundred years of Israel's history. The psalm recalls Israel's painful exile in Babylon. As mentioned above, the first reading has no thematic relationship with the gospel during the Sundays of Lent. It relates to the other first readings of the season. You can trace the story of Israel so far this year from Noah to Abraham to Moses to the prophets.

The second reading captures the theme of the paschal mystery, the passage from death to life. Here, Paul says that when we were dead in our sin, God brought us to life in Christ. We undergo a resurrection from the death of our transgressions in the same way that Christ undergoes a resurrection from the death at Calvary.

SACRAMENTARY

If the second scrutiny is celebrated today, use the prayers from the back of the sacramentary, Ritual Masses: Christian Initiation, the Scrutinies (2). Otherwise, the prayers for the Fourth Sunday of Lent take precedence. The proper preface refers to the man born blind (P 15), but if you have no scrutinies and are using scriptures from Year B, consider Lent II (P 9), with its themes of renewal and passage to a new life. For the prayer over the people, consider #13.

OTHER IDEAS

Celebrate the scrutiny the same way as last week's. It is an unusual form of prayer, and the assembly will enter its ritual more easily if it follows a predictable rhythm for three weeks. You'll help musicians, godparents and

other ministers if they know that they need not learn a new routine from week to week.

You may use the readings for the optional weekday Mass any time this week. It offers the selections from Sunday in Year A. If you have a special gathering this week, you might consider these texts.

This Sunday calls for flowers, signs of springtime and signs that we are midway through Lent and quickly approaching Easter. The traditional rose vesture rather than purple this day functions much the same way, to set the heart on the coming of Easter.

MON **31** #244 (LMC #176–184) violet
Lenten Weekday

Today begins a semicontinuous reading of John's gospel. The selections are chosen because they reveal the events that lead up to the passion. The setting for today's miracle is Galilee, prompting an ominous reminder from the evangelist that a prophet receives no esteem in the home country.

The passage from Isaiah promises the new heavens and earth that will come from God's creating hand. Even as Jesus demonstrates power over illness, we reaffirm our belief in his power over death. The psalm praises God who rescues the sinner from among those going down to the netherworld.

The first preface (P 8) invites us into the joy of the paschal mystery.

April

TUE █ #245 (LMC #176–184) violet
Lenten Weekday

Jesus cures a paralytic who is found near waters. The waters foreshadow baptism, the cure hints at Jesus' power to give eternal life, and the Sabbath provoked the enemies of Jesus to persecute

him with actions leading closer to the cross.

Ezekiel's vision of water from the temple suggests the life coming from the eternal temple by means of the water of baptism. The stream that gladdens the city of God reappears in the psalm.

The entrance antiphon invites all to the waters of God, and the communion antiphon mentions the "waters of peace."

The fourth preface (P 11) remembers the offer of everlasting life.

WED **2** #246 (LMC #176–184) violet
Lenten Weekday

Optional Memorial of Francis de Paola (+ 1507), hermit/violet ▪ The opening of today's gospel explains that the reason people were more determined to kill Jesus was that he spoke of God as his own Father. The first reading, a passage that feels more at home during Advent, foretells the salvation promised to those in darkness, hunger and thirst. In spite of the gathering gloom, the psalmist proclaims in confidence, "The Lord is kind and merciful."

Eucharistic Prayer for Reconciliation II urges peace for those who are at odds.

▪ TODAY'S SAINT: Francis came from Paola in Italy, lived the life of a hermit, and invited others into the same spiritual life. His congregation was later called the Order of Minims. He died in Tours, France. His advice to his confrères sounds very lenten: "Death is certain. Life is short and vanishes like smoke."

▪ IN VENEZUELA, today is the memorial of Blessed Mary of St. Joseph (+ 1967), recognized as the founder of the Augustine Recollects of the Heart of Jesus.

THU 3 **Lenten Weekday**

Jesus chastises those who follow the law of Moses for not accepting his own testimony. Today's passage reveals the strengthening of the enemy against Jesus. Moses pleads with God to relent from the threatened punishment against the people. Jesus, too, will plead on behalf of those who offend God. The psalm remembers Israel's adoration of a molten calf.

In the communion antiphon we hear that God will write the divine law on the hearts of the chosen people. The second preface (P 9) encourages purity of heart and controlled desires.

FRI 4 **Lenten Weekday**

Optional Memorial of Isidore (+ 636), bishop, doctor of the church / violet ▪ An attempt is made to arrest Jesus, but his hour has not yet come. His enemies still do not understand him. A plot against the righteous takes hold of the first reading. The wicked do not discern the reward offered the innocent. The verses from Psalm 34 are chosen for their affirmation of God's protection over the trials of the just.

In a spirit of contrition, Eucharistic Prayer for Reconciliation I makes a good choice on this Friday in Lent.

▪ ISIDORE WAS BISHOP OF SEVILLE, but accomplished much more in his life. A spiritual leader, a learned doctor of the faith, a man of prayer and reflection, a convener of church councils, a defender of the church, a fount of wisdom, a source of unity, an untiring example of service, he is hailed as one of the great leaders of the Western church.

SAT 5 **Lenten Weekday**

Optional Memorial of Vincent Ferrer (+ 1419), presbyter, religious / violet ▪ The enemies of Jesus seem reluctant to make their move. His teaching makes them nervous. While plotting to arrest him, they have to discuss whether or not he is the Messiah. Jeremiah, another innocent victim, trusted God like a lamb led to slaughter, and prayed to witness God's vindication over the wicked. The psalmist prays in confidence of the shelter God provides to the innocent.

The third preface (P 10) states the importance of mastering our own sinfulness.

▪ TODAY'S SAINT: For the second time, in as many days the calendar of saints honors a Spaniard. Renowned as a Dominican preacher, Vincent was pressed into service to help end the schism between the rival popes of Avignon and Rome. Throughout this painful time of the church's history, he served as a beacon of integrity.

6 **Fifth Sunday of Lent**
#35 or 34 (LMC #31 or 30)   violet

ORIENTATION

Today is the last of the scrutiny Sundays. If you have had no scrutinies, you conclude the miniseries of readings from John's gospel today.

Some remnants of calling these final two weeks of Lent "Passiontide" persist, (e.g., the shift in the prefaces), but today's celebration fits more with the previous Sundays than with the next one.

LECTIONARY

▪ YEAR A READINGS: The last and greatest sign of Jesus' ministry is also the last and greatest sign of the season of Lent: the raising of Lazarus. Jesus demonstrates in no uncertain terms his power over death. He seems to delay his arrival precisely to show the extent of God's power. For the elect, who are making their final preparation for the full commitment of their lives to Christ, this passage brings an illumination of support for their period of purification and enlightenment.

The series of passages from salvation history concludes with a proclamation from the prophets, especially fitting today with its theme of death and life. Ezekiel proclaims God's promise to open graves and have people rise from them. A great psalm of longing follows the reading today, "Out of the depths I cried to you, O Lord."

The theme reappears in the second reading in a different form. Paul writes the Romans about the "death" of the body in sin, and the "life" that comes from the Spirit.

▪ YEAR B READINGS: Concluding the short series of lenten passages from John's gospel, today's text contains another explanation of the paschal mystery. Jesus compares his future to that of a grain of wheat. Death is certain. Life will follow. But even more, fruitfulness will follow. This message of hope is also one of the optional texts for a funeral Mass.

The suffering of Jesus is the theme of the second reading also. This text from the letter to the Hebrews tells of Jesus offering "prayers and supplications with loud cries and tears," perhaps an allusion to his agony in the garden. The same text does not stop at the sad recollection of his suffering, but recalls the promise that "he was made perfect."

The series of first readings concludes today with a prophecy from Jeremiah. Having monitored many significant episodes of God's covenant in the history of Israel, today we hear the promise of the new covenant that God will write upon the hearts of the chosen people. With the psalmist we beg God to create a clean heart inside us.

SACRAMENTARY

If the third scrutiny takes place today, that Mass uses the prayers under Ritual Masses: Christian Initiation, the Scrutinies (2). Otherwise, use the prayers from the Fifth Sunday of Lent.

The preface (P 16) is proper for today, a proclamation based on the raising of Lazarus. If you have no scrutinies at Mass, consider the third lenten preface (P 10) with its theme of self-denial. The text for the communion antiphon comes from the gospel. The prayer over the people recommended for today is a good one, but so is #16.

OTHER IDEAS

You may use the texts for the optional weekday Mass for any special eucharist on a weekday this week.

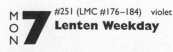

#251 (LMC #176–184)   violet
Lenten Weekday

Optional Memorial of John Baptist de la Salle (+ 1719), presbyter, religious founder/violet ▪ Jesus interrupts the stoning of a woman caught in adultery. He offers forgiveness, not punishment. Susanna, falsely accused of adultery, is freed from her punishment as well. In both cases, those who "walk through the dark valley," as the psalmist phrases it, have no fear. In one sense, the scriptures

preach the importance of forgiveness. On the other hand, they offer images of the rescue of the innocent, one of the themes of Jesus' own death and resurrection.

Do not be confused by the alternative gospel in the lectionary for today. That one comes up next year. Use the first one.

The recommended entrance antiphon stresses the same theme of rescue from enemies. The first communion antiphon is marked erroneously for Year C. It applies to this year when the correlating gospel is read.

The first preface for the passion (P 17) sets the tone.

▪ TODAY'S SAINT: John Baptist de la Salle pioneered schools for the poor and working classes, care for children with special needs, and quality education for teachers. He brought his companions together to form a religious congregation. He admonished teachers that students "must see by the way you teach that you are true ministers of God, full of true charity and sincere in carrying out your task."

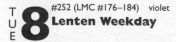

#252 (LMC #176–184)   violet
Lenten Weekday

Was Jesus' death a suicide? The thought would never cross our minds, but the Pharisees wonder about it in today's gospel. The gulf widens between Jesus and his enemies. Their origins, their future, their morality, and their identity are as far apart as belief and unbelief.

The book of Numbers tells the story of the attack of saraph serpents in the desert and the cure worked through the bronze serpent mounted on a pole. The gospels see in this story a foreshadowing of the healing Jesus works through his suffering on the cross. The psalm is a cry for help from a people in distress.

The fourth lenten preface (P 11) prays for growth in holiness.

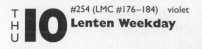

#253 (LMC #176–184)   violet
Lenten Weekday

Continuing with the passages from John's gospel that fit this season, the lectionary offers another incidence of controversy with Jesus. This time the topic concerns the legitimacy of the descendants of Abraham and the sincerity of one's devotion to God. This pairs up with a passage from Daniel, this time the story of the three young men in the fiery furnace, who retain their devotion to their own God in face of persecution. Their song in the furnace serves as today's responsory.

Rescue from enemies is the theme of the entrance antiphon. The first passion preface is in use this week (P 17), but the Eucharistic Prayer for Reconciliation I also makes a good choice.

#254 (LMC #176–184)   violet
Lenten Weekday

Another attempt is made on Jesus' life, as his enemies pick up rocks to stone him. This time, he seems to equate himself with the eternal God of Abraham. God's covenant with Abraham is told in the first reading, and the psalm remembers this eternal covenant.

The covenant is the theme of the entrance antiphon. You may use the first passion preface (P 17) today.

#255 (LMC #176–184)   violet
Lenten Weekday

Optional memorial of Stanislaus (+ 1079), bishop, martyr/violet ▪ Another attempt at stoning Jesus opens today's gospel. His enemies say he blasphemed when he claimed to be God's son. Enemies surround Jeremiah and the psalmist as well. On this, the last Friday of Lent, the cross seems closer than ever.

■ TODAY'S SAINT: Stanislaus studied canon law in Paris but refused his doctorate out of humility. After giving away his family's fortune to the poor, he was ordained for his home diocese of Kracow. A preacher and canon of the cathedral, he was the unanimous choice to succeed the bishop. Having criticized Boleslaus II for his sinful behavior, he eventually excommunicated the king, who, in turn, murdered the saint with his own hands. Today's memorial, formerly optional, became obligatory at the request of a successor to Stanislaus, Pope John Paul II. During Lent, though, all obligatory memorials are celebrated as optional ones.

■ FRIDAY OF THE FIFTH WEEK OF LENT is observed as the feast of Our Lady of Sorrows in El Salvador, and as an optional memorial in Argentina and Peru.

S A T 12 #256 (LMC #176–184) violet
Lenten Weekday

The Sanhedrin concludes that the whole world will believe in Jesus because of his signs. Caiaphas makes the unwitting prediction that it is good to have one person die for the sake of the people. The plan to kill Jesus takes shape, and the people ask a question that will be answered royally with tomorrow's liturgy: "Is he likely to come to Jerusalem for Passover?"

Ezekiel's prophecy of the gathering of all the nations resonates with the one uttered by Caiaphas. The gathering of scattered Israel also appears in today's responsory from Jeremiah.

You may use the first passion preface (P 17).

☀ 13 #38 (LMC #33) red
Palm Sunday of the Passion of the Lord

ORIENTATION

Today's gospel commemorates Jesus' entry into Jerusalem for Passover and for his own passion. Palm branches recall the day of his entry, and the proclamation of the passion recalls the day of his death. We read the passion today partly to hear another evangelist's version before John's on Friday, and partly to accommodate those of the faithful who will be unable to attend the celebration of the Lord's Passion on Good Friday this year.

Prepare for the day with an ample supply of palm branches. Let people have sizable branches of a generous quantity. Arrange a space outside the church with a suitable place for the proclamation of the gospel, plenty of holy water and a sprinkler that sprays far and wide, and sufficient equipment for good amplification of the voices of the ministers. Prepare banners for the procession. Walk the processional path ahead of time, looking for trouble spots. Will banners and cross fit through tight spaces and under low ceilings? Will the head of the procession be visible? Are there places where part of the procession can be delayed, where people can trip, get confused or take shortcuts?

LECTIONARY

During the blessing of palms, the gospel during Year B may come from either Mark or John. If you've been using John's gospel the last few Sundays and want to continue the sequence, you may find this alternative attractive.

The proclamation of the Lord's Passion is the heart of today's scriptures. This year we hear Mark's version, the shortest. It opens without the greeting "The Lord be with you" and without the crosses. No incense is used, and no candles are carried to the ambo. The passion may be sung or proclaimed with different voices: Christ, narrator, the crowd and others. Some divide the narrative into a few larger sections, each proclaimed by a different speaker. Time for silent reflection, sung acclamations, or sacred songs could set the tone.

The psalm for today is one quoted by Jesus on the cross. The first reading comes from the songs of the suffering servants, and the second reading is a classic hymn from Philippians, singing of the debasement and exaltation of Christ.

The versicle to the gospel acclamation is another gem from the chant repertoire, "Christus Factus Est." In addition to the chant, there are many choral motets based on the text, like the one by Bruckner.

A brief homily may be given. Gabe Huck gives a fine model in *The Three Days* (LTP, 1992 [revised edition], Appendix: part three).

Note that a brief homily may be given after the gospel for the blessing of palms. The liturgy allows two homilies. It also permits the homily to be given after the first gospel on that text. The advantage is that it gives the homilist a more contained text for reflection. But if the palm ceremony takes place outdoors, people will be standing through the homily and their attention will waver.

SACRAMENTARY

The commemoration of the Lord's Passion takes place at every Mass today, in one of three forms of declining solemnity. The first form includes the procession and it is envisioned for the principal Mass today. The faithful assemble in a secondary church, chapel, or other suitable place, but apart from the church to which the procession moves. All carry palms. The presider may wear a red cope or chasuble; the deacon, a red dalmatic. If you have a set of red vestments that works for Pentecost and confirmations, keep it in the closet today and use another one for martyrs and the cross.

The liturgy opens with the singing of "Hosanna to the Son of David." The original Latin chant is not difficult, but see Richard Proulx's English adaptation in *Worship.* See also Proulx's choral setting "Fanfare for Palm Sunday" (GIA, G-2829) and John Angotti's spirited "Sing Hosanna to our King" (WLP, 7432). Ann Celeen Dohms has written "Hosanna for Palm Sunday" (WLP, 5718) for choir, a singable, straightforward setting. Four procession antiphons and psalms are in *By Flowing Waters,* including a fine, new English version of the ninth-century hymn "Gloria, laus, et honor," based on Matthew 21:1–3, 8–11. The Latin chant is in the *Liber cantualis.*

The presider makes the sign of the cross, then greets the people and gives them a catechetical summary on the concluding season of Lent. This instruction may highlight some of the efforts made by the whole parish community throughout the season, while pointing them toward the upcoming celebration of the death and resurrection of the Messiah. The deacon may also give this summary.

Choose between the two prayers offered over the palms. One blesses the branches; the other acknowledges that we use them to honor Christ. The second prayer makes more sense if an earlier Mass included a blessing over all the branches used this weekend. If the people hold their branches aloft for this prayer, they will appear more united in faith, prayer and purpose. A minister could announce just before the prayer of blessing, "Let us raise our branches." The branches are then sprinkled with holy water.

Before the gospel of the palms is proclaimed, incense may be used. A deacon asks a blessing from the presider. Afterwards, a homily may be given, but it may also be omitted here.

The invitation to enter the church sounds like a direction from the deacon, but in his absence the celebrant or another suitable minister may give it.

Incense leads the way, then the minister carrying a decorated cross between two candle bearers, followed by the priest and the faithful. Meanwhile, all sing "All Glory, Laud, and Honor," or another appropriate song. "The King of Glory" is another popular choice, based on the entrance antiphon of the day. Space singers out throughout the procession to keep the music strong, but be forgiving. It probably will not go as well as you hope it will. This is one of the most difficult environments for singing in the entire liturgical year. A portable audio system may help. If the presider has been wearing a cope, he switches to a chasuble before the opening prayer.

The second form is called the solemn entrance and pertains to situations where the faithful cannot gather outside, due to constraints like lack of space. If the community must resort to the second form, it should ask when the time will come to make appropriate renovations or constructions so that the procession may occur. In the solemn form, the ministers group themselves outside the sanctuary, but in view of most of the faithful.

In the third form, the simple entrance, the entire opening rite takes place in the sanctuary.

For general intercessions, see examples in the back of the sacramentary for Holy Week.

The preface for today explains the meaning of the celebration (P 19). The suggested solemn blessing is a fitting conclusion to the celebration.

OTHER IDEAS

Cancel other activities in the parish this week. Let nothing keep people from attending the services throughout the Triduum. That may mean giving up several evenings, so encourage people to free their other evenings this week to make attendance at the community's prayer a priority.

The processional cross may be decorated with palms or otherwise festooned. See *The Sacristy Manual* pages 203–204 for more advice.

If you are still searching for a good responsorial psalm for today's liturgy, consider Richard Proulx's setting (WLP, 6225).

Catholic Household Blessings and Prayers provides prayers for Placing of Branches in the Home on Palm Sunday (page 140) and Prayers of the Triduum (page 143).

Provide a good holy week resource for people this week. Consider LTP's *What Am I Doing for Triduum This Year?* (also available in Spanish).

MON **14** #257 (LMC #176–184) violet
**Monday of
Holy Week**

The gospel reports an event six days before the Passover, the anointing of Jesus, who has his own burial on his mind. The first reading begins the series of the four songs of the suffering servant, and the psalm repeats one of its themes. God promises to make the servant a light for the nations, and we sing the psalm as Christians who identify that suffering servant with Jesus, the Lord, who is light and salvation.

See the suggested general intercessions for Holy Week in the sacramentary's first appendix, #7. The second passion preface (P 18) is used.

The 1994 *Sacramentary Supplement* includes a parish rite for the reception of the holy oils blessed at the chrism Mass. It suggests the Holy Thursday Mass as a time when this might take place, but allows other occasions. Given the complexity of the Holy Thursday Mass, you might consider receiving the oils at another celebration this week. A weekday Mass like today's would be one appropriate option—assuming, of course, that the chrism Mass has taken place and that the parish is in possession of the oils. If you have singers available, you could sing Alan Griffiths and Paul Inwood's "Procession of the Oils" (WLP, 5779), written with the chrism Mass in mind, but useful in a parish on an occasion like this.

TUE **15** #258 (LMC #176–184) violet
**Tuesday of
Holy Week**

The second song of the suffering servant assigns ministry not just to Israel, but to the Gentiles as well. The psalm sings of God's salvation. The series of passages from John's gospel concludes today at the Last Supper, where Jesus predicts one disciple's betrayal and another's denial.

The second passion preface (P 18) is good, but you may also consider using it with the first eucharistic prayer for reconciliation.

People who have taxes on their minds today might appreciate a petition in the general intercessions for the prudent usage of our country's tax dollars.

WED **16** #259 (LMC #176–184) violet
**Wednesday of
Holy Week**

On a day formerly called "Spy Wednesday," we hear Jesus identify Judas as his betrayer and predict his condemnation. The third song of the suffering servant becomes today's first reading, a text of brave endurance. The psalm takes the same attitude: "For your sake I bear insult."

The opening prayer summarizes the meaning of Lent and Passiontide. Conclude the season with the second passion preface (P 18). The communion antiphon summarizes the meaning of Jesus' ministry.

Instructions for tomorrow's Mass indicate that the tabernacle should be empty for the beginning of the liturgy. Communion ministers or the faithful may consume tabernacle breads today, reserving only a few in a pyx for emergencies.

Chrism Mass #260 white
Liturgy of the Hours violet

THU **17** **Holy Thursday
morning and
afternoon**

There is no morning Mass today, except for the gravest pastoral necessity, with permission of the diocesan bishop. The faithful gather this evening for the principal Mass of the Lord's Supper and the opening of the Triduum.

If a funeral is celebrated today, observe the form "without Mass" in the Order of Christian Funerals. Most grieving Christian families already understand the special nature of this day and may erroneously assume that no funeral may happen. They may welcome the simpler service that keeps an observance of the church's calendar while it honors the loss of a faithful Christian. They may also wish to return to the church for the opening of the Triduum.

If you have a community accustomed to gathering for a morning Mass, celebrate morning prayer with them today. You could augment it with a proclamation of the passages from the office of readings: the letter to the Hebrews on the high priesthood of Jesus and the homily of Melito of Sardis. These texts are lengthy and difficult. If you use them, be sure the reader prepares well to convey their meaning.

Communion may be brought to the sick today if necessary, but this should happen after the evening celebration of the Mass of the Lord's Supper, not during the day. The idea is to bring communion to the sick from the community's eucharist, not from the tabernacle.

If your parish school is still in session, gather the children for morning prayer and encourage their attendance at the Triduum.

Whether the chrism Mass happens today or earlier, promote attendance from your community at this diocesan event. The chrism consecrated at this Mass will be used for the Easter Vigil baptisms. Many others in the community will be anointed with it at infant baptisms and confirmation. Still more will benefit from the oil of catechumens and the oil of the sick at community prayer this year.

This year the Jewish celebration of Passover begins April 17.

MARCH 5, 2003
Ash Wednesday

Fast from Food. Repent from Your Sins.
Joel 2:12–18
"Return to me with your whole heart."

ON Ash Wednesday we stand as sinners before God. We reflect on the misdeeds of our past and on the ill habits of our present. Our frail spirits wrestle with sin, even as our frail bodies fight off death. We accept ashes as a reminder of our mortality. We fast from food as a sign of our sorrow.

Our sins weigh us down, but it could be worse. You could have a plague of locusts darkening the sky over the place where you live. That happened once before. The prophet Joel addressed a people who were losing everything because they could not stop an advancing army of locusts. They believed God was punishing them for their sins, so they fasted as a sign of their repentance.

In our lives, sin does not bring locusts, but it brings other sorrows. Sin brings estrangement from the people we love, guilt when we lift our eyes to heaven, loss to a world starved for charity.

Can you imagine yourself living your life a better way? In the quiet of your heart, do you know what sin is darkening your sky? Are you willing to name it, specifically?

Accept ashes. Fast from food. Repent.

Written by Paul Turner. © 2002 Archdiocese of Chicago, Liturgy Training Publications; 1-800-933-1800; www.ltp.org.

MARCH 9, 2003
First Sunday of Lent

The Rainbow Covenant
Genesis 9:8–15
"I set my bow in the clouds to serve as a sign."

PEOPLE give up things for Lent, but they also do some things extra. They enter into the renewal that God desires for all creation. Renewal often demands both strategies: giving up and doing extra.

Take God, for example. At the end of the story of Noah, God gave something up. You remember the story. People had behaved so badly that God sent a flood to wipe out creation. But God took pity on Noah, his family and pairs of animals. As the floods receded, God established a new covenant with Noah and set a rainbow in the sky as its sign.

What did God give up? God gave up global floods. "There shall not be another flood to devastate the earth." God gave up giving up on people.

The story of our relationship with God did not end there. We know at the beginning of Lent where that story will end—at Easter. God did more than give something up. God did something extra. God sent us a redeemer. By ending destruction and offering redemption, God set a perfect example of renewal.

Lent is like a desert. It is also like a flood. But most of all, it is like the balance of sun, water and soil that yields a bountiful harvest.

Written by Paul Turner. © 2002 Archdiocese of Chicago, Liturgy Training Publications; 1-800-933-1800; www.ltp.org.

MARCH 16, 2003
Second Sunday of Lent

Loving Self-Sacrifice
Genesis 22:1–2, 9a, 10–13, 15–18
"God put Abraham to the test."

ABRAHAM would be arrested for child abuse if he pulled a stunt like this today. He brought his son up a hill and raised a knife to kill him. No parent should do that.

We remember this story not as a model of parenting, but as a symbol of sacrifice. Both Abraham and God serve as models.

Abraham completely trusted God. God promised him a son, and according to the book of Genesis, Abraham's son Isaac was born after Abraham waited 100 years. Then God asked Abraham to sacrifice his son, his only son, the one whom he loved. Abraham continued to trust God. His trust is what inspires us in times of extreme adversity.

For Christians the story is not only about Abraham's sacrifice, but about God's sacrifice. That is why we hear it now, near the beginning of Lent, and again on the eve of Easter.

God led his Son Jesus, his only Son, whom he loved, up a hill, where he was raised high on a cross. In the story of Abraham an angel stopped the killing. In the story of Jesus the killing continues, but angels announce that the One who died has risen.

MARCH 23, 2003
Third Sunday of Lent

Other Gods
Exodus 20:1–17
"God delivered all these commandments . . ."

WE believe in one God. But it wasn't always that way. At the time of Moses, people believed in many gods. There were gods who governed the weather, gods who controlled illnesses, and gods who inspired the arts. But we believe in one God, the source of all creation and the sustainer of all that is good.

The first commandment asked people to stop offering allegiance to other gods. It asserted the supreme authority of the one God who led them out of slavery and promised them a new land.

When we review the Ten Commandments, we usually skip over number one. We don't believe in other gods. It's two through ten that cause problems. We curse and swear. We skip church on Sundays. We disobey. We destroy life, even

human life. We commit adultery. We steal and we lie. We covet everything about our neighbor's possessions and family. We sin a lot on two through ten. But we believe in one God.

Or do we? Do we substitute other gods? Do we prefer possessions, selfish pleasures and the esteem of others more than we prefer allegiance to the one God? That first commandment may cut to the heart of all our sin.

MARCH 30, 2003
Fourth Sunday of Lent

Deliverance from Exile
2 Chronicles 36:14–16, 19–23
"Those who escaped the sword were carried captive to Babylon."

WHAT did I do to deserve this? When misfortunes come our way, we instinctively suspect that God is punishing us for something. In truth, we often find out we are our own worst enemies, judging ourselves more harshly than God would. Our own bad habits, our own selfishness, and our own negligence come back to haunt us.

What did I do to deserve this? is the question residents of ancient Jerusalem asked when the city fell to the Persians and those who escaped death were carried captive to Babylon. The temple was destroyed, the city lay in ruins, and the people were made slaves. How did this happen?

God's chosen people had a lot of time to think over that question and find an answer. In captivity they came to a spiritual awakening. They realized that they and their leaders had been unfaithful to the covenant and insincere in their worship. They believed that God was punishing them. But what did God do?

In time, God spoke to Cyrus, king of Persia, and commanded the ruler to free the people. They left their captivity, returned to Jerusalem, rebuilt the temple, and dedicated themselves anew to the sacred covenant.

How has God forgiven you and set you free? What did you do to show your thanks?

APRIL 6, 2003
Fifth Sunday of Lent

Happily Complying
Jeremiah 31:31–34
"I will make a new covenant."

THERE is obedience. And then there's attitude. Sometimes we do what we're supposed to do, but we don't always like it. Sometimes we obey with anger in our hearts, resentful of our actions, unhappy with subservience.

But other times we happily comply. We obey because we agree with what has to be done. We obey because we look forward to good results. We obey because we love the one who has asked a favor.

When the exiled inhabitants of Jerusalem returned to their holy city, God promised a new covenant through the prophet Jeremiah. The old covenant was good, but people broke it and God had to show them who was their master.

This time God had a better idea. God would write the covenant on their hearts.

Now when people obeyed, they would do so with the right attitude. They would not resist. They would not wander away from the covenant when they had the chance. They would so love God that they would happily comply with what their maker asked.

And God would forgive their sins.

During Lent God is asking for your obedience. What attitude have you carried? Will you let God write the covenant on your heart? Will you happily comply and come to know the Lord?

APRIL 13, 2003
Palm Sunday of the Lord's Passion

Speaking God's Troubling Word
Isaiah 50:4–7
"My face I did not shield from spitting."

THE speaker of today's first reading is a victim. He speaks, but people beat him, pull out the hairs of his beard, slap and spit him. Why? He suffers all this because he has spoken God's rousing word. Every morning God speaks to him and enables him to speak to others. This word gets him into trouble.

But the speaker does not quit. Nor does he curse God who gives him these words. He remains firm, committed to the word God gives him, even in the face of resistance.

Although Isaiah wrote about the difficulties faced by faithful Israel in the midst of enemies, Christians read through these lines and see the image of Jesus. He received God's word, spoke it with eloquence, and suffered at the hands of his enemies.

Do your words ever get you into trouble? Does it happen even when you say the right thing? If so, you stand in a long line of those who suffer because they are servants of God.

This Friday we will come forward to show our love for the cross of Jesus Christ. Christians can face the agony of suffering as it befell Jesus, and as it comes to us, because we know there is something more.

Written by Paul Turner. © 2002 Archdiocese of Chicago, Liturgy Training Publications; 1-800-933-1800; www.ltp.org.

THE PASCHAL TRIDUUM

The Season

The Calendar

The Meaning

TRIDUUM means "three days." There should be no doubt about which three days it means. They are distinct enough from other days that we call them "the three days," and everyone should know what we mean.

Throughout his ministry, Jesus predicted his passion by referring to the "third day." Today we enter that sacred time outside of time in which we spend these days with Christ, to serve, to suffer, to die and to rise.

On these days the elect reach the climax of their initiation. The faithful bring their lenten retreat to its fulfillment.

■ HOLY SPRING: The date of Easter is calculated according to the turning of the cosmos. First we wait for spring in the northern hemisphere, Jerusalem's hemisphere. Then we wait for the first full moon. Then we wait for the first day of the week. That is when we celebrate the rising of Christ from the dead, the rising of the elect to new life in baptism, the rising of the faithful to renewed commitment to Easter faith and joy.

During these days the entire parish goes on retreat. Invite all families, staff, youth and the homebound to spend these days in a spirit of prayer and reflection. "On Good Friday and, if possible, also on Holy Saturday until the Easter Vigil, the Easter fast is observed everywhere" (*General Norms for the Liturgical Year and the Calendar,* 20). Those who fast on Good Friday should continue the fast as much as possible until the beginning of the Vigil.

To help everyone celebrate these days as fully as possible, provide copies of LTP's *What Am I Doing for Triduum This Year?* (available also in Spanish).

The Saints

THE Triduum replaces absolutely every other celebration on the liturgical calendar. It holds the highest rank on the table of liturgical days. This year this causes no changes to the general liturgical calendar. On the local calendar, however, if your community celebrates a patronal solemnity for any saint listed in the martyrology for April 17 to 20 (e.g. Kateri Tekakwitha, Ursmar, Leo IX or Anicetus, among others), it transfers to the nearest available day on the calendar. This year, because of the solemnities of the Easter octave, the first available day will be April 28.

In general, parishes with patronal days that are routinely impeded by festivals may consider locating on the calendar another regular, annual and more useful day to celebrate the patron. The general Roman calendar made use of this principle in transferring out of Lent or Advent certain saint's days; for instance, in the calendar reform of 1969, Pope Gregory the Great's memorial was moved from March 12 to September 3. The apostle Thomas's feast was transferred from December 21 to July 3.

■ ABOUT THE RANKING OF THE TRIDUUM: Notice in the *General Norms for the Liturgical Year and Calendar* that the Triduum transcends all other days, beyond "feast" or "solemnity," beyond even holy days of obligation. The liturgical spirit sees

within the Paschal Triduum a festival that gives meaning and life to all festivals, which contains within itself the mystery of all other days and seasons.

Make a concerted effort in the parish to cancel all other activities. The liturgies for the three days should be the top priority on everyone's calendar this week.

The Lectionary

NOTHING proclaims the significance of these days like the gospels assigned for their celebration. The washing of the feet, the passion and the ecstatic proclamation of the resurrection announce the meaning of our gathering and draw us into worship.

■ CHOOSE READERS WHO CAN PROCLAIM THESE TEXTS WELL. Give them ample time to practice. Rehearse the readings in church, with the microphone on—even if people usually just rehearse at home. It will remind the readers how important their proclamation is during these days and give the liturgy more focus. The first two readings on Holy Thursday are narrative and therefore easy-on-the-ears in proclamation. The first two readings on Good Friday require more skill to convey the message. The epistle for the Easter Vigil should be a centerpiece. Perhaps choose a reader from the Christian initiation team.

The seven Old Testament readings for the Easter Vigil also require readers of great skill. They may need help interpreting how their reading fits into the overall picture of the Vigil. Use a different reader for each, and avoid cutting down on their number. Although permission is granted to reduce the number of these readings, they create a sense of vigil more than any other part of the service. The church's preference is that all the readings be proclaimed on this night.

■ THE SUNDAY *LECTIONARY FOR MASSES WITH CHILDREN* includes no texts for the principal liturgies of the Triduum, and rightly so. Invite children to participate in the parish liturgies those days.

For Easter Sunday, the lectionary offers all the texts for the Mass of Easter Day, even the alternatives for the second reading.

The Sacramentary

■ THE SACRAMENTARY'S INTRODUCTION TO THE TRIDUUM develops the spirit of these days and answers some questions we often forget. A companion document, the 1988 *Circular Letter Concerning the Preparation and Celebration of the Easter Feasts* ("*Circular Letter*") also is very useful. Priceless in interpreting these is Paul Niemann's helpful work, *The Lent, Triduum, and Easter Answer Book* (Resource Publications, 1998).

■ CHRISTIAN INITIATION: For the Easter Vigil, be sure to use the *Rite of Christian Initiation of Adults.* Its description of Part III, the liturgy of baptism, replaces what is in the sacramentary. There are a few changes now if you have both elect to be baptized and baptized candidates to be received into the full communion of the Catholic church. The sequence of the Rite of Reception and the renewal of the community's baptismal promises shifted since the sacramentary was first published. Keep the *Rite of Christian Initiation of Adults* on hand for Part III of the Vigil.

■ MUSIC: Ample musical notation appears in the sacramentary for these days. They remind us of the importance of singing many parts of the rites. The *Circular Letter* frequently encourages singing the chants of the Triduum.

The Book of Blessings

BLESSINGS may be given at any time, but during this season our full attention is fixed on the primary liturgical celebrations. This is not the best time to explore the *Book of Blessings* for additions to the liturgy. Nonetheless, it does include a good one for homes during the Easter season (50) and of food for the first meal of Easter (54).

The Rite of Christian Initiation of Adults

TWO celebrations requiring your attention are the preparation rites on Holy Saturday morning and the sacraments of initiation at the Easter Vigil. If there are infants to be baptized at the Vigil, you may wish to invite the parents to bring them to the preparation rites Saturday morning.

If you have a community that gathers each morning for Mass, schedule the preparation rites at that time so they may participate. All, of course, should make every effort to attend the Vigil.

■ DISMISSAL: There are two schools of thought about dismissals during the Holy Thursday Mass of the Lord's Supper and the celebration of the passion on Good Friday. Because Thursday's gathering is for a Mass and because we dismiss catechumens and elect from any Mass, many believe that they should also be dismissed from this celebration after the liturgy of the word. Others suggest that the elect and catechumens should remain. They argue that there are no dismissals for the faithful at the conclusion of the Holy Thursday and Good Friday liturgies, and that the spirit of the Triduum just about demands that the entire church assemble as one.

The Liturgy of the Hours

A natural time to celebrate the hours at church is when the community is already in the habit of coming for a daily Mass. Holy Thursday and Good Friday both provide excellent opportunities for the celebration of morning prayer in the parish.

Those who participate in the evening Mass of the Lord's Supper do not celebrate evening prayer from the *Liturgy of the Hours,* even in private. The same applies to those who celebrate the Lord's Passion on Good Friday. Holy Saturday is the only Saturday of the liturgical year with its own evening prayer. All the other Saturday evening prayers are really the first vespers for Sunday. But there is no Evening Prayer I for Easter Sunday. Those who participate in the Easter Vigil do not celebrate the office of readings for Easter Sunday.

The psalms and scripture citations from the *Liturgy of the Hours* may be commended to the faithful as sources of meditation during the Three Days.

The Rite of Penance

THE opening rubric for Good Friday states, "According to the Church's ancient tradition, the sacraments are not celebrated today or tomorrow." The *Circular Letter* modified this statement: "except for the sacraments of Penance and Anointing of the Sick" (see 61 and 75).

Nonetheless, the celebration of reconciliation fits more with the spirit of the season of Lent than with that of the Triduum. Schedule penance services prior to the Triduum and encourage people to make this sacrament part of their preparation for Holy Week.

The Pastoral Care of the Sick

THE rubrics for Holy Thursday state that holy communion "may be brought to the sick at any hour of the day." But the *Circular Letter* says it is more appropriate to bring communion to the sick "directly from the altar" of the evening Mass (53). In this way, their communion with the faithful at the one celebration of Holy Thursday is clearer. On Good Friday, communion may be brought to the sick at any time. Others do not share communion apart from the celebration of the Lord's Passion—not even at Stations of the Cross. On Holy Saturday, communion outside the Vigil may only be given as viaticum for the dying.

The sacrament of the anointing of the sick may be celebrated during the Triduum, but other times of the year are much more appropriate. Of course, if someone is in need of this sacrament, it may be given on any day.

The Rite of Marriage

MARRIAGE is among the sacraments not to be celebrated on Good Friday and Holy Saturday. The *Circular Letter* "strictly" forbids it (61 and 75).

This becomes an issue especially if convalidations need to happen for the elect, candidates for full communion, or even among the faithful. If any of these are in a marriage that the Catholic church does not recognize, and if no canonical impediments apply, they may seek to have their marriage convalidated. This means celebrating the Rite of Marriage in the Catholic church, normally before a priest or deacon and at least two witnesses. Convalidation frees Catholics in irregular marriages to celebrate the sacraments again; notably, to receive communion.

Such convalidations should not be put off until the last moment. They may be celebrated as soon as possible for the benefit of the faithful. The Catholic partner in such marriages may then begin sharing communion right away, not waiting for Easter. If for some reason the Rite of Marriage needs to be celebrated during this time, it could take place outside of Mass during the day on Holy Thursday, or even during the Mass on Easter Sunday, but neither of these solutions frames the sacrament deservingly.

The Order of Christian Funerals

A funeral may take place on Holy Thursday, Good Friday or Holy Saturday, but not a funeral Mass. The funeral service without Mass can be found in the *Order of Christian Funerals*, (179). The *Circular Letter* says that a Good Friday funeral should be celebrated without singing, music or the tolling of bells (61), a strange rubric that tolerates the singing of psalms at morning prayer on Good Friday, but not for the death of a faithful Christian.

The Art and Environment

THESE days call for attention to the environment that will create a unique sense to each day, yet not overwhelm those who make the changes. See *To Crown the Year* (pages 74–119) and *The Sacristy Manual* (pages 207–219) for ideas and checklists.

One bit of advice regarding the many physical accoutrements of the paschal liturgy: If you wait until the final days of Lent to head out to find something that you need for the Triduum—perhaps new foot washing vessels, an improved chrism vessel, baptismal robes—odds are, you won't find what you want. If instead year-round you have your eyes open for what you need, not only are you more likely to spot it, but you just may find it on sale.

■ VESTURE: Launder the servers' vesture. Prepare the chasubles and dalmatics, as well as a humeral veil for Holy Thursday. The red vesture for Good Friday should appear to be celebrating martyrs, not Pentecost. Save the best white vesture for the Easter Vigil.

Prepare white garments for neophytes. Many communities that practice immersion also prepare non-white alb-like vesture to clothe the elect before entering the font and during their baptism. Some vest cantors and lectors to lend solemnity to these days.

■ PREPARE THE FLOWERS. Have them ready for the Vigil. If plants and flowers are to be delivered, arrange a time when the church will be open.

■ DOUBLE-CHECK THE LIGHTING AND SOUND. Replace bulbs and realign spots. Correct the sound system. Do all the mikes work, including the portable ones? Are there loose wires causing static? How about the speakers? Wouldn't this be a good time to make sure things work?

■ SPRING CLEANING: Clean up the grounds and the church. Spruce up everyplace people will see, and even places that no one ever sees. Make these days look special. Besides, cleaning the church symbolizes the cleaning of one's soul. It makes a good spiritual exercise for the conclusion of Lent and the beginning of Triduum.

Set out the vessels: the censer, the boat, containers for oil, cups and plates for communion, pitchers and bowls for washing feet. Clean and polish them as well. Iron the altar materials.

Clean the font for baptisms by immersion. Replace the water. Some communities arrange a temporary font to accommodate immersions in a visible place within the church. Praiseworthy as this is, a more permanent solution should be sought as part of the parish's long-range plans.

Prepare the place for the Easter fire. Make ready the paschal candle and the smaller ones for the assembly.

■ SET THE ENVIRONMENT FOR THE CHAPEL OF RESERVATION. To give purpose to the procession and to establish a place conducive to meditation and prayer, prepare a room apart from the church if possible, rather than a side altar within the church. Clear the path of the procession. Walk it and watch for problem areas.

The Music

CANTORS and choirs will be busy these days. Their support for the Triduum is essential to the sense of celebration. The presider should also rehearse those parts of the services that he may sing, including the eucharistic prayer on Thursday, Saturday and Sunday.

"Christ Our Light" is a complete booklet of music for the Triduum, available from World Library Publications. This intelligent presentation of the music and liturgy of the Three Days gives plenty of options for the principal liturgies as well as secondary ones like Stations of the Cross. If you like the music, this resource will save you the effort of publishing something yourselves each year.

Chants worthy of the repertoire include "Ubi caritas" and "Pange lingua" for Holy Thursday (both in the *Liber cantualis*), the opening acclamation for the Easter Vigil ("Christ Our Light"), the Exsultet, baptismal acclamations, and the Easter sequence, "Victimae Paschali laudes."

Let the choir work up a barnstormer like Handel's "Hallelujah, Amen" from *Judas Maccabaeus* (Schirmer, 304).

The Parish and Home

THE faithful should keep the spirit of these days as much as possible at home. They lead a quieter, simpler life on Friday and Saturday, and rejoice with one another on Sunday. All should keep the paschal fast between the Mass of the Lord's Supper and the Easter Vigil, joining with the elect in prayer as they prepare for baptism. Most people do not realize this, and will benefit from a reminder to fast on Saturday as well as Friday.

A sample prayer for the home is *We Watch and Pray during the Paschal Triduum* (LTP, 1995). This easy-to-follow card allows families, groups or individuals to pray in common at home or at church.

Some parishes encourage families to make or decorate their own Easter candles. These are brought to church during the Vigil, then brought home (lit!) and relighted during prayer throughout the Fifty Days of Easter. Many Greek Orthodox families do this; Roman Catholics can, too. If you have a gas stove at home, and if you can get a candle all the way home from the Vigil in safety, why not light the pilot with the blessed Easter fire? The light of Christ will bless every meal you prepare this year.

Texts

- GREETING: Sacramentaries of other language groups suggest:

  The Lord of glory and the Giver of every grace be with you.

- INTRODUCTION TO THE PENITENTIAL RITE:

  Let us call to mind our sins and call upon the Lord's mercy.

- RESPONSE TO THE GENERAL INTERCESSIONS:

  Christ our Savior, hear our prayer.

- DISMISSAL OF CATECHUMENS:

  The Lord Jesus gave us an example of service in the midst of suffering. Go in peace, and remember the example of our Savior.

April

#39   white

17 Holy Thursday Evening: The Lord's Supper

ORIENTATION

This evening's celebration opens the Triduum with the Mass of the Lord's Supper. It commemorates the institution of the eucharist and the priesthood, as well as Jesus' command of love and service. It should be the only parish Mass today.

■ ALL MINISTERS FULFILL THEIR MINISTRIES: Priests concelebrate, deacons and lay ministers assist. Some may bear the holy oils from the chrism Mass in procession. Eucharistic ministers may bring communion to the homebound at the close of the liturgy. For the washing of the feet, the seating, pitchers, bowls and towels could be prepared ahead of time, and kept in full view as part of the environment for the night.

In anticipation of tonight's celebration, check this list:

- Get holy oils.
- Prepare pitchers, bowls and towels.
- Prepare sufficient bread for tonight and tomorrow's communion.
- Prepare sufficient wine for tonight's communion.
- Prepare baskets or other receptacles for gifts for the poor.

- Prepare white altar paraments and vestments.
- Prepare humeral veil.
- Prepare place of reservation.
- Empty tabernacle, leave doors open and vigil candle extinguished.
- Tell those responsible about bells during the Glory to God: servers or choir members for small bells indoors, maintenance personnel for tower bells.
- Train servers for processions and incense.
- Arrange for stripping altar and church after Mass.

LECTIONARY

■ THE FIRST READING presents the story of the first Passover, a celebration of the freedom of God's chosen people. At the time of Passover, Jesus gathered his disciples for a meal, the Last Supper, which shaped the structure, content and themes of the Christian eucharist. Elements of prayer and the preparation of unleavened bread and wine signify a link between the first freeing of God's chosen people and the liberation of Christians from sin and death.

■ THE SECOND READING is our earliest record of the Last Supper. The letters of Paul predate the composition of the gospels. Paul passes on to the church at Corinth what he has learned about the meal on the night before Jesus died. Already in the first generation of Christians, Paul can speak about a tradition concerning the eucharist.

■ PSALM: Another verse from the same letter serves as the refrain to the responsorial psalm, which expresses thanks to God by lifting up a cup of salvation. In some ways, the psalm anticipates the second reading more than it reflects back on the first. See Marcy Weckler's "Our Blessing Cup" (WLP, 6201)

and Paul M. French's "Two Psalms for Holy Week" (WLP, 6228).

■ GOSPEL: John's account of the Last Supper features the washing of the feet. (His treatment of the eucharist occurs much earlier, in the sixth chapter of the gospel. It occurs there in a discourse, not in a story with a meal.) In hearing this gospel tonight, we reflect on the implications of the eucharist, which calls the faithful into service. Recent well-intentioned efforts to introduce signs of adoration into the communion rite of Mass threaten to overlook the important consequences of service embedded in the privilege of sharing the bread of life. The highlight of Mass is not adoration, but communion, and communion implies service.

The homily segues from John's gospel to the washing of the feet.

SACRAMENTARY

■ THE ENTRANCE ANTIPHON for this evening celebrates the cross, not the eucharist. Consider a piece like Michael Ward's arrangement of "Near the Cross" (WLP, 8526). The sacramentary antiphon, "We should glory in the cross of our Lord Jesus Christ," is set to a stirring chant in *By Flowing Waters,* 118. It widens our attention to the entire Triduum, rather than on tonight's celebration only.

Ring the bells during the Glory to God. Choir members may perform this service indoors. Someone else could handle the tower bells.

■ THE WASHING OF THE FEET is optional, but by all means include it. Jesus' words are quite strong about foot washing ("You should do what I have done"). The full meaning of tonight's celebration so hinges on this gesture, that the parish really should observe it.

This gesture of humility and service expresses the responsibilities of those who share the eucharist. Resist suggestions to replace this gesture with one more culturally expressive. Deplorably, washing hands or shining shoes have been proposed. Peter's defiant response shows that Jesus' action was not culturally attractive from the beginning. The sign expresses profound drama when presiders, the leaders of prayer, fall to their knees to serve others in the community.

In the sacramentary, no words introduce the washing of the feet, nor do they seem necessary. The celebrant's removal of the chasuble will signal strongly that the washing is about to begin. The singing may begin, and the participants, cued ahead of time, may move to their places.

If the presider needs assistance, he may consider turning to other leaders of the community. This preserves the sense of service. It hurts the sign if volunteers wash the feet of volunteers.

The sacramentary does not specify how many people get their feet washed. Some parishes have 12, others more, others less. Arrange the stations in such a way that everyone can see.

Music for the washing of the feet may include Steve Janco's "Whenever You Serve Me" (WLP, 6210) and "A New Commandment" (WLP, 5773) with verses in Polish and Spanish; Taizé's "Mandatum novum" (GIA, G-2433); Michael Ward's "A New Commandment" (WLP, 7579); Steve Warner's "The Garment of Love" (WLP, 7211); Chrysogonus Waddell's "Jesus Took a Towel" (*Worship,* #432); Christopher Walker's "Faith, Hope, and Love" (OCP, 7149); and the Ghanaian "Jesu, Jesu" (*Worship,* #431).

The dismissal of catechumens and elect may follow the washing of the feet.

■ INTERCESSIONS: Petitions from today's evening prayer in the *Liturgy of the Hours* could be adapted for the general intercessions of the eucharist.

■ GATHERING GIFTS: "At the beginning of the liturgy of the eucharist, there may be a procession of the faithful with gifts for the poor." The *Circular Letter* says that the gifts for the poor may especially include "those collected during Lent as a fruit of penance" (#52). Canned goods for a food pantry, rice bowls for Catholic Relief Services, or other gifts are appropriate today. The faithful may bring them forward from their pews, or a few may bring up a selection of gifts.

In this single instance, the sacramentary suggests a text to be sung during the procession of the gifts: "Ubi caritas." Many parishes customarily sing something during the Preparation of the Altar and Gifts, but this is the only time the liturgy actually recommends a song. The refrain of the original Latin chant from the *Liber cantualis* is not difficult and could become part of the parish's repertoire. Other versions include Taizé's (*Worship,* #604) and "Where Charity and Love Prevail" (*Gather*); one by Mark Hill (WLP, 8593); and an English translation in *By Flowing Waters* (123).

■ THE EUCHARIST: Use the first preface of the Holy Eucharist (P 47). Eucharistic Prayer I has three inserts proper for tonight's Mass. Other eucharistic prayers may be used. Singing the prayer would be very appropriate tonight. Try Richard Proulx's "Corpus Christi Mass" for unaccompanied choir, cantor and congregation, based on "Adoro Te."

The suggested communion antiphon draws its text from today's second reading. Settings of Psalm 34 also make a good selection because of the verse "Taste and see that the Lord is good." See also Robert Hutmacher's "Love Is His Word" (*Worship,* #599; and Richard Proulx's arrangement: WLP, 8677); Alan Hommerding's "Litany for the Holy Eucharist" (WLP *We Celebrate,* 29) and Lucien Deiss's "Song of My Love" (WLP, 2561).

If communion ministers bring communion to the sick, they could process out together after the faithful have shared the eucharist. They could return to the church later for adoration. The rest of the eucharistic bread should be collected in one vessel on the altar. Use a second only if necessary.

After a period of silence, the prayer after communion is sung or said. That prayer concludes the spoken texts of the liturgy. There is no greeting, no blessing, and no dismissal.

■ PROCESSION: After this prayer the presider puts incense in the thurible, kneels and incenses the Blessed Sacrament on the altar. Receiving the humeral veil, he then picks up the vessel containing the body of Christ and covers it with the veil.

Cross, candles and incense lead the procession through the church to the place of reposition. Other ministers and the assembly of the faithful follow. All sing "Pange, lingua," or another suitable song. Repeat the first four verses of "Pange, lingua" if necessary. See Frank Quinn's fine translation in *By Flowing Waters* (126 and 648).

At the place of reposition, the presider sets the vessel down before the empty tabernacle. He adds incense to the thurible, kneels, incenses the Blessed Sacrament, and all sing "Tantum ergo." The tabernacle door is then closed, perhaps by the deacon.

The *Circular Letter* notes that a monstrance is not to be used (55). Adoration will take place before the closed tabernacle, not before the exposed eucharist.

There is no dismissal of the faithful. They may remain, go home, and return as they wish. They continue their prayer and fasting before the next moment within the liturgy of the Paschal Triduum.

■ EUCHARISTIC ADORATION: The altar is stripped in silence and without ceremony. Crosses should be removed or covered in red or purple cloth. The *Circular Letter* asks that no candles burn before images of saints (57).

The materials used during the washing of the feet will require some extra housekeeping.

From the transfer of the eucharist to midnight, all should be encouraged to continue in prayer before the Blessed Sacrament. The *Circular Letter* (56) calls for John 13–17 to be read as part of this prayer time. Different groups in the parish may assemble at a given time to offer vocal prayer and song.

Many parishes conclude the period of adoration by singing night prayer from the *Liturgy of the Hours* just before midnight. In place of the usual responsory, "Into your hands," the church uses "Christ became obedient" throughout the hours of the Triduum, adding a phrase each day.

OTHER IDEAS

On Good Friday, and if possible on Holy Saturday, we abstain from meat and observe the paschal fast. In order to observe the fast, the faithful should have time to eat before tonight's liturgy. You may encourage them to finish their supper with the Lord's Supper. In a traditional Jewish seder, participants drink four cups of wine. We do not know for certain, but it is possible that if Jesus followed this protocol, he served the best wine, his own blood, last.

#40   red

☯ 18 Good Friday: The Passion and Death of the Lord

ORIENTATION

Good Friday is a celebration of the passion, the suffering and death by crucifixion of Jesus. Because this event won salvation for sinners, the day is called "Good," and the liturgy reflects on love as much as loss. For the faithful, today's commemoration drives home the full weight of our sin, even as it lifts us up by the incomparable measure of God's love. For the elect, today's dramatic reflection awakens them to the demands of discipleship, while it prepares them to receive God's love in the promise of eternal life by the waters of baptism.

■ THREE O'CLOCK IN THE AFTERNOON: The sacramentary recommends that today's celebration begin at 3:00 PM. This places the prayer closer to the traditional hour of Jesus' death, and may actually make it more accessible to many parishioners. Some will prefer daylight hours. Many communities plan all three Triduum celebrations in the evening, but some staff and parishioners may like the idea of Friday night at home. Those who take off work to attend an afternoon service give witness to the importance of the Triduum.

■ TODAY'S LITURGY IS IN THREE MAIN PARTS: the liturgy of the word, featuring John's account of the passion, the veneration of the cross, and holy communion.

■ IN ANTICIPATION OF THE CELEBRATION, check the following list:

· Practice singing intercessions.
· Set up microphones for the passion.
· Prepare the cross.
· Prepare candles and incense (with matches).
· Set altar cloth and corporal aside.
· Arrange for collection for the Holy Land.
· Prepare red vesture.
· Prepare a private place for reservation of any remaining consecrated bread.
· Prepare a central place for the cross to remain.

LECTIONARY

■ THE PASSION ACCORDING TO JOHN is the centerpiece of the liturgy of the word. Proclaim it as you did Matthew's passion on Palm Sunday. Use multiple readers and musical acclamations after the principal sections, as recommended by the Canadian lectionary. A refrain like "Be Near Me Lord, When I Am in Trouble," or even a verse of "Were You There?" make good choices.

■ OTHER SCRIPTURES: The first reading comes from the suffering servant songs of Isaiah. It concludes the series begun on Monday, Tuesday and Wednesday of Holy Week. The refrain of the psalm, actually coming from Luke's gospel, is itself a quote from the psalm: Jesus' last words on the cross. The passage from Hebrews recalls the suffering of Christ, through which he became the source of eternal life.

SACRAMENTARY

■ THE CELEBRATION BEGINS IN SILENCE. As much as possible, limit the greeting in the gathering space before Mass. This is not a day for rehearsing music with ministers and the assembly. Keep the mood somber as people enter.

The priest and deacon wear red chasuble and dalmatic. This is the only occasion on which a chasuble is worn apart from the Mass. It signifies the unity of tonight's liturgy with yesterday's eucharist and the one tomorrow.

No entrance rite is described—no cross, no candles, no song, no solo instruments. The rubrics say the ministers "go to the altar." They could actually take their places in their chairs ten or fifteen minutes before the liturgy begins. Then they could "go to the altar" and reverence it with a kiss to signal the beginning of communal prayer.

■ PROSTRATION: The priest and deacon prostrate or kneel. Prostration, the more dramatic posture, will signal the seriousness of today's prayer. "This act of prostration, which is proper to the rite of the day, should be strictly observed, for it signifies both . . . abasement . . . and also the grief and sorrow of the church" (*Circular Letter,* 65).

The assembly stands for the entrance (according to the *Circular Letter* again) and thereafter kneels in silent prayer. If space permits, other ministers and even the assembly could choose to prostrate themselves.

The silence should be long enough for the power of this gesture to sink in and for this silence to evolve into prayer. When the priest goes to the chair with the ministers, the assembly will rise. For the opening prayer, the presider does not introduce it with a greeting, nor does he say, "Let us pray." Prayer has already begun.

He extends his hands as usual and is seated afterwards.

■ THE RESPONSORIAL PSALM will be the assembly's first song of the celebration. Paul M. French has a setting in his "Two Psalms for Holy Week" (WLP, 6228). See also the effective rendering in *By Flowing Waters,* 127. The gospel acclamation should also be sung as usual.

■ IF YOU CHOOSE TO SING THE PASSION, see the setting available from GIA (G-1795). You might also divide the parts among several speakers.

A single reader with oratorical skill can also effectively proclaim the passion. Several readers may take turns in succession, each proclaiming a block of the text. A musical refrain by the assembly may separate the sections.

In any case, use no incense, no candles, no greeting and no signs of the cross. The reading begins simply with "The Passion of our Lord Jesus Christ according to John."

If several readers or singers are involved, let them practice movement, not just words. Have them come together, bow to the altar, and go to their stations before beginning the passion.

Customarily, the assembly kneels in silence for a while after the verse announcing Jesus' death. Do say, "The gospel of the Lord" at the end, but do not kiss the book (*Ceremonial of Bishops,* 319).

■ A BRIEF HOMILY MAY BE GIVEN. The theme need not stray at all from the focus of today's celebration: the love of God for us, in spite of our sin. After the homily, allow a time for silent meditation (*Circular Letter,* 66; *Ceremonial of Bishops,* 319).

■ SHOULD THE ELECT AND CATECHUMENS BE DISMISSED? Some say yes, because the intercessions are prayers "of the faithful." Others argue that they may remain

because one of the prayers is for those to be baptized. Your local community may decide.

■ THE GENERAL INTERCESSIONS TAKE ON A SOLEMN FORM. The deacon or another minister announces the intention from the ambo and the priest prays accordingly from the chair or the altar. Certainly the chair makes a better choice.

The faithful may kneel or stand throughout the prayers, but the traditional changes in posture add to the solemnity of the prayer: Stand for the intention, kneel in silence, stand for the prayer. The deacon may give these instructions, but people will catch on without repetitious directives.

As an alternative, the assembly may sing an acclamation after the intention is announced and before the prayer. Consider a Kyrie, "Oye nos, mi Dios," or another imploring refrain. The bishop may suggest additional intentions for your diocese. Is there a special need toward which your region should devote attention?

■ FOR THE VENERATION, USE ONE CROSS. This could be the main cross in the church if it can be made accessible. A processional or another devotional cross may also serve. The *Circular Letter* advises, "Let a cross be used that is of appropriate size and beauty" (68).

Choose one of the two forms for showing the cross. The first envisions a procession of a veiled cross, flanked by candles, into the sanctuary. Three times the priest unveils part of the cross, sings, "This is the wood of the cross," raises it, and all kneel in silence. (Either the deacon or the printed program may have to direct this posture.) The second envisions the procession of an unveiled cross through the church. Again, all kneel after each refrain.

For veneration, make sure the cross is accessible to the elderly and those who use a wheelchair.

Some have ministers hold it. Others place it on the ground or against a prop—but not against the altar or some other religious object. See *To Crown the Year* (98–103) for ideas.

Processions may come from several directions. Ushers may assist. When people approach, a genuflection toward the cross is most appropriate, but another sign of reverence may be given. Many kiss the cross. The *Ceremonial of Bishops* (322) has the presider remove his shoes, like Moses before the burning bush. If the presider and other ministers lead the way, the faithful will probably follow.

During the veneration, sing "We Worship You" from the sacramentary, or settings by Howard Hughes, David Isele and Michael Joncas in *Praise God in Song* (GIA, G-2270). Prepare several pieces, because the veneration may take time. Try "Pange, lingua"; "Crucem tuam" from Taizé (GIA, G-3719); "Adoramus te Domine I" from the same community (*Gather*, 221); "Jesus, Remember Me" (*Gather*, 167); and/or Owen Alstott's "Wood of the Cross" (OCP, 8826). Steven C. Warner's "Crux fidelis" (WLP, 7230) is another fine choice. Richard Felciano's four-part arrangement of "Were You There?" is available from Schirmer (4061).

Music for the reproaches is found in the sacramentary, but their text is sometimes interpreted as anti-Jewish. A revision of the verses appears in the United Methodist *Book of Worship*.

■ THE COMMUNION RITE TAKES PLACE SIMPLY. Ministers could reverently cover the altar with a cloth and corporal. The sacramentary may be placed there if needed, but a good presider should be able to lead this part of the service from memory. Candles may accompany the consecrated bread to the altar, but again, simply. Have the candles placed near the altar or on it.

The presider leads the community in the Lord's Prayer and the invitation to communion. No sign of peace is given (*Circular Letter*, 70), probably because of the scandal of the kiss of Judas. The *Circular Letter* suggests Psalm 21 for communion (probably the Latin numbering that equals Psalm 22, the responsorial psalm for Palm Sunday). Or repeat the song from last night. David Haas's "Now We Remain" (*Gather*, GIA) is appropriate. Communion is under one form for this communion service. This is not a celebration of the eucharist.

■ AFTER COMMUNION, the remaining blessed sacrament is carried without ceremony by an assisting minister to a suitable place outside the main worship space. This is a place of convenience, not really a place for adoration. A period of silence is observed, and the presider leads the prayer after communion.

The service concludes with the prayer over the people. The presider does not introduce it with the greeting, but simply extends his hands over the people for the prayer. No dismissal is given. Ministers may genuflect toward the cross and depart reverently in silence (*Ceremonial of Bishops*, 331).

Think this through: All the ministers leaving at once will appear to signal the end of prayer. Perhaps some can remain in silent prayer near the cross.

After the service, strip the altar again. Set four candles by the cross (*Circular Letter*, 71).

OTHER IDEAS

Whenever anyone enters or leaves the church, or passes in front of the cross between now and the Vigil, the proper reverence is not a bow to the altar, not a genuflection to the tabernacle, but a genuflection to the cross. This is the only time in the church's liturgy that we genuflect to anything besides the blessed sacrament (*Ceremonial of Bishops*, 69). There is no eucharist today, and the instrument of the passion becomes the center of our devotion.

■ TENEBRAE: The morning of Good Friday could include a combined celebration of the office of readings and morning prayer. The practice is recommended by the *Ceremonial of Bishops* (296), the *Liturgy of the Hours* (210) and the *Circular Letter* (40, 62). The latter recalls that this combined office used to be called *Tenebrae*, the Latin word for "darkness."

Prior to the mid-twentieth century reforms of the Roman Rite, many places of worship lit a 15-post candelabrum before the service and extinguished one candle after each of the psalms of the service, until one was left, recalling the abandonment of Jesus by his friends and the encroaching threat of death. That shining candle, signifying the light of Christ, was placed briefly behind the altar, while sounds of chaos rattled the darkness. People might have banged their hymnals against the pews, for example. Although the liturgical documents recommend the praying of readings and morning prayer on these days, they do not mention the restoration of the allegorical practices associated with the evening Tenebrae.

To combine the hours, consult *Liturgy of the Hours*, 99. Basically, start with the office of readings but use the hymn from morning prayer. Omit the final prayer of readings and the opening versicle of morning prayer, and cut to the psalms of that office, proceeding to its conclusion. The extensive prayer allows a diversity of ministers and a variety of musical interpretations of the psalms.

Be sure children are invited to attend the principal liturgy.

■ IF YOU OFFER STATIONS OF THE CROSS TODAY, they should not in any way detract from the principal celebration of the Lord's Passion (*Circular Letter,* 72).

■ NIGHT PRAYER could be offered at the end of the day, perhaps following a fasting meal.

violet

☯19 Holy Saturday Morning and Afternoon

ORIENTATION

On Holy Saturday we commemorate the day Jesus lay in the tomb. There is no Mass during the day. Communion may be given only as viaticum. Reconciliation and anointing of the sick may be celebrated today, but they make more sense on other days.

During the day today we continue the paschal fast. We continue a prayerful spirit. The climax of the Triduum, the Easter Vigil, begins when darkness arrives. The Easter Vigil launches us into the Easter season and it should not be confused with Holy Saturday itself.

■ PROPER RITES FOR THESE HOURS: The community may gather in the morning for morning prayer or with the elect for the preparatory rites (RCIA, 185–205). A combined office of readings and morning prayer may take place as it did on Good Friday. Although the community may gather for prayer at midday or evening, many will use this time to make preparations for the Easter Vigil.

The combined office of readings and morning prayer will give the faithful the opportunity to hear the patristic homily assigned for today. It depicts Christ's triumphant entrance into Sheol, his meeting with our first parents, and the beginning of the great victory procession by which the souls of the just are liberated by the conquering Savior, King Jesus. In place of the responsory, the Triduum antiphon from Philippians is chanted in its fullness.

■ NO VESTMENT COLOR IS SPECIFIED FOR HOLY SATURDAY. White is the best choice if the preparation rites are celebrated. They begin the ceremony of baptism.

■ PREPARATORY RITES BEFORE BAPTISM: If there are elect to be baptized at tonight's Vigil, be sure to conduct the preparatory rites early in the day. They form an important prelude to baptism. During Lent, the elect received the Creed from the faithful and, having meditated on it, commit it to memory. Today they recite the Creed, returning it back to the faithful, demonstrating their readiness for the questions they will hear tonight: "Do you renounce?" "Do you believe?"

If the Lord's Prayer has not yet been presented, that ceremony may take place at this time. Augustine gave testimony to this practice. But in the normal course of events, the presentation of the Lord's Prayer takes place during the fifth week of Lent.

If infants will be baptized at the Vigil, the Rite of Baptism for Children (#28) calls for preparatory rites for them as well. This should involve receiving them at the door, exorcism and anointing. (Adults, however, will not be anointed today. The elect had opportunities for anointing while they were catechumens.)

A service combining the reception of infants with preparation of the elect is possible, uniting in one assembly the prayers and expectations of the elect, the parents, the sponsors and the catechists. The format is as follows, with possible rites listed in RCIA, 185.2, and readings at #179–180, 194, 198:

- *Gathering hymn,* with entire assembly at the entrance. An appropriate text is found on page 170 of the *Triduum Sourcebook.*

- *Reception of infants* (*Rite of Baptism for Children,* 35–41)

- *Procession* of all to seating near ambo; refrain or hymn sung by all

- *Psalms, antiphon, scripture* of the appropriate hour; or a reading related to preparatory rites, followed by psalm

- *Homily*

- *Preparation rites* for infants: exorcism (RBC, 49), anointing with oil of catechumens (RBC, 50)

- One or more of the preparation rites for adults and children of catechetical age: presentation of the Lord's Prayer (RCIA, 180), ephphetha (199) or recitation of the Creed (195)

- *Hymn or gospel canticle* if part of morning or evening prayer

- *Intercessions* from morning or evening prayer of Holy Saturday, supplemented with prayers for baptized candidates for full communion

- *Lord's Prayer*

- *Prayers of blessing* (RCIA, 204)

- *Dismissal* (RCIA, 205)

Note that in the *Rite of Christian Initiation of Adults,* the ephphetha appears after the recitation of the Creed, but if both are included in the preparation rites, the ephphetha comes first.

■ SOME COMMUNITIES INVITE CHILDREN TODAY TO COLOR EGGS, hear and dramatize the scriptures from the Vigil, and to assist in preparing the worship space. Their participation in the preparation rites will be important, especially if there are children of catechetical age in this year's group.

■ EVENING PRAYER may be celebrated by the community, on its own or in conjunction with the preparation rites. This is the only Saturday of the liturgical year with vespers. Because the Vigil is to take place at night, some communities may begin the celebration in the early hours of Sunday morning. Especially in those cases, a Saturday evening prayer will be welcome. "Be Still, My Soul" (Finlandia) makes a beautiful hymn for the occasion.

🌀 19–20

#41   white
The Easter Vigil

The Easter Vigil is the most important eucharist of the year. We celebrate our faith in the resurrection, the cornerstone of our belief. Ranking highest among the celebrations of the liturgical year, it should rank highest in the spiritual life of the faithful.

■ THE FOUR PARTS OF THE EASTER VIGIL move us through a gradual unfolding of its mystery. The fire rite immediately shatters the gathering darkness. The liturgy of the word opens up the path of God's plan throughout salvation history. The liturgy of baptism draws the elect into the promise of eternal life and renews the baptismal belief of the faithful. The liturgy of the eucharist brings the celebration to its climax as we experience the presence of the risen Christ in the community.

LECTIONARY

■ READINGS: Nine scripture readings are offered for tonight's celebration. You may reduce the number of Old Testament readings, but the Exodus story must always be included. The permission to reduce the readings is given "if necessary." The sense of the liturgy is that ordinarily the readings will all be proclaimed. If this is not yet your custom, consider expanding the Vigil's word service this year.

■ LENGTH: One of the symbols of the Easter Vigil is its length. We take time for community prayer around this mystery of resurrection because nothing else matters more. Hearing the nine readings will be a challenge for communities unaccustomed to it, but they do convey more fully the mystery of God's plan of salvation, while they give the sense of what a vigil is.

■ CHILDREN: The introduction to the *Lectionary for Masses with Children* forbids a separate liturgy of the word for children (30) due to the importance of the community celebrating one Easter Vigil. But to help children through the length of the Vigil, some communities dismiss them during the scriptures to perform other activities and to reflect on the meaning of the celebration. They could, for example, rejoin the assembly for the proclamation of the gospel, in keeping with the permission to reduce the number of readings for children on Sundays and holy days (*Directory for Masses with Children,* 42).

■ THEMATICS: The scriptures work together to blend the themes of creation, covenant, baptism and resurrection.

Water appears as a theme in the first reading (the story of creation), as well as in the prophecies of Isaiah and Ezekiel in readings five and seven. The responsorial psalms with these texts repeat the water and creation imagery. They foreshadow the covenant of baptism.

Rescue is the theme of readings two and three, where God liberates Isaac and then all of Israel. The responsorial psalms with these and to the fourth reading repeat the idea. Tonight we celebrate Jesus' resurrection and our own rescue from death.

God's covenant becomes evident in readings four and six. The covenant, filled with wisdom (Baruch) and everlasting in its strength (Isaiah), reaches its fulfillment in Jesus. Again, the responsorial psalms echo these themes.

The epistle, which formerly followed the baptismal liturgy at the Vigil, plainly explains the connection between the baptism of the faithful and the resurrection of Jesus. The psalm that follows returns to the theme of rescue: the rejected stone has become the cornerstone.

The gospel announces the Good News of resurrection, the message we have longed to hear. Mark's version is perhaps the strangest, but the revised lectionary has sanitized it. Formerly in Year B, we heard the first eight verses of chapter 16. Now we just hear the first seven. Verse 8 says that after the women received the commission to announce the resurrection, they left in fear and trembling and said nothing to anyone. It hardly felt like good news. Now the proclamation ends with the commission to the women to go to the disciples—and Peter—(as if he needs to hear this more than the rest) and announce the resurrection. The disturbing verse has been omitted.

The conclusion to Mark's gospel is an unsolvable puzzle. Scholars think the original version ended with verse 8, in effect tossing to the reader the commission to tell the Good News, because the first evangelists kept quiet. A later manuscript added several more verses to the gospel, a compendium of apparitions recounted in the other gospels. The longer version is accepted as inspired and appears in the weekday lectionary next Saturday.

Use Gail Ramshaw's *Words around the Fire* (LTP, 1990) for additional reflections on these scriptures. See Rory Cooney's "Genesis Reading for the Great Vigil" (GIA, G-5018C) for an idea for the first reading. A complete set of utterly simple chant settings of the responsorial psalms—capable of being sung in the dark, without printed music for the assembly—is found in *By Flowing Waters*, 131–141.

SACRAMENTARY

■ DARKNESS: The entire Vigil takes place at night. The lateness of the hour and the length of the Vigil cause inconvenience for some of the faithful. It is hoped, however, that the Vigil is the kind of experience for which people willingly inconvenience themselves. On some special occasions you give up sleep for entertainment, shopping, family and friends. Tonight we give up sleep for faith.

Some communities start the Vigil in the early hours of Sunday morning. This is completely permissible. It makes Saturday a real day with Jesus in the tomb, a full day extending Friday's fast and heightening the anticipation for

baptism and resurrection. It rousts the faithful from slumber in the early hours of Easter Day and plunges them into an extended celebration that reaches its joy in the eucharist at dawn. Celebrating the Vigil early Sunday morning is worth considering, but think too about the needs of the ministers you will need on duty for the parish Masses as the day continues.

PART ONE IS THE SERVICE OF LIGHT.

■ BONFIRE: A blazing fire may greet the faithful as they arrive. The *Circular Letter* says this fire should be of some size, so that it actually dispels darkness and lights up the night (82). It is best to prepare the fire outdoors. It is a bonfire, not a fondue. The place need not be far from the church, but outside it. If you have the space, prepare the fire outdoors. If you do not have the space, make a five- or ten-year plan for obtaining it.

Put the fire in the hands of people who know what they are doing. A scout troop often makes the best guardian for this symbol. Most are skilled in the safe preparation of a campfire, and can douse the flame and restore the earth in such a way that you will never know they were there. Good fire builders also know how to do this in a downpour.

Fire may be prepared on asphalt or on a lawn if a thick tarp with ten inches of sand is put down. A livestock trough may also serve, with sand or cinder blocks beneath for insulation.

For safety, dried hardwood is better than pine or other softwoods. Be sure to consult with local fire marshals for whatever permissions might be required. Many municipalities have regulations about fires, even on private property. Officials are generally respectful of religious customs. Be prepared with extinguishers

in case the fire becomes too large, blankets to put out stray sparks, and hoses. Have a volunteer crew keep a careful eye on the blaze.

■ THE CHURCH SHOULD REMAIN IN DARKNESS. You need not lock the doors to keep people from entering, but you might obstruct them in some way. At the very least, have greeters on duty early enough to steer the assembly away from pews and toward the fire.

■ A LARGE NEW PASCHAL CANDLE OF WAX IS MANDATORY (*Circular Letter*, 82)—large enough, the letter continues, to evoke the truth that Christ is the light of the world.

No artificial candles may be used, and no second-use candles from previous years. Easter candles are available from a number of producers. The handcrafted quality of the Marklin Candle Company's products is noteworthy (http://www.liturgy2000.com).

Some communities rely on a local artisan to decorate the blank candle they purchase. Although the candle traditionally comes with a cross, the numbers of the year and the alpha and omega, the presider may carve these images into the wax during the preparation of the candle. If the candle comes with these symbols already in place, it lessens the argument for exercising the option of the ritual preparation of the candle during the service of light.

■ PREPARE CANDLES FOR THE ASSEMBLY. Candles inside cupped plastic shields give better protection to the flames than those with circular cardboard wheels.

■ BEGINNING: The faithful gather in the dark. Before the liturgy begins, invite members of your community to introduce their guests to the assembly, and ask visitors to say where they come from.

The ministers may assemble early together with the community or may make an entrance. Try to begin on time. It will be a long night.

The sign of the cross opens the Vigil (*Ceremonial of Bishops,* 339) and then the presider greets the people. He then may improvise an introduction for the celebration. He blesses the fire, which has been burning before his arrival.

The *Ceremonial of Bishops* says the bishop and deacon light the candle (340), but the sacramentary does not specify which minister performs this function. A member of the community might do this. The censer is also lit from the new fire (340), but this will delay the effect of incense for several minutes. Another solution is to put charcoal in the fire ahead of time. After the blessing, use tongs to place the burning charcoal in the censer.

Deacon and assembly alternate the dialogue, "Christ our light." Another acclamation may be used, but the tradition behind this one is strong. Candles should be lit when the deacon reaches the church door, but this rubric makes more sense if it refers to the candles of the principal ministers. In a larger assembly, the lighting of candles might begin after the first intonation. Have several ministers prepared to begin. The faithful will take it from there.

Lights in the church come on after the third intonation, but many communities turn them on after singing the Easter Proclamation, so that the light of the blessed fire, not artificial light, illumines the church for the first part of this great night.

■ THE EASTER PROCLAMATION (EXSULTET) is now available in several forms. The chant in the sacramentary is closest to the original idea, but it takes a skilled cantor, unafraid of setting a brisk pace and letting the joy of the season radiate from eyes, mouth and the whole face. See Robert Batastini's adaptation (GIA, G-2351) and Christopher Walker's setting (St. Thomas More, OCP, 7175). J. Michael Thompson's arrangement is available from World Library (#5716) and Everett Frese's comes from Pastoral Press. See also the much-abbreviated text and still powerful music of "This Is the Night" by Jeffrey Schneider (WLP, 5721).

Need some instrumental filler? Check out the flute solo based on the Exsultet chant in *Meditations for Unaccompanied Flute* by Richard Proulx (GIA, G-5335).

■ PACE: All in all, keep the service of light moving. Many Easter Vigils get off to a sluggish start because ministers are unaware of cues. Make sure everyone knows who is responsible for what.

What is the cue for starting the sign of the cross? For moving the procession? For starting the Easter Proclamation? Make sure the musicians and altar ministers are prepared, and let the whole service of light flow with deliberate purpose. It should set the tone for the joy of this night. If it looks confusing or amateurish from the start, you have set a tone for what follows.

The sacramentary does not say what to do with the assembly's candles, but the *Ceremonial of Bishops* says they are extinguished after the Easter Proclamation. If the presider and ministers visibly blow out their candles after the Proclamation without saying a word, the assembly may follow suit. If not, the deacon could give this instruction.

If children are dismissed to a catechetical session, that would happen here.

PART TWO IS THE LITURGY OF THE WORD.

The sequence of readings, silences, psalms and prayers sets a meditative pace for the true vigil part of the Vigil.

■ REGARDING THE NUMBER OF READINGS, the *Circular Letter* says that wherever possible, "all the readings should be read in order that the character of the Easter Vigil, which demands that it be somewhat prolonged, be respected." Some communities pride themselves on vigils under 90 minutes, or on an interpretive mixture of readings that shortens the liturgy of the word. They undermine the purpose of the Vigil.

■ TO INTRODUCE THE READINGS, the presider may give an instruction to the faithful. If you have printed programs, you may also help people by printing a summary sentence of what the reading is about, or why it was chosen for tonight's celebration. Such catechetical devices are intended to help the faithful ease into the prayerful spirit required for tonight's liturgy of the word.

The spirit is formal and yet relaxed. We are here tonight because there is nowhere else we would rather be.

Allow the moments of silence after each reading. Allow the change of posture for the prayers. All this will establish a rhythm and help the assembly enter into the spirit of the readings.

■ MUSICIANS SHOULD CHOOSE THE RESPONSORIAL PSALMS CAREFULLY. People should sense their cohesion as if they are a series of movements. Think of the psalms as a suite, as a single multi-movement musical composition with moments of excitement and moments of calm.

Many communities link the third reading directly to its responsory, which comes from the next verses of the same book of Exodus. Near the end of the reading, it says, "Then Moses and the Israelites sang this song to the Lord." There's another line of text, but it copies what will follow in the responsory. Advise the reader to omit the final line of the reading and the phrase "The word of the Lord," and then jump in with the responsory when the reading itself gives the cue.

■ GLORY TO GOD: After the prayer of the last Old Testament reading, the Glory to God rings out. As the Glory to God begins, servers light the altar candles, ring bells inside and outside the building, and turn on any lights still slumbering. Some favorites include Peter Jones (OCP), Richard Proulx "Gloria for Eastertime" based on "O filii et filiae" (GIA, G-3086 or choral version G-3087), and "Gloria of the Bells" by C. Alexander Peloquin (*Worship,* #258).

You may also decorate the worship space at this point. (See *To Crown the Year,* pages 111–112.) A procession of flowers and other items is the most orderly way. Ask volunteers, perhaps a committee or organization in the parish, to rehearse this on Holy Saturday after the flowers are delivered. Assign clusters of volunteers to zones of the space. After the rehearsal bring the materials to a side room or rear pew. During the psalm before the Glory to God, have the volunteers go quietly to the materials, pick them up, and stand ready. As the Glory to God begins, they go in procession to place the decorations as rehearsed.

■ THE OPENING PRAYER FOR THE MASS FOLLOWS. We've had plenty of prayers already, but this one parallels the typical opening prayer for the beginning of Mass.

Back in the old days, baptisms happened after the Old Testament readings and before the Glory to God. Then, after baptism, came the New Testament readings.

Now all the readings ensue in nearly uninterrupted sequence, and the liturgy of baptism follows the homily, when we usually celebrate other sacraments (for example, marriage and confirmation). Still, as a leftover from the older rites, the Glory to God appears in the midst of the liturgy of the word.

It is the Easter Vigil. A few things will be different.

■ GOOD NEWS: After the glorious epistle that compares baptism to resurrection, all rise for the gospel acclamation. Actually, the *Ceremonial of Bishops* allows for something else to happen. After this reading, one of the deacons or the reader goes to the bishop and says, "Most Reverend Father, I bring you a message of great joy, the message of Alleluia." Then all stand and the bishop intones the Alleluia. (It's hokey, but you gotta love it!)

Imagine this. A member of the catechumenate team has read the epistle. Then she or he goes to the presider and says, "Father N., I bring you a message of great joy, and the message is (*pause for dramatic effect*) Alleluia." Then a fanfare erupts from the instruments and the choir bellows out the word we have not sung for almost seven weeks. All rise and we sing three magnificent verses of acclamation.

Here's another way to do it. The one who delivers the message is the cantor, standing at the cantor stand. At the last word of the message, the cantor intones the alleluia, and all repeat. Three times. If not the traditional chant, use Christopher Walker's "Celtic Alleluia" (OCP, 7106), (and please pronounce it "Keltic" in rehearsal—

Christopher says so), with handbells if possible; "Easter Alleluia" (*Gather*), based on "O filii et filiae," verse by Marty Haugen; Richard Proulx's "Alleluia and Psalm for Easter" (GIA, G-1965), specifically written for this night, with familiar threefold Mode VI Alleluia (congregation, choir, cantor, organ and handbells) and Donald Regan's "Fanfare and Alleluia" (WLP, 7959).

If the presider sings the traditional Easter alleluia, he raises the pitch each time (*Circular Letter,* 87). For the gospel, use incense, but no candles. The Easter candle should be candle enough. Sing the introduction and conclusion. Sing the gospel! Sample tones can be found in the *Graduale Romanum.*

A homily, "no matter how brief" (*Circular Letter,* 87), is given.

PART THREE IS THE LITURGY OF BAPTISM.

Turn to the *Rite of Christian Initiation of Adults* (218–243) for this service, unless you have no one to be baptized. In that case, refer to the sacramentary.

In the *Rite of Christian Initiation of Adults* there are versions of the ritual order for the reception of baptized Christians (279–498) and for the combination of the sacraments of initiation and the Rite of Reception (566–594).

■ RESERVING EASTER FOR BAPTISM: The Rite of Reception into the Full Communion of the Catholic Church may take place at any time of year, and there are arguments for celebrating it when the candidates for reception are ready, not necessarily in conjunction with Easter. There is no connection between the Rite of Reception and any day in the liturgical year. If the Easter Vigil is reserved for the unbaptized celebrating the rites of initiation, the full significance of baptism will shine more clearly.

■ THE CELEBRATION OF BAPTISM BEGINS WITH THE PRESENTATION OF THE CANDIDATES. If the font is in view of the assembly, this rite will move there. If not, you may assemble a temporary font in the sanctuary. After Easter, you may also have discussions about a more permanent solution to the architectural needs for a baptistry visible to the assembly in your church.

Someone calls the names of the elect. The deacon or someone from the catechumenate team may do this. Be sure this person knows how to pronounce everyone's names. Godparents present the elect, and parents present infants for baptism.

■ LITANY OF THE SAINTS: The presider invites all to prayer and the litany of the saints is begun. This litany may accompany the procession to the font (219B).

You may add names to the litany. Include the patrons of the parish, the diocese and of the elect if these are not already on the list.

The litany groups the saints by category. It opens with saints from the Bible (up to Stephen), then early Roman martyrs (up to Agnes), the four great church fathers, and a group that influenced the course of church history, ending with doctors Catherine and Teresa. In general, the list is chronological. It will take a little work, but if you want to add some saints, figure out where they belong in the sequence and insert them accordingly.

Sing the litany. The traditional chant is worth having in the community's repertoire (WLP *We Celebrate,* 102). Other settings include ones by John Becker (OCP), David Haas (*Who Calls You by Name,* vol. I), Matthew Nagi (*We Celebrate,* vol. 2, cycle A), and Paul Page (vol. 1 of the same, #165).

Paul Ford has provided three petitions as the climax of the Litany of the Saints (*By Flowing Waters,* 143): "Give new life to these chosen ones by the grace of baptism: Lord, hear our prayer. Give new life to these chosen ones by the grace of baptism [pause] and pour out your Holy Spirit: Lord, hear our prayer. Give new life to these chosen ones by the grace of baptism, [pause] pour out your Spirit, [pause] and feed them with your Body and Blood: Lord, hear our prayer."

■ THE BLESSING OF THE WATER TAKES PLACE AT THE FONT. Arrange the ministers so the candle can be plunged into the water. The presider may chant the blessing.

Notation appears in the blessing (RCIA, 222A). (See *By Flowing Waters* (144) for another version.) David Haas incorporates a familiar refrain for the assembly, the alleluia from O filii et filiae (*Who Calls You by Name,* vol. II, GIA).

The assembly sings an acclamation at the end. A chant appears in the ritual text, but David Haas concludes his setting of the blessing with another option. Other versions are by Thomas Savory (GIA, G-2549), Donald Fellows (GIA, G-3639), Mike Hay (WLP *We Celebrate,* 103) and Richard Proulx (GIA, G-3097).

■ THE ELECT NOW RENOUNCE SIN AND PROFESS THEIR FAITH. Throughout Lent the elect have experienced purification and enlightenment. They have received and recited the Creed. Now they answer personally the questions of faith. Parents and godparents answer for infants.

The renunciation of sin may be made as a group (224), but each professes faith individually. This is no time for efficiency.

■ BAPTISM IN THE CATHOLIC CHURCH IS BY IMMERSION OR POURING. The options are always listed in that order. The National Statutes for the Catechumenate in the United States say, "Baptism by immersion is the fuller and more expressive sign of the sacrament and, therefore, is preferred" (17).

If the parish does not have a font, you may set up something for temporary use, but plans should be underway for a font suitable to celebrate the sacrament with adults and children.

Some parishes clothe the elect in a non-white, loose-fitting garment that they can wear over whatever clothing they don't mind getting wet. If the font is of such size that the presider also needs to enter, he removes chasuble, shoes and socks. His stole and alb and the clothing they conceal will get wet. If he wears a wireless microphone, prudence suggests he remove it before stepping into the water.

■ AFTER EACH BAPTISM the assembly may sing an acclamation. Any alleluia works well, but consider these also: Lisa Stafford, "Acclamation for Baptism" (WLP, 5229); "You Have Put on Christ" by Chrysogonus Waddell (WLP, 7249), by Howard Hughes (GIA, G-2283) and by Gary Daigle (GIA, G-5021); Arthur Hutchings, "Rejoice, You Newly Baptized" (*ICEL Resource Collection,* GIA, G-2514); Marty Haugen, "Song Over the Waters" (*Gather*); Lynn Trapp, "Rite of Christian Initiation of Adults" (Morning Star MSM-80-907A); or John Olivier, "You Have Put on Christ" (*People's Mass Book*).

You may use this acclamation at other baptisms throughout the year.

■ THE UNHAPPILY NAMED "EXPLANATORY RITES" COME NEXT. Anoint infants on the crown of the head (*Rite of Baptism for Children,* 62), but not the adults. Clothing with the white garment is optional, surprisingly. Ideally, infants would be clothed with the baptismal garment at this time, not before the baptism. Most families bring their infants to baptism already clothed in the white garment they should be receiving afterward. (Watch how the Greek Orthodox baptize babies; Roman Catholics can do likewise.)

If adults and children of catechetical age have been immersed and go to a separate room to dry off and change clothes, they receive their garments from the godparent and then put them on. If godparents present the white garment in the privacy of the changing room, give them the text to say as they make the presentation (229). Some communities do not give a white garment and allow the newly baptized to wear their Easter finest.

The presider invites godparents to light candles from the Easter candle, and they present it to the newly baptized. If the neophytes have been immersed and must leave the church to change clothes, the presider might say the text once after the last baptism. Godparents could then light the baptismal candle as the neophytes return to the church. If the presider has entered the font, he too may change into dry clothes at this time. Alternatively, the presider could recite the text for the candle at this time.

Any candle will suffice. Some companies sell special ones. Some parishes provide decorated candles. The Marklin Company makes smaller versions of its paschal candles for this rite (www.liturgy2000.com).

■ CONFIRMATION follows immediately if there are no candidates for the Rite of Reception. The link between baptism and confirmation and the mission of the Son and the outpouring of the Spirit (RCIA, 215) is better ritualized when the Rite of Reception does not interrupt the flow of the rites of initiation.

A song may begin the confirmation. If the neophytes are still changing clothes, this song will help cover the time, even as it prepares the assembly for the sacrament to follow. Try "Veni, Sancte Spiritus" or "Confitemini Domino," both ostinatos from Taizé, or Christopher Walker's "Veni, Sancte Spiritus" (St. Thomas More, OCP, 7116), or even "Come, Holy Ghost."

The newly baptized come to the font again. The priest who baptizes has the faculty to confirm all adults and children of catechetical age whom he baptizes, and he must exercise this faculty for their benefit (canon 883/2 and 885/2). He does not have the faculty to confirm infants. Many people are surprised that a presider would confirm a child younger than the diocesan age for confirmation.

The Code of Canon Law is very strict on this point. It gives the faculty to the presider directly. The faculty does not come from the bishop. The presider "must use it" for the benefit of the newly baptized, regardless of the relationship of their age to the diocesan age of confirmation. Some parents, priests and bishops prefer to defer the confirmation of baptized children of catechetical age, but they have no authority to do so. Let the sacrament benefit the child.

The presider introduces the rite and invites all to pray in silence. The next section is called "laying on of hands," but it describes an extension of hands. Still, if handlaying is possible, it offers a better symbol. The presider may sing or recite the prayer for confirmation.

Use a generous amount of chrism on the neophyte's head, and be sure to smear the forehead in the sign of the cross. If you do not, you ritualize the anointing on the crown of the head that accompanies infant baptism, not confirmation on the forehead. The priest says, "Peace be with you," but no rubric is given for a gesture. An embrace would certainly be appropriate.

■ RENEWAL OF BAPTISMAL PROMISES: All relight their candles with fire from the Easter candle or from those of the neophytes. Have ministers prepared to assist.

The faithful then renew their baptismal promises and are sprinkled with baptismal water. The presider should ask the questions in a strong voice, inviting a strong response. This ceremony signifies the climax of the assembly's period of renewal. Throughout Lent they have prepared themselves to recommit themselves to Christ. Now, at this moment, renewing their baptismal promises, they do just that.

In some communities, the faithful come to the font to sign themselves with water as they generally do upon entering the church.

A song may accompany the rite. Try Richard Hillert's "Lord Jesus, from your Wounded Side" (*Worship*) and Michael Joncas's adaptation of "O Healing River" (GIA).

For the sprinkling, be sure everyone feels the water. Ministers should walk through all the aisles to sprinkle everyone. Branches from evergreen bushes or trees make excellent sprinkling implements. Tie several together to form a generous surface. Tape the stems at the bottom to form a handle and to keep sap off of ministers' hands. Colorful ribbons may be added. An assistant carrying the bowl of water might accompany each person who sprinkles.

During the sprinkling, other ministers replenish any holy water fonts in the church.

■ RITE OF RECEPTION: If there are candidates for the Rite of Reception as well as elect to be baptized, follow the rites at 580–591 in the *Rite of Christian Initiation of Adults*. Do not follow the sacramentary, which was published earlier and observed a different sequence of ceremonies.

After the explanatory rites, the presider invites all to renew their baptismal promises. This places the candidates for reception on equal footing with the rest of the community. All share the same baptism and all renew their promises together. Sprinkling or signing with water comes next, as a ritual expression of the verbal renewal that just happened.

If in this combined rite the presider needs to change clothes after the immersions, he may do so at this time while the music for the water rite continues.

The Rite of Reception takes place in the sanctuary. The celebrant names the candidates in his opening remarks, but a member of the Christian initiation team could announce the names first, to introduce the group to the assembly. If there is a procession to the sanctuary, you may sing a song. Arrange the candidates so the assembly can see their faces. Sponsors, perhaps, stand behind them and the presider stands before, back to the assembly.

The candidates make their profession of faith by reciting the sentence of belief (585). It is best if they memorize this, and if there is a group of them, they may recite the text together. Cue one of them, though, to take the lead, so there is no hesitation.

For the act of reception, the presider speaks to each individually. The rubric says that he lays his right hand on the head of any who will not be confirmed, but it is difficult to imagine who they might be. The priest has the faculty to confirm all those he receives in this rite and is obliged to exercise the faculty. The exceptions would be people who were validly confirmed in a schismatic church, like an Orthodox congregation, but they are not to be received in a formal ceremony like this. Those who were confirmed in mainline Protestant churches or other similar ecclesial communities in the West will celebrate confirmation with their reception. Although we regard confirmation in the Eastern Orthodox traditions equivalent to that in the Roman Catholic tradition, we do not extend the same equivalency to the confirmation of churches of the West. The hand on the shoulder is a kind of reconciling gesture, and should be avoided. If some human contact feels right, the presider might try grasping the hands of the one being received.

If at all possible, the presider should memorize the text for the act of reception (586). This will enable him to look the candidate in the eye while saying the words. The words are few, but their meaning is huge.

Confirmation follows. If there are neophytes, they return at this point. If logistically possible, confirm the whole group near the font; if not, use the sanctuary.

The Rite of Reception apart from the Easter Vigil adds a sign of welcome by the presider (495) and the assembly (497). The kiss of peace in the communion rite then may be omitted, but that will seem odd. Although the texts for the Easter Vigil do not promote the sign of welcome, it would make a fitting gesture, a hand or embrace of Christian peace. Consider inviting all those who wish to step away from the seats, up to the front, and welcome the newest members of the eucharistic community.

■ THE NEOPHYTES JOIN THE COMMUNITY FOR THE GENERAL INTERCESSIONS. If they have been dismissed throughout their period of formation, this is their first time joining the prayers we call "of the faithful." Use all the languages of the community in the petitions.

PART FOUR IS THE LITURGY OF THE EUCHARIST.

The neophytes bring up the bread and wine for the eucharistic meal in which they will share for the first time. Sing a good, familiar Easter hymn to unite the voices of the assembly and to give everyone a sense of purpose as you enter the final and most familiar part of tonight's service.

■ INSERTS: If possible, the presider should sing the eucharistic prayer. When using the preface for Easter I (P 21), use the text "on this Easter night." The Ritual Mass for Christian Initiation: Baptism (3) provides inserts for four eucharistic prayers. If you use Prayer I, there are additional inserts at the bottom of the page for "In union" and "Father, accept." The first alludes to this Easter night, the second to the newly baptized. But if there were baptisms tonight, take the text for "Father, accept" from the Ritual Mass for Christian Initiation: Baptism (3) as well, because it includes an additional line.

■ ACCLAMATIONS: You might start the new set of eucharistic acclamations for the Easter season. These will be used throughout the 50 days. If you choose "Dying you destroyed our death" as the memorial acclamation, you will find it matches well with the first Easter preface (P 21), whenever it is used throughout the season.

■ COMMUNION: Before saying, "This is the Lamb of God," the presider may briefly remind the neophytes of the preeminence of the eucharist, which is the climax of their initiation and the center of the whole Christian life (RCIA, 243). Prepare a text expressing the community's joy and welcome, while affirming the centrality of our belief in and celebration of the eucharist.

Use recently baked bread and a good wine.

Music for the communion procession might include Tom Parker's "Praise the Lord, my soul" (GIA, Gather or G-2395); a setting of Psalm 34 with the refrain "Taste and see the goodness of the Lord" (suggested by the *Circular Letter,* 91); Paul Hillenbrand's "Eucharistic Litany" (WLP, 520); "I Received the Living God" (*Worship* and GIA, G-3071) by Richard Proulx or the concertato version by Ellen Doerrfeld-Coman (WLP, 7215); Taizé's "Eat This Bread" (GIA, G-2840); or Michael Joncas's "Take and Eat" (GIA).

If there is a breakfast/reception for the neophytes and all who shared the Vigil, a blessing of the food may be given after communion (*Book of Blessings,* 54).

■ THE SOLEMN BLESSING suggested for this Mass does not appear where you expect it, probably because of space, but not with the intent of omitting it. You may find it easily by turning the page to the Mass for Easter Sunday. It also appears later in the sacramentary as the sixth solemn blessing in the set.

■ TONIGHT'S DISMISSAL calls for the double alleluia. Sing the traditional chant melody, a signature acclamation of Easter.

Your choir and brass ensemble can raise the rafters with Wallace Nolin's "Fanfare for Easter Morn" (WLP, 2330), based on familiar Easter hymns. See also "Descants for Easter" by Michael Joncas (WLP, 8513) and "Festival Hymns for Organ, Brass and Timpani," Set VI–General, by John Ferguson (GIA, G-5260).

OTHER IDEAS

Work to make the entire celebration a parish event. Perhaps involve different committees in some of the preparation and celebrations. Provide written materials in advance so that everyone knows the importance of the Vigil. Keep the names of the elect and candidates for reception before the community, and find ways to introduce them at parish events.

■ MAKE EASTER WATER AVAILABLE for people to take home tonight and tomorrow. Easter eggs and fresh flowers may be given to all as they leave or during breakfast. The eggs may have been colored by children from the community or by young Catholic candidates for confirmation.

The breakfast-reception after the eucharist follows a tradition revered among many ethnic groups.

◎20 #42; afternoon or evening
#46 white
Easter Sunday
SOLEMNITY

ORIENTATION

The resurrection of Jesus from the dead demonstrates God's ultimate power over all other forces, including death. By his resurrection, Jesus opens the door of eternity to all believers. The mystery of redemption, first intimated at the incarnation, reaches its purpose in the resurrection. Belief in the resurrection is the cornerstone of Christian faith.

Today concludes the celebration of the Triduum and begins the great 50 days. After 40 days of fast, we have 50 days of feast.

Some who celebrated the Vigil or who plan to celebrate the eucharist later today may wish to celebrate morning prayer together, or to join with other Christian churches in a sunrise service.

LECTIONARY

The Easter gospel is John's account of the resurrection, but you may also choose Mark's from the Vigil. For a Mass this afternoon or evening, you may even choose Luke's account of the journey to Emmaus. These passages mark the events of Easter Day—the resurrection in the early morning, an apparition in the late afternoon.

Today's psalm is a seasonal acclamation of joy proclaiming this day as the day the Lord has made, or on which God has acted. The psalm moves the celebration of Easter away from a mere historical remembrance to one of present participation. The mystery of God's promise is proclaimed in the adage about the rejected stone.

There are two choices for the second reading. The passage from Colossians tells the effect of Jesus' resurrection on the believer, and the expectations of the believer's behavior. From First Corinthians we hear a comparison between the celebrations of the resurrection and of Passover.

The Easter sequence is sung today. We have only a few such texts in the liturgy. A sequence is a hymn that follows the second reading and precedes the gospel for certain special occasions. Musical versions can also be found under its Latin title, "Victimae Paschali laudes." The original chant is in the *Liber cantualis.* World Library's *Psalms and Ritual Music* includes several simple, effective settings. Settings include ones by Peter Scagnelli (*Worship,*

#837), by Richard Proulx (GIA, G-3088), and by Ann Colleen Dohns (WLP, 5718), a setting with congregational refrains. The hymn uses Passover imagery to proclaim the news of resurrection.

The lectionary presents only one option for the first reading, a catechetical sermon that Peter gives in the house of Cornelius. In that talk, Peter proclaims the core of Christian belief, and the message of resurrection resounds loud and clear. Peter says the prophets testified that Jesus would rise, and that believers are now called to testify by preaching.

Together, these passages proclaim the nucleus of the gospel, the resurrection of Jesus, as well as its implications for the behavior of believers and their future glory.

SACRAMENTARY

Use incense today to lend solemnity to the celebration.

■ IN PLACE OF AN INTRODUCTION TO THE MASS, the presider might lengthen the greeting and say, "Alleluia! The Lord is truly risen! His grace and peace be with you all."

Even if you plan to celebrate the rite of sprinkling in place of the Penitential Rite throughout the Easter season, wait a week to begin. The sprinkling today occurs in conjunction with the renewal of baptismal promises.

■ BOTH OPENING PRAYERS acclaim the meaning of today's solemnity while invoking divine aid in the renewal of our lives.

■ PLAN THE GOSPEL PROCESSION with a solemnity that befits the day.

■ THE HOMILY provides an opportunity to proclaim hope because of resurrection. It is not the time to intimidate once-a-year churchgoers. John Chrysostom said,

"Come, you all: Enter into the joy of your Lord. You the first and you the last, receive alike your reward. You rich and you poor, dance together. You strong and you weak, celebrate the day. You who have kept the fast, and you who have not kept the fast, rejoice today." (See *Triduum Sourcebook,* 335.)

■ RENEWAL OF BAPTISMAL PROMISES: In the United States, the Creed is replaced with the renewal of baptismal promises. This gives everyone the opportunity to state their belief as answers to questions, in repetition of one of the key moments of the Easter Vigil. A variation on the renewal suitable for home use appears in *Catholic Household Blessings and Prayers* (372).

Sprinkle with holy water as at the Vigil. Assisting ministers may carry buckets or bowls filled with water from the font to accompany those who sprinkle. Fill the bowls from the font so that the association is clear. Use evergreen branches or the traditional aspergilla. Walk all around the church and sprinkle lavishly. Be sure everyone feels the water of rebirth. All sing "Vidi aquam" or another song of baptismal character. A rousing alleluia would also be serviceable here.

■ EUCHARIST: The first Easter preface should include the phrase "on this Easter day" (P 21). When Eucharistic Prayer I is used, you may include the special Easter forms of "In union" and "Father, accept." If there are infant baptisms at Mass on Easter Sunday, you may use the inserts to the eucharistic prayers found in the Ritual Mass for Christian Initiation: Baptism (3).

The suggested entrance and communion antiphons draw on several scripture texts that refer to the resurrection or use the image of rising.

■ THE DISMISSAL today includes a double alleluia. The chant deserves to be in the repertoire of every assembly.

You'll probably want to conclude the service with a hymn everyone knows, but if you want to add something simple but jazzy to the repertoire, check out the "Dismissal Amen" by Denise Pyles (WLP, 5238). It could be used almost any time of year, but the bouncy Hallelujahs make it a good choice for Easter.

BLESSING EASTER FOOD

The blessing of food links the Easter eucharistic table to the family table. Families may bring baskets of food including children's Easter baskets to any Mass, even the Vigil.

Set up tables and ask ushers to direct people to place their baskets there, especially at the Vigil when people arrive as darkness gathers. Alternatively, household members may keep baskets with them in their places and raise them up for the blessing prayer and sprinkling (although a crowded church makes this difficult).

According to the *Book of Blessings* (54), the Order of the Blessing of Food for the First Meal of Easter could take place after the prayer after communion. Sprinkle the baskets with water from the font.

OTHER IDEAS

■ HOSPITALITY: Give a spring flower to all as they leave Mass today. Easter eggs are a traditional gift with sacred significance. Offer coffee and hot cross buns after Mass, so everyone can socialize and rejoice in their faith. If your tendency is to abandon the weekly after-worship coffee-and-doughnuts today due to the demands of home and family, reconsider. Despite the large numbers of worshipers, this is an important occasion for hospitality. An Easter egg hunt can be held for children after Mass or in the afternoon before vespers.

The community may also gather for midday prayer and an Easter meal. The blessing of the first Easter meal may take place on this occasion. Or you can provide texts for people to bless the first Easter meal at home.

■ THE PARISH BULLETIN: Be sure plenty of information is available in this week's bulletin. Visitors may want to know what other opportunities they have to share in the community's life. The schedule for getting copy to the printer no doubt was unusual this past week, and the people who ordinarily provide copy were busy with other duties. That means that the Easter Sunday bulletin, to be done well, probably required attention weeks ago. Add that duty to next year's lenten calendar.

PASCHAL VESPERS

Evening prayer to conclude the Triduum is recommended in the *Circular Letter* (98), the *Ceremonial of Bishops* (371) and the *General Instruction of the Liturgy of the Hours* (213). It reconvenes the community and the neophytes to prolong the prayer of Easter joy.

■ A PRINCIPAL PASCHAL LITURGY: As the disciples met and touched the risen Lord and received their commission, so the church gathers this evening in the peace of the risen Christ to usher out the Triduum and to begin living within the 50 days, the foretaste of our return to paradise. Thanks to its history, some people regard Paschal Vespers, along with the Mass of the Lord's Supper, the celebration of the Lord's Passion

and the Easter Vigil, as a principal liturgy of the Triduum. Like these liturgies, evening prayer on Easter Sunday is an occasion for once-a-year rites.

Afterwards be sure to have Easter treats to share. Also traditional afterwards (and through the week) at sunset time is an "Emmaus Walk," a walk through the neighborhood in search of spring—and of Christ's presence in the world.

■ THIS LITURGY IS STATIONAL: Components may be celebrated in different locations (stations) within the church complex.

According to tradition the paschal candle remains burning uninterruptedly throughout Easter Sunday, from the Vigil until this evening. It burns as people gather for evening prayer.

Here is a suggested order of service (psalms, hymns and other music may be drawn from the parish's repertory):

- *gathering:* Assembly gathers near the paschal candle.

- *service of light:* V. Christ our light. R. Thanks be to God. Assembly's candles and all church candles are lit from the paschal candle.

- *hymn:* "At the Lamb's high feast" (The ancient melody for *Ad coenam Agni providi* /*Ad regias Agni dapes* is worth the effort to learn, although the metrical version set to the carol SONNE DER GERECHTIGKEIT (*Worship,* #460) is wonderful.)

- *thanksgiving for light,* sung by cantor or presider: For Easter texts, see GIA's *Praise God in Song* or *Worship: Liturgy of the Hours* (leader's edition). The assembly's candles may be extinguished as the lights needed for psalmody are turned on.

- *psalmody:* Sunday, Evening Prayer II, Week I. The psalms should be sung.

- *canticle* from Revelation or Psalm 114: During the canticle or psalm a congregational alleluia is repeated as cantors sing verses, and the assembly processes to the font, led by

incense-bearer, minister with paschal candle, and presider. Take the route used last night. Depending on the size and location of the baptistry, all remain there until after the baptismal commemoration or until the end of the service.

- *reading:* Luke 24:13–35 (#46) or Luke 24:35–48 (#47)

- *patristic selection* from the Easter octave texts in the *Liturgy of the Hours,* or a brief homily on symbols of Easter, or silent prayer and reflection

- *sung responsory* as at Morning Prayer: "This is the day"

- *thanksgiving over the water* (adapt RCIA, 222 D or E) or form C of the rite of sprinkling in the sacramentary

- *signing:* All approach the font to sign themselves or each other while singing the antiphon, as at the blessing of water at the Vigil.

- *canticle of Mary:* sung with proper antiphon while all are honored with incense. Procession to the altar may take place during the canticle.

- *intercessions* from *Liturgy of the Hours*

- *Lord's Prayer*

- *concluding prayer* of Easter Sunday

- *solemn blessing*

- *dismissal:* Easter tone with double alleluia

- *closing hymn:* "Come, Ye Faithful, Raise the Strain" (*Worship,* #456) or "The Day of Resurrection" (*Hymnal 1982,* #210) Or, although this would be proper to night prayer, close with the Marian antiphon for the Easter season, "Regina caeli."

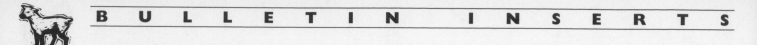

APRIL 17, 2003
Holy Thursday of the Supper of the Lord

The Night of Remembrance
Isaiah 61:1–3a, 6a, 8b–9
"It is the Passover of the LORD."

THE story of Passover is ugly. God's chosen people had been reduced to slavery in Egypt under Pharaoh's intolerable leadership. A series of plagues failed to soften Pharaoh's heart. A final, ghastly plague threatened to kill the first-born sons of Egypt. The Israelites slaughtered lambs, ate the flesh and sprinkled the blood on their doorposts. God's avenging angel committed the threatened homicides, but passed over the homes of the Israelites. They won their freedom, but it wasn't pretty.

As we enter the Triduum, the sacred three days, we remember this terrible story. Only a word of liberation could quiet the wails of sorrow. We hear this account again with all its horror and all its hope.

The church invites you into these three days unafraid of what terror you may know. You have suffered pain. You have grieved loss. You have known despair. You have tried to forgive. The dreadfulness of your story does not matter. This community gathers with you to remember and pray.

There are moments in life we would rather forget—moments of sin, moments of suffering. But there is a safe time to remember. That time is this holy night.

Written by Paul Turner. © 2002 Archdiocese of Chicago, Liturgy Training Publications; 1-800-933-1800; www.ltp.org.

APRIL 18, 2003
Good Friday of the Lord's Passion

What Wondrous Love Is This?
Isaiah 52:13—53:12
"Like a lamb led to the slaughter . . ."

HEROES risk their own lives to save someone else. Some of them live to hear accolades. Others die in the struggle. As a witness to the power of life even in death, the one who risks life for another can bring healing beyond measure.

Who has done this for you? Who raised you in the weakness of your infancy? Who taught you in a spirit of service? Who kept you from getting into trouble? Who fought for the safety of your land? Who saved your life when you were in danger? Who has redeemed you?

Isaiah recognizes a servant of God known for heroism. God laid the guilt of the people upon this servant, and the servant suffered chastisement for their sake. Christians see in Isaiah's testimony a description of Jesus: "Because he surrendered himself to death, he shall take away the sins of many."

On Good Friday we remember the wondrous love of God, whose Son suffered death so that we might have life. Jesus stands tall among the models of heroism. His death brought healing beyond measure.

Whenever you accept responsibility, whenever you admit blame, whenever you risk your popularity or your very life, you love like a hero. You love like Jesus.

Written by Paul Turner. © 2002 Archdiocese of Chicago, Liturgy Training Publications; 1-800-933-1800; www.ltp.org.

APRIL 19, 2003
The Vigil in the Holy Night of Easter

Cooperating with Resurrection
Exodus 14:15—15:1
"The Israelites marched through the midst of the sea."

ISRAEL'S exodus from Egypt tells of God's power. You remember the story. The Israelites had worked as slaves in Egypt, but God told Moses to go tell Pharaoh to let the people go. Pharaoh resisted. God sent ten plagues. After the last, the death of the firstborn sons, Pharaoh relented. The people fled.

Then Pharaoh changed his mind and sent his armies in pursuit of Israel. At evening they caught up with each other at the Red Sea. God kept Egyptians and Israelites separate throughout a watch night filled with anxiety. Then at dawn the waters of the sea stood like a wall to let Israel pass through the midst, but the waters closed upon Pharaoh's forces. God set Israel free.

This is not a story of God's power alone. It is also a story of how God used the people to cooperate in their own freedom.

The first words we hear from God in this story are surprising: "Why are you crying out to me?" God does not do this work alone. "Tell the Israelites to go forward." Tell the people to do something. "And you," God says directly to Moses, "with hand outstretched over the sea, split the sea in two."

This Easter we celebrate God's power in raising Christ from death and in rescuing us from sin. But God desires our cooperation if our freedom from sin is to stick.

Split the sea in two!

Written by Paul Turner. © 2002 Archdiocese of Chicago, Liturgy Training Publications; 1-800-933-1800; www.ltp.org.

APRIL 20, 2003
Easter Sunday of the Resurrection of the Lord

All Is New
Acts 10:34a, 37–43
"God raised Jesus on the third day."

WHAT'S new? That's what we ask when we want to hear a story. Stories celebrate the great moments of life. When you hear one, it fills you with delight. When you tell one, you fulfill an inner desire to share what has shaped your life anew.

After Jesus rose from the dead, the disciples did not wait for people to ask, What's new? They proudly proclaimed it: "God raised Jesus on the third day and granted that he be visible to us witnesses." Now, that's new!

If you have kept a good Lent, you know very well what is new with you. You are what is new! You have faced your sin, admitted your fault, and accepted your dependence on God's help. You have prayed and fasted with the commu-

nity. You have loved your neighbor. Because you have emptied a place inside yourself, you have created a space for God's Spirit to enter. Christ is risen indeed, and he has appeared to you! You are now a witness of all that God can do.

This Easter Day, tell your story. Tell your faith. Let joy radiate from your face and loosen your tongue. Jesus lives!

Written by Paul Turner. © 2002 Archdiocese of Chicago, Liturgy Training Publications; 1-800-933-1800; www.ltp.org.

These inserts may be reproduced in parish bulletins; the copyright notice must appear with the text.

EASTER

The Meaning

CHRIST is risen! Alleluia!

The resurrection has made all things new. No matter the sorrows of the human heart, the victory over sin and death has been accomplished. The hope and promise of that message is the central belief of Christianity. It takes 50 days to celebrate the resurrection of Jesus and its implications for humanity. One week is not enough. A week of weeks is not enough. It takes seven times seven days, plus one. A fullness of time observes the fullness of Easter.

■ THROUGHOUT THIS SEASON THE CHURCH REJOICES WITH THOSE BAPTIZED AT EASTER. They bring new life, new awareness, deeper prayer and renewed service to the community.

■ THE EASTER SEASON GENERALLY COINCIDES WITH THE NORTHERN HEMISPHERE'S SPRING. Easter Day comes every year on the Sunday following the first full moon of spring. We enter a natural season of new life and rebirth. As nature flowers around us, Christians enter its spirit.

The season will conclude with Pentecost, the fiftieth day. The feast of Pentecost already existed in the Jewish calendar. The coming of the Holy Spirit on that day allowed Christians to compare the giving of the covenant to Moses on the first Pentecost with the Christian sending of the Spirit on the new Pentecost. Some writers in the early church referred to the whole season of Easter as "Pentecost"—the Fifty Days.

The Saints

■ THE SOLEMNITIES OF EASTER, ASCENSION AND PENTECOST ANCHOR THE SEASON. But in the weeks ahead we will have ample opportunity to celebrate all the more. The octave of Easter itself ranks as a week of solemnities.

The date of the Ascension varies throughout the United States. In some regions it falls on a Thursday, the fortieth day of Easter, in keeping with the tradition from Acts of the Apostles. This year, that will be May 29, a few days after Memorial Day. In other areas it is transferred to replace the Seventh Sunday of Easter, so that more of the faithful may celebrate the feast. This year, that will be June 1.

■ ALL FEASTS recall people and events of the first century. The ones this season include the apostles Philip and James, Matthias the apostle, and the Visitation. The celebration of these days will replace the readings and prayers of the current day in the Easter season. Mark normally appears on April 25, but his celebration is suppressed this year due to the Easter octave.

■ WHEN AN OBLIGATORY MEMORIAL OCCURS DURING EASTER, its vestment color and presidential prayers take precedence over the Easter weekday. This year Catherine of Siena (April 29), Athanasius (May 2), Philip Neri (May 26), Charles Lwanga and companions (June 3), and Boniface (June 5) fall into this category. The preface may be drawn from the Easter weekday or from the relevant common of martyrs, pastors, doctors, virgins or holy men and women. The scriptures could be taken from the lectionary common appropriate for the saint, but most communities will benefit from observing the Easter lectionary, as the guidelines advise. (See *Introduction to the Lectionary for Mass,* 8.)

■ SEVERAL OPTIONAL MEMORIALS occur on Easter weekdays this year. Your community may elect to celebrate the Mass of the Easter weekday or of the saint whose memorial is optional.

If you wish to remember the saint of the day without eclipsing the season of Easter, consider using the saint's opening prayer as the conclusion to the general intercessions.

■ OTHER CELEBRATIONS: The liturgical books also supply texts for votive Masses and for Masses for various needs and occasions. These texts may be used during Easter only for some real need or pastoral advantage.

The Lectionary

THE Easter lectionary hugs the New Testament tightly, even on Sundays. We close the Old Testament for 50 days. The only exceptions are the daily responsorial psalm and the readings at the Pentecost vigil. In the lectionary the psalms bring the scriptures into the living, praying community that hears them. They bring us into the eternal dialogue between God and the covenanted people, mediated by the divine Word.

■ DURING THE OCTAVE OF EASTER, the gospels consistently announce the resurrection through stories of the appearances of the risen Jesus. Easter Day and its octave celebrate the resurrection in history as well as the resurrected Christ present in our midst. This week brings us not so much eight solemnities, one after another, but one eight-day-long solemnity.

■ THE WEEKDAY LECTIONARY otherwise features the semicontinuous reading of Acts of the Apostles and selections from John's gospel that open wider the mystery of the resurrection. During the final "octave" of the season, the week or more between Ascension and Pentecost, the readings continue their pattern, but the weekday psalms all sing of God's sovereignty, an Ascension theme.

■ THE GOSPELS FOR THE SUNDAYS OF EASTER EACH YEAR follow a predictable pattern. Easter Sunday, of course, features the gospel of the resurrection, and the following Sunday tells of the events "eight days later."

The Third Sunday reveals some aspect of the community's mission, while the Fourth draws on the tenth chapter of John that develops the image of Jesus as the Good Shepherd. The Fifth, Sixth and Seventh Sundays all take gospel passages from the final discourse and prayer of Jesus from John's account of the Last Supper.

■ THE FIRST AND SECOND READINGS: In the three-year cycle for the Easter season, all first readings come from Acts of the Apostles and the second readings feature one other New Testament book. This year, that book will be the First Letter of John.

Several New Testament books are attributed to John: the gospel, three letters, and Revelation. More likely, they come from the authors of a Johannine school. The first of the letters is the longest of the three, but it carries no epistolary salutation or conclusion, and the writer is not identified. It reaches out to an early Christian community and develops some very basic themes about Christ and the church that can be used effectively in mystagogic preaching.

■ THE SUNDAY *LECTIONARY FOR MASSES WITH CHILDREN* remains very faithful to the full lectionary, while abbreviating many of the longer readings. The only readings completely omitted are the second reading on the Third Sunday of Easter and the alternative second reading for Ascension. On Pentecost, only the readings for the Mass During the Day appear.

Fittingly, during the Easter season, the children's lectionary aims to do something special for the children. It offers them all three readings as one way of making this season holy.

The Sacramentary

■ NOTICE THE ATTENTION GIVEN TO THE OCTAVE OF EASTER. The gospels tell the resurrection appearances. The Easter sequence may be sung every day. In addition, each day is treated as a solemnity (*General Norms for the Liturgical Year and Calendar,* 24), and it ranks even above other feasts and solemnities. This is why St. Mark's day will not be observed this year. As a solemnity, each day calls for the Glory to God. Ordinarily, solemnities also call for the Creed (GIRM, 43), and the octave of Easter used to have it each day, but the present sacramentary has dropped the Creed from these days without explanation.

Throughout the Easter octave the first preface of Easter (P 21) may be used with the expression "on this Easter day," because every day of the octave is one with the paschal festival. The inserts to Eucharistic Prayer I may also be included. This is especially fitting if the newly baptized join the community for the daily eucharist. This custom, much encouraged in the history of the catechumenate, is urged nowhere in the *Rite of Christian Initiation of Adults.* But Mass texts like these still presume that neophytes are present for the eucharist every day for a week.

During the octave the double alleluia is added to the dismissal dialogue. If your community has not yet learned the traditional chant, this week provides an opportunity for instruction.

The octave celebrates time outside of time, a week eight days in length, a celebration that earthly time cannot measure. (Even John Lennon and Paul McCartney recognized that some love was so powerful it had to be given eight days a week.) Because of the historical interest in celebrating this week with neophytes, and the way the sacramentary texts support the former custom, you might schedule one or more evening Masses this week. Let the neophytes meet more members of the community. Swap stories. Show a video of the Vigil. And do mystagogy: Talk about the symbols of that holy night, about what they expressed and about what the neophytes experienced.

■ THE BLESSING AND SPRINKLING OF HOLY WATER MAY REPLACE THE PENITENTIAL RITE ON ANY SUNDAY. The Easter season provides an excellent opportunity for this option. Many communities sprinkle the assembly throughout the season, to highlight the symbol of baptismal water. The rite even provides a special blessing for the Easter season (C). Note the option for blessing salt to be added to the water. The prayer quotes an episode in the life of Elisha (2 Kings 2:19–22), a reference that unfortunately appears nowhere in the lectionary.

If you choose to use Penitential Rite C at any time in the season, options v, vi and vii rely on Easter themes.

■ A SAMPLE FORMULA FOR THE GENERAL INTERCESSIONS can be found in the sacramentary's first appendix. Prayers for the Easter season are at #8.

■ BESIDES P 21, OTHER EASTER PREFACES (P 22–25) may be used throughout the season. Although these additional prefaces were not found in the Roman Missal immediately before the Second Vatican Council, they all have antecedents in the liturgy prior to the eighth century.

For Ambrosian Rite prefaces, see Alan Griffiths's translations in *We Give You Thanks and Praise* (Roman P 22 resembles the one for Easter Friday, P 23 for Saturday 3 of Easter, P 27 for Wednesday 7 of Easter).

■ IN ADDITION TO THE INSERTS FOR THE EASTER OCTAVE, Eucharistic Prayer I provides texts for Ascension and Pentecost.

■ THE SOLEMN BLESSING for the Easter season is the seventh in the sacramentary's collection. It appears on the page, strangely, only for the even-numbered Sundays of the Easter season. Various prayers over the people appear on the other Sundays. But you may use the solemn blessing throughout the season.

At weekday Masses early in the season, consider prayers over the people #3, 14 and 18. Later, try #20, 23 and 24.

The Book of Blessings

SOME seasonal blessings should be noted. Homes may be blessed during the Easter season (50), and the first meal of Easter has its own blessing (54), as previously indicated. The blessing of homes could be difficult to organize, but it could also draw the community together. All pastoral ministers could be involved because the church provides forms for blessings offered by lay ministers.

■ MOTHER'S DAY will fall during this season and its blessing might conclude the general intercessions or replace the solemn blessing for its Sunday.

See also the blessings for mothers before and after childbirth (1-VIII), students and teachers (5), a new building site (10), fields and flocks (26), seeds at planting time (27), a new baptistery or font (31), holy water (41), religious articles (44), rosaries (45) and scapulars (46). For other materials contact the National Catholic Rural Life Conference, 4625 SW Beaver Drive, Des Moines IA 50310, www.ncrlc.com, NCRLC@aol.com.

The Rite of Christian Initiation of Adults

■ EASTER IS THE SEASON FOR MYSTAGOGY OF THE NEOPHYTES. The *Rite of Christian Initiation of Adults* gives precious little information about this (244–251). Primarily, the newly baptized are to continue formation through their experience of the sacraments (245). Postbaptismal catechesis is to involve the faithful as well (246).

The homily and general intercessions "should take into account the presence and needs of the neophytes" (248). Homilies that unfold the primary mysteries of creation, resurrection, baptism, eucharist and community will foster good mystagogy.

Other Sacraments of Initiation

■ CONFIRMATION: Easter may be the season in which confirmation is celebrated for Catholics baptized as infants. The sacrament may be offered any day of the year, but some bishops and diocesan worship offices prefer to schedule them during Easter as much as possible.

Celebrations should stress the gift of the Holy Spirit, not the achievement of candidates. Provide a generous amount of chrism to encourage a liberal anointing. Arrange the ministers in a way that the assembly of the faithful can see the faces of the candidates.

Avoid the use of stoles on those being confirmed. Stoles are vesture reserved for priests and deacons. The wearing of baptismal garments is entirely appropriate for those being confirmed or those being initiated in any other way—the word *candidate* comes from a Latin word meaning "clothed in shining garments."

■ FIRST COMMUNIONS ALSO MAY TAKE PLACE DURING THE EASTER SEASON. There is no universal rite of first communion, nor any recommended time of year for its celebration. Whenever the children are ready, they may join the community at the holy table.

Some parishes celebrate a special first communion Mass, apart from the regular schedule. Others incorporate the first communions—perhaps in smaller groups—into the regular Sunday celebration to honor the individual readiness of the children and to allow the whole community to rejoice with the children. In this way, first communions may appear at Sunday Mass just as catechumenate rites, baptisms and special blessings do. They keep the whole community together for important events.

The Liturgy of the Hours

Parishes are encouraged to make at least morning and evening prayer available year round. If you honored this practice during the season of Lent, it may continue throughout Easter. Some communities open evening prayer by lighting the Easter candle and repeating the Vigil's dialogue, "Light of Christ," "Thanks be to God." A special evening prayer for Pentecost will close the day and the season with appropriate festivity.

Changes in the psalms for the office of readings, begun during Lent, continue throughout Easter.

Among the fine passages in the office of readings for Easter, see Augustine's sermon for the Easter octave, where he addresses the newly baptized as "a holy seed, a new colony of bees, the very flower of our ministry and fruit of our toil, my joy and my crown."

During the octave of Easter and on the day of Pentecost, the double alleluia concludes the dismissal dialogue, as at Mass. For examples of notation, see the first and third examples in the sacramentary under Easter Vigil, 56. The Episcopal church keeps this double alleluia in all dismissals during the 50 Days.

To conclude night prayer throughout the season, sing "Regina cæli" from the *Liber cantualis*.

The Rite of Penance

Because of Lent's strong penitential character, few parishes emphasize the sacrament of reconciliation during the Easter season. Still, it is important for the community to know when the celebration happens. Some may have experienced new birth and spiritual insight as a result of this holy time of year. They may appreciate another opportunity for a communal celebration. The newly baptized need not be rushed into the celebration of the sacrament, because baptism has cleansed them for sin. But they may want to seek the opportunity to celebrate this sacrament sometime during this season, to further their experience of the Catholic way of life.

If you have a communal celebration of this sacrament during the Easter season, it would keep the spirit of the lectionary to draw the readings from the New Testament.

The Pastoral Care of the Sick

Once again, there is no season especially appropriate for this sacrament, but a communal celebration could happen during Easter. The Mass of chrism has provided a fresh stock of oil for the community, and it could be offered to the sick as a way of entering into the hope of Easter. Whenever celebrating this sacrament, or even in visiting the sick, prayer should include scripture. In keeping with the spirit of the lectionary, texts from the New Testament are most appropriate throughout the Easter season.

The Rite of Marriage

If a wedding takes place during the Mass of any solemnity (including the morning or early afternoon of Easter Saturday, April 26), or on any Saturday evening of this season (anticipating the Sunday liturgy), the readings and prayers for the day take precedence. Only one reading may come from the Mass of marriage. Throughout this season, the couple is not free to select completely alternative scripture passages for the wedding Mass unless it takes place on a weekday of lesser rank or before evening on any Saturday except April 26. The nuptial blessing, of course, is included no matter which Mass is celebrated.

If the wedding does not include a Mass, or if the wedding Mass does not take place on a solemnity, a Saturday night or a Sunday, the scriptures and prayers for marriage may be used. When choosing scripture texts, keep in mind the lectionary's preference to draw all the readings from the New Testament.

The Order of Christian Funerals

BOTH the Order of Christian Funerals and the sacramentary provide texts for a funeral during the Easter season. The sacramentary collects them under Masses for the Dead, Funeral Masses: During the Easter Season (C). The Order of Christian Funerals offers an opening prayer for a funeral Mass (164 D). The communion prayer during the Easter season from the sacramentary can also be found at 410 C, and will avoid the presider's need to switch books hastily at the end of the funeral Mass.

Even though the weekdays of the octave of Easter are treated as solemnities, the church does permit the substitution of the scriptures and prayers assigned for these days with those for a funeral Mass. Still, you may suggest that the bereaved family and friends hear the scriptures of the day, because they will eloquently proclaim the resurrection. You might conclude the rite of committal with a double alleluia during the Easter octave (223). If a funeral takes place at a Mass on a Sunday of the Easter season or on Ascension, however, the Mass of the day is celebrated and the funeral rites are included.

The Art and Environment

■ GIVE ATTENTION TO THE OUTDOORS. Let people driving by know that Easter is underway. Bunting and banners, maypoles and streamers, springtime wreaths are all possible.

■ FOR INSIDE DECORATIONS consult *The Sacristy Manual* (220) and *To Crown the Year* (122–152).

■ THE EASTER CANDLE deserves a commanding place near the ambo throughout the season. It returns to the font after evening prayer of Pentecost. Tall and stately, it should acclaim that Christ is the light of the world. Be sure it is lit for absolutely every service that takes place during the 50 days. Decorate the stand for the season.

■ WHEREVER THE FONT IS LOCATED, draw attention to it with flowers, lighting or some other means. If you used a temporary font to make Easter baptisms visible to the assembly, you may keep it for the 50 days, as long as its impermanence and construction does not distract from celebration. Better to make plans for a permanent, visible font.

An old custom invites neophytes to attend the eucharist during the octave of Easter, dressed in their white garments. They and their godparents may have a special place reserved throughout the season, perhaps near the font, the ambo or the candle. Decorate that area accordingly (RCIA, 248).

■ FLOWERS ARE "DISCOURAGED IN LENT, DEMANDED BY EASTER" (*To Crown the Year,* 149–152). If you blanket the altar and sanctuary area with lilies on Easter Sunday, have something in reserve to make it through the 50 days. Wilting flowers do not proclaim Easter promise. Peter Mazar suggests backyard flowers—perhaps flowering plum, apple and pear blossoms. Create a mood of festivity and anticipation.

Your procession cross could also be festooned during the Easter season. As it enters the liturgical space, it will announce the excitement of Easter.

If you use incense only on occasion, the Easter season is about as good an occasion as you will find.

■ AS MAY BEGINS, YOU MAY DECORATE THE IMAGE OF MARY. If your community is planning a crowning of Mary this month, consult the Order of Crowning an Image of the Blessed Virgin Mary. Rather than adding a litany or a decade of the rosary to the eucharist, plan a prayer service to honor Our Lady, including hymns and readings from scripture. For good texts, see the common of the Blessed Virgin Mary in the sacramentary, lectionary and *Liturgy of the Hours,* as well as the *Collection of Masses of the Blessed Virgin Mary.*

Beware of moving a statue front and center for the month if it would compete with the altar, ambo and Easter candle. It is better to decorate the image where it usually stands.

The Music

ONE word should predominate: Alleluia! Choose hymns and songs that let it resound throughout the 50 days.

Instrumentalists who have abstained from preludes and postludes during the previous season can offer their assemblies many delights throughout Easter. Organists can play stately trumpet voluntaries. The literature is expansive, but don't overlook choral preludes by J. S. Bach and Flor Peters, or the flashy toccatas by Widor and Vierne. Easter is the season to let the organ thrill its listeners.

■ THE SPRINKLING WITH HOLY WATER provides a good instance for the assembly's song. "Vidi aquam" from the *Liber cantualis* is a Gregorian chant written for the occasion. See also Howard Hughes's "You Have Put on Christ" (GIA, G-2283), David Hurd's "Vidi aquam" (GIA, G-2512) and Michael Ward's "I Saw Water Flowing" (WLP, 8548).

■ GLORY TO GOD: Easter is another good season for singing the Glory to God. If your community does not sing this hymn year round, now is the time to build the repertoire. Use the version from the Vigil throughout the season. Consult the musical selections in your worship aid.

■ THE COMMON PSALMS for the season of Easter are 118 and 66. Check the scripture index of your community's hymnal for suggestions. See settings of 118 by Michael Joncas in *Psalms for the Cantor,* volume 1 (World Library); by Richard

Proulx (GIA, G-1964); by Christopher Willcock in *Psalms for Feasts and Seasons* (The Liturgical Press); by Christopher Walker and by Scott Soper (OCP); by Hal H. Hopson in *10 Psalms* (Hope, HH 3930); and by Bob Hurd (OCP, 9458).

The refrain to all the responsorial psalms for the Sundays and weekdays in Easter may also be "Alleluia." *By Flowing Waters* contains 46 such "Alleluia" psalms, set to just six melodies for ease of memorization (160, 161, 169 and 170).

■ THE EASTER SEQUENCE can be sung in its original chant, or in some English adaptations. See the suggestions above at Easter Sunday.

■ THE GOSPEL ACCLAMATION should stand out throughout the season. The refrain of "O filii et filiae" is a perfect choice. See John Schiavone's version for Easter, Ascension and Pentecost (GIA, G-1262). Robert Hutmacher has a "Gospel Processional" (GIA, G-2450), J. Biery has a "Gospel Fanfare for Easter Morning" (GIA, G-2719) and Jeremy Young has verses for each Sunday of Easter (GIA, G-3175).

■ FOR THE EUCHARISTIC ACCLAMATIONS, choose festival settings with parts for brass and percussion, like Richard Proulx's "Festival Eucharist" (*Worship* or GIA, G-1960), Paul Inwood's "Coventry Acclamations" (OCP, 7117), Christopher Walker's "Festival Mass" (OCP, 7154) and Carrol T. Andrews's simpler "Easter Carol Mass" (GIA, G-1398).

In the Episcopal church, in place of the "Lamb of God" may be sung, "Alleluia. Christ our Passover is sacrificed for us; therefore let us keep the feast. Alleluia."

■ COMMUNION SONGS for the season may include Suzanne Toolan's "I Am the Bread of Life" (see Rory Cooney's arrangement, GIA, G-5016) and Richard Hillert's "Worthy Is Christ." Taizé offers "Surrexit Christus" and "Christus Resurrexit" (*Music from Taizé,* volume II; GIA, G-2788). Bob Hurd (*Gather*) and Michael Ward (WLP, 7950) offer pieces called "In the Breaking of the Bread."

■ EASTER HYMNODY could include "The Strife Is O'er;" "Hail Thee, Festival Day"; "Come, Ye Faithful, Raise the Strain"; "At the Lamb's High Feast"; "Now the Green Blade Rises" (note Hal H. Hopson's setting: GIA, G-3443); "This Joyful Eastertide"; and "That Easter Day with Joy Was Bright." Michael Joncas wrote a set of descants for six popular Easter hymns (WLP, 8513). See also Brian Wren and Carl Johengen's fine hymn, "At the Table of the World" (WLP, 2612).

Let the parish choir work up a motet like "One Fold, One Shepherd" for two-part choir, by Russell Woolen (WLP, 660), or the Hans Leo Hassler, "Quia vidisti me, Thoma" for four-part choir (WLP, 5778), especially fitting for the Second Sunday of Easter.

Your youth choir could lead everyone in a rousing rendition of John Angotti's "He Is Risen" (WLP, 7362). *With One Voice* (Augsburg/Fortress, 1995) has "There in God's Garden"; "Come Away to the Skies, My Beloved, Arise"; "Christ Is Risen! Shout Hosanna!"; and "Alleluia! Jesus Is Risen!" Ed Bolduc's setting of Psalm 16, "Show Us Your Way, Lord" (WLP, 7358) is worth learning.

The children's choir may enjoy "We Receive Power" (WLP, 7113) or "Jesus, Bread of Life" (WLP, 7855) by James V. Marchionda.

The United Church of Christ's *New Century Hymnal* has "Because You Live, O Christ, the Garden of the World Has Come to Flower"; "These Things Did Thomas Count as Real"; and "At the Font We Start Our Journey, In the Easter Faith Baptized." Hal H. Hopson has a bouncy setting of the Caribbean song "Halle, Halle, Halle" (MA 503, Hope Publishing Company). John Angotti's "On a Journey Together" might call to mind the story of Emmaus (WLP, 7482). Jerry Galipeau's "On the Wings of Change" will stir up Easter faith (WLP, 5209).

GIA's *Hymnal for the Hours* has "Sing of One Who Walks Beside Us" and *Worship* offers "Daylight Fades."

Music for Mary will be requested during the month of May. Let choirs sing a chant "Ave Maria" from the *Liber cantualis;* "Ave Maria" by David Conte (Schirmer, 4729); "Ave, Maria" by Lisa L. Stafford (WLP, 8695); and "O Mary of Graces" as arranged by William Ferris, with a text by Alan J. Hommerding.

Mary, Mother of God (362), and baptismal promises and creeds (371).

LTP's *Take Me Home* and *Take Me Home, Too* both contain activity pages for families for each week of the season.

Texts

■ GREETING: The sacramentaries of other language groups suggest,

> The grace of the Lord Jesus, who was raised for us, be with you.

■ INTRODUCTION TO THE PENITENTIAL RITE:

> Christ our hope is risen! Let us call to mind our sins.

■ RESPONSE TO THE GENERAL INTERCESSIONS:

> Risen Savior, hear our prayer.
> Hear us, Christ our Light.

■ DISMISSAL OF CATECHUMENS:

> My brothers and sisters, the love of God is this, that we keep the commandments. Go in peace that you may come to love the command of God.

The United Church of Canada recommends this prayer from India, among others, for the Easter season, in *Celebrate God's Presence:*

> Servant Christ,
> help us to follow you out of the dark tomb,
> to share daily your resurrection life,
> to be renewed daily in your image of love,
> to be used daily as your new Body
> in your service to the world.
> Servant Christ, help us to follow you. [8G006]

The Parish and Home

SEE *Catholic Household Blessings and Prayers* for a blessing at table (84), of the home (153), of children before confirmation (230) or first communion (231), for Mother's Day (197), as well as prayers for fields and gardens (166) and a prayer to complete the Easter season on the Solemnity of Pentecost (157). See also the prayers for the holy eucharist (359), in honor of

April

MON 21 #261 (LMC #185–192) white
Easter Monday
SOLEMNITY

Today begins the semicontinuous reading of Acts of the Apostles, the book that contributes the first reading virtually every day of the Easter season. The story opens today in the second chapter, on Pentecost Day, as Peter delivers a sermon about a Christian's central belief. He preaches about Psalm 16, which becomes today's responsory, and which followed the second reading of the Easter Vigil.

The gospel today begins a week-long march through the accounts of the resurrection appearances. They all agree on some points and disagree on other details. The events were so important and so different from anything else in history that the stories have been handed down to us in their unreconciled exuberance. We start in Matthew with Jesus' appearance to the women at the tomb and the gossip spread by the bribed guards.

Today's liturgy calls for the Glory to God. The sequence is optional, but by using it you will set the octave apart from other days in noble joy. The Creed is not said, probably to avoid its overuse during the week. Use the first Easter preface (P 21) with the phrase "on this Easter day." If you use Eucharistic Prayer I, include the special forms of "In union" and "Father, accept." The solemn blessing for Easter (#6) would be appropriate. Conclude the dismissal with a double alleluia. A community gathered for daily Mass this week should be able to build a musical repertoire of many of these elements, including the sequence and the solemn Easter dismissal.

In the opening prayer, note the reference to the neophytes, new members giving the church constant growth.

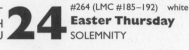

TUE 22 #262 (LMC #185–192) white
Easter Tuesday
SOLEMNITY

Peter concludes his Pentecost sermon, and the people ask how they should respond. Peter invites them to reform their lives, and three thousand step up for baptism. The psalm says that the earth is full of God's goodness, a belief evident to the early church from the numbers of those accepting Jesus.

John's gospel recounts Jesus' appearance to Mary Magdalene. She, the apostle to the apostles, brings the Good News.

Sing the Glory to God and the sequence. Omit the Creed. Use the inserts for the first Easter preface and Eucharistic Prayer I. Give the solemn Easter blessing (#6). Dismiss with the double alleluia.

In the communion prayer today we pray for the newly baptized.

WED 23 #263 (LMC #185–192) white
Easter Wednesday
SOLEMNITY

Peter and John cure a disabled man by the beautiful gate of the temple. They have already proclaimed the power of Jesus Christ. Now they demonstrate the power of his name, active still in the community. The psalm opens with the command to "invoke the name" of the Lord.

One of the most beloved stories of Easter is the resurrection appearance to the disciples on the road to Emmaus. Its two parts—discussion of scripture and breaking of bread—foreshadow the way the Christian community will celebrate its eucharist.

The suggested communion antiphon comes from today's gospel.

The Glory to God is obligatory. The sequence is optional. The Creed is omitted. Use the inserts for the first Easter preface and Eucharistic Prayer I if that prayer is your choice today. Give the solemn Easter blessing (6) if

you like. Dismiss with the double alleluia.

THU 24 #264 (LMC #185–192) white
Easter Thursday
SOLEMNITY

In the glow of the miraculous cure, Peter preaches another sermon, this time building upon the guilt of his hearers to accept Jesus as the one whom the prophets foretold. The name of God is praised again in today's psalm.

We hear Luke's sequel to the Emmaus story. While the disciples tell the others what they witnessed, Jesus appears and opens their minds to the scriptures.

Today's opening prayer and prayer over the gifts refer again to the newly baptized.

The Glory to God is sung. Try singing the optional sequence today and throughout the week. Use the insert for the first Easter preface and those in Eucharistic Prayer I if those are your choices today. The solemn Easter blessing (6) would be appropriate. The dismissal dialogue includes the double alleluia.

FRI 25 #265 (LMC #185–192) white
Easter Friday
SOLEMNITY

Peter and John are put in jail after their sermon. (Today's preachers hope their listeners don't get the same idea.) In spite of efforts to silence the word of God, five thousand put their faith in Jesus. Even on trial, Peter finds a way to preach, using a text from Psalm 118, which serves as today's responsory.

Jesus appears to the disciples again, this time by the Sea of Tiberias, fills them with joy, and cooks them some fish.

The octave continues. Sing the Glory to God. Include the sequence if you like. When singing the first Easter preface, remember this is still "Easter day" not "Easter season." If you are using Eucharistic

Prayer I you may include its inserts, one of which presumes the newly baptized are present. You may use the solemn Easter blessing (6) again. Dismiss with the double alleluia.

The suggested communion antiphon comes from today's gospel. The communion prayer is offered for those "saved" in Christ, the newly baptized.

■ THE GUATEMALAN MEMORIAL of Blessed Hermano Pedro of San José de Bethancourt is not observed this year.

S A T 26
#266 (LMC #185–192)　white
Easter Saturday
SOLEMNITY

The court recognizes that Peter and John receive their power not from education but from their experience of Jesus. They ask them to remain silent, but they will continue to proclaim what they have heard and seen. The responsory takes additional verses from yesterday's psalm of deliverance.

All week long the lectionary has presented the resurrection appearances in a kind of reconstructed chronological order. We conclude the series today with "the longer ending" of Mark's gospel. Mark's original probably ended with verse 8, and scholars believe today's passage, a pastiche of several other stories we have heard this week, was added later to give the gospel a more coherent close.

Sing the Glory to God. You may also sing the sequence. Use the inserts for the preface and eucharistic prayer (#I) and invoke the solemn Easter blessing (#6), if you like. Dismiss with the double alleluia.

The opening prayer remembers the newly baptized. You could conclude the general intercessions today with a prayer from the Mass titled "Holy Mary, Fountain

of Light and Life," from the *Collection of Masses of the Blessed Virgin Mary* (16). It would blend the themes of Mary on Saturday, and baptism.

If there is a wedding Mass this morning or early afternoon, it should use the readings of today's solemnity. One reading may be substituted from the lectionary for Masses of marriage.

■ TODAY'S GUATEMALAN OPTIONAL MEMORIAL of Isidore the bishop (+ 636), April 4 on most other calendars, is not observed this year.

27
#44 (LMC #38)　white
**Second Sunday of Easter
Octave of Easter**
SOLEMNITY

ORIENTATION

Today's celebration concludes the octave of Easter. Not only does it serve as the eighth day, but it also includes a gospel that refers to an event on the first octave day of the resurrection. This day used to be called *Dominica in albis,* because the neophytes arrived wearing their albs, the white garments of their baptism.

(When this date does not fall on a Sunday, it is observed in Argentina and Peru as the feast of Toribio de Mogrovejo, bishop and patron of the Latin American episcopacy. His optional memorial is observed on the universal church calendar on March 23,

an obligatory memorial in some countries. Today's date is an obligatory memorial for Toribio in Chile, Venezuela and the Dominican Republic, but not when it falls on Sunday.)

LECTIONARY

Today's gospel appears in all three years of the lectionary cycle. It reports an appearance of Jesus on the day of the resurrection and his reappearance a week later. Thomas, absent from the first, present for the second, makes a profound statement of Easter faith: "My Lord and my God."

The first reading begins our Sunday series of texts from Acts of the Apostles. We hear about the honeymoon era: "The community of believers was of one heart and mind." Noteworthy is the economic policy of the first disciples. They held everything in common. They sold property or houses and brought proceeds to the apostles so that the needy could be satisfied. They dared not preach without living in complete charity.

Today's psalm is seasonal and appears each year in the lectionary for this Sunday. It sings of the stone rejected by the builders that has become the cornerstone, an image the apostolic church immediately applied to Jesus. We may sing alleluia as its refrain.

Today's second reading is from the First Letter of John. We start in the fifth chapter and then backtrack to begin the semicontinuous reading of this book next week. Today's passage opens with a baptismal theme: "Everyone who believes that Jesus is the Christ is begotten by God." With compact words that proclaim the divinity of Christ, the centrality of belief and the significance of baptism, today's second reading provides much meditation for preaching and mystagogy.

SACRAMENTARY

Today concludes the octave of Easter, and the liturgy still reflects the excitement of Easter Day.

This is a good season for the blessing and sprinkling of holy water to replace the Penitential Rite. You may start the custom today and continue throughout Pentecost.

Sing the Glory to God. You may sing the optional sequence as well on this last day of the octave. When using the first Easter preface (P 21), remember this is still "Easter day" because of the octave, not yet "Easter season." Especially if neophytes are present, you may wish to use Eucharistic Prayer I with its inserts. Conclude the Mass with a double alleluia at the dismissal dialogue.

All the presidential prayers today allude to baptism, and the prayer over the gifts includes an optional phrase if the newly baptized are present for the Mass. The solemn blessing for Easter appears conveniently on the page today.

OTHER IDEAS

The *Rite of Christian Initiation of Adults* (248) suggests that the neophytes be seated with their godparents. You might have a special place for them beginning today. Many historical references urged them to wear their white garments through today. You could invite them to wear something white, or at least their Easter best once again.

A four-part choir could sing Hans Leo Hassler's "Quia vidisti me, Thoma" (WLP, 5778).

28 #267 (LMC #185–192) white
M O N
Easter Weekday

Optional Memorial of Peter Chanel (+ 1841), presbyter, religious, missionary, martyr / red ▪

Optional Memorial of Louis Mary de Montfort (+ 1716), presbyter, religious founder / white ▪ The first Christians readily perceived that even the tragic events they experienced were still in the mind and plan of God. Reflecting on the arrest, mistreatment and release of Peter and John, they remembered the words of the second psalm and recognized that the Holy Spirit was already thinking of them when inspiring the psalmist of long ago. That psalm, about the foolishness of national powers waging war against God's people, appears as today's psalm.

Today we begin a semicontinuous reading of passages from John's gospel, as we experienced during the second half of Lent. At that time, we heard the parts of the story that led up to the passion. Now we hear the parts that unfold the implications of Jesus' resurrection. We open with Jesus' conversation with Nicodemus, a Pharisee who comes at night, perhaps in embarrassment about his illicit interest in this rabbi, perhaps as a Johannine sign of his movement from the darkness of unbelief to the light of faith. Jesus speaks mystically about baptism, a theme close to the church's heart these days that follow Easter's octave.

Any Easter preface will do, but the second (P 22) refers to "children of the light."

▪ TODAY'S SAINTS: Born in eastern France, Peter Chanel became a priest and then joined the Society of Mary, the Marists. He accompanied the founder of the congregation to Rome to apply for approval of its rule. He then fulfilled a lifelong dream and became a missionary. Evangelization efforts were difficult on the island of Futuna in the South Pacific, and the king eventually turned on Peter, having a gang attack his catechumens and club the Marist to death.

Louis Mary de Montfort served France as a priest and was especially devoted to the poor. He organized a group of physically disabled women into a congregation, and wrote over the door of their community room the word *wisdom*. He founded the Montfort Missionaries (the Company of Mary) and the Daughters of Divine Wisdom.

#268 (LMC #185–192) white
Catherine of Siena (+ 1380), virgin, doctor of the church
T U E
29
MEMORIAL

We resume the story from Acts of the Apostles with the passage we heard as Sunday's first reading, a remarkable testimony of generosity by one of the new believers. The psalm is seasonal, depicting the majesty of God. Christians sing this psalm imagining the risen Jesus where the psalmist sings of "the Lord."

Today's gospel picks up the conversation between Jesus and Nicodemus. The topics include being born again, the heavenly dwelling place of the Son of Man, and the eternal life promised to believers.

▪ TODAY'S SAINT: Catherine cared for victims of pestilence, and as a Dominican she converted many people by her powerful preaching. She convinced Pope Gregory XI to leave Avignon and move the papal palace back to Rome. Her efforts to quiet the cardinals responsible for the mounting schism proved ineffective, but she is still regarded as one of the greatest minds of her age. Her visage adorns a dramatic statue at the end of Rome's Via della Conciliazione, staring up toward St. Peter's Basilica, as if commanding the popes in their Avignon exile to go home.

Take the presidential prayers from April 29 in the back of the sacramentary. You may use the preface of virgins and religious (P 68).

W E D 30 #269 (LMC #185–192)   white
Easter Weekday

Optional Memorial of Pius V (+ 1572), pope, religious/white ▪ Peter is among the apostles jailed in today's reading. His freedom through angelic intervention is the subject of a fresco by Raphael in the Vatican. The psalm recalls that the angel of the Lord delivers the faithful.

John 3:16, perhaps the most famous of all scripture quotes, opens today's gospel. Jesus explains to Nicodemus the mission of the Son, the light who entered the world.

Among the prefaces, the second (P 22) makes a good choice for its images of light and the opening of gates.

▪ TODAY'S SAINT: The pontificate of Pius V gave the church a more widespread devotion to the rosary after the battle of Lepanto and a revised Roman Missal, the fruit of the Council of Trent. With minor changes the 1570 missal remained in force until 1969.

May

T H U 1 #270 (LMC #185–192)   white
Easter Weekday

Optional Memorial of Joseph the Worker/white ▪ The Sanhedrin reminds the arrested apostles that they are forbidden to preach, and Peter simply preaches back to them. We continue singing additional verses from yesterday's psalm, which recalls how God sides with the poor and confronts those who do evil.

Jesus concludes his conversation with Nicodemus by pairing the revelation of God with the expectation of the believer's acceptance of its truth.

▪ TODAY'S MEMORIAL: After communists and others began to celebrate May Day for workers, Pope Pius XII instituted a memorial of Joseph the Worker on the same day. Of course in the United States and Canada we celebrate Labor Day in September, so celebrating the patron of workers today will make little sense. If you choose to keep the memorial, you will find recommended scriptures at #559. All the texts focus on human labor and divine creation. This is an obligatory memorial in Panama.

F R I 2 #271 (LMC #185–192)   white
Athanasius (+ 373), bishop, monastic, doctor of the church
MEMORIAL

Once again, the apostles escape punishment after an arrest. The Sanhedrin believes that if the movement is not from God, it will die out on its own. The psalm captures the reason for the apostles' spirit: "The Lord is my life's refuge. Of whom should I be afraid?"

We turn now to chapter 6 of John, the famous discourse on the bread of life. We hear the prelude today, the miracle of the loaves.

▪ TODAY'S SAINT: Athanasius, an Egyptian prelate from Alexandria, attended the Council of Nicaea and defended the divinity of Christ against Arius. Strong opposition forced him to spend 46 years of his episcopacy in exile.

Take the presidential prayers from May 2 in the back of the sacramentary, where Athanasius's defense of the faith is made clear. The preface for pastors (P 67) may be used. The sacramentary offers special musical notation for multisyllabic names like his. The lectionary offers an alternative pair of scriptures for today (#560), proclaiming the divinity of Jesus and the persecution of the disciple.

S A T 3 #561 (LMC #185–192)   red
Philip and James, apostles
FEAST

The name "James" appears frequently throughout the New Testament and it is difficult to tell if the references are to two, three, four or more personages. In the liturgy, we identify today's James as the Son of Alphaeus (not the son of Zebedee), also called "the less" (not "the greater," whose feast is July 25). In some traditions he is also the James called "the brother of the Lord," the presumed author of the letter of James in the New Testament, but this "James of Jerusalem" is probably not one of the Twelve. (Calendars of some churches of the Reformation observe a separate memorial of James the brother of the Lord.)

There was only one Philip, the one who appears throughout the gospels. A different Philip, the deacon, appears in the Acts of the Apostles. Tradition says these two are buried together in the Church of the Holy Apostles in Rome. The composer Frescobaldi is buried in the same church.

Today's first reading identifies James as the one to whom Jesus appeared after the resurrection. We hear from John Philip's naïve request, "Lord, show us the Father," and Jesus' beautiful (exasperated?) response, "Whoever has seen me has seen the Father."

Psalm 19 frequently accompanies a feast of the apostles. Their ministry tells the message of the glory of God to the ends of the earth.

Sing the Glory to God today. The presidential prayers are found under May 3 in the back of the sacramentary. Either preface for the apostles is fitting (P 64 or 65). The names of today's saints appear in Eucharistic Prayer I. The solemn blessings include one for apostles (#17).

■ In Chile, Honduras, Colombia, El Salvador, Guatemala and Venezuela, this is the feast of the Exaltation of the Holy Cross, observed in the universal calendar on September 14. In Mexico today is the feast of the Holy Cross, and in Peru it is the feast of the Veneration of the Holy Cross. In the old calendar, May 3 recognized the finding of the holy cross, and September 14 honored the exaltation, a date that fits with the dedication of the Constantinian basilicas over the sites of the crucifixion and resurrection. After the Second Vatican Council, the universal calendar eliminated the May 3 date in favor of the fall celebration, which has an older history. In some monastic traditions, the monks wore their winter garb in choir "from cross to cross," September 14 to May 3, exchanging it on this date for lighter, warm-weather attire.

In Argentina, Saturday of the second week of Easter is the memorial of Our Lady of the Valley. According to the tradition, Franciscan missionaries at Catamarca in northern Argentina hid a statue of Mary in a cave when Indians attacked them. The statue, found at the end of the sixteenth century, has been enshrined at the site.

☀ **4** #47 (LMC #41)   white
Third Sunday of Easter

ORIENTATION

Each year the scriptures for the Third Sunday of Easter offer us an example of Peter's preaching from Acts and a postresurrection appearance by Jesus that involves a meal. For mystagogic purposes, the texts give the preacher the opportunity to proclaim the divinity of Jesus and the mystery of the eucharist.

The octave of Easter ended last Sunday, so the liturgy does not include the optional sequence during the liturgy of the word or the double alleluia in the dismissal.

(When May 4 does not fall on a Sunday, the countries of Colombia, Peru, Guatemala, Venezuela and Mexico transfer to this date yesterday's feast of the apostles Philip and James.)

LECTIONARY

Today's gospel follows the story of the road to Emmaus, proclaimed last year on this date. Today, the two disciples who experienced the appearance tell the others, and Jesus appears to them all. He insists he is not a ghost, but himself. He even eats baked fish for them. Through this episode we learn more about the nature of the resurrection: the preservation of person, the transformation of life.

Speaking from Solomon's portico, Peter lays a guilt trip on an audience of unbelievers who should have known better. "The author of life you put to death," he says. "Repent," he says, "and be converted, that your sins may be wiped away." This story links the church's teachings of resurrection, forgiveness and baptism.

The psalm invokes the resurrection themes of light and sleep.

We turn to a passage early in the First Letter of John to begin our semicontinuous reading of the book. Last week we heard from the same letter, but from a later place that blended better with the themes of the Easter octave. Today's reading explains the importance of keeping God's commandments, while assuring believers of the forgiveness of sins for those who fail.

SACRAMENTARY

A communion antiphon for this year, drawn from the gospel, is proposed.

Repeat the sprinkling rite if you are replacing the Penitential Rite with it this season.

The prayer over the people suggested for today offers nothing special. You may use the solemn blessing of the Easter season (#7), or a different prayer over the people, like #18.

Easter prefaces I, III and V (P 21, 23 and P 25) refer to Christ as the Lamb, as does today's second reading. All four versions of the eucharistic prayer for various needs and occasions make a direct reference to the Emmaus story. "As once he did for his disciples, Christ now opens the scriptures for us and breaks the bread."

OTHER IDEAS

Although we are still in the season called "Easter," many people subconsciously enter a season called "May." The month of May brings devotion to Mary, graduations, first communions, weddings, ordinations, and anniversaries to families, parishes, and communities. Keep the spirit of Easter alive. "Regina cæli"; "Be Joyful, Mary"; and "Ye Watchers and Ye Holy Ones" all blend Mary's role with the celebration of resurrection.

M O N **5** #273 (LMC #185–192)   white
Easter Weekday

Acts shifts now to the story of Stephen. False witnesses accuse this innocent deacon of wrongdoing. In his trial, he goes through the same suffering Jesus experienced. The psalmist takes comfort in God, "though princes sit plotting against me." Jesus, developing the image of bread, criticizes the hunger that drives people to search for him.

The sacrifice of the cross, echoed in Stephen's arrest, appears in Easter Preface V (P 25).

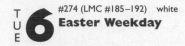

T U E **6** #274 (LMC #185–192) white
Easter Weekday

The martyrdom of Stephen imitates the martyrdom of Jesus, down to the story's quotation from the psalm that serves as today's responsory. Jesus compares himself to the manna that came down from heaven. He is the bread of life that will nourish the believer on the journey of faith. At this point of the discourse, the image of bread has not yet reached its full eucharistic intent. It more clearly signifies spiritual nourishment in these early verses.

Easter Preface I (P 21) recalls the mission of Jesus' forgiveness, a trait that Stephen embodied as well.

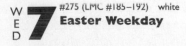

W E D **7** #275 (LMC #185–192) white
Easter Weekday

Acts of the Apostles opened with a gleaming description of church community life. But the arrest of the apostles foreshadowed future gloom. Now a persecution of the church has broken out. The martyrdom of Stephen was only the beginning. But as in those earlier cases, the persecutors only sow the seeds of evangelization. They scattered the believers, who kept right on preaching the word. The psalm, fittingly, invites "all the earth" to cry out with joy.

Jesus pursues the image of bread more deeply, this time showing its saving properties. Those who believe in him as the living bread will have eternal life.

Preface III (P 23) proclaims Christ as priest, advocate, victim

and Lamb, the one who offers salvation in the midst of suffering.

T H U **8** #276 (LMC #185–192) white
Easter Weekday

As the mission turns toward the Gentiles, one of the deacons, Philip, is involved in a remarkable story of conversion and baptism. Today's story has parallels to Emmaus, involving a journey, a discussion of scripture, baptism (in place of eucharist), and the mysterious disappearance of the protagonist. The psalm verses continue where yesterday's left off, calling on "all peoples" to bless God.

Jesus compares himself to the wisdom of God. Those who believe in him share in the bread of life.

Preface II (P 22) remembers that Christ has made us children of the light, as the Ethiopian experienced in today's episode from the book of Acts.

Today is the patronal feast of Argentina, Our Lady of Luján. Tradition holds that a Portuguese landowner in Córdoba ordered a statue of the Immaculate Conception from a friend in Buenos Aires in 1630. The friend sent two terracotta images. The oxen transporting the images stopped after two days of travel until one was removed. A local landowner built a shrine for that statue in his own house at Luján.

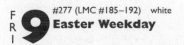

F R I **9** #277 (LMC #185–192) white
Easter Weekday

Saul, whose ominous presence appeared at the end of Tuesday's reading, reappears today, the very personification of the church's persecution. His three days of blindness signify his gradual coming to faith, under the catechetical and healing ministry of Ananias. He becomes Paul, the apostle to the Gentiles, and today's responsory could well serve as his personal anthem.

In clear, deliberate, and measured statements, Jesus tells his listeners that they must eat and drink the flesh and blood of the Son of Man. The bread of life discourse is reaching its natural conclusion, the identification of Jesus as the eucharistic bread of life.

The healing of Saul might find an echo in Easter's Preface IV (P 24), the end of sin's long reign, the restoration of humanity.

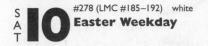

S A T **10** #278 (LMC #185–192) white
Easter Weekday

Optional Memorial of Blessed Damien Joseph de Veuster of Moloka'i (+ 1889), presbyter, religious, missionary / white ▪ All of a sudden, Luke tells us the church was at peace throughout Judea, Galilee and Samaria. In the midst of persecution, or perhaps because of it, the disciples have found peace in their belief. Peter continues to work miracles, and the number of believers increases. The mission to the Gentiles meets unparalleled success. The psalm recalls God's love for the faithful, even in death, and the thanksgiving offered by believers in their time of deliverance.

The sixth chapter of John ends on a somber note, as Jesus realizes that the core of his teaching has been rejected by some of his hearers. He wonders if even the Twelve will now desert him. Peter says there is nowhere else to go, for they have found the words of eternal life in Jesus.

The eucharistic references in Easter Preface V (P 25) make it a good choice for today.

▪ TODAY'S BLESSED: Father Damien, a Belgian priest, went to the Sandwich (Hawaiian) Islands as a missionary, where he served the leper colony and improved and tended to the physical and spiritual needs of the community. His memorial is optional throughout the world on April 15, but it is observed on this day in the United States. It was on May 10 that Damien traveled from Maui to the settlement of Kalawao on the island of Moloka'i to become the first resident priest to serve the lepers in 1873. The Diocese of Honolulu and Damien's own Congregation of the Sacred Hearts of Jesus and Mary were already observing today's date before April 15 was appointed for observance.

In Guatemala and Spain today is the memorial of John of Avila (+ 1569), priest, writer, mystic and friend of Ignatius of Loyola.

#50 (LMC #443) white
Fourth Sunday of Easter

ORIENTATION

Commonly known as "Good Shepherd Sunday," today's celebration takes its gospel from the tenth chapter of John each year of the cycle. In that chapter, Jesus develops the image of shepherd. Today, by extension, is also the World Day of Prayer for Vocations. Some parishes regard this Sunday as a good choice each year for confirmation and first communion.

■ TODAY IS MOTHER'S DAY. Prepare for extra visitors and remember mothers, both living and dead.

LECTIONARY

Not all of chapter 10 paints a clear picture of the Good Shepherd, but today's excerpt does. We hear different verses from this chapter each year on this Sunday, but none of them make it sound like Good Shepherd Sunday as

clearly as today's excerpt does. "I know mine and mine know me," Jesus says. Mystagogic preaching may explore the individual and common relationship of believers to Jesus.

The first reading gives another example of Peter's preaching. Today he is a prisoner, but not a timid one. When given the opportunity to make a defense, he simply preaches all the more. This passage shows the necessity of preaching, the power of the name of Christ in curing the disabled, and the fulfillment of scriptural prophecy in the suffering of Jesus, the stone rejected by the builders that has become the cornerstone. The text upon which that reflection is based appears as today's responsorial psalm. Still in the Easter season, we may sing alleluias for its refrain.

Today's brief second reading continues the sequence from the First Letter of John. It reveals the antagonism between the believer and the world, which does not know God. Belief has made the faithful children of God, and it will make them even more when they see who God really is. This passage inspires the insert in Eucharistic Prayer III for Masses for the dead.

SACRAMENTARY

Both opening prayers today take the image of the shepherd. Easter Preface II (P 22) might make a good choice today instead of mixing metaphors and calling Christ the Lamb (see prefaces I, III and V). The solemn blessing for the Easter season appears at the end of today's liturgy.

If you wish, continue the blessing and sprinkling of holy water in place of the Penitential Rite today and throughout the Sundays of Easter.

OTHER IDEAS

Include vocations in the general intercessions today. If your parish has a vocation committee you may honor them with blessing and approval for their work.

A two-part choir could sing Russell Woollen's "One Fold, One Shepherd" (WLP, 660).

Sample general intercessions for Mother's Day are in the *Book of Blessings,* 55, together with a prayer over the people that may conclude today's Mass.

M O N **12** **#279 (LMC #185–192)** white
Easter Weekday

Optional Memorial of Nereus and Achielleus (+ 2nd c.), martyrs / red ▪ *Optional Memorial of Pancras (+ 304?), martyr / red* ▪ Sadly, the lectionary skips chapter 10 of Acts, the great story of the conversion of Cornelius. Instead, we hear a condensed version of the proceedings in today's first reading from chapter 11. The responsory reports the soul's thirst for God. In context, we know that thirst is baptismal.

For today's gospel, choose the usual one, not the alternative, which would repeat yesterday's passage. In these opening verses of chapter 10, we hear Jesus as the gate, not the shepherd. He protects the sheep placed in his care.

Once again, Preface II (P 22) makes a good choice.

■ TODAY'S SAINTS: Romans Nereus and Achilleus were soldiers who converted to Christianity, renounced warfare and then suffered martyrdom for their faith. Their tomb is in the catacombs of St. Domitilla.

Little is known of Pancras except that he was revered as a martyr from early in church history. Gregory the Great dedicated a monastery to him, which may explain why his emissary Augustine dedicated a church in Canterbury to the same martyr. A popular legend says Pancras was 14 when he died under the persecution of Diocletian.

T U E **13** #280 (LMC #185–192)   white
Easter Weekday

Without cellular phones or e-mail, communication in apostolic days relied on labor-intensive messenger service. When the Christians in Jerusalem heard there were Christians in Antioch, they sent Barnabas to check it out. He went to Tarsus to bring Saul to Antioch, and personally vouched for his good behavior. At Antioch, the followers of Christ were called Christians for the first time. The psalm develops the theme of the universal mission of the church and the centrality of Jerusalem.

Jesus continues the shepherd theme. The sheep listening to his voice will know he is the Messiah.

The second preface (P 22) proclaims the promise of everlasting life for those who have become children of the light.

W E D **14** #564 (LMC #293, 455)   red
Matthias, apostle
FEAST

After the death of Judas the apostles decided to replace him. The story is recounted in today's first reading. A line from Psalm 113 praises God who raises a lowly servant to a seat among leaders. The gospel recalls Jesus' words to his disciples at the Last Supper, that it was not they who chose him, but he who chose them.

Sing the Glory to God. Find the presidential prayers under May 14 in the back of the sacramentary. Either preface of the apostles is fitting, but the first emphasizes that the eternal Shepherd never leaves the flock untended (P 64). Matthias appears in the first eucharistic prayer. Use the solemn blessing for the apostles (#17) if you like.

T H U **15** #282 (LMC #185–192)   white
Easter Weekday

Optional Memorial of Isidore the Farmer (+ 1130) and his wife, Maria, married couple/white ▪ Paul's missionary journey takes him to Perga in Pamphilia to Antioch in Pisidia. There he is invited to speak at the synagogue. Adjusting his script to a Jewish audience, Paul recounts the marvels God accomplished for their ancestors before announcing Jesus, the saving descendant of David. At one point he boosts his argument with a reference to Psalm 89, which then serves as today's responsory.

Our excerpts from John's gospel place us now at the Last Supper, where we will remain for the next few weeks. Having washed the feet of his disciples, Jesus instructs them about service, divine election, scriptural fulfillment, divinity, discipleship and rejection.

▪ TODAY'S SAINT: Isidore is included on the calendar of the United States as an optional memorial. Many communities also remember on this day Isidore's wife, Maria, if only because Maria and Isidore (Ysidro) are an instance of a married couple, so rarely included in the calendar of saints, whom the church has recognized for their sanctity. Born in Madrid, Isidore worked on a farm. It is said he saw visions of heaven and that angels assisted his work in the field. His wife survived him a few years. She is called "Maria de la Cabeza" because the relic of her head is sometimes carried in procession in times of drought.

Isidore is honored today with a feast in Costa Rica, an obligatory memorial in Guatemala and Venezuela, and with an optional memorial in Argentina and Mexico.

F R I **16** #283 (LMC #185–192)   white
Easter Weekday

We continue hearing from Paul's sermon in the synagogue in Antioch in Pisidia. He preaches the core of the Christian message, this time using Psalm 2 as a foundational text. The psalm appears as today's responsory.

Today we begin hearing the farewell discourse Jesus delivered at the Last Supper. Having already celebrated the death and resurrection of Jesus in the Triduum, we look backwards now while we have the time to absorb in small doses the last words of Jesus to his disciples. Thanks to Thomas's somewhat naïve question, we hear a marvelous proclamation from Jesus: "I am the way, the truth, and the life."

Penitential Rite C-vii borrows from today's gospel text. The third preface (P 23) mentions Jesus' sacrificial role as priest.

▪ MEXICO HONORS THE MARTYR JUAN NEPOMUCENO with an optional memorial today.

S A T **17** #284 (LMC #185–192)   white
Easter Weekday

First the persecution of Christians caused the spread of the gospel to the Gentiles. Now the mission to the Gentiles causes persecution. Paul and Barnabas shake the dust from their feet and rejoice still in their ministry. The gospel, as the psalm implies, goes to "all the ends of the earth."

Yesterday a question from Thomas provoked a memorable response from Jesus. Today a command by Philip produces the same. "Show us the Father" shows us the ignorance of the disciples, but Jesus seizes the opportunity to express his unity with the Father.

The fifth preface (P 25) expresses the sacrificial role of Jesus.

☼ 18 #53 (LMC 47) white
Fifth Sunday of Easter

ORIENTATION

During the second half of the Easter season the gospels are all drawn from the farewell discourse of Jesus in John's gospel. They place us back at the Last Supper, but allow us to meditate unhurriedly on these dense texts.

LECTIONARY

Jesus' facility with images becomes evident again in today's gospel about the vine and the branches. He frequently draws from his agrarian society's experience to make profound explanations of the spiritual life. Last week's image of shepherd explained something of the hierarchical relationship between Jesus and the believer. Today's image expresses the oneness of the life that flows between them.

Understandably, when Saul arrived in Jerusalem after his conversion, Christians were skeptical. It took the testimony of Barnabas to convince people that the former terrorist was now on their side. Today's second reading tells of the miraculous expansion of the gospel. The response echoes this event: "I will praise you, Lord, in the assembly of your people." It also proclaims that all the ends of the earth, all the families of nations shall turn to God. This theme of universality synchronizes with that of Paul's mission.

The mystagogic themes of belief and love come out in today's second reading from the First Letter of John. The command we have received is to believe in the name of Jesus and to love one another as he taught.

SACRAMENTARY

The suggested opening antiphon is a verse from Psalm 97 (98) that also inspired the alternative opening prayer for today.

Continue the rite of blessing and sprinkling of holy water if you wish. Easter Preface IV (P 24) speaks of renewal and restoration.

In place of the prayer over the people suggested for today, look at the solemn blessing for the Easter season (#7) or prayer over the people #20.

OTHER IDEAS

If the community is gathering for any other prayer during the next few weeks, consider using a text from John's account of Jesus' farewell discourse. It will keep the spirit of the liturgy.

19 #285 (LMC #185–192) white
Easter Weekday

On mission, the apostles shift through events with dizzying swiftness. A plot to stone Paul and Barnabas materializes. They flee and cure a disabled man. The people declare that the apostles are gods. The apostles preach the truth of their mission, but it falls on deaf ears. Psalm 115 turns the believer's attention from worship of false idols to worship of the true God.

Jude asks why Jesus limits his revelation. Jesus says he and the Father will dwell with any true believer, and that they should expect the Holy Spirit to instruct and remind them.

Easter Preface III (P 23) calls Christ the advocate who always pleads our cause.

20 #286 (LMC #185–192) white
Easter Weekday

Optional Memorial of Bernardine of Siena (+ 1444), presbyter, religious, missionary/white ▪ Not even stoning stops Paul from his mission to preach. He and Barnabas chart a successful journey, proclaiming the gospel with honor. As the psalm says, the works of God tell of glorious divine might.

Jesus gives the disciples his farewell gift of peace, a virtue they will need, considering the persecution that lay ahead.

The first Easter preface (P 21) consoles those persecuted with its words about the suffering Christ: "by dying he destroyed our death."

▪ TODAY'S SAINT: Bernardine entered the Fathers of the Strict Observance of the Order of St. Francis. His holiness gained him widespread respect and his humility kept refusing honors and appointments. Nothing gave him more satisfaction than preaching, for which he is best known.

21 #287 (LMC #185–192) white
Easter Weekday

The church in Antioch disagreed with the church in Judea about the conversion of Gentiles. The Judeans said Gentiles had to become Jews before becoming Christians. This created "much controversy" with Paul and Barnabas. They return to Jerusalem to discuss the matter as a universal church community. In response, we sing one of the Jerusalem pilgrimage psalms.

In a repeat of Sunday's gospel, Jesus explores the metaphor of the vine and the vine grower. In those images lie the unity, growth and development of the church.

The relationship of Jesus to the church appears as a theme in the second preface for the Easter season (P 22).

T H U 22 #288 (LMC #185–192) white
Easter Weekday

The resolution of the dispute over Gentile converts favors the position held by Paul and Barnabas. The dialogue is a marvelous example of early church leadership: Both sides explained their positions and James announced the conclusion. A psalm of praise follows the reading. The nations; that is, the Gentiles, sing that God is their ruler.

Love, obedience and joy intertwine as Jesus instructs his disciples to keep the commandments, live in love and find their joy.

Easter Preface IV (P 24) speaks of the new age that has dawned.

F R I 23 #289 (LMC #185–192) white
Easter Weekday

The leaders of the church meeting in Jerusalem have made their decision about Gentile converts. Now that decision, reached by the Holy Spirit and the community together, was promulgated: The church should not lay upon Gentile converts any burden greater than necessary. In short, they should not have to become Jews before becoming Christians. Our Rite of Reception for baptized Christians makes a direct reference to this passage from Acts. Those preparing baptized candidates for reception into the full communion of the Catholic church should lay on them no greater burden than necessary. The psalm foreshadows the spread of the gospel among the Gentiles: "I will praise you among the nations, O Lord."

In his farewell message, Jesus lays upon his followers his core commandment: Love one another. Easter Preface II (P 22) says God has made us children of the light.

S A T 24 #290 (LMC #185–192) white
Easter Weekday

The circumcision of Timothy seems to negate the conclusion of the meeting in Jerusalem about Gentile converts, but it may be that Paul was making a prudent, pastoral decision. His travels continue, and the gospel spreads even farther. The psalm summons all the earth to cry to God with joy.

Jesus predicts the persecution of his followers. Small comfort, but the world hated him before it hated them.

The fourth Easter preface (P 24) holds out hope for a world suffering the reign of sin.

■ IN ARGENTINA AND COSTA RICA, Mary is remembered today with an optional memorial under the title of Help of Christians. Today Venezuela has an obligatory memorial of Mary the Helper. In 1814 Pope Pius VII (+ 1823), having been imprisoned by Napoleon, was released and returned to Rome. He was restored to the papal throne on this date. Pius established the anniversary of his return as the feast of Mary, Help of Christians. The Salesians also observe this day. [See the *Collection of Masses of the Blessed Virgin Mary* (42).]

☀ 25 #55 (LMC #49)
Sixth Sunday of Easter

ORIENTATION

This Memorial Day weekend will bring some visitors to church and will cause some regulars to be absent. Be prepared to welcome the strangers.

Note two Latin American celebrations that would normally take place today were it not a Sunday. Bolivia has an optional memorial of the virgin Mariana de Jesús, celebrated by more of Latin America tomorrow. Mexico has an optional memorial of Blessed Cristóbal Magallanes and companions, martyrs (+ 1915–1937). The 22 priests and 3 laymen remembered today suffered during the persecution of the Church in Mexico associated with the Cristero uprising between 1926 and 1929. Magallanes (+ 1927), the parish priest at his home town of Totalice, established catechetical centers and schools, built a dam and created land reform. Arrested as a supporter of the uprising, though committed to nonviolence, he was shot to death by the government while declaring his innocence.

LECTIONARY

If you will celebrate Ascension not on Thursday but next Sunday, you have an option this weekend. You may choose the gospel and second reading from the Seventh Sunday of Easter. If you do, see below for comments on the texts. But be aware that you will miss this Sunday's beautiful passages about love if you exercise this option. The first reading may not be substituted because the one for the Seventh Sunday tells the story of the selection of Matthias as the apostle to replace Judas, an event that fell chronologically between Ascension and Pentecost in Luke's account.

At the Last Supper, Jesus gives the disciples his greatest commandment: to love one another. This passage, which just appeared two days ago in the weekday lectionary, is deeply moving. Jesus goes to his death as an act of love and asks his disciples for the same selfless love for one another. They will face persecutions, but he consoles them with his message of friendship. He has chosen them and now he equips them with the armor they will need the most: love.

Our semicontinuous reading of the First Letter of John reaches a point that nicely fits the same theme. The author encourages the readers to love one another. Love comes from God, and, in fact, God is love. The sending of Jesus into the world revealed that mystery most dramatically.

The amazing story of the conversion of Cornelius fills chapter 10 of Acts and we hear a truncated version of it today. Friends of the Gentile have visited Peter, disturbing his prayer, where he had a vision that the gospel would be open to the Gentiles. Peter accompanies them to the house of Cornelius, where the apostle intends to discern his readiness for baptism. The Holy Spirit takes over, another Pentecost happens, and the hapless Peter decides it would be a good idea to baptize. A psalm about the revelation of God's power to the Gentile nations follows.

Mystagogy today may highlight the role of the Holy Spirit, the universal appeal of the gospel, and the central command to love, even to the point of death.

SACRAMENTARY

If you exercise this option throughout the Easter season, continue the blessing and sprinkling of holy water at the beginning of today's liturgy. Sing the Easter Glory to God and the set of eucharistic acclamations. The solemn blessing for the Easter season appears handily on the page today. Preface III (P 23) refers to Jesus as the Advocate, or Paraclete, who pleads the cause of believers.

OTHER IDEAS

You could bless cars today (*Book of Blessings,* 21) for those planning trips this summer.

#291 (LMC #185–192)   white
26 MON
Philip Neri (+ 1595), presbyter, religious founder
MEMORIAL

Civic Holiday in the U.S.A.: Memorial Day ▪ Acts of the Apostles reports today the story of Lydia's conversion. This lovely episode reveals her as a person already leading a spiritual life, present at a place of prayer, and ready for the Holy Spirit to open her heart. After Lydia and her household are baptized, she prevails upon the apostles to stay—an opportunity for mystagogy and community. She serves as a model for catechumens, who enter the way of faith and conversion "as the Holy Spirit opens their hearts" (RCIA, 1). The psalm says the faithful delight in God, and God delights in them.

Jesus predicts the arrival of the Paraclete, the Spirit of truth, who will give them courage when they are persecuted. The memory of Jesus' words grants perseverance.

The third preface refers to Jesus as the advocate (P 23).

▪ TODAY'S SAINT: Perhaps the most joyful of saints, Philip attracted friends and admirers in his own day, including Ignatius of Loyola and Francis Xavier, and even later generations marveled at his winning personality. He developed a prayer room around which he founded the Oratorian community. The musical form known as the oratorio began as part of their apostolate in Rome.

▪ TODAY IS MEMORIAL DAY IN THE UNITED STATES. Some celebrations may take place at the cemetery. The *Book of Blessings,* 57, provides an order for visiting a cemetery today. So does *Catholic*

Household Blessings and Prayers (178, 280).

▪ ROGATION DAYS began as early as fifth-century France for protection against earthquakes. The church formerly designated the three days before Ascension Thursday as special days of prayer for protection and a fruitful harvest. They included a procession and the litany of the saints. Today bishops' conferences around the world replace these days with special days of prayer for the needs of all people, "especially for the productivity of the earth and for human labor," and to give God public thanks (*General Norms for the Liturgical Year and Calendar,* #45). In the United States each diocese chooses it own dates and intentions. Consult your diocesan office for your special days of prayer, and choose a votive Mass for various needs and occasions that suits the celebration.

▪ MARIANA DE JESÚS (+ 1645) is remembered today with a feast day in Ecuador and a memorial in Colombia and Venezuela. Also known as St. Mary Ann of Quito, or Mariana Paredes y Flores, she was born in 1618 of a Spanish family in Quito when it was part of Peru. She lived in solitude under Jesuit direction at the home of her brother-in-law, surviving on the barest of needs and receiving spiritual favors.

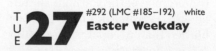

#292 (LMC #185–192)   white
27 TUE
Easter Weekday

Optional Memorial of Augustine of Canterbury (+ 604), bishop, monastic, missionary/white ▪ Another household conversion is reported in today's first reading. This time, though, the convert is not a person already practicing a spiritual life like Lydia, but a jailer fearful of the power unleashed

by an earthquake. A psalm of salvation follows the reading, affirming the rescue of the apostles and also of the jailer's soul.

The Paraclete, Jesus says, will prove the world wrong about sin, justice and condemnation. Jesus' conflict with "the world" will reach its resolution under the influence of the Holy Spirit.

Preface IV (P 24) celebrates Christ conquering the reign of sin.

■ TODAY'S SAINT: A Benedictine monk from Rome, Augustine was the first bishop of Canterbury. Part of this missionary's life is recalled in the historical work of Bede.

W
E **28** #293 (LMC #185–192) white
D **Easter Weekday**

Paul evangelizes Athens, where he brings his message to the pagan community gathered on the Areopagus, a hillock overlooking the Parthenon. His speech is a classic defense against anonymous Christianity. The psalm affirms that God is Lord of heaven and earth.

The Spirit of truth, Jesus says, will announce to the disciples the things to come. In the days of darkness ahead, the disciples will take comfort from the truth that they can never obscure.

You might return to the first Easter preface (P 21), which proclaims our central belief in salvation.

■ IN COLOMBIA, the memorial of Philip Neri is transferred to this date because of its celebration of Mariana de Jesús on May 26.

T
H **29** #294 (LMC #185–192) white
U **Easter Weekday**

Some communities in the United States celebrate Ascension today, but others celebrate this coming Sunday, June 1, in which case Thursday, May 29, is observed as an Easter weekday. All of Latin

America transfers the solemnity to the following Sunday. Adapt the following notes to your local calendar.

Paul begins his ministry in Corinth. He works as tentmaker and evangelist. His ministry to the Jewish community soured so badly he turned back to evangelize Gentiles. The psalm, overlooking Paul's outburst, placidly sings of God revealing salvation to all the nations.

The disciples remain unable to understand Jesus' sayings. He predicts his departure, the grief it will cause, but the joy that will also result.

The fifth Easter preface (P 25) sings of Jesus' departure by means of the cross. Presidential prayers for this weekday are under Thursday of the sixth week of Easter.

T
H **29☀1**
U

#58 (LMC #52) white
The Ascension of the Lord
SOLEMNITY

ORIENTATION

Not even the New Testament is consistent in dating the Ascension as an event in time, so the variance in dates around the world today need not cause scandal. Although we typically think this day commemorates an event

40 days after Easter, that chronology exists only in Acts of the Apostles. In the gospels, even in Luke's gospel, the Ascension appears to have taken place much earlier, even on Easter Day.

The meaning of the celebration is that Jesus has gone to glory with the Father, outside time and space. He intercedes for us and has sent us another Paraclete, the Holy Spirit, who advocates our cause. Meanwhile, we await Jesus' return in glory.

LECTIONARY

The first reading gives a biblical account of this event. Notice what Acts of the Apostles says, that Jesus appeared to instruct the disciples over the course of 40 days. On one of these appearances, presumably (but not conclusively) the final one, Jesus ascended to heaven, being lifted up before the eyes of witnesses in a cloud that took him from sight. This ascension to his royal throne seems foreshadowed in today's psalm refrain.

The gospel records Mark's version of the same event. This passage comes from the so-called longer ending of the gospel. It is likely that this passage was added on to the gospel in its shorter form. The longer ending of Mark seems to collect postresurrection stories from the other three gospels. After the ascension, the disciples go forth to preach everywhere, while God confirmed the word they spoke through signs.

The first chapter of the letter to the Ephesians speaks of Jesus, raised from the dead and sitting at the right hand of God in heaven. All things are at the feet of him who is head of the church and fills the universe. This year you may choose an alternative second reading, Ephesians 4:1–13, or a shorter form of the same passage. This text defines "he ascended" to mean that first Christ descended to the lower regions of the earth and then ascended above all the heavens to fill all things. In the wake of this event, the gifts of the Spirit pour forth on the church.

SACRAMENTARY

The suggested opening antiphon is taken from today's first reading. Have a festive opening procession—decorate the cross, use candles and incense. Repeat the blessing and sprinkling of holy water. If you have not been singing the Glory to God throughout Easter, revive the music again today.

If you use the first preface of the Ascension (P 26), use the bracketed word [Today.] If you choose the first eucharistic prayer, there is a special insert for the feast at "In union." The solemn blessing for the Ascension appears on the page.

OTHER IDEAS

If your celebration of the Ascension has replaced the Seventh Sunday of Easter, you may wish to rescue the alternative opening prayer from that celebration for its eloquent reflection on God, time and beauty. It might fittingly conclude the general intercessions.

The Easter candle remains burning until Pentecost.

Choose a good hymn for the feast like "Hail the Day That Sees Him Rise" (LLANFAIR) or "A Hymn of Glory Let Us Sing" (LASST UNS ERFREUEN). *By Flowing Waters* (175–183) has a complete suite of processional antiphons and psalms, including an inclusive language version of the ancient entrance antiphon.

If you sang the O Antiphons during the last part of Advent this year, you might look for an opportunity to chant the *Magnificat* antiphon for second vespers, "O rex gloriæ." It follows the same musical and textual pattern. Find it in the *Antiphonale monasticum.*

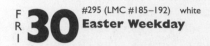

F R I **30** #295 (LMC #185–192)   white
Easter Weekday

Paul stays in Corinth a year and a half, long enough apparently for conversions to happen, but long enough also to make new enemies. Gallio refuses to hear a case against Paul because it is not a civil crime. A revolt breaks out against Sosthenes. If this is the same Sosthenes who co-authored the letters to the Corinthians, he converted to Christ as well.

Psalm 47 is seasonal for the Ascension. The psalmist sings of God mounting a royal throne as the church celebrates Christ ascending to his royal throne.

Jesus continues his warnings about persecutions. He compares the sorrow to that of a woman in painful labor. Joy will come, but at a price.

Choose the opening prayer based on the day you celebrate the Ascension.

If you have not yet celebrated the Ascension, Easter III (P 23) makes a good preface, acknowledging Jesus as priest. If you celebrated the solemnity yesterday, either Ascension preface may be used. The second (P 27) succinctly summarizes Jesus' role in heaven.

S A T **31** #572 (LMC #302)   white
The Visitation of the Virgin Mary to Elizabeth
FEAST

In the Middle Ages, the story of the visitation used to be proclaimed on July 2, to commemorate the deposition of the putative robe of Mary at a church in Constantinople. In 1389, at the urgings of the Franciscans, a feast of the Visitation became assigned to the universal church on that day. In today's calendar the feast has been moved forward, where it creates a sequence of events from the Annunciation (March 25) to the Visitation (May 31) to the Birth of John the Baptist (June 24).

Choose one of the options for the first reading, Zephaniah's cry of joy foreshadowing the child's womb-enclosed leap of joy, or Paul's admonition to hospitality from Romans. The canticle from Isaiah prophesies that the Holy One is in the midst of Zion, an image of the expectant mother of God. The gospel narrates the story of the feast.

Prayers for the feast are under May 31 in the sacramentary. Sing the Glory to God. The second preface of Mary (P 57) is based on today's gospel text, the *Magnificat.*

June

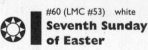   #60 (LMC #53)   white
Seventh Sunday of Easter

Some communities celebrate Ascension on Thursday, May 29, but others celebrate today, June 1. Notes for the solemnity of the Ascension are found on page 153. Adapt these notes to your local calendar.

ORIENTATION

This liminal celebration places us between the departure of Jesus in his Ascension and the arrival of the Spirit at Pentecost. We gather with the disciples in the upper room of prayerful anticipation, during the nine days that formed an original novena for the church.

LECTIONARY

Today's first reading tells of the activity of the disciples between the Ascension and Pentecost. Having lost Judas, they decide to replace him with one who accompanied them the whole time Jesus was among them. They threw dice and chose Matthias, who received the appointment instead of Judas, called Barsabbas, also known as Justus. As one wag says, Matthias won the election because no one could remember the name of his opponent. The story tells the complete trust the community placed in God.

The psalm is seasonal, proclaiming that God has a throne in heaven, a throne that Christians believe Jesus reaches today.

The gospel brings to a conclusion the series of texts we have heard from the farewell discourse of John's gospel, Jesus' final words to his chosen disciples at the Last Supper. Today, he lifts his eyes to heaven and prays that they may be one.

The series of readings from the First Letter of John concludes today. This passage returns to the theme of love. No one has seen God, but if we love one another God remains in us. Even though Jesus ascends to the heavens, God remains in us if we have love.

SACRAMENTARY

The opening prayer sets the tone for today's celebration of anticipation. The alternative is an unusually eloquent text relating time to truth and beauty.

You may choose from seven prefaces, but those for the Ascension (P 26 and 27) will keep the community in the spirit of the feast. If you used the first on Thursday, you might use the second today.

The solemn blessing for the Ascension (#8) makes a good choice for today. Prayer over the people #24 might also fit.

OTHER IDEAS

The first preface of the Holy Spirit (P 54) formerly served as the Ascension preface and refers to that feast as well as Pentecost.

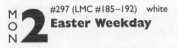

M O N
2
#297 (LMC #185–192)   white
Easter Weekday

Marcellinus, presbyter, and Peter, exorcist (+ 304), martyrs/red ▪ Paul baptizes and imposes hands on a group of disciples in Ephesus. The story implies that Apollos had delivered an incomplete catechesis and celebration. Psalm 68 is another text for the season of Ascension. It opens with the evocative expression, "God arises."

The disciples enthusiastically proclaim their faith in Jesus, but he warns them about the suffering he will endure, which will cause them to ask questions about finding peace.

You may choose from any of seven prefaces, but one of those for the Ascension (P 26 or 27) will keep the spirit of the season.

▪ TODAY'S SAINTS: Marcellinus was a priest in Rome and Peter is said to have been an exorcist. They were among the Christians martyred under Diocletian, but little is known of them. As early Roman martyrs, their names appear in the first eucharistic prayer.

#298 (LMC #185–192)   red

T U E
3
Charles Lwanga catechist, martyr; and his companions, martyrs (+ 1885–1887)
MEMORIAL

Paul addresses the elders of Ephesus like a man who knows his days are numbered. He presses on toward Jerusalem, aware that a tragic end could await him there. He reiterates his commitment to the gospel, no matter the cost. We sing more verses from yesterday's responsory, a seasonal psalm for the Ascension.

Having finished his instructions to the disciples at the Last Supper, Jesus now turns his gaze toward heaven and begins his final, high priestly prayer to God the Father, on behalf of those he called and loved. He asks the Father to glorify the divine name in the events that will follow.

▪ TODAY'S SAINTS: The faith spread throughout Africa in the nineteenth century, but it also met persecution. Charles Lwanga, a catechist and youth leader, was martyred with a group of Catholic and Anglican friends. Paul VI canonized these martyrs in 1964 in Uganda, and invited the Anglican archbishop to be present. That archbishop, Janai Luwum, later suffered martyrdom under Idi Amin.

The prayers for today are under June 3. The preface may be that of martyrs (P 66).

▪ BLESSED JOHN XXIII, POPE: "In my window," wrote Angelo Roncalli in his diary, "a little light must always shine, so that anyone may knock and enter and find a friend." That light shone one day over St. Peter's Square and the whole world found a friend in "Good Pope John."

Today is the fortieth anniversary of the death of Blessed John XXIII. His vision for the church opened windows and began a long period of transformation. On the liturgical calendar, October 11 has been set aside for remembering this holy man.

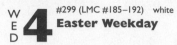

W E D **4** #299 (LMC #185–192) white
Easter Weekday

Paul's tearful departure from Ephesus provokes a lovely farewell address. This is one of a very few clear references in the Bible where a community knelt for common prayer. The context was not eucharistic. More verses from the Ascension Psalm 68 follow: "God's power is in the skies."

Jesus now prays to the Father for the well-being of his disciples. He does not ask God to take them out of the world, but to protect them in the world where they live and work.

Again, you may choose from seven prefaces, but those of the Ascension keep the feel of the week.

T H U **5** #300 (LMC #185–192) red
Boniface (+ 754), bishop, monastic, martyr
MEMORIAL

Paul is on trial before the Sanhedrin, a group he polarizes by proclaiming his Pharisaic belief in the resurrection. In a vision, Paul realizes he must go to Rome. Psalm 16, a text the lectionary associates with the resurrection (see the second reading of the Easter Vigil), follows this story.

Jesus widens his prayer. He prays not only for the disciples before him, but also for those who will come later, even us. This concludes the lectionary's presentation of Jesus' discourse and prayer at the Last Supper.

Choose from the wide options of prefaces. Those for ascension may be preferable.

■ TODAY'S SAINT: Born in England, accepted into a monastery, Boniface eventually found his vocation in preaching to those who had not yet heard the gospel in

what is today Germany. He resigned as abbot but accepted a post as bishop of Mainz. He was martyred while traveling to administer confirmation.

The opening prayer comes from June 5 in the sacramentary. Options exist for the other presidential prayers. Those for missionaries have not recently been in use, but you may also choose the prayers from the Easter weekday. The preface for pastors (P 67) could also be used in place of the one for martyrs that appeared earlier this week.

F R I **6** #301 (LMC #185–192) white
Easter Weekday

Optional Memorial of Norbert (+ 1134), bishop, religious founder / white ▪ Under arrest, Paul appeals his case so that it can go to a civil court and not be dismissed as a religious matter. His strategy gives him the opportunity to broaden his audience for the proclamation of the gospel. Another seasonal psalm for Ascension follows: The Lord has set his throne in heaven.

In a farewell conversation with Peter, Jesus asks three questions about love to the disciple who denied him three times. Predicting Peter's death, Jesus gives a command layered with suffering and promise: "Follow me."

The same choices for the preface reappear.

■ TODAY'S SAINT: Norbert, enamored of the worldly life, accepted the clerical life for its benefits. Struck by a bolt of lightning while on horseback, he completely changed his life and became an example of austerity. Founder of the Order of Premonstratensians, he became archbishop of Magdeburg and died after an illness.

■ THE JEWISH CELEBRATION OF SHAVUOT, the Feast of Weeks, is today and tomorrow. It celebrates the giving of the Torah on Mount

Sinai, an event that the Christian celebration of Pentecost also commemorates.

S A T **7** #302 (LMC #185–192) white
Easter Weekday

The lectionary texts for Saturday morning differ from those of the Pentecost vigil, assigned for later in the day today.

The first reading concludes the series from Acts of the Apostles. It follows Paul all the way to Rome, where he continues to preach from the capital city of the world. Acts ends here. It is not a biography of Paul, but a biography of the church, a story that has reached its climax by putting the proclamation of the gospel on the highest earthly pedestal, Rome.

Psalm 11 includes another seasonal reference to God on the heavenly throne.

Our series from John's gospel also concludes today, as Jesus and Peter discuss the beloved disciple. This figure, apparently an image of the believer who reads the gospel, continues to live in the world and bears witness to these events.

#62–63 (LMC #58) red
8 **Pentecost**
SOLEMNITY

ORIENTATION

Pentecost is a celebration of the coming of the Holy Spirit upon the church, as Jesus had promised. The disciples, gathered in

their upper room, experience the presence of the Spirit in such a profound way that it drives them out into the world to proclaim and preach the gospel with a courage unknown before.

Pentecost derives its name from the Feast of Weeks, a Jewish festival of the early harvest (Exodus 23:16), on which the first fruits were offered in gratitude to God. It eventually became associated with the giving of the Torah on Mount Sinai.

Paul tells the Corinthians (1 Corinthians 16:8) that he will stay in Ephesus until Pentecost, leading us to speculate that the very first generation of Christians commemorated the day every year. The name means "fiftieth" and in early Christianity it referred to the whole 50 days of Easter, culminating with the celebration of Pentecost.

LECTIONARY

An extensive and complex series of readings is arranged for the solemnity. The vigil Mass offers a selection of four Old Testament readings, one of which is to precede the second reading and the gospel. Another complete set of readings is proclaimed on Pentecost day, together with a sequence.

■ PENTECOST VIGIL: The *Circular Letter* (107) recommends "the prolonged celebration of Mass in the form of a vigil, whose character is . . . of urgent prayer, after the example of the Apostles and disciples." You could, then, choose more than one of the Old Testament passages and extend the celebration of the evening Mass.

■ OLD TESTAMENT OPTIONS FOR THE VIGIL: The Pentecost vigil marks the first time since the Easter Vigil that the first reading comes from the Old Testament. Each of the choices has special significance:

• From Genesis we hear the story of the Tower of Babel. It explained how human sin caused the development of many human languages. On Pentecost, God's grace allows people who speak many languages to understand the same preacher. The gospel translates well into the common human experience of struggling to understand another's language.

• From Exodus we hear the story of Moses receiving the sacred law from God on Mount Sinai. According to 19:1, the event took place on the third new moon, causing later interpreters to speculate that it coincided with Pentecost, the fiftieth day. The tongues of fire appear on the disciples in a mighty wind, reminiscent of the theophany on Sinai.

• Another image of wind, of God's breath, can be found in the prophecy of Ezekiel. Note how the dry bones are without "spirit," until later in the passage when "the spirit" enters the bones, and in the final lines God promises the gift of "my spirit."

• Joel prophesies that God will pour out the divine spirit upon the chosen people. This important passage appears nowhere else in the lectionary. Peter quotes it at length in his sermon on Pentecost day.

■ VIGIL PSALMODY: The psalm inviting God's spirit to renew the earth, 104, follows the first reading, no matter which one is selected. The verses vary slightly, but this is the same psalm that followed the first reading of the Easter Vigil. Settings are offered by C. Alexander Peloquin (GIA, G-1662), Robert Edward Smith (GIA, G-2122), Paul Lisicky (*Gather*), Angelo della Pica (*Psalms for the Cantor*, vol. V), Vern Pat Nelson (WLP, 2616), Dan Tucker (WLP, 7994) and bilingual settings by Charlotte Struckhoff ("Renueve la Tierra Madre") and Lorenzo Florián ("Ven, O Espiritu").

If you observe an extended vigil, use Psalm 104 after the last reading. In other places, the lectionary

recommends Psalm 33 to follow the Babel story from Genesis, Psalm 100 to follow the Sinai account from Exodus, and Psalm 130 to follow the dry bones of Ezekiel.

■ OTHER VIGIL READINGS: In the gospel we hear one occasion when Jesus promised the Spirit. John's comment, "There was no Spirit yet," makes it a serviceable passage for the Pentecost vigil.

Paul's letter to the Romans, though, reassures the community about the Spirit's ability to assist their prayer. A passage like this would have consoled the group of disciples huddled in fear, not knowing how to pray.

Although the foregoing scriptures "may be used" for the vigil, those assigned for Pentecost Sunday carry no such restriction.

The vigil readings are rich and worth hearing on any Saturday evening liturgy, even a wedding Mass, but they would not be used on Sunday. You could, though, proclaim the Sunday readings at a Saturday vigil Mass if that simplifies the preaching and preparation of music, and if you thought the assembly (who will not return on Sunday morning) would benefit from hearing the passages that most directly proclaim the event. Still, it would be a shame to lose those great vigil readings!

■ THE PENTECOST PASSAGE EVERYONE THINKS OF FIRST is Sunday's first reading from Acts. Another example of Luke's masterful writing style, this text allows the hearer to see the fire and feel the wind. Be sure the reader practices the names of the nationalities and places. The overall effect should not be one of stumbling, but of the far-flung sure-footed effect of the gospel.

The psalmist sings of the life-giving spirit. Without it we die. With it we are created.

■ THE GOSPEL OF PENTECOST DAY WILL SURPRISE PEOPLE. Even though we think of the gift of the Spirit on the fiftieth day in Luke's account from Acts, John's description of the gift of the Spirit occurs on the very day of the resurrection. He offers no account of a later Pentecost. So, according to John, the gift of the Spirit came with the resurrection, primarily for the forgiveness of sins. To remember that event is to embrace a different kind of Pentecost.

■ IN YEAR B THE LECTIONARY PERMITS AN ALTERNATIVE GOSPEL. The passage from John 15 returns us to the farewell discourse of Jesus. At the Last Supper he promised the disciples he would send the Advocate, the Spirit of truth who proceeds from the Father.

In First Corinthians, Paul explains how the gifts of the Spirit disperse throughout the community. Pentecost is a continuing, creative event.

The Year B lectionary permits an alternative for the second reading. In Galatians, Paul urges the community to live by the fruits of the Spirit: love, joy, peace, patience, kindness, generosity, faithfulness, gentleness and self-control.

■ THE SEQUENCE invites the Spirit to come upon the gathered assembly to recreate, heal and forgive. The original chant, "Veni sancte Spiritus," (*Liber cantualis* or *Worship,* #857) could be used, or the version from Taizé with the same title. Ann Colleen Dohn's version has responses for the assembly (WLP, 5718). See also Richard Wojcik's "O Holy Spirit, by Whose Breath" (*Worship,* 475); and Ralph Wright's translation in GIA's *Hymnal for the Hours,* which may be sung to a tune like PUER NOBIS. Note also Deanna Light and Paul Tate's *Come, Holy Spirit* (WLP, 7485). Dennis Fitzpatrick's and Roger Nachtwey's fine translation of the golden sequence is found in *By Flowing Waters,* 188.

SACRAMENTARY

Texts are offered for the vigil Mass and also the Mass during the day. The suggested communion antiphon for the vigil Mass comes from its gospel.

Choose resplendent red vesture for deacon and priest. The vesture should evoke Pentecost, not martyrdom. Start the procession with incense, cross and candles. Use the sprinkling rite to conclude the Easter season. Sing the Glory to God.

The opening prayers for the vigil Mass all assume we are still awaiting the celebration of the coming of the Spirit, even as they pray for that Spirit to come upon the community today. The opening prayers for the Mass during the day assume that we are now celebrating the Pentecost event.

For both Masses the preface of Pentecost is used (P 28), and if you pray the first eucharistic prayer, you may use the special insert for "In union." Sing the acclamations in use throughout the Easter season, perhaps with additional instruments or harmony.

The prayer over the people at the vigil Mass offers a simple close, but you could turn the page and use the solemn blessing printed there for Pentecost Sunday.

Easter's double alleluia returns for the dismissal dialogue.

OTHER IDEAS

After evening prayer, move the Easter candle from its place near the ambo to the baptismal font. It has been lit throughout the 50 days. Now it will burn for baptisms and funerals.

The newly baptized may want to sit together and dress for the occasion.

A strong tradition in church history made this an alternate day for baptisms. Celebrate infant baptism at today's Mass.

Decorate the space in a way that suggests the first fruits of the harvest. (See *To Crown the Year,* pages 145–148.) The use in decoration of green grasses, sweet rushes and green, leafy branches is a once universal medieval tradition shared by the synagogue and church. The custom is kept up strongly in some places in Europe, so much so that today is called "Green Sunday" from all the greenery that is carried. Pentecost greenery is a fine link with the other red-vestment Sunday eight weeks ago.

A staple in the musical repertoire should be the chant "Veni, creator" from the *Liber cantualis.* Hal H. Hopson wrote a dramatic reading of Acts 2:1–17 for singers, readers, handbells and organ (GIA, G-3442).

Encourage people at home to have a special family dinner with a decorated table. See *Catholic Household Blessings and Prayers* for texts for Pentecost (157) and the Easter season (84).

You may conclude the community's Easter celebration with Evening Prayer II. It closes with the double alleluia dismissal, signifying the end to the 50 days. Move the Easter candle to the font afterwards.

APRIL 27, 2003
Second Sunday of Easter

Share and Share Alike
Acts 4:32–35
"The community of believers was of one heart and mind."

ONE of the first lessons we learn in life is the importance of sharing what we have. Whether we receive freely or give freely, sharing brings happiness to all involved.

When the first Christians formed a community, they shared everything they owned. The followers of Jesus were not content with a personal relationship with their Savior. They craved a personal relationship with the community of believers.

Some believers had more than others. Those who owned property or houses sold them and gave the proceeds to the leaders, who distributed the money to those who needed it. Those who had more realized they could live with less. Those who had less got what they needed to live.

Today many Christians feel good if they tithe. If we give ten percent of what we earn to charities, we feel like we've done our part.

The first Christians did more. Much more. They gave until everyone in their community had the same. They gave fully in "witness to the resurrection of the Lord Jesus." Share and share alike.

Do you have more than you need of something? What would it take for you to give it away? All the early church needed was faith.

MAY 4, 2003
Third Sunday of Easter

Overcoming Blunders
Acts 3:13–15, 17–19
"The author of life you put to death."

ONCE in a while we make bad choices—really bad choices. They make us feel like all is lost. What could make us feel better? We'd feel better if we knew that other people have made worse mistakes than we did, and that they somehow overcame their bad choices.

Surely no one made worse choices than the people subjected to Peter's sermon in Acts of the Apostles. Peter tells them God gave them Jesus, but they handed him over to Pilate and missed the opportunity to grant him freedom. They asked freedom for a murderer instead.

God overcame this blunder with the mightiest act in history: God raised Jesus from the dead. Peter and others witnessed the risen Jesus.

Peter's audience had made some really bad choices. They had the chance to spare Jesus from death, but instead they were responsible for it.

All was not lost. "Repent and be converted," Peter told them, "that your sins may be wiped away." And look who's talking—a man who repeatedly denied knowing Jesus. He made a very bad choice. And now this same man is the risen Jesus' chief witness.

We have the same opportunity whenever we make bad choices. We can repent and change our ways. The God who raised Jesus has the power to forgive us. God can raise us up from despair to hope.

MAY 11, 2003
Fourth Sunday of Easter

Speaking Up
Acts 4:8–12
"In Jesus' name this man stands before you healed."

THERE are times when you just have to speak up. Something wonderful has delighted you. Or something unjust has befallen you. You may not speak eloquently, but you have to tell people about it. You might send a letter to Congress or to the editor of your paper. The word inside you has to get out. The higher it goes the better.

Peter and John healed a cripple, then preached a sermon about Jesus. Multitudes listened. The authorities grew nervous. So they arrested the apostles and locked them up overnight. Meanwhile, 5,000 new believers were baptized.

The next day, the authorities asked Peter and John for an explanation. They gave a speech about the good deed done to a cripple, the power of the name of Jesus Christ, the guilt of those who crucified him and the majesty of God who raised him from the dead.

Peter and John had experienced the wonder of God's power and the injustice of their arrest. In the wake of these events, they preached a powerful sermon.

When God's power touches us, we have to speak up about it. This Easter God has raised you up to new life in Christ. What wonders have you seen? Who will hear you proclaim them?

MAY 18, 2003
Fifth Sunday of Easter

Converting the Community
Acts 9:26–31
"Saul tried to join the disciples of Jesus, but they were all afraid of him."

IF Easter is working its wonder, you are different today than you were a year ago. Lent and Easter are seasons of renewal in the church. Each Lent we strive to face our sin, do penance and rise with Jesus. We draw on the power of these seasons to celebrate the love of God in our life, a love that accepts us in our sinfulness and calls us into grace.

Each year, if Easter works its wonder, we grow in holiness.

But there is one problem. Even though we may be different, other people may not realize it. They may treat us the same, making it hard for us to live fully the new life of grace.

Take Saul, for example. Before his conversion he persecuted Christians. After his conversion he lived for Christ alone.

But there was one problem. People didn't trust Saul. When he showed up in Jerusalem among the disciples, they were afraid of him because they didn't believe he had changed. Only when Barnabas defended Saul could he move about freely.

The mystery of renewal begins in the quiet of each person's heart, and gradually it converts the community.

MAY 25, 2003
Sixth Sunday of Easter

When Plans Go Wrong
Acts 10:25–26, 34–35, 44–48
"The believers were astounded that the gift of the Holy Spirit should be poured out on Gentiles."

SOME things don't work out the way you plan them. Even when you pray over a matter, and you decide on an action that you truly believe fits the will of God, things can turn out different from what you had in mind.

Sometimes God takes matters out of your hands.

Take Peter, for example. After the resurrection of Jesus, the Holy Spirit came upon him and other disciples. Peter preached repentance to converts from Judaism. They were baptized and then received the gifts of the Spirit. It formed a neat program: Preach to the Jews. Baptize them. Watch for the gifts of the Spirit. What could possibly go wrong?

Cornelius. Peter wasn't counting on Cornelius.

One day, while Peter was at prayer, he realized that God was calling not just Jews but Gentiles to belief in Christ. The Gentile Cornelius, who had also been praying, sent friends to find Peter.

When Peter came, his neat program fell apart. The Holy Spirit came upon the household of Cornelius before they were baptized—and before these Gentiles could even become Jews!

God had another plan.

Sometimes when things don't go our way there is a very simple reason. They are going the way God planned them.

Written by Paul Turner. © 2002 Archdiocese of Chicago, Liturgy Training Publications; 1-800-933-1800; www.ltp.org.

MAY 29 OR JUNE 1, 2003
The Ascension of the Lord

Till We Meet Again
Acts 1:1–11
"A cloud took Jesus from their sight."

WE have many ways of saying goodbye. "So long." "See you later." "Take care."

Goodbyes are softened with the promise of another meeting. "Till we meet again." The time between the goodbye and the reunion is filled with joyful hope and anxious waiting.

Surely the disciples wondered if they had the tools they needed to survive that time. Jesus had been their leader, visionary, Messiah and friend. Without him, life would lose its center.

Jesus' goodbye came with two promises. He promised the Holy Spirit would guide the disciples in his absence, and he promised that he would come again. That left them in an in-between kind of time. After the goodbye, they waited for his coming again.

In fact, that's where we are, too. We are in between the visits of Jesus, a time of hope and anxiety. We often wonder if we have the tools we need to survive. We need vision and companionship on life's long road.

We have at our disposal the first promise of Jesus, the gift of the Holy Spirit. That Spirit will guide us through times of loneliness, into good decisions, amid the sorrows of sad goodbyes. The Spirit is our center.

Written by Paul Turner. © 2002 Archdiocese of Chicago, Liturgy Training Publications; 1-800-933-1800; www.ltp.org.

JUNE 1, 2003
Seventh Sunday of Easter

Choosing Among Equals
Acts 1:15–17, 20a, 20c–26
"The lot fell upon Matthias, and he was counted with the apostles."

SOME decisions are easy. We can see the bad consequences of one choice, so we pick the option that offers better results. Some decisions are hard because the two choices seem equal. They may offer equally unhappy consequences, or they may offer two very good solutions. How do you decide when you cannot see an advantage?

This situation faced the early church as it dealt with a painful situation. Jesus had formed a core group known as "the Twelve." He probably chose that number to match the number of the tribes of Israel.

There was one problem. Among the Twelve was Judas Iscariot, who betrayed Jesus and then took his own life. The early church had to deal with the grief and exhilaration of Jesus' death and resurrection, but they also had to deal with the death of Judas.

The leadership then became known as "the Eleven." It didn't sound right.

Peter decided to replace Judas. He needed someone who was with Jesus from his baptism by John to his resurrection. The community proposed two candidates. Either would have been fine. How could they choose?

They prayed and let God choose.

JUNE 8, 2003
Pentecost

The Gift of Understanding
Acts 2:1–11
"How does each of us hear them in his native language?"

VISITORS to foreign countries are frightened if they do not know the language. It is hard to imagine how much we rely on language. We can talk with strangers, read signs and raise children with comparative ease because we have established something in common—language.

Take it away and chaos reigns. People misunderstand one another, they grow impatient or they presume others are ignorant or malicious. All this can happen when we do not speak the same language.

The book of Genesis explains the existence of multiple languages as a punishment from God. When people tried to build an enormous tower in an effort to enter heaven, God punished them by confusing their speech. Human cooperation became chaos.

God is the creator of everything and the ruler of all. God even rules over language.

When the Holy Spirit came on the first Pentecost and bestowed the gift of tongues upon the apostles, the confusion of languages ceased. Everyone could understand. The Christian message was central enough to human experience to resonate with all people, no matter what language they spoke.

Whenever we cannot understand what life is saying to us, we have only to turn to the ruler of languages. The Holy Spirit will translate.

SUMMER AND FALL ORDINARY TIME

The Meaning

THE prosaic title of Ordinary Time captures its plainness. But integral to its arrival is its sense of being ordered, not just ordinary. This long stretch of time between the Easter and Advent seasons marches silently apace, drawing no attention to itself, but quietly marking the hum of the cosmos spinning under God's powerfully creative arms. Day by day, in season and out, we celebrate the wonder of time and the hope of salvation.

■ WE RESUME ORDINARY TIME AT ITS TENTH WEEK. We interrupted the eighth week to make room for Lent and Easter. The ninth week is not observed this year. We almost always lose some of Ordinary Time because the year has to end with the thirty-fourth week. In the summer and fall span of Ordinary Time, then, we anchor the weeks where they will end and figure out what week should follow Pentecost by counting backwards. This year's casualty is week nine.

■ THIS YEAR A NUMBER OF SOLEMNITIES AND "FEASTS OF THE LORD" FALL ON SUNDAYS, AND SO ECLIPSE THE ORDINARY TIME PROPERS. You may recall this happening in February with the

Feast of the Presentation. On average, of course, that feast lands on a Sunday once every seven years. But whenever it does in a non-leap year, an unusually large number of other Sundays in Ordinary Time (this year the Fourth, Thirteenth, Twenty-fourth, Thirty-first and Thirty-second) step aside to make room for the observances of Peter and Paul, the Exaltation of the Holy Cross, All Souls, and the Dedication of the Lateran Basilica. The last time all these feasts landed on Sundays was 1997. It won't happen again until 2014.

The Saints

DURING Ordinary Time, we freely celebrate the cycle of saints' days without the extra context of a primary season of the church year.

■ SOLEMNITIES include the Assumption (August 15, a Friday and a holy day of obligation this year) and All Saints' Day (November 1, a Saturday and so not a day of obligation in 2003). Three solemnities fall during the same week in June: the Nativity of John the Baptist (June 24), the Sacred Heart of Jesus (June 27) and Peter and Paul (June 29). The last of these falls on a Sunday and takes the place of the Ordinary Time liturgy. That means that those who come on Sundays will not see green vestments this year until July.

All Souls' Day (November 2), though not called a solemnity, ranks with them. It falls on a Sunday this year and takes the place of the Ordinary Time liturgy.

If the patronal day of your city, state, parish church or religious community falls during this period, it also ranks as a solemnity. If it falls on Sunday, it takes precedence over the Ordinary Time Sunday liturgy.

■ FEASTS during this period this year include several apostles, such as Thomas (July 3), James (July 25), and Simon and Jude (October 28). Other feasts recall the Birth of Mary (September 8) and the Transfiguration of the Lord (August 6). Two events from the history of the church, the Exaltation of the Holy Cross (September 14) and the Dedication of the Lateran Basilica (November 9), fall on Sunday this year. They will replace the Ordinary Time liturgy. Other saints of note

also merit feasts, like the archangels (September 29) and Luke (October 18).

■ OBLIGATORY MEMORIALS APPEAR IN EVERY MONTH OF ORDINARY TIME. Each comes with its own vestment color and presidential prayers, including a preface. If the saint has no complete set of proper prayers, turn to the relevant common of martyrs, pastors, doctors, virgins or holy men and women. Memorials of biblical figures such as Mary Magdalene, Martha, John the Baptist, as well as the memorial of Our Lady of Sorrows and of the Guardian Angels, have proper gospels that must replace the weekday gospel. Barnabas has a proper first reading that replaces the weekday one.

It is best not to change the scriptures from the semicontinuous readings of Ordinary Time, but you may take them from the lectionary common appropriate for the saint if for some good reason it seems better that day.

■ OPTIONAL MEMORIALS APPEAR EVERY MONTH AS WELL. Your community may celebrate the Ordinary Time Mass or the saint whose memorial is optional. If you celebrate the optional saint, use the prayers from the sacramentary. You may also select readings from the lectionary commons, but it is better to follow the readings in the Ordinary Time sequence. When a Saturday in Ordinary Time calls for the weekday liturgy, a Mass for the Blessed Virgin Mary may be used. Prayers and readings may be taken from the common of the Blessed Virgin Mary or from the *Collection of Masses of the Blessed Virgin Mary*.

■ OTHER OCCASIONS: The lectionary and sacramentary also supply texts for votive Masses and Masses for various needs and occasions. These texts may be used on any Ordinary Time weekday that is not a feast or solemnity.

Several events will occur during this time, including civic holidays and back-to-school celebrations. You will find a rich collection of prayers and scripture readings in the liturgical books under headings such as "For the Church" and "For Civil Needs."

The Lectionary

THE Sunday lectionary retains the celebratory spirit of Easter for three more weeks this year. As usual, the solemnities of Trinity Sunday and the Body and Blood of Christ follow Pentecost. This year the Solemnity of Peter and Paul happens to fall on the next Sunday, giving us a longer than usual stretch before "green Sundays" return.

■ WHEN ORDINARY TIME BEGINS ITS SUNDAY SOJOURN ON JULY 6, we pick up the lectionary at week 14. We re-enter Mark's gospel at the point where Jesus meets rejection from his own family. It will feel like this incident projects him into a more intense ministry with his disciples, a mission that will unfold in the weeks ahead.

■ YOU WOULD NEED A VERY GOOD MEMORY TO RECALL THAT THE SECOND READINGS on the two Sundays before Lent this year came from Paul's Second Letter to the Corinthians. That series—if you can call it a series—concludes with one last excerpt on July 6 after a hiatus of several months. From then until Advent, the second readings of Ordinary Time Sundays will come from Ephesians, James and Hebrews. If you accept the view of many scripture scholars that the author of the letters to the Corinthians did not also write Ephesians, you will hear only one passage from the genuine letters of Paul on the Ordinary Time Sundays of summer and fall, and that single passage comes on the first green Sunday, July 6.

■ THE RESPONSORIAL PSALMS may also be drawn from the common psalms for Ordinary Time. These psalms (19, 27, 34, 63, 95, 100, 103 and 145) express different aspects of our belief, give voice and biblical foundation to the language of prayer, and provide the community the opportunity to build its musical repertoire.

■ THE SUNDAY *LECTIONARY FOR MASSES WITH CHILDREN* offers a selection of scriptures for all these Sundays, including this year's special celebrations. You will need the weekday volume to find the Masses for Peter and Paul (June 29), the Exaltation of the Cross (September 14), All Souls (November 2) and the Dedication of the Lateran Basilica (November 9). Those Masses do not appear in the volume of children's readings from Year B.

The children's lectionary offers all three readings at most of the Masses during this period. Only the Mass during the day appears for Peter and Paul on June 29, but with all the readings. The Twenty-first Sunday offers three readings, but the second is changed to lift the passage from Ephesians that speaks directly to children. In two instances, the lectionary offers three readings but changes the responsorial psalm (Sundays Fourteen and Twenty-six).

The second reading is omitted on Sundays Sixteen, Eighteen, Twenty-seven and Thirty-three. It is also omitted for the Holy Cross (September 14), when the psalm is changed to 88. On the solemnity of the Body and Blood of the Lord, the second reading and the optional sequence are both omitted from the children's lectionary.

The first reading is omitted on two occasions: the Twenty-fifth Sunday, which tells of the plot of the wicked, and the Twenty-ninth Sunday, a song of the suffering servant.

On All Souls' Day (November 2) and the Dedication of the Lateran Basilica (November 9), you may choose the number of readings from the commons of the dead and the dedication of a church, respectively. With careful planning, you can match these to the readings heard by the full assembly on those days.

The Sacramentary

■ SAMPLE FORMULAS FOR THE GENERAL INTERCESSIONS appear in the sacramentary's first appendix. See #1–2 and 9–10 for those suggested for Ordinary Time.

■ ORDINARY TIME CAN PROVIDE AN OPPORTUNITY TO EVALUATE SOME OF THE THINGS WE ORDINARILY DO. Consider, for example, the eucharistic prayer.

This prayer is the most important of the Mass, and—for goodness' sake—the most important prayer in the history of the church. We pray it each and every day at church, sometimes more than once a day. It deserves careful attention to let it stand out.

Most of the work falls to the presider, who is entrusted with almost all the text. A good presider will make every effort to be centered and to pray this prayer with intensity. A priest

prays by profession. He knows union with God through both private and public prayer. In the public arena, he unifies the prayers of the people. When he comes to know his flock, their cares and joys, he presents them to God as intercessor. But above all, he raises to God prayers of blessing and praise. To effectively pray the eucharistic prayer, the priest draws on his personal experience of a lifetime devoted to prayer, the needs of the community gathered around him, his belief in the awesome power and presence of God, and his ability to place himself in the sacramental moment of liturgical worship.

Everything ultimately depends on this. We say it so blithely: The priest prays the eucharistic prayer. But we mean it profoundly: The priest *prays* the eucharistic prayer.

The church gives us a variety of prayers. With careful planning, all of them may be used fittingly for Sunday worship. Too often presiders flip the book open to Eucharistic Prayer II, especially when the ceremony feels long, because it is the shortest. But a heartfelt rendering of any eucharistic prayer will help people lose track of time as the entire assembly loses its corporate self in this mystical moment of prayer. Do a quick mental check. Which eucharistic prayers has your community used this year? All four of the principal ones? Both prayers for reconciliation? All of the children's prayers? Those for Masses for various needs and occasions? A long stretch of Ordinary Time lies before you. You will have ample opportunity to widen the community's experience of the eucharistic prayer by exercising all the options.

The people's acclamations are meant to enhance their participation in the prayer—enhance, not restrict. These interpolations include the Holy, the memorial acclamation, the great Amen, and the other acclamations that appear in the children's eucharistic prayers and in those for various needs and occasions. But they presume that the people are praying the entire prayer quietly in union with the presider. These acclamations give voice to the prayer all are making together.

■ THE ASSEMBLY'S ACCLAMATIONS WORK BEST WHEN THEY ARE SUNG. *Sourcebook* continues to recommend that you use one set of musical acclamations for a period of time, rather than change them frequently. The liturgical books make no such recommendation, but pastoral practice has shown the wisdom of this approach.

You can develop a repertoire over a period of months. People can join in the acclamation without having to think too much about which one it will be. You can give some character and shape to the seasons of the year by following the same set of acclamations throughout. And you can give people a little variety as the church year progresses.

Instrumentalists can lend valuable support to the eucharistic prayer. Organists can change registration, keeping it light during seasons like Advent and Lent, stronger during seasons like Christmas and Easter. In planning the registration for any service, the organist could reserve some stops like reeds and mixtures for the eucharistic prayer, while relying on diapasons and even flutes for other parts of the Mass. Try to make the eucharistic prayer distinctive. On the big celebrations, and there will be several special ones during Ordinary Time this summer and fall, add extra instruments to enhance the people's acclamations and to set the big days apart.

■ DOES YOUR COMMUNITY SING THE PREFACE DIALOGUE? The presider with a gift for song can announce the solemnity of the eucharistic prayer by opening it with its dialogue and preface in song. The sacramentary gives musical settings of almost every preface, and there are over one hundred of them. Once the dialogue is in repertoire and the presider has a facility for the preface, you can start the eucharistic prayer each Sunday in song.

On some days, you may wish the presider to sing the entire prayer. Many settings are available and popular. The simple chants in the sacramentary should not be overlooked. Steve Janco's "Mass for Angels and Saints" is a gem, as is Chris Walker's "Celtic Mass." Both deserve a place in parish repertoires.

■ MOST OF THE EUCHARISTIC PRAYERS FOLLOW A SIMILAR OUTLINE, but the first has a unique structure. Many people find the first prayer ponderous and repetitive, but it was composed with a certain balance in mind. The prayers for the living in the first half of the prayer balance with those for the dead in the second half. The first list of apostles and martyrs balances with the additional saints (including several women) in the second half.

The first eucharistic prayer is called the Roman Canon. Its origins are Roman, as you can tell by the choice of saints in the second half of the prayer. It used to be "the canon"—the only way to say the eucharistic prayer in the Latin Rite. Now, it is "canon" only by tradition. That is why the church favors the title "eucharistic prayer."

■ THE TRADITIONAL POSTURE FOR THE EUCHARISTIC PRAYER IS STANDING. The Eastern Rites still observe this custom. The Roman Rite retains it universally for the opening dialogue and preface, and then has the assembly change posture to kneeling after the prayer has begun. In many parts of the Catholic world, the faithful resume standing after the memorial acclamation. In the United States we ordinarily remain kneeling until after the great Amen.

In the early church, standing for prayer expressed the faithful's belief in the resurrection. The rubrics for Mass permit the assembly to stand if the number of people is large, if the space is limited, or for "some other good reason." Good reasons might include tradition, belief in the resurrection, unity with the oriental rites, and full and active participation of the faithful.

Accommodation should always be made in our buildings and in our hearts for those who use a wheelchair or whose disabilities make any posture but sitting an extraordinary hardship. The common posture of the assembly signifies its unity, but what matters most is that all be united in prayer.

The Book of Blessings

PLAN ahead to offer blessings for certain groups in the parish. Occasions might include wedding anniversaries (1-IIIA), fathers (56), birthdays (1-XI), thanksgiving after harvest (28) and athletic events (29); people might include engaged couples (1-VI), catechists (4-I), students and teachers (5); things could include cars (21), boats and fishing gear (22), tools (24) and Thanksgiving Day food (58).

These blessings may be incorporated into Mass, or you could provide texts for people to pray at home.

The Rite of Christian Initiation of Adults

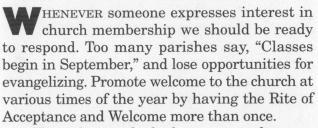

WHENEVER someone expresses interest in church membership we should be ready to respond. Too many parishes say, "Classes begin in September," and lose opportunities for evangelizing. Promote welcome to the church at various times of the year by having the Rite of Acceptance and Welcome more than once.

The unbaptized who become catechumens through the Rite of Acceptance establish an important relationship with the church supported by our liturgical and canonical documents. There is no relationship between the liturgical calendar and the Rite of Acceptance. It should be celebrated when one or more inquirers are ready to become catechumens.

The baptism of adults, however, should be reserved to the Easter Vigil, except in the most exceptional circumstances.

■ THE RITE OF RECEPTION INTO THE FULL COMMUNION OF THE CATHOLIC CHURCH, however, can be celebrated at any time of year. If baptized candidates desire communion in the Catholic church, we may receive them when they are ready. Such celebrations may take place several times a year.

When people realize that the preparation for sacraments has some fluidity, they are more likely to follow the promptings of the Spirit. They may be more receptive to our efforts for evangelization.

■ GROUPS OF CATECHUMENS may have celebrations of the Word of God throughout this period of Ordinary Time. This is the period when they may be anointed with the oil of catechumens. The anointing may be given on one or more occasions, either in a word service, or as part of the liturgy of the word at a eucharist. This ritual may take place at Sunday Mass, for example.

■ MYSTAGOGY SESSIONS may continue throughout Ordinary Time as well. The American bishops have recommended such gatherings monthly during the first year following baptism (National Statutes, 24). Attendance is usually low, but we may promote these events at Sunday Mass. Attempts should be made to give pastoral care to neophytes who are experiencing the fullness of the eucharist throughout the liturgical year for the first time.

■ THE PRESENTATIONS OF THE CREED AND THE LORD'S PRAYER may take place outside the season of Lent. This option may help parishes who find the liturgies of Lent already too rich, or whose catechumens seem ready for the presentations and would benefit by having the Creed and Lord's Prayer now as part of their formation. In the history of the catechumenate, however, these rites came shortly before baptism.

The Liturgy of the Hours

VOLUMES III and IV of the *Liturgy of the Hours* will be used throughout summer and fall. For those unfamiliar with this form of prayer, Ordinary Time is a good time to begin. The editing of the books is simpler than in the other seasons of the year, and those using the one- or four-volume set discover that the prayer requires fewer ribbons and flipping of pages these days.

If a daily Mass is not taking place on one or more days a week or a month, try using one of the offices instead of a communion service to introduce people to this prayer.

The Rite of Penance

MOST parishes will continue offering the first form of the Rite of Penance every week, usually on Saturdays. However, private confession and absolution may be celebrated any day of the week, and if the priest's schedule permits it, you could try offering reconciliation on a weekday evening or Saturday mornings.

The second form of the sacrament, a communal celebration with individual confession and absolution, frequently appears on a parish's Advent and Lent schedule of activities. But it may happen at any time of year. Although attendance may be smaller during summer or fall, you could offer the sacrament communally for those who would like this opportunity. It could be combined with an evening's retreat for the parish, a parish mission, a school service, or even during the regularly scheduled time for private confessions, to invite those who come individually to acknowledge the communal nature of sin and forgiveness.

The Pastoral Care of the Sick

THE sacrament of the anointing of the sick may take place any time of year for the benefit of the faithful. Ordinary Time is a good period to give this sacrament attention, when no other seasons are vying for our time and energy. Choose one or two weekends this summer or fall when the sacrament may be offered at a communal celebration. Or schedule it at a daily Mass for those who might benefit from it.

■ IT IS IMPORTANT THAT THE FAITHFUL RECEIVE CATECHESIS ON VIATICUM AND ON THE SACRAMENT OF THE SICK. Many times they may confuse "Last Rites" with anointing of the sick. Any lay minister may give viaticum, or "last communion," if a priest is unavailable. Prayers for the dying and prayers for the dead may be led by any lay minister. A priest can offer the anointing of the sick with its prayers for healing apart from emergency situations. Help the faithful understand when it is important for a sick relative or friend to receive the pastoral care of the church.

The Rite of Marriage

MARRIAGE may be offered any time of year, any day of the week, but Saturday weddings are still popular in the culture. If the couple comes from two different faith backgrounds, be sure to consider the option of marriage without Mass. Especially if the guests are unfamiliar with the Catholic Mass, the wedding that takes place during a word service puts the assembly on more equal footing. At Mass, the communion rite becomes an important sign of the couple's unity, but if one partner is not Catholic, the symbols of unity begin to break down.

■ This year's calendar merits special attention because of all the special days falling on Saturdays and Sundays. The readings and prayers of the wedding Mass may replace those of an Ordinary Time Sunday Mass if the wedding takes place on a Saturday evening. However, on solemnities, the Mass of the day should be used, and you may substitute one of the readings from the wedding lectionary (*Rite of Marriage*, 11). This will apply for Saturday evening weddings on June 28 (because of Peter and Paul), Saturday day weddings on November 1 (because of All Saints, not a holy day of obligation in the United States this year, but still a solemnity), Saturday evening weddings on November 1 (because of All Souls' Day), and Saturday evening weddings on November 8 (because of the Dedication of the Lateran Basilica). The Mass prayers for a wedding on those days should come from the feast, not from the *Rite of Marriage*.

But if the wedding takes place on those dates without Mass, the wedding lectionary and the prayers from the *Rite of Marriage* are used.

The Rite of Ordination or Profession

Few parishes will be responsible for the ordination rites of a diocese or the rites of profession within a religious community, but if yours has one this year it will be a time for celebration and renewal for the whole community. In planning the ritual, remember that an ordination is not a coronation. The humble, circumspect service that the candidates enter should be evident also from the liturgy.

If your parish has no candidates for the diaconate or priesthood or for religious life, this would be a good season to ask why. Does the parish have a vocations committee? Are you suggesting to men and women that they consider the religious life? Could the parish schedule an annual event, perhaps a Mass for religious vocations, to which you invite seminarians or religious leaders to speak?

The Order of Christian Funerals

During the summer months, when many in the community are on vacation, it may be difficult to offer full liturgical ministries for funerals, but it is good to make an effort. Volunteers may be available in your community to support a funeral choir, the ministry of greeter, altar servers and cooks for a post-funeral dinner. The development of these ministries will make the funeral a good celebration for the departed Christian, and it will bring much consolation to a family at a time when they need the support of faith.

■ Evaluate the wake service too. The *Order of Christian Funerals* calls for a word service. Celebrating this service at church has some advantages. The church is set up with furnishings and participation aids for a real liturgy, and will be more conducive to prayer than many funeral chapels.

If the deceased is to be buried in the earth, the funeral rite strongly recommends that the faithful be present for this action. It may take the cooperation of cemetery officials, funeral homes, parish staff and families, but the gathering of the faithful around the actual moment of burial can provide a strong statement of unity and faith in the resurrection. The interment takes place near the beginning of the service at the cemetery, and more prayers are then offered by the faithful who stand, strong in faith, above the grave.

The Art and Environment

The verdure of summer and fall make their appearance in our worship spaces as well. Be sure to decorate the places of the assembly, not just the sanctuary. The gathering area and the nave deserve attention so all feel that their space fits with the season.

■ Shifts in the liturgical environment may subtly accompany the shifts of nature. As the community makes a mental adjustment from summer's relaxation to fall's energy, the environment of the liturgical space might change to reflect the different flowers and plants of late summer and early fall. Even the vessels may change: Clay pots and planters of early summer might yield to glass vases as summer progresses, just as metal vases and then woven baskets and a cornucopia could come on the scene as autumn approaches.

▪ VESTURE SHOULD APPEAR UNOBTRUSIVE AND NEUTRAL. The very frequency of green garments during the next six months will dull our senses to the color. If the vesture tries to do too much, it will threaten the effect of more dramatic vesture for other feasts and seasons. What does your green vesture look like? Is it time for something new?

The Music

CHOOSE a set of music for the eucharistic acclamations for summer, and replace it with another set sometime in fall, perhaps over Labor Day weekend when many people make the mental shift from summer calendar to school calendar.

▪ IF YOU WOULD LIKE TO ADD SOME MUSIC TO THE REPERTOIRE, you have a long period in which this can be accomplished. The following are worth consideration:

- "Speak Now, O Lord," by Joe Mattingly (WLP, 5204), a soul-stirring prayer of openness to God's word
- "On the Wings of Change," by Jerry Galipeau (WLP, 5209), a trumpet-like statement of faith in the resurrection
- "Christ Be Near at Either Hand," by Steven C. Warner (WLP, 7200), an effective setting of the Lorica of Saint Patrick
- "Gather Your People," by Robert Schaefer (WLP, 8691), a setting of Psalm 95 that sets the tone for an important celebration by nicely accompanying a lengthy procession
- "Come to the Living Stone," by Karen Schneider-Kirner and Steven C. Warner (WLP, 7243), a rhythmic invitation to prayer
- "Where Armies Scourge the Countryside," by Herman G. Stuempfle, Jr., and Perry Nelson (WLP, 8641), a fitting setting for a beautiful text praying for peace

- "Love Is His Word," by Calvin Hampton, arranged by Richard Proulx (WLP, 8677), a lovely setting of a hymn that already was lovely
- "Open Wide the Doors to Christ," arranged by Peter M. Kolar (WLP, 8683), a quickly learned hymn that assemblies will enjoy
- "Take Courage," by Ruth Duck and Steven R. Janco (WLP, 8702), a hymn text that meets a sentiment we all need sooner or later, in a musical setting that fits perfectly
- "Go, Be Justice," by Martin Willett and Kevin Keil (WLP, 8710), a challenge to the assembly to put faith into action
- "Wisdom, My Road," by Leslie Palmer Barnhart, based on a text from Ecclesiasticus adapted by Steven C. Warner (WLP, 7263), a lovely prayer for wisdom
- "Draw Near," by Steven R. Janco, based on John M. Neale's translation of a seventh-century hymn (WLP, 8567), part of a growing body of communion hymns that finally invites the faithful to share under both forms

A youth choir could build its repertoire, too, either as a summer activity for those attending different schools, or as an opportunity in the fall when education resumes.

- "Gathered as One," by Paul A. Tate (WLP, 7452), a lightly syncopated hymn of unity
- "Journey for Home," by Ed Bolduc (WLP, 7437), a pleading song of the spiritual life
- "Sing Alleluia!" by John Angotti (WLP, 7431), a simple tune that becomes a driving statement of faith
- "God's Holy Mystery," by Paul A. Tate (WLP, 7488), a communion song of faith based on the sixth chapter of John's gospel, especially useful late this summer
- "Lay Down That Spirit," by Joe Mattingly (WLP, 3674), an energetic song of plea and praise

For music that sounds more familiar, check out your repertoire of songs by Lucien Deiss. This eminent French liturgist and musician, active during and after the Second Vatican Council, left the church a legacy of service music that has been translated into many languages. A champion also of liturgical dance, Deiss has had a profound impact on the spirit and song of the liturgy. World Library Publications continues to make many of his classic pieces available in octavo form, like "Grant to Us, O Lord" (2556); "All the Earth" (2551); "God, Full of Mercy" (2555); "Keep in Mind" (2559); "Priestly People" (2564); "The Spirit of God" (2568); "There Is One Lord" (2569); "Where Two or Three Are Gathered" (2571); and "With Eternal Love" (2572). This music has held up well over the decades since it was composed.

You may also want to expand your knowledge of music that suits particular needs, like the following:

- "Mass of Redemption," by Steven R. Janco (WLP, 3110), another fine setting of texts for the Mass that will hold up even with much repetition

- "Glory to God," by Steven R. Janco (WLP, 8559), an easily sung setting for assembly with cantor or choir

- "Vespers: A Service of Evening Prayer," by Carla J. Giomo (GIA, G-5252), a complete setting of music for evening prayer

- "Magnificat," by Alan J. Hommerding (WLP, 5208), written with a choir in mind, but immediately singable by the assembly at evening prayer

- "Canticle of Zechariah," by Carl P. Daw, Jr., and Steven R. Janco (WLP, 8708), a carefully composed text, tune and accompaniment of this song for morning prayer

- "The Guardian's Farewell," by David Haas (GIA, G-5658), an achingly moving setting of a powerful text for funerals

- "Song of Farewell," by Mary Beth Wittry (WLP, 5225), a song you could introduce on Sundays in the fall, so people can sing it throughout the year at funerals

- "May Angels Lead You into Paradise," by Richard Proulx (WLP, 5227), for those looking for a setting of *In paradisum* that closes the funeral Mass (even Michael Joncas wishes you would find something more fitting for this part of the rite than "On Eagle's Wings"!)

- "As We Forgive," by James V. Marchionda (WLP, 7117), a song for children about reconciliation

■ YOU MAY ALSO WISH TO EXAMINE SOME OTHER RESOURCES FOR HYMNS. Collections abound, too many to be numbered, but the following are worth a fresh look:

- *African American Heritage Hymnal* (GIA, G-5400)

- *Hymns, Psalms, and Spiritual Songs* (Louisville: Westminster/John Knox Press, 1990)

- *Libro de Liturgia y Cántico* (Minneapolis: Augsburg Fortress, 1998)

- *This Far by Faith: An African American Resource for Worship* (Minneapolis: Augsburg Fortress, 1999)

- *The United Methodist Hymnal: Book of United Methodist Worship* (Nashville: The United Methodist Publishing House, 1989)

- *Voices United: The Hymn and Worship Book of the United Church of Canada* (Ontario: The United Church Publishing House, 1996)

Pianists should be aware of *Fourteen American Spirituals & Hymns* by Ann Buys (GIA, G-5322).

The Parish and Home

DURING summer people may have more leisure for quiet prayer and even family prayer in common. Provide resources for summer reading and prayer. *I Will Lie Down This Night* and *I Will Arise This Day* by Melissa Musick Nussbaum are lovely introductions to prayer at evening and morning. For those who wish to do more, *Psalms for Morning and Evening Prayer* and the whole *Psalter* are fine summer books for reflection. All are available from LTP.

Families may enjoy having copies of LTP's *Table Prayer Card for Summer* and *Table Prayer Card for Autumn and Winter* (1995), an inexpensive purchase available in bulk.

Texts

■ GREETING: Sacramentaries of other language-groups include this greeting:

> The Lord of glory and the giver of every grace be with you.

The greeting that opens the letter to the Ephesians is:

> Grace to you and peace from God our Father and the Lord Jesus Christ.

■ INTRODUCTION TO THE PENITENTIAL RITE: Try an introduction inspired by the letter to the Ephesians:

> In Jesus we have redemption and the forgiveness of transgressions. Let us call to mind the riches of grace Christ lavishes even upon sinners.

■ RESPONSE TO THE GENERAL INTERCESSIONS:

> Have mercy on your people, Lord.
> God of glory, hear our prayer.

■ DISMISSAL OF CATECHUMENS:

> God has made known to us the mystery of the divine plan. May God's will be accomplished within you. Go in peace.

June

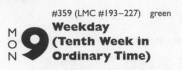

M O N 9 #359 (LMC #193–227) green
**Weekday
(Tenth Week in
Ordinary Time)**

Optional Memorial of Ephrem, deacon, poet, doctor of the church (+ 373), white • We return to Ordinary Time weekdays in just the place where the lectionary begins its semi-continuous reading of Matthew's gospel. Each year the weekday lectionary offers us daily readings from the three synoptic gospels in the order in which scholars believe they were written: Mark, Matthew, then Luke. Matthew's story begins every year during the tenth week of Ordinary Time, which just happens to be where we return to that period this year. (The week changes from year to year due to the fluctuating date of Easter.)

Many people find it helpful to think of Matthew's story as a collection of five discourses by Jesus, framed by narrative accounts of his life. We do not begin reading from Matthew at the beginning of the gospel. There we find the story of Jesus' birth, an account more fitting in December than in June. Instead, we start at the first discourse, the famous Sermon on the Mount, which begins with the well-known Beatitudes. Jesus' care for the poor in spirit stands as a manifesto for his ministry.

Matthew will serve as the gospel for daily Mass from now through the end of August.

The daily Mass first reading for the next two weeks will come from Paul's Second Letter to the Corinthians. It's not clear how many letters Paul wrote to the church at Corinth. This letter may actually be a composite of two or more, and it refers to another one that does not sound like the ones we have. But by tradition we call this letter the second. It opens with a passage dear to those who give pastoral care to the sick. God comforts us in our afflictions and enables us to comfort those who are in any trouble with the same consolation we have received from God.

The refrain of Psalm 34, "Taste and see the goodness of the Lord," makes most people assume it is a communion hymn. But its choice today relates to a different theme, thanksgiving to God for rescue from suffering. Near the end of the psalm we sing of the angel who delivers those who fear God. In the original Hebrew, this psalm is an alphabetic psalm. Each line begins with a new letter of the Hebrew alphabet. Consequently, each verse has an identity all its own, and although the verses share some thematic relationships, they do not logically follow one after another.

In Appendix VII of the sacramentary you will find a Mass for the anointing of the sick, which includes a preface reflecting on the mystery of human suffering.

■ TODAY'S SAINT: Ephrem is the only Syrian honored with the title of Doctor of the Church. His evocative poetry earned him the title, "the Harp of the Holy Spirit." A theological journal published in India today is named after him. Modern-day songwriters and poets can make good use of Ephrem's language and imagery, a model for the connections between the Bible and the liturgy.

In Argentina (and in other places) the Monday after Pentecost is a celebration of Mary, Mother of the Church, a title bestowed by Pope Paul VI at the end of the third session of the Second Vatican Council. [See the *Collection of Masses of the Blessed Virgin Mary* (25–27). See also the votive Mass in Appendix X of the sacramentary.]

T U E 10 #360 (LMC #193–227) green
Weekday

Stepping into the Sermon on the Mount, we hear Jesus' famous comparison of disciples to salt and light. Both elements can be unproductive, but put to proper use they symbolize the glory that Christians give the Father.

"Through Christ our Lord. Amen." Everyone knows that formula to conclude our prayers. Paul explains in today's reading why it is we address our Amen to God through Christ when we worship together. Jesus was always "yes" and Paul expects the same of us.

In response, we sing several verses of Psalm 119, a hymn affirming the acceptance of God's holy law. Under the category of useless trivia, note the refrains for the psalm for this day in years one and two of the lectionary. This year we sing from Psalm 119, "Lord, let your face shine on me." Next year, on the same Tuesday of week ten, we sing from Psalm 4, "Lord, let your face shine on us." Singular one year, plural the next. Go figure.

The sacramentary includes a votive Mass for the Holy Name of Jesus (4).

W E D 11 #361 (LMC #193–227) red
Barnabas, apostle
MEMORIAL

You may take the gospel from the weekday in sequence—Jesus' assurance that he has come not to abolish the law, but to complete it. Or you may draw it from June 11 (#580)—Jesus' missionary command to the disciples. The first reading, though, should come from June 11, the passage from Acts of the Apostles regarding Barnabas's ministry in Antioch. (On memorials of saints mentioned in the Bible, such as Mary Magdalene and Barnabas, a relevant passage mentioning the saint replaces one of the weekday readings.)

■ BARNABAS is an apostle, like Paul, not among "the Twelve." He is remembered with a memorial (but not a feast, like other apostles) on the liturgical calendar. So this is one apostle whose celebration does not call for singing the Glory to God. Use a preface for apostles, perhaps the first (P 64). Barnabas is mentioned in Eucharistic Prayer I.

THU 12 #362 (LMC #193–227) green
Weekday

Jesus urges his hearers to get along. If you bring your gift to the altar without forgiveness, first make peace and then offer the gift.

Remembering how Moses veiled his face to protect the people from the reflected dazzle of the glory of God, Paul says ancient Israel still has only a veiled understanding of God's word. The faithful gaze on God's glory with unveiled faces, and that glory transforms us into God's image. Psalm 85 sings of God's glory.

The second eucharistic prayer for Masses of reconciliation says, "enemies begin to speak to one another."

In Ecuador, today is the memorial of Blessed Mercedes de Jesús Molina, but this year it is suppressed: In all the dioceses of Latin American, the Thursday after Pentecost and before Trinity Sunday (and so a week before the customary date of the solemnity of the Body and Blood of Christ) is the feast of "Jesus Christ, High and Eternal Priest."

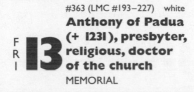

FRI 13 #363 (LMC #193–227) white
Anthony of Padua (+ 1231), presbyter, religious, doctor of the church
MEMORIAL

Jesus takes up the questions of lust, adultery and divorce. He allowed some exception, but his intent was to honor the marriage covenant.

Paul affirms the power of God that overcomes the weakness of humanity. We hold the treasure of God's glory in the earthen vessels of our bodies, to show just how strong God is. The hardships of the apostolic life only allow the life of Jesus to be revealed. A prayer of thanksgiving for deliverance from affliction serves as today's psalm, and "alleluia" is an alternate refrain.

■ TODAY'S SAINT: Anthony is one of the most popular saints in Catholic piety, frequently petitioned for the location of lost articles. A native of Portugal, his ministry as a Franciscan took him to many locations, including Padua, where he taught, preached and is buried. An endless stream of visitors prays at his shrine in Padua, where he is known simply as "the Saint."

The sacramentary offers an opening prayer for today. Others may come from the common of doctors. The preface may be that of pastors (P 67).

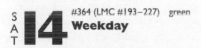

SAT 14 #364 (LMC #193–227) green
Weekday

Optional Memorial of the Blessed Virgin Mary/white ■ Jesus continues his advice on interpersonal behavior and asks his listeners not to take false oaths.

We are ambassadors of Christ, ministers of reconciliation, Paul announces. The psalmist sings that God pardons all our iniquities.

The fourth eucharistic prayer quotes today's first reading: "And that we might live no longer for ourselves but for him."

From the *Collection of Masses of the Blessed Virgin Mary,* see the texts for Holy Mary, the New Eve (#20), with its opening prayer that we may reject the old ways of sin. The Saturday following Pentecost, summer's "Ember Saturday," used to be a traditional day for the ordination of priests. You might

remember vocations, seminarians and priests in the general intercessions today.

☀15 #165 (LMC #159)
The Holy Trinity
SOLEMNITY

ORIENTATION

It's hard to imagine anyone disagreeing with the idea of a feast for the Trinity, but proposals for creating this festival met severe opposition in the Middle Ages. Pope John XXII finally declared it a feast for the universal church in 1334, while the papacy had its residence in Avignon, away from Rome, but near sites where Trinity Sunday was already an accepted practice.

The Sunday after Pentecost, in more ancient times, was observed with a nightlong vigil beginning Saturday night, using the texts in what became the Mass for Ember Saturday on the former calendar. When such "vigils" were concluded on Saturday instead of at Sunday dawn, this left no Mass formulary for Sunday morning. The "generic formulary" that focused on the Holy Trinity came to be used on this Sunday morning even before there was a festival day in honor of the Trinity.

The Byzantine calendar makes much of the festivals of Epiphany (the baptism of Christ) and Pentecost as moments of the revelation of the Holy Trinity. This Sunday is their All Saints' Day, which keeps the day grounded in Easter.

The solemnity of the Holy Trinity is a celebration of our belief in Father, Son and Spirit, one God in three divine persons. Today also is Father's Day.

LECTIONARY

The gospel for today is the traditional one for this solemnity. It served as the only gospel for Trinity Sunday each year until 1969. Even though we feature Mark on Sundays this year, we read from Matthew today. The other two years of the cycle draw from John, so this feast pays scant attention to the evangelical year. Matthew's magisterial account of the great commission stands at the end of the gospel. In his final words to the disciples, Jesus sends them out to baptize in the name of the Trinity and to teach.

Paul describes our participation in the life of the Trinity. We are adopted as children of God, whom we call Father through the Spirit.

In the first reading, Moses reminds the people that the God of all creation has come unspeakably close to them. His sermon expounds on the attributes of the God we celebrate this day.

Psalm 33 includes a prophetic verse about the Trinity. In the second stanza of today's responsory we sing, "By the word of the Lord the heavens were made; by the breath of his mouth all their host." Early Christians believed that these references to Lord, word and breath in one verse of a Hebrew song concealed the profound description of a trinitarian God, whose activity became manifest in the Word made flesh and the Spirit of life.

These texts are located in the lectionary after the Sundays of Ordinary Time. They are sometimes difficult to find, so allow extra time to set the place.

SACRAMENTARY

Prayers for today are located after the Sundays of Ordinary Time, instead of where you might expect to find them, after Pentecost. Be sure the place is marked before the eucharist begins.

The alternative opening prayer boldly addresses all three members of the Trinity. The formula is unique in the sacramentary. There is a preface for Trinity Sunday (P 43).

OTHER IDEAS

Even though a celebratory tone continues, the Easter season is over and the church year has entered Ordinary Time. This will not be immediately evident to the gathered Sunday assembly, as it would be on weekdays. But it would be appropriate to simplify the environment of the worship space to set this Sunday off from last. Certainly a simple set of white vesture (in contrast to Easter's more festive set) is an option in some parishes. You may wish to change the eucharistic prayer acclamations this week as well. If you used the sprinkling rite during the Easter season, go back to the Penitential Rite today.

This day offers us an opportunity to sing one or two of a grand collection of trinitarian hymns. If your community still observes the lamentable Catholic practice of limiting hymns to two verses (hymns are poetry set to music, and such language deserves to be kept integral), be sure not to omit a verse about the Holy Spirit!

The *Book of Blessings* includes a prayer for Father's Day (56). See also *Catholic Household Blessings and Prayers* (198). Perhaps a holy card depicting Saint Joseph, the patron of fathers, can be distributed today after Mass, and there are fine ones available from The Printery House.

Weekday (Eleventh Week in Ordinary Time)

The Sermon on the Mount continues with Jesus' advice to turn the other cheek. These simple instructions for a charitable life are difficult to observe.

The catalogue of hardships in today's first reading shows how difficult Paul's life was. But through every adversity he strives to act with patience, giving offense to no one. The psalm of salvation that follows this reading recalls Paul's acclamation, "Now is the day of salvation!"

The first eucharistic prayer for reconciliation makes a good choice today.

Weekday

Jesus' advice to be charitable reaches its climax today: "Love your enemies." This goes farther than the vengeance and tolerance proposed by other parts of the Bible and moves the Christian into a new sphere of forgiveness.

Every Christian leader eventually asks for financial support. Paul was no exception. He praised the Macedonians for supporting the needy in Jerusalem, and he asks the Corinthians to join in the effort. "I am not giving an order," he says, but testing out the church's generosity. The psalm praises God who secures justice for the oppressed and gives food to the hungry.

Use the second eucharistic prayer for reconciliation.

Weekday

Jesus suggests certain actions for his followers to perform—prayer and fasting—but more importantly he suggests the spirit with which to observe them.

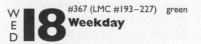

As Paul stumped for money in yesterday's passage, today he promotes the blessings afforded to those who give in the right spirit. Giving is good, but giving with the right spirit is better. God loves a cheerful giver. The psalm blesses those who give lavishly to the poor.

The fourth weekday preface (P 40) takes a humble attitude toward prayer.

THU 19 Weekday
#368 (LMC #193–227)   green

Optional Memorial of Romuald (+ 1027), abbot, monastic founder / white ▪ We call one prayer "the Lord's" because Jesus taught it to us. Shortly before the baptism of adults, we present the elect with this prayer. They receive it the way we hear it today, as a reading in the gospel. Jesus speaks through his word directly to the ears of believers today. The only part of the prayer he thought needed extra commentary was that line about forgiveness.

Was Saint Paul a lousy public speaker? He admits as much in today's first reading while he defends his knowledge of the gospel and the truthfulness of its message. Many voices compete for our attention, and sometimes the one lacking skill in delivery may actually have the most helpful content. After a reading that tries to shore up flagging faith, today's psalm affirms the reliability of God's words and works.

Again, the fourth weekday preface (P 40) takes an appropriate stance on the benefits of prayer.

▪ TODAY'S SAINT: Romuald entered a monastery near Ravenna after witnessing his father kill someone in a duel. He eventually became abbot and, as founder of the Camaldolese, was much esteemed for his spiritual life of asceticism.

In Bolivia, Cuba, the Dominican Republic, El Salvador, Mexico, Nicaragua, Puerto Rico, Venezuela

and in other places, today is the solemnity of the Body and Blood of the Lord (see this coming Sunday), and a holy day of obligation.

FRI 20 Weekday
#369 (LMC #193–227)   green

Jesus contrasts the treasures of earth with those of heaven. Every generation can examine its conscience with this reminder: Where your treasure lies, there your heart is as well.

Several times in this letter to the Corinthians, Paul has reflected on the hardships of being an apostle. Another catalogue appears today. He was whipped with 39 lashes on five separate occasions, beaten with rods three times, stoned once, and shipwrecked three times. That was just for starters. Apart from these physical sufferings, he speaks of his anxiety for the churches he loves. The psalm assures us that God will deliver the just from all their afflictions.

See the sacramentary's Mass for any need (38A) and the fourth version of the eucharistic prayer for various needs and occasions.

SAT 21 Aloysius Gonzaga (+ 1591), religious
#370 (LMC #193–227)   white
MEMORIAL

Jesus urges his hearers to put complete trust in God and turn away from other interests. God knows what we need before we do, and provides it generously.

No one knows for sure what "thorn in the flesh" Paul suffered, but his admission of this pain comes out in today's first reading, the last of our series from the Second Letter to the Corinthians. Throughout his hardships, Paul's reliance on the grace of God allowed the power of Christ to rest on him. "Therefore, I am content with weakness." How many of us

can say that? Once again, Psalm 34, with its assurance of God's deliverance, answers the theme of the first reading.

▪ TODAY'S SAINT: Aloysius joined the Society of Jesus and was praised for his simplicity and piety. During a plague he cared for the sick in the hospital. These efforts brought on the illness that claimed his life at the age of 23.

The sacramentary offers a complete set of prayers for the day, including an opening prayer. The first preface for holy men and women (P 69) is appropriate for today.

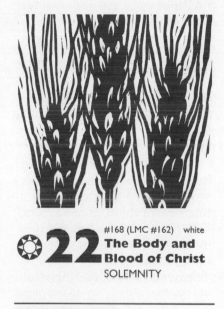

22 The Body and Blood of Christ
#168 (LMC #162)   white
SOLEMNITY

ORIENTATION

In 1208 Juliana of Retinnes, an Augustinian nun from Belgium, saw a vision of a lunar disk surrounded by rays of dazzling white light. One side of the disk appeared dark, and in her vision she heard God tell her that the darkness represented no feast on the calendar to honor the blessed sacrament. When her friend James Pantaléon became Pope Urban IV, he extended the feast of Corpus Christi to the universal church.

The festival became very popular throughout the Roman Catholic Church and, probably because the weather was finally clement in Europe, was a favorite occasion (like Pentecost and the Nativity of John) for outdoor processions, plays and fairs.

The origin of the feast shows the influence of an age when the faithful never shared the blood of Christ at communion, rarely shared even the body of Christ due to penitential practices, but adored the real presence of Christ in the reserved eucharistic host as their vicarious participation in divine life.

Today's calendar combines this medieval feast with the formerly and strangely separate feast of the Blood of Christ into a single celebration.

LECTIONARY

The texts are found just after Trinity Sunday, in the section of the lectionary following the Sundays in Ordinary Time.

The same Pope Urban IV asked Thomas Aquinas to compose several hymns for the new celebration. One of them, "Lauda Sion," still appears in the lectionary as an optional sequence after the second reading.

Our readings open this weekend with a shocking description of the covenant ritual in the book of Exodus. Moses lifts a vessel of blood from slaughtered livestock and sprinkles it on the people. "This is the blood of the covenant," he says, a line that Jesus will reinterpret at the Last Supper. It is hard for a Christian to pray Psalm 116 without thinking of the eucharistic cup: "I will take the cup of salvation and call on the name of the Lord."

Hematic symbolism figures into the second reading as well. The author says that the blood of sacrificed livestock cannot compare with the blood of Christ.

The gospel from Mark brings all these themes to their expected climax. We hear the first gospel account of the Last Supper.

SACRAMENTARY

Texts for today are found after the Sundays of Ordinary Time, and immediately following Trinity Sunday. Be sure to mark the place before Mass begins to avoid embarrassing minutes of an anxious search.

The suggested communion antiphon comes from the gospel of Year A for this solemnity. The presidential prayers all reflect on the gift of the eucharist. Of the prefaces for today, the second (P 48) explores the meaning of the eucharist more fully. Eucharistic Prayer III makes a good choice today. It is also a good day to sing the eucharistic prayer.

A solemn blessing for Ordinary Time (12, for example) could conclude the celebration if there is no eucharistic procession.

The sacramentary's first appendix includes a priest's Statement of Intention as a preparation for celebrating Mass.

OTHER IDEAS

Music for today's feast is extensive. Look for organ solos based on "Lauda Sion" and "Sacris solemniis." Jean Langlais has one on the latter text in his Livre Œcuménique, playable on the simplest of instruments with almost no demands for pedal technique.

Classic Latin hymns include "Pange lingua," "Tantum ergo," "Adoro te" and "O salutaris hostia." The sequence, "Lauda Sion," is in the *Liber cantualis*. Steve Schaubel's "Jesus Christ, Bread of Life" blends "Adoro te" with the Largo from Dvořák's Symphony No. 9 (From the New World).

Choirs may know Mozart's "Ave verum corpus," but the chant from the *Liber cantualis* also deserves a place in the repertoire.

If your community wants to learn a setting of the Lord's Prayer, try Steven C. Warner's (WLP, 7204).

Communion under both forms should be standard practice in the parish by now. If not, this is a good Sunday to begin. Because this year's scripture readings focus so much on the mystery of the blood of Christ, you could promote communion from the cup.

Holy Communion and Worship of the Eucharist Outside Mass (101–108) recommends a procession to conclude today's Mass or to follow a period of adoration. After the communion prayer of the Mass, a procession may form from the church to another place of worship, where benediction concludes the service. See also the *Ceremonial of Bishops* (387–394) for notes on the procession.

■ THIS FIRST WEEK OF SUMMER is the richest of the year with solemnities, perhaps too much of a good thing. The ancient and much-loved celebrations of the nativity of John the Baptist and the deaths of the apostles Peter and Paul are bridged by the devotional observance (that in past generations became June's theme for prayer) of the Sacred Heart of Jesus.

#371 (LMC #193–227)   green

M O N 23 Weekday (Twelfth Week in Ordinary Time)

One reason the Sermon on the Mount is so popular is the practicality of its advice. Today Jesus urges the disciples not to pass judgment on others without overcoming their own weaknesses first.

Time for Bible history. Today we start a nine-week series of readings from the first books of the Bible. They will tell the story

of God's chosen people from Abraham through Ruth. Those who reflect on these texts this summer will reconnect with the foundations of our faith in the covenant. We open today with the call of Abram. In faith, Abram leaves his homeland, takes his family and possessions, and—at the age of 75—starts out on a new life.

Because this is the story of the chosen people, we sing in Psalm 33 of the blessedness of the people that God has chosen.

Eucharistic Prayer IV, with its preface that summarizes salvation history, might be a good choice today.

T
U **24** #586/587 (LMC #316) white
E   **Birth of John
       the Baptist**
       SOLEMNITY

ORIENTATION

Six months before the birth of Jesus we celebrate the birth of John the Baptist, the midsummer nativity. Together with the preceding feasts of the Annunciation and the Visitation, this celebration demonstrates how the events recorded in the first chapters of Luke span and help form the Christian year.

In some countries this is a holy day of obligation. The liturgy includes texts for a vigil as well as for a Mass of the day. (The presence of a vigil shows the antiquity

of this festival.) Some ethnic groups have bonfires or cookouts and fireworks to honor the one who said he must decrease so that Christ may increase. Early Christians, of the northern hemisphere, saw in the summer solstice a natural response to that saying.

The sun begins its decrease so that Christ may be born at its time of increase. Those who wax romantically during Advent about the significance of darkness and long nights have cause to rejoice now in the blessedness of long days and lovely, long twilights.

LECTIONARY

Luke tells of an annunciation of John's conception, and he also gives an account of John's birth. Both stories mirror the annunciation and birth of Jesus. The first, the conception, is the gospel for the vigil Mass; the other is the gospel for Mass during the day.

The vigil includes a famous passage from Jeremiah, about having a vocation from when he was formed in the womb. The psalm uses the same image of the mother's womb to express the completeness of God's call and support. In the spirit of vigil anticipation, the second reading tells of the role of the prophets who searched for salvation. The prophets prepared the way for the birth of Jesus, but they also formed a line completed by John, who is the last of the prophets pointing the way toward Jesus.

In the Mass during the day, another passage speaks of a call from the mother's womb, this time from Isaiah. The responsorial psalm praises God for fearfully and wonderfully making the psalmist. For the second reading we hear an excerpt from a sermon of Paul, which clarifies the role of John as the herald of the coming of Jesus.

SACRAMENTARY

The suggested entrance and communion antiphons for both Masses are inspired by Luke's account of John's conception and birth.

Sing the Glory to God and the Creed. There is a preface of John the Baptist (P 61) for today. The solemn blessing for Advent (1) points toward Christ as John did. John's name appears in the first eucharistic prayer.

OTHER IDEAS

Use vestments from the Christmas season. If incense is used, bring out the Christmas scent. The *Benedictus* also comes from Luke's account of John's birth. It makes a good text for singing today.

Musicians may enjoy looking at the chant hymn for vespers, "Ut quæant laxis." The first note of each phrase forms the scale, and the Latin syllable that you sing on each of those notes spells out Ut-re-mi-fa-sol. This is the hymn that gave us the notes of the scale. Somewhere along the line they decided that "Do" was easier to sing than "Ut," and they added "Si" to finish the scale (the abbreviation for Sancte Ioannes, or Saint John), which later shifted to Ti for singability. You can find the complete hymn in the *Liber hymnarius*.

The German sacramentary proposes an insert to Eucharistic Prayer III: "In union with the whole church we celebrate that day on which John, the forerunner of Christ, was born to prepare the way for him, the redeemer of the world. We remember your saints and praise above all Mary, the glorious, ever-virgin Mother of our Lord and God, Jesus Christ."

WED **25** #373 (LMC #193–227)   green
Weekday

You know people by their deeds, Jesus says. This simple advice helps his followers to avoid false prophets who attempt to win them away.

God promises Abram land and descendants. Abram seals the covenant with a ritual sacrifice. We sing of God's faithfulness to the covenant in today's psalm.

The first eucharistic prayer remembers that God accepted the sacrifice of Abraham.

THU **26** #374 (LMC #193–227)   green
Weekday

Jesus concludes the Sermon on the Mount with a request to build faith on a strong foundation.

The octagenarian Abram and his wife Sarai have produced no children. Sarai suggests Abram try fathering a child with their servant Hagar. Hagar conceives, but incurs Sarai's wrath. Followers of Mohammed trace their ancestry to Hagar's son Ishmael, making Abraham the father of three world religions: Judaism, Christianity and Islam.

Consider the sacramentary's Mass for the spread of the gospel (#14B) and the third version of the eucharistic prayer for various needs and occasions.

FRI **27** #171 (LMC #164)   white
The Sacred Heart of Jesus
SOLEMNITY

ORIENTATION

A latecomer to the liturgical calendar, the solemnity of the Sacred Heart is a celebration not of a biblical event but of the love of God manifested in the heart of Jesus. Devotion grew throughout the late-Middle Ages and reached its climax with the visions of Saint Margaret Mary Alacoque. The feast first appeared in the universal church calendar in 1856. It occurs each year on the third Friday after Pentecost. In the United States, it is more easily reckoned as the Friday following the Solemnity of the Body and Blood of Christ.

The memorial of Our Lady of Perpetual Help, normally observed on this date in Costa Rica, Venezuela and Mexico, is suppressed this year.

LECTIONARY

Texts are found right after those for the solemnity of the Body and Blood of Christ, in the brief section of "solemnities of the Lord" that follows the Sundays in Ordinary Time. Be sure to mark the place ahead of time. Notice that, unlike many solemnities, there are texts for Years A, B and C, so B's readings and psalm are used this year.

A soldier's lance pierces the precious, loving heart of Jesus as he hangs upon the cross. This violent action opens a wound in the side of Christ from which blood and water pour forth, symbols of the life of Christ that continues to flow through the church's celebrations of baptism and the eucharist. Today's responsory comes from Isaiah, an invitation to draw water from the springs of salvation. This is one of the responsories from the Easter Vigil.

The first reading is a beautiful passage of God's love for the chosen people. The second reading is Paul's shimmering description of the love of Christ. Both passages remind us of the great power love can have, especially God's love for all of us.

SACRAMENTARY

Texts are found among the solemnities of the Lord, following the Sundays in Ordinary Time.

Choose from three opening prayers. The first explains the meaning of the day most directly. The preface is proper (P 45). Eucharistic Prayer III makes a good choice on solemnities.

OTHER IDEAS

Draw attention to the image of the Sacred Heart in your worship space through a placement of flowers or special lighting.

Many devotional hymns to the Sacred Heart have been omitted from today's hymnals because of their overly sentimental piety. But hymns like "Love Divine, All Loves Excelling" and "I Heard the Voice of Jesus Say" express the thought of the day very well.

A litany of the Sacred Heart can be found in *Catholic Household Blessings and Prayers* (339) and could be used as a devotional element for the faithful today. It could even replace the general intercessions.

S A T **28** #376 (LMC #193–227) green
Weekday

Optional Memorial of Irenaeus (+ 202), bishop and martyr / red ▪ *Optional Memorial of The Immaculate Heart of Mary / white* ▪ One of the themes of Matthew's gospel is the healing ministry of Jesus, and today's episode explains why. In healing the centurion's boy, Jesus shows that redemption is open to Gentiles as well as Jews.

Abraham's mysterious visitors promise him a child. Sarah laughs and then denies it. This comical story shows how God's plan will prevail. In response, we sing Mary's canticle from the New Testament, her hymn of praise to God as she and Elizabeth, both unlikely mothers, are expecting children to carry on God's plan.

▪ TODAY'S MEMORIALS: Irenaeus was a disciple of Polycarp, himself a disciple of John the apostle. He studied in Rome and became bishop of Lyons. His theological works, including *Against the Heresies,* are among the most important of the second century.

The Immaculate Heart of Mary entered the liturgy as a corollary to the Sacred Heart of Jesus, but takes a lesser liturgical rank. Only during the reign of Pope John Paul II was it elevated from an optional to an obligatory memorial. It is the last celebration of the liturgical year with a date computed from the date of Easter, although this year the memorial overlaps another obligatory memorial. (See *Notitiae* 392–393 March–April 1999, p. 157.)

A gospel for the Immaculate Heart can be found in the back of the lectionary, between May 31 and June 1. It tells of Mary pondering the childhood of Jesus "in her heart."

There is no proper first reading. You may choose any from the common of the Blessed Virgin Mary if you wish, together with a psalm. Or turn back to the reading of the weekday.

The presidential prayers for the Immaculate Heart are found in the sacramentary between May 31 and June 1. The preface for Mary, Mother of the Church (Appendix X of the sacramentary) says, "Mary received your word in the purity of her heart."

A Mass for the Immaculate Heart of Mary is also found in the *Collection of Masses of the Blessed Virgin Mary* (28). Lectionary and sacramentary texts are available.

Today is a solemnity in Ecuador, where Mary is patron under this title.

⊛**29** #590/591 (LMC #319) red
Peter and Paul, apostles
SOLEMNITY

ORIENTATION

This solemnity holds such importance in the church that we observe it even when it falls on a Sunday. We might call it our "Founding Fathers' Day." It's one of the ten traditional holy days of obligation on the universal calendar (although each nation alters this list), and shares the same date in the churches east and west, a sign

of its antiquity. This year Peter and Paul replace the Thirteenth Sunday in Ordinary Time.

Tradition holds that on this day Peter and Paul met and embraced before marching off to their deaths—Peter on the Vatican hill, Paul outside the city of Rome. They suffered at the hands of Nero, who persecuted Christians to distract the population from the sorrows attendant on the great fire of Rome (64–67). Together these two apostles represent the early evangelization of Jews and Gentiles.

This year the Latin American calendar is not affected. Ordinarily, Bolivia and Paraguay transfer this feast to the nearest Sunday. Nicaragua moves it to the following Sunday. It is a holy day of obligation in Peru, no matter what day of the week.

LECTIONARY

The scriptures of the vigil and the Mass during the day offer passages significant to the ministry of these two great apostles. Stories of Peter include his first miracle (vigil, first reading), his imprisonment (day, first reading), his confession of faith (day, gospel) and his final conversation with Jesus (vigil, gospel). Stories of Paul include his autobiographical comments (vigil, second reading) and prediction of his death (day, second reading).

The psalm for the vigil appears frequently with celebrations of the apostles: "Their message goes out." The psalm for the Mass during the day supports the theme of angelic protection in response to the angel's role in delivering Peter from prison.

If you are using the *Lectionary for Masses with Children* today, find the readings in the volume for weekdays, and note that the texts for the vigil Mass are omitted.

SACRAMENTARY

Separate presidential prayers are given for the vigil and the Mass during the day. The Masses call for the Glory to God and the Creed. Both suggest the preface of Peter and Paul (P 63). This pair of saints is mentioned in the first eucharistic prayer. A solemn blessing appears at the end of the Mass during the day.

OTHER IDEAS

The hymn "By All Your Saints Still Striving" has a verse for Peter and Paul. "Two Noble Saints" in *Worship* and "O Light of Lights" in *Hymnal for the Hours* are translations of traditional hymns for this feast.

June 24 and today are customary days for blessing the sea, other bodies of water, and fishing fleets, as well as those who make their living on water. The two solemnities have long been linked as part of the church's midsummer "holiday season," and this suggests a unified approach to visuals at worship at this time of year, perhaps those reflecting summer in your community. Notes for observing and for decorating for these days are found in LTP's *To Crown the Year.*

#377 (LMC #193–227)   green

MON 30 Weekday (Thirteenth Week in Ordinary Time)

Optional Memorial of the First Martyrs of the Church of Rome (+ 64–68) / red ▪ Jesus reminds those who would follow him about how much it costs to do so. This brief interlude on discipleship comes in the midst of a passage detailing a series of miracles.

Abraham tests his relationship with God by bargaining over the threatened destruction of Sodom. This popular story shows the intimate relationship between the

two, while offering believers a hopeful model of persistent prayer. The psalmist seems to have known all along that the Lord is kind and merciful.

The fourth weekday preface in Ordinary Time prays in a spirit similar to that of Abraham: "You have no need of our praise, yet our desire to thank you is itself your gift."

▪ TODAY'S SAINTS: Peter and Paul were only the best known of many who died under Nero's maltreatment. Today we remember the others who gave their lives in this first of many persecutions. Though nameless, their suffering of torture and death spilled blood that bore the fruit of a stronger faith throughout the Roman world. An alternative gospel appears in the lectionary, a passage in which Jesus predicts the harassment of his followers.

July

#378 (LMC #193–227)   green

TUE 1 Weekday

Optional Memorial of Blessed Junípero Serra (+ 1784), presbyter, religious, missionary / white ▪ Matthew has grouped a number of miracles of Jesus in this section of his gospel. This one is directed toward the wind and the sea. Jesus exercises his power over all creation.

"Fire and brimstone" sermons get their descriptor from today's first reading, the destruction of Sodom and Gomorrah. Abraham's bargaining yesterday proves fruitless as the dense corruption of these cities is revealed. Looking back, Lot's wife turns into salt. The psalmist sings, "O Lord, your kindness is before my eyes," which makes sense only when we realize that God spared Lot because of Abraham.

The sacramentary includes a prayer to avert storms (#37).

▪ TODAY'S SAINT: Junípero Serra was a Spanish missionary to Mexico and California. He founded several missions, including San Diego and San Juan Capistrano. The mission at Carmel claims his tomb. His beatification caused some controversy because of reports of the ill treatment of Indians in the missions. Remember Native Americans and the work of missionaries today. The opening prayer for this optional memorial is in the 1994 *Sacramentary Supplement.*

Today is Canada Day. Canadians may use *A Supplement to the Sacramentary* (National Liturgical Office, 1991) for special Mass texts.

#379 (LMC #452–454, 322)   green

WED 2 Weekday

One of the strangest miracles in the gospels captures our imaginations today. Jesus meets two possessed men at the Gadarene boundary. They call him Son of God, then beg him to expel them into a herd of swine. Jesus performs the miracle, and the swine commit mass suicide. When the people hear about it, they ask Jesus to leave. Not all the miracles of Jesus compelled people to become disciples.

God finally delivers on the promise to Abraham, who becomes the father of Isaac at the age of 100. Bad blood remains between Sarah and Hagar. The slave leaves after Abraham puts their son Ishmael on her back. (Wait a minute. Isn't he about 15 by now?) God promises that Ishmael will also father a great nation. The people of Islam claim him. The psalmist sings, "The Lord hears the cry of the poor."

Tomorrow's weekday reading about the sacrifice of Isaac will not be heard this year because of the feast of Thomas. You may substitute or append it today if you like.

Prayers for relatives and friends (#44) might be appropriate today.

THU 3 #593 (LMC #193–227) red
Thomas, apostle
FEAST

Although there are more exemplary stories about the apostle Thomas, he is forever remembered as the doubter, as the choice for today's gospel reinforces. Still, even in this episode of doubt, Thomas makes the most sublime proclamation of faith when he finally sees Jesus: "My Lord and my God."

Paul's letter to the Ephesians includes a generic reference to the apostles as the foundation of God's building. The psalmist encourages a spirit of apostleship with a refrain from the end of Mark's gospel: "Go out to all the world and tell the good news."

The presidential prayers for Thomas are at July 3 in the sacramentary. Sing the Glory to God today. The second preface for apostles (P 65) makes an allusion to the first reading. The apostle is mentioned in the first eucharistic prayer. There is a solemn blessing for feasts of the apostles (17).

Thomas is especially beloved by Christians from India, who regard him as their own apostle. Legend has it that he personally brought the gospel to that country. A group of Saint Thomas Christians survives in India today.

FRI 4 #381 (LMC #193–227) green
Weekday

Optional Memorial of Elizabeth of Portugal (+ 1336), married woman, queen/white ▪ *Optional Mass of Independence Day/white* ▪ You may use the scriptures for the weekday about the call of Matthew, the putative author of the gospel, and the marriage of Isaac and Rebekah with its psalm of thanksgiving.

■ TODAY'S CIVIC HOLIDAY: You may want texts that help the community in the United States to celebrate Independence Day. The sacramentary's Appendix X-6 has a Mass for this occasion with recommended readings, but see also the lectionary texts for Masses for peace and justice (831–835). The second civic preface (P 83) urges a witness to justice and peace. The fourth form of the eucharistic prayer for various needs and occasions, "Jesus, the Compassion of God," prays for a caring society. An alternative set of presidential prayers can be found in the sacramentary under July 4.

You might conclude the general intercessions with an adaptation of the prayer composed by Archbishop John Carroll for the inauguration of George Washington, as found in the *Book of Blessings,* 69. Another prayer is in *Catholic Household Blessings and Prayers,* 199.

You may sing traditional and appropriate patriotic hymns today, like "America the Beautiful." Other songs can be found in hymn indexes under "justice and peace" and "citizenship."

■ TODAY'S SAINT: Elizabeth raised a family, served as queen, cared for the poor, and later became affiliated with the Franciscans. She is a patron of Catholic charities.

In Mexico, this is the optional memorial of Our Lady of the Refuge. The Conference or Pious Union of Our Lady of Refuge is an Archsodality in Mexico. A picture of the Virgin Mary, Refuge of Sinners, moves from house to house for prayer. Members renounce drinking alcohol and practicing prostitution.

In Ecuador, the Friday following the third Sunday after Pentecost (in other words, the Friday after the solemnity of the Sacred Heart) is a commemoration of the "Consecration to the Sacred Heart of the Most Holy Virgin Mary, patron of Ecuador."

SAT 5 #382 (LMC #193–227) green
Weekday

Optional Memorial of Anthony Mary Zaccaria (+ 1539), presbyter, religious founder/white ▪ *Optional Memorial of the Blessed Virgin Mary/white* ▪ The call of Matthew, which you may have replaced yesterday, prompts today's reflection on disciples. They cannot fast while Jesus is with them. The rules are different in the presence of the Messiah.

God's plan is powerful enough to work amid fraud. Jacob deceives his father and takes the blessing destined for Esau. Rebekah, the Eleanor Roosevelt of her day, took matters into her own hands. The psalmist sings, "The Lord has chosen Jacob for himself, Israel for his own possession."

■ TODAY'S SAINT: Anthony Mary Zaccaria gave up his medical practice to become a priest. To seek collaboration between clergy and laity he founded the Barnabites. He also promoted the frequent reception of communion.

You may also consider prayers from *The Collection of Masses of the Blessed Virgin Mary.* Recalling Rebekah's role as mediator, see "Mary, Mother and Mediatrix of Grace" (30).

6 #101 (LMC #95) green
Fourteenth Sunday in Ordinary Time

ORIENTATION

Finally, we return to Sundays in Ordinary Time. Although we have observed Ordinary Time weekdays for several weeks, a series of feasts has deferred the retrieval of green vestments on Sunday. We settle in now for the long period of seasonal rest from now until Advent.

In Bolivia, the optional memorial of Blessed Ignacia Nazaria March is suppressed this year.

LECTIONARY

Throughout this year Mark's gospel dominates. We resume the semicontinuous reading from him today at a point where Jesus finds himself in trouble. In the story, Jesus has been on the other side of the lake. Today's gospel opens with the phrase "Jesus departed from there," as if we know where "there" is, but because of the interrupted sequence of readings this summer, no one will have a clue. Today's episode takes place in "his native place," which in Mark means Nazareth. Bethlehem appears only in Matthew and Luke. The point of the story is to show that even Jesus' family and childhood friends put up some resistance to his message. Very slowly, the evangelist prepares us for the terror of the cross.

In the first reading, God sends Ezekiel to a place where people will be "hard of face and obstinate of heart." Doing the will of God always implies meeting some opposition. In the psalm, we ask God for mercy, "for we are more than sated with contempt . . . with the mockery of the arrogant, with the contempt of the proud."

The second reading concludes the series begun clear back before Ash Wednesday. At daily Mass recently, we have already completed a survey of the principal texts from the Second Letter to the Corinthians. Throughout the letter, Paul has reflected on the hardships of discipleship. Today he boasts of his weaknesses, "in order that the power of Christ may dwell with me."

If you are using the *Lectionary for Masses with Children,* note that the responsorial psalm changes to 86, a song of God's mercy and forgiveness.

SACRAMENTARY

The alternative opening prayer mentions the sufferings of Christ, which appear in Jesus' ministry in the gospel today and which inspired the determination of Paul.

If you avoided using the fourth eucharistic prayer throughout the previous months in favor of the seasonal and feast day prefaces, you may wish to return to it today. Prayer over the people #17 refers to the suffering of Jesus.

OTHER IDEAS

Part of the long Independence Day weekend in the United States, this Sunday may find extra visitors to the church. Be sure the greeters are on hand to welcome all who visit today. You may offer a blessing for travelers (*Book of Blessings,* 9).

Next Sunday's gospel includes a reference to anointing the sick. If you wish to celebrate the sacrament communally, make an announcement this weekend, inviting the sick and elderly to participate.

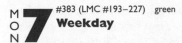

M O N **7** #383 (LMC #193–227)   green
Weekday

Returning to the miracle series from Matthew, we hear one of the rare instances where Jesus raises someone from death to life, a foreshadowing of his own resurrection.

In a dream, Jacob sees angels ascending and descending a ladder. He consecrates the site by pouring oil upon a memorial stone. The psalm, echoing Jacob's sentiment, sings of God's protection.

The second preface for the dedication of a church (P 53) honors the earthly dwelling place of God.

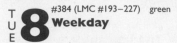

T U E **8** #384 (LMC #193–227)   green
Weekday

Matthew presents the last of the series of miracles in this section of the gospel with a general statement of Jesus' care for the needy.

Jacob wrestles with an angel until daybreak. Jacob is injured, and the divine messenger changes his name to Israel because he contended with divine and human beings and prevailed. Jacob says afterwards that he has seen God face-to-face. The psalmist says to God, "I in justice shall behold your face."

Prefaces for the Holy Trinity (P 43) and the Transfiguration (P 50) repeat the theme of beholding the glory of God.

W E D **9** #385 (LMC #193–227)   green
Weekday

Matthew turns his attention to the call, instruction and mission of the disciples. We hear today the names of the Twelve whom, in this passage, Matthew calls "apostles."

We leave the story of Jacob/Israel to enter the story of Joseph. This excerpted passage short-circuits the complex story. It presumes we know all about the near fratricidal jealousy, the coat of many colors, the sale of Joseph, his rise to power in Egypt, and the frightful famine throughout the region. Nonetheless, today's passage sets the stage for a great story of reconciliation. We hear about the emotional and physical suffering of Joseph's family. They come to him unaware of the attitude of the psalmist, who pleads for mercy, knowing that God will deliver the faithful from death "and preserve them in spite of famine."

The sacramentary's prayers for those suffering famine are in the

Masses for various needs and occasions (28A).

■ TODAY IS THE PATRONAL FEAST OF COLOMBIA, Our Lady of the Rosary of Chiquinquirá. The shrine holds a painting by Alfonso de Narváez, which was miraculously repaired in 1586 while Maria Ramos prayed before it.

In Argentina this is the memorial of Our Lady of Itatí. Tradition holds that Fray Luis de Bolaños founded a shrine at Itatí in 1615, but Indians destroyed it and removed his statue. Some days later Indian children found the statue and the locals built a new sanctuary for the wooden image.

T H U **10** #386 (LMC #193–227) green
Weekday

Jesus begins his discourse to the disciples with his slogan "The reign of God is at hand." He summarizes their work in a useful phrase: "What you received as a gift, give as a gift."

In one of the Bible's most emotional moments, Joseph reveals his identity to his brothers. His compassionate response to their need contrasts with the evil they committed against him. The whole episode is recalled in the verses selected for today's psalm.

In the second eucharistic prayer for Masses of reconciliation we acknowledge God's work when "those who were estranged join hands in friendship."

F R I #387 (LMC #193–227) white
Benedict (+ 547), monastic founder
MEMORIAL

Jesus warns the disciples that they will face persecution. These words were important to the community for which Matthew wrote the gospel. They, too, faced betrayal and hatred.

Another emotional moment brings the story of Joseph to a climax. After reconciling with his brothers, Joseph lays eyes on his father Israel after many years. The elder patriarch throws himself on Joseph's neck and weeps "a long time in his arms." The fruit of reconciliation is immeasurable. The psalm sings of God's love for those who do what is right. "In days of famine they have plenty."

■ TODAY'S SAINT: The Rule of Benedict has influenced countless numbers of men and women who chose to follow the spiritual path of community life. A founder of a dozen monasteries, he is the father of Western monasticism and a patron of Europe. Most of what we know of his life comes from the biography penned by Pope Gregory the Great.

Presidential prayers are under July 11 in the sacramentary. You may use the preface for virgins and religious (68).

S A T **12** #388 (LMC #193–227) green
Weekday

Optional Memorial of the Blessed Virgin Mary / white ▪ Again warning of persecution, Jesus offers support to the disciples who will face intimidation from human forces. He means well when he tells the disciples they are worth more than sparrows, but one would hope for a better metaphor.

Our series of readings from the book of Genesis comes to a close with the deaths of Jacob and Joseph. The psalm invites the descendants of Abraham and Jacob, whose stories we have followed these past few weeks, to give God glory.

The first eucharistic prayer for Masses of reconciliation might bring the story of Joseph to a thoughtful close.

■ CAMILLUS DE LELLIS appears on the universal calendar on July 18, but his optional memorial is transferred to this date in Bolivia.

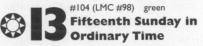

13 #104 (LMC #98) green
Fifteenth Sunday in Ordinary Time

ORIENTATION

Mark's gospel turns its attention to the mission and return of the Twelve. This Sunday's gospel forms a pair with the one for next week. After that, we will rest Mark's gospel for five weeks of John.

In Chile and Venezuela, the optional memorial of the teenage virgin Teresa de Jesús de los Andes (+ 1920) is not observed today.

On the Second Sunday of July the people of Venezuela celebrate the feast of the Consecration of the Venezuelan Republic to the Blessed Sacrament.

LECTIONARY

Although we customarily speak of the twelve apostles, the gospels rarely define the group that way. The term *apostle* is used in various ways in the New Testament. Today's passage is an example. Note how Mark simply refers to the group as "the Twelve." Their mission includes exorcism and the preaching of repentance. Their asceticism includes traveling lightly and accepting hospitality where it is offered.

Amos the prophet met opposition in his ministry, just as the Twelve would meet in theirs. There is a striking contrast between the command of Amaziah the priest, "never again prophesy," and the command of God, "Go, prophesy." The psalm, which responds to the themes of justice and truth, pertains to the overall message of Amos, not especially to today's excerpt.

Today we open the letter to the Ephesians. Still regarded as a letter by Paul in our liturgical books, commentators increasingly agree that it may have been written sometime after Paul's ministry. The opening verses that we hear today sing a hymn of praise to God for the blessings received in Christ. The Gentile audience has heard the gospel of salvation, believed in Christ and was sealed with the Spirit. Now they enjoy adoption through Jesus Christ.

SACRAMENTARY

If you celebrate the anointing of the sick at this Mass, note the preface in Appendix VII of the sacramentary. Special inserts for the eucharistic prayer will also be found there.

OTHER IDEAS

Today's gospel says explicitly that the Twelve anointed the sick with oil and cured them. This passage partially explains our inclusion of the anointing of the sick as one of the sacraments of the church. If you have not offered the communal anointing of the sick at a Sunday Mass recently, this might make a good occasion to do so. Reserve seating near the front of the assembly. Explain who is eligible for the anointing. (Consult the introduction to the *Rite of Anointing and Pastoral Care of the Sick*.) After the homily, invite forward those who wish to celebrate the sacrament. Be sure there is seating for at least some in the group who may be unable to stand even for the duration of this brief ceremony.

#389 (LMC #193–227)   white

MON 14 Blessed Katéri Tekakwitha, the Lily of the Mohawks (+1680), virgin
MEMORIAL

Jesus concludes his second discourse with bad news and good news. The disciples can expect serious divisions, even in their own families. (This probably reflects the situation of the community for whom Matthew wrote the gospel.) But he also promises rewards for those who receive the disciples well. Note the phrase that introduces the ending of today's passage: "When Jesus had finished instructing." That is Matthew's cue to the reader that a discourse has come to an end.

Continuing our nine-week survey of the history of ancient Israel, we open the second book of the Bible, Exodus. A new king "who did not know Joseph" comes to power, and that spells trouble for Israel in exile. The new leader persecutes the Israelites by increasing the burden of their labor and murdering their newborn sons. How wrong it will feel to answer, "Thanks be to God," to this reading of God's word. The psalm looks ahead to the deliverance that awaits God's chosen people: "We were rescued like a bird from the fowler's snare."

■ TODAY'S SAINT: Blessed Katéri led many in the United States and Canada to embrace the faith. Her austere life came to an untimely end at the age of 24. Remember today the contribution of Native Americans to the spiritual life of the church.

Francis Solano (+ 1610) is remembered today in Peru with a feast, in Bolivia with a memorial, and in Venezuela with an optional memorial. This Spanish Franciscan priest worked tirelessly as a missionary in Peru and other parts of Latin America.

#390 (LMC #193–227)   white

TUE 15 Bonaventure (+ 1274), bishop, religious, doctor of the church
MEMORIAL

In the narrative that precedes the third discourse, Jesus meets opposition. Today he lashes out against the towns that have failed to reform in spite of his miracles.

Moses is born of the house of Levi. His mother hides him from Pharaoh's persecution. Pharaoh's own daughter colludes to protect the child, who grows up, slays an Egyptian, and goes into hiding in Midian. From childhood, the life of Moses is already beset with adversity. The psalmist compares spiritual deliverance to rescue from watery depths. This hymn of salvation reminds us of Moses, whose name means "drawn from the water."

■ TODAY'S SAINT: Bonaventure, the Seraphic doctor, authored many treatises in his life as a Franciscan. He also served as Cardinal of Albano. He died the same year as Thomas Aquinas, causing the church to lose two immensely influential theologians at the same time.

The sacramentary gives an opening prayer for today's memorial. The other presidential prayers may be taken from doctors of the church. You may take the preface of pastors (P 67).

#391 (LMC #193–227)   green

WED 16 Weekday

Optional Memorial of Our Lady of Mount Carmel/white ▪ In a passage that sounds more like John than Matthew, Jesus expresses the union of the Father and Son by means of knowledge.

God appears to Moses in a bush that burns but is not consumed. Moses, suffering from low self-esteem, hears God's command to lead the chosen people out of slavery and back to the land of

promise. The psalm remembers that God's ways were made known to Moses.

The Masses for various needs and occasions include one for refugees and exiles (29).

■ TODAY'S MEMORIAL: This is the patronal feast of the Carmelite Order and of the Third Order laity who live the Carmelite spirituality in their secular vocations. That spirituality finds inspiration in the prophet Elijah, who saw from Carmel a cloud in the distance that would bring rain after a drought. That rain-bearing cloud became an image of the savior-bearing Mary. The *Collection of Masses of the Blessed Virgin Mary* has an expanded proper for this commemoration at #32, "Mary, Mother and Teacher in the Spirit." (The Carmelite Order, in common with the Byzantine Rite, remembers the prophet Elijah on July 20.)

■ TODAY IS THE PATRONAL FEAST OF CHILE. It is a solemnity in Chile and in Bolivia, where Mary is also a patron under this title. This is a feast in Venezuela and an obligatory memorial in Argentina, Guatemala, Colombia, Mexico and Costa Rica.

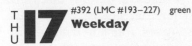
THU 17 #392 (LMC #193–227) green
Weekday

A favorite passage among the followers of Jesus, today's gospel gives us the comforting words we often imagine Jesus saying to us: "Come to me. Take my yoke. I am humble of heart. Your souls will find rest."

Even more wondrous than God's appearance in the bush is the revelation of the divine name: "I am who I am." Armed with an intimate knowledge and relationship of God, Moses receives prophecy and command to lead the people into freedom. The psalmist remembers the event: God sent Moses the servant and Aaron the chosen

one, who wrought signs among the people.

The fourth form of the eucharistic prayer for various needs and occasions is called "Jesus the Compassion of God."

FRI 18 #393 (LMC #193–227) green
Weekday

Optional Memorial of Camillus de Lellis (+ 1614), presbyter, religious founder / white ▪ Jesus meets opposition from the Pharisees who object to his disciples' disregard for the Sabbath. He uses the occasion to say he is Lord of the Sabbath.

The story of the exodus skips over the details of the plagues, but their horror forms the background for today's passage. God knows how this story will end, and commands Moses and Aaron to make preparations for the first Passover.

The votive Mass for the Holy Eucharist (3) includes many references to the "memorial," a concept common to Passover and to eucharist.

■ TODAY'S SAINT: Camillus, at 6'6", one of the tallest saints in history, suffered a gambler's addiction that reduced him to poverty. First a Franciscan, then a Capuchin, long afflicted with an infirm leg, he founded his own order of Ministers of the Sick.

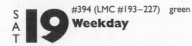
SAT 19 #394 (LMC #193–227) green
Weekday

Optional Memorial of the Blessed Virgin Mary / white ▪ The Pharisees plot against Jesus, and Matthew cites a suffering servant song from Isaiah to show Jesus' messianic heritage.

Passover night is explained in today's first reading. The people prepared unleavened bread to assist them in their hasty departure. The people of Israel still remember

this night in the annual Passover meal, the seder. Another of the historical psalms is a celebration of the details of the first Passover.

■ FROM THE *COLLECTION OF MASSES OF THE BLESSED VIRGIN MARY,* consider Mary, Image and Mother of the Church III (27) or Our Lady of Ransom (43) for the Passover motifs of pilgrimage and rescue. See also the opening prayer for the Holy Name of Mary in the sacramentary, Appendix X-5.

20 #107 (LMC #101) green
Sixteenth Sunday in Ordinary Time

ORIENTATION

Even though this year's Sunday gospels are dedicated to Mark, and even though we have not heard much from Mark this year due to the seasons and feasts that fell on Sunday, we are about to hear the last of him for a while. Mark's gospel is so short that it needs support to make it through the liturgical year. John, who has no year dedicated to his gospel, lends assistance beginning next week.

LECTIONARY

Today's gospel finishes the story we heard last week. Jesus sent the Twelve out on mission last week. Today they return and report what they have done. Jesus invites them away for some rest, but the crowd pursues them. Jesus, his heart filled with pity, teaches the crowd. Many of those involved in pastoral ministry know just what this feels like. As soon as they start to take some time off, more needs surface.

Today's passage from Jeremiah compares bad leaders to malicious shepherds. God promises to appoint shepherds who will do it right. We hear this passage today because of the line in the gospel where Jesus assesses the needs of the crowd as those of sheep without a shepherd. Predictably, the greatest of all shepherd psalms follows this reading.

The letter to the Ephesians announces the end of the division between Jew and Gentile. The Gentile Ephesians, "who once were far off," are now part of a new peace. Its theme of inclusion remains a popular one in multicultural societies.

SACRAMENTARY

The eighth preface for Sundays in Ordinary Time (P 36) praises God who reunited sinners and gathers them into a church. The fifth prayer over the people asks God to strengthen us in faithfulness.

OTHER IDEAS

Keep the pace of summer light and easy. Be sure greeters at the door know to watch for visitors. Have musicians plan some music that everyone can sing. Encourage ministers to find substitutes for the weekends they will be away.

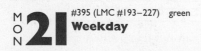

MON 21 #395 (LMC #193–227) green
Weekday

Optional Memorial of Lawrence of Brindisi (+ 1619), presbyter, religious, doctor of the church / white ▪ Jesus criticizes the scribes and Pharisees who look for signs. They are missing the sign of his teaching. Even today, people prefer to look for miracles rather than reflect on the miraculous word of God.

The Israelites begin their exodus from Egypt, but Pharaoh has a change of heart. The Israelites find themselves caught between Pharaoh's army and the sea. Through Moses, God continues to urge the people forward, no matter the adversity. The responsory anticipates the actual exodus, an excerpt from the song of the Israelites once they cross to the other side.

The second version of the eucharist prayer for Masses for various needs and occasions references the exodus in its preface.

▪ TODAY'S SAINT: Lawrence joined the Capuchins at age 16 and quickly revealed an ability for theology, philosophy and languages. He brought the gospel to Jewish converts and led an army against invading Turks. He died in Portugal as Minister General of his community while advocating on behalf of the people of Naples to their sovereign, King Philip III of Spain.

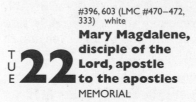

#396, 603 (LMC #470–472, 333) white

TUE 22 **Mary Magdalene, disciple of the Lord, apostle to the apostles**
MEMORIAL

Mary Magdalene was a faithful disciple of Jesus and the first to receive the news of the resurrection. She brought the Good News to the apostles, making her the "apostle to the apostles." She has been erroneously identified with the sinful woman of Luke's gospel.

The gospel is proper for the day, because Mary Magdalene is a biblical figure. The first readings proposed for her memorial are optional. You may choose the Song of Solomon, a passage in which a lover seeks the beloved, as on the day of resurrection Mary Magdalene went in search of the one she loved. But you may prefer to take the first reading from the weekday lectionary, the climax of the book of Exodus, in which Israel passes through the sea and Pharaoh's army is swallowed in the waters. The Christian community has adopted this passage as a foreshadowing of baptism, in which sin is destroyed by the waters that give new birth to those chosen by God. The relationship of baptism to resurrection makes this an unusually apt pairing of readings for the memorial. The recommended psalm foreshadows Mary's loving search for the body of Jesus, but if you choose the reading from the weekday, the continuation of yesterday's canticle from Exodus makes an appropriate response.

Presidential prayers for the day are under July 22. The male apostles are generally recognized with a feast instead of a memorial. Barnabas, not one of the Twelve, is an exception. The Glory to God is sung on feasts of the apostles, and a preface like P 65 is used on those days.

WED 23 #397 (LMC #193–227) green
Weekday

Optional Memorial of Bridget of Sweden (+ 1373), married woman, religious founder / white ▪ Our semicontinuous reading of Matthew on weekdays enters the third discourse of Jesus. Of the five discourses, this one includes the parables, beginning with the story of the sower.

After the great miracle of the exodus from Egypt, the people still have plenty to complain about. They grumble about the food in the desert. God provides quail and manna. This event is recalled in the psalm for the day: God rained manna upon them for food and gave them heavenly bread.

The sacramentary includes prayers for productive land (26A).

▪ TODAY'S SAINT: Bridget and her husband Ulfo lived a devout life and raised eight children, the last of whom, Catherine, is also a saint. After her husband's death she founded the mother house for the community that came to be known as the Brigittines. She is a patron of Sweden.

T H U **24** #398 (LMC #193–227) green
Weekday

Early in the anthology of parables, the disciples ask Jesus why he uses this literary form. Surprisingly, he says it is to confuse unbelievers as much as to illumine believers.

God appears to Moses again. This time the theophany occurs not in a burning bush, but under thunder and lightning atop a mountain. From the book of Daniel, our responsory today praises God who looks into the depths from a throne upon the cherubim.

The first preface for the dedication of a church (P 52) thanks God for this house of prayer where "you reveal your presence by sacramental signs."

■ FRANCIS SOLANO, who appears on other calendars on the fourteenth of this month, is remembered in Argentina today with a memorial.

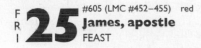

F R I **25** #605 (LMC #452–455) red
James, apostle
FEAST

This James, a son of Zebedee and brother of John, is sometimes called "the Greater." Tradition identifies him as an apostle to Spain whose martyrdom happened in Jerusalem. The first of the apostles to shed blood for Christ, his remains are said to be in Compostella, Spain. He is also a patron of Nicaragua and of Guatemala, where he is remembered with a solemnity as the patron of Guatemala City.

There are many gospel stories in which Jesus invites James among the inner circle of those who witness his miracles and prayer, but the lectionary for today chooses instead his mother's

request for a throne for her son. The cup of martyrdom, hinted at here, also plays a part in Paul's reflection on the ministry of apostle. The psalmist promises that those who go forth weeping will return in joy, just as resurrection will follow death. The psalm recalls captives proclaiming to the Gentiles that God has done great things for them, and the apostles inherited that very service.

The presidential prayers are under July 25. Sing the Glory to God today. The first preface of the apostles (P 64) speaks of their shepherd-like care. James is mentioned in the first eucharistic prayer. A solemn blessing for the apostles is at #17.

S A T **26** #400 (LMC #193–227) white
Anne and Joachim, parents of the Virgin Mary
MEMORIAL

Jesus proposes the parable of the weeds and the wheat, a lesson of God's temporary tolerance of wickedness.

Moses comes down from the mountain, reports God's words and ordinances to them, and they all respond, "We will do everything that God has told us." Moses erects an altar and sprinkles the people with blood to seal the agreement. Today's psalm sings of the covenant between God and the people.

■ TODAY'S SAINTS: The names of Mary's parents are lost. A tradition from the apocryphal gospels gives them these names. Presidential prayers are under July 26. You may choose the first preface for holy men and women (P 69).

The lectionary's readings for today's memorial (#606) are optional because Joachim and Anne are not mentioned in the Bible. The passages praise ancestors and prophets who longed to see the fulfillment of their dreams and longings.

27 #110 (LMC #104) green
Seventeenth Sunday in Ordinary Time

ORIENTATION

We interrupt Mark's gospel to bring you some good news from John. This insertion takes place just as Mark is about to tell the story of the miracle of the loaves. We turn instead to John for five weeks to hear his famous and important sixth chapter. During this time we will hear Jesus' sublime teaching about the eucharist. As we progress through these weeks, remember that in John's telling of the Last Supper, Jesus never says, "This is my body; this is my blood." Instead, it is in chapter 6 that we hear the eucharistic words of Jesus.

LECTIONARY

John's account of the miracle of the loaves sets up the motif of bread that will dominate the gospels for the next several weeks. John says the Passover was near, already making the Christian reader think ahead to the Last Supper. Seeing the large crowd, Jesus toys with the disciples: Where can we buy enough food? He takes five barley loaves and two fish and distributes them to five thousand people. John says Jesus took the loaves, gave thanks, and distributed them—actions that will remind the Christian of the eucharist.

In the first reading's story of Elisha, a similar miracle happens. Twenty loaves feed a hundred people. If you imagine them the size of buns, rather than the size of a loaf of white bread, you get the idea. Both stories concern barley loaves.

John probably included this detail to make the reader remember the similar miracle from the Second book of Kings. Whereas Elisha fed one hundred, Jesus fed five thousand, making him the greater worker of wonders. Fittingly, the psalm praises God who opens a hand and satisfies the desire of every living thing. These verses are sometimes used as a meal prayer in the Christian tradition.

The second half of New Testament epistles generally turns from theological development to exhortation. As we enter the final chapters of the letter to the Ephesians, the writer urges the readers to live in a manner that preserves the unity of the spirit: one body, one Lord, one faith, one baptism, and one God.

SACRAMENTARY

The first version of the eucharistic prayer for Masses for various needs and occasions prays for the unity of the church and recalls that Jesus broke bread for his disciples. Prayer over the people #18 asks God's help to relive the mystery of the eucharist.

OTHER IDEAS

Do not forget those who may be suffering from the summer's heat. Help the community be aware of the homeless, the needy and those too poor to provide cool shelter for themselves.

M O N **28** #401 (LMC #193–227)   green
Weekday

Jesus continues his survey of parables with short images of the reign of God based on the mustard seed and yeast. In both instances something small becomes quite large. His central teaching, that God's reign is at hand, inspires even us

latter-day disciples to spread the Good News.

The people have sinned. After Moses revealed the law to them, after they pledged their acceptance of it, after performing the covenant ritual, the people make a golden calf and worship a false god. Irate, Moses hurls the tablets containing the law to the base of the mountain and melts the false god. Even when people feel close to God they are not immune from temptation. Verses from Psalm 106 recall the incident.

The first eucharistic prayer for reconciliation says, "Time and time again we broke your covenant, but you did not abandon us."

■ PERU CELEBRATES THE FEAST OF OUR LADY OF PEACE TODAY. Benedict XV added the title "Queen of peace" to the Litany of Loreto in 1917. See the *Collection of Masses of the Blessed Virgin Mary* (45).

T U E **29** #401, 607 (LMC #193–227, 337)   white
Martha, disciple of the Lord
MEMORIAL

Today's gospel should be taken from those provided for the saint, not the weekday, because she is a biblical figure. The first option remembers Martha's belief in the resurrection on the occasion of the death of Lazarus. The second, recalling her focus on household tasks, provokes Jesus' statement praising the contemplative life.

Moses again enters conversation with God, staying 40 days and 40 nights in a fast. He then writes down the words of the covenant, the ten commandments. This fast is a precursor to Jesus' 40-day fast in the desert before beginning his public ministry. God's patience in the face of our transgressions serves as the theme for today's psalm.

The sacramentary's prayers for the saint recall her hospitality, which may alleviate some of the hurt she felt when Jesus seemed to disregard it. The second preface for holy men and women (P 70) would be appropriate.

W E D **30** #403 (LMC #193–227)   green
Weekday

Optional Memorial of Peter Chrysologus (+ 450), bishop, doctor of the church / white ▪ Jesus tells a parable about the value of the kingdom of God. It is worth more than everything else, more than buried treasure, more than fine pearls.

Moses' conversations with God have had an effect on his face. It shines so brightly that the Israelites cannot bear to look at it. Consequently, he places a veil over his face while speaking to them and removes it while speaking to God. Paul refers to this in his Second Letter to the Corinthians. Artists frequently depict Moses with rays of light shining from his face, sometimes represented as horns. Today's psalm recalls the holiness of God and the conversations between God and Moses.

The glory of God is the theme of the preface of the Holy Trinity (P 43).

■ TODAY'S SAINT: Peter Chrysologus ("golden-mouth") served as archbishop of Ravenna, practiced personal piety and rooted out heresy from his community. His sobriquet refers to his ability to preach simple, practical, gospel-based sermons.

Mexico has an optional memorial today for Blessed María de Jesús Sacramentado (+ 1959), founder of the Daughters of the Sacred Heart of Jesus.

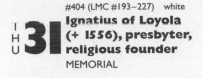

#404 (LMC #193–227) white

Ignatius of Loyola (+ 1556), presbyter, religious founder
31 THU
MEMORIAL

The final parables on the kingdom of God explain it as a separation of the good from the wicked and the source of wisdom for bringing out the new and the old.

Moses sets up the dwelling place of God, a tent for the ark of the covenant. He placed God's holy word, the ten commandments, within the ark. God led the Israelites under the form of cloud by day and fire by night. The God of all glory made a home among the chosen people throughout their pilgrimage. Today's psalm sings of the loveliness of God's dwelling place.

■ TODAY'S SAINT: The founder of the Jesuits, Ignatius was a soldier who authored the *Spiritual Exercises* and founded the Roman college. Among his followers are those silenced for their creative beliefs (for example, Teilhard de Chardin) and martyred for preaching the just word (for example, the Martyrs of El Salvador).

The presidential prayers for Ignatius are at July 31 in the sacramentary. You may use the preface for virgins and religious (P 68). The sacramentary's first appendix includes Ignatius's prayer of self-dedication to Jesus Christ. It is found without attribution among the prayers of thanksgiving after Mass.

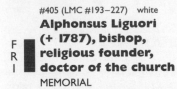

August

#405 (LMC #193–227) white

Alphonsus Liguori (+ 1787), bishop, religious founder, doctor of the church
1 FRI
MEMORIAL

Before Matthew presents the fourth discourse of Jesus, he gives a narrative section of his deeds. Today Jesus meets skepticism in his own hometown.

The story of Moses and the Israelites continues, but we move from the book of Exodus to the book of Leviticus. Today we hear the catalogue of feasts God has asked the Israelites to observe. Today's psalm was composed for a feast day.

■ TODAY'S SAINT: The founder of the Redemptorists, Alphonsus was a lawyer who mastered the field of moral theology. A school in Rome bearing his name continues instruction in this field. Presidential prayers are among those for saints. You may use the preface for pastors (P 67).

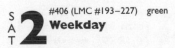

#406 (LMC #193–227) green

Weekday
2 SAT

Optional Memorial of Eusebius of Vercelli (+ 371), bishop/white ▪ *Optional Memorial of Peter Julian Eymard (+ 1868), presbyter, religious founder/white* ▪ *Optional Memorial of the Blessed Virgin Mary/white* ▪ Jesus learns of the death of John the Baptist. The hideous details are revealed in today's gospel. According to some commentators, Jesus began his spiritual life as a disciple of John, and John's death drove him into his public ministry.

Instructions for celebrating the jubilee year come from today's passage from Leviticus. People rest, and the land rests. Today's psalm is a song of harvest, thanking God for the bounty of the earth.

■ TODAY'S SAINTS: Sardinian by birth, Eusebius went to Rome as an infant and eventually Pope Sylvester made him a lector. As bishop of Vercelli he lived with his clergy, blending the clerical and the monastic lives and inspiring the canons regular of the West. Exiled for his defense of Athanasius and opposition to the Arians, he returned by the kindness of Constantine and died in peace.

Peter Julian Eymard founded the Congregation of the Blessed Sacrament and the Servants of the Blessed Sacrament, an order of sisters devoted to perpetual adoration. He influenced the establishment of world eucharistic congresses.

The sacramentary's prayers for productive land (26 B) might be appropriate today. If you choose the optional memorial of Mary, consider Mary, Temple of the Lord (23), with its allusions to the ark of the covenant.

Today is the patronal feast of Costa Rica under the title Our Lady of the Angels. It is an optional memorial in Guatemala. The date appears on the Franciscan calendar to honor the title of the beloved Portiuncula shrine where Francis of Assisi died. Tradition says that on this date in 1636 a Costa Rican Indian found a stone statue of Mary, but when he tried to move it, it returned to its original site. Believers constructed a shrine there.

☀❸ #113 (LMC #107)   green
Eighteenth Sunday in Ordinary Time

ORIENTATION

Those using the four-volume set of the *Liturgy of the Hours* switch to the last volume today. We begin the second half of Ordinary Time.

LECTIONARY

We continue our survey of the sixth chapter of John. The reading is timely this week because its interpretation depends on the story of Israel's exodus through the desert, which we have been following in the daily Mass scriptures. In today's reading, Jesus actually begins the discourse. The crowd, alert that Jesus can provide food seemingly out of nowhere, asks for a sign similar to the manna in the desert. Jesus compares himself to manna, providing nourishment for the spiritual life. Those who believe in him are like those who obtained sustenance on manna. He is promoting faith in him; he is laying the groundwork for faith in the eucharist later in the chapter.

The story from the book of Exodus is one we heard at daily Mass about ten days ago. God provides quail and manna for the wandering Israelites. The sung verses are from the same psalm we used on that Wednesday, a song about the manna God sent from heaven.

The letter to the Ephesians has already made the point that the barrier between Jew and Gentile is eliminated in Christ. Gentiles are welcome to the Christian community. Now the letter specifies that Gentile Christians are different from other Gentiles, and they should show that by their actions of righteousness and holiness.

SACRAMENTARY

Penitential Rite C-vi acclaims Jesus who feeds us with his body and blood. The sixth preface for Ordinary Time says the gift of the Spirit "is the foretaste and promise of the paschal feast of heaven." Prayer over the people #20 prays for every good gift from God.

OTHER IDEAS

The gospels these weeks provide a natural opportunity for catechesis on the eucharist and for a renewal of practices surrounding the sharing of communion. If your community needs to refine the movements of communion ministers, the posture of the assembly or the commitment to the communion song, these may be good weeks to remind people why the communion rite is so important to all of us gathered for worship.

M O N ❹ #407 (LMC #193–227)   white
John Mary Vianney (+ 1859), presbyter
MEMORIAL

Use the gospel assigned for today. During Year A this gospel is replaced because it repeats the one from Sunday, but that does not apply this year. The story that it tells, the miracle of the loaves, is one we heard a week ago Sunday are from John's gospel. Today we hear Matthew's account of the feeding of the five thousand, not counting women and children. Matthew notes that Jesus looked up to pray the blessing. The first eucharistic prayer says that Jesus looked up when he prayed at the Last Supper. The gospels never affirm that he did that. But Matthew says he raised his eyes at the miracle of the loaves. Eucharistic Prayer I thus alludes subtly to today's gospel.

We turn to the book of Numbers, continuing our nine-week survey of the early history of Israel. Just as the Sunday scriptures praise the miracle of manna in the desert, the weekday scripture reports how tired the people became of this boring food. They grumble against Moses, and he takes the complaint directly to God. So distressed is Moses over the whining about food, that he asks God either to straighten out the problem or to take his life at once. Today's psalm recalls the antagonism between God and the Israelites, in spite of its upbeat refrain. "If only my people would hear me," God moans, "I would feed them with the best of wheat."

■ TODAY'S SAINT: Better known as the Curé of Ars, Jean-Baptist Marie Vianney is the patron saint of diocesan priests. He served humbly the small community of Ars in southeastern France, and became well known for his pious spirituality, religious asceticism and pastoral care as a confessor. The architect who built the church in his honor in Ars also constructed the one in La Louvesc to honor the saint that John Mary Vianney admired, John Francis Regis.

The sacramentary gives the opening prayer for the saint. You may take the other prayers from the common of pastors and the preface for pastors (P 67) as well.

T U E ❺ #408 (LMC #193–227)   green
Weekday

Optional Memorial of the Dedication of the Basilica of St. Mary Major in Rome (c. 431)/white ■ Use the first option for the gospel today. The second is provided for Year A when the weekday and Sunday lectionaries overlap. Jesus walks on the water and invites

Peter to do the same. The miracles continue: He heals the afflicted, many of whom simply touch the fringe of his cloak. Matthew presents a Jesus in complete control over natural elements, while acknowledging the human limits of faith.

Besides dealing with complaints from his people, Moses also faced domestic quarrels. In today's reading, his marriage to a Cushite woman prompts criticism by Miriam and Aaron. God intervenes, by telling the pair to stop criticizing Moses, and by striking Miriam with leprosy. Moses asks God to leave Miriam alone. In the midst of this strange and stunningly realistic portrait of a family argument, the book of Numbers calls Moses the meekest man on the face of the earth. This encomium does not fit the irascible figure who killed an Egyptian in his youth and barks at God in today's reading. It has also caused problems for those fundamentalists who believed that Moses himself wrote the first five books of the Bible. How could Moses be the meekest man on earth if he wrote that tribute about himself? The psalm for the day helps everyone take stock of things as it leads us in prayers of contrition.

The second eucharistic prayer for Masses of reconciliation might be appropriate today.

■ TODAY'S MEMORIAL: Pope Liberius learned where St. Mary Major should be built when snow fell in the summer of 352 on Rome's Coelian Hill. After the Council of Ephesus declared Mary "Theotokos," or "God-bearer," in 431, Pope Sixtus III enlarged and consecrated St. Mary Major as the first basilica dedicated to the mother of God in the West. Beneath the altar are the supposed relics of Bethlehem's crib.

W E D 6 #614 (LMC #344)   white
The Transfiguration of the Lord
FEAST

We remember today the revelation of Jesus' glory to the disciples. Use Mark's account of the event in accord with the custom of Year B. The Second Letter of Peter remembers the event and purports to give eyewitness testimony. The passage is meant to convince people of Christian teachings and of the church's authority. Daniel's vision of the Son of Man on the clouds of heaven before the Ancient One reads like a prelude to the event we celebrate today. The psalmist also proclaims God as king upon clouds.

The sacramentary's prayers for August 6 are all inspired by the scriptural account. Sing the Glory to God. The Transfiguration has its own preface (P 50). The first solemn blessing for Ordinary Time (10) is the blessing of Aaron, a prayer that God's face may shine upon the believer.

■ ON THIS DATE IN 1890 the electric chair was used for the first time in the United States. On this date in 1945 the United States dropped the atom bomb on Hiroshima. Offer prayers for respect for human life.

This is the patronal and titular feast of El Salvador.

T H U 7 #410 (LMC #193–227)   green
Weekday

Optional Memorial of Sixtus II (+ 258), pope, martyr; and his companions, martyrs / red ▪ Optional Memorial of Cajetan (+ 1547), presbyter, religious founder / white
▪ Matthew's gospel reaches a turning point as Jesus asks the disciples who people say he is. Peter answers correctly and profoundly that he is the Messiah, the Christ, the Son of the living God. In Matthew's account of this event, Jesus goes on to entrust the keys of the kingdom of heaven to Peter. Matthew often clarifies Peter's high-ranking role among the disciples. As in the other gospels, Jesus at this point reveals to his followers the fate that awaits him in Jerusalem. They need formation in understanding just what a Messiah is and does. It isn't pretty.

Life in the desert continues to wear down the Israelites. Miriam dies. And they have no water. They complain to Moses, who prays to God, who promises to give him water from a rock. It appears that by striking the rock twice, Moses displeased God, who levels a most unfortunate prophecy against this hapless leader and faithful friend: Moses shall not lead the community all the way into the promised land. These waters of Meribah inspired the verses of the psalm we sing today.

The sacramentary includes prayers for Peter's successor in its Masses for various needs and occasions (2B).

■ TODAY'S SAINTS: Sixtus II reconciled the churches of North Africa and Rome. After one year as pope, he and several deacons were arrested while celebrating the eucharist in the catacombs during the persecution of Valerian, who had them beheaded. The archdeacon of Sixtus, Lawrence, escaped notice, but not for long.

Sixtus is mentioned in the first eucharistic prayer.

Cajetan founded the Theatines in an attempt to live like the apostles of old. A prayerful, hard-working priest, he cared for the sick and the poor.

#411 (LMC #193–227)   white

FRI 8 Dominic (+ 1221), presbyter, religious founder
MEMORIAL

Not only will Jesus suffer, but his disciples can expect the same. To follow, pick up a cross. To save your life, lose it.

We now begin a series of readings from the book of Deuteronomy, continuing our survey of the Pentateuch. Moses appeals again to the people to remain faithful to their covenant with God. He makes a glorious speech about God's nearness to them, evidenced in the past and in the wonders of creation. Today's psalm joins this theme, as it remembers the deeds of God.

■ TODAY'S SAINT: Dominic founded the Order of Preachers, devoted to contemplation, study and preaching. A contemporary of Saint Francis of Assisi, he was canonized 13 years after his death. Tradition holds that a follower of Dominic, Antonio Ghislieri, who became Pope Pius V (+ 1572), continued to wear his Dominican habit, creating the custom that popes always dress in white.

Prayers for Dominic's day are under August 8. You may use the preface for virgins and religious (P 68).

#412 (LMC #193–227)   green

SAT 9 Weekday

Optional Memorial of the Blessed Virgin Mary / white ▪ Jesus cures a child with a serious mental disability after his disciples tried and failed. He seizes the occasion to speak about the importance of faith in overcoming all obstacles.

A highlight from the book of Deuteronomy is the Shemach, the prayer that Moses reveals in today's reading. Jesus himself quotes it: You shall love the Lord your God with all your heart, soul and strength. The psalm echoes the same theme.

Remembering Jesus' ability to heal, you could include prayers for the sick today (various needs and occasions 32). If you choose the optional memorial, consider Mary, Health of the Sick (44 from the Collection of Masses of the Blessed Virgin Mary).

■ IN URUGUAY, today is the memorial of Blessed Mother Francisca Rubatto.

#116 (LMC #110)   green

◉ 10 Nineteenth Sunday in Ordinary Time

ORIENTATION

In summer's last weeks many groups will start having meetings to prepare for activities this fall. Some college students may be returning to school already. Provide opportunities for family members and friends to meet and greet.

LECTIONARY

This is the third week that we interrupt the semicontinuous reading of Mark's gospel to hear from John's chapter six. Today Jesus emphasizes his divine origin and salvific mission. He is the bread that has come down from heaven, and on the last day he will raise up those the Father sends to him. Only at the very end of this reading does he begin the theme of

eating the living bread. That more eucharistic theme will resound most clearly in next Sunday's passage.

Even so, the first reading today develops the imagery of bread, food and life. We meet Elijah fleeing for his life from Jezebel, angry with him because he bested the pagan priests in a contest. An angel gives him food and water for his journey. At daily Mass on July 29 we heard about Moses fasting for 40 days and 40 nights. Today we hear that Elijah walked 40 days and 40 nights with no more food than what this angel gives him. Both Moses and Elijah appear with Jesus in the Transfiguration episode we celebrated last week, a gospel story we read every year on the Second Sunday of Lent, while undergoing our own fast of 40 days and nights. The significance of this reading today is its image of the superphysical nourishment coming from heavenly food and drink. The psalmist sings, "Taste and see the goodness of the Lord."

The second reading appeals to the Ephesians to avoid all bitterness, fury, anger, shouting and reviling. Honest heads will hang in shame as we hear these words. Every Christian community devoted to the ideals of Jesus struggles to express compassion even for people we don't love.

SACRAMENTARY

The alternate communion antiphon for the day comes from the sixth chapter of John, albeit next week's reading. The fourth preface for Ordinary Time (P 32) praises the birth, suffering, resurrection and return of Jesus, helping us reflect on his origins and mission. The ninth prayer over the people encourages the sharing of God's love, as does today's second reading.

OTHER IDEAS

Be sure to announce the schedule of Masses for the holy day this week. Invite the faithful to celebrate our redemption as revealed in the Assumption of Mary.

If students are returning to college this week, collect e-mail addresses, and be sure they know how to access the parish website for updates.

#413 (LMC #193–227)   white

MON 11 Clare of Assisi (+ 1253), virgin, religious founder
MEMORIAL

The narrative section of Matthew's book four closes with another prediction of the passion and a story of taxes that shows the state's growing distrust of Jesus.

From Deuteronomy we hear another excerpt of Moses speaking about the law. These final, solemn speeches of the great prophet and leader still resound with wisdom, emotion and religiosity. Moses preaches the holiness of God, fidelity to the covenant, sincerity of heart, and charity toward all. The psalm praises God for the word, statutes and ordinances given to Israel.

The opening prayer for the day is in the proper of saints. It stresses Clare's love of poverty. The other presidential prayers might be taken from the commons for religious (8).

■ TODAY'S SAINT: Clare followed the example of Frances and founded a religious community for those desiring a life of poverty. Barefoot, simple and devout, she led the group of sisters at San Damiano. In a vision she could see Christmas midnight Mass although she was in a different building. She is the patron saint of television.

#414 (LMC #193–227)   green

TUE 12 Weekday

We begin hearing the fourth discourse from Matthew's gospel, this one concerning the life of the community that will form the church. Jesus speaks of the importance of childlike humility in the kingdom of God and of God's desire to rescue all the sheep of the flock.

In his last speech, the elderly Moses summons Joshua into his presence and establishes him as the people's leader. Today's responsory comes from the following chapter of Deuteronomy, the so-called Song of Moses.

Consider the texts—from the Masses for various needs and occasions—for the ministers of the church (8).

#415 (LMC #193–227)   green

WED 13 Weekday

Optional Memorial of Pontian (+ 235), pope, martyr; and Hippolytus (+ 235), presbyter, martyr / red
■ Even the church needs skills in conflict resolution. Jesus urges the disciples to work things out as best they can with the offenders, and reject them only as a last resort. He promises to be present whenever people gather in his name.

Moses, who reluctantly but faithfully responded to God's call, bravely led the people out of slavery in Egypt, daringly brought them across an immense desert, and expectantly approached the destination of God's promise, dies in today's first reading, before he has crossed the finish line of the exodus. To the Israelites, it must have seemed incredibly unfair after a full life that Moses did not get to enjoy the fruit of this intense labor. Still, God allowed him to see the promised land from the top of Mount Nebo. No matter how much we devote ourselves to God's service, we never know how much of the reward we will rejoice to see. Moses died at age 120, eyes undimmed and "vigor unabated"— probably a euphemism for his continued ability to father children. The concluding verses today, heaping praise upon Moses, brings the Pentateuch to its close. A psalm of praise honors God enthroned on high, who looks upon the heavens and the earth below.

The prayers for oppressors (#45) might harmonize with today's gospel.

■ TODAY'S SAINTS: After becoming pope, Pontian was arrested and sent to work in the mines of Sardinia under the persecution of Maximinus, who hated Christians because his opponent Alexander Severus favored them. It appears that Pontian abdicated the throne of Peter while in exile, and Anterus succeeded him as pope.

Hippolytus is remembered as a great theologian who took offense at Pope Calixtus for his too generous mercy. Hippolytus appointed himself bishop and anti-pope but also ended up in the mines of Sardinia with Pontian. The two suffered martyrs' deaths.

It is doubtful that this Hippolytus authored *The Apostolic Tradition*, as many believe, but it might still be a good day to use Eucharistic Prayer II, which was inspired by that document.

Ezekiel sees God calling on a scribe to mark the foreheads of those who bemoan the atrocities in Jerusalem. He orders the rest to be struck down. He imagines the glory of God returning to the temple after this time of purification. God's glory, the psalmist says, is higher than the heavens.

#416 (LMC #193–227) red

THU 14 Maximilian Mary Kolbe (+ 1941), presbyter, religious founder, martyr
MEMORIAL

Jesus stresses the importance for forgiving many times. The parable illustrates a different point, the importance of forgiving individual offenses, even if they are enormous.

In our nine-week survey of the early history of the Israelites, we leave the Pentateuch behind and turn to the book of Joshua, which resumes the story where Deuteronomy left off. Finally, Israel reclaims the promised land. The priests lead the way with the ark of the covenant. The Jordan stops flowing so the chosen people once more can cross a body of water on dry ground. With this miraculous intervention, the people enter the land they have yearned for since the day they left Egypt. The psalm for the day reports another version of the same story, that the Jordan turned back as Israel came out of Egypt.

■ TODAY'S SAINT: Maximilian Kolbe, a Franciscan, was among those imprisoned at Auschwitz during World War II. Founder of the Militia of Mary Immaculate, he gave up his life so that a fellow prisoner, a father of children, could live.

Presidential prayers are under August 14 in the sacramentary. The preface for martyrs could be used (P 66).

#621–622 (LMC #447–450, #352) white

FRI 15 The Assumption of the Virgin Mary into Heaven
SOLEMNITY

ORIENTATION

Today the church celebrates Mary's welcome to heaven. As we believe that Jesus was the first to rise from the dead, so we believe he has also received his mother first into eternity. Eastern traditions called this event the "Dormition" or "sleeping" of Mary, indicating that she did not die but was taken to heaven as if asleep. Pope Pius XII declared the bodily assumption of Mary into heaven as a dogma of the church in 1950.

There are two Masses for the solemnity, one for the vigil and another for the day.

Today is a holy day of obligation in the United States (except in the diocese of Honolulu).

Mary is a patron of Guatemala, Panama and Paraguay under this title. Today is also a holy day of obligation in Argentina, Costa Rica, Chile, Honduras, Nicaragua, Paraguay, Peru and Puerto Rico, but not the other Latin American countries. Bolivia transfers the solemnity to the nearest Sunday.

LECTIONARY

There is no biblical account of Mary's death, so the lectionary turns to other episodes in Mary's life. The gospel for the vigil reports Jesus hearing someone bless "the womb that bore you and the breasts that nursed him." The gospel for the Mass during the day is Mary's visit to Elizabeth. She hears her kinswoman tell her, "Blessed is the fruit of your womb."

Both second readings come from the fifteenth chapter of Second Corinthians, where Paul treats the theme of the resurrection.

The first readings draw on Marian iconography. At the vigil, we hear of the placement of the ark of the covenant with the holy tent, an image of Mary, the "ark" of divine presence, entering the holy temple of heaven. A psalm about the ark answers in responsory. These passages are especially fitting this year for those following the daily Mass readings, which highlighted the role of the ark just yesterday. In Revelation, John sees a woman clothed with the sun, the moon and the stars. Because her child does battle with the dragon, the woman has become an image of Mary in heaven. From the book of psalms we sing a wedding song, in which the queen takes her place on a royal throne—again, an image of Mary's entrance into heaven, where she rules as queen.

SACRAMENTARY

The texts for both Masses proclaim the meaning of the day's celebration, as does the proper preface (P 59). Sing the Glory and the Creed today. There is a solemn blessing for the Blessed Virgin Mary (15).

OTHER IDEAS

The German sacramentary proposes an insert to Eucharistic Prayer III: "In union with the whole church we celebrate that day on which the virgin mother of God was taken up to heaven. We praise her before all the saints, the glorious ever-virgin Mother of our Lord and God, Jesus Christ.

Display an icon of the assumption for veneration.

By Flowing Waters (355–363) includes the incomparable responsorial psalm and antiphon, "Come, my beloved, receive your crown," from the Song of Songs, and a unique alleluia psalm. In the ideal this responsorial psalm is sung from the ambo by at least four psalmists: the women of the schola sing verses 2, 4, 6 and 10— as did the bridesmaids in the Song of Songs. Male and female psalmists may represent the groom and bride on the verses.

■ HARVEST BLESSING: Some countries link this celebration to the blessing of the earth's harvest, or else the blessing of earth, sea and sky. See *Book of Blessings,* 26 or 28, and *Catholic Household Blessings and Prayers,* 170–171.

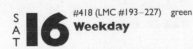

#418 (LMC #193–227)   green
Weekday
S A T 16

Optional Memorial of Stephen of Hungary (+ 1038), married man ruler/white • Optional Memorial of the Blessed Virgin Mary/white • In another instance of showing his care for children, Jesus permits them to come close over the objections of the disciples, because the kingdom of God belongs to them. This passage helps the argument that the early church practiced the baptism of children.

Our brief survey of the book of Joshua closes today with a kind of liturgy of allegiance. Joshua first obtains from the people the promise that they will forsake other gods and serve only the God who brought them up from slavery into the promised land. Then he set up a memorial stone under an oak tree to signify the stability of the covenant made at Shechem. Shechem was the first city visited by Abraham in his migration from Haran and the site of the rape of Dinah. In later years it became the religious center of the Samaritans, who built a temple on Mount Gerizim.

The first eucharistic prayer for Masses with children references today's gospel: Jesus took children in his arms and blessed them.

■ IF YOU OBSERVE THE MEMORIAL OF MARY TODAY, consider Holy Mary Handmaid of the Lord from the *Collection of Masses of the Blessed Virgin Mary* (22). Her wholehearted service of God reflects the attitude required for fidelity to the covenant.

■ TODAY'S SAINT: Stephen served as king of Hungary, yet earned a reputation for his charity to the needy. In 2000 the Orthodox church also recognized him as a saint. This marks the first time that the church east and west has agreed about a canonization since the eleventh-century schism.

■ MEXICO HAS AN OPTIONAL MEMORIAL for Blessed Bartolomé Laurel (+ 16th c.), martyr. Argentina observes an optional memorial for Saint Rock (+ 1378) today. This medieval saint is often invoked in times of pestilence because of stories that he miraculously cured others and was sustained in his own illness by a dog that brought him bread in the woods.

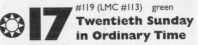
#119 (LMC #113)   green
Twentieth Sunday in Ordinary Time
17

ORIENTATION

Our detour from Mark's gospel reaches its purpose today as we behold the glorious heart of the bread of life discourse from John's gospel.

LECTIONARY

"The bread that I will give is my flesh for the life of the world." "Those who eat my flesh and drink my blood remain in me and I in them." These powerful statements from today's gospel form the beautiful heart of John's sixth chapter. For Catholics they give irrefutable evidence that the eucharist we share is a participation in the real presence of Jesus Christ.

From the book of Proverbs we hear Wisdom personified, calling people to eat and drink with her. Dining with Wisdom is like gaining understanding. Hearing this reading together with the gospel today reminds us that sharing the eucharist does more than give us a happy heart. It will have an effect on our judgment and behavior. We repeat the psalm from last week, "Taste and see the goodness of the Lord."

The letter to the Ephesians continues its exhortation to lead a moral life. As the first reading does, it equates wisdom with holiness. Avoid ignorance, it says, and understand God's will. Use psalms, hymns and spiritual songs to give thanks to God.

SACRAMENTARY

The alternate communion antiphon comes directly from today's gospel. The sixth preface for Sundays in Ordinary Time (P 34) calls the Spirit the foretaste and promise of the paschal feast of heaven, language we also apply to the eucharist. Prayer over the people #18 asks that we might desire to relive the mystery of the eucharist.

OTHER IDEAS

The gospels during this five-week period all build to the text we hear today, the heart of our eucharistic doctrine. If you have been reviewing your communion practices over the past few weeks, continue to use today's text as a foundation for catechesis. Is the cup offered to the faithful at every Mass? Do people share communion under both forms? Are communion ministers avoiding the use of tabernacle hosts as the rubrics request? Do communion ministers carry out their ministry with reverence?

M O N **18** **#419 (LMC #193–227)** green
Weekday

Optional memorial of Jane Frances de Chantal (+ 1641), religious / white ▪ "Keep the commandments," Jesus tells a would-be disciple. Jesus then recites them—well, some—of the ten commandments, and not in the correct order. To do more than these commandments, Jesus says, sell what you have and give the money to the poor.

We enter the final week of our survey of biblical texts detailing the early history of Israel. Turning now to the book of Judges, we hear the disheartening opening line: The Israelites offended the Lord by serving the Baals. They suffered at the hands of their enemies and did not grow under the leadership of their ruling judges.

Israel's infidelity is the "them" of today's psalm.

The sacramentary includes a Mass for forgiveness of sins (40).

▪ TODAY'S SAINT: Jane Frémiot became the mother of six. Widowed by a shooting accident, she took Francis de Sales as her spiritual director and founded the Visitation Nuns at Annecy in Savoy.

Chile celebrates a memorial of the priest, Blessed Alberto Hurtado, today.

T U E **19** **#420 (LMC #193–227)** green
Weekday

Optional Memorial of John Eudes (+ 1680), presbyter, religious founder, educator / white ▪ Following up yesterday's command to the wealthy young man, Jesus says how difficult it is for the rich to enter heaven. He expects total commitment from followers.

Faithful Gideon sees a divine apparition that commands him to lead a charge against the invading Midianites. A fire from a rock consumes his offering of meat and bread. As a result of his prayer, he is as fearful as he is relieved. The psalm asserts that God speaks peace to the faithful.

A Mass for peace and justice (22A) appears among those for various needs and occasions.

▪ TODAY'S SAINT: John Eudes is regarded as a founder of the Sisters of the Good Shepherd as well as the Priests of Jesus and Mary. He traveled throughout France, evangelizing and catechizing. His day is an obligatory memorial in Venezuela.

Today Mexico honors Blessed Pedro Zúñiga and Blessed Luis Flores (+ 16th c.), priests and martyrs.

W E D **20** **#421 (LMC #193–227)** white
Bernard (+ 1153), abbot, monastic, doctor of the church
MEMORIAL

One of the most difficult parables heard in a capitalist society, today's reading establishes the superiority of generosity over fairness.

At Shechem, the citizens take matters into their own hands and anoint a king for themselves. Jotham tells them a parable that basically means "You'll be sorry." He implies that they have chosen an unqualified volunteer on the mere grounds that this one was willing to take the job. The psalm seems oblivious to this dynamic as it sings of God's favor with the king.

▪ TODAY'S SAINT: Bernard joined the abbey of Cîteaux and then Clairvaux, where he served as abbot. An effective preacher, a wise and holy man, he authored hymns we still sing. "O Sacred Head Surrounded" is attributed to him.

The sacramentary has presidential prayers for today. You may use the preface for virgins and religious (P 68).

T H U **21** **#422 (LMC #193–227)** white
Pius X (+ 1914), pope
MEMORIAL

The lectionary skips well over a chapter of Matthew's gospel to today's parable, which sums up much of the preceding material: Jesus meets the same resistance from religious authority that the host of the wedding banquet meets from friends.

Why the weekday lectionary retains the story of Jephthah's daughter is a mystery. Jephthah vows that if God delivers the Ammonites into his power, he will slaughter whatever living thing first comes through the door of his house as an offering to God. The misguided fool wins the battle and returns home to be greeted by his daughter. He explains how sorry he is that she will have to die. She incredibly agrees to let him fulfill his vow, obtaining a two-month stay of execution so she can mourn her virginity. To make matters worse, the lectionary assigns as the psalm refrain, "Here am I Lord, I come to do your will," thus glorifying the daughter's decision to give up her life because of her father's rash vow. It is hard to find a shred of responsible behavior in the entire episode. You have the option of drawing the first reading from the common of pastors because of today's saint.

■ TODAY'S SAINT: With the motto, "To renew all things in Christ," Pope Pius X urged children to share communion at a younger age than the customary 12. He also urged adults to share communion frequently, a practice they were reluctant to observe.

In addition to the presidential prayers under August 21, you may use the preface for pastors (P 67).

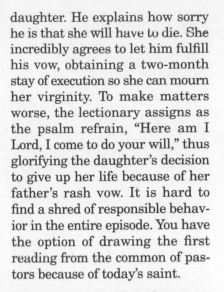

F R I **22** #423 (LMC #193–227)   white
The Queenship of the Virgin Mary
MEMORIAL

Jesus' conflict with local leadership reaches a climax in the dispute over the greatest of commandments. It gives him the opportunity to summarize his teaching by citing the great commandment of love, a commandment not much in evidence in this series of disputes.

From the ugliness of yesterday's first reading we turn to the beautiful story of the book of Ruth. Situated in the time of the judges, it forms a perfect close to our survey of early biblical history. Ruth was the Moabite daughter-in-law of the Judean Naomi, who had left Bethlehem years ago due to a famine. When prosperity returned to Bethlehem, Naomi desired to return, and Ruth, surprisingly, abandoned the pagan land of Moab to join Naomi on her return. "Your people will be my people, and your God will be my God," the Moabite Ruth says to her Israelite mother-in-law Naomi. This verse has been sung in many a wedding song, but it has nothing to do with the affection of spouses. It's a loving ode to the mother-in-law. The psalm plays off the theme of the famine, as it praises God who gives food to the hungry.

■ TODAY'S MEMORIAL: The Queenship of Mary forms an octave celebration of the Assumption. Last week's solemnity was a celebration of Mary's assumption into heaven; today's memorial is a celebration of her reign as heaven's queen. The *Collection of Masses of the Blessed Virgin Mary* (29) has a revision of today's sacramentary's texts and a new preface.

S A T **23** #424 (LMC #193–227)   green
Weekday

Optional Memorial of Rose of Lima (+ 1617), virgin, religious / white ▪ *Optional Memorial of the Blessed Virgin Mary / white* ▪ The twenty-third chapter of Matthew is laced with Jesus' criticisms of the Pharisees. We use the word *pharisaical* in English to mean hypocritical. In today's gospel we learn why.

For nine weeks we have followed the history of Israel from Abraham to Ruth. The series concludes today on a note of happiness and hope. In Bethlehem, Naomi's homeland, Ruth works the field of Boaz. He learns of her character and loves her. They marry, and Ruth bears a son whom the neighbor women name Obed. He became the father of Jesse, and Jesse became the father of David, the greatest king of Israel, from whose lineage was born a Savior. Our series of readings ends by lifting our eyes to Israel's great age of kingship and beyond, all the way to the Christian era.

Incidentally, the lectionary abridges the story of Ruth by eliminating a few verses here and there. Today's reading, for example, jumps through the second chapter from verses 1–3 to verses 8–11. Had it included verse 4, we would hear Boaz greet the reapers with the phrase, "The Lord be with you." This is the first occurrence in the Bible of a phrase that has become an integral part of Christian worship.

The sacramentary's prayers for the family (43) might be fitting today.

■ TODAY'S SAINT: The Peruvian Isabel de Oliva was nicknamed "Rose" because of her beauty. She observed personal asceticism while exercising charity for the sick and elderly. A Dominican Tertiary and a mystic, she was the first canonized saint of the Americas. She is recognized as Patron of Latin America with a feast today in Colombia and Costa Rica.

If you choose to celebrate the memorial of Mary, consider Mother of Fairest Love (36C) or Chosen Daughter of Israel (1B).

☀**24** #119 (LMC #113)   green
Twenty-first Sunday in Ordinary Time

ORIENTATION

This weekend concludes the series of readings from the sixth chapter of John. As summer draws to its close, we end this brief but important migration through a central passage of the fourth gospel.

LECTIONARY

A surprising conclusion awaits this series of readings from John, chapter six. Many of the disciples cannot accept the saying. Jesus does not budge from his point. As a result, he loses many of his followers, who go back to their former way of life. Poignantly, he asks his inner circle, the Twelve, if they also want to leave. Peter shrugs with a back-handed compliment: Where else would we go? Then he affirms his belief that Jesus is the Holy One of God. This story must have given some comfort to the first audience of John's gospel. If they were losing members, they had only to realize that Jesus lost disciples too. It will comfort us when we never again see some of the children we baptize or some of the adults who join the church. Even after some disciples rejected Jesus, the church carried on.

The first reading today repeats a passage we heard at the Saturday morning Mass just a week ago. Joshua calls on the people to reject the worship of false gods and to worship only the God who brought them to freedom. This passage has been used in the history of the catechumenate, to show the affirmation of those who desired baptism.

For the third week in a row, the psalm refrain is one we sometimes sing at communion, "Taste and see the goodness of the Lord." It is the choice refrain for Jesus' discourse on the bread of life. We sing different verses this week, which highlight the protection God grants the just. Think of Jesus' situation in the gospel as you sing the last verses of this week's psalm. Psalm 34, as mentioned earlier, is an alphabetical psalm. Each verse of the psalm in Hebrew begins with a successive letter of the Hebrew alphabet. There is no logical development from one verse to the next, and

the choice of this refrain has nothing to do with its centrality to the thematic thrust of the psalm, but everything to do with its foreshadowing of the eucharist.

Not only do we conclude the series of readings from John this weekend, we also bid farewell to the letter to the Ephesians. It ends with an admonition to husbands and wives about married life, while comparing their relationship to that of Christ and the church. "This is a great mystery," Paul says of this relationship. Another translation for mystery is "sacrament." This verse is one of the reasons we list marriage among the sacraments of our church. The lectionary of 1969 gave only the longer form of this reading. The revised lectionary now offers a shorter version, and it is no secret why. Paul's words sound absolutely unacceptable in today's society: "Wives should be subordinate to their husbands." This verse has been eliminated in the shorter version, and replaced with a new introduction from earlier in the same chapter: "Husbands, love your wives." On one level, Paul was only trying to point out that the church should be subordinate to Christ. Not a bad point. But he made it by a controversial example. Avoid the needless controversy. Opt for the shorter version of this week's second reading. Surely even Paul would not want us to let his example get in the way of our appreciating the overall message.

If you are using the *Lectionary for Masses with Children* today, note that you have a different passage from Ephesians (6:1–4). In these words, the writer addresses the children and parents of the community.

SACRAMENTARY

The second preface for marriage (P 73) says the new covenant of grace is symbolized in the marriage covenant that reflects God's plan of love. Prayer over the people #6 praises God who cares for people even when they stray, as they surely did in today's gospel.

OTHER IDEAS

More students will be returning to school this weekend. Remember them, their teachers and families in prayer.

If you have inquirers ready for the Rite of Acceptance in the catechumenate, this weekend's first reading makes an ideal passage for the ritual. It may be celebrated today and is recommended to be made available several times a year (RCIA, 18.3).

M O N **25** #425 (LMC #193–227) green
Weekday

Optional Memorial of Louis IX of France (+ 1270), married man, ruler / white ▪ Optional Memorial of Joseph Calasanz (+ 1648), presbyter, religious founder / white ▪ "Frauds!" Jesus calls the scribes and Pharisees, not burying his opinion. This is only the first part of seven woes he casts upon their heads, stretched over three lectionary days. Jesus cannot tolerate hypocrisy in general, but especially among religious leaders.

Leaving the Old Testament behind for the first time since June 23, the Ordinary Time first reading today turns to Paul's First Letter to the Thessalonians. In a playful parallel, the lectionary begins the twenty-first week of Ordinary Time in each of the two years in the weekday cycle with a letter to the Thessalonians. This is year one, and we open letter one. Both letters are very early in the Pauline corpus, possibly the first books written for the New Testament. As with all of Paul's authentic letters, they predate the composition of the written gospels. Paul thanks God for the faith of the Thessalonians, who have turned from false idols to serve the living God. The psalm echoes the theme: The Lord takes delight in his people.

Remembering the importance of praying for sincere church leadership, consider the sacramentary's Mass for ministers (8).

■ TODAY'S SAINTS: Louis IX of France fathered 11 children, led the second crusade, and built Sainte Chapelle in Paris as a reliquary for the crown of thorns. A city in Missouri is named for him.

Joseph Calasanz founded the Piarists, the Clerics Regular of Religious Schools. If your parish operates a school that makes room for the poor, Joseph is your patron. He established such a school in Trastevere, a neighborhood just south of the Vatican, across the Tiber from the heart of Rome.

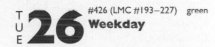

T U E 26 #426 (LMC #193–227) green
Weekday

Jesus' diatribe against the scribes and Pharisees continues. He complains again about their focus on minutiae and avoidance of actions for justice and personal sanctification.

Apparently some scandalmongers had told the Thessalonian Christians that Paul's motives had not been sincere. He stresses he came to please God, even at the cost of personal hardship, not to please people. The psalm places trust in God who scrutinizes the human heart and knows our thoughts from afar.

The first version of the eucharistic prayer for Masses for various needs and occasions prays for the ministry of the church.

Spain and Colombia celebrate today the memorial of Teresa of Jesus (+ 1897), founder of the Little Sisters of the Abandoned Aged.

■ BLESSED JUNÍPERO SERRA, remembered on July 1 in the United States, has an optional memorial today in Mexico.

W E D 27 #427 (LMC #193–227) white
Monica (+ 387), married woman
MEMORIAL

The crucifixion of Jesus becomes more comprehensible when we hear how he made enemies among the religious leaders. Today we hear the conclusion of his creed against scribes and Pharisees, calling them whitewashed tombs—pretty to look at, but filled inside with filth.

Paul defends his actions and attitudes and rejoices that the Thessalonians accepted the gospel as God's word, not as Paul's. The passage suggests that some were trying to besmirch Paul's reputation. More verses from yesterday's psalm follow this reading; they share the comfort that God knows the human heart.

The opening prayer for today's Mass can be found in the proper of saints. You may take the other presidential prayers from the common of holy women (e.g. #12). Preface 70 could be used. An optional gospel for this day appears in the lectionary, the story of Jesus raising to life the son of the widow of Naim. The story relates to that of Monica, who prayed for the salvation of her son.

■ TODAY'S SAINT: Monica the African is noteworthy just for her devotion and prayer alone, but her famous son, Augustine, brought her eternal attention. She nearly had Augustine baptized as an infant when the child took ill, but waited, an event that caused Augustine to believe that God wanted him to experience deeper

conversion later in life. By the prayers of Monica, Augustine accepted baptism. Monica died in Ostia, Italy. A freeway in California bears her name.

#428/633 (LMC #193–227)
white
T H U 28 **Augustine (+ 430), bishop, religious founder, doctor of the church**
MEMORIAL

The gospel for the weekday draws us near to the end of Matthew's story. Jesus warns the disciples in a parable to stay awake, for they know not the day God is coming.

In the midst of his trials, Paul takes comfort that the Thessalonians have remained steadfast in their faith. Paul thanks God for them and prays day and night to see them. The psalm echoes these themes of thanksgiving and daily prayer.

Alternate readings appear in the lectionary for Augustine, highlighting his role as a teacher of faith and a lover of God.

■ TODAY'S SAINT: No theologian influenced the direction of the church in the west as much as Augustine the African did. Personally, his conversion from a sinful life of a Manichean to a religious life of commitment to Christ produces a story of immense importance. As writer and preacher he put his stamp on every aspect of Christian liturgical, moral and intellectual life. A speaker of immeasurable talent, he served as bishop of Hippo in Northern Africa over thirty years.

You may use the preface for pastors (P 67) with the presidential prayers for August 28. These prayers are inspired by quotes from Augustine.

FRI **29** #429/634 (LMC #193–227/365)
red
Martyrdom of John the Baptist
MEMORIAL

Herod beheaded John at the request of the daughter of Herodias, who got the idea from her mother. Herod's wife was angered by John's dismissal of their union, even though Herod himself seemed attracted to John's words. The gospel for the day tells the morbid tale.

The first reading may come from the proper of saints (where you find the gospel) or from the common of martyrs, or you may choose the one from the weekday, which continues the series from Paul's First Letter to the Thessalonians. Paul exhorts the community to moral behavior. Do not cheat, he says, for God will punish. In the early editions of the lectionary for Mass, the editors inadvertently omitted the last word of the first reading. It should conclude with the word *you*.

Presidential prayers for August 29 will be accompanied with the preface of John the Baptist (P 61).

SAT **30** #430 (LMC #193–227)   green
Weekday

Optional Memorial of the Blessed Virgin Mary / white ▪ Our readings from Matthew conclude today with the parable of the talents. It bases God's judgment on the use and development of our gifts. The semicontinuous readings of the gospel omit those sections that pertain to seasons of the year, so we end this series not with the passion and resurrection, but with one of Jesus' last parables before his arrest.

The Thessalonians know well God's command to love one another, but Paul admonishes them to make even more progress by remaining at peace with others and minding their own business. The psalm sings of God's justice.

The second weekday preface for Ordinary Time (P 38) balances God's justice and mercy.

Consider the Mass for the Blessed Virgin Mary, the Help of Christians (42) from the *Collection of Masses of the Blessed Virgin Mary.*

▪ ROSE OF LIMA, remembered on the universal calendar on August 23, is honored with a solemnity today in Peru and the Dominican Republic as the Patron of Latin America. Today is a holy day of obligation in Peru. This is a feast in Argentina, Bolivia, Chile, Ecuador, Mexico, Panama, Paraguay and Puerto Rico. It is a memorial in Honduras, Nicaragua, El Salvador, Uruguay and Venezuela.

#125 (LMC #119)   green
☀✡ 31 Twenty-second Sunday in Ordinary Time

ORIENTATION

We finally return to Mark's gospel after our sojourn through John's sixth chapter. We left Mark at his version of the story of the miracle of the loaves. We resume today as Jesus continues his mission.

This Labor Day weekend may include prayers for workers, travelers and those affiliated with schools.

LECTIONARY

For the next two Sundays we hear excerpts from Mark's seventh chapter, detailing sayings of Jesus as part of his mission. Today, Pharisees and scribes pick on Jesus' disciples for their table manners. Jesus blasts the religious leaders for paying more attention to human rules than to divine ones. It is the evil within that makes us unclean.

Lest we get the idea that laws don't matter as much as intentions, the lectionary posts a passage from Deuteronomy to start off the readings this weekend. Moses reminds the people how important it is to observe the statutes and decrees that God has given. The psalm praises the one who does justice, not the one who mechanically observes laws.

Today we begin a series of readings from the colorful letter of James. Addressed to a wide audience, not a particular church, it is one of the so-called "catholic epistles" of the New Testament. Actually, its form does not resemble that of an epistle, but rather seems to ramble from one topic to another by means of related word. Tradition holds that the author was James, the brother of Jesus. He should not be confused with the two Jameses among the Twelve. But the Greek is highly stylized and the letter seems to know about Paul's letters, making it likely that the letter is simply a collection of exhortations preserved by late-first-century Christians under the name of James. Today's passage sounds a theme dear to the entire book: "Be doers of the word and not hearers only." This text opens with a verse made famous by a song from *Godspell.*

SACRAMENTARY

The first preface for Sundays in Ordinary Time (P 29) says that God has called us out of darkness into wonderful light. The third solemn blessing for Ordinary Time (12) asks for God's strength that we might persevere in good works.

OTHER IDEAS

This Labor Day weekend may have an assembly including some visitors and missing some regulars. Be sure people have an opportunity to greet those around them. Look for the annual Labor Day Statement from the bishops' conference as a source for the homily and bulletin inserts: www.usccb.org/sdwp/national/index.html. You will be able to download interfaith and catholic resources for worship at http://www.nicwj.org/pages/materials. The National Center for the Laity has a page (http://laity-initiatives.org/principles.html) that is always useful for preparing homilies and for bulletin quotes.

For Grandparents' Day you may include a blessing of the elderly from the *Book of Blessings* (1-XIII), but remember that some people become grandparents at a rather young age.

Intercessions for schools can be adapted from the *Book of Blessings*, 5.

September

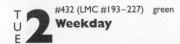

#431/907–911 (LMC #193–227)   green
Weekday

Optional Proper Mass for Labor Day/white ▪ On Labor Day you have the choice of observing the ordinary weekday or a votive Mass. The weekday readings begin the series from Luke's gospel with Jesus' self-revelation in the synagogue. Understandably, the first Christians had concerns about those who died before Jesus' return. Paul addresses these in the first reading, which is followed by a psalm of God's judgment.

The lectionary offers a selection of texts for the Blessing of Human Labor, and it would be fitting to choose from these today. Choose from the Genesis accounts of creation if you like. Paul's exhortation to the Thessalonians to work for their food is also good. Both psalm options sing of human labor. The first choice for the gospel helps people put work into its perspective. The second option for the gospel is a text that should have appeared last Friday but was replaced by the gospel of the martyrdom of John the Baptist.

The sacramentary includes prayers for the blessing of human labor (25).

#432 (LMC #193–227)   green
TUE 2 Weekday

The gospels for weekdays in Ordinary Time give us a semicontinuous reading of the three synoptics in what scholars believe are the chronological order of their composition. Mark opens the series each year after the Christmas season. Matthew governs the summer. And Luke takes over for the final third of the year. This week we begin hearing the passages from Luke. As with Matthew, Luke's infancy account is omitted, as will be his version of the passion. Today we hear of Jesus' powerful teaching and his ability to expel demons. Luke establishes the dynamic traits of his protagonist from the beginning of the story.

Today we conclude the series of readings from Paul's First Letter to the Thessalonians. He considers questions about the end of time. He warns them not to be complacent, but to be watchful at all times, continually comforting and building up one another. One thing the psalmist seeks is to dwell in the house of God forever.

Prayers for a happy death (46) might be appropriate today.

Mexico remembers Blessed Bartolomé Gutiérrez (+ 1632), priest and martyr, today with an optional memorial.

#433 (LMC #193–227)   white
WED 3 Gregory the Great (+ 604), pope, monastic, doctor of the church
MEMORIAL

Jesus cures Simon's mother-in-law and expels a host of demons who call him the Son of God. He begins his career as an itinerant preacher.

The authorship of the letter to the Colossians remains a point of dispute among scholars, but its spirituality and insight into the Christian life have made it a classic of early Christian literature. Typical of New Testament letters, a thanksgiving begins the text. Throughout this series of readings from Colossians, the lectionary makes little attempt to link a theme from the first reading with the psalm. Instead, it chooses a series of psalms of praise to link with the thrust of the letter as a whole. Today, verses of thanksgiving from a psalm make the response.

■ TODAY'S SAINT: Gregory the Great came from a noted Roman family but humbly entered monastic life. Still, at election time, the people and clergy of Rome unanimously chose him to be their pope. His treatises have earned him the rank of one of the four great fathers of the Latin church. To him has been attributed some of the chants of the early church, and a large repertoire of chant is still called Gregorian in his honor.

Presidential prayers are under September 3. You may use the preface for pastors (P 67). Sing some chant today in Gregory's honor.

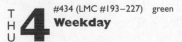

#434 (LMC #193–227)   green
THU 4 Weekday

Jesus borrows Peter's boat to preach to a crowd, then thanks Peter by pointing out a catch of fish. Peter first makes excuses for not following Jesus, but he then leaves everything and follows.

The letter includes a prayer for the Colossians to grow in perfect wisdom and spiritual insight, the kind that will have spirituality at its root. It praises God who offers redemption, as the psalm praises God who reveals salvation.

The sacramentary has texts for the spread of the gospel (14A). The alternative opening prayer asks for the Spirit to sow the truth in people's hearts so that all may be born again to new life and communion.

F R I **5** #435 (LMC #193–227) green
Weekday

Early on in Luke's story, Jesus already meets controversy with scribes and Pharisees. Today they object that his disciples do not fast. He uses images of a new coat and new wine to proclaim a new age.

Today's first reading appears weekly as a canticle for Wednesday evening prayer in the *Liturgy of the Hours.* The song acclaims Christ as the visible image of the invisible God. He is firstborn of creation, and all was made through him. A psalm of praise follows.

The saving mission of Jesus is a theme of preface 6 for weekdays in Ordinary Time (P 42).

S A T **6** #436 (LMC #193–227) green
Weekday

Optional Memorial of the Blessed Virgin Mary/white ▪ Jesus faces another controversy with the Pharisees as they challenge the disciples' behavior on the Sabbath. Jesus asserts his superiority over the Sabbath.

The letter to the Colossians is addressed to a Gentile Christian audience. They were once alienated from God because of their exclusion from the covenant. But now Christ has reconciled them, and the psalm today sings of God's help.

The first eucharistic prayer for Masses of reconciliation says that now is the time of grace and reconciliation.

Consider the texts for Mary, Image and Mother of the Church I (P 25) in the *Collection of Masses of the Blessed Virgin Mary.*

⊛7 #128 (LMC #122) green
Twenty-third Sunday in Ordinary Time

ORIENTATION

We are approaching a turning point in Mark's gospel. Throughout the first half of his gospel, one theme that unites his work is an attempt to answer the question, Who is Jesus? After the miracle today, the answer is becoming clearer.

LECTIONARY

The miracle told in today's gospel shows Jesus as a wonderworker with extraordinary power. He cures a deaf man with a speech impediment. The story retains an Aramaic word, *ephphatha,* indicating its antiquity and importance. Disciples retold this story with the Aramaic word in place, as if it had become a word of some significance to them. The word remains in our liturgical vocabulary to name the ritual we perform after the baptism of infants and before the baptism of adults. The priest or deacon performing the rite asks that God will open the ears so the new Christian may hear the divine word, and open the lips to profess it. The gospel story includes another interesting detail: Some people bring the disabled person to Jesus. This supports the theory that the story may have been used in preparing people for baptism even before the gospels were written down,

especially if someone like sponsors introduced them to the body of Christ, the church.

In a prophecy from Isaiah, God promises to open the eyes of the blind and clear the ears of the deaf. The first reading makes a direct preparation for the proclamation of the gospel. In the psalm, we praise God who gives sight to the blind.

James accuses people of showing prejudice to the poor. Our society falls to the same temptation. James says God chose those who were poor in this world to be rich in faith. His words will embarrass many who reflect on them in honesty.

SACRAMENTARY

The fourth eucharistic prayer says that Jesus proclaimed good news to the poor. The second prayer over the people prays for health of mind and body.

OTHER IDEAS

As the season subtly shifts, you may introduce some changes in the environment if you like—a different tone of green vesture, different plants, even a different musical setting of eucharistic prayer acclamations.

M O N **8** #636 (LMC #447-451) white
Birth of Mary
FEAST

No one knows for sure when Mary was born, but today has been chosen for the feast because it marks the anniversary of the dedication of a church building to Mary's mother, traditionally known as Saint Ann. (No one knows for sure the name of Mary's mother either.)

There is no biblical reference to Mary's birth. The lectionary instead gives us Matthew's account of the birth of Jesus. You may include the genealogy, if the assembly is patient, because it places Mary into the long history of the ancestors of Jesus from Abraham to Joseph. You have a choice for the first reading. The passage from Micah includes a prophecy about Bethlehem, used to interpret the significance of that city in the story of Jesus' birth. The passage from Romans speaks of those whom God predestined to share the image of the Son. Mary, preserved from the stain of original sin from the moment of her conception according to the Catholic tradition, fulfills this description of those God predestined for glory. The exceptionally brief responsory psalm for the day sings only one verse of scripture. Its theme resonates with that of Mary's *Magnificat.*

Penitential Rite C-iii calls Jesus "Son of God and Son of Mary." Presidential prayers can be found in the proper of saints. If you use the first preface of the Blessed Virgin (P 56), insert the words "the birth" in the third line.

■ TODAY IS THE PATRONAL FEAST OF CUBA, Our Lady of Charity of El Cobre. Tradition holds that conquistador Alonso de Ojeda's ship wrecked on Cuba in 1508 and he vowed to present a statue of Mary to the first village he reached. After his rescue, he gave the statue to the town of El Cobre, a site of pilgrimage today.

#438 (LMC #193–227)   white
Peter Claver (+ 1654), presbyter, religious, missionary
MEMORIAL

Luke's gospel is sometimes called the gospel of prayer, because he describes Jesus praying on several occasions. Today his prayer precedes the calling of the Twelve.

Many early Christians faced temptations to revert to their former unbelief. The letter to the Colossians urges its readers to be rooted in Christ and built up in him, growing ever stronger in

faith. Through baptism, they now enjoy the power of Christ. A psalm of praise follows.

■ TODAY'S SAINT: Every Episcopal conference may establish some optional memorials as obligatory ones on the local calendar. That is the case with Peter Claver, a Jesuit missionary to the new world who worked for the salvation and freedom of slaves. Colombia and Venezuela also have established this date as an obligatory memorial.

The opening prayer is under September 9. Other prayers may come from the common of pastors, notably those for missionaries. You may use the preface for virgins and religious (P 68).

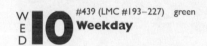

#439 (LMC #193–227)   green
Weekday

Although we are more familiar with Matthew's version of the Beatitudes, Luke's is also a lovely passage. Jesus delivers this sermon from the plain, not from the mount. He has four beatitudes and four woes. Jesus blesses not the poor in spirit, but the poor. This may be the more original form of this sermon.

The letter to the Colossians now asks them to live in accordance with the baptism they have received: "Since you have been raised up in company with Christ, set your heart on what pertains to higher realms." Too often we think of more mundane things. With slight variation, we repeat yesterday's psalm of praise.

The third preface for weekdays in Ordinary Time repeats some themes we find in Colossians: creation and restoration through the Son, and the praise of all creation, the church on earth and the saints in heaven.

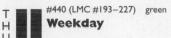

#440 (LMC #193–227)   green
Weekday

Jesus encourages love for enemies, a striking change from past law and a demonstration of the great challenge that his followers face. He favors more than just getting along. He seeks real demonstrations of care for others.

Today's first reading is one of the options for the Rite of Marriage. It speaks of the Christian community, not specifically of a married couple, but the command to love applies to both. The letter to the Colossians suggests that we wear our virtues like clothing, and over them all, wear love. This concludes the series of this epistle. Another psalm of praise follows.

Prayers for charity can be found at #41.

On this date in 2001, hijacked planes crashed into the World Trade Center and the Pentagon. Thousands lost their lives in a grave assault by terrorism. Pray for peace.

■ TODAY IS THE PATRONAL FEAST OF VENEZUELA, Our Lady of Coromoto. Tradition holds that Mary appeared to an Indian chief of the Cospes, a tribe considering conversion to Christianity. While he vacillated, she appeared to him repeatedly. Finally the chief lost his temper and witnesses saw him attempt to strangle the Virgin. She disappeared, leaving him a statue of herself, now venerated in the parish church at Guanare, near Coromoto.

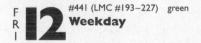

#441 (LMC #193–227)   green
Weekday

Disciples who want to lead others will have to scrutinize their own behavior first. Jesus says take the log out of your own eye before removing a splinter from someone else's.

The New Testament includes three letters known as "pastoral epistles." Two are addressed to Timothy, one to Titus. The letters are pastoral because of the church leaders to whom they are addressed, but also because of their content: practical advice on how to govern, asceticisms to accept, adaptations to make in a pagan world while preserving the heart of the gospel. The letters presume that the ecclesial community has a fairly advanced hierarchical structure, making it unlikely that Paul is the author of these missives. The vocabulary is unlike that of the classic Pauline letters to the Romans and the Corinthians. But they are filled with useful advice and interesting glimpses of the nascent church. The author starts the letter with a thanksgiving, a form we have seen at the beginning of other New Testament letters. Strangely, though, the focus of the thanksgiving is not on the church, but on the author. Usually a letter thanks God for something in the church to whom the correspondence is written, but in this case, the author, who claims to be Paul, thanks God for personal conversion. The psalm, also in the first person, echoes the theme of thanksgiving to God for protection.

#442 (LMC #193–227)　white

John Chrysostom (+ 407), bishop, monastic, doctor of the church

S A T 13

MEMORIAL

Jesus wants results. You can tell good persons by the results they achieve. He disparages those who call him Lord but do not put into practice what he teaches.

The First Letter to Timothy proclaims a truth much repeated in the gospels: Jesus came into the world to save sinners. The psalm praises God who raises up the lowly from the dust.

Presidential prayers for the day are under September 13. You may use the preface for pastors (P 68).

■ TODAY'S SAINT: John led a life of solitude and asceticism even before pursuing priesthood. He was named bishop of Constantinople, but suffered at the hands of powerful enemies and spent many years in painful exile. His eloquent preaching, however, earned him the nickname "Golden-Mouth."

#638 (LMC #370)　red

⚹ 14 The Triumph of the Cross

FEAST

ORIENTATION

Today's feast takes the place of the Twenty-fourth Sunday in Ordinary Time.

This day is a celebration of the dedication of the church of the Holy Sepulcher in Jerusalem. It houses the sites of Calvary, the empty tomb, and the discovery of the wood of the cross. This basilica, still an unfortunate bevy of intra-Christian conflict, remains nonetheless one of the most important shrines in the world.

LECTIONARY

The first reading is essential for understanding the gospel. Serpents attack the Israelites wandering in the desert. Moses makes a bronze serpent and mounts it on a pole. All who look upon it are healed. This talisman became a symbol of the cross of Christ, which offers salvation to all those in need. The psalm remembers the struggles surrounding that event in the desert.

In the gospel, then, Jesus compares himself to the lifting up of the bronze serpent. His mission is to save those who suffer the torments of evil. Just as the bronze serpent resembles the source of evil, so Jesus on the cross resembles a source of suffering. But it is an illusion. The cross offers salvation to all who gaze upon it in faith.

The second reading is the classic text from Philippians, singing of the debasement and exaltation of Jesus. This passage likely existed before Paul wrote the letter, as a hymn text sung by the faithful. It was incorporated into the letter, preserved for eternity, and now summarizes well the incarnation and ministry of Jesus. Part of this text is much used throughout the holy week liturgies, because it captures the theme of the self-emptying of Jesus for the sake of our salvation.

The *Lectionary for Masses with Children* changes the psalm today to 88, a passage that includes this verse: "Ever since I was a child, I have been sick and close to death."

SACRAMENTARY

Sing the Glory to God. The presidential prayers are under September 14. The day has its own preface (P 46), but that of the passion (P 17) may also be used. A solemn blessing is recommended, but see also the one for the passion (5).

The sacramentary's first appendix includes a priest's prayer to our redeemer as a thanksgiving after any Mass. The same section includes a prayer to Jesus Christ crucified.

OTHER IDEAS

You may wish to decorate the crucifix in the church in some way today. Draw attention to it as the source of glory. Make the sign of the cross at the beginning of the Mass slowly and deliberately. This feast would make another opportunity for celebrating the Rite of Acceptance into the Order of Catechumens, because of the centrality of the image of the cross.

If you have new liturgical ministers or new staff to commission, you may wish to do so this weekend. See the *Book of Blessings,* 60–65.

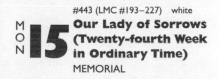

M O N 15 #443 (LMC #193–227) white
Our Lady of Sorrows (Twenty-fourth Week in Ordinary Time)
MEMORIAL

You may use the weekday readings if you wish. When Jesus finishes his "sermon on the plain" in Luke's gospel, he returns to his ministry of healing. A centurion approaches seeking the cure of his servant, and Jesus assists the Gentile.

The First Letter to Timothy encourages prayers for everybody, but especially for those in civil authority. The last line of the reading probably alludes to the early Christian practice of praying with hands raised, a gesture the presider of liturgical prayer still uses. The psalm shows that the same gesture was used in the pre-Christian era, "I cry to you, lifting up my hands."

You may also use the readings from the memorial of Our Lady of Sorrows. The idea for the feast comes from the two alternative gospels allowed for the day: Mary at the foot of the cross and Mary hearing the prophecy that a sword of sorrow shall pierce her heart.

More tears and sorrow appear in the first reading. This time it is Christ who offers mournful prayers that God would spare him from

death. The psalm is a desperate prayer for rescue.

This is one of the few dates on the liturgical calendar that has retained its sequence. The sequence is a hymn that may be used after the first reading and before the gospel acclamation. Easter and Pentecost and Corpus Christi all come with sequences. It is unusual that a day that pales in comparison has retained one. But the text for this day is the "Stabat mater," made popular in the Stations of the Cross. You can find the chant in the *Liber cantualis.* These texts come up so rarely that it is a good idea to use them, but they are optional.

Presidential prayers are in the proper of saints. The second preface for the Blessed Virgin Mary (P 57) may sound too gleeful given the tone of today's feast. Consider the first preface (P 56) instead.

The sacramentary's first appendix includes a priest's prayer before Mass to the Virgin Mary. It acknowledges that she stood by her Son "as he hung dying on the cross."

T U E 16 #444 (LMC #193–227) red
Cornelius (+ 253), pope, martyr; and Cyprian (+ 258), bishop, martyr
MEMORIAL

None of Jesus' miracles is more memorable than when he raises the dead to life. Among the few but insistent accounts of this ability is today's gospel, a story in which he casts favor on the only son of the widow of Naim.

The First Letter to Timothy explains the traits it expects in a bishop: irreproachable, married

only once, even-tempered and hospitable, to name a few. The bishop should even earn the respect of those outside the church. Deacons, women and all who have a role in the church should lead blameless lives. We sing the psalm of one who wants to walk in integrity.

■ TODAY'S SAINTS: These two saints had a serious disagreement about the proper procedures for readmitting those who had fallen from the faith. Still, their more serious enemies were outside the church. Novatius claimed to be pope as soon as Cornelius was elected. Cyprian suffered under the persecution of Decius. Both accepted martyrdom for the faith.

Presidential prayers can be found at September 16. The preface for martyrs (P 66) is appropriate. Both saints are mentioned in the first eucharistic prayer.

W E D 17 #445 (LMC #193–227) green
Weekday

Optional Memorial of Robert Bellarmine (+ 1621), bishop, religious, doctor of the church / white ■ Jesus associates his ministry with that of John the Baptist, and chides those who reject the message that both of them brought.

The "mystery of faith" that we proclaim at every Mass is expressed in the First Letter to Timothy today in another form. It summarizes the incarnation, resurrection and evangelization. The psalm sings of God's great works.

■ TODAY'S SAINT: Robert Bellarmine, an Italian Jesuit and cardinal, wrote vigorously in defense of the church in the years following the Reformation. A teacher, scholar and canonist, he found himself part of the Galileo controversy.

The fifth preface for weekdays in Ordinary Time proclaims the mystery of faith in words very similar to the memorial acclamation of every Mass (P 41).

THU 18 #446 (LMC #193–227) green
Weekday

Jesus gives a powerful lesson on forgiveness while dining at the home of Simon the Pharisee. A woman known to be a sinner approaches him with kindness, and he proclaims the forgiveness of her sin. Tradition unfairly associates this woman with Mary Magdalene.

Today's first reading cautions a young bishop to be a continuing example of love, faith and purity. Church leaders should devote themselves to reading scripture, preaching and teaching. How are we doing as pastoral workers when held up to the scrutiny of today's first reading? The psalm continues the one we began yesterday, praising the prudent who live by the fear of God.

The second eucharistic prayer for reconciliation says, "We had wandered far from you, but through your Son you have brought us back."

■ IN PERU, today is the feast of Saint John Macías (+ 1645), who left Spain for the Americas, lived in austerity and served the poor, following the example of his friend Martin de Porres.

FRI 19 #447 (LMC #193–227) green
Weekday

Optional Memorial of Januarius (+ c. 305), bishop, martyr / red ■ Jesus returns to his preaching ministry, accompanied by the Twelve and a group of women, whose names are noted.

Not just the content of teaching, but the manner of teaching will also evangelize. The letter today advises Timothy to seek after the virtues that lead to a good life, avoiding "the root of all evil" and "fighting the good fight." A psalm about the just follows, attended by a refrain from the Beatitudes.

You could offer a prayer for your own bishop today from the Masses for various needs and occasions (3B) and pray the first version of the eucharistic prayer for those Masses, which allows a prayer for the local church by name.

■ TODAY'S SAINT: Januarius was bishop of Benevento and suffered martyrdom under the persecution of Diocletian after he visited other Christians in prison. Thrown to bears, the wild beasts would not destroy the saint, according to the legend, so executioners beheaded him. A vial of his blood, kept in Naples, is said to liquefy when placed near the relic of his head on this day.

■ IN MEXICO, Blessed José Maria de Yermo y Parres (+ 1904) is remembered today.

#643 (LMC #452–454, 376) red
Andrew Kim Taegon (+ 1846), presbyter, martyr; Paul Chong Hasang (+ 1839), catechist, martyr; and their companions, martyrs (+ 1839–1867)

SAT 20
MEMORIAL

In Luke's version of the parable of the sower, Jesus tells the parable, explains why he uses the form, and then interprets the meaning of his saying. Some will accept the word of God. Others will not.

Readings from the First Letter to Timothy conclude today. In the doxology you can hear the church's firm belief that Jesus will return, probably in the face of some late-first-century impatience.

■ TODAY'S SAINTS: Andrew Kim of Taegu and Paul Chong of Hasang are among 103 Korean martyrs of all ages whose sanctity is recognized collectively on this day. Ninety-two were lay people, the single largest group of laity in the history of the church to be canonized. The martyrs are included in the general calendar so all the

world may recognize the universality of faith and witness.

Prayers for the day are under September 20. The suggested scripture readings on that page are optional, as they would be for any nonbiblical memorial. A preface for martyrs is at P 66.

#134 (LMC #128) green
21 Twenty-fifth Sunday in Ordinary Time

ORIENTATION

We resume the semicontinuous but much interrupted reading of Mark's gospel. Last week's celebration of the cross gave the community the opportunity to reflect on the instrument of our salvation, but it replaced an important passage from Mark's gospel that usually falls on that Sunday during Year B. Jesus asks the question, "Who do you say that I am?" The question marks a turning point in the gospel. From now on, the disciples know better who Jesus is, and the gospel begins its headlong descent toward the "folly of the cross."

LECTIONARY

The contrasting episodes of today's gospel show the abiding disparity between the mission of Jesus and its acceptance by the disciples. He reveals his upcoming passion. They argue over who is the greatest.

The first reading recounts some of the trials of the prophet Jeremiah. Reluctant to become a prophet, Jeremiah found himself beset by enemies. Today he hears his enemies plotting evil against him. Although this is another passage where answering, "Thanks be to

God" seems woefully out of place, it perfectly prepares us to hear Jesus predict his own passion. The psalm repeats a similar theme: Ruthless people seek the life of the psalmist, whose helper is God.

Today's passage from James includes a verse beloved by those who advance the church's causes of justice: "The fruit of righteousness is sown in peace for those who cultivate peace." James encourages the reader to put away discord and accept the wisdom that comes from above. That will help restrict war and limit unrestricted human passion.

SACRAMENTARY

Eucharistic Prayer II's own preface summarizes the incarnation and mission of Jesus. The solemn blessing for the Passion of the Lord (5) repeats themes from today's gospel.

OTHER IDEAS

Today is Catechetical Sunday. We remember the service of our catechists. You may include a blessing for them (Book of Blessings, 4). Be sure to include all sorts of catechists: those who provide religious education for children, formation for sacraments for children and adults, and athletic coaches who instill Christian principles on the playing field.

MON 22 #449 (LMC #193–227)   green
Weekday

Jesus makes several statements to the crowds today in a compact speech of aphorisms drawn together by Luke. He speaks of different properties of light: helping those in the dark and exposing what is hidden.

We return to the Old Testament for our first readings for the next few weeks. The books excerpted all come from the historical and prophetic literature pertaining to the reconstruction of the temple. We begin today with the opening of the book of Ezra, a report of the return of the Jewish community from exile. In today's passage, Cyrus, king of Persia, a pagan inspired by God, frees the exiles. Neighbors contribute in-kind gifts to help them. A psalm about the return from exile follows the reading.

Eucharistic Prayer IV develops the theme of light.

TUE 23 #450 (LMC #193–227)   green
Weekday

There is a hint of separation between Jesus and his family when he learns that his relatives wish to see him. Jesus imagines a much larger family: all those who hear the word of God and act upon it.

King Darius orders the reconstruction of the destroyed Temple on its former site. The exiles will have a geographical and a spiritual homeland.

Eucharistic Prayer II comes with its own preface that presents Jesus as the Word through whom God made the universe.

■ MEXICO REMEMBERS Blessed Cristóbal (+ 1527) and Antonio y Juan (+ 1529) today. These children accepted the Christian faith and encouraged others to believe. They suffered brutal martyrdoms.

WED 24 #451 (LMC #193–227)   green
Weekday

Jesus instructs the Twelve and sends them out to overcome demons and cure the sick. They proclaim the Good News and move on from those places that will not receive them.

In this last excerpt from the book of Ezra we meet the priest who gives the book its name. This passage portrays one of the prayer postures of the time: Ezra kneels and stretches out his hands toward God. The prayer that he offers confesses the guilt of the people and the mercy of God. The responsory comes from the book of Tobit, an acclamation of God's mercy.

The first eucharistic prayer for Masses of reconciliation carries the theme of repentance and God's mercy.

■ OUR LADY OF MERCIES is patron of the Dominican people, who celebrate today with a holy day of obligation. The devotion is associated with the Mercedarians, was added to the universal calendar in 1696, and removed in 1969, but it is still celebrated today in the Dominican Republic as a solemnity, and in Argentina, Guatemala and Venezuela as a memorial. See the *Collection of Masses of the Blessed Virgin Mary* (39).

THU 25 #452 (LMC #193–227)   green
Weekday

Herod, who had been attracted to the words of John, has a similar curiosity about the words of Jesus. He asks the question that underlies the gospel: Who is this man?

Haggai prophesied at the same period that the Temple was being rebuilt. In today's passage, the opening of his book, he speaks God's command that in building the Temple, they reform their wayward habits. Today's psalm praises God's delight in the faithful.

The first preface for weekdays of Ordinary Time (P 37) proclaims the essence of Jesus' ministry.

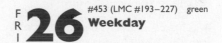

FRI 26 #453 (LMC #193–227)   green
Weekday

Optional Memorial of Cosmas and Damian (+ 300), martyrs/red ■ Yesterday's passage had Herod wondering who Jesus is. Today Jesus takes the same question to the disciples: Who do people say he is? Peter comes up with the reply:

the Messiah of God. And Jesus tells them of his upcoming sufferings.

Haggai calls upon those who remembered the splendor of the former Temple and inspires them to create a better home for God. In response, we sing of going up to the altar of God, our gladness and joy.

The second preface for the dedication of a church (P 53) includes themes found in today's first reading and psalm.

■ TODAY'S SAINTS: The Syrian brothers Cosmas and Damian were physicians who generously cared for the sick, remaining untainted by the desire for personal gain. They were beheaded under the persecution of Diocletian. Both of their names appear in Eucharistic Prayer I.

■ THE JEWISH HOLIDAY of Rosh Hashanah begins at sunset tonight, celebrating the New Year of 5764.

S A T #454 (LMC #193–227)   white
27 Vincent de Paul (+ 1660), presbyter, religious founder
MEMORIAL

Jesus articulates the teaching on the passion to his incredulous disciples. They fail to grasp his meaning.

Zechariah the prophet picked up where his contemporary Haggai left off. In today's vision he sees the measuring of Jerusalem and its coming role of glory. The responsory comes from Jeremiah today, a canticle about the return of God's people to the heights of Zion.

■ TODAY'S SAINT: Vincent de Paul founded the Congregation of the Missions, serving the poor and staffing seminarians. With Saint Louise de Marillac he also founded the Daughters of Charity. In the office of readings today, we hear him say not to feel bad if you have to put down your prayer book to serve the poor.

Prayers for this day are at September 27. You may use the preface for virgins and religious (P 68).

#137 (LMC #131)   green
⚹**28 Twenty-sixth Sunday in Ordinary Time**

ORIENTATION

This weekend concludes the series of second readings from the letter of James. The coming week will include festivals of several popular saints: Thérèse of Liseux and Francis of Assisi, as well as the archangels and guardian angels.

■ IN CHILE, the last Sunday of September is the solemnity of Our Lady of Carmel, Mother and Queen of Chile. (See July 16.)

LECTIONARY

The two episodes of today's gospel show Jesus' range of tolerance and intolerance. An exorcist from outside the community expels demons using Jesus' name, and Jesus tolerates that. Someone else causes an innocent person to sin, and Jesus will not tolerate that. The one causing the evil influence will suffer all the more. The text should warn us about the prejudices we hold against others outside our community who still use the name of Jesus.

Today's passage from the book of Numbers prepares us for the episode that opens the gospel. Eldad and Medad receive the spirit of prophecy, even though they were in the wrong place. Over the objections of a young man, Moses tolerates the prophecy because it comes from the Spirit. If only we

had the problem that the Spirit of God were falling on too many people! Today's psalm sings praise of God's law and asks for cleansing from unknown faults.

The letter of James concludes with a diatribe against the rich. Not only have they placed their trust in wealth that corrodes, but they have obtained it through unjust practices against workers: "The wages you withheld from works are crying aloud." Many global companies still take advantage of poor workers in many parts of the world.

The *Lectionary for Masses with Children* changes the responsorial psalm today to 66, a song of praise for all that God has done.

SACRAMENTARY

The second preface for the Holy Spirit (P 55) speaks about the manifold gifts of grace that God gives the church. The third prayer over the people prays that we might cherish the heavenly gifts we have received.

OTHER IDEAS

Alert your social justice committee about the hard-hitting passage in today's second reading. What actions on behalf of the poor can your parish take? What are the economic issues right in your own community?

#647 (LMC #381)   white
M O N 29 Michael, Gabriel and Raphael, archangels
FEAST

We celebrate the feast of three angels mentioned in the Bible by name. But the lectionary includes stories about only one of them, Michael. This feast day originally belonged to him alone, and vestiges remain. Michael appears in the alternate choices for the first reading today. His takes a dominant role in the vision from the book of Daniel and reappears in the conflict with the dragon in Revelation.

In the gospel, Jesus promises Nathanael that he will see the angels of God ascending and descending on the Son of Man. The vision seems to recall Jacob's ladder. In the psalm, we sing praises of God in the sight of the angels.

Prayers for the feast are in the proper of saints. Sing the Glory to God today and use the preface for the angels (P 60).

#456/648 (LMC #193–227) white

TUE 30 Jerome (+ 420), presbyter, doctor of the church
MEMORIAL

Luke 9:51 is an important verse in the gospel. Jesus turns his face toward Jerusalem, and with him the entire story moves from a description of his ministry to the preparation for the cross. Although we continue hearing about Jesus' sayings and miracles in this second half of the gospel, Luke reminds us several times that Jesus is heading toward Jerusalem, the ominous, yet awesome, place of the story's fulfillment.

In a vision, Zechariah sees all the nations streaming toward Jerusalem. They take hold of the hem of every Jew's garment, and together they march toward the city. The climactic verse that concludes this reading, "We have heard that God is with you," inspires the refrain for a psalm that sings of the glory of Zion.

■ TODAY'S SAINT: Jerome served God as an ascetic monk, and is frequently depicted as a cardinal. He translated the Bible from Hebrew and Greek into Latin, making it more understandable to ordinary people. He is one of the four great doctors of the Latin church. "Ignorance of scripture is

ignorance of Christ," he said. He died in Bethlehem.

Presidential prayers can be found at September 30. You may use the preface for pastors (P 67). There is an alternate first reading in the lectionary for Jerome's day, a passage that praises the scriptures Jerome loved.

October

#457/649 (LMC #384) white

WED 1 Thérèse of the Child Jesus (+ 1897), religious, doctor of the church
MEMORIAL

Would-be disciples approach Jesus as he begins his ascent to Jerusalem. He discourages all of them from joining. He will not sugarcoat the message of the cross.

For a week or so we have heard the prophets encourage the rebuilding of the temple. Today, Nehemiah obtains letters from King Artaxerxes that will allow him to go to Judah and to oversee the building of the temple, the city wall and his residence. The saddest psalm of exile follows this reading, which places Jerusalem ahead of every other joy.

■ TODAY'S SAINT: Thérèse joined a Carmelite monastery in her native Normandy and made a strong impression on the community. Her autobiography, written under obedience, reveals the simplicity and profundity of her faith. Only 24 when she died, she was named a doctor of the church at the end of the twentieth century.

Alternate readings for today's saint can be found in the lectionary. The first reading contains a metaphor for the maternal role of Jerusalem, and the gospel praises those who are like little children. Beware, though, that this same gospel reappears for tomorrow's memorial.

Prayers for the Mass are in the proper of saints. You may use the preface for virgins and religious (P 68).

#458/650 (LMC #193–227) white

THU 2 The Guardian Angels
MEMORIAL

The lectionary has readings for this day, but only the gospel is expected. Matthew says of children that their angels constantly behold God's face. This text has been used to justify the belief in guardian angels.

Angels appear in the optional first reading and psalm for October 2, but you may also turn to the weekday for those texts today. There, Ezra opens the book of the law and reads it for people who have not heard it. The event crystallizes the people's recommitment to the God who has brought them home.

Today's memorial has been on the calendar since 1670 as a way of proclaiming God's protection for those who are helpless. The preface for angels (P 60) is used with the presidential prayers for October 2.

#459 (LMC #193–227) green

FRI 3 Weekday

Jesus prophesies ill for those who hear and reject his message. His disciples will be icons of his presence: When people hear them, they hear Jesus. When people reject them, they reject Jesus and the One who sent him.

From the book of Baruch, we hear the people's admission of their sin. As they resettle in their homeland and become aware of God's insistent care for them, the people recognize their sin and make a communal confession of it. It is nearly inconceivable that a nation today would make such a beautiful statement.

The first eucharistic prayer for Masses of reconciliation might make a good choice today.

■ IN GUATEMALA AND SPAIN, today is an optional memorial of Francis Borgia (+ 1572), a priest, writer and general of the Society of Jesus.

#460 (LMC #193–227)   white

SAT 4 Francis of Assisi (+ 1226), religious founder
MEMORIAL

The 72 return from their mission, rejoicing at what they have accomplished. Jesus prays in thanksgiving, another example of how Luke's gospel frequently shows Jesus at prayer.

The comforting words from the prophet Baruch assure Israel that the God who brought disaster upon them will bring them enduring joy. Their restoration will bring the peace they have hoped for. For the psalm response we sing several verses that specifically promise that God will rebuild the cities of Judah and that the people will inherit the land. We hear in these texts the promise and joy of the end of exile and the reconstruction of the homeland.

■ TODAY'S SAINT: Francis pursued a life of voluntary poverty. He formed a religious community with other like-minded friars. His simple approach to life and his love for God's creation have made him a charismatic figure to every generation. Canonized just two years after his death, he has made Assisi a popular place of pilgrimage. Sing music inspired by his writing: the "Canticle of Creation," "All Creatures of Our God and King" or "Lord, Make Me an Instrument of Your Peace."

In the optional first reading in the lectionary, Paul says he bears the brand marks of Jesus on his body. It is unclear if Paul is referring to a physical share in the wounds of Christ, but the reading is suggested because the story of Francis reports that this saint did receive the stigmata.

The preface for virgins and religious (P 68) could accompany the presidential prayers for October 4. Some communities have a blessing of animals or of fields and flocks today (*Book of Blessings,* 25–26, or *Catholic Household Blessings and Prayers* 174). If celebrating this day with children, see LTP's *School Year, Church Year.*

#140 (LMC #134)   green

☀ 5 Twenty-seventh Sunday in Ordinary Time

ORIENTATION

Our long march through Ordinary Time advances. Today's second readings shift to the letter to the Hebrews. A difficult book to read aloud and interpret on first hearing, it contains affirmations about the faith that deserve studied attention.

LECTIONARY

Jesus' teachings on marriage and divorce have had an effect on an enormous number of families throughout the Christian era. He stresses that the union of husband and wife is sacred. In this passage he does not tolerate divorce; the parallel passage in Matthew seems to allow an exception. The longer form of the gospel this weekend includes Jesus' tolerance of little children. The shorter form of the gospel keeps the first part, not the second. It eliminates the warmhearted Jesus in favor of the stern Jesus.

The reading of Genesis also explains the sacredness of marriage. In fact, Jesus quotes from this passage in the gospel to make his point. The psalm is a celebration of the blessings of married life. It is one of the recommended psalms for marriage.

Paul promises peace to those who direct their thoughts to what is true, honest and worthy of praise. He wants the Philippians to be freed from anxiety so they can present their prayer to God in gratitude.

SACRAMENTARY

The first eucharistic prayer for reconciliation confesses, "Time and time again we broke your covenant." The second solemn blessing for Ordinary Time (#11) comes from today's second reading.

OTHER IDEAS

Today's gospel and first reading are popular choices at weddings. Choose music today that will also work for the celebration of marriage. Let people know that these are some selections they can consider for a Catholic wedding.

This can be a busy time of year for parishes. If you have a lot of announcements, you can just give headlines and keep the details in the printed bulletin, in a voice mailbox, and on the parish website.

■ THE JEWISH DAY OF ATONEMENT, Yom Kippur, begins at sundown tonight.

#461 (LMC #193–227)   green

MON 6 Weekday

Optional Memorial of Blessed Marie Rose Durocher (+ 1849), virgin, religious founder, educator / white ▪ Optional Memorial of Bruno (+ 1101), presbyter, hermit, religious founder / white ▪ Luke is probably the most literary writer of the New Testament. Today's parable of the Good Samaritan is a good example of why this is true. The story reflects not just Jesus' skill as a storyteller, but Luke's as a writer. The powerful message of this parable has brought the expression "Good Samaritan" into the English language.

This week will conclude our survey of some of the minor prophets associated with the restoration of Israel and the rebuilding of the Temple. Ask people to tell you the story of the book of Jonah, and they'll say it's about a whale. Well, yes, it does include a large water mammal, but the story is much more a story of preaching and repentance, a fitting episode in this period of Israel's self-scrutiny and sorrow. In today's passage, Jonah flees God's call, wreaks havoc on the getaway ship, gets tossed overboard, is swallowed by that large creature, and, after three days, is spit up on the shore of the very place he told God he would refuse to visit. As a responsory, we sing a canticle from the book of Jonah, a hymn of praise to God who preserves in singer in time of distress.

Among the Masses for various needs and occasions is one for charity (41).

■ TODAY'S SAINTS: A native of Quebec and the youngest of ten children, Marie Rose Durocher founded the Congregation of the Sisters of the Most Holy Names of Jesus and Mary for the purpose of bringing Catholic education to Canada. Her sisters are at work even outside of Canada in countries like the United States, Lesotho, Peru, Brazil and Haiti.

Bruno directed a school at Reims and became chancellor of the diocese there. But he sought the solitary life of prayer and founded the monastery of La Chartreuse, from which the monks are called Carthusians. The monks live an austere life in a remote setting

visible not from the main road, but only from the peaks of nearby mountains. They gained fame for their secret recipes for a variety of strong but tasty after-dinner liqueurs.

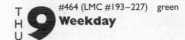

7 TUE #462 (LMC #193–227)   white
Our Lady of the Rosary
MEMORIAL

Although Martha is busy with hospitality, Jesus tells her that Mary listening at his feet has chosen the better part. A passage that still rankles many a devoted Martha, it has often been used to compare the active and contemplative spiritual life. Nevertheless, when he comes again, Jesus will have some explaining to do with a lot of hard-working homemakers.

Jonah finally announces the prophecy God asked him to give. The message is rather brief: "Forty days more and Nineveh shall be destroyed." But everybody repents at the pronouncement. In response, we sing one of the great penitential psalms.

■ TODAY'S MEMORIAL: Today was dedicated to Our Lady of the Rosary after Christians won the Battle of Lepanto over Muslim forces on this date in 1570. The victory was attributed to Mary's intercession, after people prayed the rosary. Although this history is disturbing, the rosary continues to offer comfort to those who make it a part of their daily prayer.

The second Marian preface (P 57) goes well with today's presidential prayers, which are found in the proper of saints.

8 WED #463 (LMC #193–227)   green
Weekday

Luke's version of the Lord's Prayer is briefer than Matthew's, and many scholars believe it is more original. Its simple directness and its divine source have made it one

of the most well-known prayers in the world.

The enigmatic epilogue to the book of Jonah shows us a prophet disappointed that God did not carry out the threatened punishment. God gives Jonah a plant for shade, and then it withers, making Jonah angry enough to die. God says that if Jonah was concerned about a plant, he should not have been surprised that divine mercy extends to people and cattle. The psalm sings of God's abundant kindness.

The second eucharistic prayer for Masses of reconciliation announces that God's Spirit changes our hearts.

9 THU #464 (LMC #193–227)   green
Weekday

Optional Memorial of Denis (+ 258), bishop, martyr; and his companions, martyrs/red ▪ *Optional Memorial of John Leonardi (+ 1609), presbyter, religious founder/white* ▪ Following yesterday's revelation of the Lord's Prayer, Jesus encourages the disciples to pray frequently, and to ask God persistently for their needs.

Our survey of the minor prophets writing at the time of Israel's return from exile contains one passage devoted to the work of Malachi. The prophet predicts that the day of judgment is coming and evildoers will be set on fire. But those who fear God will behold the sun of justice with its healing rays. This passage refers to the restoration of Israel, but it has been interpreted as a reference to the coming of the Messiah. In the Christmas carol "Hark! the Herald Angels Sing," we hail the newborn Sun of Righteousness, "ris'n with healing in his wings." The psalm today describes the divergent paths of the just and the wicked.

The sacramentary includes prayers for any need (38A).

■ TODAY'S SAINTS: Denis is honored as the first bishop of Paris. He was beheaded with several companions at the instigation of pagan priests. According to legend, Denis was beheaded on the site of Sacre Coeur on Montmartre in Paris, then picked up his head and walked two miles, where he died and was buried. The church of St. Denis, built on the site of his grave, is the first Gothic church in history, enclosing the world's oldest rose window of stained glass. France's royalty was buried there. Denis is the patron saint of those with headaches.

As a priest, John Leonardi took on youth ministry and founded the Congregation of Clerics Regular of the Mother of God to provide better education. He is considered a founder of the Society for the Propagation of the Faith.

Luis Beltrán (+ 1581) is remembered in Colombia and Venezuela today with a memorial, and with an optional memorial in Bolivia. A Spanish Dominican priest who preached the fear of God, Beltrán traveled to Spanish America and baptized enormous numbers of natives, especially in Colombia, where he is a patron saint.

F
R   **10**   #465 (LMC #193–227)   green
I   **Weekday**

Jesus meets opposition on his way to Jerusalem, this time in the form of demonic possession and a disbelieving crowd.

Our quick survey of the minor prophets concludes today and tomorrow with passages from Joel. The prophet warns the people that a great and terrible day of judgment is coming. A plague of locusts is attacking the city like an army. This passage inspired lines in the sequence of the former requiem Mass, "Dies irae." The psalm contrasts the loss of nations with the mighty throne of God.

"All your actions show your wisdom and love," says Eucharistic Prayer IV, before it details the revelation of the new covenant.

■ THOMAS OF VILLANOVA (+ 1555), an Augustinian friar, served as archbishop of Valencia. He is remembered with an optional memorial today in Guatemala and Spain.

■ THE JEWISH FESTIVAL OF SUKKOT, or Tabernacles, begins at sundown tonight.

S
A   **11**   #466 (LMC #193–227)   green
T   **Weekday**

Optional Memorial of the Blessed Virgin Mary / white ■ The spirit of opposition hovers behind today's gospel, where Jesus implies some distance between his family's approval and his ministry. Someone blesses his mother, but Jesus blesses those who hear and keep God's word.

Joel has prophesied the coming day of God's judgment. In today's reading it sounds imminent. Nations shall be destroyed, and Judah and Jerusalem will last forever. The psalm envisions the majesty of God in language reminiscent of the reading.

There are prayers for oppressors among the Masses for various needs and occasions (#45).

■ IF YOU ARE CELEBRATING THE MEMORIAL OF MARY TODAY, consider Mary, Pillar of Faith from the *Collection of Masses of the Blessed Virgin Mary* (35), which uses the gospel of the day.

■ THIS IS THE LITURGICAL DAY for observing the memory of Blessed John XXIII, the beloved, humble pope who catapulted the church into the modern age by opening the Second Vatican Council. You have the option of celebrating a Mass from the common of pastors.

■ MARY SOLEDAD (+ 1887) of Spain founded the Handmaids of Mary Serving the Sick, a community

that expanded to Latin America. She is remembered today with an optional memorial in Spain and Guatemala.

#143 (LMC #137)   green
☸ **12**   **Twenty-eighth Sunday in Ordinary Time**

ORIENTATION

In some parts of the country, autumn leaves are reaching their peak color. As we become aware of the cycle of seasons again, Mark's gospel imperceptibly slips into its final chapters.

■ TODAY IS THE PATRONAL FEAST OF SPAIN, OUR LADY OF THE PILLAR. According to a twelfth-century legend, the apostle James had a vision of Mary carrying the infant Christ, and of angels carrying a pillar. Mary asked for a church to be built on the site. A shrine honors the story at Zaragoza. When this date does not fall on a Sunday, it is an optional memorial in Argentina and Guatemala.

LECTIONARY

Unique to this gospel is the expression "Jesus, looking at him, loved him." Who does Jesus love? The rich young man, the dreamer who wants eternal life, the obedient observer of God's commands— this man receives the master's loving look. And then Jesus blasts him: "Sell what you have and give to the poor." The disciples learn a hard lesson that having wealth is not the same as attaining salvation. This lesson is hard for anyone to learn in an affluent society.

The speaker in the first reading prefers wisdom to all riches. This

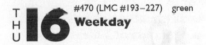

is not "smarts" wisdom. This is divine wisdom, knowledge of the mysteries of God. In the psalm, we ask God that we may gain wisdom of heart.

In a famous analogy, the letter to the Hebrews says the word of God is sharper than any two-edged sword. God's word is like wisdom. It penetrates between soul and spirit, joints and marrow.

SACRAMENTARY

The first communion antiphon fits the theme of the gospel: The rich suffer want and go hungry, but nothing shall be lacking to those who fear God. The fifth preface of Ordinary Time says we are stewards of creation. Prayer over the people #19 prays that God will enrich people with grace.

OTHER IDEAS

Some parishes find autumn a good season for conducting a special campaign for funds. This weekend's readings will give the faithful much to think about as they consider their gifts to the church.

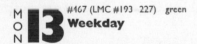

M O N **13** #467 (LMC #193–227) green
Weekday

Thanksgiving Day, Canada/ white ▪ In the face of opposition, Jesus reminds the crowds about Jonah and the queen of the south. The Ninevites reformed their lives at Jonah's preaching, and the queen traveled a great distance to listen to Solomon. But this generation does not listen and does not reform. As we know from the recent weekday readings, Jesus is referring to the part of the story concerning the effectiveness of Jonah's preaching, not to the prophet's three days in the belly of the great fish.

Paul's letter to the Romans is one of the greatest epistles in the New Testament. Filled with insight, sweeping in its themes, it draws the believer into a deeper union with God. It is one of the undisputed letters of Paul. Today Paul introduces the letter with his greetings. He establishes his position as an apostle, affirms the incarnation as a fulfillment of God's plan, proclaims the resurrection as a sign of Jesus' divinity, and recognizes the holiness of the community to which he writes. A general psalm of thanksgiving follows the reading.

The first eucharistic prayer has roots in the early Christian community of the city of Rome.

T U E **14** #468 (LMC #193–227) green
Weekday

Optional Memorial of Callistus I (+ 222), pope, martyr/red ▪ Even when Jesus responds favorably to a dinner invitation, he cannot avoid opposition. The Pharisee who hosts him complains that he did not perform the proper ablutions. For Jesus, it was a prophetic sign that allowed him to preach.

Paul introduces an important verse that he will analyze: The just shall live by faith. He criticizes those who have known of God but did not give God thanks. The psalm of praise that we sing in response is frequently used on days that honor apostles and evangelists: Their message resounds to the ends of the world.

▪ TODAY'S SAINT: Callistus extended forgiveness toward those who had lapsed from their faith but wanted to return. He started Ember Day fasts and opened the first Christian cemetery in Rome.

W E D **15** #469 (LMC #193–227) white
Teresa of Jesus (+ 1582), religious, doctor of the church
MEMORIAL

The ill feelings between Jesus and his enemies break out into harsh words. Jesus criticizes the Pharisees and the lawyers for their hypocrisy.

Paul rails against those who judge others, warning them that God's just judgment is waiting for them. God will bring affliction and glory to people with no favoritism. The psalmist puts complete trust in God, who gives to all what they deserve.

▪ TODAY'S SAINT: Born in Avila, Spain, Teresa entered a Carmelite convent and became the author of many spiritual writings that remain very popular. Giovanni Lorenzo Bernini captured her rapturous ecstasies in a remarkable stone sculpture. Presidential prayers for Saint Teresa are under October 15. You may use the preface for virgins and religious (P 68). An alternative first reading appears in the lectionary to remind us of her experiences of mystical prayer.

T H U **16** #470 (LMC #193–227) green
Weekday

Optional Memorial of Hedwig (+ 1243), married woman, monastic/white ▪ *Optional Memorial of Margaret Mary Alacoque (+ 1690), religious/white* ▪ Jesus continues his bleak assessment of hypocritical lawyers. His speech causes his enemies to set traps for him.

Paul says that we are justified by faith, not by a strict observance of the law, and that God belongs to Jews and Gentiles alike. This passage became a point of dispute at the time of the Reformation, but since then the mainline Christian churches have reached substantial agreement on its interpretation. The mercy of God is sung in the psalm today.

■ TODAY'S SAINTS: Hedwig, duchess of Silesia, was a wife and mother of seven children. She donated her fortune to the church and the poor and retired to a Cistercian convent after her husband's death.

Margaret Mary Alacoque of France promoted first Friday devotions in honor of the Sacred Heart, due to her mystical visions as a Visitation sister. She bore many trials of rejection and contempt with patient love.

■ ON THIS DAY in 1978, Karol Wojtyla, cardinal of Krakow, Poland, was elected the youngest pope in over a century and the first non-Italian bishop of Rome in 450 years.

FRI 17
#471 (LMC #193–227) red
Ignatius of Antioch (+ c. 107), bishop, martyr
MEMORIAL

The crowd following Jesus has reached soccer-game and rock-concert status. Thousands were walking over one other. Luke strings together a series of aphorisms about avoiding hypocrisy, secrecy and groundless fears.

■ TODAY'S SAINT: Ignatius authored seven letters to early church communities, similar in style to the New Testament epistles, but composed a generation later. He bravely prepared for his death before wild beasts in the amphitheatre under the persecution of Trajan.

You may use the preface for martyrs (P 66) with the presidential prayers for Ignatius. He is among the saints listed in the first eucharistic prayer. The suggested communion antiphon for the day is lifted from his letters. The lectionary provides optional readings that offer hope to those who suffer martyrdom.

SAT 18
#661 (LMC #452–454, 396) red
Luke, evangelist
FEAST

The third gospel and the Acts of the Apostles are attributed to Luke, a companion of Paul. In some sections of Acts, the author writes in the first person plural, putting himself into the story. He is called a physician in the New Testament, an occupation associated with artists in the Middle Ages. A late tradition proposed that Luke was also a painter, and that he actually created some works of religious art in possession. His combined work takes up nearly a third of the New Testament, and the style of writing is acclaimed for its excellence.

The first reading identifies Luke as a companion of Paul. The psalm is one used for apostles and evangelists because it says the works of creation proclaim God's glory. The gospel, taken from Luke, tells of the appointment of the 72 disciples, of whom tradition numbers this saint.

Sing the Glory to God. The second preface for apostles is recommended (P 65) because of its reference to "the living gospel." But the fourth version of the eucharistic prayer for various needs and occasions, "Jesus, the Compassion of God," refers to stories of Luke's gospel. Take the presidential prayers from Luke's feast. You may use the solemn blessing for apostles (17).

◯19
#146 (LMC #140) green
Twenty-ninth Sunday in Ordinary Time

ORIENTATION

Take a look at the Alleluia verses for Sundays in Ordinary Time (163). Any of them may be used on any week, but three of them are reserved for the last Sundays of Ordinary Time. These Sundays are not specified, but if you judge that the period of Ordinary Time is reaching its climax, you may switch to those verses.

LECTIONARY

The sons of Zebedee have completely missed the point of the gospel. Jesus patiently dialogues with them about their desires. He tricks them into asserting their willingness to drink his cup and be baptized with his baptism. But Jesus has martyrdom in mind. The gravity of discipleship is revealed again as he instructs all the Twelve to a life of service.

The first reading comes from the "Songs of the Suffering Servant" at the end of the book of Isaiah. They are frequently interpreted as prophetic utterances of the passion of Jesus. As Jesus foretells his passion today, it is fitting to hear its prophecy. In the psalm we sing that God looks upon the faithful, "to deliver them from death."

The letter to the Hebrews contrasts Jesus with the high priest of the Temple. Jesus can sympathize with our weaknesses because he was one like us. But he has passed through the heavens and we can approach him with confidence.

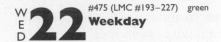

SACRAMENTARY

The first communion antiphon is a quote from today's psalm, and the second comes from today's gospel. The fourth preface for Sundays in Ordinary Time (P 32) summarizes the birth, suffering and glory of Jesus. Look at the solemn blessing for the Passion of the Lord (5).

OTHER IDEAS

Today is Mission Sunday, a Roman Catholic observance. Choose a hymn to draw attention to the day and include intercessions for the mission of the church. The Mass texts for the spread of the gospel (14) may be used today.

Although the liturgical observance is suppressed because it falls on a Sunday, today the church remembers Isaac Jogues, John de Brebeuf and their companions, martyrs of the North American missionary movement.

MON 20 Weekday
#473 (LMC #193–227)   green

Optional Memorial of Paul of the Cross (+ 1775), presbyter, religious founder / white ▪ To settle a dispute about property ownership, Jesus tells about a rich person who stores up everything only to die early. The story reflects the urgency surrounding Jesus' message ("Reform your lives") and the thoroughness of conversion he seeks.

Abraham, who lived before Moses, is a model of faith. And his faith, Paul argues, was credited to him as justice. The same, he holds, is true for Christians. The fulfillment of God's promise is remembered in the responsory today: the canticle of Zechariah, drawn from Luke's gospel.

The first eucharistic prayer for Masses of reconciliation confesses that we broke our covenant, but God brings us back.

■ TODAY'S SAINT: In the United States we offer the optional memorial of Paul of the Cross a day later than almost everyone else in the world. Paul's day (October 19) coincides with that of Isaac Jogues, John de Brebeuf, and their companions, martyrs on the continent we inhabit. Consequently, we have permanently displaced Paul of the Cross, not off the calendar, but to the next day. This year it seems a little odd because the memorial of the North American martyrs got completely replaced by the Twenty-ninth Sunday in Ordinary Time. That leaves us with a surprisingly resilient optional memorial for Paul of the Cross, who hangs onto the calendar this year even when our local martyrs take the year off! Paul led an austere life and preached to the poor. He founded the Discalced Clerks of the Most Holy Cross and Passion of Our Lord Jesus Christ, more popularly known as the Passionists.

TUE 21 Weekday
#474 (LMC #193–227)   green

In another saying reminiscent of yesterday's warning about the brevity of life and the importance of vigilant readiness, Jesus tells the disciples to be like those waiting the master's return from a wedding. Be prepared at all times.

Paul contrasts Adam with Jesus. Through one man sin entered the world. Through another came acquittal and life. Grace surpasses sin. In the psalm we can imagine hearing Jesus sing, "To do your will, O God, is my delight." Where Adam failed in the face of temptation, Jesus remained faithful.

The second preface for weekdays in Ordinary Time (P 38) says that God condemned humanity in justice but redeemed us in mercy.

Twenty-five years ago today John Paul II became the bishop of Rome.

In Bolivia, today is the optional memorial for Miguel Febres Cordero (+ 1910). (See February 9.)

WED 22 Weekday
#475 (LMC #193–227)   green

We hear another saying about being prepared. People do not know when the thief is coming, nor when the master will return. Jesus proposes that all must be ready for the return of the Son of Man.

Paul has been preaching freedom from the law in Christ, but he wants no one to misunderstand. He is not advocating sin. Christ has freed us from slavery to sin, but now we are slaves of justice. The psalm recalls God's rescue of Israel from persecution. Today it applies to the way Christ has rescued us from sin.

The third preface for weekdays in Ordinary Time (P 39) speaks of God's restoration of creation.

THU 23 Weekday
#476 (LMC #193–227)   green

Optional Memorial of John of Capistrano (+ 1456), presbyter, religious, missionary / white ▪ Although we like to think of Jesus in his role as peacemaker, he says today that he has come not for peace but for division. His message will cause people to join his cause or reject it. Even families will be divided. Divided families must have troubled the early church community for whom Luke wrote the gospel.

Paul builds on his theme from yesterday's reading. When the Romans were under the old law, they were slaves to it, and they had freedom from justice. They performed acts of degradation. Now they are ashamed of those actions. But in the new life of grace, God brings them sanctification. The first psalm contrasts the way of the wicked and the way of the just.

The first preface for weekdays (P 37) says God has renewed all things in Christ and has given us all a share in his riches.

■ TODAY'S SAINT: John was born in Capistrano and educated in Perugia. He joined the Franciscans and became a student of Bernadine of Sienna, who encouraged his love for the Holy Name of Jesus. Renowned for his preaching, he led a crusade against invading Turks and has become the patron of military chaplains. One of the California missions is named for him.

FRI 24 #477 (LMC #193–227) green
Weekday

Optional Memorial of Anthony Mary Claret (+ 1870), bishop, religious founder / white ▪ People can make the simplest of weather predictions, Jesus says, but they cannot interpret the present age. As a sign of living in urgent times, people should settle with their accusers without going to court. In Jesus' view, there is no time for long cases.

Paul describes a classic moral dilemma. The desire to do right is there but not the power. He wants to do good, but does evil instead. Only Christ can free him. From the longest psalm, we sing several verses about fidelity to God's law.

Prayers for the progress of peoples (#21) will help the community build on the grace God gives us.

■ TODAY'S SAINT: Anthony Mary Claret served as archbishop in Cuba, laboring for spiritual and social reforms and championing the rights of indigenous peoples. He founded the Claretians, the Missionary Sons of the Immaculate Heart of Mary. Today is an obligatory memorial in Bolivia and Venezuela.

■ ON THIS DAY, Mexico honors Blessed Rafael Guizar y Valencia (+ 1938), bishop of Veracruz and resister of government-sponsored anticlericalism.

SAT 25 #478 (LMC #193–227) green
Weekday

Optional Memorial of the Blessed Virgin Mary / white ▪ Jesus calls on his listeners to reform their lives by recalling disasters that befell their comrades. The care of the soul should at least resemble the care given a barren fig tree. Jesus does not wish judgment, but conversion.

Paul assures the Romans that the Spirit who raised Jesus from the dead now lives in them. They have power in God to overcome sin. The psalm recognizes the qualities of the just.

See the votive Mass for the Holy Spirit (7B) for prayers that acknowledge the effect of the Spirit in the church.

■ THIS IS ONE OF THE DATES ON WHICH YOU MAY CELEBRATE THE ANNIVERSARY OF THE DEDICATION OF YOUR CHURCH, if the date is unknown. Use the sacramentary and lectionary texts for the common of the dedication of a church, sing the Glory to God, and recite the Creed.

■ IF YOU OPT FOR THE MEMORIAL OF THE BLESSED VIRGIN, consider Mary, Mother and Teacher in the Spirit from the *Collection of Masses of the Blessed Virgin* Mary, which makes a reference to our baptismal promises.

#149 (LMC #143) green

✹26 Thirtieth Sunday in Ordinary Time

ORIENTATION

Daylight saving time ends this weekend for many people. Trees in many locales are losing their leaves. In the midst of gathering darkness, we meet blind Bartimaeus, who recognizes hope in Jesus.

LECTIONARY

The story of Bartimaeus is a classic description of discipleship. When he hears that Jesus is near, he calls out in faith and asks for mercy. Anti-sponsors try to quiet the new disciple, but he calls only louder. Then Jesus calls him and asks what appears to be the stupidest question a miracle worker could ask a blind man: "What do you want me to do for you?" Bartimaeus makes his request, and Jesus gives him sight. In language filled with meaning, Mark says Bartimaeus "received his sight" and followed Jesus "on the way." The sight he receives is the sight of faith. The way is the way of discipleship.

From Jeremiah we hear a prophecy of Advent spirit that looks to a day when God will bring back the blind and the lame from the ends of the earth. This passage, which looks forward to Israel's return from exile, is followed by a post-exilic psalm. It sings of how God brought back the captives of Zion.

Melchizedek is a type of Jesus. He is king of justice and peace. He appears and disappears in the book of Genesis without indication of his origins or destiny. He offers bread and wine. The letter to the Hebrews says Jesus is closer to the priesthood of Melchizedek than he is to the high priest in the temple, who is taken from among people. Jesus is a greater priest.

SACRAMENTARY

The preface for the fourth version of the eucharistic prayer for various needs and occasions says Jesus was moved with compassion for the sick and the sinner. The first solemn blessing for Ordinary Time (10) is the blessing of Aaron, and prays that the face of God may shine upon us with graciousness and kindness.

OTHER IDEAS

The last Sunday of October is Reformation Sunday, the anniversary of the beginning of the Protestant Reformation by Martin Luther, an opportunity for us to affirm the common mission of Christians to reform our lives by the gospel and to celebrate the unity of our baptism.

If the date of your church dedication is unknown, you may celebrate it this Sunday (or October 25) with the common Mass for the dedication of the church. Both the sacramentary and the lectionary texts may substitute for those assigned for the Ordinary Time Sunday. See *General Norms for the Liturgical Year* and Calendar, the note to 52C, and consult your diocesan offices for local regulations. It is important to celebrate this anniversary each year. If the date is known, be sure to include it in the parish's calendar of events. If unknown, celebrate it well this week.

Be sure to announce the upcoming holy day.

MON 27 #479 (LMC #228–231) green
Weekday

Today's gospel unfortunately does not appear in the Sunday cycle of readings. It is a marvelous miracle story. Jesus cures a woman stooped by 18 years of illness when he lays a hand on her. She praises God. The chief of the synagogue is indignant that Jesus healed on the Sabbath, and blames the congregation! Jesus is baffled by the tactlessness of his opponents, and the crowd rejoices at the marvels he does.

Paul encourages the Romans to live by the Spirit, putting to death what is evil. Through the Spirit we call God "Father." The psalm praises God who controls the passageways of death.

The fourth version of the eucharistic prayer for various needs and occasions asks God to keep our service of others faithful to the example and command of Christ.

The *Lectionary for Masses with Children* has a special section devoted to the weeks at the end of the liturgical year. If you like, you could start using them in Masses with children. The regular lectionary has a common psalm (175) and verses to the gospel acclamations (164 and 509) that may be used for the last weeks of the year.

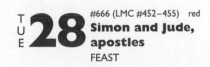

TUE 28 #666 (LMC #452–455) red
Simon and Jude, apostles
FEAST

Simon and Jude were among the Twelve, but Simon is the Zealot or the Cananaean, not Simon Peter; and Jude (short for Judas) is known as Thaddaeus in Matthew and Mark, and is not the same as Judas the betrayer.

The gospel for today is Luke's listing of the Twelve, which mentions both of them. The first reading from Ephesians tells the Gentile Christians they are no longer strangers, but members of

the household of God, built upon the foundation of the apostles. The psalm today is frequently used for apostles because it says the works of God let their voice resound through all their earth, and the message carries to the end of the world. The psalm seems to prophecy the work of apostles.

The presidential prayers come from October 28. Sing the Glory to God. You may use either preface for the apostles, but the second (P 65) relies on today's first reading. Both apostles are mentioned in the first eucharistic prayer.

■ TODAY IS THE PATRONAL FEAST OF PERU, the Lord of Miracles (El Señor de los Milagros).

WED 29 #481 (LMC #228–231) green
Weekday

Today's gospel opens with the reminder that Jesus is making his way toward Jerusalem. Throughout the second half of Luke's gospel, Jesus is on a physical and spiritual journey toward the city of his death. Luke has planted reminders in the text so we do not lose our way with Jesus, as he heads toward the cross. A discussion about salvation arises. Jesus suggests that even the Gentiles will find a place at God's feast.

One of the benefits of life in the Spirit is prayer. The Christian, Paul argues, profits from the support of the Spirit, who helps us pray when we do not know how or what to say. A prayerful life is a sign of the presence of God's Spirit. The psalm today sings of God's goodness: Our hope is in God's loving kindness.

The preface for the second eucharistic prayer says Christ fulfilled God's will and won a holy people.

■ IN PERU, yesterday's feast of the apostles Simon and Jude is transferred to this date.

T H U **30** #482 (LMC #228–231)   green
Weekday

Pharisees warn Jesus that Herod is trying to kill him, but he insists he will continue toward Jerusalem. He wails over the city like a mother bird. The church of Dominus Flevit outside the Mount of Olives in the Holy Land has an artistic depiction of Jesus as a mother hen, gathering her young.

Today's passage from the letter to the Romans is a high point of this book and of the entire Bible. Paul asks two beautiful rhetorical questions: If God is for us, who can be against us? Who will separate us from the love of Christ? The psalmist, praying in distress, relies on God's kindness.

The second preface for weekdays (P 38) says God created us in love, condemned us in justice, and redeemed us in mercy.

■ IN GUATEMALA, today is the solemnity for celebrating the dedication of individual churches throughout the Republic.

F R I **31** #483 (LMC #228–231)   green
Weekday

Today's gospel is omitted from the Sunday cycle of readings. It tells the story of Jesus curing a man with dropsy. The cure takes place on the Sabbath in the house of a leading Pharisee in the presence of all the religious leaders. They keep silent while he cures the diseased man and lectures them about the law of love.

Paul expresses his deep love for the Israelites. He desires that they share his faith. His desire is so strong that he would willingly separate himself from Christ for their sake. We respond with a psalm of praise to God who has proclaimed statutes and ordinances to Israel.

The mission of Jesus to the poor, the prisoner and the sorrowful is one of the themes of Eucharistic Prayer IV.

■ HALLOWEEN is the eve of All Saints. See *Take Me Home* for ideas. LTP's *School Year, Church Year* makes several recommendations, as does *Preparing Liturgy for Children and Children for Liturgy.*

November

S A T **1** #667 (LMC #402)   white
All Saints
SOLEMNITY

ORIENTATION

Today we recognize all the saints of heaven in a universal celebration, a festival of the triumphant church of the resurrection in the new and holy city of Jerusalem. The saints, in a way, are God's harvest. God has reaped the fruits of good sowing and gathered the mature faithful into the eternal storehouse.

November opens a season of the year when our thoughts turn toward the fear of death, the hope of eternal life, the gratitude we feel for God's gifts, and the charity we owe to others. In the northern hemisphere, trees turn barren and the chill of late fall settles in to stay.

All Saints' Day is a holy day of obligation in the United States (except in the diocese of Honolulu), but the obligation does not apply today because it falls on a Saturday. Today is also a holy day in Chile, Honduras, Peru and Puerto Rico, but not the other Latin American countries. Bolivia transfers the observance to the nearest Sunday.

LECTIONARY

The gospel for All Saints' Day is the account of the Beatitudes from Matthew. When Jesus opened the Sermon on the Mount, he proclaimed the reign of God for those who were virtuous in poverty, spirituality and persecution. The beatitudes are a job description for sainthood.

In the second reading, John proclaims that we are God's children now, and what we shall later be has not yet come to light. But John proclaims the hope of an eternal reward, which we celebrate today as it shines in the saints.

John's vision in Revelation sees an immense crowd of holy ones gathered before the throne and the lamb. Dressed in white are the martyrs who have survived the period of trial and washed their robes in the blood of the lamb. One reason we wear white baptismal garments and white albs and drape caskets with a white pall is to stand among the blessed who worship at the eternal throne of God. The psalm describes the sinless who long to see the face of God.

SACRAMENTARY

The prayers for the day are under November 1. They include a solemn blessing. The preface is proper to the day (P 71) and the first eucharistic prayer will name a number of saints we rarely talk about. The recommended communion antiphon is based on the gospel.

Beginning today, you may want to favor Penitential Rite C-ii, or texts like it. Its spirit will move us through this season and on into Advent.

OTHER IDEAS

On the present liturgical calendar there is no vigil Mass for All Saints, even though the culture celebrates the vigil with the secular observance of Halloween. Mass may certainly be celebrated on Halloween night, but it has no special texts. If you are looking for another kind of vigil celebration, check the vigil for the Eve of All Saints' Day and the Service for All Hallows' Eve in the Episcopal *Book of Occasional Services* for ideas. Of course, you may build a vigil service from the office of readings, or sing a more solemn setting of Evening Prayer I from the *Liturgy of the Hours*.

For the environment, use the harvest motif. See *To Crown the Year* (192–197). Set up a parish book of the dead, like the one published by Liturgy Training Publications. Record the names of all who have died in the past year, and arrange the book near the font and lit Easter candle. If your parish has a cemetery, you might decorate the entranceway and set out special prayers to encourage visits to the graves of loved ones and strangers.

For prayer at home, see *Catholic Household Blessings and Prayers* (178–183) for prayers for this month and a visit to a cemetery. LTP's *Sourcebook about Death* (1989) has 30 sections for day-by-day reading that families may find useful this month.

#1011–1016 (668) (LMC #531–535)
white, violet, or black

✵2 All the Faithful Departed (All Souls)
COMMEMORATION

ORIENTATION

We remember the deceased among the faithful who await their entrance to eternal glory. These two days together honor the dead. Yesterday's celebration remembered the saints whose excellent lives make them sure models of redemption. Today we pray for the rest, those who need forgiveness for their sins, who yearn to see the face of God.

LECTIONARY

Readings are taken from the commons for the Masses for the dead. You are completely free to choose the passages you wish. The text from Second Maccabees, for example, says it is good to pray for the dead for the forgiveness of their sins. That passage is one of the scriptural foundations for the Catholic traditional belief in purgatory and to justify prayer for the dead as we do today.

If you are using the *Lectionary for Masses with Children* today, you have fewer selections. Try to coordinate the parish Mass readings with these.

SACRAMENTARY

Priests are allowed to celebrate three Masses today, but they need not.

Any of the sacramentary's texts for the All Souls' Day Masses may be used. Any preface of Christian death (P 77–81) may accompany these prayers. The Glory to God is not included in this Mass. Ordinarily the Creed is also omitted today, but it would be appropriate this year because this is Sunday. A solemn blessing is recommended.

■ SAMPLE FORMULAS FOR THE GENERAL INTERCESSIONS appear in the sacramentary's first appendix. See #11 for those suggested for Masses for the dead.

OTHER IDEAS

Sing music from the parish's funeral repertoire. Does the community know a setting of the "In Paradisum"? The chants from the funeral Mass are among the most beautiful and best remembered of the church's Latin music.

The *Book of Blessings* has an order for visiting a cemetery on All Souls' Day (57). Display the parish book of the dead near the font.

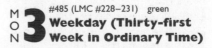

M O N **3** #485 (LMC #228–231)   green
Weekday (Thirty-first Week in Ordinary Time)

Optional memorial of Martin de Porres (+ 1639), religious / white ■ Jesus announces a new order of community. Invite to your table not the wealthy who can repay you, but the needy who cannot.

Paul gives a remarkable explanation for the existence of sin. It is to let God's mercy be known. God's ways are inscrutable. In the psalm, we praise God who helps us in times of affliction.

The fourth version of the eucharistic prayer for Masses of various needs and occasions honors Christ who "made himself neighbor to the oppressed."

■ TODAY'S SAINT: Martin was born in Peru of a Spanish father and a Black mother freed from slavery. As a teenager he apprenticed in medicine, the Doogie Howser of his day. As a Dominican, his gift for healing was exceeded only by his charity in sharing it with the poor. Because of his power as an intercessor in the Hispanic culture, Martin's image appears on many an altarcito. Today is a solemnity in Peru and an obligatory memorial in Bolivia, Colombia, Costa Rica, Panama and Venezuela.

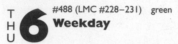

TUE 4 #486 (LMC #228–231)   white
Charles Borromeo (+ 1584), bishop
MEMORIAL

At a banquet himself, Jesus uses the setting to tell a parable of people who refuse invitations to a banquet. He criticizes those who make excuses not to accept his teaching, especially those from among God's chosen people who should know better.

"We, though many, are one body." Today's first reading is one of several places where Paul expounds on the image of the body of Christ. He honors the different gifts in a community and urges the Romans to make their love sincere. In response we sing of the humblest songs in the psalter: "I have stilled and quieted my soul like a weaned child on the mother's lap."

■ TODAY'S SAINT: "Humility" was the motto for Charles Borromeo, a bishop of Milan whose pastoral mind made him extremely influential in applying the teachings of the church after the Council of Trent. He held numerous provincial councils and diocesan synods. Karol Wojtyla, the future Pope John Paul II, was named for this saint.

The preface for pastors (P 67) may accompany the presidential prayers for this saint.

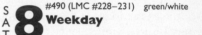

WED 5 #487 (LMC #228–231)   green
Weekday

In sayings and parables, Jesus stresses the importance of complete conversion and the willingness to accept the pain of the cross. He also explains the virtue of thinking ahead.

Paul focuses on love in the Christian community. Pay off all your debts, he says, except for one: the debt to love. Live by love. The psalm praises those who are merciful and give lavishly to the poor.

The preface for the first version of the eucharistic prayer for various needs and occasions says, "Your church bears steadfast witness to your love."

THU 6 #488 (LMC #228–231)   green
Weekday

The fifteenth chapter of Luke contains Jesus' beautiful teaching on forgiveness and reconciliation. He speaks of God's love for the lost sheep and the lost coin, comparing God's care to that of shepherd and woman.

Today's first reading is one of the options for a funeral Mass. Whether we live or die, we belong to God, Paul says. We will all have to give an account of ourselves before God. With the psalmist we sing in faith that we will see good things in the land of the living.

The first eucharistic prayer for reconciliation says, "When we were lost and could not find the way to you, you loved us more than ever."

FRI 7 #489 (LMC #228–231)   green
Weekday

Probably because the story appears so frequently elsewhere in the lectionary, the weekday readings skip the story of the prodigal son and move to another parable. Jesus praises a devious employee who cheats his master in order to win

support from others in the community. The parable praises the industriousness of the oppressed.

Approaching the conclusion of his letter to the church at Rome, Paul expresses his desire to help convert the Gentiles. In the psalm we sing that God has revealed salvation to all the nations.

The preface for the first version of the eucharistic prayer for various needs and occasions says, "you have brought together in a single Church people of every nation, culture, and tongue."

■ IN COSTA RICA, today marks the solemnity of the dedication of all individual churches except cathedrals.

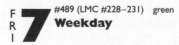

SAT 8 #490 (LMC #228–231)   green/white
Weekday

Optional Memorial of the Blessed Virgin Mary/white ▪ Jesus counsels finding friends because the goods of this world fail. Love God, he says, pricking the conscience of the Pharisees; do not love money.

Paul's great letter to the Romans comes to its close today. Paul gives greetings to a large number of members of the church there. And this is an abbreviation of the complete list, astonishing in its length. The name of Paul's secretary, Tertius, is given. The letter concludes with a doxology highlighting some now-familiar themes: the gospel of Jesus, the mystery hidden from ages, the revelation of God, the command made known to the Gentiles, and the glory due to God alone. Fittingly, a psalm of praise follows the reading. This is another alphabetical psalm. It does not develop a logical thought. It simply presents a series of independent verses praising God, each one beginning with a successive letter of the Hebrew alphabet.

In the first version of the eucharistic prayer for various needs and occasions you may pray for the local church by name.

■ IF YOU CELEBRATE THE MEMORIAL OF MARY TODAY, consider Mary, Image and Mother of the Church II (26) from the *Collection of Masses of the Blessed Virgin Mary*.

■ ON THE SATURDAY PRECEDING THE SECOND SUNDAY OF NOVEMBER, Uruguay celebrates its patronal feast, "Our Lady of the Thirty-Three" (Nuestra Señora de los Treinta y Tres Orientales). The title refers to Mary's protection of 33 insurrectionists, led by Juan Antonio Lavalleja, in 1825. They all prayed for her help in the city of Florida in the church of Our Lady of Luján, and then signed Uruguay's Declaration of Independence from Brazil in the parish office.

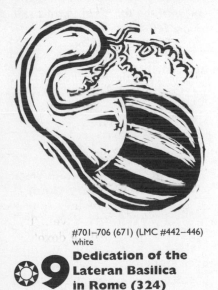

#701–706 (671) (LMC #442–446) white

☸9 Dedication of the Lateran Basilica in Rome (324)
FEAST

ORIENTATION

All churches are invited to celebrate the anniversary of their dedication on the liturgical calendar. Your parish church and your cathedral church should have their days. The cathedral church of Rome and hence of the entire Roman church has its dedication day today. We celebrate it as a feast throughout the Catholic world.

When it falls on a Sunday, it replaces the Ordinary Time liturgy.

The church is dedicated to John the Baptist and John the Evangelist. It sits on the hill that bears the name of its former owners, the Lateran family. When Constantine won the battle of the Milvian Bridge in the fourth century, he made Christianity an acceptable religion in the empire and eventually accepted baptism. The first church to take advantage of the permission for Christianity to go public was the one set up on property given by the Laterans. The original building has undergone many renovations, but it still bears its basic floor plans for the church and the baptistry. The Lateran is the mother church of Rome, and hence of all the world. It is the cathedral church of Rome, and one of the four major basilicas in the city.

LECTIONARY

Scriptures may be taken anywhere from the common of the dedication of a church. The passage from First Corinthians, for example, places the emphasis not just on the building but on the people it represents.

If you are using the *Lectionary for Masses with Children* today, you have fewer selections. Try to coordinate the parish Mass readings with these.

SACRAMENTARY

Texts come from the Anniversary of Dedication, outside the dedicated church (unless you celebrate this day at St. John Lateran in Rome!). The preface is proper (P 53). Sing the Glory to God. Proclaim the Creed together because this is Sunday. The solemn blessing for the dedication of a church (19) implies that you are in the church recalling its anniversary.

It could be used if you adapt one phrase: "to recall the dedication of the Lateran church."

See also Appendix VIII in the sacramentary for the prayers for the dedication of a church.

OTHER IDEAS

Today is truly a celebration of cathedrals. Let people know something about the cathedral of your diocese. Encourage them to visit, or organize a parish pilgrimage there to help them claim it as the mother church.

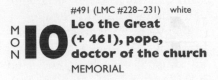

#491 (LMC #228–231) white

MON 10 Leo the Great (+ 461), pope, doctor of the church
MEMORIAL

In a series of short sayings, Jesus criticizes scandals, promotes forgiveness and encourages faith.

To close out the liturgical year the weekday readings turn to some of the last books written for the Old Testament: Wisdom, the Maccabees, and Daniel. The book of Wisdom may date from the last century before the time of Christ. It seeks to strengthen the Jewish community in the face of persecution and against the temptations of idolatry. In the opening chapter, which we hear from today, the community is encouraged to love justice and accept the kindly spirit of God's wisdom. The psalm suggests that God's wisdom is too lofty for humans to attain. Like the all-embracing wisdom of the first reading, God is present everywhere.

You may use the preface for pastors (P 67) with the presidential prayers for Leo the Great.

■ TODAY'S SAINT: Leo was the first pope claiming to be Peter's heir, exercising authority over not just Rome, but over other bishops as well. The Eastern Church was less disposed to accept his claims. He reigned during the time of the

Council of Chalcedon. He confronted Attila the Hun and diverted his invasion—according to the legend—with the help of Peter and Paul, who appeared in the sky. Algardi captured the incident in a bas-relief that presides above the tomb of Leo in St. Peter's in Vatican City.

T U E 11 #492/673 (LMC #228–231) white
Martin of Tours (+ 397), bishop, monastic
MEMORIAL

Jesus appreciates good servants, but implies they can be treated as mere servants unless they do more than their duty. He expects more of us than we might imagine.

Today's first reading is a popular choice for funerals. It shows an unusual pre-Christian vision in a life after death. Only the foolish think death is an affliction or destruction. The souls of the just are in peace. In the psalm, we acknowledge that God has eyes for the just and ears for their cry. God saves those who are crushed in spirit.

■ TODAY'S SAINT: Martin of Tours was still a catechumen when he severed his garment and gave half to a shivering beggar. Later, in a dream, he saw Christ with the beggar's face. He founded the first monastery in the west and became bishop of Tours. He was the first non-martyr to have a day on the calendar, and the *Liturgy of Hours* honors him with a special set of antiphons and the psalms and canticles from Sunday morning prayer of week one. That distinction is generally reserved for feast days. He appears in the litany of the saints just before Benedict, who wrote the influential rule of monastic life.

You may use the preface of pastors (P 67) with the prayers for Martin's day. The lectionary includes an optional gospel for today, a choice inspired by Martin's care for the poor.

■ VETERANS' DAY IN THE UNITED STATES AND REMEMBRANCE DAY IN CANADA coincide with the anniversary of the conclusion of World War I. You might invite veterans who are present for the liturgy today to receive the blessing and gratitude of the community for their service.

W E D 12 #493 (LMC #228–231) red
Josaphat (+ 1623), bishop, religious, martyr
MEMORIAL

The first line of today's gospel reminds us that Jesus is on his journey to Jerusalem. This is the third reference to the journey that Luke has mentioned, all the while keeping the reader's view searching for the looming cross.

Wisdom, personified, speaks to the rulers of the earth and challenges them to reject their ways and accept divine wisdom. The psalm contrasts God's judgment with those who afflict the destitute.

■ TODAY'S SAINT: Josaphat worked for the union of churches east and west. His own people nominated him as archbishop, but he suffered martyrdom at the hands of those who opposed his efforts. Like Leo the Great, whom we commemorated on Monday this week, Josaphat is buried in St. Peter's Basilica in Rome.

The preface for martyrs (P 66) may accompany the presidential prayers for his day.

T H U 13 #494 (LMC #228–231) white
Frances Xavier Cabrini (+ 1917), religious founder, missionary
MEMORIAL

Jesus returns to his theme, the reign of God. He says you cannot tell when it is coming, but you must be ready for it at all times.

Today's first reading sings praise of divine Wisdom. It imagines Wisdom as a holy, intelligent spirit, penetrating all things. It is an aura of the might of God, the refulgence of eternal light. The first O Antiphon of the Advent season quotes this passage with its image of Wisdom reaching mightily from end to end. As a response, we sing excerpts from a lengthy psalm praising the wisdom of God's law.

■ TODAY'S SAINT: Mother Cabrini founded the Missionary Sisters of the Sacred Heart, left her native Italy and worked for immigrants in the New World, where she attained citizenship. After serving the needy and providing hope to the desperate, she was the first United States citizen to be canonized.

Today's memorial is obligatory in the United States. The opening prayer can be found at November 13. Others may come from the common of virgins. You may pray the preface for virgins and religious (P 68).

■ LEANDER (+ c. 600), the learned and conciliatory bishop of Seville, is remembered with an optional memorial today in Spain and Guatemala.

F R I 14 #495 (LMC #228–231) green
Weekday (Thirty-second Week in Ordinary Time)

Jesus predicts that in the days before the coming of the Son of Man, people will be living sinful lives and only the just will be redeemed. It will resemble the situation of Noah's day.

The book of Wisdom criticizes those who study nature but do not discern the artisan. Today's passage argues for the existence of God from the evidence in the world around us. The psalmist says the heavens declare the glory of God.

The third preface for weekdays in Ordinary Time praises God for creating the human family, and asserts it is God's right to receive the obedience of all creation.

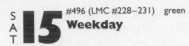

S
A
T
15 #496 (LMC #228–231)   green
Weekday

Optional Memorial of Albert the Great (+ 1280), bishop, religious, doctor of the church / white ▪ *Optional Memorial of the Blessed Virgin Mary / white* ▪ Jesus tells a parable of the benefits that come from persistent prayer. He has asked for complete commitment and vigilant readiness from his disciples. Now he offers help through prayer.

Our final passage from the book of Wisdom this week recounts the story of the exodus. In poetic language it describes the coming of God's all-powerful word from heaven's royal throne, bearing a sharp sword. The reference is to the final plague, the loss of the first-born children. The same passage also describes the crossing of the Red Sea. These incidents are also recalled in the excerpts from today's psalm.

The fourth preface for weekdays of Ordinary Time (P 40) says God does not need our praise, and our prayer only helps us grow in God's grace.

▪ TODAY'S SAINT: A Dominican, Albert was the teacher of Thomas Aquinas. Himself a student of Greek philosophy, natural sciences, Jewish and Arabic studies, he serves as a model of blending the intellectual with the spiritual life.

▪ IF YOU CELEBRATE THE MEMORIAL OF MARY TODAY, consider Mary, Seat of Wisdom (24), in the *Collection of Masses of the Blessed Virgin Mary.*

#158 (LMC #152)   green
16 Thirty-third Sunday in Ordinary Time

ORIENTATION

The last Sundays of the year independently form a miniature season. The end of the liturgical year leads us into deeper reflection on the end of all time.

For a lectionary year dedicated to the gospel of Mark, this year comes up short. Mark's gospel is so brief that it steps aside for five weeks of summer while we listen to the sixth chapter of John, just to fill up a normal liturgical year. But this happens to be a year when several Sundays in Ordinary Time are replaced by other celebrations, as happened the last two weekends, so we've heard even less of Mark than we usually do in Year B of the cycle. The on-again off-again semicontinuous reading of Mark comes to an abrupt finish today, because John returns next Sunday for the final solemnity of the liturgical year.

LECTIONARY

Today's passage comes from chapter 13. Few will remember that we heard from this chapter on only one other Sunday all year: the First Sunday of Advent. This apocalyptic chapter brackets the second year of the lectionary's cycle. The vision in today's gospel is not pretty. The sun and the moon will be darkened, stars will fall from the sky, and the Son of Man will come on clouds. Heaven and earth will pass away, Jesus says, but his words will not.

The first reading is another eschatological passage, this time from Daniel. When Michael the great angel arises, it shall be a time "unsurpassed in distress." The righteous among the dead shall rise, and others shall go to disgrace. In the psalm we sing confidently, "you will not abandon my soul to the netherworld, nor will you suffer your faithful one to undergo corruption."

The last passage from the series of readings from Hebrews returns to the image of priesthood. Jesus differs from earthly priests who offer sacrifice daily and never remove sins. Jesus offered one sacrifice for sins and has made perfect forever those who are being consecrated. The passage enthrones Jesus at the right hand of God.

SACRAMENTARY

Eucharistic Prayer IV comes with its own irreplaceable preface. If you are planning to use the seasonal prefaces with other eucharistic prayers on Sundays for the next two months, you might use Prayer IV today. The fifth solemn blessing for Ordinary Time (14) asks that the faithful may walk in God's ways, "always knowing what is right and good."

OTHER IDEAS

Keep the parish book of the dead visible this week, as a reminder to pray for those who have died in the past year, and of the mortality we face in the scriptures of this month.

#497 (LMC #228–231)   white
M
O
N
17 Elizabeth of Hungary (+ 1231), married woman, religious
MEMORIAL

Luke tells the story of the blind beggar on the road to Jericho. Jesus hears his plea for help and grants him vision. As Jesus moves

closer to Jerusalem, all the disciples will need the eyes of faith.

The Maccabees were a political family that led Judea through the first two centuries before Christ. When Antiochus IV Epiphanes of Syria promoted Hellenization, it threatened the observance of Jewish belief. The Maccabeean rebellion against these influences is recounted in the two books that bear the family name. In the opening passage today, Antiochus comes to power and profanes the altar of the temple in Jerusalem. Many Israelites renounce their religion, but others resolve to stand firm in the face of persecution. From the psalm that best praises God's commands, we sing selected verses—not sequential ones—that show the law under attack by the wicked, the malicious, sinners and apostates.

The opening prayer for Mass comes from the proper of saints. You may choose the other prayers from those for the common of saints who worked for the underprivileged. The preface for virgins and religious (P 68) may be used.

■ TODAY'S SAINT: Born into Hungarian royalty, Elizabeth eschewed the trappings of the wealthy and lived a simple, austere life. She married, then bore three children. After her husband died, she made arrangements for the care of the children and entered a Franciscan community. Notable for her sacrifice and charity toward the sick, she died at the age of 24. Although Elizabeth's life certainly deserves praise, it points out the lack of saints' days honoring married women who raised families.

■ IN PARAGUAY, today is the feast of Roque González of the Holy Cross, Juan del Castillo, and Alonso Rodríguez, Jesuit priests and martyrs (+ 1628). All worked on the reductions in Paraguay, where natives were housed, acculturated and instructed in the

faith. An apostate led a revolt against the priests, and they were tomahawked to death. Although there were earlier martyrs in the Americas, these were the first to be beatified. They are remembered in Argentina and Bolivia today with a memorial.

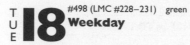

TUE 18 #498 (LMC #228–231)   green
Weekday

Optional Memorial of the Dedication of the Basilicas of the Apostles Peter (324) and Paul (390) in Rome/white ▪ *Optional Memorial of Rose Philippine Duchesne (+ 1852), religious, missionary, educator/white* ▪ Too short to see over the crowd, Zacchaeus climbed a tree to see Jesus. When Jesus invites himself over to the tax collector's home, Zacchaeus professes his conversion from sin.

During the persecution, Eleazar is forced to eat pork, against his Jewish beliefs. He spat out the meat, accepting torture and death, in order to give an example to the young. In response we sing a psalm praying for help against adversaries: "When I lie down in sleep, I wake again, for the Lord sustains me."

The first eucharistic prayer for reconciliation admits, "we broke your covenant."

■ TODAY'S MEMORIALS: The basilicas of Peter and Paul are built over the tombs of the two great apostles. Together with St. Mary Major and St. John Lateran they constitute the four major basilicas of Rome. All the dedication days are optional, except for St. John Lateran, which we observed as a feast on a Sunday earlier this month. Optional readings for the dedications are in the lectionary, stories of Paul and Peter, and a psalm of praise.

Rose Philippine Duchesne was born in Grenoble, France, and died in St. Charles, Missouri. A member of the Religious of the Sacred

Heart, she founded a house in the United States and opened the first free school west of the Mississippi. Among native Americans, she was called "the woman who prays always." The opening prayer for this optional memorial is in the 1994 *Sacramentary Supplement.*

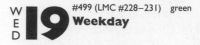

WED 19 #499 (LMC #228–231)   green
Weekday

Today's gospel opens and closes with references to Jerusalem. For several weeks we have walked with Jesus on his journey to that city, throughout the second half of Luke's gospel. The story today opens by saying he is near Jerusalem, and closes by saying he is about to enter. The parable in the middle tells a story of judgment based on responsible usage of the gifts God entrusts to us.

Similar to yesterday's story of the persecution of Eleazar, today's episode concerns a mother and seven sons forced to eat pork in violation of the Jewish law. They all valiantly remain faithful to God in the face of torture and death. In the psalm we sing, "I in justice shall behold your face; on waking, I shall be content in your presence."

Among the prayers for various needs and occasions are those for oppressors (#45).

■ TODAY IS THE PATRONAL FEAST of Puerto Rico, The Blessed Virgin Mary, Mother of Divine Providence, celebrated as a solemnity on their local calendar. The devotion began with the Barnabites, and its Mass was celebrated on the Saturday before the third Sunday of November. See the *Collection of Masses of the Blessed Virgin Mary* (40).

Argentina transfers the memorial of Elizabeth of Hungary from November 17 to this date.

THU 20 #500 (LMC #228–231)   green
Weekday

Seeing the city of Jerusalem now, Jesus weeps over it because the people have lost their way and enemies threaten to bring war. *Jerusalem* means "city of peace." It still promises God's peace even in the midst of its international struggles.

The first reading skips around between the two books of the Maccabees this week, but it actually makes the story more coherent. Officers enforcing the persecution appeal to the Maccabeean leader Mattathias to end the resistance. Bad idea. Mattathias kills an apostate Jew and rallies the remaining faithful into a band that flees to the mountains and waits. In response we sing about offering praise as a sacrifice to God.

Among the Masses for various needs and occasions is one in time of war or civil disturbance (23).

FRI 21 #501 (LMC #228–231)   white
The Presentation of the Blessed Virgin Mary
MEMORIAL

Entering Jerusalem, Jesus makes his way to the temple where he throws out the traders. His prophetic action announces a sea change in the religious center.

The Maccabees do indeed crush their enemies. They rededicate the temple, celebrating the event for eight days. Their actions gave birth to the observance of Hanukkah. The responsory comes from the First Book of Chronicles, a hymn of praise to God, who holds dominion over all.

■ TODAY'S MEMORIAL: A story of the presentation of Mary appears in one of the apocryphal gospels. Today is the anniversary of the dedication of the basilica of St. Mary the New, in Jerusalem. This date was therefore chosen to honor this otherwise nonbiblical

event in Mary's life. In the Christian east, this day and the day of Mary's conception are regarded as advental "fore-feasts" of the Nativity of the Lord.

The opening prayer is in the sacramentary under November 21. But see more texts in the *Collection of Masses of the Blessed Virgin Mary* (#23: Mary, Temple of the Lord). If you use the first preface for Mary (P 56), you may insert "we celebrate the presentation of the Blessed Virgin Mary."

■ TODAY IS THE PATRONAL FEAST OF ECUADOR, Our Lady of El Quinché, celebrated as a solemnity. A shrine was founded there in 1586.

El Salvador celebrates this as the solemnity of Our Lady of Peace, Patron of the Republic of El Salvador.

SAT 22 #502 (LMC #228–331)   red
Cecilia, martyr (+ 3rd c.?)
MEMORIAL

As his death draws closer, Jesus meets a group of Sadducees who do not believe in the resurrection. They pose an absurd question to him, permitting him to proclaim the living God. Some scribes give him support.

The story of the Maccabees reaches a happy ending of operatic proportions. Antiochus hears that the Jews have retaken the temple, and sees it as a sign that he has sinned. On his deathbed he confesses his evil and bewails the sorrow of his dying in a foreign land. The psalm sings of triumph over enemies.

The fifth preface for weekdays in Ordinary Time (P 41) proclaims the resurrection and the anticipated return of Jesus in glory.

■ TODAY'S SAINT: Cecilia, an early Roman martyr, is patron of church musicians. There is little reliable information about her life, less about her musicianship, but her complete dedication to Christ even

to death will resonate with the dedication felt by many church musicians. Cecilia and the other virgin martyrs are compared in the liturgy to the parable of the bridesmaids who bear their lamps in expectation of the groom.

Use the preface for martyrs. Cecilia is mentioned in Eucharistic Prayer I. You may use other prayers for martyrs to go with the opening prayer for her day, a text which tells virtually nothing of her life because so little can be said. However, since today's memorial is well-loved by many musicians, much can be said about the value of music and the other arts in human life and in the life of the church.

☀23 #161 (LMC #155)   white
Christ the King: Thirty-fourth and Final Sunday in Ordinary Time
SOLEMNITY

ORIENTATION

Today is the last Sunday of Ordinary Time. As the church year comes to its end our thoughts turn to the end of all time. The faithful Christian reflects not with fear but with confident hope that Christ will come again as the supreme ruler over all.

■ IN MEXICO AND THE UNITED STATES, today's optional memorial of the priest and martyr, Saint Miguel Agustín Pro, is not observed this year.

LECTIONARY

To conclude the church year we turn again to John to supply the gospel. The choice will surprise many expecting a text about Jesus reigning as king over all. He is a prisoner on trial before Pilate over the question of his kingship. His kingdom is not of this world.

Throughout his ministry, Jesus frequently referred to himself as the Son of Man. The reference comes from today's first reading from the book of Daniel. He comes on clouds of heaven and receives kingship as all nations serve him. The everlasting dominion of the Son of Man is the dominion Jesus applies to himself. It is a kingdom not of this world. "The Lord is king," we sing in the psalm.

The opening of the book of Revelation has the same vision from Daniel in mind when it says Jesus is coming amid the clouds and every eye will see him. This doxology captures the spirit of today's solemnity, a grand proclamation of the kingship of Jesus Christ.

SACRAMENTARY

The prayers for the day are in the part of the book marked Solemnities of the Lord During Ordinary Time. Christ the King follows the Sacred Heart.

The preface for the day is at P 51. The first solemn blessing for Ordinary Time prays that God will look upon the faithful with kindness (10), but see also the solemn blessing for beginning a new year (3) and for the Passion of the Lord (5).

The entrance antiphon for the celebration comes from Revelation and inspired hymns like "Crown Him With Many Crowns," "All Hail the Power of Jesus' Name" and "To Jesus Christ our Sovereign King." *By Flowing Waters* (296–301) has a complete suite of processional antiphons and psalms. The majestic Canticle of David (I Chronicles 29:10–18) is sung during the communion procession.

OTHER IDEAS

You might end the Sundays of Ordinary Time with evening prayer tonight. Sing again a hymn to Christ the King and ring bells during the *Magnificat* or at the close of the celebration.

As a kind of "Ember Day" observance, the church of the United States recommends setting aside the next three days for deeds of charity, penance and economic justice. See *Catholic Household Blessings and Prayers,* 188–189 for ideas.

Choirs may enjoy learning "Christus vincit" from the *Liber cantualis.*

#503 (LMC #228–231) red

Andrew Dung-Lac (+ 1839), presbyter, martyr, and his companions, martyrs

MON 24

MEMORIAL

Still at the temple, Jesus sees a woman put in two copper coins and is moved by her complete generosity. He praises those who give everything to God, as he himself is about to do.

For the final week of the year we turn to the book of the prophet Daniel. The first half of the book contains stories of the Babylonian and Persian courts. The second half contains apocalyptic revelations with a first person narration. The visions in the latter half of the book seem contemporary with the stories from the books of the Maccabees. The opening chapter introduces Daniel as an Israelite who makes a favorable impression in the Gentile court. All week long the responsory is taken from the same source, a canticle from the book of Daniel, praising the God of Israel. The canticle is quite long, so it is divided among the six days this week. The verses have little to do with the theme of the first reading. They simply present a lovely song from the same book from which the first readings are drawn.

The presidential prayers for Andrew Dung-Lac and companions are in the Sacramentary Supplement of 1994. Use the preface of martyrs (P 66) today.

■ TODAY'S SAINTS: The Catholic church in Vietnam suffered a series of sadistic persecutions between 1745 and 1862. Andrew Dung changed his name to Lac to avoid recognition, but still suffered martyrdom together with another Vietnamese priest, Peter Thi, on December 21, 1839. The emperor who authorized that particular persecution, Minh Mang, believed that Christian missionaries were attempting revolts against him. In 1988, 117 martyrs from several different persecutions were canonized. Ninety-six of them were Vietnamese, 59 were lay people, one of the largest groups of laity to be canonized in history. Only one was a woman, Agnes De (+ 1841). We remember the entire group of martyrs today.

TUE 25

#504 (LMC #228–231) green

Weekday

Although people admire the construction of the temple, Jesus announces that it will all be destroyed. He predicts a dire future of warfare, earthquake and famine.

Daniel interprets a vision for Nebuchadnezzar. He foresees a series of wars that will dismantle the king's rule, and God will establish a kingdom that shall never be destroyed. We sing more verses of praise to God from the canticle of Daniel.

The prayers of Christ the King replaced those for the thirty-fourth week in Ordinary Time yesterday. You can find the presidential prayers for this week right after those for the thirty-third week. See also the sacramentary's prayers for after the harvest (27).

WED 26 #505 (LMC #228–231) green
Weekday

Jesus warns his disciples that they will be persecuted for their loyalty to him. He promises to give them wisdom that will befuddle their adversaries and to preserve them from harm.

Today's first reading gave the English language an expression of doom, "the handwriting is on the wall." When King Belshazzar sees the fingers of a human hand writing on the wall of his palace, Daniel interprets the vision to mean the days of his kingship are numbered. The responsory today continues with verses from the Canticle of Daniel.

The fourth weekday preface for Ordinary Time (P 40) raises a hymn of thankful praise to God.

THU 27 #506 or #943–947 (LMC #228–331) green
Weekday

Thanksgiving Day, U.S.A. / white

ORIENTATION

Throughout the United States, citizens set aside this as a day of thankful prayer. Our church gathers for its eucharist, a celebration with a name that means "thanksgiving."

LECTIONARY

You have a wide selection of readings to choose from. You may even use those assigned for the weekday, but they are not appropriate to the spirit of the day. (Those readings treat the upcoming desolation of Jerusalem and the rescue of Daniel from the lion's den.)

Readings may come from the Masses in thanksgiving or from the appendix to the lectionary. Jesus' cure of the ten lepers, for example, strikes home with many of us who often forget to say thanks.

SACRAMENTARY

The prayers for Thanksgiving Day appear after those for November 30. The well-intentioned patriotism of the recommended preface (P 84) manages to denounce Europe ("the desert") and justify aggression ("destiny"). The previous preface may make a better choice. Or use the fourth version of the eucharistic prayer for various needs and occasions, "Jesus, the Compassion of God," with its own preface.

The *Book of Blessings,* 58, uses as a greeting, "May the Lord, who fills you with his bounty, be with you always."

OTHER IDEAS

Encourage the assembly to bring food for the hungry today. Stock the parish food pantry or give the groceries to a neighborhood food bank.

An order of blessing Thanksgiving food is in the *Book of Blessings,* 58. The *Book of Common Prayer* has a litany of thanksgiving (836–387).

Hymns may include "Come, Ye Thankful People, Come"; "We Plow the Fields"; "We Gather Together"; and "For the Beauty of the Earth." "Father, We Thank Thee" comes from the *Didache* prayer for the eucharist. Frank Schoen's responsorial psalm for Thanksgiving is "May God Have Pity on Us" (GIA).

A table prayer for use at home is in *Catholic Household Blessings and Prayers,* 200.

FRI 28 #507 (LMC #228–231) green
Weekday

In the parable of the fig tree, Jesus expects his disciples to be able to read the signs that God is near. His words, the words of life we have heard all year, will never pass away.

Moving to the second half of the book of Daniel, we hear the full apocalyptic vision whose abridgment served as the first reading for Christ the King. Four immense beasts are no match for the coming of the Son of Man. Human nations are no match for the reign of Jesus. We sing more verses from the canticle of Daniel.

Consider the prayers among the votive Masses for the Holy Name of Jesus (4).

SAT 29 #508 (LMC #423) green
Weekday

Optional memorial of the Blessed Virgin Mary / white ▪ We close the series of gospels from Luke and the entire liturgical year with Jesus' admonition to be on the watch and pray constantly to stand secure before the Son of Man.

Daniel, who interpreted visions in the first half of the book, has one of his own. The last of the beasts seems very powerful, but it represents a mighty kingdom that also will fade at the coming of the Most High. All week long the canticle of Daniel has invoked all creation to praise God. The litany of created things reaches a climax today as the song calls on people, the faithful of Israel, to praise God forever.

Prayers from the Mass for a happy death (46) might bring the year to an appropriate close.

■ IF YOU CELEBRATE THE MEMORIAL OF MARY TODAY, consider Mary, Gate of Heaven (46), from the *Collection of Masses of the Blessed Virgin Mary.*

JUNE 15, 2003
The Holy Trinity

God's Story
Deuteronomy 4:32–34, 39–40
"Did anything so great ever happen before?"

EVERY family has its own unique story. Some speak of the immigration of their forebears. Others trace their ancestry back many generations within the place where they live. Some have endured great hardship. Others have received countless blessings. Every family has stories that make it different from every other family.

On his way to the promised land, Moses reminded his people of their story. They used to live in Egypt, but by many signs and wonders, and by war, they left their place of slavery and stood poised to enter a new home. They shared ancestry, persecution, victory, freedom and a long journey. Those events had made them the unique family they now were.

But there was something more about their story. God played a central role. God spoke to them. God claimed them. God worked the wonders that brought them freedom. They could not tell their own family story without also telling a story of God.

God has played a central role in our story, too. When you review the history of your family and your parish, where has God been active? How has God shown power and presence? How has God shown love?

Written by Paul Turner. © 2002 Archdiocese of Chicago, Liturgy Training Publications; 1-800-933-1800; www.ltp.org.

JUNE 22, 2003
The Body and Blood of Christ

The Blood of the Covenant
Exodus 24:3–8
"Moses took the blood and sprinkled it on the people."

To drink the blood of Christ is to perform a strong act of faith. Drinking human blood would be repulsive in any culture. But drinking divine blood is an act of faith.

Jesus specifically asked us to do this. "Take and drink," he said. "This is my blood." And, "If you do not drink my blood you have no life in you." These are strong words.

Like Abraham and others before him did, Moses used blood as a sign of the covenant between Israel and God. After relating God's commands to the people, they all answered with one voice, "We will do everything that the Lord has told us." Moses had some young men slaughter young bulls as a peace offering. He

sprinkled some of the blood on an altar. He sprinkled more of it on the people. Blood, the symbol of life, united the people with God in a committed covenant.

Moses told the people, "This is the blood of the covenant." Jesus told those gathered at the Last Supper, "This is the blood of the new and everlasting covenant."

When we drink the blood of Christ, we drink the source of life. We make firm our commitment with God. We say in our sip, "We will do everything that the Lord has told us."

Written by Paul Turner. © 2002 Archdiocese of Chicago, Liturgy Training Publications; 1-800-933-1800; www.ltp.org.

JUNE 29, 2003
Saints Peter and Paul

God Never Gives Up on Us
Acts 12:1–11
"The chains fell from Peter's wrists."

SOME of the stories about Peter are not complimentary. Peter tried to talk Jesus out of suffering. He refused to have his feet washed at the Last Supper. He denied Jesus three times later that night. Peter made a lot of mistakes.

The story of Peter's miraculous release from prison is all the more remarkable, given this background. The story takes place after the resurrection, at Passover time. King Herod persecuted Christians and discovered that this pleased their enemies. He had the apostle James killed by the sword. Then he arrested Peter, chained him up and locked him in jail behind an iron gate and watched by 16 guards. All this happened without a trial.

At night, an angel appeared to Peter, broke the chains, and led him to freedom. Peter just assumed he was dreaming. But when the angel left, Peter was free.

God never gave up on Peter. Even though Peter had sinned many times during his years of discipleship, God was always ready to give him another chance and to reward him for persistently growing in faith.

You have confessed your sins before God. When did God last send you an angel to free you from your chains?

JULY 6, 2003
Fourteenth Sunday in Ordinary Time

Speaking When No One Listens
Ezekiel 2:2–5
"Hard of face and obstinate of heart are they to whom I am sending you."

WHENEVER you have something to say, not everyone is going to listen. Some people will roll their eyes. Others will wait until you're done and then change the subject. You don't always get the admiring audience you want.

For some reason, this never stops God from putting passion into the human heart. Our faith becomes a part of us. We link our identity to it. When we see someone challenging something we believe in, we cannot keep quiet. We have to speak up.

It feels good to say what we think. It feels good to let the strongest beliefs inside us have voice and air. It feels good to have other people know what matters the most to us.

But some people don't listen. They do not heed the word we speak. They patronize us with kind looks or light applause.

But God keeps putting the word into the human heart, and we keep speaking up.

When Ezekiel spoke God's word to people who were hard of face and obstinate of heart, God knew the word might not change them. But some good would come. "They shall know that a prophet has been among them."

Even if people do not listen to our words, they know that a prophet was there.

JULY 13, 2003
Fifteenth Sunday in Ordinary Time

God-given Words
Amos 7:12–15
"Off with you, visionary!"

"**G**ET out of here!" No one likes to hear those harsh words. Wherever we go, we like the assurance that the place where we have arrived is hospitable. Sometimes we trespass. Sometimes we say offensive words. Sometimes we perform an action that separates us from the community. If we upset the host, we may hear those awful words, "Get out of here!"

That was the command that Amaziah the priest of Bethel leveled against the prophet Amos. Amos came from Tekoa of Judah in the southern part of the kingdom. At God's command he traveled to Bethel in the north to prophesy. He warned the people of God's judgment against them. The local priest didn't like hearing the message Amos brought. So Amaziah gave Amos a blunt and derisive retort: "Go home. Get out of Bethel. Go back to Judah. Prophesy there. Leave us alone."

There was one problem. Prophesying in Bethel wasn't Amos's idea in the first place. It was God's idea. God sent Amos from Judah to Bethel to bring divine judgment on the people.

Sometimes when people tell us to leave them alone, they are wrong. If God has given us words to speak, we stay and deliver them.

Written by Paul Turner. © 2002 Archdiocese of Chicago, Liturgy Training Publications; 1-800-933-1800; www.ltp.org.

JULY 20, 2003
Sixteenth Sunday in Ordinary Time

Uniting the Flock
Jeremiah 23:1–6
"Woe to the shepherds who scatter the flock."

WHEN parents hand children over to other caretakers for the day, they rightly expect that those in authority will dutifully watch the kids. When religious and civil leaders accepted responsibility for the people of Israel, God rightly expected that they would watch the people with care.

It didn't happen. They failed. Through Jeremiah, God told the leaders of Israel that they were like hired shepherds who scattered the sheep and drove them away.

Several consequences resulted. God punished the irresponsible leaders, gathered the remnant of the chosen people back together, and appointed new leaders who would do the job right. God also promised something more. God promised to raise up a righteous shoot to David, a king who would govern wisely and do what is just. We Christians believe that that prophecy was fulfilled in the coming of Jesus, who rules as a righteous king and a good shepherd.

God is no happier with bad leadership than parents are when caretakers mistreat their children.

Whom has God placed in your care? If God were to assess your leadership, how would you score? If God could use you to unite rather than scatter, what actions would you take?

Written by Paul Turner. © 2002 Archdiocese of Chicago, Liturgy Training Publications; 1-800-933-1800; www.ltp.org.

JULY 27, 2003
Seventeenth Sunday in Ordinary Time

Much from Little
2 Kings 4:42–44
"A man brought Elisha twenty barley loaves."

ALMOST any Christian can tell you the story of Jesus' miracle of the loaves. But very few can tell you the story of Elisha's miracle of the loaves.

Elisha was one of the first prophets to appear in the Bible. The Second Book of Kings records a series of ten legends about Elisha's power. One of them concerns bread.

In this story, a man travels a distance to bring the prophet a gift of 20 barley loaves and fresh grain. Elisha told him to give it to the people. The man objected that there would not be enough for 100 people. Elisha told him to give it anyway.

There was enough. And there was bread left over.

When John tells the story of Jesus' miracle of the loaves, he includes some details that remind us of this story about Elisha. The loaves were made of barley. And after everyone had eaten, there was bread left over.

When Jesus' story reminds us of Elisha's story, we realize that the same God has been at work all along, choosing prophets to speak the divine word, and providing food for body and spirit in abundance.

If what you have to give is only a little, God can use it to do a lot.

AUGUST 3, 2003
Eighteenth Sunday in Ordinary Time

What's This?
Exodus 16:2–4, 12–15
"I will now rain down bread from heaven for you."

MANNA probably didn't look very appetizing, but it was the only food the Israelites could find in the desert—besides quail, that is.

The dramatic exodus from Egypt became a dim memory for people who escaped destruction by the waters of the Red Sea only to face the unforgiving desolation of a long trip on aching legs through the dry desert. They did what any of us would do under the circumstances. They grumbled about it.

They had no bread. Grain won't grow in deserts. Water is hard to find. There's plenty of heat for baking, but nobody could make fresh bread.

Except for God, that is. In the morning they discovered something like bread on the ground. With hungry, disappointed, fearful eyes, they looked at the substance and asked the question many children have asked, suspicious of something unrecognizable on the dinner plate: What's this?

So that's what they called it. "What's-this?" "Manna."

Crossing the desert days of life, we may take no pleasure in the food we eat, the companions we share, or the place where we live. God provides for us in ways that may not be appetizing, but at least they offer rescue.

AUGUST 10, 2003
Nineteenth Sunday in Ordinary Time

Food for the Journey
1 Kings 19:4–8
"Elijah prayed for death."

THE reason Elijah was hungry is that he was traveling through the desert. The reason he was traveling through the desert is that Jezebel was chasing him. The reason Jezebel was chasing him is that she wanted to kill him. The reason she wanted to kill him is that Elijah had just embarrassed the priests of Baal, whose god couldn't send rain on command and Elijah's God could.

God got him into this mess, and at one point, Elijah gave up. He sat exhausted in the desert and prayed for death. God gave him a snack instead.

An angel appeared with cake and water. It doesn't sound like much, but on the strength of that food, Elijah walked 40 days and 40 nights more. Then he climbed the mountain of God.

There, he discovered God not in the wind, earthquake or fire, but in silence.

On days when we would like to give up, when we can't figure out the mess we are in, when we have wished for more useful companions, when we feel hungry and lost, God finds us. In the simplest of meals, we receive strength to meet God at last on the holy mountain of life, shrouded in silence.

Written by Paul Turner. © 2002 Archdiocese of Chicago, Liturgy Training Publications; 1-800-933-1800; www.ltp.org.

AUGUST 15, 2003
The Assumption of the Blessed Virgin Mary

The Ark of the Covenant
1 Chronicles 15:3–4, 15–16; 16:1–2
"David pitched a tent for the ark."

CHRISTIANS honor Mary as the mother of Jesus and as our mother. She was the chosen vessel of our redemption. She agreed to bear the child who would save the world. The Catholic church believes that God has taken Mary, body and soul, into heaven.

One way of explaining this belief is to consider the story of the ark of the covenant. The ark was a portable shrine that represented the divine presence for Israel. With the ark in their midst, God was in their midst.

The ark resembled an ornate chest. Among the sacred objects it enclosed was some of the manna from Israel's sojourn in the desert. Eventually David prepared a place for it within a specially designated tent.

One of Mary's titles is "the Ark of the New Covenant." As the original ark became a symbol of God's presence, so has Mary. As the original ark contained manna, so Mary enclosed the Son of God, the Bread of Life, in her womb. As David prepared a home for the original ark, so Jesus, descendent of David, prepared a place for Mary. As the original ark found a home in a special tent, so God brought Mary to her final home in heaven.

Written by Paul Turner. © 2002 Archdiocese of Chicago, Liturgy Training Publications; 1-800-933-1800; www.ltp.org.

AUGUST 17, 2003
Twentieth Sunday in Ordinary Time

You Are What You Eat
Proverbs 9:1–6
"Wisdom calls, 'Come, eat of my food.'"

PEOPLE who reflect on their diet learn a lot about themselves. They discover their passions and temptations. They learn what they cannot tolerate and what they cannot avoid. They discover the effect their choice of food has on others. It may hurt the family farmer and help global distributors.

People who do not eat healthy food pay a price more dear than the grocery bill. You are what you eat.

The book of Proverbs envisions divine Wisdom as a woman who has prepared a lavish meal. She has built a house and spread a table within it. She invites to this table not those who are hungry for physical food, but those who are simple. Those who lack understanding may come to this meal.

Those who dine at Wisdom's table nourish their mind, not their belly.

The meal we share at church is small: a bit of bread, a sip of wine. But this food and drink is much more. It is the body and blood of Christ, the source of all wisdom.

When we make the eucharist a part of our lives, we grow in wisdom. We make room for God.

When we eat the bread of life, we become what we eat. We are the body of Christ.

Written by Paul Turner. © 2002 Archdiocese of Chicago, Liturgy Training Publications; 1-800-933-1800; www.ltp.org.

AUGUST 24, 2003
Twenty-first Sunday in Ordinary Time

An Uncompromised Choice
Joshua 24:1–2a, 15–17, 18b
"As for me and my household, we will serve the LORD."

SOONER or later you have to decide. Faced with a difficult decision, you have to decide what to do.

Our choices reveal what we really prize. Before making a choice, then, it helps to review our values. Which choice gives the strongest affirmation to the principles we hold dear? If we take a different choice, we doom ourselves to living with compromised values. We are not who we thought we were. We hold other things precious.

When Joshua gathered all the tribes of Israel at Shechem, he told the people they had to make a choice. God brought them up out of the land of Egypt, performed miracles before their very eyes and protected them along their entire journey.

This God wanted to be their only God. They no longer serve other gods. They had to decide.

Joshua said, "As for me and my household, we will serve the LORD."

The people answered the same.

Before you make a difficult choice, think about how God has brought you to this day. God brought you and your family to safety, performed miracles before your very eyes, and protected you thus far. Remember, then make your choice.

"As for me and my household, we will serve the LORD."

Written by Paul Turner. © 2002 Archdiocese of Chicago, Liturgy Training Publications; 1-800-933-1800; www.ltp.org.

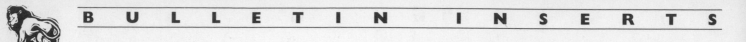

AUGUST 31, 2003
Twenty-second Sunday in Ordinary Time

Follow Directions
Deuteronomy 4:1–2, 6–8
"I am teaching you to observe the commandments that you may live."

IF you follow the directions good things will happen. But if you take short cuts or disobey the rules, you will fail.

When Moses read the statutes and decrees of God before the people, he told them to follow the directions—the statutes of the covenant. If they did, they would enter the promised land. They would give evidence of their intelligence. And God would remain close to them.

If the people did not follow directions, Moses could not promise anything.

Throughout their relationship, God asked Israel only to keep the covenant. When Israel strayed, God sent prophets to remind the people.

God never abandoned Israel, but remained in relationship with them.

Many times we do not follow God's directions. Sometimes we think they are too hard or that they won't give us the results we want. But the commands of God remain firm for a reason. They bring the best results.

The commands of God are not hard to find nor difficult to remember. They are as close as our Bible and as familiar as friends. They signify God's love for us. They demonstrate God's desire to be present to us.

When we follow directions, when we bend our will to match God's will, good things will happen.

Written by Paul Turner. © 2002 Archdiocese of Chicago, Liturgy Training Publications; 1-800-933-1800; www.ltp.org.

SEPTEMBER 7, 2003
Twenty-third Sunday in Ordinary Time

Fear Not
Isaiah 35:4–7a
"Be strong, fear not! Here is your God."

THE uncontrollable forces of nature cause uncontrollable fear. If we cannot overcome them, they can make us fear the future. A natural disaster can cause destruction and harm. If we cannot control it, we fear it could happen again, and the fear can be crippling, as serious as any disaster.

We experience fear when we do not understand the sources of infirmity, or when we cannot control the future.

God spoke through Isaiah to Israel, "Fear not." The blind, the deaf, the lame and the mute suffer uncontrollable infirmities. But God is stronger than disability, and God is coming to save.

The desert yielded no water. It offered no chance for crops to grow or life to thrive. But God is stronger than death, and God is coming to save.

In moments of fear, it may help to remember the source of our strength. God is the author of creation. God is our destiny in redemption. All creation suffers weakness, and imperfection causes fear. But creation is not equal to the Creator. The Creator knows no weakness. The Creator knows no fear.

The fear we feel need not overpower us. The one who made us, sustains us and calls us home gives us strength when we are weak.

Written by Paul Turner. © 2002 Archdiocese of Chicago, Liturgy Training Publications; 1-800-933-1800; www.ltp.org.

SEPTEMBER 14, 2003
The Triumph of the Cross

Staring Death in the Face
Numbers 21:4b–9
"Moses made a bronze serpent and mounted it on a pole."

IT is hard to look death in the eye. We cannot bear to look at the remains of one we loved. We cannot think too long or hard about our own mortality. But those who keep death before their eyes can make peace with life.

However, staring death in the face comes with a risk. It can cripple a soul. It can poison the heart. What is the balance between facing death and embracing life?

When the Israelites in the desert complained to Moses about the terrible food on their journey, they faced a new peril. Poisonous serpents bit them. Many people died. Moses appealed to God. Strangely, God told Moses to make a serpent out of bronze and to mount it on a pole.

Those who looked at the bronze serpent lived. They had to look death in the eye. Once they did, they were saved.

The cross of Christ is a thing of beauty, but also a thing of fear. It reminds us of our mortality, but it promises redemption for those who raise their eyes, look upon it, believe in it and live.

Written by Paul Turner. © 2002 Archdiocese of Chicago, Liturgy Training Publications; 1-800-933-1800; www.ltp.org.

SEPTEMBER 21, 2003
Twenty-fifth Sunday in Ordinary Time

The Wicked Reveal the Just
Wisdom 2:12, 17–20
"The wicked say: Let us beset the just one."

FOR churchgoers who strive to do what is right, it is hard to understand why some people strive to do what is wrong. But those people exist. They steal to support a drug habit. They hack websites to cause confusion. They lie. They murder. They have no respect for human life.

Malicious people have been around throughout the history of the world. Jesus predicted that his life would end in their hands. Jeremiah faced them in his ministry.

Jeremiah overheard the collusion of the wicked. They targeted him because he was just, and righteous people were obnoxious to them.

Whenever the just reproach the wicked, the two sides grow further apart. The just become more just and the wicked conceive more wickedness in retaliation.

To the untrained eye, evil people seem to win. They achieve the wrong they try to do, sometimes with spectacular success. But to eyes of faith, the wicked never win. Agents of death and destruction, they are eternally conquered by the God of might. Their misdeeds reveal the goodness of the just.

Jeremiah did not live to see the final victory that Jesus achieved over death. Jeremiah lived to see revilement. In the light of the resurrection, we know now what prophets only hoped for: that wickedness can never overcome what is good.

Written by Paul Turner. © 2002 Archdiocese of Chicago, Liturgy Training Publications; 1-800-933-1800; www.ltp.org.

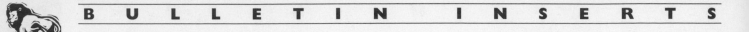

SEPTEMBER 28, 2003
Twenty-sixth Sunday in Ordinary Time

The Annoying Choices of the Spirit
Numbers 11:25–29
"Are you jealous of God's choice?"

WHEN people overstep their boundaries, we usually object. We don't need the inexpert help of well-meaning busybodies who get in the way.

The problem is especially strong when people step into our own area of expertise. If you have devoted your life to a craft or skill, it's not right for some amateur to take more attention than you receive. If you trust your own advisors, you don't need help from someone who does not fully understand the situation.

However, the Holy Spirit has a very annoying habit of offering us help through people who otherwise shouldn't have much influence at all.

Take Eldad and Medad, for example. In the book of Numbers, God sent some of the spirit that was on Moses to the 70 elders, and they prophesied. But Eldad and Medad were not in the gathering at the time. The spirit came to rest on them anyway.

When Eldad and Medad came back to the camp, they prophesied, too, but a young man complained about it to Moses. They had overstepped their boundaries. "Stop them," he pleaded.

But Moses wished that God would send the spirit of prophecy on all the people.

Sometimes God speaks to us through people we'd rather not listen to at all.

Written by Paul Turner. © 2002 Archdiocese of Chicago, Liturgy Training Publications; 1-800-933-1800; www.ltp.org.

OCTOBER 5, 2003
Twenty-seventh Sunday in Ordinary Time

Try, Try Again
Genesis 2:18–24
"The LORD God built the rib up into a woman."

GOD keeps trying. If things don't work out the way God wants them to, our creator never gives up. God keeps trying.

The book of Genesis tells the story of God's attempt to create a partner for the solitary man. God tried everything. Out of the ground came various wild animals. Out of the air came various birds. God brought each of them to the man, hoping one might make a good partner. The man gave names to all of them. But none proved to be a suitable partner.

You can almost sense the disappointment that God and the created man must have felt. The earth is filled with wondrous creatures. In the view of the writer of the book of Genesis, all those creatures were made for delight. But none ultimately satisfied.

Finally, God reached not into the ground, not into the air, but into the man himself, withdrew a rib, and fashioned it into a woman. God kept trying.

When the man saw her, he recognized that she was his partner.

God desires our happiness. Sometimes we move from friend to friend, house to house, school to school, and job to job, looking for the right source of satisfaction. God never gives up on us. God keeps trying.

Written by Paul Turner. © 2002 Archdiocese of Chicago, Liturgy Training Publications; 1-800-933-1800; www.ltp.org.

OCTOBER 12, 2003
Twenty-eighth Sunday in Ordinary Time

The Desire for Wisdom
Wisdom 7:7–11
"All good things together came to me in Wisdom's company."

THERE are many things we can possess. Advertisers remind us of this hundreds of times every day. When we read the morning news, ads borrow the attention of our eyes. When we watch television, go to the movies, drive the highway, go to the ballgame, or pick up a program, we see ads suggesting that the purchase of certain goods can make us happy, ads encouraging us to shop.

Testimony from the book of Wisdom speaks in favor of something else, though. The speaker asks for possessions, but not for things. The speaker asks for prudence and a spirit of wisdom.

Many of us have other goals. We work hard at our job to earn what we need to pay for home and food. We work hard in school to earn the grades that win us a degree and the chance for a job. But the book of Wisdom envisions something else. It envisions people working hard to learn God's wisdom first.

Throughout this past week, what did you shop for? What kind of possessions did you want to bring home? What sacrifices are you making to obtain what you desire?

Do you desire something deeper? Do you desire prudence? A spirit of wisdom? What sacrifices are you making to fulfill those desires?

Written by Paul Turner. © 2002 Archdiocese of Chicago, Liturgy Training Publications; 1-800-933-1800; www.ltp.org.

OCTOBER 19, 2003
Twenty-ninth Sunday in Ordinary Time

Communion in Suffering
Isaiah 53:10–11
"My servant shall bear the guilt of many."

THE mystery of human suffering haunts every life. No one likes to endure suffering. We feel better about it if it produces some good. But for those who suffer needlessly and pointlessly, life seems bitter.

The prophet Isaiah speaks words that offer little consolation. "The Lord was pleased to crush him in infirmity." That sounds like our worst nightmare. It sounds like God took pleasure in crushing someone with illness. It appears to support the perverse belief that God takes delight in human suffering.

But Isaiah goes on. God has given a task to those burdened with miseries. If they give their lives as an offering, they shall obtain their reward. God can work wonders through the heavy-hearted who place themselves at the service of others.

If someone else has the same sorrows we have, we can give them hope. Our weakness shows them that they are not alone. All humans share the same condition, a condition that leads to life through death.

Not everyone can bear burdens with hope. But infirmity need not bring despair. It can be a source of connection with others, an occasion for insight into the meaning of life, and a glimpse at the pleasure of God.

Written by Paul Turner. © 2002 Archdiocese of Chicago, Liturgy Training Publications; 1-800-933-1800; www.ltp.org.

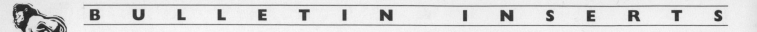

OCTOBER 26, 2003
Thirtieth Sunday in Ordinary Time

Homecoming
Jeremiah 31:7–9
"Behold, I will bring them back."

THE survival of the fittest is a merciless principle of life. It bestows more offspring to those who are stronger, swifter and smarter than to those who are weaker.

In the lives of species, this principle eliminates those who cannot compete. In the marketplace, it impoverishes those who can be duped. But in the spiritual life, it does not work at all. In the eyes of God, the fit and the lame both survive.

When Israel went into exile, they lost homeland and hope. After years of suffering, they reflected more deeply on their covenant, and eventually God brought them back.

But God brought back not only the fittest. The healthiest of mind, body and spirit did not return to Jerusalem alone. It must have been quite a procession. The blind and the lame marched in the midst of the remnant who returned. Those offering care and those needing care took their place within the immense throng. God brought them all back on a level road, so that none might stumble.

In many ways we are all unfit to enter the house of God. Our sins make us feel unworthy.

But God has opened the doors. We may be blind to grace. We may be lame in charity. But God has made us filled with hope in receiving the love that heaven so bountifully bestows.

Written by Paul Turner. © 2002 Archdiocese of Chicago, Liturgy Training Publications; 1-800-933-1800; www.ltp.org.

NOVEMBER 1, 2003
All Saints

Seeing into Heaven
Revelation 7:2–4, 9–14
"I had a vision of a great multitude."

A lot of the good you do goes unnoticed. You care for family. You donate to charity. You pray for the needy. Perhaps you perform civic services that few people ever see. You might even do some things in secret precisely to avoid the attention that a reward would bring. Your satisfaction is often its own reward.

You believe that God sees, and that is enough.

You are not alone. The good that many people do can never be fully rewarded. Society owes a debt of gratitude to everyday heroes who improve life for the masses by performing the simplest of deeds for the sake of giving care.

Imagine that multitude of good people gathered together. Imagine them before the throne of the Lamb, worshiping God. Imagine them wearing as reward the uniform of heaven— white garments washed in the blood of the Lamb.

That is the vision that John sees in the book of Revelation. The throng of the blessed gathers to give praise, only to be counted among those who survived the trials of life and persevered in their faith.

On All Saints' Day we remember the numberless who host. They inspire us to continue the good we do, even if no one notices.

Written by Paul Turner. © 2002 Archdiocese of Chicago, Liturgy Training Publications; 1-800-933-1800; www.ltp.org.

NOVEMBER 2, 2003
All Souls

In God's Hand
Wisdom 3:1–9
"The souls of the just are in the hand of God."

EVEN if we know that someone we loved was dying, death catches us off guard. No one feels the grief we feel in exactly the same way. Sorrow leads some people to deeper levels of despair, but for others it gives way to hope.

The book of Wisdom was written before the birth of Jesus. The writer faced the same questions we face about death. But the writer had no knowledge of the resurrection. Even so, the book offers remarkable wisdom for all who grieve.

The book of Wisdom says the foolish see death differently than the wise do. The foolish see the death of the just as an affliction, as a complete destruction. But the wise know otherwise.

The wise know that the souls of the just are in the hand of God, where no torment shall touch them. Those souls are at peace.

Some people suffer greatly in life, but Wisdom believes that God uses their suffering as a trial, to discover who is worthy. God proves people like gold in a furnace. Then God gathers them up like a sacrificial offering.

We will always miss our loved ones who die. But their death can be a sign of hope to those who believe in the providence of God.

Written by Paul Turner. © 2002 Archdiocese of Chicago, Liturgy Training Publications; 1-800-933-1800; www.ltp.org.

NOVEMBER 9, 2003
The Dedication of the Lateran Basilica in Rome

Waters of Life
Ezekiel 47:1–2, 8–9, 12
"I saw water flowing out from beneath the temple."

WHEN you offer water to someone who is thirsty, you give more than a drink. You give a kindness that can bring peace to the recipient, a peace that inspires other acts of charity. Sometimes a dribble of water can gush into a river of good will.

Ezekiel envisions a trickle of water streaming from the Temple in Jerusalem. This sweet water swells into a mighty river that transforms the salty sea into a place of healing and life. In this vision, the Temple of God provides the source of life and transformation.

We hear this reading on the day we remember the dedication of the cathedral church of Rome, the basilica of St. John Lateran. From that temple has streamed a river of life in the sacraments, the community, and the mission of the church around the world. That river splashes into your church and your home, where you have received the Spirit of God and offered its refreshment to others in need.

Imagine your church as Ezekiel's Temple. How does the water of life stream from it? How does it touch the homes of your community? How does it reach out to the city? To the needy of the world?

Written by Paul Turner. © 2002 Archdiocese of Chicago, Liturgy Training Publications; 1-800-933-1800; www.ltp.org.

NOVEMBER 16, 2003
Thirty-third Sunday in Ordinary Time

Rise and Shine
Daniel 12:1–3
"Many who sleep in the dust of the earth shall awake."

DEATH scares people. It even scares believers. It shouldn't, of course, because believers hope in a life of bliss with our redeemer. But death still scares us.

Like students awaiting a report card, like employees awaiting a performance review, the faithful believe that God will judge our acts after we die. Nothing will be concealed. God may be merciful, but God is also just.

The vision of the judgment that appears in the book of Daniel strikes as much fear as hope. Michael, the archangel, the prince and guardian of God's people, will come at a time of unsurpassed distress. Those who inhabit the graves of the earth will awaken. Some will live forever, but others will be in everlasting horror and disgrace. That is Daniel's vision.

Those who escape the tribulation are those whose names are found written in the book. The hope of every believer is that his or her name will show up there.

In daily prayer, many people review what they have done and place it in judgment before God. God's Spirit can help scrutinize our actions each day. Then the day of reckoning will come as no surprise. Those who lead others to justice shall be like the stars forever.

Written by Paul Turner. © 2002 Archdiocese of Chicago, Liturgy Training Publications; 1-800-933-1800; www.ltp.org.

NOVEMBER 23, 2003
Our Lord Jesus Christ the King

The Source of Security
Daniel 7:13–14
"I saw one like the Son of man coming on the clouds of heaven."

EVERY day we seek security. We fasten the safety belts in our cars. We set alarms to prevent theft. We help watch our neighbors' homes. We take care of our health. We take what measures we can to help us feel secure.

There are few guarantees. Tragedy can befall even those who take precautions. The things of this world can provide supports for safety, but none of them can make us totally secure.

Security ultimately comes from God alone. The power of God is stronger than any theft, accident or injury. It rules over illness and death. The power that created us will re-create us in love.

Jesus, our Savior, had a favorite image for himself. He called himself the Son of Man. He took that expression from the book of Daniel, where the prophet envisioned one like a Son of Man coming on the clouds of heaven. He receives dominion, glory and kingship. All nations served him. His dominion extended over all lands and times.

In borrowing that image, Jesus gave his disciples a message of hope. He himself would lose security, suffering torment and death. But he himself would reign over all.

The church year ends with a vision of hope for each of us who seeks security: the coming of the Son of Man.

Written by Paul Turner. © 2002 Archdiocese of Chicago, Liturgy Training Publications; 1-800-933-1800; www.ltp.org.

These inserts may be reproduced in parish bulletins; the copyright notice must appear with the text.

■ WHAT FOLLOWS ARE LISTS OF TITLES that communities have found useful in preparing the liturgy. Your favorites may be missing, but the list is a start. Each community needs to keep up to date with the vast world of liturgical literature. Many parishes have found it helpful to elect or appoint someone to serve as "librarian" who maintains published resources, orders new materials, gets on mailing lists, and devises a proposed budget for each project.

Here is a list of abbreviations of publishers. A more complete list of publishers with addresses follows on page 255.

CB: Catholic Book Publishing Co.
CCCB: Canadian Conference of Catholic Bishops
ICEL: International Committee for English in the Liturgy
LP: The Liturgical Press
LTP: Liturgy Training Publications
USCC: United States Catholic Conference
WLP: World Library Publications

LITURGY DOCUMENTS, COMMENTARIES AND HISTORY OF LITURGICAL REFORM

The Code of Canon Law (1983, Canon Law Society of America) contains a significant amount of legislation pertaining to the liturgy.

Documents of Christian Worship: Descriptive and Interpretive Sources (1992, White, James F., Westminster John Knox). This thorough compilation is traced from the beginning (scripture, fathers, councils) and across the traditions (Jewish, Catholic, Orthodox, Anglican, Reformed), and grouped by "area": space, time, sacraments, word, etc. It is a look within but beyond Roman Catholicism toward where we have come from and what we have in common, as well as where we differ.

Documents on the Liturgy, 1963–1979: Conciliar, Papal and Curial Texts (1982, LP). A fine translation and compilation of everything official. The massive index makes this a gold mine of information.

The Liturgy Documents: A Parish Resource (1991, LTP). The most recent translations of Roman liturgical documents, along with documents of the Bishops' Committee on the Liturgy. An introduction by a liturgical scholar is provided for each document.

The Liturgy Documents: A Parish Resource, Volume 2 (1999, LTP). A companion to the first volume, which includes *Dies Domini, Plenty Good Room* and *Comme le prévoit.*

Bugnini, Annibale. *The Reform of the Liturgy (1948–1975)* (1992, LP). The man who worked on the reform of Holy Week under Pius XII went on to be one of the principal, practical architects of the massive reform that followed Vatican II. Rite by rite, meeting by meeting, Archbishop Bugnini takes us through the high points and low points, collaboration and intrigue that attended this tumultuous time of which we are the heirs.

Fenwick, John, and Bryan Spinks. *Worship in Transition: The Liturgical Movement in the Twentieth Century* (1995, Continuum). This is meant to give a sense of historical context to those engaged in the liturgical enterprise at the end of the twentieth century. Written by two Anglicans from England, this concise and comprehensive volume gives us a sense of the liturgical movement beyond Roman Catholicism and outside the United States. A particularly helpful chapter is entitled "Snapshots of the Movement in North America."

Hughes, Kathleen, RSCJ, ed. *How Firm a Foundation Volume I: Voices of the Early Liturgical Movement* (1990, LTP). A history of the decades of wisdom, humor, patience and frustration before Vatican II.

Tuzik, Robert L. *How Firm a Foundation Volume II: Leaders of the Liturgical Movement* (1990, LTP). A book about the lives and work of more than forty pioneers and recent leaders from the last three generations.

GENERAL LITURGY RESOURCES

Finn, Peter, and James Schellman, eds. *Shaping English Liturgy* (1990, Pastoral Press). An investigation of the challenges and processes by which ICEL is crafting a contemporary vernacular liturgy for the church. Especially timely in light of present debate on and future publication of ICEL's revised sacramentary.

Huck, Gabe, ed. *A Liturgy Sourcebook* (1994, LTP). This volume contains favorite texts of artists, pastors, scholars, musicians and educators, all about liturgy.

Irwin, Kevin W. *Context and Text: Method in Liturgical Theology* (1994, LP). The author begins with a historical overview of the relationship between liturgy and theology. His thesis: context is text—text shapes context. All those seriously engaged in liturgical planning and ministry will find the subsequent chapters translating theory into practical and pastoral considerations. Especially helpful are Irwin's observations about liturgical texts (euchology) and the liturgical arts.

Jones, Cheslyn, Geoffrey Wainwright, Edward Yarnold, and Paul Bradshaw. *The Study of Liturgy,* Revised Edition (1992, Oxford). An encyclopedic presentation of issues in liturgy, Catholic and Protestant. Extensive illustrations and bibliography. Good background on various elements of calendar, eucharist, vesture, etc.

Leonard, John K., and Nathan D. Mitchell. *The Postures of the Assembly during the Eucharistic Prayer* (1994, LTP). A scholarly, yet practical discussion, in light of the ongoing debate that is sure to continue in the United States beyond the revised sacramentary's publication. Chapter titles bespeak the breadth of presentation:

The Anthropology of Posture and Gesture, The Sociological and Religious Significance of Standing and Kneeling, Ritual Posture in the Context of Meals and the Meal Ministry of Jesus, Posture during the Eucharistic Prayer.

Mazar, Peter. *To Crown the Year: Decorating the Church through the Seasons* (1995, LTP). This resource will help those responsible for church decorations to make a wide variety of seasonal choices. Included are "pep talks" to get a team in the right spirit for thinking about the seasons.

Ryan, Thomas G. *The Sacristy Manual* (1993, LTP). The finest (and nearly only) book on the market that covers the history and use and appointing of the many materials and settings required by the liturgical rites. Those who prepare the liturgy will find the book's many checklists handy.

Schmemann, Alexander. *Introduction to Theology* (1966, 1986, St. Vladimir's Seminary Press). This is an Orthodox theologian's masterful attempt, many years back now, to do what Irwin does more extensively, from the Roman Catholic and contemporary perspective, in *Context and Text*. A classic introduction to the art of theologizing liturgically and looking at liturgy from a theological perspective.

White, James. *Roman Catholic Worship: Trent to Today* (1995, Paulist Press). Like the authors of the preceding volume, White feels that before plunging into the task at hand, liturgical planners and ministers need to know at least something of the movement with which they stand in continuity. This book provides that orientation from the Catholic experience.

THE LITURGY OF THE HOURS AND COMMENTARIES

The Liturgy of the Hours (1975, 4 volumes, CB; 2 volumes, Daughters of Saint Paul). A treasure for all Catholics.

Christian Prayer (1977, CB) is a one-volume excerpt from the full collection.

Shorter Christian Prayer (1987, CB, LP) is a simplified, pocket-sized edition to help introduce the assembly to this form of liturgical prayer.

Supplement with new memorials to be observed in the United States (1987, CB).

Campbell, Stanislaus. *From Breviary to Liturgy of the Hours: The Structural Reform of the Roman Office, 1964–1971* (1995, LP). For anyone helping to revive and plan the parish celebration of the Hours.

Cones, Bryan. *Daily Prayer 2003* (2002, LTP). A one-volume, handy companion to daily prayer through the calendar year that focuses on scripture reading.

Storey, William G. *An Everyday Book of Hours* (2001, LTP). A four-week cycle of morning and evening prayer using the classic patterns of prayer. *A Seasonal Book of Hours* (2001, LTP) complements *An Everyday Book* with material for feasts and seasons.

Zimmerman, Joyce Ann. *Morning and Evening: A Parish Celebration* (1996, LTP). This work gives a clear explanation of the Liturgy of the Hours and offers practical ideas for its implementation in parishes.

RITUAL BOOKS FOR MASS

The Roman Missal has been published in several parts, mostly to distinguish the various ministries. These volumes form the core of any parish's liturgical library.

Sacramentary (1985, CB, LP). Although a two-volume revision of the sacramentary has been prepared, with revised translations from the Latin, this hard and good work has been in limbo the past decade.

Eucharistic Prayer for Masses for Various Needs and Occasions (1996, CB, LP)
　　Four thematic variations:

- Form I or A: The Church on the Way to Unity
- Form II or B: God Guides the Church on the Way of Salvation
- Form III or C: Jesus, Way to the Father
- Form IV or D: Jesus, the Compassion of God

Sacramentary Supplement (1994, CB, LP)

- Propers for saints added to calendar since 1985 sacramentary
- Proclamation of the Birth of Christ
- Proclamation of the Date of Easter on Epiphany
- Reception of Holy Oils

Collection of Masses of the Blessed Virgin Mary (1992, CB, LP)

- Volume I: Sacramentary (only volume needed in most communities)
- Volume II: Lectionary (needed only at Marian shrines)

Lectionary for Mass for Use in the Dioceses of the United States of America: Volume 1: Sundays, Solemnities, Feasts of the Lord and the Saints, Second Typical Edition (1998, CB, LP, LTP). Volume 2 (2002): Weekdays of Year 1 and the sanctoral cycle with commons. Volume 3 (2002): Weekdays of Year 2 and the sanctoral cycle with commons. Volume 4 (2002): Ritual and votive Masses and Masses for special needs and occasions.

The Sunday volume is available in separate editions for Years A, B and C, as well as a one-volume study edition for all years. The Canadian Revision (1992, CCCB) uses the NRSV translation.

Lectionary for Masses with Children, Contemporary English Version (1993, various publishers).

Introduction to the 1981 Latin revision of the Sacramentary, English translation (see LTP's *The Liturgy Documents*).

Book of the Gospels (2000, LP, CB; 2001, LTP, WLP).

Revised Common Lectionary (from the Consultation on Common Texts) (1992, Abingdon Press). The Protestant adaptation of the Roman three-year lectionary.

ON THE EUCHARIST AND SUNDAY MASS

Baker, J. Robert, and Barbara Budde. *A Eucharist Sourcebook* (1999, LTP). An anthology that explores what eucharist means. Topics include hungering, gathering, remembering, healing and offering.

Griffiths, Alan, trans. *We Give You Thanks and Praise.*

Huck, Gabe, ed. *Preaching about the Mass* (1992, LTP). Includes sample homilies and reflection questions with reproducible bulletin inserts.

Mazza, Enrico. *The Origins of the Eucharistic Prayer* (1995, LP) and *The Eucharistic Prayers of the Roman Rite* (1986, LP). Both volumes are treasures for those who choose, those who proclaim, and those who affirm in assembly, the great eucharistic prayer. The first volume brings us through the history and multi-faceted developments of eucharistic praying; the second examines the prayers now in use (including the early version of our newest eucharistic prayer: for special needs and occasions).

Philippart, David. *Savings Signs, Wondrous Words* (1996, LTP). The words and actions we use when we pray as an assembly are probed in short essays.

Ramshaw, Gail. *Words around the Table* (1991, LTP). These reflections on the words and deeds of the Mass will help the reader enter more deeply into its mystery.

SCRIPTURES OF YEAR B

The New Jerome Biblical Commentary (1990, Prentice Hall). This should be in every Catholic library. This year see especially the chapters on Mark by Daniel J. Harrington, SJ, and on John by Pheme Perkins.

Blain, Susan A., ed. *Imagining the Word: An Arts and Lectionary Resource* (several volumes) (1995, Cleveland: United Church Press). Rich illustrations in all styles and for all periods. Suitable for placement at the entrance of the worship space as a contemporary icon.

Bonneau, Norman. *The Sunday Lectionary: Ritual Word, Paschal Shape* (1998, Collegeville: The Liturgical Press).

Brown, Raymond E. *An Introduction to the New Testament,* especially chapter 7 (1997, Doubleday).

Capel Anderson, Janice, and Stephen D. Moore, eds. *Mark and Matthew: New Approaches in Biblical Studies* (1992: Minneapolis: Fortress).

Deeley, Mary Katherine, Michael Cameron, and Kathy Hendricks. *At Home with the Word 2003* (2002, LTP). Families, parish staffs and individuals can use this book to prepare themselves to hear the scriptures Sunday after Sunday and to act on them week by week.

Donahue, John R., SJ, and Daniel J. Harrington, SJ. *The Gospel of Mark* (2002: Collegeville, The Liturgical Press).

Juel, Donald H. *Mark: Augsburg Commentary on the New Testament* (1992, Minneapolis, Augsburg).

Powell, Mark Allan. *Fortress Introduction to the Gospels* (1998, Minneapolis: Fortress).

"Reading Guide to the Gospel of Mark," in *The Catholic Study Bible.* (1992, New York, Oxford University Press).

Rhoads, David, and Donald Michie. *Mark as Story: An Introduction to the Narrative of a Gospel* (1982, Philadelphia: Fortress).

Tolbert, Mary Ann. *Sowing the Gospel: Mark's World in Literary-Historical Perspective* (1989, 1996, Minneapolis: Fortress).

West, Fritz. *Scripture and Memory: The Ecumenical Hermeneutic of the Three-Year Lectionaries* (1997, Collegeville: The Liturgical Press).

Wold, Wayne L. *Tune My Heart to Sing: Devotions for Choirs Based on the Revised Common Lectionary* (1997, Minneapolis: Augsburg Fortress). Brief reflections for all three cycles in one volume. Each entry is coordinated with the gospel of the Sunday and refers to a hymn text appropriate to that gospel.

INTERCESSIONS AND OTHER LITURGICAL TEXTS

Borg, Robert, ed. *Together We Pray* (1994, LP). These intercessions are based on the biblical texts for Sundays and solemnities, and follow liturgical norms.

Cormier, Jay. *Lord, Hear Our Prayer* (1995, LP). This collection of texts for general intercessions on Sundays and major feasts for all three cycles as well as for Masses, reflecting themes and language of the lectionary readings.

Griffiths, Alan, trans. *We Give You Thanks and Praise: The Ambrosian Eucharistic Prefaces* (2000, Sheed & Ward).

Scagnelli, Peter. *Prayers for Sundays and Seasons: Year A* (1998, LTP). This useful pastoral resource contains scripture-related collect prayers, most translated from European sacramentaries. Also included are lectionary references for the Roman and Revised Common Lectionary (used by the other Christian churches), suggested texts for general intercessions based on the readings, introductions to the Lord's Prayer, invitations to holy communion, and dismissal texts. This book is a companion to *Sourcebook for Sundays and Seasons*.

PRIESTLESS SUNDAYS

United States version: *Sunday Celebrations in the Absence of a Priest* (1994, CB, LTP). Canadian version: *Sunday Celebrations of Word and Hours* (1995, CCCB). Extensive pastoral notes

face difficult questions raised by this rite and present carefully crafted rites for celebration. The Canadian version contains more extensive and creative resources than the U.S. edition.

Dallen, James. *The Dilemma of Priestless Sundays* (1994, LTP). Before we charge naively into any resolution of the "priest shortage," Dallen asks us to reflect carefully on its impact on Catholic identity and mission, and to consider alternatives.

RITUAL BOOKS FOR SACRAMENTS OTHER THAN EUCHARIST

The Roman Ritual, published in one volume before Vatican II, has since been published in several volumes, one for each sacrament or rite. The increased number of options and adaptations made this necessary. Every parish, every presider and every planning group needs a full set of the current editions at hand—with the possible exception of the *Rite of Religious Profession.* For the celebration of the rites, beautifully bound editions of these books are to be used. These reflect the dignity of the assembly and its worship. Paperback editions are published for study and preparation only.

Rite of Christian Initiation of Adults (1988, LTP, LP, USCC, CB). This includes the Rite for the Reception of Baptized Christians, formerly published in a separate booklet. Study editions are available, as well as Spanish volumes.

Book of the Elect (1999, CB) is an enrollment book for the RCIA.

Rite of Baptism for Children (1970, CB, LP). The Canadian bishops published a handsome edition of this book with separate rites "within Mass" and "outside Mass" and with slight revision of ICEL text for inclusive language. Copyright restrictions prohibit bulk sales in the United States, but individual copies can be obtained from the Canadian Catholic Conference.

Rite of Marriage (1970, CB, LP, Ave Maria Press). The Canadian edition, published by the Canadian Catholic Conference, includes suggested texts for the Rite of Reception at the entrance, table and anniversary blessings, and other texts that make it the best volume currently available.

The Vatican issued a new edition in 1990. ICEL and the U.S. Bishops' Conference are working on the U.S. translation and adaptation.

Presumably this will be the next section of the ritual to be published.

Order of Christian Funerals (1989 CB, LP, LTP). A study edition of the entire rite and ritual editions of the wake and rite of committal are also available from LTP. The Canadian edition (1990, CCCB) includes a fine re-ordering of the "Vigil and related rites and prayers," placing them in chronological order. It also contains important appendices: prayers for the end of the day, after vigil and visitation, norms for cremation and ritual directives for a funeral liturgy in the presence of ashes. There is also a laminated card with a practical adaptation entitled "Shorter Rite of Committal for Use in Inclement Weather."

Vigils and Related Prayers (1989, LTP), excerpts from the complete rite.

Rites of Committal (1989, LTP), excerpts from the complete rite.

Book of the Names of the Dead (1991, LTP), in which Christian communities may record and remember the names of their dead; especially for use during November.

Cremation Rite Appendix (1997, LTP). Cremation rite and the U.S. Bishops' statement on cremation.

Rite of Penance (1975, CB, LP). Published in both "sanctuary size" for penance services and "confessional size" for individual penance.

Pastoral Care of the Sick: Rites of Anointing and Viaticum (1983, LTP [Spanish and English], CB, LP). Published in "sanctuary" and "pocket" sizes.

A Ritual for Laypersons: Rites for Holy Communion and Pastoral Care of the Sick and Dying (1993, LP). Rites that may be led by a layperson in the absence of a priest or deacon.

Communion of the Sick (1984, LP). The official texts for bringing the eucharist to the sick.

Holy Communion and Worship of the Eucharist outside Mass (1976, CB).

Order for the Solemn Exposition of the Holy Eucharist (1993, LP):

- for exposition over one or several days
- liturgy of the hours during the period of exposition
- eucharistic services of prayer and praise during exposition
- closing celebration (two forms: with Mass, outside Mass)
- scripture readings, litanies, music resources

Rite of Religious Profession (1988, LTP).

ON THE SACRAMENTS

Fink, Peter, sj, ed. *The New Dictionary of Sacramental Worship* (1990, Michael Glazier). A vast theological and pastoral resource, whose entries run the whole gamut from theological to practical liturgical, including the pastoral dimension and the insights of the social sciences.

ON BAPTISM/CHRISTIAN INITIATION

Baker, J. Robert, Larry J. Nyberg, and Victoria M., eds. *A Baptism Sourcebook* (1993, LTP). Prose, poetry, scripture and liturgical and patristic texts that help to unfold the mystery of baptism.

Fitzgerald, Tim. *Infant Baptism: A Parish Celebration* (1994, LTP) encourages baptism to be understood as the action of the entire community.

Jackson, Pamela. *Journeybread for the Shadowlands* (1993, LP). Unusual and useful reflections on readings for the various rites of the RCIA throughout the year.

Johnson, Maxwell E. *The Rites of Christian Initiation: Their Evolution and Interpretation* (1999, LP). This study surveys the development and theology of those rites from their New Testament origins to their current shape in the Roman Catholic, Episcopal and Lutheran churches.

Morris, Thomas H. *The RCIA: Transforming the Church: A Resource for Pastoral Implementation* (1997, Paulist). A revised and updated edition of the standard primer for implementing and perfecting the rites of initiation for adult believers in the Catholic church.

Nelson, Gertrud Mueller. *Child of God* (1997, LTP). A "baby book" that commemorates days from birth to age 6 with places to record memories and sacraments.

Ramshaw, Gail. *Words around the Font* (1995, LTP). Reflections on 13 words about the font, arranged in the order of the catechumenate.

Tufano, Victoria M. *Celebrating the Rites of Adult Initiation: Pastoral Reflections* (1992, LTP). Essays about the scrutinies, the Rite of Acceptance, taking a new name and more.

Turner, Paul. *The Hallelujah Highway: A History of the Catechumenate* (2000, LTP). Stories of people and documents that played a role in developing and recording the rites.

Turner, Paul. *Your Child's Baptism* (1999, LTP). What parents should know in preparation for infant baptism.

_____. *The Catechumenate Answer Book* (2000, Resource Publications). Answers the 101 most-asked questions.

ON MARRIAGE

Baker, J. Robert, Kevin Charles Gibley and Joni Reiff Gibley, eds. *A Marriage Sourcebook* (1994, LTP). Scripture, prayer, poetry, fiction, song and humor expressing the joys and sorrows, deaths and resurrections of the mystery of marriage.

Covino, Paul. *Celebrating Marriage: Preparing the Wedding Liturgy: A Workbook for the Engaged Couple* (1994, Pastoral Press). This workbook walks the engaged couple through each step of the wedding liturgy and offers practical and proven suggestions.

Fleming, Austin. *Parish Weddings* (1987, LTP). A guide for good liturgy at weddings.

Fleming, Austin. *Prayerbook for Engaged Couples* (1990, LTP). An invitation for couples to pray the scriptures that will be heard at their wedding.

Kunde-Anderson, Mary Beth, and David Anderson. *Handbook for Church Music for Weddings* (1992, LTP). A guide for planning wedding music.

Marcheschi, Graziano, and Nancy Seitz Marcheschi. *Scripture at Weddings: Choosing and Proclaiming the Word of God* (1992, LTP). Readings and commentaries appropriate for Christian wedding liturgies.

Nelson, Gertrud Mueller, and Christopher Witt. *Sacred Threshold: Rituals and Readings for a Wedding of the Spirit* (1998, Doubleday). This book is written for the bride and groom who are searching for more meaningful, gracious and sacred wedding traditions.

Turner, Paul. *The Catholic Wedding Answer Book* (2001, Resource Publications). Answers the 101 most-asked questions.

ON THE SACRAMENT OF RECONCILIATION

Dallen, James, and Joseph Favazza. *Removing the Barriers: The Practice of Reconciliation* (1991, LTP). A call to rethink the way the church reconciles while expanding our ideas about our mission as church.

Hughes, Kathleen, RSCJ, and Joseph A. Favazza, eds. *A Reconciliation Sourcebook* (1997, LTP). The parable of the Prodigal Son is the framework for the texts about division, alienation, penance, mercy and celebration.

Kennedy, Robert, ed. *Reconciling Embrace: Foundations for the Future of Sacramental Reconciliation* (1998, LTP). Seven major presentations from the 1995 symposium on reconciliation sponsored by the North American Forum on the Catechumenate.

ON FUNERALS

Sloyan, Virginia, RSCJ, ed. *A Sourcebook about Christian Death* (1990, LTP). Topics include the communion of saints, prayer for the dead, images of heaven, rest, pilgrimage, reckoning and resurrection. For November or for the period of mourning after death.

Smith, Margaret. *Facing Death Together: Parish Funerals* (1998, LTP). This is a guide for celebrating the order of Christian funerals in a context of pastoral care.

BLESSINGS

Book of Blessings (1989, CB, LP). This book contains numerous blessings and prayers, including several rites once published separately: the orders for crowning an image of the Blessed Virgin Mary, for the commissioning of extraordinary lay ministers of the eucharist, for the installation of a pastor.

Catholic Household Blessings and Prayers (1988, USCC). This is the first attempt by the U.S. bishops since *A Manual of Prayers,* issued by the Baltimore Council of 1888, to provide a standard domestic prayer book for the whole country.

Shorter Book of Blessings (1990, CB, LP) is an abridged form of the *Book of Blessings.* It contains most of the blessings that take place outside of Mass. Study editions are also available.

PONTIFICAL

The Roman Pontifical includes those rites normally celebrated by a bishop. The *Blessing of Oil and Consecration of Chrism* has been included in the sacramentary. The rites for confirmation and for the dedication of a church are published separately and should be in every liturgical library.

Roman Pontifical, Part I (1978, ICEL) contains the now outdated rites of initiation, confirmation, the institution of readers and acolytes, the various ordination rites, and several blessings of persons (blessing of an abbot/abbess and consecration to a life of virginity).

Confirmation (1973, USCC). Excerpted from fuller pontifical. The Canadian version (1973, CCCB) incorporates helpful notes from the *Ceremonial of Bishops*.

Dedication of a Church and an Altar (1989, USCC). An important resource for parishes undergoing renovation or construction; useful for parishes as they prepare for each year's anniversary.

Ceremonial of Bishops (1989, LP). While not a liturgical book of texts, it is an official compilation of rubrics, with liturgical and historical orientation to feasts, seasons and services, and of emendations made since the various ritual books were published. The notes are useful for charting liturgical celebrations in any parish.

HISTORY AND OBSERVANCE OF THE LITURGICAL YEAR

Adam, Adolph. *The Liturgical Year: Its History and Its Meaning After the Reform of the Liturgy* (1981, LP). Contains some "received wisdom" that has been superseded by recent scholarship. One of the best studies available.

Baldovin, John. *Worship: City, Church and Renewal* (1991, Pastoral Press). See chapters on feasting the saints and on a calendar for a just community—all founded on careful scholarship of our ancient Christian heritage.

Bishops' Committee on the Liturgy, National Conference of Catholic Bishops, *Holy Days in the United States: History, Theology, Celebration* (USCC, 1984). With additional notes on the days in the American proper calendar as of 1984.

Bishops' Committee on the Liturgy, National Conference of Catholic Bishops, *Study Text 9: The Liturgical Year: Celebrating the Mystery of Christ and His Saints* (1984, USCC).

Carroll, Thomas, and Thomas Halton. *Liturgical Practice in the Fathers* (1988, LP). Carefully chosen quotations and commentary on the various seasons and feasts as they developed in the first centuries.

Days of the Lord: The Liturgical Year, 7 volumes (1990–1994, LP). This is an in-depth commentary on the riches of the liturgical year and companion to the sacramentary, lectionary and *Liturgy of the Hours.* This series comprehends the totality of the liturgical year, its structure and meaning. It is a sort of updated Church's Year of Grace.

Guéranger, Abbot. *The Liturgical Year.* The most-available English edition was published by Newman Press (Westminster, MD) in 1948 and 1949 (15 volumes). Though written through the entire second half of the nineteenth century, readers might search this out in libraries for its plethora of details and for its witness to the liturgical renewal leading to Vatican II.

Hynes, Mary Ellen. *Companion to the Calendar* (1993, LTP) is a daily and seasonal guide to saints and mysteries that make up the Christian calendar, with additional notes on the calendars of Jews and Muslims and the national days of the United States and Canada. It is designed for homes, schools and parishes.

Martimort, A. G., et al. *The Church at Prayer,* 4 volumes, but especially volume 4: "The Liturgy and Time," (1986, LP; one-volume edition 1993). See especially the essays by Pierre Jounel on Sunday and the year.

Metford, J. C. J. *The Christian Year* (1991, Crossroad, 1991). A masterful summary, with many nuggets of fascinating detail, organized season by season.

Nelson, Gertrud Mueller. *To Dance with God: Family Ritual and Community Celebration* (1986, Paulist Press). A helpful collection of essays on celebration and suggestions for family rituals for each season.

Nocent, Adrian. *The Liturgical Year,* 4 volumes (1977, LP). One of the architects of Vatican II's reform takes us Sunday-by-Sunday and season-by-season through the church's liturgy and lectionary with excellent commentaries.

Parsch, Pius. *The Church's Year of Grace,* 5 volumes (1957 and various editions, LP). While commenting on the old calendar, these volumes still offer enormous assistance to readers, especially when looking for guidance to the previous generation's approach to seasons and saints.

The Saint Andrew Bible Missal (1982, Hirten). Contains insightful introductions to the liturgical seasons and to the readings, as well as attention to Christian initiation.

Stuhlman, Byron David. *Redeeming the Time: A historical and theological study of the church's rule of prayer and the regular services of the church* (1992, Church Hymnal Corporation). Taking inspiration from Schmemann's "liturgy of time," but approaching things differently, Stuhlman, writing from an Episcopalian perspective, articulates the theological connections between the various cycles and the rites proper to them.

Talley, Thomas J. *The Origins of the Liturgical Year* (LP, 1986). Challenges much of the "received wisdom" about the development of the liturgical year. Groundbreaking insights into the development of the calendar and the role of the word of God in the lectionary in shaping the framework of our worship. Difficult going, but greatly rewarding for the serious reader.

Turner, Paul. *What Am I Doing for Lent this Year?* and *What Am I Doing for Triduum this Year?* (both also available in Spanish, LTP, 2001). Short booklets used to accompany a person's keeping of Lent and in the celebration of the Triduum.

Walsh, Mary Caswell. *The Art of Tradition: A Christian Guide to Building a Family* (2000, LTP). This book will help to explore the practical wisdom of the ages and apply it to everyday life.

Weiser, Francis X. *Handbook of Christian Feasts and Customs* (various editions, including 1963, Paulist Press). Contains abridged materials from his earlier volumes: *The Christmas Book, The Easter Book* and *The Holy Day Book.* All are invaluable for their references to once-popular traditions.

CALENDAR

Roman Calendar. When the current (1969) calendar was implemented in the dioceses of the United States, several dates proper to this country were added. That list continues to grow. The calendar and the *General Norms for the Liturgical Year and the Calendar* are reprinted at the front of the sacramentary.

Liturgy Documentary Series, #6: Norms Governing Liturgical Calendars (1984, USCC). The General Norms and the calendar are accompanied by the commentary released by the Vatican in the early 1970s and updated to 1984 by the principles for particular calendars and by clarifications issued by the Vatican.

Roman Calendar: Text and Commentary (1976, USCC) has much of the same, but in an earlier version. It is one of the few places in English to find the Litany of the Saints. Several versions are printed in various volumes of the *Roman Ritual,* but here one can find the full version "for solemn intercessions," the version for consecrations and solemn blessings, and special invocations for various sacraments.

Dioceses are mandated to issue annual calendars, with local feasts and norms. Many publishers issue annual calendars and *ordos,* some with regional editions.

Roman Martyrology. This is a particular kind of calendar, cataloguing all the saints according to their date of observance. This includes not only the scores that are on the current universal (Roman) calendar, but also the thousands of others who might be part of national, diocesan or religious community calendars. A new edition that takes the revisions of the calendar into account is in the works.

As the Roman martyrology is prepared for issuance, local churches and orders are encouraged to prepare local martyrologies to supplement the universal listing.

THE LORD'S DAY

Pope John Paul II. *Guide to Keeping Sunday Holy* (the apostolic letter *"Dies Domini"*) (1998, LTP).

Porter, Harry Boone. *The Day of Light: The Biblical and Liturgical Meaning of Sunday* (1987, Pastoral Press). A new edition of a classic examination of the primacy of the Lord's Day.

ADVENT AND CHRISTMAS

Advent and Christmastime Table Prayer (1998, LTP). These stand-up cards contain a variety of seasonal prayers for before and after meals.

Alexander, J. Neil. *Waiting for the Coming: The Liturgical Meaning of Advent, Christmas, Epiphany* (1993, Pastoral Press). Combines scriptural insights of Raymond Brown (*Birth of the Messiah*), liturgical research of Thomas

Talley (*Origins of the Liturgical Year*), with his own pastoral experience and insights.

Erspamer, Steve, SM, *Fling Wide the Doors: An Advent and Christmastime Calendar* (1992, LTP). This three-dimensional calendar comes with a booklet of prayers for each day from November 30 to January 6.

Irwin, Kevin. *Advent & Christmas: A Guide to the Eucharist and Hours* (1986, LP). Volume one of a guide to liturgical texts in the seasons.

Mazar, Peter. *Keeping Advent and Christmastime* (1996, LTP). This seasonal pocket booklet helps prayer and scripture reading throughout the day.

Mazar, Peter. *Winter: Celebrating the Season in a Christian Home* (1996, LTP). This delightful book helps families celebrate winter in all its shifting moods from Advent through Christmas and carnival.

Mazar, Peter, and Gabe Huck. *Amazing Days: All the Days of Christmas* (1998, LTP).

O'Gorman, Thomas, ed. *An Advent Sourcebook* (1988, LTP). A wonderful collection of texts for reflection throughout this season.

Simcoe, Mary Ann, ed. *A Christmas Sourcebook* (1984, LTP). This delightful collection of historical texts will offer many moments of reflection throughout this holy season.

Welcome, Yule! (2002, LTP). These Sunday handouts unify the observance of Advent and Christmas and link prayer at church to prayer in the household.

Wild Goose Worship Group, *Cloth for the Cradle: Worship Resources and Readings for Advent, Christmas, and Epiphany* (2000, GIA). This book's main purpose is to allow the adult world to rediscover the stories of Christ's birth, speaking from and to adult experience.

LENT, THE PASCHAL TRIDUUM AND EASTER

Alexander, J. Neil. *Time and Community* (1990, Pastoral Press). Serious essays on such topics as the lenten lectionary in the fourth century and the origins of Candlemas.

Baker, J. Robert, Evelyn Kaehler, and Peter Mazar, eds. *A Lent Sourcebook: The Forty Days,* two volumes (1990, LTP). An outstanding collection of texts for each day of Lent, suitable for meditation and inspiration.

Congregation for Divine Worship, "Circular Letter concerning the Preparation and Celebration of the Easter Feasts" (USCC). Issued by the Vatican in 1988, it is an excellent compendium of liturgical principles applicable in these weeks.

DePaola, Tomie. *The Garden of the Good Shepherd: A Sticker Calendar to Count the Fifty Days of Easter* (2001, LTP). Counts the 50 days from Easter Sunday to Pentecost with images drawn from scripture.

Halmo, Joan, and J. Frank Henderson, eds. *A Triduum Sourcebook,* three volumes (1996, LTP). These volumes are an excellent anthology for the holiest of days.

Huck, Gabe, Gail Ramshaw, and Gordon Lathrop, eds. *An Easter Sourcebook: The Fifty Days* (1988, LTP). This is an outstanding collection of historical texts suitable for reflection and inspiration every day of the season.

Huck, Gabe. *An Introduction to Lent and Eastertime* (1988, LTP). This popular pamphlet will help your community understand the meaning of these holy seasons and to observe them with devotion.

Huck, Gabe. *The Three Days: Parish Prayer in the Paschal Triduum* (1992, LTP). This book offers wonderful advice to parishes on how to get the most out of the Triduum. Suggestions range from scheduling liturgies to cutting baptismal garments.

Huck, Gabe. *Three Days to Save* (1991, LTP). This inexpensive flyer can be slipped into your bulletin on Palm Sunday to explain the Triduum to the assembly and to encourage their participation.

Huck, Gabe. *Los Tres Días para Guardar* (1991, LTP). This is the Spanish translation of *Three Days to Save.*

Irwin, Kevin. *Easter, A Guide to the Eucharist and Hours* (1991, LP). Along with Advent/ Christmas and Lenten volumes, this forms a trilogy of exhaustive guides to every day, to every liturgical text.

Irwin, Kevin. *Lent: A Guide to the Eucharist and Hours* (1985, LP).

Jarrett, Judy. *Forty Days and Forty Nights: A Lenten Ark Moving toward Easter* (1995, LTP). An Advent-type calendar for Lent.

Mazar, Peter. *Keeping Lent, Triduum and Eastertime* (1996, LTP). This popular booklet contains prayers and reflections for everyone to enrich their celebration of these holy days.

Mazar, Peter. *We Watch and Pray during the Paschal Triduum* (1996, LTP). This pamphlet contains an order for prayer and scripture reading for different times throughout the Triduum.

Nussbaum, Melissa Musick. *Bible Stories for the 40 Days* (1997, LTP). Children will enjoy reading these stories (or having them read to them) and studying the illustrations by Judy Jarrett. Each day of Lent comes with its own story from the Bible.

Paschal Mission (2002, LTP). Give away this set of inexpensive flyers to the assembly week by week throughout the quarter of the year that is Lent, the Paschal Triduum and Eastertime. They contain blessings and reflections to sanctify these holy seasons at home.

Ramshaw, Gail. *Words around the Fire* (1994, LTP). Reflections on the scripture readings of the Easter Vigil.

Schmemann, Alexander. *Great Lent: Journey to Pascha* (1974, St. Vladimir's Seminary Press, 1974). A classic, with universally applicable meditations on fasting, discipline, celebration and Lent as pilgrimage.

Stevenson, Kenneth. *Jerusalem Revisited: The Liturgical Meaning of Holy Week* (1988, Pastoral Press). Incorporates the latest liturgical scholarship regarding the evolution of this core of the liturgical year.

Table Prayer for Lent and Eastertime (1988, LTP). Provide multiple copies of this card for all the tables throughout your community. They contain a variety of prayers for before and after meals.

Wild Goose Worship Group, *Stages on the Way: Worship Resources for Lent, Holy Week & Easter* (2000, GIA). An inventive "book of bits" from the Iona Community in Scotland, containing litanies, meditations, monologues, poems and actions for the 90 days.

SAINTS

McGrath, Michael O'Neill. *Patrons and Protectors: Saints and Occupations* (2001, LTP). This book presents images of the saints as patrons of particular occupations with fresh, contemporary interpretations.

Reynolds, Stephen, compiler. *For All the Saints: Prayers and Readings for Saints' Days* (1994, Anglican Book Centre). Produced by the Anglican Church of Canada, most of the Roman Calendar Saints are represented in close to 800 pages.

Thurston, Herbert J., SJ, and Donald Attwater. *Butler's Lives of the Saints,* 4 volumes (1956, Christian Classics). The most complete publication on the saints in English, reprinted from a 1956 edition. While the changes in the Roman calendar have shifted several observances, this is invaluable for researching additions to the litany of the saints and for discovering the dates of saints not appearing in the current Roman calendar.

Walsh, Michael. *Butler's Lives of the Saints: Concise Edition* (1991, Harper Collins). This has about a seventh of the material found in the full edition, but all recent canonizations and calendar shifts are listed in the complete index of saints.

JEWISH AND CHRISTIAN CONCERNS

Bishops' Committee on the Liturgy, National Conference of Catholic Bishops, *God's Mercy Endures Forever: Guidelines on the Presentation of Jews and Judaism in Catholic Preaching* (1988, USCC). Includes specific notes on the various liturgical seasons.

Eskenazi, Tamara, Daniel Harrington, and William Shea. *The Sabbath in Jewish and Christian Traditions* (1991, Crossroad).

Fisher, Eugene. *The Jewish Roots of Christian Liturgy* (1990, Paulist Press). The chapters on the Sabbath and Sunday show their similarities and differences. The bishops' document, *God's Mercy Endures Forever,* is reprinted as an appendix.

Jegen, Carol F., BVM, and Rabbi Byron L. Sherwin. *Thank God: Prayers of Jews and Christians Together* (1989, LTP). Prayers and brief orders of service to be used at home, in small groups or in interfaith services.

Pawlikowski, John, and James A. Wilde. *When Catholics Speak about Jews* (1987, LTP). Notes for homilists, catechists and intercession writers, arranged by the liturgical year.

MUSIC RESOURCES

■ HYMNALS

Cantate Domino (1980, Oxford). The European ecumenical hymnal (the first edition was produced in the 1920s). An invaluable resource.

Catholic Book of Worship, III (1994, Canadian Conference of Catholic Bishops). The Canadian national Catholic hymnal.

The Catholic Liturgy Book (1975, Baltimore: Helicon Press, Inc.). A fine, early attempt at a service book, well edited.

The Collegeville Hymnal (1990, LP). Contains new seasonal psalm settings and contributions by many Benedictine authors and composers.

The Hymnal 1982 (1985, Church Publishing). The Episcopal hymnal. There's more chant in this volume than in any Catholic hymnal.

Hymnal for Catholic Students (1988, GIA and LTP, 1988). A basic book for grade-school students in parochial schools and religious education programs. Children can learn this repertoire and then carry it with them throughout their lives. The leaders' manual of this book, *Preparing Liturgy for Children and Children for Liturgy,* is fundamental reading for anyone interested in public worship.

Hymnal for the Hours (1989, GIA). A gold mine of hymnody.

ICEL Resource Collection (1981, GIA). Hymns in the public domain and settings of service music for the rites by contemporary composers.

Lead Me, Guide Me, A Hymnal for African American Parishes (1987, GIA).

Lutheran Book of Worship (1978, Augsburg).

Peoples Mass Book (1984, WLP). A basic collection with lots of Lucien Deiss.

Songs of Zion (1982, Abingdon). Music from the Black gospel and spiritual traditions.

We Celebrate: Worship Resource (published every three years, WLP). Hymnal and missal form a complementary pair; the missal includes weekly liturgical catechesis.

With One Voice: A Lutheran Resource for Worship (1985, Augsburg). While much of this material will be familiar to Roman Catholics, there are some fine new texts and tunes in this collection.

Worship, Third Edition (1986, GIA). Well-rounded American Catholic service book and hymnal.

■ MUSICAL RESOURCES FOR LITURGY OF THE HOURS

The publications listed here provide settings for the Liturgy of the Hours. (Titles listed in the hymnals section may also offer orders of service, prayer texts and musical settings of invitatories, office hymns, psalms, intercessions and canticles.)

Christian Prayer, organ accompaniment. Various composers (1978, ICEL).

Haas, David. *Light and Peace: Morning Praise and Evensong* (1986, GIA).

Haugen, Marty. *Holden Evening Prayer* (1990, GIA). This setting of vespers follows the traditional form while using contemporary and inclusive language.

Hughes, Howard. *Nightsong: Music for Evening Prayer* (1989, WLP).

Hymnal for the Hours (1989, GIA).

Joncas, Michael. *O Joyful Light* (1985, North American Liturgy Resources).

Melloh, John Allyn, SM, and William G. Storey, eds., with original music by David Clarke Isele, Howard Hughes, SM, and Michael Joncas. *Praise God in Song: Ecumenical Daily Prayer* (1979, GIA).

Melloh, John Allyn, SM, and William G. Storey, eds., with original music by David Clarke Isele, Howard Hughes, SM, and Michael Joncas. *Praise God in Song: Ecumenical Night Prayer* (1982, GIA).

Worship, Third Edition: Liturgy of the Hours Leaders' Edition (1989, GIA).

■ PSALM RESOURCES

These collections of responsorial psalmody are available as individual publications. Many contain reprintable refrains.

Alstott, Owen. *Respond and Acclaim* (1991, Oregon Catholic Press).

Cosley, Thomas M. *Six Psalms for Sundays and Seasons* (1995, WLP). Simple refrains and psalm tones make these very effective.

Garcia, Manuel F. *Salmos* (1984, OCP).

The Gelineau Gradual (1977, GIA). Responsorial psalms for the lectionary for Mass for the Sundays and principal feasts of the liturgical year.

The Gelineau Gradual, Volume II (1979, GIA). Responsorial Psalms from the lectionary for Mass for the rites of the church.

Grail/Gelineau Psalms (1972, GIA). 150 Psalms and 18 Canticles.

The Grail Psalms: Inclusive Language Version (text only) (1993, GIA).

Haas, David, and Jeanne Cotter. *Psalms for the Church Year,* Volume III (1989, GIA).

Hansen, Jim. *Psalms for Sundays and Seasons* (1984, Chancel). Twelve psalms for soloist, choir and congregation.

Haugen, Marty, and David Haas. *Psalms for the Church Year* (1983, GIA).

Haugen, Marty, and David Haas. *Psalms for the Church Year,* Volume II (1988, GIA).

Hopson, Hal H. *Eighteen Psalms for the Church Year* (1990, Hope).

Hopson, Hal H. *Ten Psalms* (1986, Hope).

ICEL Lectionary Music, various composers (1982, GIA). Psalms and alleluia and gospel acclamations for the liturgy of the word.

Isele, David Clark. *Psalms for the Church Year* (1979, GIA).

Kreutz, Robert. *Psalms and Selected Canticles* (1983, OCP).

Psalms for All Seasons: From the ICEL Liturgical Psalter Project, various composers (1987, NPM).

Psalms for the Cantor, Volumes I–VII. Various composers (1985–1987, WLP).

Psalms and Ritual Music: Music for the Liturgy of the Word (1999, WLP). A fine collection of responsorial psalmody that offers simple, effective musical settings that do not intrude on the meaning of the text and keep the spirit of the psalm together with that of the liturgy of the word.

Somerville, Stephen. *Psalms for Singing* (1976, WLP).

Warner, Steven. *Psaltery* (1990, GIA).

Willcock, Christopher, SJ. *Psalms for Feasts and Seasons: Reformed, Anglican, Lutheran & Wesleyan Rites* (1999, LP).

■ MISCELLANEOUS MUSIC RESOURCES

Dalles, John A. *Swift Currents and Still Waters* (2000, GIA). This collection of new hymn texts can be sung to familiar tunes.

Ford, Paul F. *By Flowing Waters: Chant for the Liturgy: A Collection of Unaccompanied Song for Assemblies, Cantors and Choirs* (1999, LP).

Hommerding, Alan J., and Diana Kodner. *A Music Sourcebook* (1997, LTP). A rich anthology containing the texts of hymns, the thoughts of mystics and the words of musicians throughout the ages that sing the praises of music.

Hopson, Hal H. *The Creative Use of the Organ in Worship* (2000, Hope). This volume is part of a series of arrangements of hymns for choirs and instruments.

Petrunak, Stephan, and Kathleen Felong. *Beyond Strumming: A Liturgical Guitar Method Series* (2000, GIA). This useful series helps the liturgical musician play more effectively. It comes with a CD.

Richer, Linda S., and Anita Stoltzful Breckbill, eds. *Chatter with the Angels* (2000, GIA). This delightful collection puts classical hymns and fun songs into the hands and onto the lips of children.

Service Music for the Mass, Volumes 1–5. Various composers (1988–1989, WLP).

Stuempfle, Jr., Herman G. *Awake Our Hearts to Praise! Hymns, Songs and Carols* (1998, WLP). This resource collects hymns popular with young Catholics. The entire community could build its repertoire with some of these selections.

PERIODICALS

Assembly (Notre Dame Center for Pastoral Liturgy, available from LTP). Five times a year. Each issue explores the tradition, meaning and practice of some aspect of the liturgical event in order to help the community and its ministers enter more deeply into the spirit of the liturgy.

The Bible Today (LP). Provides insights, evaluations and reflections on the word of God that can be readily understood and applied to serve those in ministry.

Catechumenate: A Journal of Christian Initiation (LTP). This bi-monthly publication presents articles on a variety of topics to enhance your understanding and celebration of the rites of initiation.

Celebration: An Ecumenical Worship Resource (NCR). Published monthly, it consists of a magazine section and two resource units: one on scripture and one on ritual.

Chicago Studies (LTP). Published three times a year, it is edited by priests of the archdiocese of Chicago and faculty members of St. Mary of the Lake Seminary for the continuing theological development of priests and other religious educators.

Environment & Art Letter: A Forum on Architecture and Arts for the Parish (LTP). Published monthly, this full-color newsletter explores issues concerning the environment for worship, both permanent and seasonal.

¡Gracias! (LTP). This journal, published six times a year, will assist the formation of pastoral liturgy for the Hispanic-Latino community of the United States. It has articles in both English and Spanish.

Liturgical Ministry (LP). Quarterly. A new publication, each issue focuses on a single topic, aiming to bridge the academic and pastoral approaches to liturgical ministry.

Liturgy (The Liturgical Conference). Quarterly. The Journal of the Liturgical Conference, an ecumenical organization. Each issue explores a single aspect of liturgy, usually taking in many disciplines and many church traditions. Back issues are available and are excellent resources.

Ministry and Liturgy (Resource Publications). This liturgical magazine includes a planning guide for seasons, as well as features, bulletin inserts, etc.

National Bulletin on the Liturgy (Canadian Catholic Conference). Published four times a year with helpful background on many liturgical topics, each issue exploring one topic in detail, often with extensive bibliographies. Many of the "thematic" back issues of this fine journal are still available.

Newsletter of the Bishops' Committee on the Liturgy (USCC). Timely information on liturgical developments and regulations in the United States. Published ten times a year.

Pastoral Music (NPM). Published six times a year. Often contains several major articles on a single theme together with reviews and announcements. Centers on music but touches on all areas of liturgy.

Rite (formerly *Liturgy 90*) (LTP). Published eight times a year, this magazine features articles on the seasons and sacraments, regular columns on music, environment and art, questions and answers.

Worship (LP). Published six times a year. Scholarly journal which, since 1926, has been the primary support of liturgical renewal throughout the English-speaking world.

VIDEOGRAPHY

Lift Up Your Hearts: The Eucharistic Prayer (1993, LTP) (30 min.). Because liturgical texts function in the context of public worship, this videocassette provides an opportunity to "see" the words of the liturgical texts enacted in their "lived setting" of communal worship.

Liturgies of the Triduum: Holy Thursday, Good Friday, Easter Vigil (2000, LTP). These three videos explore what we do on each day of the Triduum and help to discover what these days can and should be in each parish. Approximately 30 minutes each, they are available individually or as a set.

Our Catholic Wedding (2001, LTP). This video helps anyone to better understand how to prepare a wedding liturgy that is a celebration for the entire community.

Proclaiming the Word: Formation for Readers of the Liturgy (1994, LTP). Comprises two 20-minute sections, this video includes expert demonstrations and thoughtful commentary by readers. A Spanish version, *Proclamadores de la palabra,* filmed and recorded in Spanish (not a voiceover) is also available.

Say Amen! To What You Are: The Communion Rite (1994, LTP) (30 min.). The texts of the communion rite (from the Lord's Prayer through the prayer after communion) are "seen" in their natural setting in this inspirational video. The need to wed ritual gesture and movement to the formal text is illustrated by these powerful images of an inner city worship community.

Video Guide for Ministers of Communion (1997, LTP). This video explores the spiritual dimensions and meaning of this ministry as well as the practical aspects of holy communion at Mass.

We Will Go Up with Joy: The Entrance Rite (1996, LTP) (30 min.). The entrance rite of the Sunday eucharist happens within the context of a living community and comes at the end of a lot of other "entrances" into the orbit of the word and sacrament.

The Word of the Lord (1996, LTP) (30 min.). What elements are woven together into a strong and effective celebration of the liturgy of the word? Some are obvious: good proclamation. Some are preparatory: prayer over the text, communal study of that text in some scriptural, liturgical and practical (proclamatory) detail. Some celebrative: the context of community, silence, song, attentive and focused listening within which the text is proclaimed.

SOFTWARE

Clip Art for Parish Life (1998, LTP). A collection of images with art by Suzanne Novak depicting events and topics for every month and season. Includes a book and CD-ROM.

Clip Notes for Church Bulletins, Volume I (2000, LTP). Seventy-five articles, each with an illustration for use in bulletins, handouts and flyers. Includes a book and CD-ROM.

Liturgy Plus ABC, Version 3.2 (2000, Resource Publications).

LitPlan 2002 (2002, OCP). Liturgy planning software. Includes song suggestions, dismissals and readings.

Religious Clip Art for the Liturgical Year (1997, LTP). Contains all of Steve Erspamer's images from LTP's three clip art books (years A, B and C) in CD-ROM format for Windows and Macintosh.

Schedule Maker for Ministers and Volunteers (2000, LTP). Create, view and print liturgical ministry schedules for lectors, eucharistic ministers, altar servers, ushers, greeters, cantors, etc., and also print minister lists and labels.

WEBSITES

The URLs given below were accurate at the time of *Sourcebook*'s going to press. Because of the evolving nature of this resource, always work with your web browser to do a net search using the keyword *liturgy* (or other appropriate words). Even sites that do not at first appear relevant may provide links to helpful sites.

Publishers' websites are listed beginning on page 255, along with their snail-mail addresses and telephone numbers.

Order of Saint Benedict: http://www.osb.org/ liturgy (a particularly rich site for reference links).

Notre Dame Center for Pastoral Liturgy: http:// www.nd.edu/~ndcpl/

North American Forum on the Catechumenate: http://www.naforum.org

Liturgical Studies: http://www.music.princeton. edu/chant_html/liturg.html

The Catholic Calendar Page, with scripture readings for the day, saints and other useful information: www.easterbrooks.com/personal/ calendar/

Online study Bible with 16 different translations, searchable by words and phrases: http:// bible.crosswalk.com

Catholic Internet Directory with links to many resources: http://catholic.net/RCC/Indices/ index.html

Internet lists related to topics in religion: http://www.alapadre.net (more than 2,500 links of Catholic interest)

Times of Masses throughout the United States: www.masstimes.org (not only Mass times but information about reconciliation, devotions, handicapped accessibility, non-English services, etc.)

PUBLISHERS

Abingdon Press
201 Eighth Avenue S.
Nashville TN 37202
800-251-3320; fax: 800-836-7802
e-mail: info@abingdon.org

Anglican Book Centre Publishing
600 Jarvis Street
Toronto, Ontario M4Y 2J6, Canada
416-924-1332
fax: 416-924-2760
e-mail: abcpublishing@national.anglican.ca
www.abcpublishing.com

Ave Maria Press
PO Box 428
Notre Dame IN 46556-0428
800-282-1865 x 1; fax: 800-282-5681
e-mail: avemariapress.1@nd.edu
www.avemariapress.com

Augsburg Fortress Publishers
426 S. Fifth Street
PO Box 1209
Minneapolis MN 55440-1209

800-328-4648; fax: 800-772-7766
e-mail: info@augsburgfortress.org
www.augsburgfortress.org

Canadian Conference of Catholic Bishops
90 Parent Avenue
Ottawa, Ontario K1N 7B1, Canada
800-769-1147; fax: 613-241-5090
e-mail: publi@cccb.ca
www.cccb.ca

Canon Law Society of America
431 Caldwell Hall
Catholic University of America
Washington DC 20064-0002
202-269-3491; fax: 202-319-5719
e-mail: clsa@tidalwave.net
www.clsa.org

Catholic Book Publishing Company
77 W. End Road
Totowa NJ 07512
973-890-1844; fax: 800-890-1844
e-mail: cbpcl@bellatlantic.net
http://.catholicbkpub.com

Chancel Music
(See Oregon Catholic Press)

Christian Classics, Inc.
(See Thomas More Publishing)

Church Publishing Incorporated
(formerly Church Hymnal Corporation)
445 Fifth Avenue
New York NY 10016
800-242-1918; fax: 212-779-3392
e-mail: churchpublishing@cpg.org
www.churchpublishing.org

Cokesbury
PO Box 801
Nashville TN 37202
800-672-1789; fax: 800-445-8189
e-mail: cokes_sew@cokesbury.com
www.cokesbury.org

The Continuum International Publishing Group
370 Lexington Avenue
New York NY 10017-6503
800-561-7704; fax: 703-661-1501
e-mail: info@continuum-books.com
www.continuum-books.com

The Crossroad Publishing Company
481 Eighth Avenue, Suite 1550
New York NY 10001
212-888-1801; fax: 212-868-2171

Doubleday Religious Publishing
Division of Random House
1540 Broadway
New York NY 10036
800-223-5780; fax: 212-302-7985
e-mail: customerservice@randomhouse.com
www.randomhouse.com

Evangel Publishing House
PO Box 189
Nappanee IN 46550-0189
800-253-9315; fax: 219-773-5934
e-mail: sales@evangelpublishing.com
www.evangelpublishing.com

Farrar, Straus & Giroux, Inc.
FSB Associates
19 Union Square West
New York NY 10003
212-206-5326; fax: 212-206-5340
e-mail: sales@fsgee.com
www.fsbassociates.com

Fortress Press
(See Augsburg Fortress Publishers)

GIA Publications, Inc.
7404 S. Mason Avenue
Chicago IL 60638
800-442-1358; fax: 708-496-3828
e-mail: custserv@giamusic.com
www.giamusic.com

Michael Glazier, Inc.
(See The Liturgical Press)

HarperCollins Publishers
10 East 53rd Street
New York NY 10022
800-242-7737; fax: 800-822-4090
e-mail: orders@harpercollins.com
www.harpercollins.com

Hendrickson Publishers
PO Box 3473
Peabody MA 01961-3473
800-358-3111; fax: 978-531-8146
e-mail: orders@hendrickson.com
www.hendrickson.com

William J. Hirten Company
6100 17th Avenue
Brooklyn NY 11204
718-256-4801

Hope Publishing Company
389 S. Main Place
Carol Stream IL 60188
800-323-1049; fax: 630-665-2550
e-mail: hope@hopepublishing.com
www.hopepublishing.com

ICEL (International Committee on English
in the Liturgy)
1522 K Street NW, Suite 1000
Washington DC 20005-1202
202-347-0800; fax: 202-347-1839

The Liturgical Conference
415 Michigan Avenue NE
Washington DC 20017-1518
202-832-6520
e-mail: litconf@sol.com
www.litconf.org

The Liturgical Press
St. John's Abbey
PO Box 7500
Collegeville MN 56321-7500
800-858-5450; fax: 800-445-5897
e-mail: sales@litpress.org
www.litpress.org

Liturgy Training Publications
1800 N. Hermitage Avenue
Chicago IL 60622-1101
773-486-8970, 800-933-1800
fax: 800-933-7094
e-mail: orders@ltp.org
www.ltp.org

NPM (National Association of Pastoral Musicians)
225 Sheridan Street NW
Washington DC 20011-1492
202-723-5800; fax: 202-723-2262
e-mail: npmsing@npm.org
www.npm.org

NCR (National Catholic Reporter Publishing
Company)
115 E. Armour Boulevard
Kansas City MO 64111-1203
816-968-2266
e-mail: patmarrin@aol.com
www.ncrpub.com

New Dawn Press
(See Oregon Catholic Press)

North American Liturgy Resources
(See Oregon Catholic Press)

Notre Dame Center for Pastoral Liturgy
PO Box 81
Notre Dame IN 46556-0081
219-631-5435; fax: 219-631-6968
www.nd.edu/~ndcpl

OCP Publications, Inc.
(Oregon Catholic Press Publications)
5536 NE Hassalo
Portland OR 97213
800-548-8749; fax: 503-843-8181
e-mail: retail@ocp.org
www.ocp.org

Oxford University Press
198 Madison Avenue
New York NY 10016-4314
800-451-7556; fax: 212-726-6446
www.oup-usa.org

The Pastoral Press
(See Oregon Catholic Press)

Pauline Books & Media
Daughters of St. Paul
50 St. Paul's Avenue
Boston MA 02130
800-876-4463; fax: 617-524-8035
e-mail: orderentry@pauline.org
www.pauline.org

Paulist Press
997 Macarthur Boulevard
Mahwah NJ 07430
800-218-1903; fax: 800-836-3161
e-mail: info@paulistpress.com
www.paulistpress.com

Prentice-Hall
Division of Schuster, Inc.
The Simon & Schuster Building
1230 Avenue of the Americas
New York NY 10020
800-282-0693; fax: 800-835-5327
www.vig-prenhall.com

Pueblo Publishing Company
(See The Liturgical Press)

Resource Publications, Inc.
160 E. Virginia Street, #290
San Jose CA 95112-5876
800-273-7782; fax: 408-287-8748
e-mail: orders@rpinet.com
www.rpinet.com

St. Vladimir's Seminary Press
575 Scarsdale Road
Crestwood NY 10707-1699
914-961-8313; fax: 914-961-4507
e-mail: svspress@svots.edu
www.svots.edu

Sheed & Ward
7373 S. Lovers Lane Road
Franklin WI 53132
800-booklog; fax: 419-281-6883
e-mail: sheed@execpc.com
www.bookmasters.com/sheed

Society of Biblical Literature
825 Houston Mill Road, Suite 350
Atlanta GA 30329
877-725-3334; fax: 802-864-7626
e-mail: sblexec@sbl-site.org
www.sbl-site.org

Thomas More Publishing
An RCL Company
200 E. Bethany Drive
Allen TX 75002
800-527-5030; fax: 800-688-8356
e-mail: rcl@rclweb.com
www.rclweb.com

USCC (United States Catholic Conference)
3211 Fourth Street NE
Washington DC 20017-1194
800-235-8722; fax: 202-541-3089
www.nccbuscc.org

Westminster John Knox Press
Presbyterian Publishing Corporation
100 Witherspoon Street
Louisville KY 40202-1396
800-227-2872; fax: 502-569-5113
www.ppcpub.org

World Library Publications
A division of J. S. Paluch
3825 N. Willow Road
PO Box 2703
Schiller Park IL 60176-0703
800-566-6150; fax: 888-957-3291
e-mail: wlpcs@jspaluch.com
www.wlpmusic.com